Astrologers at Work

Time, Astronomy, and Calendars

TEXTS AND STUDIES

VOLUME 14

The titles published in this series are listed at *brill.com/tac*

Helena Avelar (1964–2021)
PHOTO BY LUÍS RIBEIRO

Astrologers at Work

Essays on the Practices and Techniques of Astrology in Memory of Helena Avelar

Edited by

Luís Campos Ribeiro
Charles Burnett

BRILL

LEIDEN | BOSTON

Cover illustration: Folio from William Lilly's workbooks displaying four consultation charts. Oxford, Bodleian Library, Ashmole 427, fol. 4r. (with kind permission of the Bodleian Library)

The Library of Congress Cataloging-in-Publication Data is available online at https://catalog.loc.gov

Typeface for the Latin, Greek, and Cyrillic scripts: "Brill". See and download: brill.com/brill-typeface.

ISSN 2211-632X
ISBN 978-90-04-74531-5 (hardback)
ISBN 978-90-04-74532-2 (e-book)
DOI 10.1163/9789004745322

To Helena Avelar (1964–2021)
For her inspiring and enthusiastic dedication
to the history of astrology

⁙

Contents

Preface: Charting the Practice of Astrology Across Time and Culture

In November of 2018, *The Astra Project* was born from the shared vision of Helena Avelar and Luís Campos Ribeiro. Conceived as a space for advancing the historical study of astrology, it was established to promote rigorous research into astrological doctrines, techniques, and practices. What began as a focused scholarly initiative has since grown into a dynamic international enterprise, currently based at the CIUHCT (Interuniversity Centre for the History of Science and Technology, University of Lisbon), in partnership with The Warburg Institute (University of London). It was also supported in its early stages by the now-concluded IKGF—The International Consortium for Research in the Humanities (University of Erlangen-Nuremberg).

At its core, *Astra* is devoted to the history of astrology—specifically the analysis of astrological technique. It seeks to complement existing historical scholarship by delving into the internal logic of astrology itself: how it was practised, how its principles were formulated, and how its methods of judgement were applied. This technical perspective is not pursued in isolation but in dialogue with adjacent fields such as the history of astronomy, medicine, natural science, magic, geography, and philosophy.

The project's underlying conviction is that, to fully understand astrology's place in cultural history, one must understand how astrology actually worked. By focusing on the practical and theoretical dimensions of astrological craft, *Astra* sheds light on its broader historical and intellectual significance. It explores not only astrology's scientific foundations but also the cultural implications of its use—how it emerged from natural knowledge and how it, in turn, influenced pre-modern conceptions of the world and humanity's place within it. In doing so, *The Astra Project* seeks to re-establish astrology as a central thread in the fabric of the history of science and ideas.

In many ways, it continues the work that Helena Avelar herself championed: a deep, methodical engagement with astrology's technical heritage, pursued with scholarly integrity and intellectual openness. This volume stands as both a contribution to that vision and a tribute to the enduring legacy of her work.

As part of its ongoing commitment to this field, *The Astra Project* inaugurated its first international academic conference, 'The Tools of the Art'. At first delayed because of the global pandemic, it finally took place in May 2023. It was, sadly, held in memory of Helena Avelar who had passed away suddenly in early 2021. This meeting brought together twelve scholars to assess the current state of research on astrological techniques to explore new lines of inquiry. The conference marked a significant milestone in advancing the systematic study of astrology's inner workings and methods.

'The Tools of the Art' was generously hosted by the Monastery of Batalha, in collaboration with *The Astra Project*, and with the support of CIUHCT, the Monastery of Batalha, the Batalha Municipality, CEPAE (Centro do Património da Estremadura), and M. Moleiro Editor. The conference venue—the Monastery of Batalha itself—offered a fitting setting for such reflection. A masterpiece of late Gothic architecture, the monastery is one of Portugal's most iconic monuments and a UNESCO World Heritage site. A note of immense gratitude must be presented to Joaquim Ruivo, the director of Batalha Monastery, without whom this event would not have happened, as well as to Pedro Redol and the rest of the monastery's team.

Taking part in this remarkable place, 'The Tools of the Art' offered a space for meaningful scholarly exchange and honoured the enduring legacy of Helena Avelar. Her vision, dedication, and intellectual clarity continue to inspire and guide the work of *The Astra Project* and all those who strive to understand astrology's role in the intellectual heritage of the West.

The original speakers at the conference were Jean-Patrice Boudet (Université d'Orléan), Steven Vanden Broecke (Universiteit Ghent), Charles Burnett (The Warburg Institute), Martin Gansten (Lunds Universitet), Dorian Gieseler Greenbaum (University of Wales Trinity St David), Stephan Heilen (Universität Osnabrück), David Juste (Bayerische Akademie der Wissenschaften), Jeffrey Kotyk (Università di Bologna), Levente László (Eötvös University), Günther Oestmann (Technische Universität Berlin), Luís Campos Ribeiro (Universidade de Lisboa), and Petra Schmidl (Friedrich-Alexander-Universität Erlangen-Nürnberg). During two days they offered their lectures in front of an enthusiastic international audience.

This book, *Astrologers at Work*, is one of the outcomes of that gathering. Many of the chapters originated as papers presented at 'The Tools of the Art', and have since been revised, expanded, and peer reviewed. As such, the volume captures both the spirit of scholarly exchange that defined the conference and the shared commitment to deepening our understanding of astrology as an intellectual and cultural practice. Unfortunately, Martin Gansten was not able to participate in this book, and the volume was enriched with the contributions of Darrel Rutkin, Christopher Lucken and Susan Ward.

Astrologers at Work stands as a landmark contribution to the historiography of astrology. It gathers thirteen essays by leading scholars, each delving into the working practices, techniques, and intellectual frameworks of astrologers in varied historical and cultural contexts. Conceived in memory of Helena Avelar—herself a dedicated historian of astrology and a practitioner deeply engaged with the craft—this volume is more than an academic tribute. It is an affirmation of the historical relevance of astrology as a living and evolving discipline, rooted in ancient traditions yet constantly reshaped by its interpreters. Its title also honours Helena's own master research—*An Astrologer at Work in Late Medieval France* (Brill, 2021)—which focused on the workbook of fifteenth-century astrologers S. Belle.

This curated collection of essays reflects the diversity, rigour, and richness of the field. From the oracles of Mesopotamia to the private notebooks of William Lilly, the book reveals astrology not merely as a set of abstract systems but as a human and interpretive enterprise—where cosmological viewpoints meet practical necessity.

Recovering the Depths of Astrological Practice

Helena Avelar's legacy lies in her profound engagement with the inner mechanics and meanings of historical astrology. As a scholar, she was attuned to the nuances of technique, focusing in an internalist study of astrology and highlighting the subtle negotiations between doctrine and application in the astrologer's daily work. This volume honours that methodological approach by foregrounding the *practice* of astrology—how charts were constructed, how methods were applied, and how answers were interpreted, recorded, and received. What emerges is a multifaceted picture of astrologers not as detached theoreticians but as deeply embedded cultural actors—interpreters of fate, professional advisers, intellectuals, and sometimes agents of political influence. Each contribution in the collection, which includes both studies as well as edition of significant astrological texts, shows astrology as a dynamic interplay between technical skill, philosophical worldview, and lived experience.

Dorian Gieseler Greenbaum opens the volume with a groundbreaking essay on the origins of interrogational astrology, addressing a long-standing debate in the historiography of astrology. She challenges the dominant scholarly position, that horary astrology emerged primarily in Indian or Arabic contexts, presenting compelling evidence of its roots in ancient Mediterranean traditions. Drawing on oracles, omens, and katarchic astrology, Greenbaum argues for a continuous divinatory tradition from Babylon to Greece and beyond. Her work reframes astrological interrogations as foundational to the way humans have historically sought meaning from the heavens, rather than as a marginal or late development.

In the second chapter, David Juste explores the concept of the Almuten, or ruling planet, within the Latin astrological tradition, revealing a nuanced intellectual tradition around planetary authority in astrological charts. Through close examination of manuscript tables and examples, Juste provides new perspectives into the methods used by medieval astrologers to calculate and interpret the Almuten of the Nativity. His contribution highlights how this method may be among one of the most important novelties in post-Hellenistic horoscopic astrology, showing up among the first generation of Arabic astrologers and embraced by Latin astrologers which included it as a central element in their practice since the twelfth century.

Charles Burnett, contributes with a critical and comparative edition of Sahl ibn Bishr's *50 Precepts*, examining the transformations of this influential text across languages and centuries. This chapter shows how foundational principles of astrological judgment were transmitted to successive generations of astrologers, preserving knowledge but also reconfiguring it in new cultural contexts, and reaffirming the centrality of Arabic astrology in shaping the practices in medieval Europe. Next, Petra Schmidl turns to thirteenth-century Yemen with her study of al-Ashraf ʿUmar's *Kitāb al-Tabṣira*, framing the practice of astrological elections. It describes the election table included in the *Tabṣira* and its contents, comparing it with other examples of this practice in offered in the book and assessing the skill required from the astrologer to put them into practice.

Continuing the medieval tradition, Jeffrey Kotyk presents in chapter 5 a unique cross-cultural perspective with his study of a twelfth-century Japanese horoscope interpreted by a Buddhist monk. His work provides crucial insights into how astrological knowledge was practiced and interpreted in East Asia, reconstructing the monk's interpretation of planetary positions through the lens of spiritual and physical well-being. This contribution shows how horoscopic astrology as a wide-ranging phenomenon with diverse epistemological foundations, rather than solely a Greco-Islamic-European enterprise.

Levente László follows with an examination of the horoscopes attributed to the anonymous astrologer of Emperor Zeno, a corpus that only recently has been addressed more systematically. Building on his doctoral research, László deciphers the technical and conceptual foundations of these charts, on the border between Hellenistic and early Byzantine astrological thought. This chapter combines a rigorous philological analysis with a description on how astrological theory accommodated to imperial and educational settings, and how every terrestrial phenomenon was judged as astrologically verifiable and thus unfalsifiable, reflecting astrology's fundamental aim of offering an all-encompassing explanatory framework.

In a collaborative effort, Jean-Patrice Boudet and Christopher Lucken conduct in chapter 7 a sophisticated study on the astrology of Richard de Fournival's *Nativitas*, revisiting the attribution of the *Speculum Astronomiae* to him. Their study explores in particular the technical vocabulary of birth horoscopes used by Fournival, offering an edition of his *Nativitas* text and a glimpse into Latin medieval practice.

Moving to the end of the medieval and beginning of the early modern periods, Stephan Heilen focuses on a little-known prediction of the Antichrist by John of Lübeck in 1474. His essay serves as both a historical recovery of a unique episode and a theoretical reflection on astrology's eschatological dimensions. Through careful chart analysis, Heilen shows how astrology facilitated bold theological claims and intervention in political discourse, challenging assumptions about astrology's secularization in the later Middle Ages and revealing its persistent entanglement with religious and apocalyptic thought.

Chapters 9 and 10, offer two views on a preeminent figure in Renaissance astrology, Marsilio Ficino. In the first, Darrel Rutkin offers a comprehensive survey of Ficino's astrological writings within his Neoplatonic framework, examining his views on nativities, planetary cycles, and revolutions. Rutkin argues that Ficino's engagement with astrology was both sustained and complex, marked by critical distance and strategic appropriation, deepening our understanding of Renaissance astrology as a site of philosophical innovation and cultural negotiation. Continuing the Renaissance theme, Steven Vanden Broecke provides an incisive study of astrological elections in Ficino's *Disputatio contra iudicium astrologorum* and *De vita*. He examines how Ficino reconceptualized election regarding individual agency, spiritual freedom, and philosophical ethics. Vanden Broecke illustrates that Ficino did not reject astrology outright; rather, he sought to redefine its purpose and scope, especially concerning health and happiness, situating Renaissance astrology within broader debates about autonomy, providence, and the limits of knowledge.

Günther Oestmann addresses challenges related to historical horoscopes in chapter 11. By discussing errors, pitfalls, and scribal mistakes, his essay warns against uncritical source acceptance, illustrating how miscalculations can distort our understanding of historical practice. Examining charts from figures like Johannes Schöner and Kepler, Oestmann advocates cross-disciplinary methods combining historical astronomy, philology, and technical astrology to accurately reconstruct past interpretations, providing vital methodological guidance for historians of science.

In chapter 12, Luís Campos Ribeiro returns to the issue of planetary power. By analysing technical sources from the sixteenth to the seventeenth century, he investigates the methodology for the quantification of planetary strengths and debilities in early modern astrology. He compares tables of essential and accidental dignities from various authors, revealing how astrologers sought to systematize this judgment numerically. Ribeiro connects this trend to broader developments in early modern scientific cultures, positioning astrology within the history of quantification.

Susan Ward concludes the volume with a detailed exploration of the daily practices of William Lilly, England's most renowned astrologer. Utilising Lilly's casebooks, correspondence, and political writings, she reconstructs the rhythms of his consultations and his involvement in seventeenth-century political landscape. Ward's engagement with Lilly's archive allows her to depict a vivid portrait of an astrologer negotiating public authority, private belief, and professional identity, bridging scholarly and practitioner perspectives and grounding astrological history in the lived experiences of one of its key figures.

Together, these chapters create a comprehensive and interdisciplinary portrait of astrologers at work—spanning time, space, and culture. From the ancient Mediterranean, through medieval Europe, and the Islamic regions to Renaissance Italy and early modern England, and including East Asian religious traditions, these contributions connect fields such as classics, manuscript studies, religious history, science studies, and philosophy.

This volume reflects the breadth of Helena Avelar's interests and commitment: historical rigour, and a respect for astrology as an intellectual and practical discipline. The essays are unified not by a single thesis but by a shared concern for the historical *craft* of astrology—its tools, contexts, and practitioners.

Astrologers at Work does more than honour a life. It carries on Helena Avelar's legacy by engaging the sources she loved, asking the questions she asked, and gathering a community of scholars who share her curiosity, discipline, and generosity of spirit. It is a living project, one that recognises the value of astrology as a historical object, a cultural practice, and a field of intellectual inquiry. For those interested in the technical, cultural, and conceptual dimensions of astrology—whether an academic or a practitioner—this volume offers essential insights and foundational research. It invites the reader into the astrologer's world, not only to observe but to understand. And in doing so, it keeps alive the work to which Helena Avelar devoted her life.

Luis Campos Ribeiro
Charles Burnett

List of Figures and Tables

Figures

Tables

Abbreviations

Aberdeen, UL	Aberdeen University Library
Bergamo, BCAM	Biblioteca Civica Angelo Mai
Berlin, SBPK	Staatsbibliothek Preußischer Kulturbesitz
Bernkastel-Kues, CSB	Cusanusstiftsbibliothek
Bologna, BU	Biblioteca Universitaria di Bologna
Bordeaux, BM	Bibliothèque municipale de Bordeaux
Cambridge, UL	Cambridge University Library
Cambridge, MC	Magdalene College Library
Cambridge, TC	Trinity College Library
Cambrai, BM	Bibliothèque municipale de Cambrai
Cambridge (Mass.), HU-HHL	Harvard University Library–Houghton Library
Catania, BU	Biblioteca Regionale Universitaria di Catania
Cracow, BJ	Biblioteka Jagiellońska
Dijon, BM	Bibliothèque municipale de Dijon
Erfurt, UFB	Universitäts- und Forschungsbibliothek
Escorial	Real Biblioteca de Monasterio de San Lorenzo de El Escorial
Fermo, BC	Biblioteca Civica di Fermo
Florence, BML	Biblioteca Medicea Laurenziana
Gotha, FB	Forschungsbibliothek Gotha
Innsbruck, UB	Universitäts- und Landesbibliothek Tirol
Klagenfurt, ADG-BM	Archiv der Diözese Gurk—Bischöfliche Mensalbibliothek
Laon, BM	Bibliothèque municipale de Laon
Leiden, UB	Universitaire Bibliotheken Leiden
Leipzig, UB	Universitätsbibliothek Leipzig
Lüneburg, RB	Ratsbücherei Lüneburg
London, BL	British Library
Melk, SB	Stiftsbibliothek
Munich, BSB	Bayerische Staatsbibliothek
Oxford, BL	Bodleian Library
Paris, BnF	Bibliothèque nationale de France
Prague, NKCR	Národní knihovna České republiky
Princeton, UL	Princeton University Library
San Marino (Ca), HHL	Huntington Library
Uppsala, UB	Uppsala universitetsbibliotek
Vatican, BAV	Biblioteca Apostolica Vaticana
Vienna, ÖNB	Österreichische Nationalbibliothek

Vicenza, BCB	Biblioteca Civica Bertoliana
Warsaw, BN	Biblioteka Narodowa
Wiesbaden, HLB	Hochschul- und Landesbibliothek
Wolfenbüttel, HAB	Herzog August Bibliothek

Astrological Symbols

Planets

♄	Saturn
♃	Jupiter
♂	Mars
☉	Sun
♀	Venus
☿	Mercury
☽	Moon

Aspects

☌	Conjunction
✶	Sextile
□	Square
△	Trine
☍	Opposition

Signs

♈	Aries
♉	Taurus
♊	Gemini
♋	Cancer
♌	Leo
♍	Virgo
♎	Libra
♏	Scorpio
♐	Sagittarius
♑	Capricorn
♒	Aquarius
♓	Pisces

Other symbols

☊	North Node
☋	South Node
⊗	Lot of Fortune
℞	Retrograde
⚸	Black Moon

Notes on Contributors

Jean-Patrice Boudet
is emeritus professor of medieval History at the University of Orléans. His book, *Entre science et* nigromance. *Astrologie, divination et magie dans l'Occident médiéval (XIIᵉ–XVᵉ siècle)*, Paris, Publications de la Sorbonne, 2006, is a reference work in these fields. His last book, *Astrologie et politique entre Moyen Âge et Renaissance*, was published in 2020 (Florence, SISMEL, Ed. del Galluzzo).

Steven Vanden Broecke
is Professor at Ghent University's Department of History, specializing in early modern intellectual history and the history of science, and co-director of the Sarton Centre for the History of Science and the Humanities. His recent research has explored topics such as astrology, astronomy in the Catholic context, and the intersections of medicine and religion.

Charles Burnett
(BA, PhD Cambridge), Professor Emeritus of Arabic/Islamic Influences in Europe at the Warburg Institute, University of London and Fellow of the British Academy. His research has concentrated on the translations of Arabic texts into Latin in the Middle Ages, in the fields of philosophy, science, religion and magic. Among his publications are *The Introduction of Arabic Learning into England* (1997); *Arabic into Latin in the Middle Ages: The Translators and their Intellectual and Social Context* (2009), *Numerals and Arithmetic in the Middle Ages* (2010), and *The Great Introduction to Astrology by Abū Maʿšar* (with Keiji Yamamoto, 2019).

Dorian Gieseler Greenbaum
is an historian of astrology who teaches post-graduates at the University of Wales Trinity Saint David. She received her PhD from the Warburg Institute, University of London. Her book, *The Daimon in Hellenistic Astrology: Origins and Influence* (Brill 2016) was based on her PhD research. She has written numerous articles on the history of astrology and its practices.

Stephan Heilen
is Professor of Classics at the University of Osnabrück, Germany. His main field of research is the history of astrology from Greco-Roman antiquity to the Renaissance. He edited various Greek and Latin texts, especially the two Neo-

Latin didactic poems by Laurentius Bonincontrius (15th c., publ. 1999) and the fragments of the Greek astrological manual of Antigonus of Nicaea (2nd c. AD; publ. 2015, with translation and substantial commentary). A monograph on Hartmann Schedel's astral texts is forthcoming. Moreover, he is working on a three-volume project *Konjunktionsprognostik in der Frühen Neuzeit* (vol. 1, publ. 2020) and preparing, together with Claudio De Stefani, an anthology of Greek astrological poetry for the series *Oxford Classical Texts*.

David Juste

is research leader of the projet Ptolemaeus Arabus et Latinus at the Bayerische Akademie der Wissenschaften in Munich. His publications deal primarily with Latin astrology and astronomy in the Middle Ages and the Renaissance.

Jeffrey Kotyk

(PhD, Leiden University, 2017) is presently a postdoctoral researcher at the Max Planck Institute for the History of Science in Berlin, Germany, where he is examining the history of astral iconography in historical East Asia. His past studies have broadly examined the transmission of astrology and related astral lore in premodern China and Japan. His recent monograph (Brill, 2024) is titled *Sino-Iranian and Sino-Arabian Relations in Late Antiquity China and the Parthians, Sasanians, and Arabs in the First Millennium*.

Levente László

is a classicist with a current research interest in the history of astrology. He received his PhD in 2023 with a dissertation on Hellenistic inceptional astrology and the horoscopes of the emperor Zeno's anonymous astrologer. An independent scholar and a translator of Hellenistic and Byzantine astrological texts, he has published on the textual history of various Hellenistic astrological works.

Christopher Lucken

is Professor emeritus at the University of Paris 8 and former lecturer at the University of Geneva, Christopher Lucken is in particular a specialist of Richard de Fournival. He has recently published a monography devoted to this author, entitled *Les portes de la mémoire. Richard de Fournival and the Arriereban d'Amours* (Droz, 2024).

Günther Oestmann

(b. 1959) has been trained as a clockmaker and received a PhD with a study on the astronomical and astrological significance of the clock in Strasbourg Cathedral in 1992. In 2013 the Musée international d'horlogerie (La Chaux-de-Fonds) awarded the 'Prix Gaïa' to him, and in 2014 he was elected as corresponding member of the International Academy of the History of Science (Paris). Three years later Oestmann was appointed as extraordinary professor for history of science at Technical University Berlin. Fields of research: History of scientific instruments and clocks, history of astronomy/astrology and mathematical geography, maritime history.

Luís Campos Ribeiro

is a historian of science and art and a researcher at CIUHCT, University of Lisbon. He has been awarded a PhD in History and Philosophy of Sciences by the University of Lisbon, published by Brill with the title *Jesuit Astrology: Prognostication and Science in Early Modern Culture* (Brill, 2023). His research focuses on the history of astrology, astronomy and medicine (Medieval and Early Modern) as well as scientific illustration. Luís is the head of the *Astra Project: Historical research on astrological techniques and practices*, hosted by the CIUHCT, University of Lisbon and The Warburg Institute.

H Darrel Rutkin

is a historian of science with a focus on the history of astrology in Europe, ca. 1250–1800. He is currently completing volume II of his three volume treatment of the history of astrology and magic, which is focused on the Renaissance and treats primarily Marsilio Ficino (1433–1499) and Giovanni Pico della Mirandola (1463–1494), both in themselves and in relation to each other.

Petra G. Schmidl

is a historian of science with a focus on pre-modern astronomy, astronomical instruments, and astrology, prognostic practices, and occult sciences in Islamicate societies. She is mainly interested in procedures and methods that help people in orienting themselves in every day life, e.g., timekeeping and prognostic practices. Her recent research project aims at the edition, English translation, commentary and study of the *Kitāb al-Tabṣira fī ʿilm al-nujūm* ("Enlightenment in the science of the stars") written by the future Rasūlid sultan al-Ashraf ʿUmar in thirteenth century Yemen.

Susan Ward

is an independent researcher specializing in the history of astrology, with a particular focus on its practical applications and broader significance. Her work primarily focuses on the early modern period, and for over forty years, she has studied the life and works of the astrologer William Lilly (1602–1681) and his contemporaries. She earned a first-class degree in history from the University of East Anglia, where she specialized in the British Civil Wars. Currently, Ward is engaged in a major project—a three-volume edition of William Lilly's work and relationships, offering essential primary sources for researchers.

CHAPTER 1

The Origins of Questions in Astrology

Dorian Gieseler Greenbaum

Abstract

The origin of the practice of 'interrogations' in western astrology has been a topic of debate within scholarship and amongst practitioners. This chapter makes a thorough investigation of the history and practice of asking questions in astrology. Katarchic astrology, including elections, event interpretation, interrogations and decumbitures, is the platform through which questions are asked of the astrologer, either implicitly or explicitly; its strong ties to divination provide a *modus operandi* in forms of divination such as astral omens, extispicy, oracles and augury. A critical motivation for divination is for humans to be in harmony with the gods, discovering what they want humans to do. Therefore the essay will, first of all, explore divinatory practices in the Mediterranean region that can be related to astrological practice. Next, it will look at astrology's specific intersections with practices such as extispicy and ritual, the relationship of katarchic astrology to the right moment (*kairos*) for beginning a ritual or an action for best results; and the similarities between oracular and astrological practice. There is a questioning mode inherent in these forms of divination, not just literally expressed by the asking of a question, but in the unspoken questions katarchic astrology aims to answer, based on its links to divination and the human wish to act in harmony with the gods. Finally the essay will note specific examples of asking questions in astrological texts beginning in the first century CE, ending with a brief look at later manuscripts that reflect earlier practices.

Keywords

Interrogations – katarchic astrology – divination – oracles – *kairos*

1   Introduction

The initial impetus for this essay arose from a prevalent scholarly view that interrogational astrology was never a part of astrological practice in Mediterranean antiquity, but rather appeared as an import from Indian sources, or developed within the evolution of Arabic astrology in the early eighth century.[1] For someone who has extensively studied Greco-Roman and late antique astrology, and has been investigating the origins of interrogational astrology since 2006, this view seemed misguided. In exploring its history in more depth, it became more and more clear that its origins indeed lay in the Mediterranean world in which western astrology developed and thrived. Its roots lie within a broader context of asking questions within all forms of astrological theory and practice, and also draw notably on related divinatory practices within the ancient Mediterranean world.

The history of questions in astrology, furthermore, cannot be separated from other divinatory practices, including sky omens, extispicy, oracles and augury.[2] This essay will therefore consider relevant divinatory models and practices in the ancient Mediterranean region, and examine divination and astrology along with the topic of questions in astrology during its long history in antiquity. A final, though non-exhaustive, section will examine some material in the afterlife of interrogational astrology in the medieval period.

We shall start from the premise at the heart of the practice of divination, which asks what the gods want humans to do, and how they may achieve it.

---

1   David Pingree, arguably the foremost scholar on astrology at the time, was instrumental in promoting this view. This is somewhat odd, because until 1997, his view about the origins of interrogational astrology was that it had 'developed naturally from catarchic astrology', referring to Dorotheus, *Carmen Astrologicum*, Book 5 ('Astrology', in *Dictionary of the History of Ideas: Studies of Selected Pivotal Ideas*, vol. 1, ed. Philip P. Wiener (New York: Charles Scribner's Sons, 1973), 124); and 'as far as the "Indian" passages are not commonplaces of interrogational astrology they are also not specifically Indian in character' ('The Indian and Pseudo-Indian Passages in Greek and Latin Astronomical and Astrological Texts', *Viator: Medieval and Renaissance Studies* 7 (1976):177); also that '*praśna* was introduced to India from the Hellenistic world' in the Yavanajātaka (*Jyotiḥśāstra: Astral and Mathematical Literature*, Wiesbdaden: Harrassowitz, 1981, 110). However, by 1997 his new view claimed that 'nor is there any other ancient Greek example of this form of astrology [i.e. interrogational], which first appears in India in the third century ...' and 'the Indians invented it as an extension of divination, using the techniques of catarchic astrology' ('Māshā'allāh: Greek, Pahlavī, Arabic and Latin Astrology', in *Perspectives arabes et médiévales sur la tradition scientifique et philosophique grecque. Actes du colloque de la SIHSPAI, Paris, 31 mars–3 avril 1993*, vol. 79, eds A. Hasnawi, A. Elamrani-Jamal and M. Aouad (Leuven/Paris: Peeters/Institut du Monde arabe, 1997), 135); also 'interrogational astrology was developed in India in the 2nd and 3rd centuries A.D. on the basis of Greek catarchic astrology ...' (*From Astral Omens to Astrology: From Babylon to Bīkāner* (Rome: Istituto italiano per l'Africa e l'Oriente, 1997), 21). This remained his contention in later work: see, e.g., 'The Byzantine Transmission of Māshā'allāh on Interrogational Astrology', in *The Occult Sciences in Byzantium*, eds Paul Magdalino and Maria Mavroudi (Geneva: La Pomme d'or, 2006), 232–233.

2   I would like this essay to also make a final tribute in memory of Geoffrey Cornelius, whose life's work on this topic inspired my own inquiry.

The role of questioning in order to obtain such information is crucial in divinatory models, whether stated as an explicit question or implied; it includes as well the ritual practices associated with asking the gods for answers. Therefore it is important to examine this divinatory foundation before turning to the way in which astrology addressed these issues within its own practices.

In looking at this history, we shall draw on evidence from the periods in which it developed, using sources from Mediterranean cultures within and outside of astrology proper. Relevant material both prior to and during the development of Hellenistic astrology will be included. Within this framework, astrology's divinatory background will be explored in its connections with other forms of divination and relationships to its practitioners and its methods in practice. A key component within this milieu is the genre of katarchic astrology and the implicit and explicit questions that lie at its core. Katarchic astrology will, therefore, be a focus throughout this investigation.

The essay has three main areas of investigation. Part 2, Asking the Gods for Answers, will examine the forms of Mediterranean divination that are relevant to this topic. Part 3, Divination and Astrology, will look more closely at astrology's intersections with divinatory practices. Part 4, Asking Questions in Astrology, will look specifically at the evidence from astrologers. Before beginning, though, I must acknowledge my debt to two astrologers whose work has stimulated my own thoughts and research on this topic: Geoffrey Cornelius and Deborah Houlding.[3] I have corresponded with both over many years, discussed topics that will be investigated in this chapter, and benefitted immensely from their insights. It is not hyperbolic to say that without their previous work, this contribution to the subject of questions in astrology could not exist.

1.1   *The Forms of Astrology*

Katarchic astrology, mentioned above, is an essential element in understanding the role of questions in astrology. It is one of three main branches of astro-

---

3 Cornelius's seminal work, *The Moment of Astrology* (London: Arkana/Penguin, 1994, 2nd ed. Bournemouth: Wessex Astrologer, 2003) was critical to this endeavour, as were other publications of his on this topic, such as 1982's 'Astrology and Divination (the Oslo paper)', in *A Paper and a Series of Articles by Geoffrey Cornelius*, Foreward by Kirk Little, Cosmocritic, 2016, Reprint at https://cosmocritic.com/wp-content/uploads/2023/12/cornelius_geoffrey_oslo_and_moment.pdf (accessed 20 September 2025); and 'Is Astrology Divination and Does it Matter?', 1998, http://cura.free.fr/quinq/01gfcor.html (accessed 16 April 2024). My discussions with Houlding beginning in late 2006, and her 2012 public presentation of 'Ancient Enquiry Charts' (United Astrology Conference, New Orleans, LA, 26 May 2012), in which she included some of my evidence for interrogations in Hellenistic astrology, were instrumental in furthering my own investigation.

logy, here outlined in order to orient the reader who may be unfamiliar with the ways in which astrology is organised.[4] Each branch—natal, universal and katarchic—is concerned with particular topics relevant to the various concerns of humans living in and experiencing the world.

- **Natal** astrology gives an interpretation of the chart cast for the place and time of the birth, providing a general view of the characteristics of the person born at that date, place and time. Natal astrology can also be connected to the 'conception' chart.[5]
- **Universal**, also called 'mundane' or 'general' (*katholika*) astrology, is the astrology for groups, countries, cities or states, and the general population. It also includes weather prediction. This kind of astrology uses repeating celestial patterns like the conjunctions of outer planets (Jupiter through Pluto), solar and lunar eclipses, charts for equinoxes and solstices for a specific place connected with a population, daily and yearly solar motions and phases of the Moon.[6]
- **Katarchic** astrology is really an umbrella term that includes four different, but related, kinds of astrology: elections, events, interrogations (also known as horary, the preferred modern term) and decumbiture.
  - *elections* are casting a chart for the best astrological time to begin something
  - Related directly to elections are the interpretation of *event* charts. This is a chart cast for the time an event occurs but after it has taken place, which is interpreted to understand the meanings of the event and outcomes arising from it.
  - The third category, *interrogations*, are charts cast for the time a question is asked. Related to these are charts cast for the time when someone *found out* about an event, such as when a husband discovered his wife had left:[7]

---

4 For a more complete picture of this schematic, see Dorian Gieseler Greenbaum, 'The Hellenistic Horoscope', in *Hellenistic Astronomy: The Science in Its Contexts*, eds Alan C. Bowen and Francesca Rochberg (Leiden/Boston: Brill, 2020), 448–449; other authors may have different schemes, but cover the same forms, e.g. Levente László, 'The Inceptions of the Emperor Zeno's Anonymous Astrologer', PhD Thesis, Eötvös Loránd University, 2023, 18–19.

5 See Katrin Frommhold, *Die Bedeutung und Berechnung der Empfängnis in der Astrologie der Antike*, Vol. 38, Orbis antiquus (Münster: Aschendorff, 2004); Claudius Ptolemy, *Tetrabiblos*, trans. F.E. Robbins, Loeb Classical Library (Cambridge, MA: Harvard University Press, 1940, repr. 1994), III, 1; Claudius Ptolemy, Ἀποτελεσματικά, ed. Wolfgang Hübner, Opera quae exstant omnia III, 1 (Stuttgart/Leipzig: B.G. Teubner, 1998), III, 2.

6 See, e.g., Ptolemy, *Tetrabiblos* trans. Robbins, Book II.

7 These are not quite the same as a typical event chart, which is cast for the time the event occurred, but rather the moment of *discovering* the event had occurred.

these are interpreted in the same way as a question about, say, whether a wife will return to her husband; or whether a slave will be captured.
– A decumbiture is a chart cast for the time that an ill person takes to her bed, or becomes sick enough to have to lie down (from Latin *decumbo*, noun *decubitus*; Greek κατακλίνω, κατάκλισις).[8]

It is important to keep in mind that these sub-sets of katarchic astrology use similar rules and are connected in similar ways by a common goal: to find out what is going to happen, what can be done about it, and how to obtain the best outcome. Katarchic astrology is concretely connected to divination, religion and ritual; it may well be the oldest kind of astrology to be practised (as we will see), and it derives directly from astral omens that were interpreted as messages from the gods, and used to ask for assistance from the gods. It is also connected to oracles, and some kinds of questions asked of oracles are not dissimilar to the kinds of questions asked in a katarchic setting.

This then, is our starting place: the idea of asking the gods for answers about the past, present and future—with omens and oracles, and other ways of finding out what the gods want humans to do, and how they communicate with them. The following section will explore Mediterranean cultures and practices that reflect this and are relevant to the objectives of this essay.

2   Asking the Gods for Answers

2.1   *The Babylonian Tradition*
The tradition of Mesopotamian celestial omens is the oldest in the Mediterranean world. It is fundamentally connected with signs—a sign in the sky, correctly interpreted, correlates with an event on the earth. The world is a 'system of signs',[9] waiting to be interpreted. In this case, the sky is divine, and the signs are from the gods. The general practice of omens uses conditionals in the 'protasis'/ 'apodosis' form: If x is in the sky, then y will happen.[10] Thousands of examples exist in Mesopotamian omen literature, one of which is the following:

---

8   For Galen, the moment when someone develops a fever; see Dorian Gieseler Greenbaum 'Divination and Decumbiture: Katarchic Astrology and Greek Medicine', in *Divination and Knowledge in Greco-Roman Antiquity*, ed. Crystal Addey (Abingdon, UK: Routledge, 2022), 118–119.
9   Stephan Maul, 'Divination Culture and the Handling of the Future', in *The Babylonian World*, ed. G. Leick (New York/London: Routledge, 2007), 362.
10   Francesca Rochberg, 'Conditionals, Inference and Possibility', *Science in Context* 22, no. 1 (2009): 14–15; Amar Annus, 'On the Beginnings and Continuities of Omen Sciences in the Ancient World', in *Divination and Interpretation of Signs in the Ancient World*, ed. Amar

MUL DIL-BAT ANA SIN IS-NIQ AN.M[I] LUGAL. URI^{KI} B[E]

If Venus comes near the Moon: eclipse, the king of Akkad will die.[11]

Some important considerations of the 'if x then y' format should be kept in mind. First, this format is a common trope not only in Mesopotamia, but in other cultures in the Mediterranean such as Egypt and Greece, as we shall see below.

In the case of the Mesopotamians, the two circumstances designated in the protasis and apodosis had *resemblance* to one another. In this format, the logic appears in putting the two statements together, thus elaborating a basic idea. In addition, every cuneiform sign can have multiple meanings, which must be determined by context, and these different meanings also had relationships with each other. Yet the causality, or the predictive nature, that one might automatically assume for 'y' being dependent on 'x', or even dependent on 'x' in linear time, is not straightforward: a connection may be physical or not; it will likely have a divine component, but the relationship between the two is an implication, in the sense that 'x' implies 'y'.[12] Thus, at least in Mesopotamia, conditionals are relational, neither causal nor predictive, and they do not even have to have a physical basis.[13]

This correlation and interrelationship between the omen and the event on earth is the foundation of any kind of divinational attitude, including the basis for astrology itself. Astrology will also cover the opposite direction: an event on earth will correlate with a celestial pattern in the sky.

These practices are not forecasting an immutable future, in fact the opposite. The future revealed by the omen opens a dialogue between gods and humans in which an outcome could be changed or ameliorated by human action in response to the omen. (And this is an underlying premise of katarchic astrology as well—the katarchic rationale exists because of the possibility of changing the future by understanding it in the context of both past and present, and finding a way to negotiate being in harmony with the heavens while obtaining the best possible outcome.) As Stefan Maul writes,

Annus, (Chicago: University of Chicago Press, 2010), 3; Francesca Rochberg, 'If P, then Q: Form and Reasoning in Babylonian Divination', in *Divination and Interpretation of Signs in the Ancient World*, ed. Amar Annus (Chicago: University of Chicago Press, 2010), 19.

11 VAT 10218, Omen 36, in Erica Reiner and David Pingree, *Babylonian Planetary Omens*, Part Three (Groningen: Styx Publications 1998), 44–45.
12 Rochberg, 'Conditionals, Inference and Possibility', 10–11.
13 Rochberg, 11.

Divination was not an expression of fatalism or a listless resignation. Instead, it allowed shape to be given to an amorphous, in many situations threatening, future. This deprives the at first unfathomable future of some of its dread. After all, the perspective towards the future as revealed by the omen marshalls a human response, a directive that was needed especially when the portents were bad. Omina concretized the future which could then be furthered or prevented by specific actions.[14]

Liver divination and extispicy were significant forms of divination in Mesopotamia. They were developed by the last quarter of the third millennium BCE,[15] and continued throughout the history of ancient Mesopotamia. They provided rulers with an ultimate legitimacy for actions, whether political, military, religious or personal. As the Sumerian King Shulgi proclaimed, acting as a diviner, 'In the insides of a single sheep I, the king, / Can find the (divine) messages for the whole universe'.[16]

Thus an interpreted extispicy could contain messages that could be universally applied. Furthermore, liver divination can also be correlated with celestial omens, and conclusions based on astral observation could also be refined through extispicy. All parts of the cosmos were linked to each other, so that each star or region of the sky might have a terrestrial counterpart and vice versa. The sky was seen as the earth's mirror image, so signs from the sky could be related to the entire world.[17] Entrails of the animal were frequently called a '"tablet" inscribed by the gods',[18] just as the sky was inscribed, its heavenly writing a 'tablet with the stars of the heavens'.[19] The sky and its movements were

---

14   Maul, 'Divination Culture', 363.
15   Krzysztof Ulanowski, 'Mesopotamian Divination. Some Historical, Religious and Anthropological Remarks', *Miscellanea Anthropologica et Sociologica* 15, no. 4 (2014): 15–16.
16   Hymn Shulgi B, ll. 148–149, in Ulanowski, 'Mesopotamian Divination', 15–16, in the translation of Piotr Michalowski, 'How to Read the Liver—In Sumerian', in *If a Man Builds a Joyful House: Assyriological Studies in Honor of Erle Verdun Leichty*, eds Ann K. Guinan, Maria deJ. Ellis, A.J. Ferrara, Sally M. Freedman, Matthew Rutz, Leonhard Sassmannshausen, Steve Tinney and M.W. Waters (Leiden/Boston: Brill, 2006), 248.
17   Maul, 'Divination Culture', 362.
18   Maul, 369.
19   The Gudea cylinders speak of the *dub mul-an-kù*, 'tablet star of the heavens' consulted by the goddess Nisaba; this *mul-an* can be both a heavenly star and a cuneiform sign on a tablet: see Francesca Rochberg, *The Heavenly Writing: Divination, Horoscopy, and Astronomy in Mesopotamian Culture* (Cambridge: Cambridge University Press, 2004), 2; also the metaphor *šiṭir šamê*, heavenly writing, 1. Gudea, the king of Lagash, has a dream vision in which he sees Nisaba, the goddess of grain and scribal arts, consulting a lapis 'tablet with the stars of the heavens' (*dub mul-an-kù*) to find the best time for building a tem-

seen as stellar writing to show the evidence of divine intentions to those initiated into its secrets. Erica Reiner notes an Uruk tablet that correlates the parts
of the liver with a god, a month and a constellation, including zodiacal ones,
thus reinforcing the connection between sky and earth, and the importance of
considering the heavenly counterpart.[20] (We shall find a similar relationship
between the liver and the sky in Etruscan hepatoscopy.) A well-known statement from a Babylonian diviner's manual makes clear the relationship between
the two types of divination: 'The signs on earth together with those of the sky
give us signals. Sky and earth both bring us portents, each separately but not
different, since sky and earth are interconnected'.[21]

In addition to hepatoscopy, extispicy, astral omens and astrology, another
Mesopotamian divinatory practice is also relevant for this study. Hemerologies and menologies were used to find favourable days for performing certain
actions or rituals, by finding the 'right' or 'propitious' days for these. The Assyrian word *adannu*/Sumerian UD.DA.KAM is the word for this 'propitious' or 'fate-
ful' day. There is an interesting similarity of meaning here with the Greek word
kairos, which is also associated with divination and proper time of beginning
a ritual (see below, pp. 17–18). Earlier hemerologies were later correlated to
zodiac signs in the Persian period (ca. 5th c. BCE). More will be said about the
kairos in connection with katarchic astrology later in this essay.

Our focus until now has been mainly on omens, but oracles as well have great
relevance for the origins of questions in astrology. There is evidence of oracle
practice in Mesopotamia after the eighth century BCE, most often directed to
the sun god Shamash, who was also the god of oracles. However, the tradition
begins much earlier in Egypt, ca. 1500 BCE (the New Kingdom).[22]

---

ple to Ningirsu. See Ulla Koch-Westenholz, *Mesopotamian Astrology: An Introduction to Babylonian and Assyrian Celestial Divination* (Copenhagen: Museum Tusculanum Press, 1995), 32–33. This tablet, as well as being a lapis model of the heavens (see W.C. Horowitz, *Mesopotamian Cosmic Geography* [Winona Lake, IN: Eisenbrauns 1998], 180), could be interpreted as a 'tablet of heavenly writing', as Åke Sjöberg suggested: see Rochberg, *Heavenly Writing*, 64, citing Å. Sjöberg and E. Bergmann, *The Collection of the Sumerian Temple Hymns*, Texts from Cuneiform Sources 3 (Locust Valley, NY: J.J. Augustin, 1969), 138b.

20   Erica Reiner, *Astral Magic in Babylonia*, vol. 85 no. 4 (Philadelphia: Transactions of the American Philosophical Society, 1995), 78. I thank Deborah Houlding for this reference.

21   Trans. Koch-Westenholz, *Mesopotamian Astrology*, 138, lines 36–40, modified. Cuneiform Tablet, K. 2847, in the British Museum.

22   Jean-Marie Kruchten, 'Oracles', in *The Ancient Gods Speak: A Guide to Egyptian Religion*, ed. Donald B. Redford (New York: Oxford University Press, 2002), 299; Françoise Dunand and Christiane Zivie-Coche, *Gods and Men in Egypt: 3000 BCE to 395 CE*, trans. David Lorton (Ithaca, NY: Cornell University Press, 2004), 121, 311.

2.2 The Egyptian Tradition

Egyptian oracles are similar to the later Greek ones, in that they are public events in which common people could participate to ask questions of a deity. However, the circumstances under which they occur, and the specific practices and personnel involved, are different. We should note at the outset the difference between oracles and omens: an oracle is initiated by a human to a god who answers the question of a human, an answer which may require interpretation. An omen, by contrast, originates from god to human via a sign understood as such by humans, and which is then interpreted to determine the answer.[23]

In Egypt, oracles often took place in public processions, where a god, represented by a statue, was paraded on a ceremonial barque. People therefore asked questions of the god in public, in a public ritual. The interpretation of the question and answer was provided by priests of the god. Often that god was Amun, the premier god of the New Kingdom, who was called *Nb-nṯrw*, 'lord of gods'. The earliest attestation of this practice is during the reign of Queen Hatshepsut, (ca. 1479–1457 BCE), when she asks Amun the best way to go to Punt. In another example her nephew, Thutmose III, was chosen by the god in his barque, who 'perambulated' and 'settled' in front of the prince (a stela from Karnak describes this).[24] Descriptions of oracles can be found both on stelae and papyri, and in Ptolemaic and Roman Egypt we find Oracular Amuletic Decrees that were protective in a medical context.

Oracle practice contrasts with more private forms of divination such as dream interpretation, also an important concern in Egypt. Dream books were used to interpret the events and characters in a dream, of which the oldest examples come from the late Ramesside period, though they may reflect earlier practices. Parallel characteristics, symbolism, or even wordplays connect the thing dreamt of and the prediction.

An example of interpretation is:

> If she gives birth to a cat, she will have many children
> If she gives birth to a dog, she will have a boy
> If she gives birth to an ass, she will have an idiot child
> If she gives birth to a crocodile, she will have many children[25]

---

23   von Lieven, Alexandra, 'Divination in Ägypten' *Altorientalische Forschungen* 26, no. 1 (1999): 78.

24   Kruchten, 'Oracles', 299; for Thutmose's relationship to Hatshepsut, see Ann Macy Roth, 'Genealogy of Hatshepsut's Family', in *Hatshepsut: From Queen to Pharaoh*, ed. Roehrig et al. (New York/New Haven: Metropolitan Museum of Art/Yale University Press, 2005), 7.

25   Dunand and Zivie-Coche, *Gods and Men*, 135; trans. based on Serge Sauneron, 'Les songes

What is interesting about such interpretations for our purposes is their word-ing in the form of an if/then statement, just as we saw in the Mesopotamian *protasis/apodosis* practice for the interpretation of astral omens. This format will continue to be important as we move into astrology.

The Egyptians, like the Mesopotamians and Greeks, also used hemerologies and menologies from the Middle Kingdom onwards, and their use extended well past the Greco-Roman period.[26] Days were classified as lucky or unlucky, and each day was divided into thirds (morning, middle of the day, and dusk/evening; it is unclear whether night was included). Each part was designated as good (*nfr*), dangerous (*ꜥḥꜣ*), or uncertain (*ꜥḥꜥ*).[27] A further divinatory use of days and months is described by Herodotus, who writes that 'The Egyptians, too, found out to which god every month and day belongs, and to tell by the day of a man's birth what fortune he will have, when he will die and what manner of man he is'.[28] This description could have been based on Egyptian practices such as deities of good fortune being connected to a particular month (Shepset).[29] The five epagomenal days at the end of the year were seen as unfortunate and dangerous.[30] We can compare the practices of assigning qualitative values to days, and assigning them to deities, to the astrological techniques of electing fortunate times to begin something, and the assignment of days of the week and hours of the day to specific gods.

---

et leur interprétation dans l'Égypte ancienne', in *Les songes et leur interprétation*, collected by Serge Sauneron et al. (Paris: Éditions du Seuil, 1959), 37; see also Luigi Prada, 'Dreams, Rising Stars and Falling Geckos: Divination in Ancient Egypt', *Egyptian Archaeology* 51 (2017): 5–6.

26 Examples include the Cairo Calendar (P. Cairo JE 86637), P. Sallier IV recto, BM 10474 and even Coptic hemerologies such as P. Heidelberg Inv. Kopt. 236. See, e.g., Christof-fer Theis, 'Searching for a Source of the Coptic Hemerology: Diachronic and Synchronic Approaches', *Mythos* 16 n. s. (2016): 66–67 (history of Egyptian Pharaonic and Coptic hemerologies); also Franziska Naether and Micah Ross, 'Interlude: A Series containing a Hemerology with Lengths of Daylight', *Egitto e Vicino Oriente* 31 (2008): 52–91; Rolf Krauss, 'Egyptian Calendars and Astronomy', in *Cambridge History of Science*, Volume 1, *Ancient Science*, eds Alexander Jones and Liba Taub (Cambridge: Cambridge University Press, 2018), 140–141.

27 See Theis, 'Coptic Hemerology', 67; also Christian Leitz, *Tagewählerei. Das Buch ḥꜣt nḥḥ pḥ.wy ḏt und verwandte Texte, Part 1*. Vol. 55, Ägyptologische Abhandlungen (Wiesbaden: Harrassowitz, 1994), e.g. 51–52, ꜣḥt [Akhet] 25', for examples of the three types.

28 Herodotus, *The Histories of Herodotus of Halicarnassus*, trans. Harry Carter (London: Oxford University Press, 1962), II, 82.1, 123.

29 See Dorian Gieseler Greenbaum, *The Daimon in Hellenistic Astrology: Origins and Influ-ence* (Leiden/Boston: Brill, 2016), 53, 101 and n. 115.

30 Dimitri Meeks, 'Demons', in *The Ancient Gods Speak*, ed. Donald B. Redford (New York: Oxford University Press, 2002), 105; Anne-Sophie von Bomhard, *The Naos of the Decades: From the Observation of the Sky to Mythology and Astrology*, trans. Ludwig von Bomhard (Oxford: Institute of Archaeology, University of Oxford, 2008), 181 n.c, 183.

2.3   *The Greek Tradition*

When we move across the Mediterranean to Greece, the practice of assigning positive or negative values to days is also present, in a system of propitious and unpropitious days promoted by Hesiod in the last section of his *Works and Days* (the 'days' part of the poem, lines 764–828). For example, Hesiod associates propitious days with Zeus, saying 'Mark the days which come from Zeus, duly telling your slaves of them, and that the thirtieth day of the month is best for one to look over the work and deal out supplies. For these are days which come from Zeus the all-wise, when men discern aright'.[31] In *L'Astrologie grecque*, Bouché-Leclercq extensively analyses Hesiod's system, including the specific days and times of day for specific actions, by specific gods, and its implications for later astrological practice, calling Hesiod's times and works the 'berceau de la théorie des Initiatives'[32] The examples outlined here and above show that this kind of practice was fairly common in the Mediterranean region.[33]

For the Greeks, though, and for the purposes of this study, it was oracles that became a significant and enduring divinatory legacy through more than a millennium of Greek civilisation. As we shall see, oracle practice also had a lasting impact on the practice of katarchic astrology and the genre of asking questions that became known as interrogations. For now, it will suffice to present the typical topics (see Table 1.1 below, p. 12) and questions asked of oracles, in this case examples from the Oracle at Dodona:

Typical examples of questions are:[34]

- 'God ... Good Luck. About possessions and about a place to live: whether (it would be) better for him and his children and his wife in Kroton?' Response: 'In Kroton'
- 'God ... Good Luck. Archonidas asks the god whether I should sail into Sicily?'
- 'And if it would be better for me to work with Diotimos, in Megara?'
- 'God. Fortune. Lysias asks the god whether he will do better by sticking with the sea and taking a share of a ship? Answer: You should do nothing by land'.
- [asked by a slave] 'What will happen to me if I leave?/Shall I make it happen?' Answer: 'The woman remains/O woman, stay!'
- 'God. Fortune. Alkinoos asks Zeus Naios and Dione if it will be to the advantage of Nikeas to build the workshop?'

---

31   Hesiod, *Works and Days*, 764–769, in *Hesiod, Homeric Hymns, Epic Cycle, Homerica*, trans. Hugh G. Evelyn-White, Loeb Classical Library (Cambridge, MA/London: Harvard University Press, 1914 (1995)), 58–59.

32   Auguste Bouché-Leclercq, *L'astrologie grecque* (Paris: E. Leroux, 1899) 459–461, quotation on 459.

33   See also Bouché-Leclercq, 461–462.

34   Esther Eidinow, *Oracles, Curses and Risk among the Ancient Greeks* (Oxford: Oxford University Press, 2007) 76–120.

- 'Did Dorkilos steal the cloth?'
- 'Lysanias asked Zeus Naos and Dione whether the child with which Annyla is pregnant is not from him?'

TABLE 1.1   Topics of Oracle Questions, from Dodona*

Travel (sea journeys, moving house, moving for a job)
Women, marriage
Children
Work (various occupations)
Slavery
Health and disease
Property
Prosperity and Safety
Ritual Activity
Military Campaigns
Judicial Activity
City Affairs and Politics
Crime (especially stolen property)
Questions Concerning an Inquiry (what the petitioner may have in mind)

Eidinow, *Oracles*, 72–121.

We shall return to the subject of Greek oracle practices in comparison with astrological practices in Part 3 of this essay.

2.4   *Etruscan Traditions*

The Etruscan tradition of liver divination, as mentioned above, had commonalities with Mesopotamian hepatoscopy, from which it derives in part. A connection between Mesopotamian hepatoscopy and Etruscan hepatoscopy has long been known;[35] recent research reveals the details of the connections and influence from practices carried by emigrants from Anatolia into Etruscan lands.[36]

---

35   Reiner, *Astral Magic*, 63, citing Jean Nougayrol, 'Les rapports des haruspicines étrusque et assyro-babylonienne, et la foie d'argile de *Falerii Veteres* (Villa Giulia 3786)', *Comptes rendus des séances de l'Académie des Inscriptions et Belles-Lettres* 99 no. 4 (1955): 509–519; Walter Burkert, *The Orientalizing Revolution: Near Eastern Influence on Greek Culture in the Early Archaic Age* (Cambridge, MA: Harvard University Press, 1992, repr. 1995), 46–48; Derek Collins, 'Mapping the Entrails: The Practice of Greek Hepatoscopy', *American Journal of Philology* 129, no. 3 (2008): 325–327; K. Ulanowski, *Neo-Assyrian and Greek Divination in War*, Vol. 3, Ancient Warfare (Leiden/Boston: Brill, 2021), 478–479.

36   Mary R. Bachvarova, 'The Transmission of Liver Divination from East to West', *Studi Micenei ed Egeo-Anatolici* 54 (2012): 143–164.

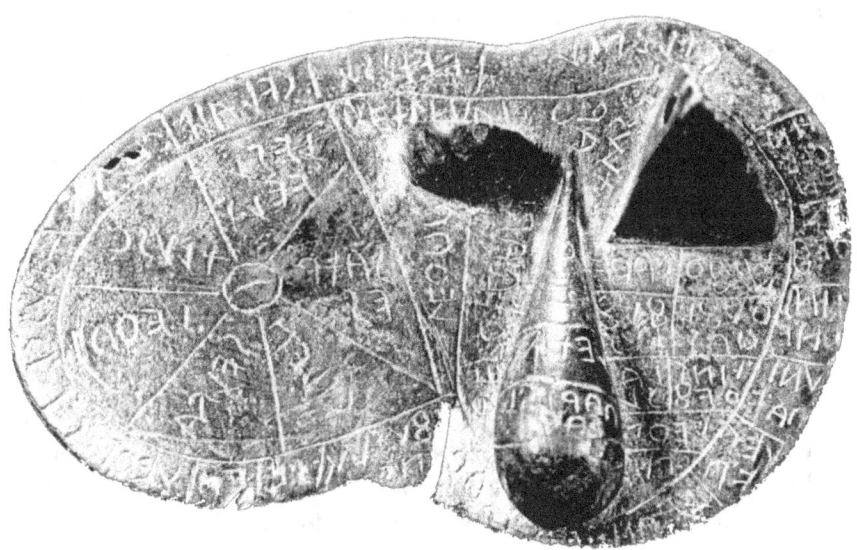

FIGURE 1.1   The Piacenza Liver
FROM LAMMERT BOUKE VAN DER MEER, *THE BRONZE LIVER OF PIACENZA:
ANALYSIS OF A POLYTHEISTIC STRUCTURE*, 1987

Using the Piacenza liver as an example, the liver is divided into sixteen sections, each correlated with a divinity and a portion of the sky. It demonstrates
the connection between liver divination and celestial divination, especially
through lightning, an Etruscan specialty. Both Pliny (*NH* II, 55.142–144) and
Cicero (*De div*. II.xviii.42)[37] mention 16 regions of the heavens and their connection with divination by lightning. In an astrological context, the divinities of
certain regions correlate with places in the 'Circle of Athla', a doctrine outlined
in Manilius.[38] In his *Marriage of Philology and Mercury*, Martianus Capella
(ca. 420–490) speaks of sixteen regions linked to divinities, and his list has been
shown to have both Etruscan and astrological connotations.[39] We shall be looking later at the Circle of Athla in connection with katarchic astrology.

37   Pliny the Elder. *Natural History*, Vol. 1, trans. Harris Rackham, Loeb Classical Library (Cam-
      bridge, MA: Harvard University Press, 1938); Cicero, *De divinatione*, trans. W.A. Falconer,
      in *On Old Age, On Friendship, On Divination*, Loeb Classical Library (Cambridge, MA/Lon-
      don: Harvard University Press, 1923, repr. 2001).

38   Bouché-Leclercq, *L'astrologie grecque*, 298n2; Greenbaum, *Daimon in Hellenistic Astrology*,
      294–296.

39   Stefan Weinstock, 'Martianus Capella and the Cosmic System of the Etruscans', *Journal of
      Roman Studies* 36.1 and 2 (1946): 101–129.

By the second century BCE, we begin to find astrologers connected with both liver or entrail divination and astrology.[40] Sudines served either Attalus I (241–197 BCE) or Eumenes II (187–159 BCE) as an entrail diviner at the court in Pergamon (there are accounts of this by Polyaenus (*Stratagems* 4.20) and Frontinus (*Stratagems* I, XI.15)); Vettius Valens quoted a Soudines on lunar tables.[41] He was also mentioned by Strabo (*Geography*, 16.1.6) as an astrologer.[42]

Posidonius (135 BCE–51 BCE), the Stoic philosopher and astrologer born in Apamea, Syria, is cited by Cicero on entrail divination in his treatise *On Divination*, saying: '… I am ashamed of Chrysippus, Antipater and Posidonius, who say exactly the same as you've said: "The guiding hand to the choice of a victim is a divine sentient force that permeates the whole universe".'[43] In the first century BCE, Nigidius Figulus (d. 45 BCE), a friend of Cicero, was an astrologer and intellectual[44] who, among other works, also transcribed an Etruscan calendar on thunder omens ('brontoscopic calendar').[45] A fragment of his on Egyptian astrology survives.[46] He was also likely an astrological source, through Cornelius Labeo, for Martianus Capella.[47]

---

40   Note: Geoffrey Cornelius used the following examples in showing connections between extispicy and astral omens; see *Moment of Astrology* 2003, 134.

41   Vettius Valens, *Anthologiarum libri novem*, ed. David Pingree (Leipzig: B.G. Teubner, 1986), IX, 12.10, 339.21.

42   For more on Sudines and his connections with liver divination and astrology, see Kathryn Stevens, *Between Greece and Babylonia: Hellenistic Intellectual History in Cross-Cultural Perspective* (Cambridge: Cambridge University Press, 2019), 57, 88, 92, 163, 231–236. See also Franz Cumont, *Astrology and Religion among the Greeks and Romans* (New York/London: G.P. Putnam's Sons, 1912), 56–57: 'Another Chaldaean, Soudines, invited to the court of Attalus I., king of Pergamus, practised there, about the year 238, the methods of divination in vogue in his native land, such as the inspection of the liver (ἡπατοσκοπία), and he continued to be an authority frequently quoted by the later "mathematici".'

43   Cicero, *De div.*, II.xv.35, responding to Quintus's assertions about this in I.lii.118 f.

44   Alun Hudson-Williams and Anthony J.S. Spawforth, 'Nigidius Figulus, Publius', in *Oxford Classical Dictionary*, 3rd ed., eds Simon Hornblower and Anthony Spawforth (Oxford/New York: Oxford University Press, 1996), 1044; see also Stephan Heilen, 'Ancient Scholars on the Horoscope of Rome', *Culture and Cosmos* 11 (2007): 64–67.

45   Nigidius Figulus, *P. Nigidii Figuli Operum Reliquiae*, ed. A. Swoboda, Prague 1889, fr. 83, 93–106 (in Greek); John Lydus, *Ioannis Laurentii Lydi Liber de Ostentis et Calendaria Graeca Omnia*, ed. C. Wachsmuth, Leipzig 1897, 62–88. See also Jean MacIntosh Turfa, *Divining the Etruscan World: the Brontoscopic Calendar and Religious Practice* (Cambridge: Cambridge University Press, 2012).

46   See Nigidius Figulus ed. Swoboda, 128.

47   Weinstock, 'Martianus Capella', 116n87.

2.5   *Augury and the Sky*[48]

One more divinatory practice relevant for the purposes of this essay is the Roman tradition of augury—looking at the sky for omens, especially the flights of birds, but also clouds, lightning and other celestial phenomena. Augury was the premier state-sanctioned form of divination in Rome. Cicero, in fact, was a member of the college of augurs, despite his criticisms of divination generally. Looking for omens in the sky was a practice traceable even to the early kings of Rome. It is worth reviewing this practice, as it illustrates the process showing the connections between sky and earth that make the divination possible. The augury took place in an open rectangular space, divided by lines into four regions, called a *templum*. Within that space was the *auguraculum*, a small rectangular space where the augur was; there he marked out in imaginary lines a corresponding space in the sky with a special staff called a *lituus*.[49] This celestial space was also designated as a *templum*. The signs given in the sky corresponded with the earthly space to produce the augury.[50] It is worth noting that *templum* is the word Manilius often uses for the astrological places in his *Astronomica*.

Both Romulus, the first king of Rome, and Numa Pompilius, the second, used augury to sanctify their accessions in accordance with the will of the gods. For Romulus,

> ... when the time was come, he rose at break of day and went forth from his tent. Then, taking his stand under the open sky in a clear space and first offering the customary sacrifice, he prayed to King Jupiter and to the other gods that he had chosen ... that, if it was their pleasure he should be king of the city, some favourable signs might appear in the sky.[51]

---

48   In this section, I am indebted to Deborah Houlding's previous work on this topic, in her lecture 'Ancient Enquiry Charts', UAC 2012.

49   Described by Livy, *The History of Rome*, Vol. 1, trans. W.M. Roberts (New York: E.P. Dutton, 1912), I, 18.5–10; see below.

50   Smith, William, William Wayte and G.E. Marindin, eds., *A Dictionary of Greek and Roman Antiquities*, London: John Murray, 1890, s.v. TEMPLUM. At the Perseus Digital Library, https://www.perseus.tufts.edu/hopper/text?doc=Perseus%3Atext%3A1999.04.0063%3Aalphabetic+letter%3DT%3Aentry+group%3D1%3Aentry%3Dtemplum-cn (accessed 2 Dec 2023).

51   Dionysius of Halicarnassus, *The Roman Antiquities*, Vol. 1, trans. Earnest Cary, Loeb Classical Library (Cambridge, MA/London, 1937), II, 5.1–2.

Likewise, Numa's augur prayed: 'Father Jupiter, if it be heaven's will that this Numa Pompilius, whose head I hold, should be king of Rome, do thou signify it to us by sure signs within those boundaries which I have traced'.[52]

The orientation of the places used in the augury is also significant:

> [7] After surveying the prospect over the City and surrounding country, he [Numa's augur] offered prayers and marked out the heavenly regions by an imaginary line from east to west; the southern he defined as 'the right hand,' the northern as 'the left hand.' [8] He then fixed upon an object, as far as he could see, as a corresponding mark ... [10] Then he described in the usual formula the augury which he desired should be sent. They were sent, and Numa being by them manifested to be king, came down from the 'templum.'[53]

As the historian Dionysius of Halicarnassus remarked: '... the best seat and station for those who take the auspices is that which looks toward the east, from whence both the Sun and the Moon rise as well as the planets and fixed stars'.[54] This eastern orientation fits well, in fact, with the layout of an astrological chart, where east is the point of the Ascendant (the sign rising on the eastern horizon). If one looks east, then south (where the culminating point, the Midheaven, is located) is on the right and north is on the left.

The next part of this essay will show how these forms of divination become adapted within the practice of Hellenistic astrology, especially within the branch of katarchic astrology.

3   Divination and Astrology

The divinatory traditions in the previous section show similarities with the development of an astrological system that includes techniques to relate events on earth to events in the sky. We have already seen this correlation explicitly laid out in the quotation from the Babylonian Diviner's Manual. The heavens as divine, and the associations of gods with parts of the sky—planets as gods are the obvious example here—and the urge for humans to connect with the

---

52   Livy, *History of Rome*, Vol. 1, I, 18.9.
53   Livy, Vol. 1, I, 18.7–8, 10.
54   Dionysius of Halicarnassus, *Roman Antiquities* Vol. 1, II, 5.2.

divine in the cosmos, occur in all Mediterranean cultures. As Plato remarks in the *Timaeus*, '... we are not an earthly but a heavenly plant'.[55]

As astrology develops in the Mediterranean world from the Hellenistic period, and elements from both Babylon[56] and Egypt[57] begin to be incorporated into a system that now is called Hellenistic astrology, the divine components of the desire to know what the gods want us to do, and that they have a means to communicate this to us through the sky, come into astrology as well. These produced what the ancients came to call katarchic astrology, and what we call, usually by separate names, elections, events, interrogations and decumbiture. There are two important words associated with this development: *katarchē* and *kairos*.

3.1   *Katarchē, Kairos and Ritual*

The word *katarchē* (καταρχή), which can mean just 'beginning'—or 'initiative' or 'inception'—is the word used specifically for the beginning of a ritual,[58] and this is associated with *kairos* (καιρός), the right and proper time to begin a sacred process. *Kairos* was briefly mentioned above when discussing a similar concept in Mesopotamian divination, *adannu* (UD.DA.KAM).[59] This prac-

---

55   Plato, *Timaeus*, trans. R.G. Bury, in *Plato*, IX, Loeb Classical Library (Cambridge, MA: Harvard University Press, 1929, repr. 1989), 90ᵃ–c, trans. R.G. Bury, modified. The full quotation is: '... we say god has given each of us, as his daimon, that which is housed at the summit of our body, and which raises us from earth to our kindred in heaven, since we are not an earthly but a heavenly plant.'

56   These include the sexagesimal system, astral events portending the health of the king and the state, and the eventual development of personal natal astrology not only for the king but for anyone (see, e.g., Rochberg, *Heavenly Writing*, 35 and Chapter 4).

57   Including the Ascendant, Midheaven and the places (houses) of the chart representing areas of life experience and decans (see Alexandra von Lieven, *Grundriss des Laufes der Sterne. Das sogennante Nutbuch*, Vol. 1, *Text*, Vol. 31, Carsten Niebuhr Institute Publications, The Carlsberg Papyri 8 (Copenhagen: Museum Tusculanum Press, 2007), 146; Dorian Gieseler Greenbaum and Micah Ross, 'The Role of Egypt in the Development of the Horoscope', in *Egypt in Transition: Social and Religious Development of Egypt in the First Millennium BCE*, eds L. Bareš, F. Coppens and K. Smolarikova (Prague: Faculty of Arts, Charles University in Prague, 2010), 146–182.

58   LSJ, s.v. κατάρχω: in its middle form, 'begin the sacrificial ceremonies' or 'begin the rite'.

59   See Daniel Bodi, 'Akkadian and Aramaic Terms for a "Favorable Time" (*ḫidānu, adānu*, and *'iddān*): Semitic Precursors of Greek *kairos*?', in *Time and History in the Ancient Near East. Proceedings of the 56th Rencontre Assyriologique Internationale at Barcelona 26–30 July 2010*, eds L. Feliu, J. Llop, A. Millet Albà and J. Sanmartín, 47–56, (Winona Lake, IN: Eisenbrauns, 2013), 47, 52–56; Greenbaum, 'Hellenistic Horoscope', 355; Greenbaum, 'Divination and Decumbiture', 112.

tice comes to intersect with astrology, specifically in creating an astrological *katarchē* for a ritual.

Porphyry, the philosopher, Neoplatonist and astrologer, (232–c. 305 CE) wrote about the usefulness of astrology in determining the moment for a ritual on consecrating statues. His *Letter to Anebo* contains a passage which suggests that astrology as divination is being used in an interrogational manner to predict whether rituals will be successful:

> 'But these [who generate effective images],' the letter says, 'observe the movement of the heavenly bodies, and they tell, from the presiding[60] of a given star with another or others around the heavens, whether the divination will be true or false, and whether the rites performed will be of no purpose, or have annunciatory power and bring about the [desired] effects (ἀποτελεστικά[61]).'[62]

This passage is quoted by Porphyry's contemporary and fellow Neoplatonist Iamblichus in *On the Mysteries*,[63] who also mentions what is obviously katarchic astrology in association with beginning a ritual. Taking his cue from the Egyptian astrologers, Iamblichus knows of the opportune moment (*kairos*) at which theurgic rituals should be 'begun ... without ... bringing to bear anything other than the observation of the opportune moment. (*kairos*)'.[64] Thus

---

60   Iamblichus, *On The Mysteries*, ed. trans, and comm. E.C. Clarke, J.M. Dillon and J.P. Hershbell. (Atlanta: Society of Biblical Literature, 2003). Clarke/Dillon/Hershbell have 'ranging' but the verb is πολεύω, an astrological term referring to planets which preside over a birth or even over times of the day; this is where the idea of planetary hours arises. (See Paulus Alexandrinus, *Elementa Apotelesmatica*, ed. E. Boer (Leipzig: B.G. Teubner, 1958), ch. 21, pp. 41–42; D.G. Greenbaum, *Late Classical Astrology: Paulus Alexandrinus and Olympiodorus with the Scholia from Later Commentators*, trans. and annot. D.G. Greenbaum, ed. Robert Hand (Reston, VA: ARHAT, 2001), 39 and n. 1).

61   This word is very close to the astrological 'apotelesmatika'.

62   Porphyry, *Lettera ad Anebo*, ed. A.R. Sodano (Naples: L'arte tipographia, 1958), 2.6c Sodano = *DM* III.30 [173.7–10] trans. Clarke/Dillon/Hershbell, modified. Ἀλλὰ παρατηροῦσιν οὗτοι, φησί, τὴν τῶν οὐρανίων φοράν, καὶ λέγουσι τίνος τῶν κατ' οὐρανὸν μετὰ τίνος ἢ τίνων πολεύοντος ἔσται ψευδῆ τὰ μαντεῖα ἢ ἀληθῆ, καὶ τὰ δρώμενα ἀργὰ ἢ ἀπαγγελτικὰ ἢ ἀποτελεστικά.

63   This is the modern title given by Marsilio Ficino to the work originally entitled *The Reply of the Master Abamon to the Letter of Porphyry to Anebo, and the Solutions to the Questions it Contains* (Ἀβάμμωνος διδασκάλου πρὸς τὴν Πορφυρίου πρὸς Ἀνεβὼ ἐπιστολὴν ἀπόκρισις καὶ τῶν ἐν αὐτῇ ἀπορημάτων λύσεις): see Clarke/Dillon/Hershbell, xlviii and n. 110, 2–3.

64   The full quotation in *DM* VIII, 4, 267.6–10, trans. Clarke, Dillon, Hershbell, slightly modified: 'but they recommend that we ascend through the practice of sacred theurgy to the regions that are higher, more universal and superior to fate, towards the god who is the creator, without calling in the aid of matter or bringing to bear anything other than the

additional evidence in this Neoplatonic text by Iamblichus shows that these rituals were elected astrologically.

Even more evidence appears in the late 4th c.-early 5th c. astrologer Hephaestio, where two passages in Book III of his *Apotelesmatika* describe what parts of the chart represent a ritual—one for making supplication with a prayer (III, 7.18) and one for an animal sacrifice (III, 6.11). The supplication through prayer reads:

> [20] The supplications and prayers are known as follows: [21] The Hour-marker is the supplicant; the Setting place, the sacrifice [22] which he offers; the Midheaven, the god; and the Underground [23] centrepin signifies whether the prayers may be heard and the [24] matter about which the person is praying and inquiring.[65]

The second example designates the places in the chart that show the components of the ritual for a sacrifice:

> The composed *katarchē* points out each [part of the ritual] before the opening of the animal: the Hour-marker reveals the one making the sacrifice; the Setting [place] that which is sacrificed or the sacrificial victim; the Midheaven the god or gods; the Underground [place] the reason for the altar,[66] the completion of the matter and how it is sacrificed. One must carefully consider the stars—in what places they are, their position and phase, and the four lots—Fortune, Daimon, Necessity, Eros ...[67]

---

observation of the opportune moment (*kairos*).' ἀλλὰ καὶ διὰ τῆς ἱερατικῆς θεουργίας ἀναβαίνειν ἐπὶ τὰ ὑψηλότερα καὶ καθολικώτερα καὶ τῆς εἱμαρμένης ὑπερκείμενα παραγγέλλουσι πρὸς τὸν θεὸν καὶ δημιουργόν, μήτε ὕλην προσποιουμένους μήτε ἄλλο τι προσπαραλαμβάνοντας ἢ μόνον καιροῦ παρατήρησιν]. For more on the topic of katarchic astrology in Iamblichus, see Gregory Shaw, *Theurgy and the Soul: The Neoplatonism of Iamblichus* (University Park, PA: The Pennsylvania State University Press, 1995), 201; and discussion of this passage in Crystal Addey, *Divination and Theurgy in Neoplatonism: Oracles of the Gods* (Farnham, Surrey/Burlington, VT: Ashgate, 2014), 105–106.

65   Hephaestio of Thebes, *Apotelesmaticorum libri tres*, ed. David Pingree, 2 vols. (Leipzig: B.G. Teubner, 1973), vol. 1, Book III, 7.18, p. 259.20–24, my translation. Αἱ δὲ προσελεύσεις καὶ εὐχαὶ γιγνώσκονται οὕτως· / ὁ μὲν ὡροσκόπος ἐστὶν ὁ εὐχόμενος, τὸ δὲ δῦνον τὸ θῦμα / ὃ προσφέρει, τὸ δὲ μεσουράνημα ὁ θεός, τὸ δὲ ὑπὸ γῆν / κέντρον σημαίνει εἰ ἐπήκοοι τῶν εὐχῶν εἶεν καὶ περὶ τοῦ / πράγματος οὗ τις εὔχεται καὶ πυνθάνεται.

66   I.e., why a sacrifice is needed.

67   Heph. III, 6.11, pp. 253.20–254.4 Pingree (my translation). Ἀποδείκνυσι δὲ ἕκαστα πρὸ τῆς ἀναπτύξεως τοῦ ζῴου / διατεθεῖσα ἡ καταρχή, καὶ μηνύουσιν ὁ μὲν ὡροσκόπος τὸν / θύοντα, τὸ δὲ δῦνον τὸ θυόμενον ἢ τὸ ἱερεῖον, τὸ δὲ μεσουράνημα τὸν θεὸν ἢ τοὺς θεούς, τὸ δὲ ὑπόγειον τὴν /

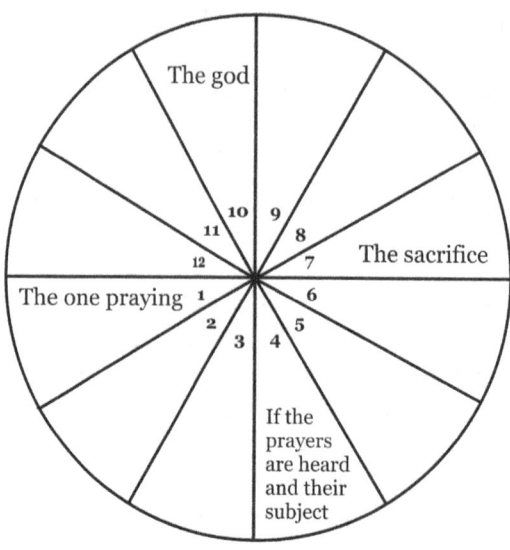

The god

The one praying

The sacrifice

If the prayers are heard and their subject

FIGURE 1.2
Diagram showing the places of the chart representing the prayer and supplication ritual

Instructions for interpretation follow in III, 6.12–17, where the parts of the animal (called both innards [σπλάγχνα] and liver [ἧπαρ]) are correlated to the planets and the zodiac; these are a kind of sacrificial melothesia. The right and left parts of the entrails correlate with the upper and lower hemispheres of the chart respectively, and the planets and signs are each assigned parts of the body.

We see, therefore, the same coordination of entrails/liver and sky as in Etruscan and Babylonian hepatoscopy, but now in a specifically astrological setting. This provides yet another connection between other forms of divination and astrological *katarchai* that is present throughout a millennium of history. In addition, this practice is reminiscent of an Uruk text of the Seleucid period (late 4th–1st c. BCE) mentioned by Erica Reiner, that makes the same kinds of correlations between the liver and gall bladder (in this instance), with months of the year, zodiacal signs and heliacal risings of constellations.[68] It takes only a small step to imagine that the culmination of such an arrangement lies here in Hephaestio's *katarchê* for a sacrifice, melding liver, signs and planets together. Other Babylonian texts combine the Moon and the zodiac in determining the best time for beginning an activity (e.g. BRM 4, 19 and 20), causing Reiner

---

(254) τῆς ἑστίας αἰτίαν καὶ τὴν ἔκβασιν τοῦ πράγματος καὶ δι' / ὃ θύεται· τούς τε ἀστέρας ἐπιθεωρητέον ἐν οἷς γέ εἰσι / τόποις καὶ τάξει καὶ φάσει καὶ τοὺς τέσσαρας κλήρους—/ τύχης, δαίμονος, ἀνάγκης, ἔρωτος.

68　　See Reiner, *Astral Magic*, 77–79.

The god or gods

The sacrificial victim

Person making the sacrifice

Reason for the sacrifice and how it is done

FIGURE 1.3
Hephaestio of Thebes, *Apoteles-matika*, III, 6.11. Diagram showing the places of the chart representing a ritual of animal sacrifice

to remark that 'By determining the propitious time for initiating an activity, the genre represents an early example of the process known as catarchic astrology'.[69]

Bouché-Leclercq had already considered the relationships of the Mesopotamian and Egyptian material to the Greek and Latin, and suggested that katarchic astrology, in the form of choosing the right moment to begin something, is the oldest form of astrology in those places, based on the practices of its divinatory and omen-interpreting forbears, and that natal astrology developed from it:

> clients who asked them [astrologers] if the moment was favourable or not for such an enterprise. This kind of method, known by the name 'Initiatives' (Καταρχαί) or opportunities, was the normal occupation and sustenance of popular astrology. It contains the germ of genethlialogy, which emerged from it and returned as a hybrid combination, as we will see in due course. (My translation.)[70]

69   Reiner, 110–111; see also Amar Annus's summary of Reiner at the Melammu Project, 'The beginnings of catarchic astrology', http://www.melammu-project.eu/database/gen_html/a0001339.html (accessed 5 Dec 2023).

70   Bouché-Leclercq, *L'astrologie grecque*, 83, '... clients qui leur demandaient si le moment était ou non favorable pour telle enterprise. Ce genre de calculs, connu sous le nom d'"Initiatives" (Καταρχαί) ou opportunités, a été l'occupation normale et l'aliment de l'astrologie populaire. Il contient en germe la généthlialogie, qui en est sortie et qui y est

In using the words 'Initiatives' (his translation of καταρχαί) or 'opportunités', Bouché-Leclercq means elections, that is, selecting the most opportune time (*l'opportunité*) for doing something. He brings up the related practice of interrogations, but is of the not implausible opinion that these follow from elections, and came about as a way to compete with other forms of divination for clients, who could ask any question they liked of the haruspex, dream interpreter or lot caster (to mention three of his examples).[71] If astrology could find a method for answering such queries, it could be more lucrative for its practitioners (though Bouché-Leclercq questions the logic of the theory behind it).[72] It is, however, clear enough that whether the practice of katarchic astrology literally asks a question or seeks the best time to begin an action, the questioning attitude is intrinsic to the process, and the rationale and methods underlying an election or an interrogation are similar and related. It is also clear that the practices are happening within the same historical timeframes. We find Propertius, Juvenal, Tacitus, Petronius and others writing about the uses of katarchic astrology in all of its forms from the 1st c. BCE to the 2nd c. CE and beyond.[73]

We shall next look more closely at the Greek oracle tradition, which in this writer's view had an important impact on the practice of katarchic astrology.

---

rentrée à l'état de combinaison hybride, comme nous le verrons en temps et lieu.' Cited in Tim Hegedus, *Early Christianity and Ancient Astrology* (New York/Oxford: Peter Lang, 2007), 7n57. See also Bouché-Leclercq, 462 (re the principle of a god as planet ruling a moment of time astrologically, i.e. a *katarchē*): 'C'est la même principe qui a engendré la généthlialogie, ses signes et planètes natales et ses oecodespotes.'

71 Bouché-Leclercq, 469–470.

72 Bouché-Leclercq, 469. And rightly so, since the two are ontologically different.

73 Propertius, *Elegies*, ed. and trans. G.P. Goold, Loeb Classical Library (Cambridge, MA/London: Harvard University Press, 1990), Book IV, 1.71–150; and see, especially, the reconstruction in D.A. Kidd, 'Propertius Consults His Astrologer', *Greece & Rome* 26, no. 2 (1979): 169–180. Juvenal, *Satire* VI.553–591: *Juvenal. Satire 6*, eds Lindsay Watson and Patricia Watson (Oxford Classical Texts. Cambridge: Cambridge University Press, 2014). Tacitus, *Annals*, vol. 5, trans. John Jackson, Loeb Classical Library (Cambridge, MA/London: Harvard University Press, 1937), XVI.30, 1–33, 2 (the case of Servilia)—I am indebted to D. Houlding for this reference—and *Annals*, vol. 4, trans. John Jackson, Loeb Classical Library (Cambridge, MA/London: Harvard University Press, 1937), XII.68–69; see also Josèphe-Henriette Abry, 'Who was Agrippina Waiting For?', in *Horoscopes and Public Spheres: Essays on the History of Astrology*, eds Günther Oestmann, H Darrel Rutkin and Kocku von Stuckrad, (Berlin/New York: Walter de Gruyter, 2005), 39. Petronius, *The Satyricon*, trans. P.G. Walsh (Oxford: Oxford University Press, 1997), Section 30, which, though not necessarily katarchic, mentions calendars of lucky and unlucky days.

3.2   *Oracles and Astrology*

We have already seen the topics typically asked of oracles in Part 2, along with a sampling of the questions petitioners asked of them. Now we shall expand on the reasons for this, and elaborate their connections with katarchic astrology.[74]

First, the following table (Table 1.2) compares these oracle topics with typical topics common to katarchic astrology (this list comes from Dorotheus, *Carmen Astrologicum*, with correlations in Hephaestio, *Apotelesmatica*,).[75]

It should not be inferred that the similarity of topics in astrology directly results from the topics appearing in oracles, but that both forms of divination will naturally address the chief concerns of human life. Astrology provides perhaps a more accessible means to address these concerns. The typical questions asked in katarchic astrology illustrate the personal interests of the questioner in these topics, and are not dissimilar from the questions asked of oracles:

- Will my child live or die? (fol. 57^r [Mysteries 1])[76]
- Is the unborn child mine or from another? (fol. 66^r [Mysteries 1])

---

74   Note that I am not the first scholar to make comparisons between oracles and astrology, and especially katarchic astrology: see, e.g. Bouché-Leclercq, *L'astrologie grecque*, 470–471: 'C'était [katarchic astrology] une concurrence directe aux oracles qui répondaient à des questions cachetées.' See also J.L. Lightfoot, *Pseudo-Manetho Apotelesmatica Books Two, Three, and Six* (Oxford: Oxford University Press, 2020), 17–18: 'so that catarchic astrology is rather like day-to-day transactions with oracles in which cities and individuals sought advice on a projected course of action'; and 231, where she found affiliations between oracular and astrological poetry. On the superiority of katarchic astrology's rational methods over oracular pronouncements, see Richard Gordon, ' "Will my child have a big nose?": Uncertainty, authority and narrative in katarchic astrology', in *Divination in the Ancient World: Religious Options and the Individual*, ed. Veit Rosenberger (Stuttgart: Franz Steiner Verlag, 2013), 95–96, 110. Kristin M. Heineman, *The Decadence of Delphi: The Oracle in the Second Century AD and Beyond* (Abingdon UK/New York: Routledge, 2018), 142–172 suggests the popularity of astrology significantly affected the decline of the oracles between the first century BCE and the second century CE, but she does not take into consideration the many other factors affecting their decline, and her arguments are somewhat simplistic.

75   Oracle topics: Eidinow, *Oracles*, 72–121. Katarchic topics: Dorotheus of Sidon, *Carmen Astrologicum*, ed. David Pingree (Leipzig: B.G. Teubner, 1976), Book V; and Hephaestio of Thebes. *Apotelesmaticorum libri tres*, ed. David Pingree, 2 vols. (Leipzig: B.G. Teubner, 1973), Book III. These are abbreviated in Table 2: Dorotheus (Arabic version) = Dor., Hephaestio = Heph., and E. = Eidinow, followed by their respective book/chapter/sentence numbers, or page numbers. Note that Bouché-Leclercq, *L'astrologie grecque*, 469n1, also mentions connections between astrological queries and the oracle at Dodona; see also 471, on the oracle knowing the contents of sealed questions or knowing whether the client will succeed or not at the topic he is thinking of.

76   Folio numbers in this list are from Laur. plut. 28.33 (see below, Section 4.2.4, The 'Palchus' Material and Material from the 'Mysteries', pp. 44–47); Erasistratus in *CCAG* I, 94–97; Dor.

TABLE 1.2   Topics of Katarchic Questions and Oracle Questions

Katarchic Topics	Oracle Topics
Building Dor., v. 6; Heph. III, 7	*Property; buying property; construction of buildings* E. 108–109
Buying and Selling Dor., v. 9–10	*Business; trade; buying or selling property* E. 95–99
Marriage Dor. v, 16; v, 17.11; Heph. III, 9	*Marriage (to women, about women)* E. 83–87
Children Dor. v, 16.22–26	*Children* E. 89–93, 120
Journeys Dor. v, 21–22	*Travel (moving house, moving for a job)* E. 72–74; examples 75–81
Ships; Voyages Dor. v, 23–25; Heph. III, 17, 30	*Travel; sea voyages* E. 73
Letters Dor. v, 15, 26; Heph. III, 27	
Sickness Dor. v, 29, 31, 38–41; Heph., III, 31–32	*Health and disease* E. 104–107, 120
Exile; foreign journeys Dor. v, 34	*Journeys abroad* E. 74–75, 80
Fugitives; Slaves Dor. v, 11, 13, 36; Heph. III, 16, 21, 47	*Slavery* E. 101–103
Theft Dor. v, 35; Heph. III, 42–46	*Crime (especially stolen property)* E. 117–118
Rituals Heph. III, 4; III, 6.11; III, 7.18	*Ritual activity* E. 112–113
Thought-reading Heph. III, 4	*Inquiry questions/What client is thinking* E. 121.1–3
Adversaries/Who will win (later Military) Dor. v, 33; Heph. III, 4.24, 30–32	*Military campaigns* E. 113–114
Judicial activity Dor. v, 33; Heph. III, 37–38	*Judicial activity* E. 114–115
Truth of a report Heph. III, 5.12–14	*Requests for truth* E. 119.1–2
	Treasure E. 120

- What good or bad things will happen to me? (fol. 199ʳ ['Palchus'])
- Reading a sealed letter (fol. 206ᵛ ['Palchus'])
- Finding a thief (Erasistratus, fol. 210ᵛ ['Palchus'])
- If you are asked about a time when goods are stolen ... (Dor. v 35, 1)
- Moving house (fol. 220ʳ ['Palchus']); moving residence abroad (fol. 223ᵛ ['Palchus'])
- If two adversaries argue and plead before a judge, which will be successful (Dor. v 33 title)
- Will I find the slave/Will the slave return? (Serapion, fol. 226ᵛ ['Palchus'])
- Buying land and residing there (fol. 230ʳ ['Palchus'])

The popular awareness of this astrological method of asking questions can be shown by another passage from Porphyry's *Letter to Anebo*, who deplores such a frivolous use of the practice. He says, speaking of those who ask trivial questions of the divine rather than seeking knowledge of the good, and divine

---

= Dorotheus, *Carmen Astrologicum*; Serapion in *CCAG* I, 101; I have drawn these, with their folio numbers, from the helpful list in Gordon, 'Big Nose', 99–101.

TABLE 1.3   A Sampling of Katarchic Questions Compared with Oracle Questions

'What good or bad things will happen to me?' ['Palchus' fol. 199 ʳ]	'of safety and fortune' [E, p. 111]
'Is the unborn child mine or from another?' [*Mysteries* 1, fol. 66 ʳ]	'Whether the child with which Annyla is pregnant is not from him?' [E, p. 120]
'If you are asked about a man, whether he will depart from his land and his city or travel from it' [Dor. v, 34.1]	'Whether he will do better if he migrates to Alyzea?' [E, p. 76]
'the one inquiring about freeing slaves' (slave's viewpoint) [Heph. III, 21.2–3]	[asked by a slave] 'What will happen to me if I leave?' [E, p. 102]
'To know what someone wants to ask, from the Lot of Fortune' ['Palchus', fol. 200ᵛ, ch. 7]	'Whether ... what he has on his mind you also foretell as an oracle' [E, p. 121]
'To know the name of the thief' [*Mysteries* 1, fol. 21ᵛ]	'Did Dorkilos steal the cloth?' [E, p. 117]

union: 'Vain has their study of wisdom been, who worried the divine mind about finding a runaway slave, or buying a farm, or if a marriage or business deal should happen ...'[77] Be that as it may, he did not succeed in suppressing these kinds of queries.

We can see that these questions being asked of astrologers track well with those asked of oracles (see above, p. 11), as compared in Table 1.3 above.

3.3   *Astrology and Oracular Language*

The similarities of topics and questions between oracle practice and katarchic astrology are not the only links between these two forms of divination; some of the language and style used in katarchic astrology, especially within a format of implied or direct question, reflect the way in which questions are asked of the oracle. This is significant for katarchic practice. We find evidence of it in at least two important texts: Dorotheus's Carmen Astrologicum and Maximus of Ephesus's fourth century CE text, *On Initiatives* (Περὶ καταρχῶν).[78] First, it should be noted that both Dorotheus and Maximus wrote mostly in dactylic hexameter, the typical metre of oracles.[79]

---

77   Porphyry ed. Sodano, p. 30: 11, 19ᵇ: ... μάτην αὐτοῖς ἡ σοφία ἐξήσκηται περὶ δραπέτου εὑρέσεως ἢ χωρίου ὠνῆς ἢ γάμου, εἰ τύχοι, ἢ ἐμπορίας τὸν θεῖον νοῦν ἐνοχλήσασιν. The same in Porphyry, *Lettre à Anébon l'Égyptien*, eds H.D. Saffrey and A.-P. Segonds (Paris: Les Belles Lettres, 2012), 44 (Eusebius, PE, V 10.11).

78   Maximus of Ephesus, *Des initiatives*, ed., trans. and annot. Nicola Zito (Paris: Les Belles Lettres, 2016). On Maximus of Ephesus as the author of the work, see xix–xxii.

79   See Joseph Fontenrose, *The Delphic Oracle* (Berkeley/Los Angeles: University of California Press, 1978), 186; H.W. Parke and D.E.W. Wormell, *The Delphic Oracle*, 2 vols (Oxford: Basil Blackwell, 1956), vol. 2, xxii, xxix; the metric analysis of Pseudo-Manetho in Light-

Nicola Zito, in his recent edition of Maximus's *Περὶ καταρχῶν*, noticed characteristics of oracular style, including tone, Homeric allusions and wordplays, that were hallmarks of Maximus's style as well.[80] The formulaic phrase ʼλώιον καὶ ἄμεινον ἐστιν/ἔσται' (*lôion kai ameinon estin/estai*)[81] or similar, also appears in Maximus.[82] It is commonly translated as 'It is/will be better and more good' to do X. The use of the comparative form here 'presupposes alternatives' for the god who considers the answer.[83] It makes clear that an absolute is not the goal: as Walsh puts it, 'The god's response presents human goodness not as a matter of what is ultimately ideal, but as steering the best course through life's contingencies',[84] Eidinow notes that, rather than this wording compelling a yes or no answer akin to a lot oracle, it

> is asking its recipient to make an objective judgment about the future potential of his possible action, and the use of comparatives highlights this aspect. The god is not asked simply to provide information, but to make a judgment. (It is crucially important that the phrasing does not make explicit the basis for the judgment to be made, and so leaves some cognitive room to create the explanation when events proceed in a way that may seem less than 'better and more good' to the mortal consultant).[85]

Making judgments about future potential is not foreign to astrological practice.

Another word used in oracles, the present imperative φράζεο (*phrazeo*), meaning 'take care', 'pay attention to' or 'beware' in this context,[86] is also found in Maximus's poem, advising the reader to beware when the Moon is in the first decan of Taurus.[87]

---

foot, *Manetho* 2020, Part 2, ch. 7. See the use of hexameters in ritual, especially including oracles, in C.A. Faraone, *Hexametrical Genres from Homer to Theocritus* (New York: Oxford University Press, 2021): he posits, at 18, that 'at least until the end of the classical period, dactylic hexameters remained a special kind of meter, because they alone were thought to be capable of bridging the gap between gods and mortals as a kind of "ritualized communication."'

80   Zito, *Maximus*, lvi.
81   Eidinow, *Oracles*, 51, 65, 74; P&W I, 2; Fontenrose, *DO*, 192, 195, 221–222.
82   Zito, *Maximus*, lvii.
83   Lynda Walsh, 'The Rhetoric of Oracles', *Rhetoric Society Quarterly* 33, no. 3 (2003): 59.
84   Walsh, 'The Rhetoric of Oracles', 60.
85   Esther Eidinow, 'Oracular Consultations, Fate, and the Concept of the Individual', in *Divination in the Ancient World*, ed. Veit Rosenberger (Stuttgart: Franz Steiner Verlag, 2013), 34.
86   See Fontenrose, *DO*, 170–171.
87   Zito, *Maximus*, lvii, 26: 'beware the path of Taurus up to the tenth degree' (Φράζεο δ' ἐς δεκάτον τόδε μοι Ταύροιο κέλευθον).

Though Zito does not mention other astrologers in this discussion, I have subsequently found these phrases and/or words in Dorotheus, in quotations by Hephaestio and in other Dorothean fragments. Ἄμεινον and λῷον appear in Hephaestio's chapter on buying and selling (III, 16), where he first paraphrases and then quotes Dorotheus directly.[88] The paraphrase explains that when the Moon is waxing, with the (ascending) North Node and moving fast, a buyer will pay more than he should; but when waning, slow in motion and with the (descending) South Node, there are bargains to be had (III, 16.11). Dorotheus expresses this poetically:

9   When the Moon is present with the ascending node,

10   if in her full light and increasing in numbers her course,

11   for what you wish to buy you'll pay more than you should.

12   But the minute she wanes, moving toward the descending [node] on the paths which I've mentioned,

13   small will the purchase be.

14   And if you perceive the phase of the Moon when she goes

15   from Concurrence[89] to pass into first square

16   with the fiery Sun, **more good** will it be for those who are more even-handed,

17   for the money you'll pay is as much as it was worth to buy

18   and the amount you'll put down **will be better**, neither too little

19   nor much too much.   ...

23   When the goddess in the fourth quarter's going toward Concurrence,

24   you should pay little for something high-priced—**it'll** surely **be more good** for you[90]

---

88   III, 16.11–17; the two words appear in lines 16, 18 and 24 (p. 271.8–24 ed. Pingree).

89   I.e. conjunction with the Sun; see a description of the entire cycle in Paulus, ed. Boer, ch. 16, 'On the Figures the Moon Makes to the Sun' (33–35).

90   Heph. III, 16.13–14, 17; 271.9–19, 23–24 Pingree. My translation (with gratitude to Stephan Heilen for his advice, though remaining errors are mine). συνδέσμῳ δ' ἀνάγοντι Σεληναίης παρεούσης / εἰ μὲν πλησιφάεσσα δρόμον τ' αὔξησιν ἀριθμοῖς / ὅττι κεν ὠνήσει δώσεις πλέον ἢ δόμεναι χρή, / ὅττι κεν ὠνήσει δώσεις πλέον ἢ δόμεναι χρή, / αὐτίκα δ' ἐν κατάγοντι πορεύμασιν οἷσιν ἔλεξα / ἐρχομένης ἐπὶ μεῖον ἐλαφρὴ ἔσσεται ὠνή. / καὶ δὲ Σεληναίης φάσιν αἱ λεύσσης κεν ἰούσης / ἐκ συνόδου πρῶτον μετανισσομένης τετράπλευρον / αἴθοπος Ἠελίοιο δικαιοτέροισιν ἄμεινον· / χρήματα γὰρ δώσεις ὅσον ἄξιον ἦν ἀγοράζειν / καὶ πρῆγμα λῷον καταθήσεαι οὔτε μὲν ἧσσον / οὔτε λίην τι περισσόν. / ... / τετρατίῃ πλευρῇ δὲ θεῆς σύνοδόν δε κιούσης / βαιὸν ἂν ἐκ πολλοῦ δοίης τό τοι ἔσσετ' ἄμεινον.

The use of *phrazeo* also appears once in Dorotheus, when speaking of the lords of the Ascendant and Descendant in the same sign and their own faces: 'beware of [or consider] these as opponents'.[91]

In addition, the optative mood is common both in oracles and in katarchic astrology.[92] Dorotheus has numerous examples; here two samples are quoted by Hephaestio, using φράσσαιο (*phrassaio*) in the aorist optative middle second singular (oracles as well often use the second person in response).[93] The first, at III, 9.1 (on marriage), assesses the potential bride, writing: 'the maiden, lovely in spirit, you should consider from the [7th] setting zodiacal sign,[94] and Kythereia (Aphrodite) of the lovely hair'.[95] A second, about someone going away from home to a foreign land, uses both φράσσαιο and τεκμήραιο (*tekmēraio*) (both in the second person aorist optative middle):

9   If now someone should go from his fatherland to foreign soil

10   For him **you should consider** well the hour regulator, the country into which he departs

11   from the setting centrepin, his business from the midmost

12   height; and further, what the end to his life will be

13   **you should judge** clearly and well from the Underground[96]

These grammatical and word styles all emphasise choice, alternatives, and contingencies, just as we saw with oracles.

We should note as well the optative being used within an if/then format, as in the above example, which is not uncommon in Dorotheus and well-nigh

---

91   'φράζεο νείκεα ταῦτα', Dorotheus ap. Heph., III, 38.33, p. 300.4 Pingree = Dorotheus Pingree, p. 407.10.

92   For its use in oracles and katarchic astrology, see the apt comment of Lightfoot, *Pseudo-Manetho* 2020, 143: '... optatives are familiar from the Sibylline oracles, which favour the -ειε ending; more to the point, they are well established in catarchic astrology, with examples in Dorotheus ... and Maximus ... for catarchic astrology deals with theoretical contingencies which, were they to come about, would produce the stated outcome, which the addressee ponders when choosing the best course of action.'

93   See Zito, *Maximus*, lvii and n. 137.

94   Manuscripts have '9th', but the app. crit. says 'ϛ ζ' in marg. **P**' (ed. Pingree).

95   Heph. III, 9.1, p. 260.3–4 Pingree, 'αὐτὴν δ' ἐκ ζῳδίου θ' ἱμερόφρονα δυομένοιο κόρην ἂν φράσσαιο καὶ ἠυκόμου Κυθερείης.'

96   Heph. III, 30.1, p. 280.9–13 Pingree. My translation. Εἰ δέ νύ τις πάρτηθεν ἐπ' ἀλλοδαπὴν χθόνα βαίνοι / αὐτὸν ἀφ' ὡρονόμου, χῶρόν γε μὲν εἰς ὃν ἄπεισιν / ἐκ δυτικοῦ κέντρου, πρῆξιν δέ τοι ἐκ μεσάτοιο / ὕψεος εὖ φράσσαιο, τί δ' αὖ τέλος ἔσσεται αὐτῷ / ζῴῳ ὑποχθονίῳ σάφα κεν μάλα τεκμήραιο. A similar example, with φράζοιο, at Heph III, 40.18, p. 303.1 Pingree.

pervasive in Maximus.[97] Plutarch, the long-time priest at Delphi, also has some-thing to say about the use of 'if'. In his essay 'On the E at Delphi', he speaks of the religious and prayerful quality present in the use of the word, εἰ in Greek, in the questions petitioners make to the god, and their optative nature (386C3–D1) (the English word 'optative' comes from Latin *optare*, to wish, implying a respectful wish to a deity, and the Greek εὐκτικός, 'optative' is the same). For Plutarch, this quality underlies every oracular use of εἰ, even if not followed by a verb in the optative mood: 'IF they will be victorious, IF they shall marry, IF it is to their advantage to sail the sea, IF to take to farming, IF to go abroad' (my emphasis).[98] That katarchic questions use this same format (here in the exam-ples of Maximus, Dorotheus and Hephaestio) demonstrates how the astrologi-cal milieu mimics the oracular one. And again we see the similarities between oracle questions and katarchic ones.

To end Part 3 of this essay, I wish to stress again a point relevant to the ques-tioning mode in katarchic astrology. It is that questions are *inherent* in these practices, not only literally the asking of a question, but in the unspoken ques-tions applied to an election (what is the best time for this?), to the chart of an event (what will the outcome of this event be?), or decumbiture (what is the progress of the illness, and will the patient recover?). In katarchic astrology of whatever kind, questions are the main way in which this astrology is prac-ticed. Of course, as we have seen, the genre itself develops out of a divinatory milieu—religious ritual and oracles—to answer the ultimate question: what shall I do, and how do I obtain the sanction and advice of the gods? So to limit the 'origin date' of interrogational astrology only to the chart that literally asks a question, and to separate it from this cultural milieu, is to ignore the complex interweaving of these different but related kinds of astrological practices, and the history of *katarchē*. It is clear, I think, from what we have now seen in this section, that a questioning mode is present in astrological contexts from a very

97   The examples in Maximus are too numerous to list; in Dorotheus, see among others Dorotheus v, 21.8 (= Heph. III, 30.10) and v, 27.21 (= Heph. III, 40.21) On this also see Lightfoot, *Pseudo-Manetho* 2020, 143, who comments: 'Unlike natal astrology, in which the apodosis happens whether one likes it or not, catarchic astrology involves a contingency which the potential optative is well calculated to express.'

98   Plutarch, *The E at Delphi*, trans. Frank Cole Babbitt, in *Moralia*, V. Loeb Classical Library. Cambridge, MA: Harvard University Press, 1936, repr. 2003, 386C2–3: εἰ νικήσουσιν, εἰ γαμή-σουσιν, εἰ συμφέρει πλεῖν, εἰ γεωρτεῖν, εἰ ἀποδημεῖν, as in Zito, *Maximus*, lviii; see also simi-larly at *De Pythiae oraculis* (*The Oracles at Delphi No Longer Given in Verse*) (in the same volume as *The E at Delphi*), 408C, 'εἰ γαμητέον', 'εἰ πλευστέον', 'εἰ δανειστέον' (if one ought to marry, to sail, to make a loan).

early stage. Nevertheless, for the sake of completeness, the last section of this essay will explore the evidence for asking a question in astrological texts.[99]

4   Asking Questions in Astrology

This section's main focus will be on Greek and Latin texts of katarchic astrology that contain evidence of specifically asking questions, as opposed to those dealing with katarchic astrology in its other forms of elections, event interpretation and decumbiture. Early evidence, aside from Dorotheus, is sparse for the asking of a question in astrological texts, and the chronology is often difficult, since not all astrologers who wrote on these topics can be securely dated. However, to provide some context on the prevalence of katarchic astrology in the astrological literature of the Greco-Roman period and late antiquity, we shall begin with a section on astrologers who wrote on katarchic astrology but do not include question words. This will be followed by a section on those who explicitly do.

4.1   *A Selective Survey of Astrological Writers on Katarchic Astrology*[100]
4.1.1   Early Katarchic Astrologers
Few astrologers before the first century CE whose writings are extant, or can be securely dated, provide any evidence about the asking of questions along with their discussions of other forms of katarchic astrology. For example, we find the technique of electing the time of the founding of a city in the work of Varro and Tarutius on the founding of Rome in the 1st c. BCE.[101] Mentioned by Pliny the Elder,[102] Timaeus Praxidas (probably early to middle 1st c. BCE) writes on runaways and thieves, presumably based on interpreting an event chart.[103]

---

99   Even though it seems myopic, given what we have already explored, to privilege only the
        date when one specific kind of chart was cast for the time a question was asked.
100   For reasons of space, this section will necessarily be truncated, but it should be noted
        that the practice of katarchic astrology was not meagre in the Greco-Roman era and late
        antiquity. For a more complete listing, see László, *Inceptions*, 24–26, 238–261.
101   See Heilen, 'Horoscope of Rome'; for other foundings of cities, see Jean-Patrice Boudet
        'From Baghdad to *Civitas Solis*: Horoscopes of Foundations of Cities', in *From Masha'allah
        to Kepler: Theory and Practice in Medieval and Renaissance Astrology*, eds Charles Burnett
        and Dorian Gieseler Greenbaum (Ceredigion, Wales: Sophia Centre Press, 2015), 49–76;
        László, *Inceptions*, 63–76.
102   Who calls him 'Timaeus mathematicus'. Pliny the Elder, *Natural History, Books 3–7*, Vol. 2,
        trans. H. Rackham, Loeb Classical Library (Cambridge, MA/London: Harvard University
        Press, 1942), *NH* 5, X.55–56.
103   See Wolfgang Hübner, *Raum, Zeit und soziales Rollenspiel der vier Kardinalpunkte in der*

A fragment ascribed to 'Petosiris' (ca. 1st c. BCE) on decumbiture may relate to Juvenal's mention of that name in Satire 6 (see above, p. 22).[104]

4.1.2   Katarchic Authors of Contested or Uncertain Dates

Furthermore, accurate dating for a number of writers on katarchic astrology is difficult. Texts were collected or transcribed much later than when they may have been written, so even though they may contain katarchic practices that correspond to the known early practices of, say, Dorotheus, their dates may well be later. Writers such as Protagoras of Nicaea may well have written before the common era, but suggested dates for him range from the third century BCE to the third or fourth century CE.[105] According to Hephaestio (III, 47.52), he wrote on ships and runaway slaves. Demetrius is another writer of uncertain date.[106] He is mentioned in the text of 'Palchus'[107] as writing on buying and selling, asking for something, marriage, runaways, sailing, leaving home, and tribunals.[108] His work has correlations with topics in Dorotheus and Hephaestio. A 'Zoroaster' (also mentioned by Pliny the Elder, clearly pseudepigraphical) writes on the reception of a letter, its intention and contents (CCAG I, 192–195); and when a war or evil thing will happen (CCAG V/3, 87). Erasistratus (200–300 CE?),[109] who also appears in 'Palchus', discusses loss and theft (CCAG I, 94–97).

---

antiken Katarchenhoroskopie, Band 194, Beiträge zur Altertumskunde (Munich/Leipzig: K.G. Saur Verlag, 2003), 28; Stephan Heilen, Hadriani genitura. Die astrologischen Fragmente des Antigonos von Nikaia. Edition, Übersetzung und Kommentar, 2 vols, Band 2, Kommentare (Berlin: De Gruyter, 2015), 691 and n. 1473; a date 'in the early 1st century CE at the latest' (because of the elder Pliny's citation) is preferred in László, Inceptions, 257–258.

104 See László, Inceptions, 248.

105 From the 3rd c. BCE: W. Gundel and H.G. Gundel, Astrologumena. Die astrologische Literatur in der Antike und ihre Geschichte (Wiesbaden: Steiner, 1966), 106; Richard Gordon, 'Quaedam Veritatis Umbrae: Hellenistic Magic and Astrology'. In Conventional Values of the Hellenisti Greeks, eds Per Bilde, Troels Engberg-Pedersen, Lise Hannestad and Jan Zahle (Aarhus: Aarhus University Press, 1997), 131 and n. 8, including a possible 2nd c. BCE date also. From the 3rd or 4th c. CE: David Pingree, ed., trans. and comm., The Yavanajātaka of Sphujidhvaja. 2 vols. (Cambridge, MA/London: Harvard University Press, 1978), vol. II, 439; but Hübner, Raum, Zeit, 27, suggests an earlier time based on Protagoras's statements about the four centrepins.

106 László, Inceptions, 241, suggests his work is 'probably before the 5th [century]'.

107 See Pingree, Yavanajātaka, II, 426; Hübner, Raum, Zeit, 30; For more on 'Palchus' and his texts, see below, 'The Palchus Material ...'.

108 See a summary of his work in CCAG VIII/3, 98 (the topic of 'asking for something', περὶ αἰτούντων, should not be assumed to be a literal question); and sections on sailing, leaving home and running away in CCAG VIII/3, 98–99 and CCAG I, 104–106.

109 Paul T. Keyser, 'Erasistratus (Astrol.)', in The Encyclopedia of Ancient Natural Scientists, eds Paul T. Keyser and Georgia L. Irby-Massie, 294 (Abingdon, UK/New York: Routledge, 2008).

Serapion, whose dates are also problematic,[110] wrote at least five chapters on katarchic astrology, dealing with elections and events; one of his pet methods seems to be using the planet presiding or managing at the time the chart is cast (he mentions this in all extant fragments, whether the topic is the success of a *katarchē* in general, intercourse with women, running away, confinements or decumbitures, or associations of various kinds).[111]

4.1.3   General and Natal Astrologers Writing on Katarchic Astrology

It is also useful to point out the common awareness of katarchic astrology, even by authors whose work is not specifically focused on that branch of astrology. Two examples are Vettius Valens and Paulus of Alexandria. Valens differentiates between katarchic and natal astrology (e.g. IV, 16.25), connects *kairos* and *katarchē* (V, 2.22, 23) (also see above, Section 3.1, 'Katarchē, Kairos and Ritual') and combines the two with following one's daimon to achieve the best result (IX, 12.28–31).[112] Within Chapter 2 of Book V (ed. Pingree) is a section called 'On Inceptions' (Περὶ καταρχῶν), which is treated as a separate chapter in Kroll's critical edition.[113] Here Valens applies a method of using the Moon and its nodes specifically to katarchic practice, stressing that no chart for any action should be made when the Moon conjoins or squares the ascending node, noting that under these circumstances 'one must guard against beginning anything …'![114]

Book IX, 6, 'On decumbiture and katarchic charts', offers a numerical method for investigating decumbitures using the distance between the new moon prior to the birth and the natal Moon, the distance between the current new moon and the birthdate, and the distance between the new moon preceding the decumbiture and the date of the decumbiture. These distances are divided by four and the remainders are compared. If they are the same, the illness will be fatal, but if different, the patient will survive. This arcane process appears unique to Valens.[115] In the next paragraph he makes the odd statement that his experience has led him to consider that not only decumbitures are operative

---

110   See Susanne Denningmann, 'Die Datierung des Astrologen Serapion', *MHNH* 9 (2009): 159–174; and László, *Inceptions*, 250–252, for two different analyses.

111   Respectively in *CCAG* I, 99–100 and *CCAG* V/3, 87.4–15; *CCAG* V/1, 179.16–180.11; *CCAG* I, 101 (F. 107, 38.1–10); *CCAG* I, 101 (F. 107, 39.1–7) and 102 (F. 107, 39.1–14); *CCAG* V/1, 180.12–27, and see also László, *Inceptions*, p. 252, unedited mss. for F5B.

112   For an analysis of these last two points, see Greenbaum, *Daimon in Hellenistic Astrology*, 40–43.

113   Vettius Valens, *Anthologiarum libri*, ed. Wilhelm Kroll (Berlin: Weidmann, 1908), V, 3, p. 212.

114   V, 2.19, p. 202.3–5 Pingree: 'φυλακτέον … μὴ κατάρχεσθαί τινος …'. Seemingly this advice is based on his personal experience (explained at V, 2.22).

115   IX, 6.1–5, pp. 325.26–326.7 Pingree.

(*chrēmatistikos*) but all katarchic practices, as if the doctrine of the decumbiture had preceded general *katarchē*. The end of the chapter is a screed against
those he calls 'cheats' (γόητες), a pejorative word also meaning 'sorcerer',[116] who
think one katarchic chart can supply answers for every topic of someone's life
and experience, contrasting it with the longer and harder work of interpreting
a nativity and the timing techniques that can be applied to it.

Paulus, like Valens, also treats katarchic astrology as separate from natal and
universal astrology. In the following passage he differentiates between a birth
chart and a chart of a 'day' (which by context we can deduce as katarchic,
through the topics being mentioned).[117] It is not explicit whether these are
event charts, elections or interrogations.

> It will be necessary to examine the one which presides and the one which
> manages for each nativity and for every day ... For it is through these that
> events which occur concerning agreements, contracts, favors and gifts
> are comprehended. The examination itself is useful for success both in
> alliance with ruling or prominent people, and with lawsuits or blackmail,
> and imprisonments, oppressions, accusations, slanders, entanglements,
> losses, thefts, and testaments which are coming to be; and for sailing
> voyages, commerce and travel we will learn to know [also] about battle,
> tumults, decumbitures and things similar to these. For doctors, it also con-
> tributes to inquiry both in diagnoses of the sick and in considerations of
> surgeries or medical treatments, in order to make a perfect inception in
> the aforesaid things.[118]

---

116 The word *goeteia* is used pejoratively in Neoplatonic texts, to contrast it with the more
legitimate practice of *mageia*.

117 A common word by metonymy for a katarchic chart is *pragma*, 'matter': see, e.g., Valens IV,
29.7, p. 195.6–7 Pingree; V, 3.20, p. 202.10; V, 3.21, p. 202.15 Pingree; Scholion 56 to Ch. 24 in
Paulus ed. Boer, p. 120.23; Olympiodorus, *Eis ton Paulon ⟨Heliodorou⟩. Heliodori, ut dicitur,
in Paulum Alexandrinum Commentarium*, ed. Emilie Boer (Leipzig: B.G. Teubner, 1962),
Ch. 16, p. 30.4, 12, 18; p. 32.16, 21.

118 Paulus, *Introduction*, ch. 21, p. 39 Greenbaum trans., in Boer pp. 41.18–19, 42.2–15: Τὸν πολεύ-
οντα καὶ διέποντα ἐφ' ἑκάστης γεννήσεως καὶ ἐπὶ πάσης ἡμέρας σκοπεῖν δεήσει ... δι' αὐτῶν γὰρ
τὰς γινομένας ἀθρόως συντυχίας ἐπί τε συνθηκῶν καὶ ἐπὶ ὑποσχέσεως καὶ χάριτος καὶ δωρεᾶς
ἔστιν συλλαβεῖν· ἐπί τε ἐπιτυχίας χρήσιμος ἡ σκέψις αὕτη, συστάσεώς τε πρὸς ἄρχοντας ἢ ὑπερέ-
χοντα πρόσωπα, πρός τε δίκας ἢ συκοφαντίας καὶ δεσμοὺς καὶ συνοχάς, ἐγκλήματα καὶ διαβολὰς
καὶ συμπλοκὰς καὶ ἀπώλειας καὶ κλοπὰς καὶ τὰς γινομένας διαθήκας, ἐπί τε πλοῦ καὶ ἐμπορίας
καὶ ὁδοιπορίας, μάχης καὶ θορύβων καὶ κατακλίσεων καὶ τῶν τούτοις παραπλησίων ἐπιγνωσό-
μεθα. συμβάλλεται δὲ καὶ ἰατροῖς πρὸς ἐπίσκεψιν καὶ ἐν ταῖς τῶν νοσούντων καὶ ἐν ταῖς τῶν
χειρουργιῶν ἢ θεραπειῶν ἐπιβολαῖς πρὸς τὸ ἀδιαπτώτως ἐν τοῖς προειρημένοις τὴν καταρχὴν
ποιεῖσθαι.

It is interesting to discover that the emphasis on the presiding and managing planets found in Serapion appears again in Paulus's writing on katarchic practice. The topics he mentions are, as we have seen earlier, common in katarchic astrology (see Table 1.2 above, p. 24).

4.1.4 A 'Manethonian' Text

A text of questionable authenticity from a fourteenth-century manuscript claiming to be from Manetho the astrologer (b. 80 CE),[119] in prose, not poetry, illustrates principles that are common in writings on *katarchai*, here concentrating on outcomes when the Moon is unconnected to other planets. In the passage regarding Mercury, we find: 'The Moon unconnected to Hermes makes every *katarchē* become more unsuccessful, and especially as regards those asking for [something] or sending letters'.[120] (Like the earlier passage from Demetrius, this should not necessarily be interpreted as the literal asking of a question.)

4.2 *Interrogatory Words in Katarchic Texts*

We shall now examine those texts which do mention questions directly and by implication (such as using phrases like 'whether'—or not—'to do something').

4.2.1 'Hermes' Mystical Method'

I shall begin with a fragment written by 'Hermes Trismegistus', the date of which may be sometime in the mid-fourth century: its *terminus ante quem* is the death of Constantine in 337 CE, because it mentions crucifixion and that practice ended in his reign.[121] Crucifixion is mentioned in other Hellenistic astrological texts, including Pseudo-Manetho (1.148–149, 4.196–200 Lightfoot), Dorotheus (Gr. frg., 362.11 Pingree), Ptolemy (IV, 9, 434–435 Robbins), Firmicus (*Mathesis*, VI, 31.58–59; VIII, 22.3 KSZ) and the *Liber Hermetis* (XXV, 1.21, p. 82.61i; XXVI, 77, p. 156.402 Feraboli);[122] its popularity among the Roman occupiers at the turn of the millennium should also not be ignored.

---

119 Cod. Marcianus 334, fol. 205ᵛ, in Robert Lopilato, 'The "Apotelesmatika" of Manetho', Ph.D. Thesis, Brown University, 1998, Appendix I, an apograph by Pingree, 444. See the listing in *CCAG* II, 16, no. 6, and 37 (what may be a variant at fol. 27, ζ' p. 17).

120 Ἡ Σελήνη τῷ Ἑρμῇ ἀσύνδετος ἀπρακτοτέρον ποιεῖ πᾶσαν καταρχὴν γενέσθαι, καὶ μάλιστα τῶν αἰτούντων χάριν ἢ γράμματα πεμπόντων. In Lopilato, 'Manetho', 444.

121 *CCAG* VIII/1, 172–177, here 176.16; Cumont notes this in his introduction to the text on 172; László, *Inceptions*, 247–248, also mentions it. On this topic, see John Granger Cook, *Crucifixion in the Mediterranean World* (Tübingen: Mohr Siebeck, 2014), 398–406; David Potter, 'Constantine and the Gladiators', *Classical Quarterly* 60, no. 2 (2010): 602–603 and n. 20.

122 For Manetho, see J.L. Lightfoot, *Pseudo-Manetho Apotelesmatica: Books Four, One, and Five*

The title of the fragment is 'A Mystical Method of Hermes Trismegistus suitable in every initiative'.[123] It begins with a statement ascribed to this 'Hermes' that states his method can be used for those asking questions about offspring:

> Before all, the one preparing beforehand and seeking to inquire by initiatives must, if he should wish to be successful and not mistaken in whatever the initiative is, make the arrangement of the centrepins and stars precise; that is, *whenever you should be asked* about the sowing of seed, is it human or beast ...[124]

The 'mystical method' itself, which allows the astrologer to determine information about a *katarchē* by different queries (such as whether the offspring is human or bestial, male or female, able to be reared or not, etc.), involves an unusual lot-like technique in which the degree-arc from the Sun to the Moon is divided by 6, and the number that is the remainder from that is projected, by one degree per whole sign, from the Moon's sign. The sign that results is used to answer the questions being asked about the offspring.[125]

In addition to the one cited above, four other passages in the text employ question words:

(Oxford: Oxford University Press, 2023), 585–586, 799–800 and, for dating, 178, with a likely *terminus ante quem* for Book 4 in the 3rd c. CE. See also Franz Cumont, *L'Égypte des astrologues*, (Brussels: La Fondation Égyptologique Reine Élisabeth, 1937), 196 and n. 5. For Firmicus, Julius Firmicus Maternus, *Matheseos libri VIII*, eds Wilhelm Kroll, Franz Skutsch and Konrat Ziegler, 2 vols (Leipzig: B.G. Teubner, 1897–1913), here vol. 2. For the *Liber Hermetis, Hermetis Trismegisti: De triginta sex decanis*, ed. Simonetta Feraboli, Hermes Latinus IV/1 (Corpus Christianorum) (Turnhout, Belgium: Brepols, 1994).

123 Par./Ven. in CCAG 8/1, 172–177, here 172; an alternate title is 'Method of Hermes Trismegistus in every initiative' (Flor.: 173). The text was previously translated by Robert Schmidt, *The Astrological Record of the Early Sages in Greek*, Project Hindsight Greek Track Vol. x, Berkeley Springs, WV: The Golden Hind Press, 1995, 7–11; see also László, *Inceptions*, 247–248 (without translation).

124 CCAG 8/1, 172.4–173.1 (left column), from Par. gr. 2419, fol. 69ᵛ and Marc. gr. 334, fol. 49ʳ. My trans. and italics. Πρὸ πάντων δεῖ τὸν σκεπτόμενον καὶ ζητητικῶς ἔχοντα περὶ τὰς καταρχὰς ⟨ποιεῖσθαι τὰς⟩ μεταθέσεις τῶν κέντρων καὶ τῶν ἐποχῶν τῶν ἀστέρων, εἴπερ βούλοιτο ἐπιτευκτικὸς εἶναι καὶ μὴ σφάλλεσθαι ἐν οἱᾳδήποτε καταρχῇ, ἤγουν ὅταν ἐρωτηθῇς περὶ καταβολῆς σπέρματος ἀνθρώπου ἐστὶν ἢ κτήνους ...

125 Other katarchic texts that use lots, mainly the Lot of Fortune for learning information about what the questioner is thinking, are Heph. III, 4.14–18, pp. 233.23–234.7 Pingree; and a similar text in 'Palchus', Laur.plut. 28.33, fol. 200ᵛ, 7 with a copy in Escorial Φ.I.5, fol. 322 in CCAG XI/1, 202–203, for knowing what the questioner is thinking about asking, from the Lot of Fortune. These examples will be discussed in more depth below, in 'Hephaestio: What is the client thinking', pp. 41–44.

– (parallel text to that in the previous quotation, in) '... **if he should be asked** about the sowing of seed, whether the offspring will be human or bestial ...'[126]

– '... take the ascensional time in the zone **where the question** is set ...'[127]

– '... the conduct of **each one of those questioning** is known, whether inferior or able, through this very means of approach; if you find the zodiacal sign declining, but witnessed by benefics, not together with malefics, say **the questioner** is sceptical and meddlesome ...'[128]

This fourth-century text makes clear that its methods are being used to answer specific questions. But examples from earlier authors give evidence of asking questions as well. The next sections will focus on allusions to the asking of questions in astrology, as well as actual topics, methods and interpretations used by these astrologers.

4.2.2　　Manilius and the Circle of Athla

I begin with someone who has not been mentioned much in discussions on interrogational astrology: Manilius, the early 1st century CE astrologer (fl. 10 CE), whose poem *Astronomica* was written during the reigns of the Roman emperors Augustus and Tiberius. Manilius writes on an interesting practice called the 'Circle of Athla' in Book 3 of his poem. This practice uses the Lot of Fortune as a beginning point for the places of the chart, and each place deriving from the beginning point of Fortune has its own set of parameters that are different from the places deriving from the Ascendant.

The interpretation of these 'lot houses' can be used for astrological assessment of a nativity, but the description of two of these places contains a very interesting reference to what can only be referring to forms of katarchic astrology, namely elections and interrogations. As in Figure 1.4 above, the 11th place from Fortune covers health, remedy and the *time for administering it*, clearly a reference to an election in the service of astrological medicine. 'Outstanding is the portion located in the eleventh lot', Manilius says.[129] And he adds,

---

126　My translation. Florence, Laur. pl. 28.14, fol. 241ʳ= *CCAG* VIII/1, 172.10–173.1: εἰ ἐρωτηθείη περὶ καταβολῆς σπέρματος, πότερον ἀνθρωποειδὲς ἔσται τὸ γεννηθησόμενον ἢ κτηνοειδὲς.

127　My translation. *CCAG* VIII/1, 174.16–17: λάμβανε τοὺς ἑκάστου ἀναφορικοὺς / χρόνους, ἐν ᾧ κλίματι γίνεται ἡ ἐρώτησις.

128　My translation. *CCAG* VIII/1, 175.17–20: ἡ ἀγωγὴ ἑνὸς ἑκάστου τῶν ἐρωτώντων, εἴτε φαύλη / εἴτε χρησίμη, διὰ τῆσδε τῆς ἐφόδου· ἐὰν εὕρῃς τὸ ζῴδιον τοῦτο / ἀποκεκλικός, μαρτυρούμενον δὲ ὑπὸ ἀγαθοποιῶν, κακοποιῶν μὴ / συμπαρόντων, λέγε τὸν ἐρωτῶντα ζητητικὸν εἶναι καὶ πολυπράγμονα·.

129　Manilius, *Astronomica* III, v. 138 Goold, my trans. 'praecipua undecima pars est in sorte locata'.

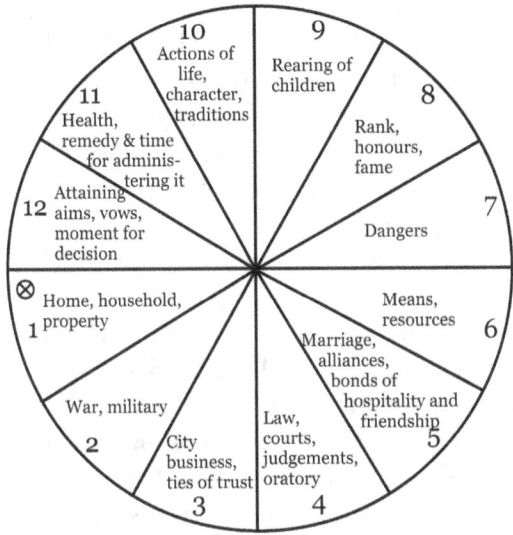

FIGURE 1.4
Manilius' Circle of Athla, or Astrological Places from the Lot of Fortune (Book 3.96–164)[a]

[a] Manilius, *Astronomica*, ed. and trans. G.P. Goold, Loeb Classical Library, Cambridge MA: Harvard University Press, 1977, repr. 1997.

of this eleventh place from Fortune, 'There is no other seat that claims *the choice of remedy and the moment for administering it, or in whose hour therapy and the mixing of life-saving potions have greater efficacy*',[130] The twelfth place's functions are more overtly interrogatory, effectively answering questions about success in a number of different areas, and whether one should initiate an action or not:

> 'Whether one is to offer one's services and submit to another's every beck and call, whether to embark on a bitter dispute by litigation in the courts, whether to seek fortune on the sea and pursue it with the winds, whether to put one's hopes on a crop that with huge harvest will exceed one's outlay or a vintage that will overflow with the rich must—*this is the portion in which day and hour for decision shall be given, if the planets as they move through the zodiac are favourably situated*'[131]

---

130 Manilius, *Astronomica* III, vv. 142–144 Goold (my italics). 'non alia est sedes, tempusve genusve medendi / quae sibi deposcat vel cuius tempore praestet / auxilium et vitae sucos miscer salubris.'

131 Manilius, *Astronomica* III, vv. 150–155 Goold (my italics). 'seu ferat officium nutus blanditus in omnis, / aspera sive foro per litem iurgia temptet, / fortunamve petat pelago ventisque sequatur, / seu Cererem plena vincentem credita mess /aut repetat Bacchum per pinguia musta fluentem, / hac in parte dies atque had momenta dabuntur, / si bene convenient stellae per signa sequentes;'. For more discussion of this topic, see also Greenbaum, *The Daimon in Hellenistic Astrology*, 292–294 (with the diagram).

It is quite clear that these examples of katarchic astrology appearing in another text from the first century CE besides that of Dorotheus, and particularly with the interrogatory word 'whether'—or not—to seek fortune on the sea, etc., again provide evidence that this type of astrology was being practised by at least the turn of the millennium. As Wolfgang Hübner remarks, 'Since at least the middle of the 1st c. CE the doctrine [of katarchic astrology] is essentially fully developed',[132] And questions are part of that doctrine.

4.2.3   Dorotheus and Hephaestio: The Transmission of Questions

We can now turn to Dorotheus with a more informed view about the use of interrogatory practices in the first century CE. As a well-known practitioner of katarchic astrology in his time, Dorotheus devotes Book v of his *Carmen Astrologicum* entirely to katarchic practice. The following example shows evidence of asking a question in an astrological context that dates at least to the 1st c. CE, given that its text, in the Arabic version of Chapter 17 of Dorotheus's Book 5, is duplicated in Greek, in Hephaestio's *Apotelesmatica*, III, 11:[133]

> Dorotheus v, 17.t-1:
> The courtship of a woman, and what occurs between a wife and her husband when she quarrels and scolds and departs from her house publicly. If you want to know, if she returns to him, whether he will profit from her or will see joy and happiness or other than this in her, then *look at the hour in which you are asked about this* at the position of the Sun and of Venus.[134]

> Hephaestio of Thebes, *Apotelesmatika*, III, 11.t-2:
> On separations [of married couples]. One must look at their separations and returns in this way: [According to] the inception (*katarchē*)

---

132   Hübner, *Raum, Zeit*, 245 (my trans.). 'Spätestens seit der Mitte des ersten Jh. n. Chr. ist die Lehre im wesentlichen voll entwickelt.'

133   I first noticed this in late 2006, when Deborah Houlding and I were discussing the origins of interrogational astrology, and she publicized the following example, credited to me, in her 2012 United Astrology Congress lecture 'Ancient Enquiry Charts'. Benjamin Dykes, who also cites this example in Hephaestio's Book III, seems to have arrived at it independently (*Hephaistion of Thebes: Apotelesmatics Book III: On Inceptions*, ed. B.N. Dykes, trans. E.J. Gramaglia (Minneapolis: Cazimi Press, 2013), 11, 15–16, 17).

134   Dorotheus of Sidon, *Carmen Astrologicum*, ed. and trans. Pingree, v, 17.t-1, p. 275 Pingree; also the quotation in Greek, 393.29–394.1 = v 17.2 = frs. 87a and 88 Stegemann.

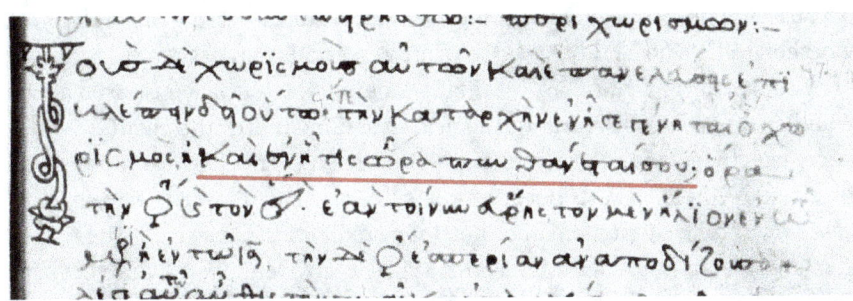

FIGURE 1.5   BnF, Parisinus graecus 2417, fol. 161ʳ, lines 20–23 (note, on the left side, the decoration for this section in the manuscript)

in which the separation has come to be, or *even in which hour someone inquires of you* [my italics], look at Aphrodite and the Sun.[135]

We can assess the reliability of this evidence in several ways. One of the main manuscripts Pingree used in his critical edition, P (Par. gr. 2417, fol. 161ʳ, ll. 20–23), contains this passage, using the verb *punthanomai* (πυνθάνομαι), inquire (of someone)[136] (Figure 1.5).

In addition, two of the three epitomes of Hephaestio's treatise where this chapter appears contain this crucial phrase—and the third is similar, although it appears to contain a scribal error that incorrectly writes *peithetai* for *puthetai*:

καὶ ἐν ᾗ πύθεταί σου ὅρα Ἀφροδίτην καὶ τὸν / Ἥλιον· (Ep. I.35.2, vol. 2, p. 17.24–18.1)

καὶ / ἐν ᾗ ὥρᾳ πείθεταί σου ὅρα γοῦν τὴν Ἀφροδίτην καὶ τὸν / Ἥλιον ... (Scribal error in Ep. II, III 20.2, vol. 2, p. 121.2–4)

ἢ καὶ τὴν ὥραν ἐν ᾗ πύθοιτο ἂν τις σου περὶ | τούτου / καὶ σκέπτου τὴν Ἀφροδίτην καὶ τὸν Ἥλιον ... (Ep. IV.85.2 [in V = Vat. gr. 1056], vol. 2, p. 294.25–26)

This evidence supports its textual reliability. Clearly these texts are relying on the same source, seemingly information from the original Greek text of Dorotheus. It may even be that Hephaestio is more faithful to the original,

---

135   My translation. Heph. III, 11.1–2, p. 266.11–15 Pingree (the Greek phrase is underlined): Περὶ χωρισμῶν. / Τοὺς δὲ χωρισμοὺς αὐτῶν καὶ ἐπανελεύσεις ἐπιβλέπειν / δεῖ οὕτως. ⟨κατὰ⟩ τὴν καταρχὴν ἐν ᾗ γεγένηται ὁ χωρισμὸς / ἢ καὶ ἐν ᾗ τις ὥρᾳ πυνθάνεταί σου ὅρα τὴν Ἀφροδίτην καὶ / τὸν Ἥλιον·

136   See LSJ s.v. A.4.

because it plainly states at the beginning *two* ways of addressing the problem of whether a wife who left home will return: by an event chart cast for the moment of her departure; or by a chart cast at the moment the astrologer is asked about whether the wife will return. It is logical to assume that *if* the client does not know exactly when the wife left, and therefore an event chart cannot be cast, that a question to the astrologer on the subject would allow the astrologer to cast a chart for that moment and then interpret it for the answer.[137] The Arabic version of Dorotheus has a title which suggests an event chart, but a first sentence which clearly depicts an interrogation. Yet in sentences 7–10, it appears that the Arabic version has returned to the interpretation of an event chart for the departure. Hephaestio, being closer in time to Dorotheus, and writing in the same language, may have retained more of the original Dorotheus, while the Arabic version has slightly adjusted the paragraph, talking about both interrogational and event charts (note that these were separate categories in Arabic astrology), but not specifically saying that at the beginning of the chapter. We should also note that the same rules of interpretation apply for both kinds of charts.

I have mentioned before the major reliance on Dorotheus that Hephaestio has in his third book on *katarchē*; Table 1.4, below, p. 41, is a breakdown of the correlations (somewhat truncated for reasons of space). Of the forty-three chapters in Book v of Dorotheus, only five chapters (in the Pingree edition) have no counterpart in Hephaestio, as can be seen in the table.[138]

As one can easily see in Table 1.5, p. 41, although the only *literal* asking of a question is in Hephaestio III, 11.1–5, the chapters on thievery (III, 42-III, 46) show clearly that the event chart is being queried in several different ways: What is the thing lost? (III, 43). Who is the thief? (III, 44). [What is] the appearance of the thief? (III, 45). In which way is it lost? (III, 46). All of these have a direct equivalent with the sentences in Dorotheus's v, 35 that set up the different things the querent is trying to find out: 35.1–44 deals with the theft in general (= Heph. III, 42); 35.45–74, is covered by 'what is the thing lost?' in Heph. III, 43; 35.75–133 matches the thief's appearance in Heph. III, 45; and 35.134–138 matches 'in which way is it lost?' in Heph. III, 46.

---

137   We shall not go into the ontological issue of a physical moment in time for the event being replaced by a time which has no physical connection to the event; but see Cornelius, *Moment of Astrology*; and D.G. Greenbaum, 'Modern Western Astrology, Prediction and Divination: An Autoethnography', in ~~preparation~~ press.

138   This information in Pingree, *Heph.*, x–xi; *Yavanajātaka*, II, 402–403.

TABLE 1.4   Correlations between chapters in Dorotheus and chapters in Hephaestio

Dorotheus	Hephaestio	Dorotheus	Hephaestio	Dorotheus	Hephaestio
V 1–2	III 1	V 16	III 9	V 30	
V 3	III 1	V 17	III 11	V 31	III 31
V 4	III 1	V 18	III 12	V 32	III 41
V 5	III 1	V 19		V 33	III 38
V 6	III 7.1, 9–10	V 20	III 28	V 34	III 39
V 7	III 7.11–12	V 21	III 30.1–13	V 35	III 42–III 46
V 8		V 22	III 30.37–71	V 36	III 47
V 9	III 16	V 23	III 17	V 37	III 33
V 10	III 16	V 24	III 17	V 38	III 34
V 11	III 16	V 25	III 30.38–65	V 39	III 32
V 12	III 19	V 26	III 27	V 41	III 32,5
V 13	III 21	V 27	III 40	V 40	
V 14	III 20, III 25	V 28		V 42	App. II.1–6
V 15	III 27	V 29	III 31	V 43	III 16.11–17

TABLE 1.5   Correlating Questions in Dorotheus with Questions in Hephaestio

Dorotheus question	Topic	Hephaestio	Question in Hephaestio?
V 17.t–1	Wife leaves	III 11.1–5	Yes
V 18.t	Pregnant woman: if child will die in womb	III 12.1–2	No
V 28.2–3	What may be or not: if query is about …	–	–
V 29.t–2	If the querist asks about a sick person	III 31	No
V 32	If you want to know when property increases or decreases	III 41.1–4	Question implied
V 33.1	Adversaries: 1. If you want to know this at hour in which you are asked/ 8. If at the hour you are asked about it	III 38	No
V 33.8			
V 34	Exile: If you are asked about a man whether he will depart	III 39 (but content not really the same)	–
V 35. 1–44	Goods stolen: (1) 'if you are asked about this'	III 42	If the lost thing will be found
	(45) 'If at that hour in which you are asked	III 43	
45–74	about the theft'	III 44	What is the thing lost?
	Characteristics of the thief	III 45	Who is the thief?
75–133	Details of the theft	III 46	Thief's appearance
134–138			In what way is it lost?
V 36.77	Runaway: if master does not know time of flight, use time he/she heard of it	III 47	No

In my view, what this comparison shows is the innate interrogational stance of katarchic astrology, that we have seen earlier in the evidence from oracles and their commonalities with this branch of astrology. We should not assume that because there is not a literal question, no such concept exists until later in the tradition. The evidence of even one or two examples of this, as in the Hephaestio-Dorotheus correlation of III, 11 to V, 17, and the passages in Manilius, as well as the 'Mystical Method', are proof of the approach used in this kind of astrology, and well before the Arabic period.

To round out this examination of the relevant katarchic material in Hephaestio, we shall look at a chapter in Book III that is certainly interrogatory, but not in the typical ways in which interrogational astrology is presented.

Hephaestio: What is the Client Thinking?

III, 4. How one may learn beforehand the inquiries of those wishing to investigate from *katarchē*

'One may learn the prior circumstances of those approaching and wanting to know beforehand [i.e. predictions] from a *katarchē*, by making the inspection according to a general and panoramic form similar in method, especially, to that used for nativities'.[139]

This chapter is about discovering what the questioner has in mind when he or she consults the local katarchic astrologer. A chart is cast, presumably in advance of the consultation, for the astrologer to investigate the client's thoughts or intentions, which we could describe as 'thought-reading'.[140] In this case, it may be that the astrologer is casting his own 'question' chart to find out what the circumstances are behind the client's wish for a *katarchē*, and even what the motives may be behind this request. One of the methods for interpretation uses the *dodekatēmorion* of the Ascendant and where it lies (Heph. III, 4.19–34, including an interpretation for each *dodekatēmorion*).[141]

---

139   Heph. III, 4. t-1, p. 231.12–17 Pingree. ⟨δ'⟩ Πῶς ἄν τις προγνοίη τὰς πεύσεις τῶν / βουλομένων σκέψασθαι ἐκ καταρχῆς / Γνοίη δ' ἄν τις τῶν προσιόντων καὶ προγνῶναι βουλο-/μένων ἐκ καταρ-χῆς τὸ προγινόμενον κατὰ καθολικὸν καὶ / συνοπτικὸν εἶδος ὁμοιοτρόπως μάλιστα ταῖς γενέσεσι τὴν / ἐπίσκεψιν ποιησάμενος.

140   The term is Deborah Houlding's, which I am adopting here. It is called 'thought interpretation' or 'consultation chart' by Dykes, *Hephaestion Apotelesmatics Book III*. See more about its later tradition in Hermann of Carinthia, *The Search of the Heart*, trans. and ed. Benjamin N. Dykes (Minneapolis, MN: The Cazimi Press, 2011).

141   Pingree, *Yavanajātaka*, II, 371, discusses this passage and its relationship to Ch. 52, verses 7–10.

Another method uses places from the Lot of Fortune to ascertain topics of the *katarchē* and the people involved with it (Heph. III, 4.14–18); earlier we discussed a lot-like technique in the Mystical Method of 'Hermes' (pp. 25–26). In addition, 'Palchus' explains how someone may know 'from the Lot of Fortune what the questioner wishes to ask'.[142] This two-page transcribed passage is ascribed to Dorotheus. As László notes, its similarity in wording to Heph. III, 4.14–18 demonstrates that 'Palchus' and Hephaestio were drawing from the same original source, and the manuscript sources in this example explicitly say that person is Dorotheus: '... and these issues concerning people are collected by Dorotheus'.[143]

In the same chapter we find an additional method relevant for our purposes, involving the places of the chart (mainly the centrepins), a part of which is concerned with past, present and future:

> Also one must observe the two places on either side (that is the decline and the post-ascension of the Midheaven), and one must inspect the stars in them, those in the decline as showing the past, and those on the post-ascension the future, but those in the Midheaven, things in the present time itself.[144]

This ability to use the chart not only to know what is occurring in the present, but also to interpret past and future, is interesting because this, too, is a function of divination: not only to see the future, but to learn as well about the past and the present.

The concept of casting a chart beforehand to discover what is on the client's mind was taken up in the *Yavanajātaka* (chs. 52–63 are all concerned with the thoughts of the client).[145] However, we can find some earlier evidence for this

---

142 In Laur. plut. 28.33, *CCAG* I, 53, fol. 200ᵛ, no. 7: Περὶ τοῦ γνῶναι, ἀπὸ τοῦ κλήρου τῆς τύχης τὸν πυνθανόμενον περὶ τίνος θέλει ἐρωτᾶν. As I write this up for publication, I see that László, *Inceptions*, 55, has discussed this very text, using a transcription by Zuretti from Escorial Φ.I.5, fol. 322 in *CCAG* XI/1, 202–203; see 53–56 for his full examination. One could also observe the use of the Lot of Fortune places in Manilius in a katarchic framework.

143 *CCAG* XI/1, 203.22–23, my translation. '... συμπεριλαμβάνεται δὲ καὶ τὰ περὶ προσώπων Δωροθέου.' László, *Inceptions*, also notes this passage and the similarity of wordings in the Escorial manuscript with those of Hephaestio: see 55 and n. 42.

144 Heph. III, 4.3, p. 231.21–27 Pingree, my translation. 'καὶ τοὺς παρ' ἑκάτερα δύο τόπους ἐφορατέον (τουτέστι τό τε ἀπόκλιμα καὶ τὴν ἐπαναφορὰν τοῦ μεσουρανήματος), τούς τε ἐν αὐτοῖς ἀστέρας ἐπισκοπητέον τοὺς μὲν ἐπὶ τοῦ ἀποκλίματος ὡς δηλοῦντας τὰ παρῳχηκότα, τοὺς δὲ ἐπὶ τῆς ἐπαναφορᾶς τὰ μέλλοντα, τὰ δὲ ἐν αὐτῷ τῷ ἐνεστῶτι καιρῷ τοὺς ἐν τῷ μεσουρανήματι.'

145 For commentary on this, see esp. Pingree's comments in *Yavanajātaka*, vol. II, 371. Pingree thought the origin date of the 'original' Greek version of the Yavanajātaka was ca. 150 CE,

kind of practice both in Babylon and in the oracle tradition. In Babylon, in the texts of the medical omen series called Sakikku, Tablets 1 and 2 of this series deal with the omens seen by the doctor/exorcist [ašipu] on his way to the patient's house.[146] These omens give a preview of the outcome of the illness, for example: 'If he sees either a black dog or a black pig: that patient will die',[147] In the evidence of petitioners to Greek oracles, some clients concealed the topic of their questions, or had a sealed letter whose contents they wanted to know[148] and thought the god should know it.[149] The evidence of these two examples is not conclusive, to be sure, but at least it shows the concept was not unheard of.

For a final look at interrogational astrology, which later would be expanded and embraced in Arabic astrology, let us turn to documents ascribed to an author called 'Palchus' and another text containing a large collection of material on katarchic astrology, including interrogations.

4.2.4   The 'Palchus' Material and Material from the 'Mysteries'

The material ascribed to 'Palchus' contains katarchic charts including interrogations dated in the fifth century CE, which at least provides a *terminus ante quem*. These charts, and more, are covered in the contribution of Levente László elsewhere in this volume, so I will mainly summarise the material from both 'Palchus' and the 'Mysteries', and make a few remarks on the contents relevant to this particular investigation. The name 'Palchus' is a toponym, 'from Balkh' (now in present day Afghanistan); because he was also from Balkh, it has been (erroneously) ascribed to Abū Ma'shar.[150] But despite the uncertain author-

---

written by Sphujidhvaja ca. 270 CE (but see Bill M. Mak, 'The Date and Nature of Sphujidhvaja's Yavanajātaka Reconsidered in the Light of Some Newly Discovered Materials', *History of Science in South Asia* 1 [2013]: 1–20). We have seen above, n. 1, that Pingree considered interrogational astrology to be an Indian invention.

146 A.R. George, 'Babylonian Texts from the Folios of Sidney Smith. Part Two: Prognostic and Diagnostic Omens, Tablet 1', *Revue d'Assyriologie* 85 (1991): 138. I thank Francesca Rochberg for this reference.

147 George, 'Babylonian Texts', 143, Tablet 1, line 5.

148 Bouché-Leclercq, *L'astrologie grecque*, 471.

149 Eidinow, *Oracles*, 121, 126, 136.

150 See discussions in David Pingree, 'The Astrological School of John Abramius' *Dumbarton Oaks Papers* 25 (1971): 203–204; and László, *Inceptions*, 2022, 238–239. For the *nisba* al-Balkhī as part of Abū Ma'shar's full name, see the biographies in David Pingree, 'Abū Ma'shar Al-Balkhī, Ja'far ibn Muhammad', in *Dictionary of Scientific Biography*, Vol. 1, ed. Charles Coulston Gillispie, 32–39. Vol. 1, (New York: Scribner, 1970) 32, 36; and Charles Burnett, in Keiji Yamamoto and Charles Burnett, eds. *Abū Maʿšar, The Great Introduction to Astrology* (Leiden/Boston: Brill, 2019), Vol. 1, 1.

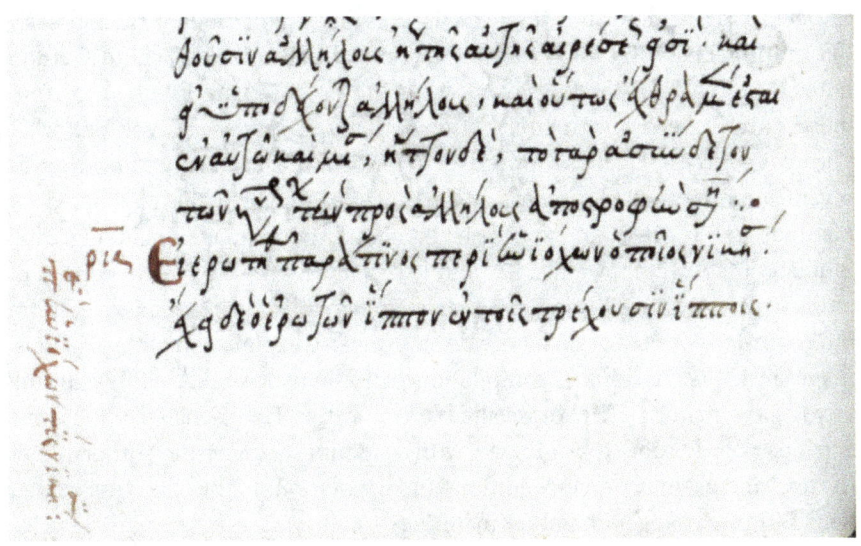

FIGURE 1.6   On Which Charioteer will Win (Title on the side in red)
Note: Laur. Plut. 28.33, fol. 52ᵛ, line 21, my translation. Εἰ ἐρωτηθῇς παρά τίνος περὶ ἡνιόχων ὁ ποῖος νικήσει This chapter is edited in CCAG XI/1, 170.19–171.8 (Escorial Φ.1.5, fol. 237ᵛ. In Angel. gr. 29, it is fol. 31ʳ, lines 1–12).

ship, the material it contains has been noted as deriving from earlier sources by more than one writer.[151] Thus the material covered by these texts is clearly older than the date of its supposed author, and likely earlier than the fifth century. This is immediately obvious because the questions covered in the multiple page texts[152] devoted to interrogations include things like 'Which charioteer will win?'—a question unlikely to be asked by an Arabic astrologer of the early Middle Ages.

Just as we saw in Serapio and Paulus, this passage uses the managing planet,[153] and its condition and location, to answer the question; the outcomes range from the charioteer coming in first to predicting his injury or death.

---

151   E.g., Gordon, 'Big Nose', 99, 101; and Roger Beck, 'Thus Spake Not Zarathuštra: Zoroastrian Pseudepigrapha of the Greco-Roman World', in *A History of Zoroastrianism. Zoroastrianism under Macedonian and Roman Rule (vol. 3)*, edited by Mary Boyce and Frantz Grenet (Leiden: E.J. Brill, 1991), 534 n. 132: 'Much of the material ascribed to Palchus is of course considerably earlier.'

152   In Angel.gr. 29, 60 folia, with apographs in Laur. plut. 28.33 and Escorial Φ.1.5.

153   That is, the planet ruling the planetary hour when the chart was cast; see Paulus, *Introduction*, Chapter 21, p. 42.16–45.9 Boer; and for a table of planetary hours, Greenbaum, *Daimon in Hellenistic Astrology*, 135, Table 4.1.

David Pingree describes the texts as '... a mixture of Hellenistic and early Byzantine texts with Greek translation from the Arabic'.[154] Richard Gordon notes that Book 1 of the 'Mysteries', whose three books are ascribed to 'Apomasar', are 'spliced with material from other sources by a Greek editor',[155] The two sources, 'Palchus' and the 'Mysteries' were transcribed together in several manuscripts, the oldest and main one, Angelicus gr. 29, copied by Eleutherius Elius in 1388 (from which apographs were made, including Laur. Plut. 28.33 (shown above, Fig. 1.4) and Escorial Φ.1.5.)[156] No critical edition of either 'Palchus' or the 'Mysteries' has been fully published in a modern edition, but recently, Levente László has made an extensive exploration of the 'Palchus' material, which he calls 'a compilation of Hellenistic and Arabo-Byzantine astrological material ... with invaluable content'.[157] He discusses manuscript versions not mentioned by Pingree, with a stemma, assesses the authorship of the text, and usefully provides editions and translations of the charts associated with Zeno's astrologer and other material.[158]

The contents of the original compilation in Angelicus graecus 29 include a letter of Manuel Komnenos defending astrology (fols. 1–9), the Greek version of the aforementioned 'Mysteries' (fols. 10–91), and 'from the Apotelesmatic Book of Palchus' (fols. 91–152). The first and second books of the 'Mysteries' and this last 'Apotelesmatic Book of Palchus' is where the katarchic material, including interrogations, is found.

The texts themselves are collections and compilations of various astrological doctrines. They mention a number of authors on interrogations and *katarchē* in general, with instructions on how to interpret each question following the question itself. The excerpts on *katarchē* from earlier authors include Dorotheus, Timaeus, Serapion, Demetrius and Julian of Laodicea.[159] The collection contains the famous interrogation charts of the 5th century CE (Leontius crowned at Antioch, charts of fear of shipwreck, the linen of the slave girl, etc.). It would not be unreasonable, then, to call this part of the collection a 'katarchic reader' or a primer on *katarchē* for astrologers interested in learning the techniques of this genre.

---

154   Pingree, 'Abramius', 204.
155   Gordon, 'Big Nose', 132.
156   Pingree, 'Abramius', 202–204; László, *Inceptions*, 81, 239–240.
157   László, *Inceptions*, 239.
158   László, 81–103, 238–239.
159   See *CCAG* V/1, 4–57, incipits for the folia in Angelicus graecus 29. Dorotheus (fol. 26ʳ [Mysteries 1], 125ᵛ ['Palchus']), Timaeus (fol. 102 ['Palchus']), Serapion (fols. 103ʳ, 106ʳ, 107ʳ⁻ᵛ ['Palchus']), Demetrius (113ʳ ['Palchus']), Julian (113ʳ ['Palchus']).

TABLE 1.6   Examples of topics and texts in 'Mysteries' Books 1 and 2, and 'Palchus'

Folio Number Laur. plut. 33	Folio Number Angel. gr. 29	Topic
18ʳ, 19ʳ	16ᵛ, 17ʳ, ch. 40–41	'If you are asked about ... theft'
19ᵛ	17ᵛ, ch. 42	'If he wishes to know the image ... of the thief'
20ᵛ	17ᵛ, ch. 43	'If you are asked about the stolen item'
21ᵛ	18ʳ, ch. 47	'What is the name of the thief?'
28ᵛ	21ᵛ, ch. 69	'On the quality of the battle and who will win'
52ᵛ	31ʳ, ch. 111	'Which charioteer will win?'
56ʳ	34ᵛ, ch. 134	'Will my child have a big nose?'
56ᵛ	34ᵛ, ch. 138	'Will it have a squint?'
57	34ᵛ, ch. 139	'Will it live or die?'
58	35ʳ, ch. 141	'Will it be a single birth or twins?'
66	38ᵛ, ch. 154	'Is the unborn child mine or from another?'
199	96ʳ, ch. 4	'What good or bad things will happen to me?'
200, ch. 7	97ᵛ, ch. 7	'What is someone asking about?' ('from the Lot of Fortune')
210ᵛ, ch. 17	100ᵛ, ch. 17	Erasistratus on theft
213ᵛ, ch. 18	102ʳ, ch. 18	Timaeus on fugitives
215ᵛ, ch. 19	103ʳ, ch. 19	Serapion on *katarchai*
235ᵛ, ch. 57	112ʳ, ch. 57	A voyage by ship (event)
235ᵛ, ch. 58	112ʳ, ch. 58	Question on a *katarchē* on fear about a voyage to Athens
235ᵛ, ch. 59	112ᵛ, ch. 59	Question in Smyrna on fear about a ship from Alexandria

What is perfectly clear is that 1) the material is older than the date of the compilation and 2) it was an important enough topic that it survived in two major manuscripts on astrological topics.[160] In correlating and looking at the two texts and their topics, two things become immediately evident: 1) the top-

---

160   Angel. gr. 29 also contains the Greek version of Abū Maʿshar's *Great Introduction*; see David Pingree in Yamamoto/Burnett, *Abū Maʿšar Great Introduction*, vol. 2, 1–3. Laur. plut. 28.33 (the apograph of Angel. gr. 29) contains 'Apomasar's *Book of the Mysteries*' (3 books *in total*), including sections on *katarchē* containing interrogations (folios 18–67).

ics are very similar across centuries and authors; and 2) much of the material being covered is very Hellenistic in tone.

The compiler of the texts is keen on presenting a Hellenistic history of *katarchē*, including that which is in the form of questions. That this person comes from the Byzantine period is not all that important; what is relevant is that the doctrine and its topics are maintained over hundreds of years, from Dorotheus to Byzantium. Certain practices may be adapted over time, other interpretative practices may arise, or the emphasis on one practice or another changed, but the foundation is stable.

5   Some Final Observations

In investigating these texts, the points that should be stressed are that there is much material on all forms of *katarchē*, the sections on interrogations fit right in with the other forms, and the techniques for all of these branches are the same. Furthermore, the idea of 'questioning' is present in many of these texts, whether it is a typical interrogation, i.e. a question about something asked of the astrologer, who then casts a chart for that time for the answer; or the questioning of an event chart (what will the outcome be?), the questioning involved in the casting of an election (what are you trying to elect for? what results are you looking for?), or asking questions about the intentions and thoughts of the questioner. All of these kinds of charts, under the general rubric 'katarchai', are therefore intimately connected by 1) the fact that they are charts cast for something other than a birth; 2) each of them can be elucidated by asking either one or a series of questions about the topics concerned; and 3) the same astrological rules are used in interpreting these processes. This again shows the innate and inextricable connection between questions and *katarchē*. To separate the different forms these take, to divorce them from one another, or to emphasise a hierarchy among them, misses the point about the common theoretical, and even cultural, basis under which they are conceived.[161] That interrogations

---

161   Although he claims not to privilege one branch over another, ('I take it for granted that questions, elections and event charts ... are all valid', Dykes, *Hephaistion Apotelesmatics Book III*, 10) refers to explicit questions as 'second best alternatives' to a timed event chart (Dykes, 17). He states that the different kinds of katarchic charts use 'different assumptions and procedures', and therefore should not be grouped together 'uncritically' (Dykes, 16), but they *are* related all the same. The fundamental impetus for any kind of katarchic chart is to interpret the outcomes of actions and/or events, whether they are in the form of an elected time for an event, an event unelected, a question about something in the client's

specifically have a different ontological basis, in that they are not cast for a physical space and time moment in which an event occurred, but for the moment that a questioner asks a sincere and respectful question, does not seem to be an issue as far as interpretation is concerned[162]—though it certainly connects them with their divinatory roots.

This explicit, as opposed to what we could say is sometimes an earlier *implicit*, differentiation of interrogations from other kinds of *katarchai* can be viewed in two ways. It seems to be a later development, in that earlier texts, like the Greek fragments of Dorotheus, do not make a distinction in method for treating the different branches (in Dorotheus's case, elections, events and questions about events are handled using the same methods).[163] But, as Robert Hand points out,[164] and I have also mentioned earlier, the word 'katarchē' contains the idea of a beginning in its etymology and meanings, a moment in time when something begins, and often with the sense of a proper or right time. A question does not have the physical space and time basis of an event; its beginning is in the querent's mind and intention. Its rationale is coming, instead, from something like the oracle tradition in which the question *as posed* is the impetus for divine response, a question that in its very framework and language shows its prayerful stance and plea for the god to supply the answer, as we saw earlier with Maximus and Plutarch. This is not so far off the early modern horary stricture that the client must ask the question with a sincere and respectful attitude and no hint of frivolity in order to get a proper answer from the astrologer.[165] And ultimately, it connects with the oracular and ritual strictures that a petitioner must also approach the god with her question in a pious and sincere manner. This route through divination, then, is the ultimate origin of questions in astrology.

---

life, or the process and outcome of an illness. *Katarchai* can be, and are, subdivided, but their basic rationale is the same.

162   Similar methods are used for both events and interrogations, as we saw in Heph. III, 11.2.

163   See examples of this in medieval Latin texts, esp. Bonatti, in Robert S. Hand, 'The Use of Military Astrology in Late Medieval Italy' (PhD Thesis, The Catholic University of America, 2014), 170–173.

164   Hand, 'The Use of Military Astrology', 49.

165   See William Lilly, *Anima Astrologiae: or, A Guide for Astrologers* (London: B. Harris, 1676), 4–5 (Consideration 2). This is Lilly's annotated version of Guido Bonatti's 146 Considerations on Judgements, translated by Henry Coley; also Guido Bonatti, *De astronomia tractatus X* (Basle: n.p., 1550), Tractate V, col. 162.53–163.18. Translation in Benjamin N. Dykes, *Book of Astronomy Guido Bonatti*, 2 vols (Golden Valley, MN: Cazimi Press, 2007), vol. 1, 265.

Bibliography

Manuscripts

Angelicus graecus 29, 14th cent. Rome: Biblioteca Angelica (Digital: https://www.intern
etculturale.it/it/16/search/detail?id=oai%3Awww.internetculturale.sbn.it%2FTeca
%3A20%3ANT0000%3ACNMD%5C%5C0000116644&mode=all&teca=MagTeca+-
+ICCU)

Escorial Φ.I.5, 16th cent. Madrid, San Lorenzo de el Escorial: Real Biblioteca (Digital:
https://rbme.patrimonionacional.es/s/rbme/item/15953#?xywh=-3640%2C-250%2
C10453%2C4990)

Laurentianus Pluteus 28.33, 16th cent. Florence: Biblioteca Medicea Laurenziana
(Digital: https://tecabml.contentdm.oclc.org/digital/collection/plutei/id/735327/re
c/1491)

Parisinus graecus 2417, 13th cent. Paris: Bibliothèque nationale de France (Digital:
https://gallica.bnf.fr/ark:/12148/btv1b107223308/f169.planchecontact)

Vaticanus graecus 1056, 14th cent. Vatican City: Vatican Apostolic Library (Digital Vatican Library: https://digi.vatlib.it/view/MSS_Vat.gr.1056)

Primary Sources

Abū Maʿšar. *Abū Maʿšar, The Great Introduction to Astrology*. Edited by Keiji Yamamoto
and Charles Burnett. Leiden/Boston: Brill, 2019.

Bonatti, Guido. *De astronomia tractatus X*. Basle: n.p., 1550. http://hardenberg.jalb.de/
display_dokument.php?elementId=5257 (accessed 9 March 2025)

Bonatti, Guido. *Book of Astronomy Guido Bonatti*. Translated by Benjamin Dykes, PhD.
2 vols. Golden Valley, MN: Cazimi Press, 2007.

Catalogus Codicum Astrologorum Graecorum. Edited by Franz Cumont et al. 12 vols.
Brussels: Henri Lamertin, 1898–1953. Abbreviated as CCAG.

Cicero, Marcus Tullius. *De senectute. De amicitia. De divinatione*. Translated by W.A. Fal-
coner, Loeb Classical Library. Cambridge, MA: Harvard University Press, 1923, repr.
2001.

Dionysius of Halicarnassus. *The Roman Antiquities*, Vol. 1. Translated by Earnest Cary.
Loeb Classical Library. Cambridge, MA/London, 1937.

Dorotheus of Sidon. *Carmen Astrologicum*. Edited and translated by David Pingree.
Leipzig: B.G. Teubner, 1976.

Dorotheos of Sidon. *Die Fragmente des Dorotheos von Sidon, Lieferung IV*. Edited, translated and annotated by Viktor Stegemann. Unpublished, manuscript held in the
Berliner Staatsbibliothek.

Firmicus Maternus, Julius. *Matheseos libri VIII*. Edited by Wilhelm Kroll, Franz Skutsch
and Konrat Ziegler. 2 vols. Leipzig: B.G. Teubner, 1897–1913.

Hephaestio. *Apotelesmaticorum libri tres*. Edited by David Pingree. 2 vols. Leipzig:
B.G. Teubner, 1973.

Hephaistion of Thebes: Apotelesmatics Book III: On Inceptions. Edited by B.N. Dykes, translated by E.J. Gramaglia. Minneapolis: Cazimi Press, 2013.

Hermann of Carinthia. *The Search of the Heart*. Translated and edited by Benjamin N. Dykes. Minneapolis, MN: The Cazimi Press, 2011.

Hermetis Trismegisti: De triginta sex decanis. Edited by Simonetta Feraboli. Hermes Latinus IV/1 (Corpus Christianorum). Turnhout, Belgium: Brepols, 1994.

Herodotus. *The Histories of Herodotus of Halicarnassus*. Translated by Harry Carter. London: Oxford University Press, 1962.

Hesiod. *Works and Days*. Translated by Hugh G. Evelyn-White. In *Hesiod, Homeric Hymns, Epic Cycle, Homerica*. Loeb Classical Library. Cambridge, MA: Harvard University Press, 1914, repr. 1995.

Iamblichus. *On The Mysteries*. Edited, translated and commentary by Emma C. Clarke, John M. Dillon and Jackson P. Hershbell. Vol. 4, Writings from the Greco-Roman World. Atlanta: Society of Biblical Literature, 2003.

Juvenal. *Satire 6*. Edited by Lindsay Watson and Patricia Watson. Oxford Classical Texts. Cambridge: Cambridge University Press, 2014.

Lightfoot, J.L. *Pseudo-Manetho Apotelesmatica Books Two, Three, and Six*. Oxford: Oxford University Press, 2020.

Lightfoot, J.L. *Pseudo-Manetho Apotelesmatica: Books Four, One, and Five*. Oxford: Oxford University Press, 2023.

Lilly, William, and Henry Coley. *Anima Astrologiae; or, a Guide for Astrologers, Being the considerations of the Famous Guido Bonatus Faithfully rendred into English. As Also The Choicest Aphorisms of Cardan's Seaven Segments*. London: B. Harris at the Stationers' Arms, 1676. https://wellcomecollection.org/works/s7p7dhv4 (accessed 9 March 2025).

Livy. *The History of Rome*. Translated by William Masfen Roberts. Vol. 1. New York: E.P. Dutton, 1912.

Lopilato, Robert. 'The "Apotelesmatika" of Manetho'. Ph.D. Thesis, Brown University, 1998.

Lydus, John. *Ioannis Laurentii Lydi Liber de Ostentis et Calendaria Graeca Omnia*. Edited by Curt Wachsmuth. Leipzig: B.G. Teubner, 1897.

Nigidius Figulus, Publius. *P. Nigidii Figuli Operum Reliquiae*. Edited by Anton Swoboda. Prague: F. Tempsky, 1889.

Manilius, Marcus. *Astronomica*. Edited and translated by George P. Goold, Loeb Classical Library. Cambridge, MA/London: Harvard University Press, 1977, repr. 1997.

Maximus of Ephesus. [Maxime.] *Des initiatives*. Edited, translated and annotated by Nicola Zito. Paris: Les Belles Lettres, 2016.

Olympiodorus. *Eis ton Paulon ⟨Heliodorou⟩. Heliodori, ut dicitur, in Paulum Alexandrinum Commentarium*. Edited by Emilie Boer. Leipzig: B.G. Teubner, 1962.

Parke, H.W., and D.E.W. Wormell. *The Delphic Oracle*. 2 vols. Oxford: Basil Blackwell, 1956.

Paulus Alexandrinus. *Elementa Apotelesmatica*. Edited by Emilie Boer. Leipzig: B.G. Teubner, 1958.

(Paulus and Olympiodorus) Greenbaum, Dorian Gieseler. *Late Classical Astrology: Paulus Alexandrinus and Olympiodorus with the Scholia from Later Commentators*. Translated and annot. Dorian Gieseler Greenbaum. Edited by Robert Hand. Reston, VA: ARHAT, 2001.

Petronius Arbiter. *The Satyricon*. Translated by P.G. Walsh. Oxford: Oxford University Press, 1997.

Pingree, David, ed., trans. and comm. *The Yavanajātaka of Sphujidhvaja*. 2 vols. Cambridge, MA/London: Harvard University Press, 1978.

Plato. *Timaeus*. Translated by R.G. Bury. In *Plato*, IX. Loeb Classical Library. Cambridge, MA: Harvard University Press, 1929, repr. 1989.

Pliny the Elder. *Natural History*. Vol. I. Translated by Harris Rackham. Loeb Classical Library. Cambridge, MA: Harvard University Press, 1938.

Pliny the Elder. *Natural History, Books 3–7*. Vol. II. Translated by H. Rackham. Loeb Classical Library. Cambridge, MA/London: Harvard University Press, 1942.

Plutarch. *The E at Delphi*. Translated by Frank Cole Babbitt. In *Moralia*, V. Loeb Classical Library. Cambridge, MA: Harvard University Press, 1936, repr. 2003.

Porphyry. *Lettera ad Anebo*. Edited by A.R. Sodano. Naples: L'arte tipografica, 1958.

Porphyry. *Lettre à Anébon l'Égyptien*. Edited by Henri Dominique Saffrey and Alain-Philippe Segonds. Paris: Les Belles Lettres, 2012.

Propertius. *Elegies*. Translated by G.P. Goold, Loeb Classical Library. Cambridge, MA/London: Harvard University Press, 1990.

Ptolemy, Claudius. *Ptolemy, Tetrabiblos*. Trans. F.E. Robbins. Vol. 435, Loeb Classical Library. Cambridge, MA: Harvard University Press, 1940, repr. 1994.

Ptolemy, Claudius. *Ἀποτελεσματικά*. Edited by Wolfgang Hübner. Opera quae exstant omnia III, 1. Stuttgart/Leipzig: B.G. Teubner, 1998.

Reiner, Erica, and David Pingree. *Babylonian Planetary Omens*. Vol. 3, Bibliotheca Mesopotamica 2. Groningen: Styx, 1998.

Schmidt, Robert. *The Astrological Record of the Early Sages in Greek*. Vol. X, Greek Track. Berkeley Springs, WV: The Golden Hind Press, 1995.

Sjöberg, Å., and E. Bergmann. *The Collection of the Sumerian Temple Hymns*, Texts from Cuneiform Sources 3. Locust Valley, NY: J.J. Augustin, 1969.

Stegemann, Viktor. ed., trans. and comm. *Die Fragmente des Dorotheos von Sidon, Lieferung IV*. Unpublished, manuscript held in the Berliner Staatsbibliothek.

Tacitus, *Annals*, vol. IV. Translated by John Jackson. Loeb Classical Library. Cambridge, MA/London: Harvard University Press, 1937.

Tacitus, *Annals*, vol. V. Translated by John Jackson. Loeb Classical Library. Cambridge, MA/London: Harvard University Press, 1937.

Vettius Valens. *Anthologiarum libri*. Edited by Wilhelm Kroll. Berlin: Weidmann, 1908.

Vettius Valens. *Anthologiarum libri novem*. Edited by David Pingree. Leipzig: B.G. Teubner, 1986.

Secondary Sources

Abry, Josèphe-Henriette. 'Who was Agrippina Waiting For?' In *Horoscopes and Public Spheres: Essays on the History of Astrology*, edited by Günther Oestmann, H Darrel Rutkin and Kocku von Stuckrad, 37–48, Berlin/New York: Walter de Gruyter, 2005.

Addey, Crystal. *Divination and Theurgy in Neoplatonism: Oracles of the Gods*, Ashgate Studies in Philosophy & Theology in Late Antiquity. Farnham, Surrey/Burlington, VT: Ashgate, 2014.

Annus, Amar. 'On the Beginnings and Continuities of Omen Sciences in the Ancient World'. In *Divination and Interpretation of Signs in the Ancient World*, edited by Amar Annus, 1–18, Chicago: University of Chicago Press, 2010.

Bachvarova, Mary R. 'The Transmission of Liver Divination from East to West'. *Studi Micenei ed Egeo-Anatolici* 54 (2012): 143–164.

Beck, Roger. 'Thus Spake Not Zarathuštra: Zoroastrian Pseudepigrapha of the Greco-Roman World'. In *A History of Zoroastrianism. Zoroastrianism under Macedonian and Roman Rule (vol. 3)*, edited by Mary Boyce and Frantz Grenet. Leiden: E.J. Brill, 1991.

Bodi, Daniel. 'Akkadian and Aramaic Terms for a "Favorable Time" (*ḥidānu, adānu*, and *'iddān*): Semitic Precursors of Greek *kairos*?' In *Time and History in the Ancient Near East. Proceedings of the 56th Rencontre Assyriologique Internationale at Barcelona 26–30 July 2010*, edited by L. Feliu, J. Llop, A. Millet Albà and J. Sanmartín, 47–56, Winona Lake, IN: Eisenbrauns, 2013.

Bomhard, Anne-Sophie von. *The Naos of the Decades: From the Observation of the Sky to Mythology and Astrology*. Translated by Ludwig von Bomhard, Oxford Centre for Maritime Archaeology, Monograph 3. Oxford: Institute of Archaeology, University of Oxford, 2008.

Bouché-Leclercq, Auguste. *L'astrologie grecque*. Paris: E. Leroux, 1899.

Boudet, Jean-Patrice. 'From Baghdad to *Civitas Solis*: Horoscopes of Foundations of Cities'. In *From Masha'allah to Kepler: Theory and Practice in Medieval and Renaissance Astrology*, edited by Charles Burnett and Dorian Gieseler Greenbaum, 49–76, Ceredigion, Wales: Sophia Centre Press, 2015.

Burkert, Walter. *The Orientalizing Revolution: Near Eastern Influence on Greek Culture in the Early Archaic Age*. Cambridge, MA: Harvard University Press, 1992, repr. 1995.

Collins, Derek. 'Mapping the Entrails: The Practice of Greek Hepatoscopy'. *American Journal of Philology* 129, no. 3 (2008): 319–345.

Cook, John Granger. *Crucifixion in the Mediterranean World*. Vol. 327, Wissenschaftliche Untersuchungen zum Neuen Testament. Tübingen: Mohr Siebeck, 2014.

Cornelius, Geoffrey. 'Is Astrology Divination and Does it Matter?' 1998. http://cura.free .fr/quinq/01gfcor.html.

Cornelius, Geoffrey. *The Moment of Astrology: Origins in Divination*. London: Arkana/ Penguin, 1994.

Cornelius, Geoffrey. *The Moment of Astrology: Origins in Divination*. 2nd ed. Bourne-mouth: The Wessex Astrologer, 2003.

Cornelius, Geoffrey. *A Paper and a Series of Articles by Geoffrey Cornelius*. Foreward by Kirk Little, Cosmocritic, 2016. Reprint, https://cosmocritic.com/wp-content/upload s/2023/12/cornelius_geoffrey_oslo_and_moment.pdf.

Cumont, Franz. *Astrology and Religion among the Greeks and Romans*. History of Religions Series 1911–1912. New York/London: G.P. Putnam's Sons, 1912.

Cumont, Franz. *L'Égypte des astrologues*. Brussels: La Fondation Égyptologique Reine Élisabeth, 1937.

Dunand, Françoise, and Christiane Zivie-Coche. *Gods and Men in Egypt: 3000 BCE to 395 CE*. Translated by David Lorton. Ithaca, NY: Cornell University Press, 2004.

Eidinow, Esther. *Oracles, Curses and Risk among the Ancient Greeks*. Oxford: Oxford University Press, 2007.

Eidinow, Esther. 'Oracular Consultations, Fate, and the Concept of the Individual'. In *Divination in the Ancient World*, edited by Veit Rosenberger, 21–39, Stuttgart: Franz Steiner Verlag, 2013.

Faraone, Christopher Athanasious. *Hexametrical Genres from Homer to Theocritus*. New York: Oxford University Press, 2021.

Fontenrose, Joseph. *The Delphic Oracle*. Berkeley/Los Angeles: University of California Press, 1978.

Frommhold, Katrin. *Die Bedeutung und Berechnung der Empfängnis in der Astrologie der Antike*. Vol. 38, Orbis antiquus. Münster: Aschendorff, 2004.

George, A.R. 'Babylonian Texts from the Folios of Sidney Smith. Part Two: Prognostic and Diagnostic Omens, Tablet I'. *Revue d'Assyriologie* 85 (1991): 137–163.

Gordon, Richard. 'Quaedam Veritatis Umbrae: Hellenistic Magic and Astrology'. In *Conventional Values of the Hellenisti Greeks*, edited by Per Bilde, Troels Engberg-Pedersen, Lise Hannestad and Jan Zahle, Aarhus: Aarhus University Press, 1997.

Gordon, Richard. '"Will my child have a big nose?"; Uncertainty, authority and narrative in katarchic astrology'. In *Divination in the Ancient World: Religious Options and the Individual*, edited by Veit Rosenberger, 93–137, Stuttgart: Franz Steiner Verlag, 2013.

Greenbaum, Dorian Gieseler. *The Daimon in Hellenistic Astrology: Origins and Influence*. Vol. 11, Ancient Magic and Divination. Leiden/Boston: Brill, 2016.

Greenbaum, Dorian Gieseler. 'The Hellenistic Horoscope'. In *Hellenistic Astronomy: The Science in Its Contexts*, edited by Alan C. Bowen and Francesca Rochberg, 443–471, Leiden/Boston: Brill, 2020.

Greenbaum, Dorian Gieseler. 'Divination and decumbiture: Katarchic astrology and Greek medicine'. In *Divination and Knowledge in Greco-Roman Antiquity*, edited by Crystal Addey, 109–137, London/New York: Routledge, 2022.

Greenbaum, Dorian Gieseler, and Micah T. Ross. 'The Role of Egypt in the Development of the Horoscope'. In *Egypt in Transition: Social and Religious Development of Egypt in the First Millennium* BCE, edited by Ladislav Bareš, Filip Coppens and Kveta Smolarikova, 146–182, Prague: Faculty of Arts, Charles University in Prague, 2010.

Gundel, Wilhelm, and Hans Georg Gundel. *Astrologumena. Die astrologische Literatur in der Antike und ihre Geschichte*. Wiesbaden: Steiner, 1966.

Hand, Robert S. 'The Use of Military Astrology in Late Medieval Italy'. PhD Thesis, The Catholic University of America, 2014.

Hegedus, Tim. *Early Christianity and Ancient Astrology*. New York/Oxford: Peter Lang, 2007.

Heilen, Stephan. 'Ancient Scholars on the Horoscope of Rome'. *Culture and Cosmos* 11 (2007): 43–68.

Heilen, Stephan. *Hadriani genitura. Die astrologischen Fragmente des Antigonos von Nikaia. Edition, Übersetzung und Kommentar*. 2 vols. Vol. 43, Texte und Kommentare. Berlin: De Gruyter, 2015.

Heineman, Kristin M. *The Decadence of Delphi: The Oracle in the Second Century AD and Beyond*. Abingdon UK/New York: Routledge, 2018.

Horowitz, Wayne C. *Mesopotamian Cosmic Geography*. Winona Lake, IN: Eisenbrauns, 1998.

Houlding, Deborah. 'Ancient Enquiry Charts'. United Astrology Conference, New Orleans, Louisiana, 26 May 2012.

Hübner, Wolfgang. *Raum, Zeit und soziales Rollenspiel der vier Kardinalpunkte in der antiken Katarchenhoroskopie*. Band 194, Beiträge zur Altertumskunde. Munich/Leipzig: K.G. Saur Verlag, 2003.

Hudson-Williams, Alun, and Anthony J.S. Spawforth. 'Nigidius Figulus, Publius'. In *Oxford Classical Dictionary*, 3rd ed., edited by Simon Hornblower and Anthony Spawforth, 1044, Oxford/New York: Oxford University Press, 1996.

Keyser, Paul T. 'Erasistratus (Astrol.)'. In *The Encyclopedia of Ancient Natural Scientists*, edited by Paul Keyser and Georgia Irby-Massie, 294, Abingdon, UK/New York: Routledge, 2008.

Keyser, Paul T., and Georgia Irby-Massie. *The Encyclopedia of Ancient Natural Scientists: The Greek Tradition and its Many Heirs*. Abingdon: Routledge, 2008.

Kidd, D.A. 'Propertius Consults His Astrologer'. *Greece & Rome* 26, no. 2 (1979): 169–180.

Koch-Westenholz, Ulla. *Mesopotamian Astrology: An Introduction to Babylonian and Assyrian Celestial Divination*. Copenhagen: Museum Tusculanum Press, 1995.

Krauss, Rolf. 'Egyptian Calendars and Astronomy'. In *Cambridge History of Science, Vol-*

ume 1. Ancient Science, edited by Alexander Jones and Liba Taub, 131–143, Cambridge: Cambridge University Press, 2018.

Kruchten, Jean-Marie. 'Oracles'. In *The Ancient Gods Speak: A Guide to Egyptian Religion*, edited by Donald B. Redford, 298–302, New York: Oxford University Press, 2002.

László, Levente. 'The Inceptions of the Emperor Zeno's Anonymous Astrologer'. PhD Thesis, Eötvös Loránd University, 2023.

Leitz, Christian. *Tagewählerei. Das Buch ḥȝt nḥḥ pḥ.wy ḏt und verwandte Texte, Part 1*. Vol. 55, Ägyptologische Abhandlungen. Wiesbaden: Harrassowitz, 1994.

Lieven, Alexandra von. 'Divination in Ägypten'. *Altorientalische Forschungen* 26, no. 1 (1999): 77–126.

Lieven, Alexandra von. *Grundriss des Laufes der Sterne. Das sogennante Nutbuch*. Vol. 1. *Text*. Vol. 31, Carsten Niebuhr Institute Publications. The Carlsberg Papyri 8. Copenhagen: Museum Tusculanum Press, 2007.

Mak, Bill M. 'The Date and Nature of Sphujidhvaja's Yavanajātaka Reconsidered in the Light of Some Newly Discovered Materials'. *History of Science in South Asia* 1 (2013): 1–20.

Maul, Stefan M. 'Divination Culture and the Handling of the Future'. In *The Babylonian World*, edited by G. Leick, 361–372, New York/London: Routledge, 2007.

Meeks, Dimitri. 'Demons'. In *The Ancient Gods Speak*, edited by Donald B. Redford, 102–106, Oxford/New York: Oxford University Press, 2002.

Michalowski, Piotr. 'How to Read the Liver—In Sumerian'. In *If a Man Builds a Joyful House: Assyriological Studies in Honor of Erle Verdun Leichty*, edited by Ann K. Guinan, Maria deJ. Ellis, A.J. Ferrara, Sally M. Freedman, Matthew Rutz, Leonhard Sassmannshausen, Steve Tinney and M.W. Waters, 247–258. Vol. 31, Leiden/Boston: Brill, 2006.

Naether, Franziska, and Micah Ross. 'Interlude: A Series containing a Hemerology with Lengths of Daylight'. *Egitto e Vicino Oriente* 31 (2008): 52–91.

Nougayrol, Jean. 'Les rapports des haruspicines étrusque et assyro-babylonienne, et la foie d'argile de *Falerii Veteres* (Villa Giulia 3786)'. *Comptes rendus des séances de l'Académie des Inscriptions et Belles-Lettres* 99, no. 4 (1955): 509–519.

Pingree, David. 'Abū Maʿshar Al-Balkhī, Jaʿfar ibn Muhammad'. In *Dictionary of Scientific Biography*, edited by Charles Coulston Gillispie, 32–39. Vol. 1, New York: Scribner, 1970.

Pingree, David. 'The Astrological School of John Abramius'. *Dumbarton Oaks Papers* 25 (1971): 189–215.

Pingree, David. 'Astrology'. In *Dictionary of the History of Ideas: Studies of Selected Pivotal Ideas*, edited by Philip P. Wiener, 118–126. Vol. 1, New York: Charles Scriber's Sons, 1973.

Pingree, David. 'The Indian and Pseudo-Indian Passages in Greek and Latin Astronomical and Astrological Texts'. *Viator: Medieval and Renaissance Studies* 7 (1976): 141–195.

Pingree, David. *Jyotiḥśāstra: Astral and Mathematical Literature*. Edited by Jan Gonda. Vol. 4, A History of Indian Literature. Wiesbaden: Otto Harrassowitz, 1981.

Pingree, David. 'Māshā'allāh: Greek, Pahlavī, Arabic and Latin Astrology'. In *Perspectives arabes et médiévales sur la tradition scientifique et philosophique grecque. Actes du colloque de la SIHSPAI, Paris, 31 mars–3 avril 1993*, edited by Ahmad Hasnawi, Abdelali Elamrani-Jamal and Maroun Aouad, 123–136. Vol. 79, *Orientalia Lovaniensia Analecta*, Leuven and Paris: Peeters and Institut du Monde arabe, 1997.

Pingree, David. *From Astral Omens to Astrology: From Babylon to Bīkāner*. Rome: Istituto italiano per l'Africa e l'Oriente, 1997.

Pingree, David. 'The Byzantine Transmission of Māshā'allāh on Interrogational Astrology'. In *The Occult Sciences in Byzantium*, edited by Paul Magdalino and Maria Mavroudi, 231–243, Geneva: La Pomme d'or, 2006.

Potter, David. 'Constantine and the Gladiators'. *Classical Quarterly* 60, no. 2 (2010): 596–606.

Prada, Luigi. 'Dreams, Rising Stars and Falling Geckos: Divination in Ancient Egypt'. *Egyptian Archaeology* 51 (2017): 4–9.

Reiner, Erica. *Astral Magic in Babylonia. Transactions of the American Philosophical Society*, 85, no. 4. Philadelphia: Transactions of the American Philosophical Society, 1995.

Rochberg, Francesca. *The Heavenly Writing: Divination, Horoscopy, and Astronomy in Mesopotamian Culture*. Cambridge: Cambridge University Press, 2004.

Rochberg, Francesca. 'Conditionals, Inference and Possibility in Ancient Mesopotamian Science'. *Science in Context* 22, no. 1 (2009): 5–25.

Rochberg, Francesca. ' "If P, then Q": Form and Reasoning in Babylonian Divination'. In *Divination and Interpretation of Signs in the Ancient World*, edited by Amar Annus, 19–27, Chicago: University of Chicago Press, 2010.

Roth, Ann Macy. 'Genealogy of Hatshepsut's Family'. In *Hatshepsut: From Queen to Pharaoh*, edited by Catherine H. Roehrig, Renée Dreyfus and Cathleen A. Keller, 7, New York, New Haven: Metropolitan Museum of Art and Yale University Press, 2005.

Sauneron, Serge. 'Les songes et leur interprétation dans l'Égypte ancienne'. In *Les songes et leur interprétation. Égypte ancienne—Babylone–Hittites–Canaan–Israël–Islam–Peuples altaïques–Persans–Kurdes–Inde–Camboge–Cnine–Japon*, collected by Serge Sauneron et al., 17–61, Paris: Éditions du Seuil, 1959.

Shaw, Gregory. *Theurgy and the Soul: The Neoplatonism of Iamblichus*. University Park, PA: The Pennsylvania State University Press, 1995.

Smith, William, William Wayte and G.E. Marindin, Eds. *A Dictionary of Greek and Roman Antiquities*, London: John Murray, 1890, s.v. TEMPLUM. At the Perseus Digital Library, https://www.perseus.tufts.edu/hopper/text?doc=Perseus%3Atext%3A1999.04.0063%3Aalphabetic+letter%3DT%3Aentry+group%3D1%3Aentry%3Dtemplum-cn

Stevens, Kathryn. *Between Greece and Babylonia: Hellenistic Intellectual History in Cross-Cultural Perspective*. Cambridge: Cambridge University Press, 2019.

Theis, Christoffer. 'Searching for a Source of the Coptic Hemerology: Diachronic and Synchronic Approaches'. *Mythos* 16 n. s. (2016): 61–79.

Turfa, Jean MacIntosh. *Divining the Etruscan World: the Brontoscopic Calendar and Religious Practice*. Cambridge: Cambridge University Press, 2012.

Ulanowski, Krzysztof. 'Mesopotamian Divination. Some Historical, Religious and Anthropological Remarks'. *Miscellanea Anthropologica et Sociologica* 15, no. 4 (2014): 13–28.

Ulanowski, Krzysztof. *Neo-Assyrian and Greek Divination in War*. Vol. 3, Ancient Warfare. Leiden/Boston: Brill, 2021.

van der Meer, L. Bouke. The Bronze Liver of Piacenza: Analysis of a Polytheistic Structure. Vol. 2, Dutch Monographs on Ancient History and Archaeology. Amsterdam: J.C. Gieben, 1987.

Walsh, Lynda. 'The Rhetoric of Oracles'. *Rhetoric Society Quarterly* 33, no. 3 (2003): 55–78.

Weinstock, Stefan. 'Martianus Capella and the Cosmic System of the Etruscans'. *Journal of Roman Studies* 36.1 and 2 (1946): 101–129.

CHAPTER 2

Calculating the Almuten (Ruling Planet) with Medieval Latin Astrologers

David Juste

Abstract

The almuten (Arabic *al-mubtazz*) is the most powerful planet in a given zodiacal degree of the chart. This is typically determined by adding up the points of essential dignities owned by the planet in the degree concerned, counting 5 points for the domicile, 4 for the exaltation, 3 for the triplicity, 2 for the term and 1 for the decan. This paper explores the various methods of calculation of the almuten encountered in Latin manuscripts from the thirteenth to the fifteenth century.

Keywords

Astrology – almuten – al-mubtazz – ruling planet – Latin Middle Ages

1 The Almuten

The 'almuten' is a central concept in medieval and early modern astrology. Briefly stated, it is the most powerful planet in a given degree of the zodiac. In most cases, this is determined by adding up the points of essential dignities owned by the planet in the degree concerned, counting 5 points for the domicile, 4 for the exaltation, 3 for the triplicity, 2 for the term and 1 for the decan or face (*facies*). Astrologers resort to the almuten in a variety of contexts. In nativities, it is used (1) to rectify the birth chart by the method of the animodar, one parameter of which is the almuten of the degree of the syzygy preceding birth, (2) to calculate the alcochoden, which is the almuten of the degree of the hyleg; and (3) to determine the general ruler of the chart, which is the almuten of the five 'hylegiacal' places, i.e., the degrees of the Sun, the Moon, the Part of Fortune, the ascendant and the syzygy preceding birth. The almuten is also more or less often used in chart interpretation, in nativities as well as in revolutions, elections and interrogations, as the significator of the question dealt with, of the querent or of the period of time under consideration.

The name *almuten* derives from the Arabic *al-mubtazz* ('the predominant one'), variously transliterated *almubtaz, almubtez, almubtec, almutaz, almutez, almutas* etc., which in turn became *almutam, almutem* or *almuten*, most probably by copying mistake (*z* and *m/n* being easily confused when they stand as the last letter of a word). *Almuten* seems to be the most common form among Latin authors and it is the form which will be used here. It should be noted that the word was also variously latinised as *dominator, dispositor, gubernator, significator, victor, dux, dominus, dominus vigoris*, and other such terms which may take several meanings in astrology, so that it is not always easy to trace the concept of almuten in Latin texts.

The 'weighted' almuten (1–5) as described above appears to be a medieval invention. Hellenistic astrologers display multiple methods—and virtually no consensus—for determining the ruling planet.[1] The closest account to our weighted almuten is given by Ptolemy in his *Tetrabiblos*:

> In general the mode of domination is considered as falling under these five forms: when it is trine, house, exaltation, term and phase or aspect; that is, whenever the place in question is related in one or several or all of these ways to the star that is to be the ruler.[2]

There are, however, two significant differences between Ptolemy's system and the weighted almuten. First, Ptolemy speaks of the planet that is the most powerful as regards triplicity, house (i.e., domicile), exaltation, term and 'phase' or 'aspect', but without giving further explanation, so suggesting that these five conditions are of equal strength. Second, Ptolemy does not refer to the decan (the decans are absent from the *Tetrabiblos* altogether) and speaks instead of the 'phase' (φάσις) or 'aspect' (συσχηματισμός), two terms whose exact meaning is not immediately clear in the present context.

We do not know who invented the weighted almuten, but if we trust the Latin sources, it was already used by the first generation of Arabic astrologers around the late eighth or early ninth century. From the twelfth century onwards, many Latin texts, both translations and original compositions, detail the mode of calculation. Without trying to be exhaustive, these texts include:

---

1 See Greenbaum, *The Daimon in Hellenistic Astrology*, pp. 255–266.

2 Ptolemy, *Tetrabiblos*, III.2 (ed. and tr. Robbins, pp. 232–233) or III.3 (ed. Hübner, p. 174). See also *Tetrabiblos*, II.7 (ed. and tr. Robbins, pp. 168–171) or II.8 (ed. Hübner, p. 129): 'The one [planet] which has the greatest number of relationships [...] both by virtue of the nearest visible applications or recessions and by those of the aspects which bear a relation, and furthermore by rulership of the houses, triangles, exaltations, and terms, that planet alone will hold the dominance'.

- *Aomar, *De iudiciis astrorum*, 2 (MS Dijon, BM, 449, f. 25ra–25rb)
- *Alkindi, *Iudicia astrorum*, 137 (ed. Burnett, p. 40)
- Albubater, *De nativitatibus*, 162 (ed. 1540, sig. q$_1$r)
- Alcabitius, *Introductorius*, I.22 and I.77 (ed. Burnett/Yamamoto/Yano, pp. 239–240 and 265–266)
- *Haly Abenragel, *De iudiciis astrorum*, I.9 (ed. 1485, sig. b$_1$rb)
- *Hermann of Carinthia, *De occultis* or *De indagatione cordis* (ed. Low-Beer, pp. 276 and 338–339)
- *Liber novem iudicum*, A.129 (ed. 1509, sig. 1vb)[3]
- *Pseudo-John of Seville, *Epitome totius astrologie*, I.2 (ed. 1548, sig. F$_2$r)
- Abraham Avenezra, *Liber de nativitatibus* (anonymous tr.), I.20–21 (ed. and tr. Sela, pp. 268–269) and *Liber nativitatum et revolutionum earum* (tr. Peter of Abano), 8 (ed. 1507, sig. XLVI$^{va–vb}$)[4]
- *Guillelmus Anglicus, *De urina non visa*, 6 (ed. Moulinier-Brogi, pp. 153–154)[5]
- The *De impressionibus aeris* attributed to Robert Grosseteste (ed. Baur, pp. 42 and 49)
- *Leopold of Austria, *De astrorum scientia*, IV.1 and VIII (ed. 1489, sig. [c$_5$]r and [l$_6$]v)[6]
- Guido Bonatti, *Liber introductorius ad iudicia stellarum*, II.2.19 (ed. 1491, sig. C$_6$v)
- John of Eschenden, *Summa iudicialis de accidentibus mundi*, I.12.5 (ed. 1489, sig. 76rb–76va)

These texts basically agree on the procedure as described above, assigning 5 points to the domicile, 4 to the exaltation, 3 to the triplicity, 2 to the term and 1 to the decan. An alternative count, represented by the texts marked with an asterisk, ascribes 3 points to the term and 2 points to the triplicity.[7] Alcabitius

---

3   The author borrows this section verbatim from Aomar's *De iudiciis astrorum*, as acknowledged in the title 'De eligendo querentis et questionis duce Aomar'.

4   These texts are respectively an adaptation and a translation of Ibn Ezra's *Sefer ha-moladot* ('Book of Nativities'), III.1.3 (ed. and tr. Sela, pp. 100–101).

5   Guillelmus borrows this section verbatim from Hermann of Carinthia's *De occultis* and acknowledges his source: 'Ducem illum cui nomen almubtaz via qua Messahallach et post ipsum Hermannus in Libro de indagatione cordis et occultis indagabimus'. For the attribution to Messahallach [Māshāʾallāh], see n. 7 below.

6   Leopold's two passages are very brief, but nevertheless clear: 'Et planeta in domo sua fortitudines habet 5, in exaltatione 4 et sic descendendo usque ad unam' (sig. [c$_5$]r, in a section where dignities are listed in the order house-exaltation-term-triplicity-face) and 'recipe almutam, cuius cognitio habetur, ut in introductoriis expeditum est, per dignitates domus vel exaltationis vel termini vel triplicitatis vel faciei' (sig. [l$_6$]v).

7   This alternative seems to prevail chronologically among the Arabs, with ʿUmar ibn al-Farrukhān al-Ṭabarī (Aomar) and al-Kindī. It is also attributed by Hermann of Carinthia to

and Guido Bonatti show themselves aware of this alternative, but they make it clear that they do not advocate it.[8] What I render here by 'points' for convenience is variously called *fortitudines, dignitates, virtutes, potestates, testimonia* or *partes*.

The calculation of the almuten is not necessarily limited to scoring the essential dignities. Several of the texts listed above also take into account additional conditions, three of which are likewise subject to mathematical quantification:

> 1) The position of the planets in the twelve houses. 12 additional points are allocated to the planets standing in the first house, 11 points in the tenth house, and so on, down to 2 points in the twelfth house and 1 point in the sixth house, but the sources disagree on the values assigned to the intervening houses, as shown in the table below. This rule is given by Hermann of Carinthia (*De occultis*, two occurrences, ed. Low-Beer, pp. 276–277 and 339; the second occurrence is repeated verbatim in Guillelmus Anglicus's *De urina non visa*, 6, ed. Moulinier-Brogi, p. 155), Pseudo-John of Seville (*Epitome*, I.2, ed. 1548, sig. F_2r-F_2v), Abraham Avenezra (*Liber de nativitatibus* I.21.3, ed. and tr. Sela, pp. 268–269, and *Liber nativitatum et revolutionum earum*, 8, ed. 1507, sig. XLVI^{vb}), and Leopold of Austria (*De astrorum scientia*, IV.3 and VIII, ed. 1489, sig. d_2r and $[l_6]v$).[9]

Māshā'allāh, in a book entitled *Septem claves* (no such book appears to have survived in Latin, but see Pingree, 'Māshā'allāh', p. 162, no. 27), cf. 'sequentes viam quam Messehalla in libro suo qui Septem claves intitulatur hoc artificium ordinat [...] initio a domicilii domino sumpto cui primum 5 partibus dicatis, principatus domino 4 concedunt, termini domino 3, primo trigoni domino 2, decano unam' (*De occultis*, ed. Low-Beer, pp. 338–339) and 'Messehalla vero inter omnia providendum est inquid quis in oriente plures habeat dignitates. Domicilii siquidem sunt 5, principatus 4, termini 3, primi dominorum trigoni 2, decani unus' (p. 276). Guido Bonatti also attributes this alternative to Māshā'allāh (see following note). Haly Abenragel attributes it to al-Kindī: 'Almutez secundum opinionem Alkindi' (*De iudiciis astrorum*, I.9, ed. 1485, sig. $b_1$rb). It should be noted that Alkindi's *Iudicia astrorum* was translated twice, by Hugo Sanctelliensis and by Robert of Ketton, and that the latter modified the text at that place, allocating 3 points to the triplicity and 2 to the term (see the edition in two columns in Burnett, p. 40—that Hugo's translation is correct seems to be confirmed by Haly Abenragel).

8 Alcabitius, *Introductorius*, I.22 (ed. Burnett/Yamamoto/Yano, p. 240): 'Et quidam preponunt terminum triplicitati, id est volunt ut dominus termini fortiori sit domino triplicitatis, set iam superius exposuimus in quo valet unusquisque'; Guido Bonatti, *Liber introductorius*, II.19 (ed. 1491, sig. C_6v): 'Unde Messala preposuit dominum termini domino triplicitatis [...], sed non est ita que a Messala locutus est'.

9 Hermann attributes the rule to Māshā'allāh and refers to the same book *Septem claves* (see n. 7 above). Ibn Ezra's two Latin texts correspond to *Sefer ha-moladot*, III.1.3.5 (ed. and tr. Sela, pp. 100–101). Leopold's two passages disagree regarding the house which is allocated 9 points

houses	1st	2nd	3rd	4th	5th	6th	7th	8th	9th	10th	11th	12th
Hermann I	12	4	5	7	9	1	8	3	6	11	10	2
Hermann II / Guillelmus	12	3	5	7	8	1	9	4	6	11	10	2
Pseudo-John of Seville	12	4	5	9	7	1	10	3	6	11	8	2
Abraham, *Liber de nativitatibus*	12	6	3	9	7	1	10	4	5	11	8	2
Abraham, *Liber nativitatum*	12	6	3	9	7	1	10	5	4	11	8	2
Leopold of Austria	12	3	5	7/9	8	1	10	4	6	11	9	2

2) The ruler of the day and the ruler of the hour. One Latin version of Abraham Avenezra's *Book on Nativities*, the *Liber de nativitatibus*, allocates 7 points to the ruler of the day and 6 points to the ruler of the hour,[10] presumably the planetary ruler of the day and of the hour of the nativity. Haly Abenragel also mentions this rule, but only to say that some astrologers, who are not named, give 1 point to the ruler of the hour.[11]

3) The position of the three superior planets in their synodic period. According to Pseudo-John of Seville, Saturn, Jupiter and Mars receive 12 points when they are located within 1°–30° after their conjunction to the Sun, 11 points within 31°–60°, 10 points within 61°–90°, 9 points from there to the first station, 8 points to the second station, 7 points within

---

'Respectus planetarum est secundum domos: in domo prima potestates habent 12, in medio celi 11, in septima 10, in quarta 9, et hoc minime per succedentes et remotas' (sig. d_2r) and 'Item per fortitudinem vel respectum domorum. Nam prima domus habet dignitates 12, decima 11, septima 10, undecima 9, inde quinta, quarta, nona, tercia, octava, ⟨secunda,⟩ duodecima, sexta, semper minuendo usque ad unum. Hic est ergo almutam seu dux qui plures in his obtinet dignitates quod considera per totum circulum' (sig. $[l_6]$v, immediately after the second passage quoted n. 6 above). This rule was used by the astrologer who cast the horoscope of Louis x (see § 2.1 below) and also occurs in three witnesses of Table 1 (see Notes to the edition #5) and in Conrad of Dyffenbach (Table 5, MS V).

10   'Domino diei 7 virtutes attribue, domino hore 6' (Abraham Avenezra, *Liber de nativitatibus*, I.21.4, ed. Sela, p. 268). No such rule is found in Abraham Ibn Ezra's original Hebrew text, as noted by Sela, p. 379. This rule is also reported by Conrad of Dyffenbach (Table 5, MS V).

11   'Et sunt qui dant unam dignitatem domino hore, sicut domino faciei' (Haly Abenragel, *De iudiciis astrorum*, I.9, ed. 1485, sig. $b_1$va). A vaguely similar statement occurs in Aomar, *De iudiciis astrorum*, 2 (MS Dijon, BM, 449, f. 25rb), and is repeated verbatim in the *Liber novem iudicum*, A.129 (ed. 1509, sig. 1vb): 'Astrologorum etiam nonnulli quamdam huiusmodi dignitatis portionem hore domino ascribere volentes, a quorundam aliorum sentencia longe videntur aberrasse'. Hermann of Carinthia also mentions the rulers of the hour and of the day briefly, but without assigning points: 'Deinde conpetentia adhibenda sunt testimonia, domini scilicet hore, dominique diei ...' (*De occultis*, ed. Low-Beer, p. 277).

1°–30° from the second station, then 6 points within 31°–60°, 5 points to the first station, 4 points within 1°–30° from the first station, 3 points within 31°–60°, 2 points to the opposition to the Sun, then 1 point up to the conjunction to the Sun.[12]

The calculation of the almuten supposes the knowledge of the five essential dignities, whose standard version is shown in the table below. This table, or some variant thererof, is ubiquitous in Latin texts and manuscripts and provides all the necessary data to calculate the almuten over any degree of the zodiac. The procedure is not complicated, but it is somewhat cumbersome, as one has to add the points of essential dignities for each of the seven planets and select as almuten the planet which obtains the most points. For example, the almuten over 1° Aries is the Sun by day (exaltation + triplicity = 7 points) and Mars by night (domicile + decan = 6 points).

There is, however, one difficulty regarding the triplicities. The triplicities have three rulers, one by day, one by night and an additional ruler called the 'participant' (*particeps*). None of the texts listed above tell us which ruler(s) to use in the calculation of the almuten. A straighforward interpretation would have it that the ruler by day must be chosen in diurnal charts (when the Sun is above the horizon) and the ruler by night in nocturnal charts (when the Sun is below the horizon), but, as we shall see, this is not that simple. Our texts also remain silent as to whether and when the participant should be counted. Yet, this is not a trivial question, for the choice of counting or ignoring the participant would affect the almuten in a significant number of cases.[13]

---

12   'Porro Saturnus, Iupiter, Mars distantes a luce Solis usque ad triginta gradus orientales habent duodecim virtutes, ab inde usque ad sexaginta undecim, usque ad nonaginta decem, usque ad primam stationem novem. Stando in secunda statione habent octo, deinde usque ad triginta gradus septem, inde usque ad sexaginta gradus sex. In prima statione quinque, inde uque ad triginta gradus quatuor, inde usque ad sexaginta tres, usque ad oppositionem Solis duas, hinc venientes ad combustionem unam tantum habent' (Pseudo-John of Seville, *Epitome*, I.2, ed. 1548, sig. F$_2$v). The author adds a similar rule for Venus and Mercury, but without being specific regarding the allocated points: 'Venus et Mercurius cum separantur a Sole et sunt occidentales, fortes sunt, ut praedicti tres superiores orientales, et cum separantur a luce Solis et sunt retrogradi sunt tales ut praedicti opposti Solis'. This rule is also reported by Conrad of Dyffenbach (Table 5, MS V).

13   By day, 50 degrees throughout the zodiac are disputed: Gemini 7°–10° (Jupiter if counting the participant vs Mercury if ignoring the participant), Cancer 8°–10° (Moon vs Venus), Cancer 11°–13° (Moon vs Moon and Venus), Cancer 20° (Moon vs Jupiter), Cancer 21°–26° (Moon vs Moon and Jupiter), Scorpio 11° (Mars vs Mars and Venus), Sagittarius 22°–

Essential dignities

	D5	E4	T3			T2					F1		
			d	n	p						1–10	11–20	21–30
♈	♂	☉	☉	♃	♄	♃1–6	♀7–12	☿13–20	♂21–25	♄26–30	♂	☉	♀
♉	♀	☽	♀	☽	♂	♀1–8	☿9–14	♃15–22	♄23–27	♂28–30	☿	☽	♄
♊	☿	—	♄	☿	♃	☿1–6	♃7–12	♀13–17	♂18–24	♄25–30	♃	♂	☉
♋	☽	♃	♀	♂	☽	♂1–7	♀8–13	☿14–19	♃20–26	♄27–30	♀	☿	☽
♌	☉	—	☉	♃	♄	♃1–6	♀7–11	♄12–18	☿19–24	♂25–30	♄	♃	♂
♍	☿	☿	♀	☽	♂	☿1–7	♀8–17	♃18–21	♂22–28	♄29–30	☉	♀	☿
♎	♀	♄	♄	☿	♃	♄1–6	☿7–14	♃15–21	♀22–28	♂29–30	☽	♄	♃
♏	♂	—	♀	♂	☽	♂1–7	♀8–11	☿12–19	♃20–24	♄25–30	♂	☉	♀
♐	♃	—	☉	♃	♄	♃1–12	♀13–17	☿18–21	♄22–26	♂27–30	☿	☽	♄
♑	♄	♂	♀	☽	♂	☿1–7	♃8–14	♀15–22	♄23–26	♂27–30	♃	♂	☉
♒	♄	—	♄	☿	♃	☿1–7	♀8–13	♃14–20	♂21–25	♄26–30	♀	☿	☽
♓	♃	♀	♀	♂	☽	♀1–12	♃13–16	☿17–19	♂20–28	♄29–30	♄	♃	♂

D5 = Domicile (house), E4 = Exaltation, T3 = Triplicity, three rulers: by day (d), by night (n) and the participant (p), T2 = Term (with degrees), F1 = Facies/decan (with degrees)

In the rest of this article, I will present practical examples of the calculation of the almuten in the Latin tradition from the thirteenth to the fifteenth century, with occasional ventures into the sixteenth century.

26° (Saturn vs Jupiter), Capricorn 1°–10° (Mars vs Saturn), Capricorn 11°–14° (Mars vs Saturn and Mars), Capricorn 15°–20° (Mars vs Saturn, Mars and Venus), Capricorn 21°–22° (Mars vs Saturn and Venus) and Capricorn 23°–26° (Saturn and Mars and Saturn). By night, 69 degrees are disputed: Aries 26°–30° (Mars and Saturn vs Mars), Cancer 1°–7° (Moon vs Moon and Mars), Cancer 20° (Moon vs Jupiter), Cancer 21°–26° (Moon vs Moon and Jupiter), Leo 12°–18° (Sun and Saturn vs Sun), Libra 15°–20° (Venus, Saturn and Jupiter vs Venus and Saturn), Libra 21° (Jupiter vs Venus), Sagittarius 22°–26° (Saturn and Jupiter vs Jupiter), Capricorn 1°–10° (Mars vs Saturn), Capricorn 11°–20° (Mars vs Saturn and Mars), Capricorn 23°–26° (Saturn and Mars vs Saturn) and Aquarius 14°–20° (Saturn and Jupiter vs Saturn). If we count both rulers by day and by night, 20 degrees are disputed, all in Cancer: 1°–7° (Moon vs Moon and Mars), 8°–10° (Moon vs Venus), 11°–13° (Moon vs Moon and Venus), 20° (Moon vs. Jupiter) and 21°–26° (Moon vs Moon and Jupiter).

2   The Almuten of the Nativity: Three Examples

The almuten as the ruler of the nativity is often mentioned in birth chart readings (judgements on nativities), but in most cases the author is satisfied with stating which planet is the almuten without explaining how they arrived at that result, which leaves some uncertainty about the method they followed.[14] But in a few cases, we have a full account. I present here three such cases.

2.1   *Louis X*

Our first example is the nativity horoscope of King Louis X of France (reigned 1314–1316), which was cast by a Parisian astrologer, probably Peter of Limoges or William of Saint-Cloud, soon after the future king was born on 7 October 1289.[15] This horoscope is preserved in MS Paris, BnF, lat. 15971, f. 233ʳ, together with a table for the calculation of the almuten (reproduced below).[16]

This table provides for each planet (column 1) the points of essential dignities in each of the five hylegiacal places, the Sun, the Moon, the Part of Fortune, the ascendant and the syzygy preceding birth (columns 2–6). The sum of these is given for each planet in column 7. The astrologer also took into account the rulers of the hour (Saturn 6) and of the day (Jupiter 7) of the nativity (column 8), as well as the points allocated to each planet according to their position in the twelve houses (column 9), following two of the additional conditions mentioned above (pp. 62–63), which the astrologer found in Abraham Avenezra's *Liber de nativitatibus*.[17] The grand total is indicated in column 10.

---

14   For such examples, see Juste, 'A Sixteenth-Century Astrological Consultation', p. 163; Avelar de Carvalho, *An Astrologer at Work*, pp. 194–195; Juste, 'Reading Birth Horoscopes', pp. 567 (no. 8), 571 (no. 13), 579 (no. 21), 581 (no. 23), 586 (no. 29) and 592 (no. 34).

15   This horoscope has been analysed by Poulle, 'L'horoscope de Louis X', who confesses (p. 264) that he could not make sense of the almuten table. On the context of this horoscope, see now Steel/Vanden Broecke/Juste/Sela, *The Astrological Autobiography*, p. 68 n. 194.

16   The page containing the horoscope and the almuten table is reproduced in Juste, *Catalogus*, Planche 8. For the sake of clarity, I have slightly edited the table by giving the astrological symbols in lieu of plain text and by adding the positions of the five hylegiacal places in square brackets (all five positions are displayed in the horoscope, including the syzygy preceding birth—here an opposition—in the ninth house). The word 'Diei' as header of column 8 is crossed out.

17   As shown not only by the values 7 and 6 allocated to the rulers of the day and of the hour, but also by the value 4 given to Saturn, which is found in the eighth house in the horoscope. Abraham Avenezra was especialy popular among late-thirteenth century Parisian astrologers, including Peter of Limoges, see Steel/Vanden Broecke/Juste/Sela, *The Astrological Autobiography*, pp. 72–74.

Almuten of Louis x

	☉	☽	⊕	AS	♂		D̶i̶e̶i̶	Domorum
	[21° ♎]	[10° ♋]	[23° ♏]	[12° ♌]	[15° ♈]			
♄	4	0	0	2	0	6	6 hore	4	16
♃	1	4	2	1 3	3	14	7 diei	8	29
♂	0	3	5 3	0	5	16		6	22
☉	0	0	0	5	1 4	10		3	13
♀	5 2	1	1	0	0	11		9	20
☿	3	0	0	0	2	5		9	14
☽	0	0	0	0	0	5		1	6

Columns 2–7. The indicated figures are straightforward. For example, the points allocated to the position of the Sun at 21° Libra (column 2) are for Saturn 4 (exaltation), Jupiter 1 (decan), Mars and the Sun 0, Venus 5 (domicile) + 2 (term),[18] Mercury 3 (triplicity by night) and the Moon 0. As can be seen in this example, the astrologer counted 3 points for the triplicity and 2 points for the term. For the triplicity, only the ruler by night is taken into account (this is a nocturnal nativity, with the Sun in the third house) and the participant is ignored. The table contains two mistakes in column 3 (indicated in bold). Venus should be given 2 points (term) instead of 1 and the Moon 5 points (domicile) instead of 0. The total indicated for the Moon in column 7 is however correct (5), while the total indicated for Venus is garbled and should read 9 or 10 (depending on whether the mistake just mentioned was taken into account or not) instead of 11.

Column 8. 7 points are allocated to Jupiter as the ruler of the day and 6 points to Saturn as the ruler of the hour. No date is provided in the horoscope, but the positions of the planets and houses are correct for 7 October 1289 at 00:03 (which agrees with 'Hora estimata media nox' in the central panel) in Paris, i.e., still 6 October by astronomical reckoning. 6 October 1289 was a Thursday, i.e., the day of Jupiter. It is unclear how the planetary hour was determined, but the astrologer indicated Saturn in the central panel ('Dominus hore Saturnus').[19]

Column 9. One mistake: the Moon in the twelfth house should be given 2 points (not 1).

---

18   21° Libra is the last degree of the term of Jupiter, but 21° is here understood as the 22nd degree of Libra.

19   Poulle's recalculations of the horoscope using the Tables of Toulouse do not seem correct.

Almuten of Eleanor of Portugal

	Gradus	Domus	Exaltatio	Triplicitas	Terminus	Facies
☉	2 ♎	♀	♄	☿ ♃	♄	☽
☽	14 ♐	♃	☋	♃ ♄	♀	☽
AS	11 ♍	☿	☿	☽ ♂	♀	♀
⊕	29 ♊	☿	☊	☿ ♃	♄	☉
☌	27 ♍	☿	☿	☽ ♂	♂	☿

2.2 *Eleanor of Portugal*

The nativity of Eleanor of Portugal, future Holy Roman Empress (reigned 1452–1467) was cast in 1451 or early 1452 by Johannes Regiomontanus or by his master.[20] This is part of a full judgement on Eleanor's nativity, which includes a table for the calculation of the almuten (reproduced above).[21]

This table provides for each hylegiacal place (column 1), with indication of their position (column 2), the ruler(s) of the five essential dignities (columns 3–7). This table is correct throughout. The points are not allocated but it is not difficult to work them out. The order in which the dignities are listed suggests that the astrologer allocated 3 points to the triplicity and 2 points to the term. Two rulers are here given for the triplicity, namely the ruler by night (this is a nocturnal nativity, with the Sun in the first house) and the participant, which, as we can surmise, was taken into account in the calculation. With these precisions in mind, Mercury is the almuten with 30 points, followed by Jupiter with 14 points. This is confirmed by the astrologer's remark: 'Super loca autem hilegialia victorem invenio Mercurium, ceteros enim omnes numero auctoritatum et dignitatum in his excellit. Principalem igitur huius nativitatis rectorem Mercurium esse pronuntio'.[22]

Poulle states that the horoscope was cast for 8 October 1289 at 0:00 (p. 262) and inexplicably writes that 'l'horoscope porte sur le 8 mars (!) 1289, dont la férie fut effectivement un samedi' (p. 261), whereas it is made clear in the horoscope that the birth occured on the day of Jupiter (Thursday) and at the hour of Saturn.

20 The authorship of this nativity is disputed, see Juste, 'Reading Birth Horoscopes', 580–582 (no. 23).

21 This judgement is edited, together with a facsimile of the earliest manuscript (Munich, BSB, Clm 453, f. 78^{r}–85^{v}, in Regiomontanus's hand), by Schmeidler, *Joannis Regiomontani Opera*, 1–33. See pp. 4–5 for the horoscope and pp. 6–7 for the table, entitled 'Dignitates autem in quinque locis hilegialibus fuerunt ut hec tabula continet'. Here too, I have given the astrological symbols for the planets and signs in lieu of plain text.

22 Schmeidler, 10–11.

Almuten of Maximilian I

☉	11 ♈	♂	☉	☉ ♄	♀	☉
☽	19 ♏	♂	–	♀ ☽	☿	☉
AS	26 ♍	☿	☿	♀ ♂	♂	☿
⊕	04 ♉	♀	☽	♀ ♂	♀	☿
☍	08 ♈	♂	☉	☉ ♄	♀	♂

		Domus	Exaltatio	Triplicitas	Terminus	Facies
♄	♃	♂	☉	♀	☿	☽
6	6	27	16	20	13	13

2.3 Maximilian I

This is the nativity horoscope of Emperor Maximilian I (1459–1519) found in Johannes Schöner's *De iudiciis nativitatum*, a didactic treatise on the interpretation of nativities taking as the guiding example Maximilian's nativity, which Schöner published in Nürnberg in 1545. Maximilian's horoscope is given at the beginning (1.1, sig. Iᵛ) and two tables (reproduced above) for the calculation of the almuten a few pages later on (1.1, sig. VIIIᵛ).

The first table is identical in structure with the table for Eleanor of Portugal above and is correct throughout. For the triplicity, two rulers are given, the ruler by day (this is a diurnal nativity, with the Sun in the seventh house) and the participant. The total of points owned by each planet is then given in the second table. This second table requires some comment, for it seems to contain three mistakes, with Jupiter being given 6 points instead of 0 (Jupiter is completely absent from the first table), Mars 27 points instead of 24 and the Moon 13 points instead of 7. These three mistakes can however be explained if one assumes that Schöner also counted the ruler of the triplicity by night, i.e., Jupiter for both the Sun and the syzygy (☍) in Aries, Mars for the Moon in Scorpio, and the Moon for both the ascendant in Virgo and the Part of Fortune in Taurus. The inconsistency between the two tables is hard to explain, but since the numbers in the second table are repeated in the accompanying text,[23] it seems that Schöner did take into account the three rulers of the trip-

---

23 'Victorem igitur huius nativitatis supra 5 loca hylegialia. Martem cum participatione Veneris invenio. Nam numero dignitatum in dictis locis, Mars habet 27, Venus vero 20, caeteros in hoc vincendo, ut hic apposita tabella dignitatum eorundem ostendit. Principem itaque nativitatis huius propositae Martem esse censeo, Venerem sibi coniungendo. Nec Solem ab hac participatione secludendum puto, quod in perfecta ac amicabili cum Marte commixtione reperiatur, cum in dictis locis quoque 16 dignitates habeat' (sig. VIIIᵛ).

licity regardless of whether the nativity is diurnal or nocturnal and despite the fact that the ruler of the triplicity by night is omitted in the first table.

3   Tables for the Calculation of the Almuten

Another way of assessing the method followed by medieval astrologers is provided by a variety of tables specifically designed for the calculation of the almuten. As far as I can tell, these tables have gone almost entirely unnoticed in modern studies, despite the fact that they were extremely popular from the thirteenth to the late fifteenth century, with well over 100 extant manuscripts altogether. In this section, I will review and edit six of these tables from the simplest to the most complex one, which also roughly corresponds to the chronological order of their appearance in Latin. I do not know whether these tables have their counterparts in Arabic or in other languages.

3.1   Table 1

A Aberdeen, UL, 123, s. XV, f. 69^r

B Bergamo, BCAM, MA 388, s. XV, f. 139^r

B_1 Berlin, SBPK, lat. oct. 44 (962), s. XIV, f. 10^r

B_2 Bernkastel-Kues, CSB, 209, s. XIV, f. 71^r

C Cambridge, UL, Mm 3.11 (2327), s. XV, f. 104^v

C_1 Cracow, BJ, 593, s. XV, f. 146^v

C_2 Cracow, BJ, 601, s. XV, f. 121^v

C_3 Cracow, BJ, 617, s. XV, f. 1^r

C_4 Cracow, BJ, 2495, s. XV, f. 28^r

C_5 Cracow, BJ, 2729, s. XV, f. 49^v

E Erfurt, UFB, Dep. Erf. CA 4° 371, s. XIV, f. 45^v

F Fermo, BC, 85, s. XIII, f. 56rb

F_1 Florence, BML, Ashburnham 203, s. XVI, f. 1^v

L Laon, BM, 425, s. XIII, f. 89^r

L_1 Leiden, UB, Scaliger 64, s. XIII–XIV, f. 127^v

L_2 London, BL, Harley 7402, s. XIV, f. 101^r

L_3 London, BL, Royal 12.C.IX, s. XIV, f. 30^v

L_4 London, BL, Sloane 780, s. XV, f. 54^r

M Munich, BSB, Clm 214, s. XV, f. 2^v

M_1 Munich, BSB, Clm 14783, s. XV, f. 523^v

P Paris, BnF, lat. 7406, s. XIII, f. 55^v

P_1 Paris, BnF, lat. 7411, s. XIII, f. 61^r

P_2 Paris, BnF, lat. 7421, s. XIII–XIV, f. 221^r

P_3 Paris, BnF, lat. 16658, s. XIII, f. 112^r
P_4 Prague, NKCR, III.C.2 (433), s. XV, f. I^v
V Vatican, BAV, Pal. lat. 1399, s. XVI, f. 20^v
V_1 Vatican, BAV, Pal. lat. 1399, s. XVI, f. 27^v
V_2 Vienna, ÖNB, 5239, s. XIV, f. 96^v
V_3 Vienna, ÖNB, 5251, s. XV, f. 145^r
W Bartholomaeus Marisiensis Slesita de Paczków, *Commentum in Ephemeridem Regiomontani*[24]
X Johannes Regiomontanus, *Ephemerides*[25]
Y Johannes de Glogova, *Summa astrologie*, I.3.6[26]
Z Luca Gaurico, *Isagogicus in totam astrologiam praedictivam tractatus*, I.6.6[27]

	Saturnus	Iupiter	Mars	Sol	Venus	Mercurius	Luna
Aries	5^2	5	8	8	3	2	0
Taurus	3	2	5^2	0	10	3	8
Gemini	5	6^3	3	1	2	10	0
Cancer	2	6	5	0	6	3	9^6
Leo	6^3	6	3	8	2	2	0
Virgo	2	2	5^2	1	6	12	3
Libra	10	6^3	2	0	7	5	1
Scorpio	2	2	11	1	6	2	3^0
Sagittarius	6^3	10	2	3	2	3	1
Capricornus	7	3	10^7	1	5	2	3
Aquarius	10	5^2	2	0	3	6	1
Pisces	3	8	6	0	9	2	3^0

24 Ed. 1481, sig. a$_2$r. This text is also extant is at least 13 MSS, of which I checked Munich, BSB, Clm 25005, s. XV, f. 69^v; and Paris, BnF, lat. 10271, s. XV, f. 63^v.

25 Ed. 1484, sig. a$_3$v (reprinted 1488, sig. a$_3$v; Augsburg, 1492, sig. a$_3$v; Venice, 1492, sig. a$_3$v). The table occurs among astrological material found in the introduction to the *Ephemerides* in those four editions, but it should be noted that it was not part of the original edition of the *Ephemerides* published by Regiomontanus himself in Nürnberg in 1474.

26 I have used MSS Cracow, BJ, 570, s. XV–XVI, f. 168^v; and Dresden, SLSUB, N. 100, s. XV, f. 256^r. Other MSS include Cracow, BJ, 1963, s. XVI, f. 246^v; Jena, TULB, El. f. 77, s. XVI, f. 33^r; Paris, BnF, lat. 7443C, s. XV, f. 32^r; Vatican, BAV, Pal. lat. 1439, s. XV, f. 230^r.

27 Ed. 1575, sig. 885. The date of this work, which does not seem to have been printed separately, is unknown to me.

Title om. C_1EY; Quot dignitates habent (habeant L_3) planete in signis AL_1L_3; Potestates vel testimonia planetarum in signis B; Iste sunt fortitudines et dignitates planetarum in signis secundum Alkabicium B_1; Tabula dignitatum omnium planetarum B_2; Tabula ... (?) quot dignitates habent planete in signis C; Hec tabula ostendit tibi quot dignitates habeat unusquisque planetarum in quolibet signorum C_2; ... (?) ens testimonia planetarum essentialia C_3; Tabula continens testimonia essentialia planetarum C_4V_1; Tabula dignitatum planetarum in signis (planetarum dignitatum M_1; in signis *om.* P_4V_3) $FM_1P_4V_2V_3$; Dignitates planetarum in signis F_1; Quot in signo planeta dignitates habeat LP_3; Quot dignitates habet quilibet planeta in quolibet signo L_2; Hee dignitates planetarum in signis notande sunt permaxime in iudiciis faciendis (faciendis *add.* L_4) L_4VWX; Tabula generalis continens dignitates essentiales planetarum M; Quot in quo signo dignitates habeat quilibet planeta P; Tabula fortitudinum planetarum in signis P_1; Tabula numeri virium dignitatum planetarum in signis naturalium P_2; Planetae habentes plures dignitates in signis per numerum secundum quosdam, sed mihi non fit verisimilis Z.

Aries (Saturnus) 5] 2 C_2; *corr. in* 2 L_2 (Venus) 3] 8 F **Taurus** (Saturnus) 3] 2 F (Iupiter) 2] 3 FP_2 (Mars) 5] 2 C_2; *corr. in* 2 L_2 (Mercurius) 3] 4 $ACC_1FLL_1L_2P_1P_2P_3P_4V_2$ **Gemini** (Iupiter) 6] 3 C_2 (Mars) 3] 5 B_1 (Venus) 2] 3 L_4 **Cancer** (Saturnus) 2] 5 B_1 Luna 9] 6 C_2 **Leo** (Saturnus) 6] 3 C_2; *corr. ex* 8 L_1 (Mercurius) 2] 5 F (Luna) 0] 3 B_1 **Virgo** (Saturnus) 2] 5 B_1 (Iupiter) 2] 5 B_1L_4; 0 C_2 (Mars) 5] 2 C_2 (Sol) 1] 0 L_1; 6 L_2 (Mercurius) 12] 11 B_1 (Luna) 3] 0 B_1 **Libra** (Iupiter) 6] 3 C_2 (Mars) 2] 5 B_1 (Venus) 7] 6 $C_2F_1L_4VWXZ$ (Mercurius) 5] 6 V_1 **Scorpio** (Saturnus) 2] 5 B_1; 3 C_5 (Iupiter) 2] 5 B_1 (Mercurius) 2] 5 B_1 (Luna) 3] 0 C_2 **Sagittarius** (Saturnus) 6] 3 C_2 (Iupiter) 10] 9 P_2 (Mars) 2] 5 $B_1CFLL_1L_2P_2P_3V_2$ (Venus) 2] 3 C_1P_4 **Capricornus** (Mars) 10] 7 C_2 (Mercurius) 2] 5 B_1 **Aquarius** (Iupiter) 5] 2 C_2 **Pisces** (Venus) 9] 6 V_1 (Mercurius) 2] 5 B_1; 6 L_1L_2 (Luna) 3] 0 C_2.

Notes to the edition: 1. The table has been edited on the basis of all witnesses listed above and all variant readings are reported in the apparatus. Numbers in superscript give the alternative version of C_2 (see below). — 2. Layout: the layout is identical in all witnesses, except in L_3P_4, where the columns are for the signs and the rows for the planets, and in P, where the planets are listed from Sun-Venus to Mars. — 3. Lunar nodes: several witnesses (BF_1L_4VWXZ) have two more columns for the Head and the Tail of the Dragon, which receive 4 points (exaltation) in Gemini and Sagittarius respectively. — 4. Several witnesses ($C_3C_4C_5MV_1Y$) add the corresponding dignities in superscript and in abbreviated form, e.g. Saturnus in Aries = 5 [ter(minus) tri(plicitas)] etc. In a similar, although different, way, the scribe of L_2 gives the value of the corresponding dignities, e.g. Jupiter in Aries = 5 [2.3] etc., even though he did so for the first two signs only. — 5. Three witnesses (BV_2Z) include a second table, showing the points allocated to the planets according to their position in the twelve houses (pp. 62–63 above), under the titles 'Potestates planetarum in domibus' (B), 'Tabula scientie virtutum duodecim domorum' (V_2) and 'Dignitates accidentales domus coeli' (Z). B has the same values as Hermann II / Guillelmus. V_2 is also closer to Hermann II / Guillelmus, except that 4 points are allocated to the second house, 8 to the fourth, 7 to the fifth and 3 to the eight. Z (Gaurico) gives the same values as Abraham Avenezra's *Liber de nativitatibus*.

Table 1 gives the total of points of essential dignities owned by each planet in each of the twelve signs.[28] The indicated values show that all three rulers of the triplicity (including the participant) have been taken into account. Thus, Saturn is allocated 5 points in Aries, because it is the participant of the triplicity and the ruler of one term ($3 + 2$). An exception to this is C_2, whose values have been corrected so as to omit the participant in all cases (these values are noted in superscript in the table above). Another interesting case is MS London, BL, Harley 7402 (L_2), whose scribe made corrections in the first two signs, changing the values of Saturn in Aries 5 into 2 and Mars in Taurus 5 into 2, evidently as a way of excluding the participant, but he gave up after Taurus. Only ten witnesses provide the correct values throughout ($B_2 C_3 C_4 EL_3 MM_1 PV_3 Y$—$L_3$ after correction by the scribe or by another hand) and the variants found in the other witnesses can be explained as mistakes in copying or calculation, some of which are recurring, especially Mercury in Taurus = 4 instead of 3 and Mars in Sagittarius = 5 instead of 2 (see apparatus).

The origin of Table 1 is not known. The earliest manuscript seems to be L, copied in the early 1220s in France, where the table occurs among the Tables of Toulouse (an adaptation of the Toledan Tables). The other early manuscripts originated in the late thirteenth century in Paris ($FPP_1P_2P_3$). In the late fifteenth century, the table enjoyed considerable success, for it was borrowed by Bartholomaeus Marisiensis Slesita de Paczków in his *Commentum in Ephemeridem Regiomontani* (printed in 1481), by Johannes de Glogovia in his *Summa astrologie* (dating probably from the 1480s), and especially in the four editions of Regiomontanus's *Ephemerides* printed between 1484 and 1492. In the first half of the sixteenth century, Luca Gaurico inserted it into his *Isagogicus in totam astrologiam praedictivam tractatus*, although he did so with reservation, expressing doubts about the relevance of this table, whose caption or title reads: 'Planets having the most dignities in the signs by number according to some ⟨astrologers⟩, but it does not seem likely to me'.

---

28   This table was noticed by Fritz Pedersen, who edited it from five witnesses (CLL_1PP_3), where it occurs among the Toledan Tables, see Pedersen, *The Toledan Tables*, IV, pp. 1598–1599 (RE11). Pedersen could not explain the structure and purpose of the table.

FIGURE 2.1   Table 1 from Paris, Bibliothèque nationale de France, lat. 7411, f. 61r

The purpose and use of this table are nowhere explained and one may wonder why a table giving the almuten of the whole sign, without consideration for specific degrees, would be needed. Yet, as it turns out, this table in fact provides the (almost) complete picture of the almuten in all 360 degrees of the zodiac, at least if ones takes into account all three rulers of the triplicity, as it is the case here. For example, Mercury is not only the almuten of Gemini with 10 points, but also the almuten over all 30 degrees of Gemini, and the same goes for the other signs, with the sole exception of four degrees in Pisces (13°–16°), where Jupiter, not Venus, is the almuten.[29] The drawback of this table, however, is that it gives good results only if all three rulers of the triplicity are taken into account. In other situations, including when the user wishes to distinguish between the tripicity by day and by night (as in the three examples above), the results are less reliable and sometimes largely wrong, as is the case for the signs of Taurus and Pisces by night.

3.2   *Table 2A*
E   Erfurt, UFB, Dep. Erf. CA 4° 345, s. XIV[in], f. 51[v]
L   London, BL, Royal 12.E.XXV, s. XIII[ex]–XIV[in], f. 168[v]
M   Munich, BSB, Clm 267, s. XIV[in], f. 101[r]
P   Paris, BnF, lat. 7413-II, s. XIII[ex], f. 47[r]
V   Vatican, BAV, Pal. lat. 1414, s. XIII[2], f. 219[v]

	Saturnus	Iupiter	Mars	Sol	Venus	Mercurius	Luna
Aries	2	2.3	1.5.2	3.4.1	2.1	2	0
Taurus	3.2.1 [2.1]	2	2	0	2.5 [5.3.2]	1.2.3 [2.1]	4.1 [4.3.1]
Gemini	2 [3.2]	1.2	1.2	1	3.2 [2]	2.5 [5.3.2]	0
Cancer	2	4.2	2.3	0	1.2 [3.2.1]	1.2	5.1
Leo	1.2	3.1.2	1.2.3 [2.1]	5 [5.3]	2	2	0
Virgo	2.3 [2]	2	2	1	1.2.3	1.5.2.4	0 [3]
Libra	1.2.4 [4.3.2.1]	1.2	2	0	5.2	2 [3.2]	1
Scorpio	2	3.2 [2]	1.5.2 [5.3.2.1]	1	1.2 [3.2.1]	2	3 [0]

---

29   To give a full picture, we may add that there are four cases where the almuten is shared by two planets, i.e., in Aries 21°–25° (Sun and Mars—but note that the Sun and Mars are also co-almuten of the whole sign of Aries, with 8 points each), Taurus 11°–20° (Venus and Moon), Libra 22°-28 (Saturn and Venus) and Capricorn 23°–26° (Mars and Saturn).

(cont.)

	Saturnus	Iupiter	Mars	Sol	Venus	Mercurius	Luna
Sagittarius	1.2	5.2 [5.3.2]	3.2 [2]	3	2	1.2	1
Capricornus	2.5	1.2	4.1.2	1	3.2	2.3 [2]	0 [3]
Aquarius	5.2 [5.3.2]	2	2	0	2.3.1 [2.1]	3.2.1	1
Pisces	1.2	1.2.5	1.2.3	0	2.4 [4.3.2]	2	3 [0]

Aries (Iupiter) 2.3] 2 *E* (Mars) 1.5.2] 2.3.5.1 *M* **Taurus** (Mercurius) 1.2.3] 2.3 *ELP* **Gemini** (Venus) 3.2] 3 *P* (Mercurius) 2.5] 2 *P* **Cancer** (Mars) 2.3] 2 *EM* (Sol) o] 1 *P* (Luna) 5.1] 5.1.3 *M* **Leo** (Sol) 5] 5.3 *M* **Virgo** (Venus) 1.2.3] 1.2 *EM* (Mercurius) 1.5.2.4] 1.2.5 *LP*; 4.2.3.5.1 *M* **Libra** (Venus) 5.2] 5 *LP*; 5.2.3 *M* **Scorpio** (Iupiter) 3.2] 2 *M*; 1.2 *E* (Mercurius) 2] 1.2 *L* (Luna) 3] o *L* **Sagittarius** (Iupiter) 5.2] 5.2.3 *M* **Capricornus** (Saturnus) 2.5] 5.3.2 *M* (Venus) 3.2] 2 *M* **Aquarius** (Sol) o] 1.2.3 *M* (Venus) 2.3.1] 1.2 *M* **Pisces** (Mars) 1.2.3] 1.2 *M* (Sol) o] 2.4 *M*.

Notes to the edition: 1. I had originally prepared the edition on the basis of all MSS accessible to me (see n. 31 below), but this had no other effect than creating an embarrassingly large apparatus. I have chosen to use instead the five earliest MSS accessible to me, which turned out to be sufficient to confidently reconstruct the original table. The readings of *V* (the earliest MS, copied in or shortly before 1266) have been followed and all variants from the four other MSS have been reported in the apparatus. The only value for which *V* is challenged by more than two MSS is Mercury in Taurus (2.3 in *ELP* against 1.2.3 in *VM*), but verification in other MSS confirms that *V*'s value is original (and also correct, for that matter). — 2. In bold: the 26 'anomalies' (see below), with the expected values in superscript. — 3. All five MSS (and many of the other MSS) have a blank space for o. — 4. The order in which the points are listed is inconsistent in *V* and greatly varies in the MSS without any discernible logic. These variations are ignored in the apparatus insofar as they do not affect the result.

Table 2A consists of a circular figure made of eight concentric circles giving the names of the zodiacal signs in the outer circle, the seven following circles being assigned to the planets from Saturn to the Moon. Like Table 1, this figure gives the total of points owned by each planet in each of the twelve signs, except that each dignity is separately numerated. Thus Saturn is allocated 2 points in Aries (term), Jupiter 2 + 3 points in Aries (term and triplicity by night) etc. Another difference with Table 1 is that the participant of the triplicity is ignored.

A puzzling feature of Table 2A is that it contains 26 anomalies (in bold), for which I find myself unable to provide an explanation. These anomalies are clearly not mistakes in copying or calculation, for in all cases, we are dealing with an addition or subtraction of 3, which would suggest some bearing on the triplicities. However, these anomalies do not seem to be related to the participant or to the rulers by day and by night in any way. Two cases (Moon in Scorpio and Pisces, with 3 points instead of 0) might be interpreted as counting the participant, but seeing that the participant is otherwise consistently ignored, including for the Moon in Cancer, these two cases must be considered anomalies.

Table 2A is found in the *De impressionibus aeris* (1249) commonly attributed to Robert Grosseteste (c. 1170–1253). Ludwig Baur edited this text in 1912 from eight manuscripts,[30] but he inexplicably omitted the figure and failed to mention even its existence, whereas it is present in most manuscripts[31]

---

30   Baur, *Die philosophischen Werke*, pp. 41–51 (and introduction, pp. 72*–75*).

31   Bordeaux, BM, 531, s. XV, f. 69ᵛ–74ᵛ (figure on f. 74ᵛ); Cambridge (Mass.), HU-HHL, Lat. 361, s. XIII, f. 104ʳᵇ–107ᵛᵇ (107ʳ); Cambridge, UL, Gg 6.3 (1572), s. XIV, f. 134ʳ–138ᵛ (136ᵛ); Catania, BU, 87, s. XV, f. 263ᵛ–264ʳ (263ᵛ, the text is incomplete); Cracow, BJ, 1843, s. XV, f. 267ʳ–271ʳ (270ʳ); Cracow, BJ, 1915, s. XV, f. 62ᵛ–65ᵛ (61ʳ, so before the text); Erfurt, UFB, Dep. Erf. CA 4° 345, s. XIV, f. 50ʳᵃ–52ʳᵇ (51ᵛ); Leipzig, UB, 1469, s. XV, f. 1ᵛ–2ᵛ (1ʳ, so before the text); London, BL, Harley 5311, s. XV, f. 1ʳ–1ᵛ (1ʳ); London, BL, Royal 12.E.XXV, s. XIII–XIV, f. 166ᵛ–169ᵛ (168ᵛ); London, BL, Sloane 1620, s. XV, f. 80ʳ–84ᵛ (84ʳ); Lüneburg, RB, Miscell. D 4° 46, s. XIV, f. 20ʳᵃ–22ʳᵃ (21ᵛ); Munich, BSB, Clm 267, s. XIV, f. 101ʳᵃ–101ᵛᵇ (101ʳ); Naples, BN, VIII C. 45, s. XV, f. 170ʳ–175ᵛ (175ᵛ); Nürnberg, SB, Cent. V 64, s. XV, 175ᵛ–176ᵛ (f. 176ʳ); Oxford, BL, Ashmole 191, s. XV, f. 48ʳ–49ᵛ and 55ᵛ (49ᵛ); Oxford, BL, Bodley 464, s. XIV, f. 122ᵛ–125ᵛ (125ʳ, incomplete); Oxford, BL, Digby 57, s. XIV, f. 144ʳ–145ᵛ (144ᵛ, as a table); Oxford, BL, Digby 98, s. XIV–XV, f. 156ʳ–157ᵛ (157ᵛ); Oxford, BL, Laud. Misc. 594, s. XIV, f. 159ᵛᵇ–160ʳᵇ (160ʳ); Oxford, BL, Rawlinson D.1227, s. XIV, f. 44ʳᵃ–45ᵛᵇ (45ᵛ, as a table); Oxford, BL, Savile 17, s. XV, f. 46ʳ–49ᵛ (49ᵛ, incomplete figure); Oxford, UC, 41, s. XIV, f. 33ʳ–34ᵛ (32ᵛ); Paris, BnF, lat. 7413-II, s. XIII, f. 44ʳᵃ–48ʳᵇ (47ʳ); Paris, BnF, lat. 7443, s. XV, f. 143ᵛ–147ʳ (144ᵛ, as a table); Paris, BS, 1037, s. XV, f. 188ʳ–191ʳ (190ᵛ); Prague, NKCR, I.G.6 (280), s. XV, f. 258ᵛ–260ʳ (258ʳ, before the text); Princeton, UL, Garrett 95, s. XV, f. 131ᵛ–134ᵛ (134ᵛ); San Marino (Ca), HHL, HM 83, s. XV, f. 21ᵛ–22ʳ (22ʳ); Uppsala, UB, C 653, s. XIV, f. 72ʳ–74ʳ (73ᵛ); Vatican, BAV, Barb. lat. 303, s. XIV, f. 3ᵛᵃ–4ʳᵇ (4ʳ); Vatican, BAV, Pal. lat. 1414, s. XIII, f. 216ᵛᵇ–220ʳᵃ (219ᵛ); Vatican, BAV, Pal. lat. 1438, s. XV, f. 29ᵛ–34ᵛ (33ʳ, as a table); Vienna, ÖNB, 5239, s. XIV, f. 29ᵛ–31ᵛ (31ʳ); Wiesbaden, HLB, 79, s. XVI, f. 47ʳᵃ–49ʳᵇ (48ᵛᵇ, incomplete). The following MSS omit the figure: Bologna, BU, 132 (154), s. XIV, f. 28ᵛ–31ʳ (blank space for the figure); Cambridge, MC, Pepys 2329, s. XV, f. 184ʳᵃ–186ʳᵇ; Cracow, BJ, 566, s. XV, f. 43ᵛ–45ʳ; Cracow, BJ, 573, s. XV, f. 186ᵛ–190ʳ; Cracow, BJ, 1843, s. XV, f. 247ᵛ–249ᵛ; Cracow, BJ, 1857, s. XV, pp. 160–161; Cracow, BJ, 2495, s. XV, f. 6ʳ–6ᵛ and 8ʳ; Erfurt, UFB, Dep. Erf. CA 2° 394, s. XIV, f. 147ᵛᵇ–148ʳᵃ; Erfurt, UFB, Dep. Erf. CA 4° 366, s. XIV, f. 94ʳ–96ʳ; Erlangen, UB, 434, s. XIV, f. 262ʳᵃ–265ᵛᵇ; Gloucester, CL, 21, s. XV, f. 224ᵛ–228ᵛ; London, BL, Harley 1612, s. XIV, f. 10ʳ–12ᵛ; London, BL, Sloane 636, s. XV, f. 89ᵛ–90ʳ and 97ᵛ–98ʳ; London, WL, 531-VIII, s. XIV, f. 32ʳᵃ–34ᵛᵇ; Oxford, BL, Canon. Misc. 517, s. XV, f. 28ᵛᵇ–31ʳᵇ; Paris, BS, 1037, s. XV, f. 131ʳ–136ᵛ; Prague, NKCR, VI.F.7 (1144), s. XV, f. 101ʳ–102ʳ; Vatican, BAV, Pal. lat. 1340, s. XV, f. 205ʳᵃ–207ᵛᵇ; Vatican, BAV, Pal. lat. 1367, s. XV,

and explicitly referred to in the text ('describam tibi figuram octo circulorum', ed. Baur, p. 49, line 9). The figure was later excerpted from the text and
circulated independently in a number of manuscripts, the earliest of which
I am aware of is Vatican, BAV, Pal. lat. 1398, f. 32ʳ, copied in France c. 1300,
where the figure (here in the form of a table) occurs among the Toledan
Tables.[32]

The *De impressionibus aeris* explains how to predict the weather on the basis
of the position of the planets at any desired time. The text is fully relevant
to us, for the planet which has the most points of essential dignities, i.e., the
almuten, at that time will be the guiding planet in making the forecast ('Qui
enim planeta plura testimonia habuerit, dispositor illius temporis erit', p. 49,
l. 20–21). The calculation of the almuten is standard, as made clear in the figure
(minus the anomalies) and twice in the text (pp. 42, l. 28–29, and 49, l. 14–16).
The author provides a full description of the five essential dignities and their
rulers (pp. 42–44), omitting, however—and perhaps not unintentionally—, to
name the rulers of the triplicities (p. 43, l. 14–18). Then, the author describes at
some length a number of strengths (*fortitudines*) and weaknesses (*debilitates*)
of the planets which must also be taken into account, such as their aspects
and their position along both their epicycle and their deferent (pp. 44–49), but
without clear explanations as to how to account for these in either calculating
the almuten or making predictions. The author nevertheless concludes 'These
are the essential and accidental dignities which are necessary to our purpose'
('Haec igitur sunt testimonia planetarum essentialia et accidentalia quae necessaria sunt ad propositum nostrum insinuandum', p. 49, l. 6–7) and introduces
at this point his 'figura octo circulorum', meant to help understand without

---

f. 120ᵛᵇ–123ʳᵇ; Vatican, BAV, Rossi 732, s. XV, f. 81ʳ–83ᵛ; Vienna, ÖNB, 5508, s. XIV, f. 202ʳᵃ–
204ʳᵃ; Vicenza, BCB, 208 (132), s. XV, f. 103ᵛ–111ʳ (empty figure f. 109ᵛ); Warsaw, BN, Rps 12634
II, s. XV, f. 22ᵛ–25ʳ. I have not seen the following MSS: Boston, CML, 7 (20), s. XIV, f. 156ʳ–159ʳ;
London, BL, Cott. Otho D.X, s. XIV, f. 57ᵛ–58ᵛ; London, BL, Royal 6.E.V, s. XIV–XV, f. 240ʳᵃ–
241ʳᵃ; Oxford, BL, Digby 48, s. XV, f. 182ʳ–188ᵛ; Oxford, BL, Digby 92, s. XIV, f. 5ʳ–9ʳ; Oxford,
BL, Savile 25, s. XIV–XV, f. 200ʳ–201ᵛ; and Paris, BA, 1127, s. XIV, f. 75ʳ–81ᵛ.

32   The table from the Vatican MS has been edited by Pedersen, *The Toledan Tables*, IV, p. 1599
(RE21)). The other MSS are Berlin, SBPK, lat. fol. 192, s. XV, f. 6ʳ; Cambridge, TC, R.15.21, s.
XV, f. 70ʳ (ed. Friedman, *John de Foxton's Liber cosmographiae*, p. 285); Copenhagen, KB,
Add. 447 fol., s. XIV–XV, f. 140ᵛ; Cracow, BJ, 1864, s. XV, f. 108ᵛ; London, BL, Harley 531, s. XIV,
f. 133ᵛ (as a table); Madrid, BN, 3349, s. XIV, f. 11ᵛ (in Portuguese, ed. Chabás and Goldstein,
A Survey of European Astronomical Tables, p. 218 (Table 18.3B)); Oxford, BL, Ashmole 191,
s. XV, f. 10ᵛ; Prague, NKCR, III.C.2 (433), s. XV, f. 59ᵛ; Vatican, BAV, Pal. lat. 1373, s. XV, f. 109ᵛ
(as a table); Vatican, BAV, Pal. lat. 1381, s. XV, f. 82; Vatican, BAV, Pat. lat. 1446, s. XIV, f. 69ᵛ
(as a table).

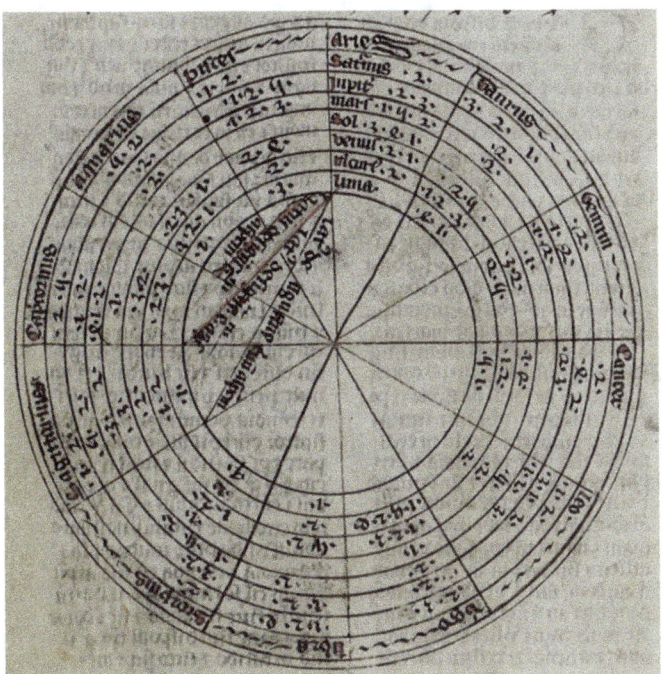

FIGURE 2.2   Table 2A from Vatican, Biblioteca Apostólica Vaticana, Pal.
     lat. 1414, f. 219ᵛ

effort all the things seen so far ('Ut ergo omnia predicta sine labore et tedio possis comprehendere, describam tibi figuram octo circulorum', p. 49, l. 8–9). The
rest of the text is devoted to specific examples, starting with one for 15 April
1249. The author lists the positions of the planets (in the sidereal zodiac)[33] for
that date and states that the Sun at 22° Aries gets 7 points (exaltation+triplic-
ity), Venus at 17° Taurus 5 points (domicile—note that Venus is also the ruler of
the triplicity by day, but the author ignored this in agreement with his 'anomaly'
for Venus in Taurus, where the triplicity is ignored), Mercury at 14° Taurus 2
points (term), while the other planets (Saturn at 10° Scorpio, Jupiter at 1° Aquarius, Mars at 28° Aquarius and the Moon at 21° Aries) get no points. The Sun is
therefore the leading planet and because it is not impeded by any planet, the
judgement must be made from it, which leads the author to conclude that the
weather should be judged to be temperate, and also hot and dry, at that time,
which indeed happened, as the author informs us ('Quod et factum est', p. 50,

---

33   As shown by Nothaft, 'Sidereal Astrology', pp. 63–64.

l. 18). The text closes with further forecasts based on configurations to come, when the Sun will reach its domicile in Leo in July 1249 and when Saturn will reach its domicile in Capricorn in 1255.

3.3   Table 2B

C	Cracow, BJ, 610, s. XV, f. 1r
E	Erfurt, UFB, Dep. Erf. CA 2° 395, s. XIV, f. 74vb
G	Gotha, FB, Chart. B 386, s. XVI, f. 36v
I	Innsbruck, UB, 750, s. XV, f. 110r
K	Klagenfurt, ADG-BM, XXXI b. 7, s. XIV–XV, f. 27r
L	Leipzig, UB, 1496, s. XV, f. 76v
L_1	London, BL, Addit. 10362, s. XIV, f. 29v
M	Melk, SB, 601, s. XV, f. 269v
O	Oxford, BL, Ashmole 369, s. XV, f. 4v
V	Vatican, BAV, Pal. lat. 1390, s. XIV, f. 183r
V_1	Vatican, BAV, Vat. lat. 3104, s. XV, f. 110v
W	Wolfenbüttel, HAB, 65 Aug. 2° (2637), s. XV, f. 232v
Z	Pierre d'Ailly, *Tractatus de figura inceptionis mundi et coniunctionibus mediis sequentibus*[34]

	Saturnus	Iupiter	Mars	Sol	Venus	Mercurius	Luna
Aries	3.2	3.2	5.2.1	4.3.1	2.1	2	0
Taurus	2.1	2	3.2	0	5.3.2	2.1	4.3.1
Gemini	3.2	3.2.1	2.1	1	2	5.3.2	0
Cancer	2	4.2	3.2	0	3.2.1	2.1	5.3.1
Leo	3.2.1	3.2.1	2.1	5.3	2	2	0
Virgo	2	2	3.2	1	3.2.1	5.4.2.1	3
Libra	4.3.2.1	3.2.1	2	0	5.2	3.2	1
Scorpio	2	2	5.3.2.1	1	3.2.1	2	3

---

34 I used Pierre d'Ailly's autograph copy (Cambrai, BM, 929, f. 103v), which is correct through-out, except for one mistake (Mercury in Pisces = 3.2 instead of 2). The same mistake is also found in the three other MSS I have checked: London, BL, Addit. 29969, s. XV, f. 70r; Vienna, ÖNB, 5266, s. XV, f. 49r; and Vienna, ÖNB, 5318, s. XV, f. 97r. Unlike the other astrological works by Pierre d'Ailly, the *Tractatus* was never printed.

(*cont.*)

	Saturnus	**Iupiter**	**Mars**	**Sol**	**Venus**	**Mercurius**	**Luna**
Sagittarius	3.2.1	5.3.2	2	3	2	2.1	1
Capricornus	5.2	2.1	4.3.2.1	1	3.2	2	3
Aquarius	5.3.2	3.2	2	O	2.1	3.2.1	1
Pisces	2.1	5.2.1	3.2.1	O	4.3.2	2	3

Title om. CEIKLOV$_1$; Tabella omnium potestatum planetarum omnium in singulis signis *G*; Tabula testimonorum sive potestatum 7 planetarum *L$_1$*; Tabula continens digni-tates planetarum in 12 signis *M*; Tabula de fortitudinibus planetarum *V*; Hec tab-ula ostendit testimonium planetarum in quibuscumque signis *W*; Hec figura docet domos, exaltationes et dignitates planetarum in signis *Z*.

Aries (Saturnus) 3.2] 2 *V$_1$* (Mars) 5.2.1] 5.2 *V$_1$* (Sol) 4.3.1] 4.3 *V$_1$* (Venus) 2.1] 2 *V$_1$* (Mer-curius) 2] 2.1 *L$_1$* **Taurus** (Saturnus) 2.1] 2 *V$_1$* (Iupiter) 2] 3.2 *L$_1$* (Mars) 3.2] 3 *L$_1$*; 2 *V$_1$* (Mercurius) 2.1] 2.4.1 *O*; 2 *V$_1$* (Luna) 4.3.1] 4.3 *V$_1$* **Gemini** (Saturnus) 3.2] 1.3.2 *L$_1$*; 1.3 *W* (Iupiter) 3.2.1] 2 *V$_1$* (Mars) 2.1] 2 *L$_1$V$_1$* **Cancer** (Saturnus) 2] 1 *M* (Iupiter) 4.2] 2 *L$_1$* (Venus) 3.2.1] 3.2 *V$_1$* (Mercurius) 2.1] 2 *V$_1$* (Luna) 5.3.1] 5 *V$_1$* **Leo** (Saturnus) 3.2.1] 2 *V$_1$*; 1.3 *W* (Iupiter) 3.2.1] 3.1 *W*; 3.2 *V$_1$* (Mars) 2.1] 3.2 *G*; 1.2.3 *L$_1$*; 2 *V$_1$* **Virgo** (Saturnus) 2] 3.2 *C* (Iupiter) 2] 3 *L$_1$* (Mars) 3.2] 2 *V$_1$* (Sol) 1] o *V$_1$* (Venus) 3.2.1] 3.2 *V$_1$* (Mercurius) 5.4.2.1] 5.4.3.2.1 *C*; 5.4.2 *V$_1$* (Luna) 3] o *CL$_1$* **Libra** (Saturnus) 4.3.2.1] 4.2.1 *C*; 4.3.2 *V$_1$* (Iupiter) 3.2.1] 2 *V$_1$* (Luna) 1] *om. M*; o *V$_1$* **Scorpio** (Mars) 5.3.2.1] 5.1.3 *K*; 5.3.2 *V$_1$* (Sol) 1] 1.2.3 *M*; o *V$_1$* (Venus) 3.2.1] 1.2 *corr. in* 1 *M*; 3.2 *V$_1$W* (Mercurius) 2] 2.1 *I* (Luna) 3] o *V$_1$* **Sagittarius** (Saturnus) 3.2.1] 2 *V$_1$* (Mars) 2] 3.2 *C* (Mercurius) 2.1] 2 *V$_1$*; 1 *W* (Luna) 1] o *V$_1$* **Capri-cornus** (Iupiter) 2.1] 1.5.2 *L$_1$*; 2 *V$_1$* (Mars) 4.3.2.1] 4.3.1.3 *K*; 4.2 *V$_1$* (Sol) 1] o *V$_1$* (Luna) 3] 3.1 *C*; 4.3 *L$_1$* **Aquarius** (Iupiter) 3.2] 2 *V$_1$* (Venus) 2.1] 2 *V$_1$* (Mercurius) 3.2.1] 3.2 *V$_1$* (Luna) 1] o *MV$_1$* **Pisces** (Saturnus) 2.1] 2 *V$_1$*; (Iupiter) 5.2.1] 1.5 *L$_1$*; 5.2 *V$_1$* (Mars) 3.2.1] 3.2 *V$_1$* (Mercurius) 2] 3.2 *Z* (Luna) 3] o *V$_1$*.

Notes to the edition: 1. The table is edited from all witnesses, except *EL*, whose values have been ignored, because they are mostly missing (most of the figure is blank). — 2. Like in Table 2A, the order in which the points are listed greatly varies between the MSS. These variations are ignored in the apparatus.

Table 2B is a recomputed version of Table 2A, where all anomalies have been corrected and the participant of the triplicity added. The result is a table which is correct throughout, allowing for mistakes in copying or calculation. Only one manuscript (*V*) has all correct values, while *GIOZ* have one mistake each, *KL$_3$* have two mistakes each and the other manuscripts three or more mistakes each (see apparatus). *V$_1$* is a special case, where both the participant of the triplicity and the decan have been omitted (the value 1 is absent from the figure).

The dependence of Table 2B on Table 2A is also shown by the use of the same circular figure (*EIKLOV₁Z*), even though almost half of the manuscripts made it a rectangular table (*CGL₁MVW*). The origin of Table 2B is otherwise unknown. All that can be said is that its earliest manuscripts were copied in England in 1366–1367 (L_1) and 1373 (E). In 1414, the table was inserted by Pierre d'Ailly (Petrus de Aliaco) in his *Tractatus de figura inceptionis mundi et coniunctionibus mediis sequentibus*, a work extant in at least ten manuscripts.

3.4   Table 3

John of Eschenden, *Summa iudicialis de accidentibus mundi*, I.12.5 (ed. 1489, sig. 76va)

	♄	♃	♂	☉	♀	☿	☽
♈	3• ♄ 21 / 2 26 30	3↑ / 2 1 6	5↑ 2 1↓ / 21 25	4 19 / 3↓ 1•	2 7 12 / 1↑ ς	2 13 20	0
♉	2 23 27 / 1↑	2 15 22	3• ς / 2 28 30	0	5↑ 3↓ 2 / 1 9 / 8 14	1↓	4 3↑ 1• / 3
♊	3↓ 25 30 / 2	3• ς 2 1↓ / 7 12	2 18 24 / 1•	1↑	2 13 17	5↑ 3↑ 2 / 1 6	0
♋	2 / ς 27 / 30	4 15 / 2 20 26	3↑ ♄ 28 / 2 1 7	0	3↓ 2 1↓ / 8 14 / 13 19	2 / 1•	5↓ 3• 1↑
♌	3• ς / 2 12 18 / 1↓	3↑ / 2 1 6 / 1•	2 25 30	1↑	5↓ 3↓ / 2 7 11	2 19 24	0
♍	2 29 30	2 18 21	3• / 2 22 28	1↓	3↓ 2 1• / ♄ 8 / 27 17	5↓ 4 2 1↑ / 15 1 / 7	3↑
♎	4 2 21 / 3↓ 1 6 / 1•	3• 2 1↑ / 15 21	2 / ς 29 / 30	♄ 19	5↓ 2↓ / 22 28	3↑ / 2 7 14	1↓
♏	2 25 30	2 20 24	5↓ 3↑ 2 1↓ / 2 1 / 7	1•	3↓ 2 1↑ / ς 8 / 11	2 12 19	3• ♄ 3
♐	3• 2 1↑ / 22 26	5↓ 3↑ 2 / 1 12	2 27 30	3↓ r	2 13 17	2 18 21 / 1↓ ς	1•

(*cont.*)

	♄	♃	♂	☉	♀	☿	☽
♑	5↓ 2 (23 26)	ↄ (15) 2 (8 14) 1↓	4 (28) 3• 2 (27 30) 1•	1↑	3↓ 2 (15 22)	2 (1 7)	3↑ ς
♒	5↑ 3↓ 2 (26 30)	3• 2 (14 20)	2 (21 25)	ς	2 (8 13) 1↓	3↑ 2 (1 7) 1•	1↑
♓	2 (29 30) 1↓	5↑ 2 (13 16) 1•	3↑ 2 (20 28) 1↑	o	4 (27) 3↓ 2 (1 12)	ↄ (15) 2 (17 19) ς	3•

Note to the edition: the table has been reconstructed following John of Eschenden's instructions (n. 36 below). All the witnesses I have seen, whether of John's *Summa* or the five MSS listed below, contain mistakes and misuses of the symbols.

5↓ Primary domicile	3↓ Triplicity ruler by day
5↑ Secondary domicile	3↑ Triplicity ruler by night
ς Detriment	3• Triplicity participant
4 Exaltation (with degree written underneath)	2 Term (with first and last degrees underneath)
ↄ Fall (with degree underneath)	1↓ First decan
	1• Second decan
	1↑ Third decan

This table occurs in John of Eschenden's *Summa iudicialis de accidentibus mundi*, written at Oxford in 1347–1348. The text is extant in at least 36 manuscripts and was printed in Venice in 1489. The table takes place at the end of the long chapter I.12.5, dealing with the essential dignities, and it is preceded by a full set of instructions, in which John of Eschenden explains that he provided this table to show at a glance the number of dignities owned by each planet in any degree of any sign. This is indeed what the table offers, by means of a series of innovations. First, John introduces three symbols, the *punctus elevatus* (↓), the *punctus simplex* (•) and the *punctus depressus* (↑), to distinguish between the three rulers of the triplicities, as well as between the three rulers of the decans. Second, he provides the exact position of the terms by listing their first and last degrees. Additionally, John also uses the *punctus elevatus* and the *punctus depressus* to distinguish between the primary and secondary domiciles and introduces two more symbols, an inverted 5 (ς) to denote the detriment and an inverted 4 (♄) to denote the fall.[35] The table includes three rows for each sign. The first row gives the points of essential dignities (these points are identical with those of Table 2B) and the two following rows provide the additional information as needed, i.e., the first and last degrees of each term (underneath '2'), the detriment (ϛ), the fall (♄) and the exact degree of both the exaltation (underneath '4') and the fall (underneath '♄').[36]

---

35   Although John remains silent about this, the detriment and fall have a bearing on the calculation of the almuten in some cases where the planet that has the most essential dignities is found in its detriment or fall, something which would probably be considered a disqualifying factor by many astrologers. This happens in three cases when the participant of the triplicity is counted: for Saturn in 26°–30° Aries by night (co-almuten with Mars); for Jupiter in 7°–10° Gemini by day; and for Saturn in 12°–18° Leo by night (co-almuten with the Sun); and in two cases when the participant is not counted: for Mars in 1°–7° Cancer by night (or counting both the rulers by day and by night); and for Venus in 11° Scorpio by day (co-almuten with Mars).

36   Here is the full text of the instructions: 'Et ponam tibi unam tabulam notabilem in qua statim videbis quot dignitates habet planeta in quocumque gradu cuiuscumque signi fuerit. Nam figura significans quinque significabit tibi domum et si iuxta istam figuram inveneris punctum elevatum significabit tibi domum planetae principalem et si inveneris punctum depressum significabit domum planetae secundariam. Item figura designans 4 significabit tibi exaltationem planetae et sub illa figura inveniemus quis sit gradus exaltationis illius signi. Et ubicumque inveneris figuram significantem exaltationem eversam, significabit ibidem fore depressionem sive casum et ponetur gradus depressionis sub figura. Et eodem modo ubi inveneris figuram domum significantem eversam, significat fore exilium planetae sive detrimentum. Item figura significans 3 significabit tibi triplicitatem planetae et ubicumque iuxta illam figuram punctus elevatus fuerit, significat quod in illa triplicitate dominatur planeta de die. Et ubi ponitur depressus punctus iuxta figuram significantem triplicitatem, significat quod in illa triplicitate dominatur planeta de nocte. Sed si iuxta predictam figuram ponitur punctus simplex significat participationem planetae in illa triplicitate de die et de nocte. Item figura significans 2 significabit tibi terminum planetae et quantitas terminorum in gradibus ponetur sub illa figura. Et nota quod termini qui ponentur in ista tabula erunt termini Egiptiorum eo quod maior pars astrologorum consentit in eis. Sed si volueris operari per terminos Ptolemei, invenies eos primus in hoc capitulo in quadam tabula. Item nota quod domini triplicitatum qui ponuntur in hac tabula sunt illi quod ponit maior pars astrologorum. Item figura designans unitatem significabit tibi faciem planetae. Et si iuxta illam figuram ponatur punctus elevatus significat ibidem fore faciem, scilicet primam, illius signi in quo fuerit illa facies. Et si iuxta illam figuram fuerit punctus simplex, scilicet nec elevatus nec depressus, significabit ibidem fore faciem secundam illius signi. Et si iuxta hanc figuram fuerit punctus depressus, significabit ibidem fore faciem tertiam illius signi. Nomina vero planetarum ponuntur in capite tabule et nomina signorum ponuntur in fine eius. Unde in hac tabula invenies omnes dignitates essentiales praedictas cuiuscunque planetae volueris in quocumque signo volueris in concursu duarum linearum tabule quae scilicet procedunt ab illo planeta de quo queris et ab illo signo de quo queris etc.' (John of Eschenden, *Summa iudicialis de accidentibus mundi*, I.12.5, ed. 1489, sig. 76rb; the table follows immediately on sig. 76va).

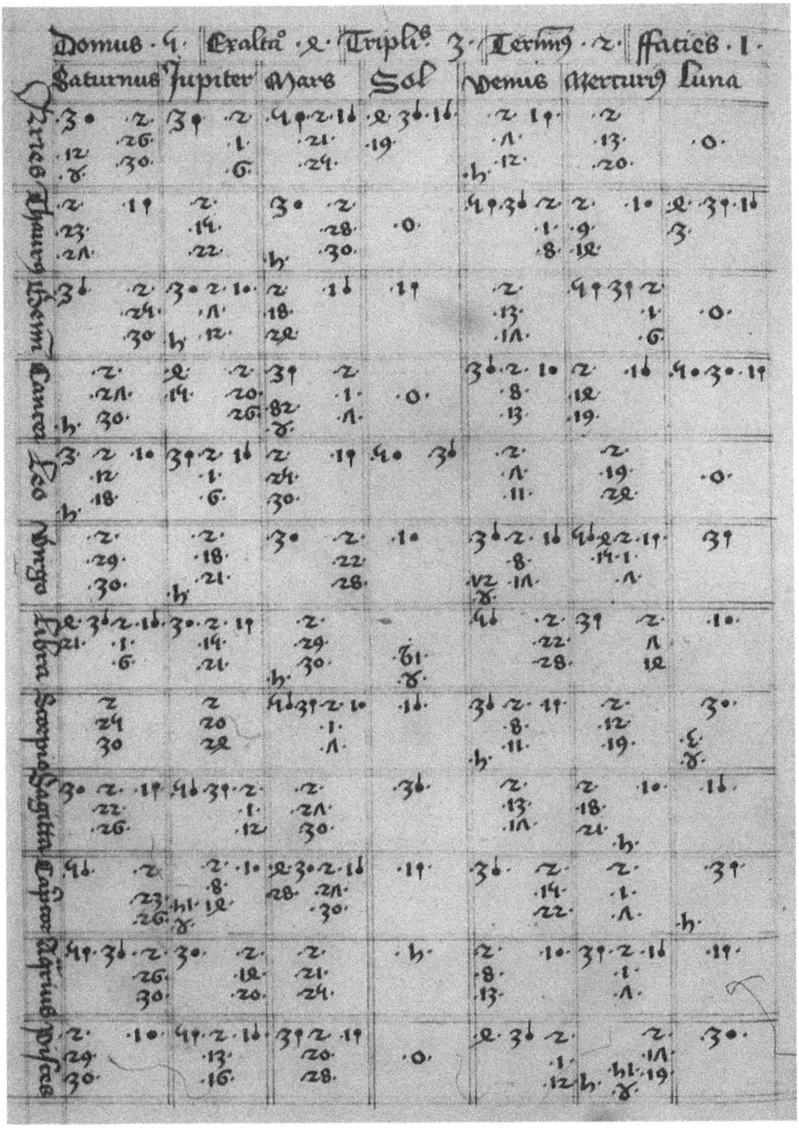

Domus · 5 ·	Exaltā · 4 ·	Triplic̄ 3 ·	Terminus · 2 ·	facies · 1 ·
Saturnus	Jupiter	Mars	Sol	Venus	Mercurius	Luna

FIGURE 2.3 Table 3 from London, British Library, Addit. 24071, f. 76ᵛ

The advantage of this table is evident, as it allows the user to calculate the almuten for any degree of the zodiac at a glance. Another advantage is that it leaves all options open to the user, including which triplicity ruler(s) should be taken into account. The disadvantage is that the table is somewhat cumbersome, forcing the user to get acquainted with a network of unusual symbols. This disadvantage, however, did not deter later astrologers who excerpted the table from the *Summa* and copied it, together with the instructions, in their own manuscripts. I am aware of five such manuscripts: Klosterneuburg, SB, 683, s. XV, f. 18ʳ (with instructions f. 18ᵛ); London, BL, Addit. 24071, s. XV, f. 76ᵛ (with instructions f. 77ʳ); London, BL, Harley 2269, s. XVI, f. 70ᵛ (with instructions f. 71ʳ); Oxford, BL, Ashmole 191, s. XV, f. 122ᵛ (without instructions); and Vienna, ÖNB, 5251, s. XV, f. 39ʳ (with instructions f. 38ᵛ).

3.5   Table 4
Oxford, BL, Rawlinson D.1227, s. XIV, f. 63ᵛ

		♄	♃	♂	☉	♀	☿	☽				♄	♃	♂	☉	♀	☿	☽
	5	0	0	5	0	ſ	0	0			5	0	0	ſ	0	5	0	0
	4	ħ	0	0	19	0	0	0			4	21	0	0	ħ	0	0	0
	3	3	n	0	d	0	0	0			3	d	3	0	0	0	n	0
♈	2	26	1	21	0	7	13	0	♎		2	1	15	29	0	22	7	0
		30	6	25	0	12	20	0				6	21	30	0	18	14	0
	1	0	0	1	11	21	0	0			1	11	21	0	0	0	0	1
		0	0	10	20	30	0	0				20	30	0	0	0	0	10
	5	0	0	ſ	0	5	0	0			5	0	0	5	0	ſ	0	0
	4	0	0	0	0	0	0	3			4	0	0	0	0	0	0	ħ
	3	0	0	3	0	d	0	n			3	0	0	n	0	d	0	3
♉	2	23	15	28	0	1	9	0	♏		2	25	20	1	0	8	12	0
		27	22	30	0	8	14	0				30	24	7	0	11	19	0
	1	21	0	0	0	0	1	11			1	0	0	1	11	21	0	0
		30	0	0	0	0	10	20				0	0	10	20	30	0	0
	5	0	ſ	0	0	0	5	0			5	0	5	0	0	0	ſ	0
	4	0	0	0	0	0	0	0			4	0	0	0	0	0	0	0
	3	d	3	0	0	n	0	0			3	3	n	0	d	0	0	0
♊	2	25	7	18	0	13	1	0	♐		2	24	1	28	0	13	18	0
		30	12	24	0	17	6	0				27	12	30	0	17	23	0
	1	0	1	11	21	0	0	0			1	21	0	0	0	0	1	11
		0	10	20	30	0	0	0				30	0	0	0	0	10	20
	5	ſ	0	0	0	0	0	5			5	5	0	0	0	0	0	ſ
	4	0	15	ħ	0	0	0	0			4	0	0	28	0	0	0	0
	3	0	0	n	0	d	0	3			3	0	0	3	0	d	0	n
♋	2	27	21	1	0	8	14	0	♑		2	23	8	27	0	15	1	0
		30	26	7	0	13	20	0				26	14	30	0	22	7	0
	1	0	0	0	0	1	11	21			1	0	1	11	21	0	0	0
		0	0	0	0	10	20	30				0	10	20	30	0	0	0
	5	ſ	0	0	5	0	0	0			5	5	0	0	ſ	0	0	0
	4	0	0	0	0	0	0	0			4	0	0	0	0	0	0	0
	3	3	n	0	d	0	0	0			3	d	3	0	0	0	n	0
♌	2	12	1	25	0	7	19	0	♒		2	26	14	21	0	8	1	0
		18	6	30	0	11	24	0				30	20	25	0	13	7	0
	1	1	11	21	0	0	0	0			1	0	0	0	0	1	11	21
		10	20	30	0	0	0	0				0	0	0	0	10	20	30

(*cont.*)

		♄	♃	♂	☉	♀	☿	☽			♄	♃	♂	☉	♀	☿	☽
	5	o	S	o	o	o	5	o		5	o	5	o	o	o	S	o
	4	o	o	o	o	ŧ	15	o		4	o	o	o	o	27	ŧ	o
	3	o	o	3	o	d	o	n		3	o	o	n	o	d	o	3
♍	2	29	18	22	o	8	1	o	♓	2	29	13	20	o	1	17	o
		30	21	28	o	17	7	o			30	16	28	o	12	19	o
	1	o	o	o	1	11	21	o		1	1	11	21	o	o	o	o
		o	o	o	10	20	30	o			10	20	30	o	o	o	o

5 (domicile): 5 = domicile; S = detriment
4 (exaltation): with indication of the degree; ŧ = fall
3 (triplicity): d = ruler by day; n = ruler by night, 3 = participant
2 (term): first and last degrees
1 (decan): first and last degrees
Note to the edition: the table has been edited as it occurs in the Oxford MS, except that I have used the symbols for the planets and signs instead of their full names. The table includes nine mistakes (or deviations from the standard theory), which are indicated in bold.

Table 4 occurs under the title 'Tabula dignitatum omnium planetarum' in MS Oxford, BL, Rawlinson D.1227, f. 63ᵛ, a manuscript copied in Oxford around the middle of the fourteenth century and containing, among others, the Oxford Tables for 1348 (f. 64ʳ–101ʳ). Like Table 3, this table allows the user to calculate the almuten for any degree of the zodiac at a glance. It is perhaps based on Table 3, with which it shares the symbols ŧ (fall) and S (detriment), but it has the advantage of sparing the other unusual symbols. Each sign is given five rows labeled 5-4-3-2-1, corresponding to the five essential dignities. Each row provides the relevant information, including the domicile and detriment, the degree of the exaltation (under '4'), and the first and last degrees for both the terms (under '2') and the decans (under '1'). For the triplicities (3), the authors simply used the letters 'd' for the ruler by day and 'n' for the ruler by night, and the number '3' for the participant.

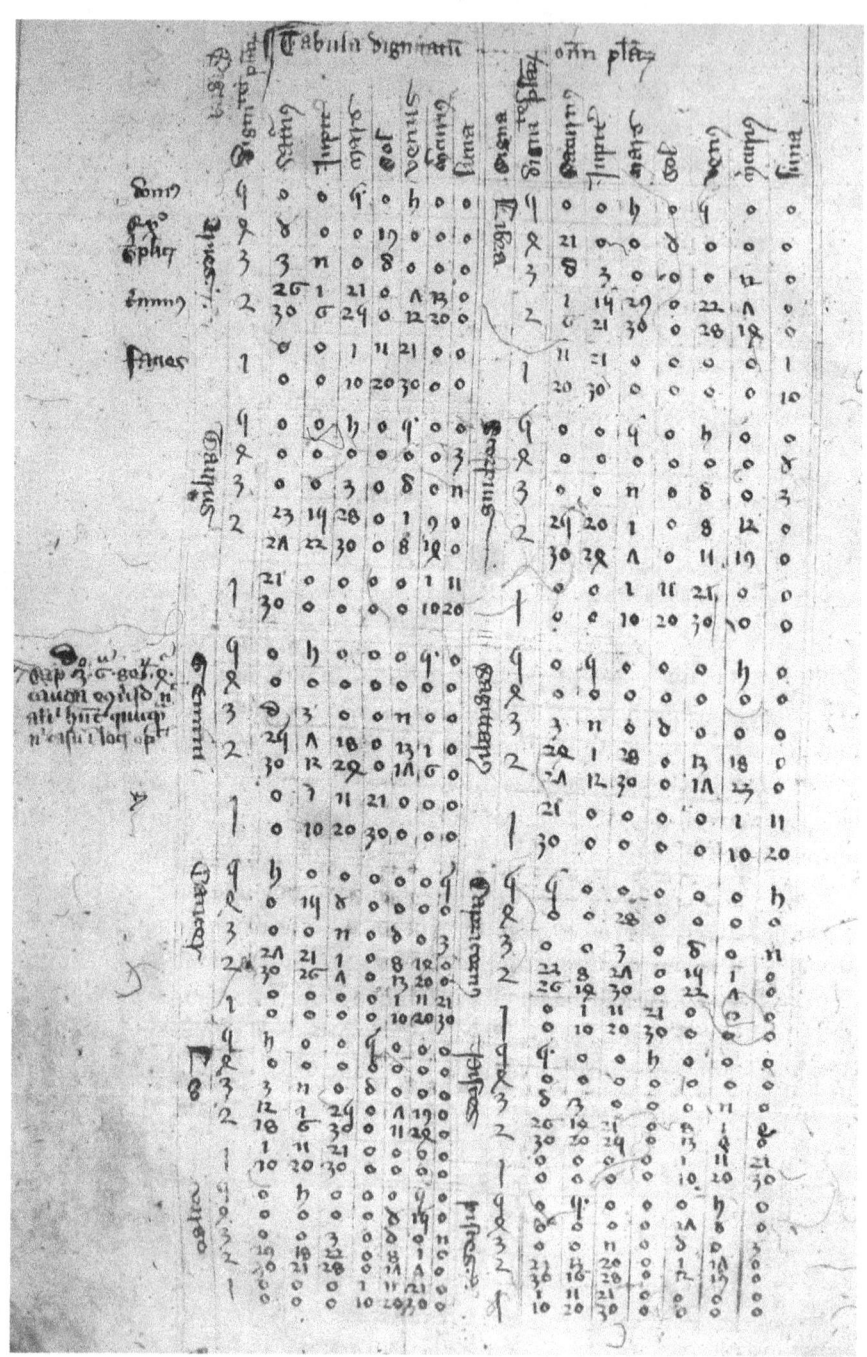

FIGURE 2.4 Table 3 from Oxford, Bodleian Library, Rawlinson D.1227, f. 63ᵛ

3.6   *Table 5*

L   Leipzig, UB, 1496, s. XV, f. 142^r–144^v
L1   London, BL, Arundel 88, s. XV–XVI, f. 51^r–53^v
P   Paris, BS, 1037, s. XV, f. 74^r–79^v
V   Vatican, BAV, Pal. lat. 1368, s. XV, f. 49^v–50^r
V1   Vicenza, BCB, 208, s. XV, f. 20^r–20^v

Aries	♄	♃	♂	☉	♀	☿	☽
1°	3	5	6	7	0	0	0
2°	3	5	6	7	0	0	0
⋮	⋮	⋮	⋮	⋮	⋮	⋮	⋮
7°	3	3	6	7	2	0	0
⋮	⋮	⋮	⋮	⋮	⋮	⋮	⋮
11°	3	3	5	8	2	0	0
⋮	⋮	⋮	⋮	⋮	⋮	⋮	⋮
13°	3	3	5	8	0	2	0
⋮	⋮	⋮	⋮	⋮	⋮	⋮	⋮
21°	3	3	7	7	1	0	0
⋮	⋮	⋮	⋮	⋮	⋮	⋮	⋮
26°	5	3	5	7	1	0	0
⋮	⋮	⋮	⋮	⋮	⋮	⋮	⋮

Title om. LP; Quot dignitates essentiales (puta domus, exaltatio, triplicitas, terminus et
     facies) habeant singuli planetae in singulis gradibus uniuscuiusque signi *L1*; Tabule
     fortitudinum seu dignitatum septem planetarum in omnibus gradibus 12 signorum
     zodyaci *V*; Pro almutaz *V1*

In the fifteenth century, we find yet more detailed tables. Table 5 shows the
points of essential dignities of each planet in each of the 360 degrees of the
zodiac. This table is arranged by sign, with 30 rows per sign, and runs over two
to twelve pages. For reasons of space and simplicity, I have edited here only the
significant rows of Aries, showing the first two degrees and each subsequent
degree where change occurs, i.e., the 7th, 11th, 13th, 21st and 26th degrees.[37]

---

37   It should be noted that, with the exception of *V1*, all MSS have additional columns pro-
      viding further information on the zodiacal degrees. *L* has one additional column giving
      the quality of groups of degrees, e.g., 1°–19° Aries are 'indifferens', 20° Aries to 2° Taurus
      'sicca', 3°–15° Taurus 'humida' etc. *L1* has two additional columns giving the sex and type

All three triplicity rulers are taken into account, as can be seen immediately in the values displayed under 1° Aries, with 3 points allocated to Saturn (triplicity participant), 5 to Jupiter (triplicity ruler by night + term) and 7 to the Sun (exaltation + triplicity ruler by day). The advantage of this table is that it allows the user to grasp the almuten for any degree of the zodiac not only at a glance, but also without any effort. The disadvantage is that it can be used only by astrologers who take into account all three triplicity rulers (but see MS V_1 below).

L was copied in 1486–1487 by Virgilius Wellendörffer, then a master student at the University of Leipzig.[38] L_1 is the well-known manuscript of Giovanni Battista Boerio, copied between 1484, when he was a student at the University of Pavia, and the early years of the sixteenth century, when he had become physician and astrologer to Henry VII and Henry VIII in London.[39] The values given in the edited table above are those of these two manuscripts, which generally provide correct values.[40]

The three other manuscripts have distinctive features. In V, whose f. 34–68 were copied around 1426 by Conrad of Dyffenbach in Worms or thereabouts, the table displays basically the same values as LL$_1$, except that Conrad granted a bonus of 2 points to the Sun in the northern signs (Aries-Virgo) and to the Moon in the southern signs (Libra-Pisces), so that, in the table above, the values indicated for the Sun are 9, 9, 9, 10, 10, 9, 9. Conrad applied this rule consistently throughout the twelve signs and explains, in a note added in the top margin of the double page, that he followed the opinion of a certain 'Gwido'.[41] In the

---

of degree ('lucidus', 'tenebrosus', 'fumosus', 'vacuus', 'putealis', 'azemena'). V has three additional columns giving the position of the lunar mansions and of a selection of stars in the northern and southern hemispheres. P has nine additional columns giving the rulers of the decans, novenaries and duodenaries, the lunar mansions, the sex and type of degree (four columns), and the degree of exaltation and fall. See also n. 44 below.

38   Virgilius also copied Table 2B on f. 76^v.

39   On him and his MS, see Azzolini, *The Duke and the Stars*, pp. 29–40 and 48–49.

40   I only note three mistakes in L (in Scorpio 11°, Venus is given 3 points instead of 5; in Sagittarius 30°, the Sun 3 points instead of 2; and in Capricorn 7°, Mercury 7 points instead of 2) and two mistakes in L_1 (in Cancer 11°–13°, Mercury is given 0 point instead of 1; and in Leo 12°–18°, Venus 2 points instead of 0).

41   'Et sunt fortitudines planetarum in locis: compute videlicet pro domo 5, pro exaltatione 4, pro triplicitate 3, pro termino 2 et pro facie 1. Et Gwido dicit quod fortitudo Solis ut in termino sit ab initio Leonis in finem Capricorni, et eodem modo dicit quod fortitudo Lune ut in termino sit a principio Aquarii usque in finem Cancri, et pro Sole in signis septentrionalibus, scilicet a principio Arietis usque in finem Virginis, pro fortitudine 2, et eodem modo in signis meridionalibus, scilicet a principio Libre in finem Piscium, pro eius fortitudine similiter 2' (V, f. 49^v–50^r, top margin). The first part of this rule (another 2-point

bottom margin of the same double page, he noted additional conditions which affect the calculation of the almuten, including (1) 1–12 points allocated to the planets according to their position in the twelve houses, where the values are identical with those of Abraham Avenezra's *Liber de nativitatibus*; (2) 6 points to the ruler of the hour; (3) 1 point if the planet is in its *hayz*;[42] (4) 7 points to the ruler of the day; and (5) 1–12 points to the superior planets according to their position in their synodic pedioid.[43] With the exception of the third one, we are familiar with these additional conditions (pp. 62–64 above).

In V_1, a rich astrological manuscript copied in 1467–1470 by Bartolomeo Valdizocco of Padua, the table is arranged by triplicity. The first page (f. 20^r) includes the signs Aries, Leo and Sagittarius, with the captions 'Prima triplicitas' and 'Domini prime triplicitatis: Sol in die, Iupiter in nocte, Saturnus particeps'; and the second page (f. 20^v) includes the signs of Taurus, Virgo and Capricorn, with the captions 'Secunda triplicitas' and 'Domini secunde triplicitatis: Venus in die, Luna in nocte, Mars particeps'. The third and fourth triplicities are not (or no longer) found in the manuscript. A striking peculiarity of Bartolomeo's table is that no points are allocated to the triplicity rulers, probably, as I suspect, as a way of leaving the question open to the user, as the arrangement of the table by triplicity suggests. The table includes further peculiarities or errors: in Aries 1°–30°, the Moon is given 2 points (instead of 0) and in 21°–30°, Venus 0 point (instead of 1); in Taurus, the Moon receives 3 additional points (as if the triplicity by night was counted); in Leo, the Sun receives 3 additional points (as if the triplicity by day was counted); in Leo 25°–30°, Mars is given 1 point (instead of 3); in Virgo 18°–20°, Venus 0 point (instead of 1); in Sagittarius 1°–30°, the Sun 2 points (instead of 0—or 3 if we were to count the triplicity) and in 21°, Mercury 0 point (instead of 2); in Capricorn 23°–26°, Saturn 5 points (instead of 7), and in 1°–19°, the Sun 2 (instead of 0) and in 20°–30°, the Sun 3 (instead of 1).

In *P*, an anonymous manuscript copied c. 1437–1438 in France and/or Germany, three features stand out: (1) each dignity is numerated separately as in Tables 2A–2B, so that in 1° Aries, Jupiter gets 2.3, Mars 1.5 and the Sun 3.4; (2) the points allocated to the triplicity rulers are given only in the first row of the

---

bonus to the Sun from 1° Leo to 30° Capricorn and to the Moon from 1° Aquarius to 30° Cancer) was not applied in the table. This Gwido does not seem to be Guido Bonatti, who does not offer any such rule in his *Liber introductorius ad iudicia stellarum*.

42   On the *hayz*, see Alcabitius, *Introductorius*, II.78 (ed. Burnett/Yamamoto/Yano, p. 266).

43   This fifth condition is garbled: 'Item tres superiores post combustionem usque ad 30 gradus habent virtutes ut 12, demum ad 90 gradus fortitudines ut 10, demum ad stationem primam ut 9, demum fit retrogradus'. Compare with Pseudo-John of Seville's text quoted in n. 12 above.

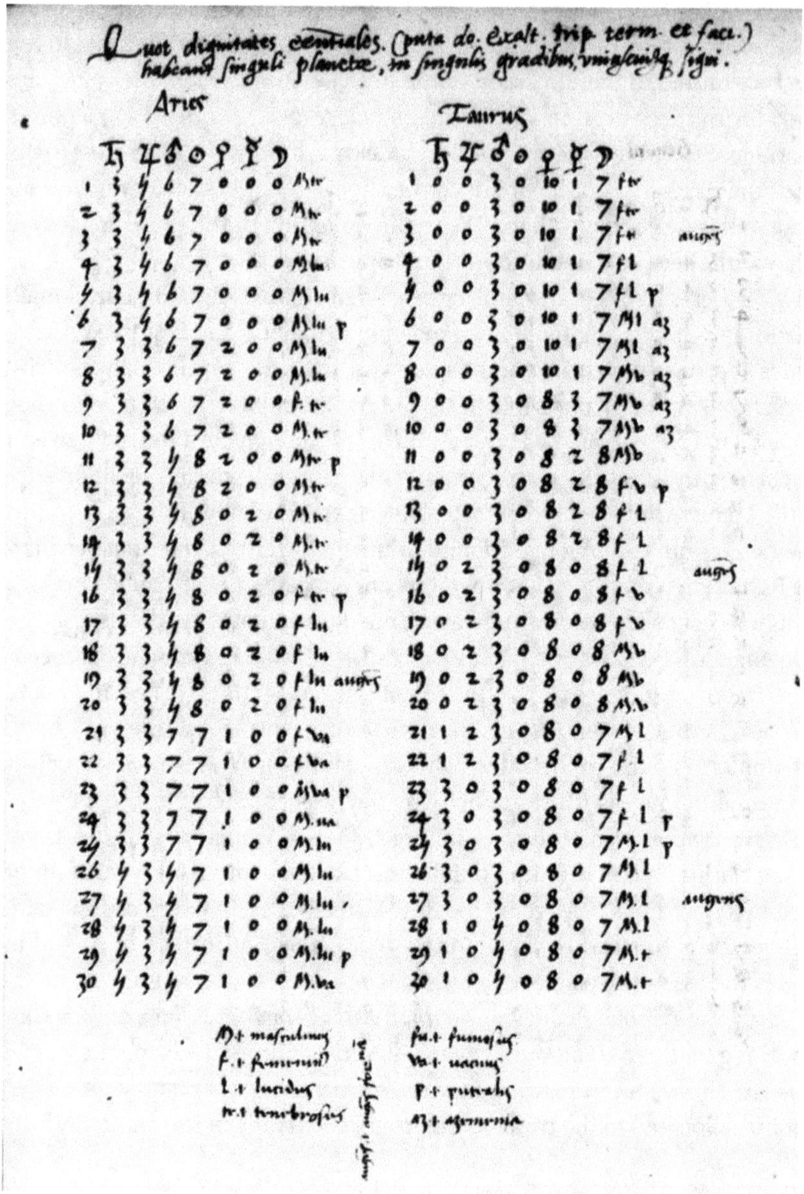

Quot dignitates essentiales (puta do. exalt. trip. term. et faci.) habeant singuli planetae, in singulis gradibus, uniuscuiusque signi.

Aries	♄	♃	♂	☉	♀	☿	☽			Taurus	♄	♃	♂	☉	♀	☿	☽		
1	3	5	6	7	0	0	0	M tr		1	0	0	3	0	10	1	7	f tr	
2	3	5	6	7	0	0	0	M tr		2	0	0	3	0	10	1	7	f tr	
3	3	5	6	7	0	0	0	M tr		3	0	0	3	0	10	1	7	f tr	augens
4	3	5	6	7	0	0	0	M lu		4	0	0	3	0	10	1	7	f l	
5	3	5	6	7	0	0	0	M lu		5	0	0	3	0	10	1	7	f l	p
6	3	5	6	7	0	0	0	M lu	p	6	0	0	3	0	10	1	7	M l	az
7	3	3	6	7	2	0	0	M lu		7	0	0	3	0	10	1	7	M l	az
8	3	3	6	7	2	0	0	M lu		8	0	0	3	0	10	1	7	M v	az
9	3	3	6	7	2	0	0	f tr		9	0	0	3	0	8	3	7	M v	az
10	3	3	6	7	2	0	0	M tr		10	0	0	3	0	8	3	7	M v	az
11	3	3	5	8	2	0	0	M tr	p	11	0	0	3	0	8	2	8	M v	
12	3	3	5	8	2	0	0	M tr		12	0	0	3	0	8	2	8	f v	p
13	3	3	5	8	0	2	0	M tr		13	0	0	3	0	8	2	8	f l	
14	3	3	5	8	0	2	0	M tr		14	0	0	3	0	8	2	8	f l	
15	3	3	5	8	0	2	0	M tr		15	0	2	3	0	8	0	8	f l	augens
16	3	3	5	8	0	2	0	f tr	p	16	0	2	3	0	8	0	8	f v	
17	3	3	5	8	0	2	0	f lu		17	0	2	3	0	8	0	8	f v	
18	3	3	5	8	0	2	0	f lu		18	0	2	3	0	8	0	8	M v	
19	3	3	5	8	0	2	0	f lu	augens	19	0	2	3	0	8	0	8	M v	
20	3	3	5	8	0	2	0	f lu		20	0	2	3	0	8	0	8	M v	
21	3	3	7	7	1	0	0	f va		21	1	2	3	0	8	0	7	M l	
22	3	3	7	7	1	0	0	f va		22	1	2	3	0	8	0	7	f l	
23	3	3	7	7	1	0	0	M va	p	23	3	0	3	0	8	0	7	f l	
24	3	3	7	7	1	0	0	M va		24	3	0	3	0	8	0	7	f l	p
25	3	3	7	7	1	0	0	M lu		25	3	0	3	0	8	0	7	M l	p
26	5	3	5	7	1	0	0	M lu		26	3	0	3	0	8	0	7	M l	
27	5	3	5	7	1	0	0	M lu		27	3	0	3	0	8	0	7	M l	augens
28	5	3	5	7	1	0	0	M lu		28	1	0	5	0	8	0	7	M l	
29	5	3	5	7	1	0	0	M lu	p	29	1	0	5	0	8	0	7	M tr	
30	5	3	5	7	1	0	0	M va		30	1	0	5	0	8	0	7	M tr	

M. i. masculinus
f. i. femininus
l. i. lucidus
tr. i. tenebrosus

fu. i. fumosus
va. i. vacuus
p. i. puteales
az. i. azemena

FIGURE 2.5 Table 5 from London, British Library, Arundel 88, f. 51r (Aries-Taurus) sign (in 1° Aries, we read for Saturn 'Part. 3', evidently for 'Particeps 3', for Jupiter 2.3 and for the Sun 3.4), but these are irregular and sometimes entirely omitted, like in Taurus, Virgo, Libra, Aquarius and Pisces; (3) above the planetary symbols at the top, the author indicated the total of points of essential dignities as in Table 1, with, however, two mistakes: Mercurius in Taurus = 4 (instead of 3) and Mars in Sagittarius = 5 (instead of 2). Besides these features, the table is replete with mistakes.

3.7   *Table 6*
F   Florence, BML, Ashburnham 1697, s. XV, f. 36ʳ–41ᵛ
P   Paris, BnF, lat. 7432, s. XV, f. 259ᵛ–262ʳ

Aries	Domus	Exaltatio	Triplicitas	Terminus	Facies	Almuten
1°	♂	☉	☉♃♄	♃	♂	☉
2°	♂	☉	☉♃♄	♃	♂	☉
⋮	⋮	⋮	⋮	⋮	⋮	⋮
7°	♂	☉	☉♃♄	♀	♂	☉
⋮	⋮	⋮	⋮	⋮	⋮	⋮
11°	♂	☉	☉♃♄	♀	☉	☉
⋮	⋮	⋮	⋮	⋮	⋮	⋮
13°	♂	☉	☉♃♄	☿	☉	☉
⋮	⋮	⋮	⋮	⋮	⋮	⋮
21°	♂	☉	☉♃♄	♂	♀	☉♂
⋮	⋮	⋮	⋮	⋮	⋮	⋮
26°	♂	☉	☉♃♄	♄	♀	☉
⋮	⋮	⋮	⋮	⋮	⋮	⋮

Table 6 is similar in structure to Table 5, showing all 360 degrees, with 30 rows per sign, but the organisation is different. The first five columns give the planetary ruler(s) of each of the five essential dignities, including the three rulers of the triplicity, and a sixth column is specifically devoted to the almuten.[44]

---

44   Here too (see n. 37 above), the MSS include additional columns, eight in the case of *F* (sex and type of degree, novenaries, denaries and duodenaries) and nine in the case of *P* (sex, novenaries and duodenaries, quality of degrees, position of degrees on the eighth sphere, and position and quality of the lunar mansions).

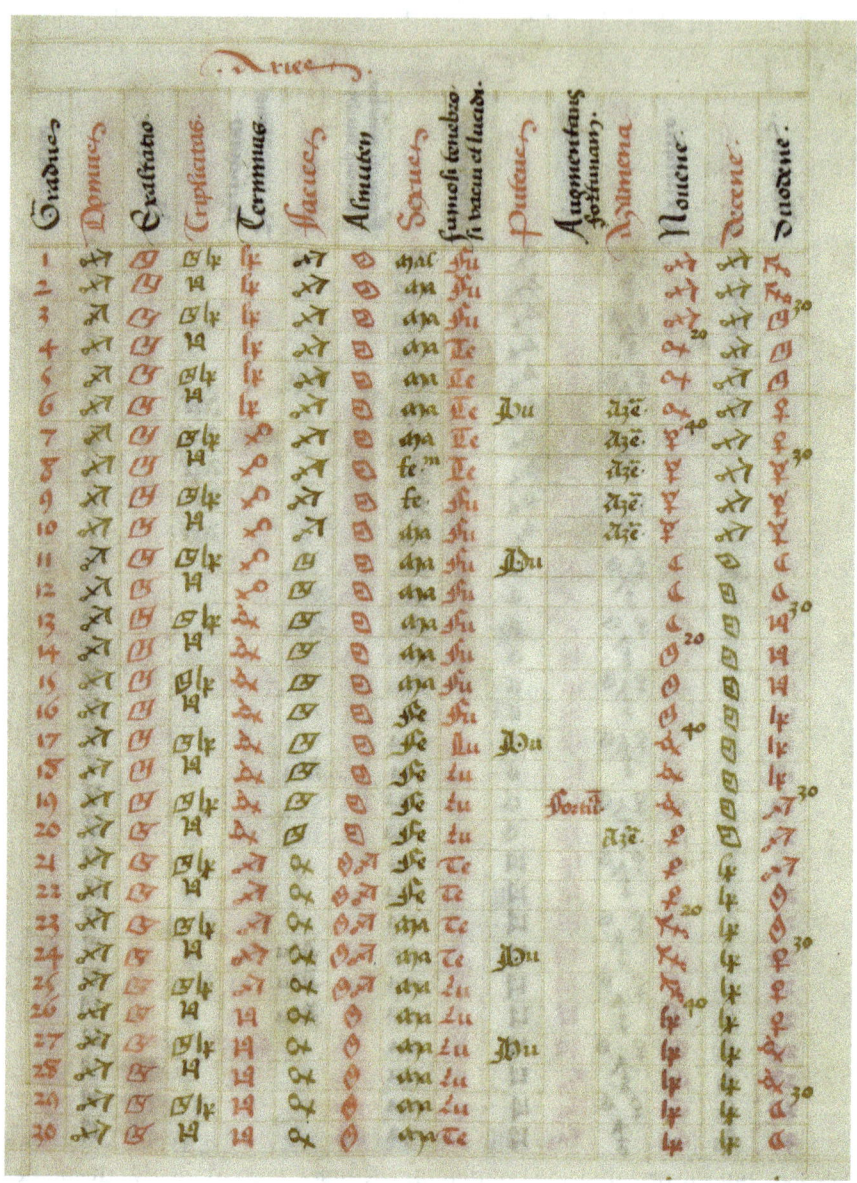

FIGURE 2.6 Table 6 from Florence, Biblioteca Medicea Laurenziana, Ashburnham 1697, f. 36ʳ
(Aries)

The table is edited here from *F* in the same simplified form as Table 5, that is, showing only the significant rows of Aries. In *P*, the columns for domicile, exaltation and triplicity are omitted, because the relevant information is supplied in the headers (e.g., for Aries, 'Aries: none spere, domus Martis, exaltatio Solis, triplicitas Solis, Iovis et Martis, alii Saturni').

F is a splendid manuscript filled with the Alphonsine Tables with John of Saxony's canons. *P* is another splendid manuscript prepared between c. 1468 and 1485 by the famous astrologer Conrad Heingarter for Duke Jean II of Bourbon. Both manuscripts basically agree on the almuten, which was calculated taking into account all three triplicity rulers. Thus, in Aries 1°–20°, the almuten is the Sun, in 21°–25° the Sun and Mars, and in 26°–30° the Sun (as shown in the table above); in Taurus 1°–10° Venus, in 11°–20° Venus and the Moon, and in 21°–30°[45] Venus; in Gemini 1°–30°, Mercury; in Cancer 1°–30° the Moon; in Leo 1°–30° the Sun; in Virgo 1°–30° Mercury; in Libra 1°–21° Saturn, in 22°–28° Saturn and Venus, and in 29°–30° Saturn;[46] in Scorpio 1°–30° Mars; in Sagittarius 1°–30° Jupiter; in Capricorn 1°–22° Mars, in 23°–26° Saturn and Mars, and in 27°–30° Mars;[47] in Aquarius 1°–30° Saturn; in Pisces 1°–12° Venus, in 13°–16° Jupiter, and in 17°–30° Venus. The advantage and disadvantage of Table 6 are the same as with Table 5: on the one hand, it allows the user to grasp the almuten for any degree at a glance and without any effort, but, on the other, it can be used only by astrologers who take into account all three triplicity rulers.

4   Conclusions: Points of Contention / A Pessimistic View of the World

The weighted almuten should probably be counted among the important post-Hellenistic innovations to horoscopic astrology. Attested since at least the first generation of Arabic astrologers around 800, it was enthusiastically adopted by Latin astrologers and enjoyed considerable success in Europe from the thirteenth to the late fifteenth century.

---

45   So in *P*, whereas *F* has Venus alone in 1°–30° Taurus. This would be correct if counting the ruler of the triplicity by day only, but this is not what *F* (nor *P*) did in the other places.

46   So in *P*, whereas *F* has, incorrectly, Saturn in 1°–20°, Saturn and Venus in 21°–25°, and Saturn in 26°–30° Libra.

47   So in *F*, whereas *P* has Saturn in 1°–30° Capricorn. This must probably be interpreted as a mistake, which the author attempted to correct in a note added at the bottom of the page (f. 261ᵛ): 'Alii ponunt Martem almuten usque ad 22°, deinde Martem et Saturnum usque ad 26° et depost (!) iterum Martem'.

The basic procedure is accepted by most, if not all, Latin practitioners. The almuten over a given zodiacal degree is the planet that has the most points of essential dignities in that degree, counting 5 points for the domicile, 4 points for the exaltation, 3 points for the triplicity, 2 points for the term and 1 point for the decan. Several authors allocate 3 points to the term and 2 points to the triplicity, but this alternative was not followed in practice, at least judging from the sources presented here.

Yet, there are points of contention. The three examples of the almuten of the nativity examined above follow three different methods. The main problem concerns the three rulers of the triplicity, that is, which ruler(s) should be taken into account and when. In most cases, the triplicity participant is counted, but there are exceptions, including the astrologer who cast the nativity of Louis X and the author of Table 2A, as well as one manuscript of Table 1 (C_2) and one manuscript of Table 2B (V_1). The use of the triplicity rulers by day and by night is not entirely straightforward either. While some astrologers select the ruler by day in diurnal charts and the ruler by night in nocturnal charts, as did the astrologers who cast the nativities of Louis X and of Eleanor of Portugal, Johannes Schöner shows hesitation before finally choosing to include both rulers in his treatment of the diurnal nativity of Maximilian I. Likewise, Tables 1, 2, 5 and 6 were designed to be used in situations where both rulers by day and by night are counted (as well as the participant for that matter) and would be virtually useless in other situations. Another issue concerns the additional conditions advocated by one or several authors, including the 1–12 points allocated to the twelve houses, the 6–7 points allocated to the rulers of the hour and of the day, and the 1–12 points allocated to the superior planets in their synodic period. The astrologer who cast the horoscope of Louis X took into account the first two of these conditions[48] and Conrad of Dyffenbach reports all three conditions in the margins of his almuten table (Table 5, MS V). The first condition is also the subject of a table appended to Table 1 in three witnesses (BV_2Z). To be complete, we may also mention a number of specific choices which confirm that the calculation of the almuten is not fixed once and for all, like the 26 anomalies of Table 2A (all of which were corrected in Table 2B), the rejection of the decan by one manuscript of Table 2B (V_1) or the idiosyncrasies displayed by Conrad of Dyffenbach (Table 5, MS V) and Bartolomeo Valdizocco of Padua (Table 5, MS V_1). In short, the calculation of the almuten was not a trivial and straightforward operation among medieval astrologers. Various efforts were deployed to facilitate the procedure, essentially by means of tables, but

---

48   The fifteenth-century French astrologer S. Belle also takes into account those two additional conditions, see Avelar de Carvalho, *An Astrologer at Work*, pp. 194–195.

none of these tables are perfect. Tables 1, 2, 5 and 6 are easy to use, but they force the astrologer to take into account all three rulers of the triplicity. Tables 3 and 4 leave all options open, but they are difficult to handle.

A final point that deserves to be highlighted is that neither the inventor nor the users of the weighted almuten seem to have realised that it carries with it a pessimistic view of the world. The reason is that, regardless of which method of calculation is applied, the almuten is much more likely to be a malefic planet (Mars or Saturn) than a benefic planet (Jupiter or Venus). An ultimate table will illustrate this point:[49]

	Counting the triplicity participant			Ignoring the triplicity participant		
	Day	Night	Day+night	Day	Night	Day+night
♂	65 17.0%	98 22.4%	65 16.8%	49 11.9%	89 20.6%	72 17.8%
♄	75 19.6%	62 14.2%	64 16.6%	92 22.4%	72 16.7%	64 15.8%
☿	56 14.7%	75 17.2%	60 15.5%	60 14.6%	75 17.4%	60 14.8%
♀	63 16.5%	43 09.8%	63 16.3%	78 19.0%	44 10.2%	69 17.0%
☉	60 15.7%	40 09.2%	60 15.5%	60 14.6%	40 09.3%	60 14.8%
♃	33 08.6%	59 13.5%	34 08.8%	46 11.2%	53 12.3%	41 10.1%
☽	30 07.9%	60 13.8%	40 10.4%	26 06.3%	59 13.7%	39 09.6%

Bibliography

Primary Sources

Abraham Avenezra [Abraham Ibn Ezra]. *Liber de nativitatibus* (anonymous adaptation), edited and translated by Shlomo Sela, *Abraham Ibn Ezra Latinus on Nativities. A Parallel Latin-English Critical Edition of Liber Nativitatum and Liber Abraham Iudei de Nativitatibus*. Leiden-Boston: Brill, 2019, pp. 249–351.

---

49 This table gives the total number of degrees owned by each planet throughout the zodiac, together with the corresponding percentage in superscript, according to the six modes of calculation, i.e. counting the participant or not, and in each case, counting the ruler by day only, the ruler by night only or both the rulers by day and by night. The standard procedure is assumed, i.e., 3 points for the triplicity and 2 points for the term. When two or three planets share ownership in the same degree, each of them is given 1 point, hence the number of degrees exceeds 360 in each category. The planets are listed from the most to the least powerful following the mean percentage obtained in all six categories: Mars 17.8%, Saturn 17.6%, Mercury 15.7%, Venus 14.8%, Sun 13.2%, Jupiter 10.8%; Moon 10.3%.

Abraham Avenezra [Abraham Ibn Ezra]. *Liber nativitatum et revolutionum earum* (tr. Peter of Abano). Venice: Petrus Liechtenstein, 1507, sig. XLIIII^v–LVIII^v.

Abraham Ibn Ezra. *Sefer ha-moladot*, edited and translated by Shlomo Sela, *Abraham Ibn Ezra on Nativities and Continuous Horoscopy. A Parallel Hebrew-English Critical Edition of the Book of Nativities and the Book of Revolution.* Leiden: Brill, 2013.

Albubater [Abū Bakr al-Ḥasan ibn al-Khaṣīb]. *De nativitatibus.* Nürnberg: Johannes Petreius, 1540.

Alcabitius [al-Qabīṣī]. *Introductorius*, edited by Charles Burnett, Keiji Yamamoto, Michio Yano, *Al-Qabīṣī (Alcabitius): The Introduction to Astrology. Editions of the Arabic and Latin Texts and an English Translation.* London-Torino: The Warburg Institute—Nino Aragno Editore, 2004.

Alkindi [al-Kindī]. *Iudicia astrorum, Al-Kindi: The Forty Chapters (Iudicia astrorum).* Edited by Charles Burnett. London, 1993 [unpublished, copy available at the Warburg Institute Library].

Aomar ['Umar ibn al-Farrukhān al-Ṭabarī], *De iudiciis astrorum*, unpublished, MS Dijon, BM, 449, f. 25ra–33vb.

Bartholomaeus Marisiensis Slesita de Paczków. *Commentum in Ephemeridem Regiomontani.* Venice, 1481.

Gaurico, Luca. *Isagogicus in totam astrologiam praedictivam tractatus*, in Gaurico's *Opera omnia*, vol. II, Basel: ex officina Henricpetrina, 1575, sig. 859–1103.

Guido Bonatti. *Liber introductorius ad iudicia stellarum.* Augsburg: Erhard Ratdolt, 1491.

Guillelmus Anglicus. *De urina non visa.* Laurence Moulinier-Brogi, *Guillaume l'Anglais, le frondeur de l'uroscopie médiévale (XIIIe siècle).* Genève: Droz, 2011.

Haly Abenragel [Abū al-Ḥasan ʿAlī ibn Abi al-Rijāl]. *De iudiciis astrorum.* Venice: Erhard Ratdolt, 1485.

Hermann of Carinthia. *De occultis.* In M. Low-Beer. 'Hermann of Carinthia: The *Liber imbrium*, the *Fatidica*, and the *De indagatione cordis*'. PhD dissertation, City University of New York, 1979, pp. 260–344.

Johannes de Glogova, *Summa astrologie*, unpublished (MS Cracow, BJ, 570, pp. 147–176).

John of Eschenden. *Summa iudicialis de accidentibus mundi.* Venice, 1489.

John of Seville (Pseudo-). *Epitome totius astrologie.* Nürnberg: Johannes Montanus & Ulricus Neuberus, 1548.

Leopold of Austria. *De astrorum scientia.* Augsburg: Erhard Ratdolt, 1489.

Liber novem iudicum. Venice: Petrus Liechtenstein, 1509

Pierre d'Ailly (Petrus de Aliaco). *Tractatus de figura inceptionis mundi et coniunctionibus mediis sequentibus*, unpublished (MS Cambrai, BM, 929, f. 99^r–104^v).

Ptolemy, Claudius. *Tetrabiblos.* Edited and translated by Frank E. Robbins. Cambridge (Mass.): Loeb, 1940.

Ptolemy, Claudius. *Claudius Ptolemaeus: Apotelesmatica.* Edited by Wolfgang Hübner. Stuttgart-Leipzig: Teubner, 1998.

Regiomontanus, Johannes. *Ephemerides*. Venice: Erhard Ratdolt, 1484 (reprinted Augsburg: Erhard Ratdolt, 1488; Augsburg, 1492; Venice, 1492).

Robert Grosseteste (?). *De impressionibus aeris*. In *Die philosophischen Werke des Robert Grosseteste, Bischofs von Lincoln*. Edited by Ludwig Baur. Münster: Aschendorffsche Verlagbuchhandlung, 1912, pp. 41–51.

Studies

Avelar de Carvalho, Helena. *An Astrologer at Work in Late Medieval France. The Notebooks of S. Belle*. Leiden-Boston: Brill, 2021.

Azzolini, Monica. *The Duke and the Stars. Astrology and Politics in Renaissance Milan*. Cambridge (Mass.)-London: Harvard University Press, 2013.

Chabás, José, and Bernard R. Goldstein. *A Survey of European Astronomical Tables in the Late Middle Ages*. Leiden-Boston: Brill, 2012.

Friedman, John B. *John de Foxton's Liber cosmographiae (1408). An Edition and Codicological Study*. Leiden-New York: Brill, 1988.

Greenbaum, Dorian. *The Daimon in Hellenistic Astrology. Origins and Influence*, Leiden: Brill, 2016.

Juste, David. 'A Sixteenth-Century Astrological Consultation'. In *Astrologers and Their Clients in Medieval and Early Modern Europe*, edited by W. Deimann and D. Juste. Köln-Weimar-Wien: Bohlau, 2015, pp. 151–204.

Juste, David. *Catalogus Codicum Astrologorum Latinorum*, vol. II: *Les manuscrits astrologiques latins conservés à la Bibliothèque nationale de France à Paris*. Paris: Éditions du CNRS, 2015.

Juste, David. 'Reading Birth Horoscopes in the Middle Ages. Latin Judgements on Nativities 1100–1450'. In *Le Moyen Âge et les sciences*, edited by D. Jacquart, A. Paravicini Bagliani. Firenze: SISMEL, 2021, pp. 549–593.

Nothaft, C. Philipp E. 'Sidereal Astrology in Medieval Europe (Twelfth and Thirteenth Centuries): Traces of a Forgotten Tradition'. *International Journal of Divination & Prognostication* 3 (2021), pp. 45–84.

Pedersen, Fritz S. *The Toledan Tables. A Review of the Manuscripts and the Textual Versions with an Edition*. København: C.A. Reitzels Forlag, 2002, 4 vols.

Pingree, David. 'Māshā'allāh'. In *Dictionary of Scientific Biography*, IX. New York: Charles Scribner's Sons, 1981, pp. 159–162.

Poulle, Emmanuel. 'L'horoscope de Louis X'. In *Finances, pouvoirs et mémoire. Mélanges en l'honneur de Jean Favier*. Paris: Fayard, 1999, pp. 256–268.

Schmeidler, Felix. *Joannis Regiomontani Opera collectanea. Faksimiledrucke von neun Schriften Regiomontans und einer von ihm gedruckten Schrift seines Lehrers Purbach*. Osnabrück: O. Zeller Verlag, 1972.

Steel, Carlos, Steven Vanden Broecke, David Juste and Shlomo Sela. *The Astrological Autobiography of a Medieval Philosopher. Henry Bate's* Nativitas *(1280–1281)*. Leuven: Leuven University Press, 2018.

CHAPTER 3

A Popular *Vademecum* for the Practice of Astrology

Sahl ibn Bishr's The Choice Nuggets of Judgement *or 50* Precepts, *in Arabic and Its Latin and Hebrew Versions*

Charles Burnett

Abstract

A well-used astrological tool in the Middle Ages was the set of fifty precepts composed by the early ninth-century Baghdadi astrologer, Sahl ibn Bishr. These precepts provided easy-to-memorize key statements concerning the practice of astrology. The precepts contain astrological doctrine that is relevant to all branches of astrology. Their popularity is attested by the number of translations (into Latin and Hebrew and later on into the European vernaculars) that were made. This article provides a selection of these translations (in Latin and Hebrew) and investigates the significance of their differences.

Keywords

Arabic astrology – aphorisms – Sahl ibn Bishr – 50 precepts – transmission of astrology

1 Introduction

In the early ninth century Sahl ibn Bishr al-Isrāʾīlī wrote texts on each of the different astrological genres, which were evidently meant to be read consecutively. First, an introduction to astrological doctrine, called the *Introduction* (*kitāb al-mudkhal*, *Introductorium*), secondly, a collection of astrological aphorisms, called the *Choice Nuggets of Judgement* (*Nawādir al-qaḍāʾ*, *Quinquaginta præcepta*), which refers back to the *Introduction*.[1] This, in turn, introduces the

---

1 The Arabic titles vary, and a consensus is needed. The first three books, as a collection, should probably be called *kitāb al-aḥkām* (+ʿalā al-nisba al-falakīya/fī ʿilm mīqāt/bi-l-kawākib = 'The book of judgements (according to the celestial set-up (?)/concerning the science of times/by the planets') as reflected in the Latin title *Liber De iudiciis* (+ .lvi. *capitulis distinctus*): see Fuat

On Interrogations (*kitāb al-masā'il, De interrogationibus*), which gives judgements on a large range of questions asked by the astrologer's client. Further
books address 'choices' (*kitāb al-ikhtiyārāt, De electionibus*), the best time for
an action (*kitāb al-awqāt, liber temporum*), and world (or general) astrology
(*kitāb taḥāwīl al-'ālam, Pronostica*), which is described by its translator, Hermann of Carinthia, as 'the sixth book'.[2] The *50 Precepts* is self-contained, and
belongs to a recognizable genre of astrology (aphorisms), which includes the
Centiloquia of Pseudo-Ptolemy, Hermes, and Bethen, the 150 *propositiones* of
Almansor, the 122 aphorisms of Pseudo-Aristotle, the 200 of Pseudo-Eutocius
and 65 surviving aphorisms of 'Uṭārid b. Muḥammad al-Ḥāsib.[3] The choice of
a 'semi-centiloquium' (*50* precepts) may have been deliberate on the part of
Sahl. Most of the precepts are convenient summaries of astrological doctrine
given elsewhere (e.g., in Sahl's *Introduction*). The homely illustrations (e.g., the
man at the door of his house, the 'household' of the Sun), may be specific to
this text. The collated transcriptions of the Arabic, Latin and Hebrew texts are
meant to show the progressive development of the text from the Arabic original through a literal translation of this text, to an interpretation in a literary
style of Latin and its revision, and its consequences in Hebrew and Latin. The
following information is given:

Sezgin, *Geschichte des arabischen Schrifttums VII: Astrologie-Meteorologie und Verwandtes bis
ca. 430 H*, Brill, Leiden, 1979, pp. 125–128. For convenience, they can be called the Three Books.
For excerpts from the *Introduction*, in three languages (Arabic, Latin and Greek), see Viktor
Stegemann, *Dorotheos von Sidon und das Sogenannte Introductorium des Sahl ibn Bišr*, Druck-
erei des Protektorates Böhmen und Mähren in Prag, Prague, 1942. For further information see
Julio Samso, 'Sahl ibn Bishr and the Rise of Astrology in Abbasid Times', *Qatar Digital Library*
https://www.qdl.qa/en/sahl-ibn-bishr-and-rise-astrology-abbasid-times [accessed 27 November 2024].

2   The title of the text translated by Hermann of Carinthia is *Fatidica, Pronostica* or the *Liber sextus astronomie*: see Charles Burnett, 'Arabic into Latin in Twelfth-Century Spain: The Works
of Hermann of Carinthia', *Mittellateinisches Jahrbuch*, 13 (1978), pp. 100–134.

3   For the *Centiloquium* of Pseudo-Ptolemy see Emanuele Rovati, *'Pseudo-Ptolemy, Kitāb al-
Thamara'* (update: 08.11.2024), *Ptolemaeus Arabus et Latinus. Works*, URL = http://ptolem
aeus.badw.de/work/190. The Latin versions of *Centiloquia* of Hermes and Bethen and the
Propositiones of Almansor were all published by Iohannes Hervagius in Basel in 1533.'Uṭārid
b. Muḥammad al-Ḥāsib's aphorisms are edited and translated in José Maria Parra Perez, 'El
"Sirr al-asrār" de 'Uṭārid b. Muḥammad al-Ḥāsib y sus aforismos', *Anaquel de Estudios Arabes*
20 (2009), pp. 165–186. For Pseudo-Aristotle and Pseudo-Eutocius see Sezgin, *Geschichte des
arabischen Schrifttums VII*, p. 62 and p. 48. For the significance of this genre in particular
see Geoffrey Cornelius, 'Interpreting Interpretations: the Aphorism in the Practice of the
Renaissance Astrologers', in *From Māshā'allāh to Kepler: Theory and Practice in Medieval and
Renaissance Astrology*, ed. Charles Burnett and Dorian Gieseler Greenbaum, Sophia Centre
Press, Ceredigion, Wales, 2015, pp. 101–121.

1.   The Arabic text, based on Escorial, Real Bibl. del Monasterio de San Lorenzo, ar. 918, fols. 47^v–49^v (E),[4] collated with Leipzig, Universitäts-bibliothek, Vollers 799, fols 9^r–12^r (L) (this largely corresponds with an anonymous on-line transcript—D), and Istanbul University, A 6141 (A), fols. 35^r–36^v, for *præcepta* 38–50. LD number the *præcepta* with alphanu-merical numerals; EA spell out the numbers in full. Each *præceptum* starts with a facsimile of the relevant lines of the Escorial manuscript.

2.   An English translation of the Arabic text. This is deliberately literal, at the expense of being elegant, in order to aid the comparison between texts.[5]

3.   The Latin text of John of Seville's translation, based on Paris, BnF, lat. 16204, pp. 441^a–445^a (P), collated with British Library, Harley 5402, fols. 23^v–26^v (H) and Sloane 2030, fols. 45^r–47^r (S), and Munich, BSB, clm. 13201 (M), fols. 83rb–87rb and 18927, fols. 48^v–49^v (T = Tegernsee), and the printed edition in Ptolemy, *Quadripartitum* (Venice, 1519), fols. 114rb–115va, transcribed by Lenka Jiroušková for the Arabic and Latin Corpus (https://www.arabic-latin-corpus.philosophie.uni-wuerzburg.de/). In each case the *50 Precepts* occurs between Sahl's *Introduction* and his *Interrogations*. The orthography follows that of the Sloane manuscript, which includes the digraph for Classical Latin 'ae': 'æ' (as does T occasionally):[6] hence-forth 'John of Seville'.

4.   The separately occurring abbreviated translation of Sahl ibn Bishr's *Three Books*, either preceding or derived from the version used for the *Liber*

---

4   This is a manuscript of works on astronomy, astrology and trigonometry written in Maghrebi script. The description in Hartwig Derenbourg, *Les manuscrits arabes de l'Escurial*, II.3, Libraire orientaliste Paul Geuthner, Paris, 1941, pp. 18–25 is superseded by that of Emanuele Rovati, 'MS Escorial, Real Biblioteca del Monasterio de San Lorenzo, ár. 918' (update: 29.07.2023) *Ptolemaeus Arabus et Latinus. Manuscripts*, URL = http://ptolemaeus.badw.de/ms/957. The last work copied into this manuscript dates from 1483 AD. Sahl's *50 Precepts* has been copied into this manuscript on its own, and not as part of his astrological corpus.

5   For another English translation from the Arabic see Benjamin Dykes, *The Astrology of Sahl b. Bishr*, vol. I: *Principles, Elections, Questions, Nativities*, The Cazimi Press, Minneapolis, 2019, pp. 76–88. This is based on Arabic MSS Yale, Beinecke 523, Hathi Trust 1707 (fols. 18–23?), Leipzig, Vollers 799 and London, British Library, Or. 12802 (but not Escorial 918 or Istanbul University, A 6141).

6   Note that an English translation by Benjamin Dykes of the Latin version in Paris, BnF, lat. 16204 and the 1493 edition, has been published in his *Works of Sahl and Māshā'allāh*, The Caz-imi Press, Minneapolis, 2008, pp. 51–66 (see also p. lxxiii where Dykes points out the 'mess' in parts of the work and the lack of consistency in the witnesses to this Latin version); this translation is revised in his *The Book of the Nine Judges*, The Cazimi Press, Minneapolis, 2011, pp. 644–658.

trium iudicum, edited from Erfurt, Universitäts- und Forschungsbibliothek, 4° 377 (= E), s. xiv, fols. 61^r–61^v, and Munich, BSB, Clm 588 (= N),
s. xvi^1, fol. 233rb–233vb: henceforth 'EN-Text'.[7]

5. The first of the *Libri iudicum*: The *Liber trium iudicum*, which shows signs
of being Hermann of Carinthia's translation, based on Dublin, Trinity College, 368 (D), fols. 54^v–56^r: henceforth '*Liber trium iudicum*'. Except for the
first two precepts, this text is abbreviated in respect to the Arabic text and
John of Seville's translation.

6. The second of the *Libri iudicum*: The *Liber novem iudicum*, which is evidently Hugo Sanctelliensis's revision of 5) above, based on Vatican, Vat.lat.
6766 (v), fols. 10^v–11^v. The revision involved a rearrangement of the order
of the *præcepta*, as indicated here by the numbers preceding each *præceptum*: henceforth '*Liber novem iudicum*'.[8]

7. Abraham Ibn Ezra, in chapter 8 of his *Reshit Ḥokhmah* paraphrases most
of the *50 præcepta*, as the first part of a collection of 120 judgements,
and following chapter 7 which is modelled on, and indebted to, Sahl's
Introduction.[9] It is likely that he was using an Arabic text directly, but he
shares his rearrangement of Sahl's *præcepta* and certain distinctive passages with the revised Latin text in the *Liber novem iudicum* (no. 6) above).
The English translation is that of Shlomo Sela. The order of the *præcepta*
in Abraham's work is given in the numbers preceding each *præceptum*:[10]
henceforth 'Abraham Ibn Ezra'.

8. Henry Bate's translation of Ibn Ezra, made in 1292, taken from the edition in Shlomo Sela,[11] to which readings from MS Gloucester, Cathedral,
21 (= Gl), fols. 60^v–68^r have been added: henceforth, 'Henry Bate's translation'.

---

7   See Appendix II below for an attempt to locate this version textually.
8   This version is the origin of the French translation of the '.L. commandemenz' which
is included in *L'Introductoire d'astronomie* in Paris, BnF, fr. 1353, fols. 59rb–61va (ed. Jean-
Patrice Boudet, in press).
9   Edited and translated in Shlomo Sela, *Abraham Ibn Ezra's Introductions to Astrology: A
Parallel Hebrew-English Critical Edition of the Book of the Beginning of Wisdom and the
Book of the Judgments of the Zodiacal Signs*, Brill, Leiden, 2017, pp. 210–235 (commentary
pp. 459–464).
10   The identity of the scholars responsible for the *Liber trium iudicum* and *Liber novem
iudicum*, and the relation of the Hebrew and Latin astrological works of Abraham Ibn
Ezra to the activity of Hugo Sanctelliensis are subjects of separate studies.
11   Shlomo Sela, *Abraham Ibn Ezra Latinus: Henry Bate's Latin Versions of Abraham Ibn Ezra's
Astrological Writings*, Brill, Leiden, 2022, pp. 300–312. Bate is translating from Hagin the
Jew's French translation from the Hebrew, commissioned in 1273.

9.   Pietro d'Abano's translation of Ibn Ezra, made in 1293, transcribed from
       Paris, Bibliothèque de la Sorbonne, 640, fol. 91vb–92va (= S), checked with
       ed. Venice 1507, fos. XXVI^{ra}–XXVII^{rb}: henceforth, 'Pietro d'Abano's transla-
       tion'.

10.   The text unique to Gloucester, Cathedral Library, 21, s. xv², fols. 72^v–
       75^r.[12] Most of this manuscript was copied (and some parts composed) by
       John Argentine, Royal physician and provost of King's College, Cambridge
       (d. 1508). The *50 Precepts* are preceded by Sahl's *Introduction* and followed
       by his *De interrogationibus*, all in the same translation. The *50 Precepts*
       are provided with the running head 'De regulis (astronomie)'. Henceforth
       '*Gloucester Text*'.

In the following editions italics indicate 1) divergences from the immediately
previous versions: e.g. in John of Seville's version, the *Liber trium iudicum*, Abraham ibn Ezra's Hebrew version, and the *Gloucester Text*, relative to the Arabic
text; in the *Liber novem iudicum* relative to the *Liber trium iudicum*; and the
Latin translations relative to Abraham Ibn Ezra's Hebrew text. Bold font 1) in the
Arabic, indicates the readings from the other manuscripts which are more correct, when the Escorial 918's reading is dubious; 2) in the Latin transcriptions,
the readings which correspond to the Arabic but are not in the base manuscript; 3) coincidences between the EN-Text and the *Liber trium iudicum*. Red
words and phrases draw attention to similarities between Ibn Ezra's Hebrew
version and other versions. ⟨⟨...⟩⟩ indicates a significant omission in regard to
a previous version. ⟨ ⟩ indicate editorial additions; [ ] editorial deletions; *corr.
ex* = corrected from; ( ) the realization of abbreviations, where dubious; *supra*
= written above the word; *in marg.*= written in the margin.

2   **Text Edition**

       Title

1.

كتاب لنوادر القضاء وهي خمسون بابا من كلام سهل بن بشر الاسرائيلي ه

(+ وهذا LY) ابتداء نوادر القضاء وهي (فيه Y) خمسون بابا من كلام سهل بن بشر
الاسرائيلي (- من سهل ... الاسرائيلي L)

---

12   I am indebted to David Juste for alerting me to this version, and for his full description of
      the manuscript in an as yet unpublished volume of his *Catalogus codicum astrologorum
      Latinorum*.

2. The beginning of the Choice Nuggets of Judgement, and they are fifty chapters, from the words of Sahl ibn Bishr al-Isrāʾīlī.

3. John of Seville: Liber secundus zehel de 50 preceptis P; Et hec sunt initia precipuorum iudiciorum et sunt capitula .l. H; Incipiunt precipua iudicio-rum capitula M; Incipiunt præcipua iudicia et sunt .l. S;–T

4. EN-text: Ex .50. principalibus iudiciis.

5. *Liber trium iudicum*: Quinquaginta loci sunt ex quibus iudicandi certa procedit ratio D *in marg.* Followed by an introduction (see Appendix I below).

6. *Liber novem iudicum*: Descriptio .50. preceptorum que in omnibus nego-tiis et questionibus notanda occurrunt, çæl. Followed by an introduction which amplifies that of the *Liber trium iudicum* (see Appendix I below).[13]

7. Abraham Ibn Ezra. All of the judgments related to nativities, anniver-saries, and interrogations ....

8. Henry Bate: Universalia quidem qui iudicia quedam sive regule sunt in nativitatibus et revolutionibus ac interrogationibus ...

9. Pietro d'Abano: Sunt autem .120. iudicia ...

10. *Gloucester Text*: De iudiciis hoc loco ordiendum est. Et primum quedam iudiciorum pars proponenda qua diligenter expedita iudicia sequentia facilius intelligamus. Hec pars in quinquaginta partes dividitur, quarum prima est de Luna.

1

1.

الباب(Y-) الاوال اعلم أن الدليل أعني القمر هو أقرب الكواكب فلكا من (إلى LDY) الأرض وهو أشبه الكواكب بأمر الدنيا ألا ترى أن الإنسان يبدا (يبدو LY) صغيرا ثم يكبر ثم يفنى وكذلك القمر فاتخذه دليلا على كل أمر فإن (فY) صحته صحة كل شيء وفساده

---

13 See Appendix I below for the introductions in the *Liber trium iudicum* and *Liber novem iudicum*.

فساد كل شيء وهو يدفع تدبيره إلى أول من يلقى ويتصل به من النجوم وينتقل حاله الى
ذلك النجوم فيسمى ذلك الكوكب قابل التدبير (- من النجوم ... للتدبير LDY) لأنه قبل
ما دفع إليه فهو كمال (خال L، حمال DY) لهذه الكواكب والمصلح بينها والناقل (+ من
YDL) بعضها إلى بعض.

2. The first chapter. Know that the indicator—i.e., the Moon—is the closest of the planets in its sphere to the earth, and it is the most similar of the planets to the matter of our world. Do you not see that man begins small, then becomes bigger, then comes to an end? Similarly, the Moon. So take it ⟨as⟩ the indicator of every matter. For, its soundness is the soundness of every thing and its harm is the harm of every thing. It is pushing its management onto that star which it first meets and joins with, and changes its condition to that star. And that planet is called the receiver of the management, because it receives what is pushed onto it. And it is the perfection (كمال)/ bearer (حمال)/ releaser (حالّ؟) of these planets and the saviour between them and the carrier of one of them to another.

3. John of Seville: Primum capitulum (Primum de receptione dispositionis per Lunam pr). Scito quod significatrix (+ id est HMSTpr) Luna cuius circulus est (e.c. S) omnium planetarum *circulis* propior terræ, est (- HSpr) pre omnibus planetis (+ est pr) consimilis rebus mundi. Nonne vides quod (quia H) homo incipit esse parvus (+ esse M), deinde crescit, donec consum⟨m⟩atur (d.c.] **deinde finitur** H, donec finiatur MSTpr). Similiter facit Luna. Hab/P p. 441b/eto ergo eam (Lunam MSTpr) significationem (**significatricem** MSTpr) omnium rerum, quia sanitas illius (ipsius pr) sanitas est (e.s. S) omnis rei, et eius detrimentum est detrimentum omnis rei. Et ipsa pulsat *id est* (- pulsat id est S) *committit* dispositionem suam ei super quem (quam MT) proicit radios suos (ei ... suos] **ei cui primum occurrit** H) et cui iungitur ex (de pr) planetis et (- MT) mutat esse suum ad ipsum planetam. Nominaturque ipse planeta receptor dispositionis, quia recipit (recepit T) quod sibi commissum fuerit (fuerat HMTpr). Ipsa ergo (quoque S) Luna est **delatrix** (= *ḥammāl*?; significatrix H) horum planetarum et ipsa pacificat eos et defert a quibusdam eorum ad alios.

4. EN-text: *Primo nota* quod ducatus celestis in rebus humanis est Luna, quia ea salva, *salvantur res*, et ea corrupta, *corrumpuntur*.

5. *Liber trium iudicum: Nam in iudiciis prima est ducatus speculatio.* **Ducatus** *autem* **celestis in rebus humanis** *atque mundi huius accidentibus quasi universalis princeps* **est Luna.** Quoniam et citima terris *ceterarumque*,

velociori discursu, internuntia familiarius ad occiduam accedit naturam, *ut eius recte mutatione nature series ire videatur.* Nascimur enim, crescimus et deficimus. *Qua ratione indagatrix vetustas tangat universalem et principalem Lune ducatum inter omnes celestes motus omnibus in negotiis experta est, ut,* si **salva** sit Luna, *spem atque fiduciam et securitatem promittat,* **corrupta,** *dubitandum incidet et metuendum.* Nam et ceterarum cui proxime conferat consilium *statim notandum est. Illa siquidem est que lunare legit consilium. Que etiam sit causa quare principalius sequenda sit* Luna, quoniam velut internuntii et mediantis vicem optinet.

6. *Liber novem iudicum*: Prima *namque* est in iudiciis ducatus speculatio. *Celestis* quidem ducatus in rebus *mundanis* atque huius accidentibus quasi *suprema et* universalis princeps est Luna, quoniam et *vicina* terris ceterarum et velociori discursu, nuntia familiarius ad occiduam accedit naturam, ut eius recta mutatione nature series ire videatur. Nascimur enim, crescimus atque deficimus. Ad hanc ergo rationem *omnium Antiquissimorum* **indagatrix vetustas** inter omnes celestium motus *corporum* et processus universalem et principalem Lune ducatum experta est, ut, si salva sit Luna, spem, fiduciam atque securitatem promittat, corrupta, dubitandum *esse* indicet atque metuendum. *Set etiam* cui ceterarum proxime conferat consilium notandum videtur. Illa siquidem est que *luminare* lunare legit consilium. Que etiam sit causa quare principalius sequenda sit Luna, quoniam *valde* internuntium mediantis vicem *creditur* optinere.

7. Abraham Ibn Ezra: i The Moon is close to the Earth **and quick in its motion**; it is more mixed with the planets, because it gives power to them *and no planet gives its power to it*; it transfers light from one to another; it resembles the native in that its light increases gradually and grows until it is complete and then decreases gradually until it is invisible and departs from the world. **Consequently all the Ancients said that it signifies every thing and every thought and the beginning of every action.** If it is in its strength and in auspicious conditions, everything that a person begins doing at this moment will succeed; but the opposite applies if it is with malefics. *They said that you should observe for the querent the ascendant sign and its lord and for the thing he is posing a question about, the seventh sign and its lord, and you should always make the Moon its partner.*

8. Henry Bate's translation: ... quarum una est quia Luna propinqua terre est, et velox in motu suo et multiplicat commixtionem *sive multotiens commiscetur* cum planetis. Ipsa namque dat eis virtutem et nullus planeta illi. Et ipsa transfert lumen unius ad alium et assimilatur *etiam* nato, quia

lumen eius paulatim et paulatim crescit, donec sit perfectum, et postmodum paulatine diminuitur quousque nichil de illo videatur et a mundo
auferatur. Idcirco dixerunt Antiqui quod Luna super omnem rem significat et super cogitationes et super principia omnium operationum. Si igitur in fortitudine sua fuerit et eius dispositiones bone, perficietur omnis
res qua (**quam** Gl) incipiet homo in hora illa. Et econtrario (econverso Gl),
si fuerit cum nocivis *seu impedita.* Dixerunt /Gl 61^r/ *etiam* quod querente
seu interrogatore considerandum est ad signum ascendentis (ascendens
Gl) et ad eius dominum, pro re vero quesita ad septimum signum et ad
eius dominum (et dominum eius Gl), semper (**semperque** Gl) ponenda
est Luna particeps cum illo.

9.   Pietro d'Abano's translation: ... unum quia Luna propinqua est terre et cita
motu, simul planetarum /S 92ra/ commiscet (miscet pla/pr xxvib/neta-
rum) naturas, eo quod ipsa dat omnibus (+ suam pr) dispositionem *vel
fortitudinem dat illis* (- vel fortitudinem dat illis pr) et nullus dat ei fortitudinem suam (n.d.e.f.s.] nullusque ei pr) et transfert lumen unius ad
alium (alterum pr). Et proportionatur *vel similatur* nato, eo quod ipsius
lumen paulatim ⟨⟨...⟩⟩ et (- pr) paulatim minuitur donec ipsius nichil
poterit videri, et sit a seculo (secundo pr) remota. Et de hoc dixerunt
Antiqui quod ipsius est omne cogitatum (cogitativum pr) et cuiuslibet
(cuiusque pr) initium (+ operis pr), et si fuerint in sua fortitudine et suum
esse bonum, proficiet homo in omni illa hora incepto, et contrarium erit si
cum malis fuerit. Et dixerunt te (se S) aspicere pro querente signum ascendens et eius dominum, et pro re quesita .7. signum et dominum ipsius, et
semper facias Lunam participem eius.

10.   *Gloucester Text*: Ti(tulus) primus. Luna in eventibus terrenis validius argu-
mentum est, quia planetis omnibus hec sola *inferior et* terre proximior
est. Est et patens ratio quare Luna prosit terrenis eventibus quia, sicut res
terrene nascuntur, crescunt et vadunt ad interitum, sic et Luna nascitur,
crescit et diminuitur. Hec eadem regiminis sui administrationem quam
habet in terrenis planete proximo transmittit. Stelle vero regiminis huius
receptrix gubernaculi receptaculum appellatur, hic inde planeta gubernaculum quod a Luna recipit planetis aliis transmitit ut per ipsos terreno-
rum administratio moderetur.

2

1.

الثاني (و LY) النحوس تدل على الفساد والشر بإفراطها وجورها (جواهرها L؛ جوهرها

DY) فبرد غالب أو حر غالب (--فبرد غالب أو حر غالب LDY) فإن (فإذا YI) كان الكوكب

في بيت النحس (+ واتصل به من بيته D) أو شرفه (+ Yقد) قبله وكفّ عنه شره أو يكون

نظر النحوس من تثليث أو تسديس فإنها أيضا تكفّ عن ذلك لأنها نظرت (ناظرة D) من

مودة بلا عداوة فأما (وأما DL) السعود فإنها معتدلة الطبيعة فممتزجة من الحرارة والبرودة

(الرطوبة LD) فهي تنفع قبلت أو (أم DL) لم تقبل، والمقبول فيها (منها LD) أمثل وأجود.

2.   The second. Malefics indicate harm and badness, because of their excess and oppression (properties L), and thus predominant cold or predominant heat. If the planet is in the house of a malefic or (applies to it from its house or D) its exaltation, it receives it and it averts its badness from it, or ⟨if⟩ the aspect of the malefics is from trine or sextile, they are also averted from this (the badness), because they are aspected from love without enmity. And as for the benefics, they are tempered in their nature, and mixed from hot and cold; thus they give benefit, whether they receive ⟨a planet⟩ or not, but being received in them is more exemplary and better.

3.   John of Seville: Secundum (.2. M, *lacuna pro numero hic et passim* T, quid mali quidve boni planete significent pr). Mali planetæ significant detrimentum et malum *propter* (+ *accidentia sua ac* **proprietates** *propter* H) excedentiam (excedentia T) *vel* (- e.v. H) *superfluitatem* vis frigoris vel (ac H) caloris in eis vincentis *et* (*vel* M) *impedientis*. Set si fuerit planeta (+ bonus pr) in domo mali vel in exaltatione eius, recipit eum, et refrenat malitiam suam ab eo (a deo P), aut si fuerit aspectus malorum a trino vel a sextili aspectu, refrenatur (**refrenantur** HMS) etiam (et pr) ab hoc, eo quod sit aspectus amicitiæ absque ulla inimicitate. Fortunæ vero, quia sunt temperatæ naturæ *atque æqualis complexionis, id est quia sunt temperatæ ex calore et frigore, semper* proficiunt (per- M) et præstant si alium

planetam (- **s.a.p.** HMSpr,—a.p. T) receperint (- receperint T) an non. Set receptio in eis est utilior ac melior.

4.   EN-text: –

5.   *Liber trium iudicum*: Secundus locus est pro metu corruptionis *infortunio-rum* speculatio. Excedunt enim in calore et frigore (unde dicantur infortunia D *in marg.*). Si tamen acciderit stella (aliqua D) in domicilio aut principatu infortunii consistere, pro receptione (recipiat D supra) non adeo ledit, sic quoque si trigono sive exagono stella infortunium respexerit, minus officit. Fortunate vero ut sunt nature temperate, salubres etiam si non recipiant, firmiores tamen cum receptione, *optimeque prospera figura.*

6.   *Liber novem iudicum*: *18* est infortuniorum pro metu corruptionis speculatio. Excedunt enim in calore et frigore. Si tamen acciderit stellam in domicilio aut principatu *malivolarum* consistere, **si recipiatur**, **non adeo ledet**, *ad hunc quoque modum* si trigono *vel* exagono *stellam quamlibet* infortunium respexerit, minus *obest*. Fortunate vero ut sunt temperate nature, salubres etiam si non *recipiantur*, firmiores tamen cum receptione, *set* optime prospera figura.

7.   Abraham Ibn Ezra: ix Benefic planets are balanced and beneficial, whether or not they receive ⟨another planet⟩, although it is better if they receive it. Malefics are destructive by their nature, although its **harm is diminished if the planet is received by it** (a benefic), and the same holds true if it (a benefic) aspects it (a malefic) in trine or sextile.

8.   Henry Bate's translation: .9m. Planete benevoli et temperati *ipsi semper valent* (*valeant Gl*), sive recipiant sive non. Si *tamen* receperint tanto melius est. Malivoli *vero* dissipantes sunt secundum ipsorum naturam. Si *tamen* ab eis receptus fuerit planeta, alleviabitur eorum nocumentum. Et consimiliter est de aspectu eorum ad illum sextili aut (vel Gl) trino.

9.   Pietro d'Abano's translation: Planete fortu/pr xxvi^{va}/nati directi (directe pr) prosunt, sive sint recepti sive non. Mali destruentes natura, si receperint planetam, ipsorum alleviabitur malus. Et similiter si sextili aut trino aspexerint aspectu.

10. *Gloucester Text*: Titulus 2us. Planete nocivi rerum detrimentum et venenosum excidium designant, quia extra moderamentum calidi vel frigidi sunt. Set si planeta aliquis in alicuius planete nocivi domicilio recipiatur, planeta nocivus fervorem suum temperat. Nec quicquam mali ei administraret si extra /73^r/ esse domicilium hospitalitatis consortio administrat. Item, si nocivus planeta planetam aliquem a 3 vel a 6 angulis respiciat, minus adversitatis ei inserit quam naturaliter ei posset inserere, quia aspectus talis aspectus amoris sine omni odio est. Set planete prosperi

quia inter caliditatem et frigiditatem temperati sunt, sive recipiant planetas in domiciliis suis sive non, prospera eis administrant. Et tamen si quos
in domibus receperint, magis prospera eis inserunt.

3

1.

الثالثُ ———— أنجموع على جودوميز جيمه وشرن محيث ما رأيت النجومِ فَصَـلِ
الجِّمَ وحينَما رأيتَ الهمعود يقلِالجَّبَرِه

الثالث النجوم (الكواكب D) على حدين خير وشر فيثما رأيت النحوس فقل الخير (الشر
corr. D، L) وحيثما رأيت السعود (الخير L) يقل (فقل LD) الخير.

2. The third. The stars (planets D) are according to two definitions: good and
bad. Wherever you see malefics say 'bad', and wherever you see benefics,
one says 'good'.

3. John of Seville: Tertium (Capitulum tertium incipit M, De impedimento
planetarum tria iudicia pr). Duo modi sunt stellarum, bonus scilicet et
malus. Quocumque ergo videris malos, *id est malos planetas* (m.i.e.m.p.]
malos planetas MSTpr), dic malum, et quocumque videris fortunas (fortunam pr), dic bonum.

4. EN-Text: –

5. *Liber trium iudicum*: Tertius est duplex stellarum inter /D 55^r/ bonum et
malum affectus, planetarum scilicet consilium pro benivolis, boni, pro
noxiis, adversi (*supra*: -tis = adversitatis D) iudicium.

6. *Liber novem iudicum*: 28 duplex stellarum inter bonum et malum *effectum*,
planetarum scilicet consilium pro benivolis, *bonum*, pro noxiis, *adverse*
iudicium *for⟨tun⟩e*.

7. Abraham Ibn Ezra: viii The planets are of two sorts, benefic and malefic.
In every position where you find a benefic planet, pronounce ⟨that the
outcome will be⟩ fortunate, and vice-versa.

8. Henry Bate's translation: .8m. Stellarum *seu* (- Stellarum seu Gl) *planetarum* quidem due sunt species, una bona, alia *vero* (- Gl) mala, ubicumque ergo planetam bonum inveneris, dic bonum, et econtrario dic (contrarium Gl) ubi contrarium.

9. Pietro d'Abano's translation: Planetarum duplex est modus, bonus unus,
malus alter, et ubicumque inveneris fortunam, dicas bonum, si contrarium, malum.

10. *The Gloucester Text*: 3 Planetarum finis duplex est: bonitas et malitia. Ubi
enim planeta bonus invenitur, bonum significat. Ubi malus, malum.

4

1.

الرابـــــع ولا يسمى الكوكب محنوشًا حتى يلقى النحس

fol. 48ʳ

الرابع و(- D) لا يسمى الكوكب منحوسا حتى يلقى النحس على نوره وشعاعه (نور الشعاع على LD) قدر ما وصفت من أبوابها (أنوارها LD) فإذا جاوز حد النحوس (النور LD) سمى ناظرا إلى النحس ولم يقدر على الفساد فإذا جاوز النحس الكوكب (الكوكب النحس LD) بدرجة تامّة أدخل الروعات (المروعات D) بلا إيقاع في البدن ولم يقدر النحس على أكثر من ذلك لأنه عنه (- LD) منصرف وكذلك السعد إذا جاوز الكوكب وانصرف عنه بدرجة تامّة يطمع ولا يتمّ الامر (- LD) وكل نحس ينحس وهو ساقط عن الطالع (- ساقط عن الطالع D) يدخل الروعات (المروعات D) ولا يضر وكذلك السعود إذا كانت ساقطة عن الطالع تطمع ولا يتمّ الأمر.

2. The fourth. The planet is not called unfortunate until a malefic throws its rays onto its light (omitting و; the light of the rays LD), according to what I have described of their lights (?). So, when it has passed the limit of the malefics (the light LD), it is called 'aspecting the malefic' and is not able to harm. And when the malefic has passed the planet (the planet has passed the malefic LD) by a complete degree, it brings in fears without an effect on the body, and the malefic is not able to do more than that because it has separated from it. Similarly the benefic, when it passes the planet and separates from it by a complete degree, desires but does not complete the matter. And every malefic that brings harm when it is falling from the ascendant brings in fears but does not harm. Similarly, the benefics, when they are falling from the ascendant, desire but do not complete the matter.

3. John of Seville: /H 24ʳ/ Quartum (4 M). Et non (- Tpr) nominatur plan-
    eta impeditus (i. p. M) donec malus super (supra T) lumen suum (l.s.]
    eum H) proiiciat radios (implying حتى يلقى النحس على نوره شعاعه), secundum
    quantitatem quam dixi tibi de eorum orbibus (implying ادوارها). Cumque
    transierit terminum malorum, vocatur aspiciens malum, et non poterit
    impedire. Et cum transierit malus planetam (planeta pr) per gradum per-
    fectum, immittit timorem absque impedimento (implying آفة?) corporis,
    et non potest malus (+ planeta pr) plus (- pr) *agere* quia separatus est ab
    eo. Similiter, fortuna cum transierit planeta (**planetam** HMSTpr) et sepa-
    ratus (**separata pr**) fuerit ab eo (ab eo f. H) per gradum integrum, sperat,
    set non perficitur res. Et omnis malus (- HMSpr) impediens, cum fuerit
    cadens ab ascendente, mittit timorem et non impedit. Similiter, fortuna
    (**fortunæ** HSTpr), cum (c.fortune M) fuerit (**fuerint** HMSTpr) ab ascen-
    dente cadentes (cadens T), separatur (**speratur** HSpr), set (et M) non per-
    ficitur res (- set non perficitur res T).

4. EN-text: *Item*, non est stella corrupta nisi infortunii lumine lumen eius
    excipiatur.

5. *Liber trium iudicum*: Quartus, quoniam **non est stella corrupta nisi infor-
    tunii lumine lumen eius excipiatur**, quomodo supradictum est. Nam si
    transivit iam lumen infortunii, *licet adhuc respiciat*, non tamen prevalet
    infortunium, excepto timore. Sic quoque quando fortunate lumen tran-
    scursum est, *licet respiciat*, spes quidem datur, set vacua.

6. *Liber novem iudicum*: 29, quoniam non est stella corrupta nisi lumen eius
    lumini infortunii excipiatur, quomodo supradictum est. Nam si transivit
    iam lumen infortunii, licet *ad hoc* respiciat, non tamen prevalet infortu-
    nium, excepto timore. Sic quoque quando fortunate lumen transcursum
    est, licet respiciat, spes quidem datur, set vacua.

7. Abraham Ibn Ezra: x A planet is said to be harmed only if the ray of a
    malefic reaches it, in keeping with the power of its (malefic's) body; if it
    (the malefic's ray) is less than that (the malefic's body) it signifies only
    slight harm. After it separates from its aspect, even if only by one degree
    and particularly if by more degrees, it will cause *fear that will not come to
    pass*. The same holds true for a benefic planet and the planet that signifies
    what will be in the future. If it does aspect the ascendant sign, what the
    querent is hoping for will not come to pass.

8. Henri Bate's translation: .1om. Non vocatur planeta impeditus donec
    super ipsum (illum Gl) radii sint planete malivoli secundum fortitudinem
    corporis eius; et si minus fuerint quam ita, non significat nisi parvum noc-
    umentum. Postquam *autem* ab illo separatus (superatus Gl) fuerit, etiam
    per unum gradum et adhuc melius si plus, terrebit terrore qui ad opus

non perveniet. Consimilisque (consimilis quoque Gl) modus est in planeta benevolo; planeta vero significans omnem rem que ad effectum veniet *et erit*, nisi aspiciat signum ascendens, non exibit in lucem spes querentis.

9. Pietro d'Abano's translation: Non dicetur unde (- pr) planeta dampnificatus *vel infortunatus* donec ipsum radii mali attingant vigore corporis eius, et si minus isto fuerit, non nisi modicum dampnatur. Et postea, cum separatur ab eo per unum gradum planetarum (planeta pr), ac melius si ad hoc plus distaverit (distiterit pr), significat timorem et non egredientem ad effectum. Et similis est modus fortune.

10. *Gloucester Text*: 4 Nullus planeta a planeta nocivo corrumpitur quousque radios sue claritatis super ipsum inserit, *sicut in Isagogis expeditum est*. Notandum quod quando planeta a planeta nocivo uno gradu pleno removetur, contagione nocivi planete commaculari non potest. Et tamen sui contagii maculam ne commaculetur ab ea admodum perhorrescit. Simili modo quando letus planeta planetam prosperum respicit, sue prosperitatis participationem ei largitur. Quando vero uno gradu ab eo recedit, sue bonitatis prosperitatem expectans, frustra letatur. Bonam enim spem sine aliquo fructu coniectat. Idem enim de omni planeta nocivo affirmamus, quod si in aliquo locorum 4, id est in 2°, 6° vel 8° vel 12 ab orientali inventus fuerit, mortalibus timorem inferre poterit, set nichil nocere.

5

1.

الخامس (+ و DL) الكوكب إذا كان في أوتاد النحس أعني إذا كان معه أو في الرابع منه (D -) أو (+) في (D) السابع أو العاشر فهو (وهو D) مثل (.L post corr) المقاتل عن نفسه لما نزل به (D -) من البلاء (- من البلاء LD) فإذا جاوز النحوس وانصرف عنه بدرجة تامّة كما وصفت فقد فاته أضرار النحوس ولم يقدر النحس (النحوس D) أن يدخل أكثر من الروعات (المروعات D) فأحفظ هذه الأبواب فإنها من أسرار المسائل (+ والمواليد DL).

2. The fifth. When the planet is in the cardines of the malefic, i.e., when it is with it or in the fourth from it, or the seventh or the tenth, it is like one who fights for himself against what distress descends on him. And when it is passing the malefic and separated from it by a complete degree, as I

have described, then the compulsions of the malefics have passed him by and the malefic is not able to bring in more than fears. Keep these chapters in mind, as they belong to the secrets of interrogations.

3. John of Seville: Quintum (.3. M). Planeta /P p. 442a/, cum fuerit in angulis *malorum* (+ planetarum H), id est, cum fuerit cum eo aut in quarto ab eo aut in septimo aut (vel HSpr) in decimo (undecimo M), erit sicut qui pugnat pro semetipso in (**contra** HMSTpr) tribulationem *et malum* quod descendit super eum. Cumque transierit eum et separatus fuerit ab eo per gradum integrum, sicut predixi *tibi*, iam evasit *impedimentum illius mali*, et nichil poterit malus præter timorem inmittere. Serva ergo hæc capitula, quia sunt ex secretis interrogationum (+ et nativitatum H).

4. Hermann, EN-Text: –

5. *Liber trium iudicum*: Quintus, cum est stella in cardine infortunii, id est, conventu aut tetragono *sive oppositione*. Sic enim existens, assimilatur pro adversis casibus seipsum excrucianti, que valde servanda precipimus. Sunt enim de *intimis celestium* secretis, ad iudiciorum rationem magnopere attinentia.

6. *Liber novem iudicum*: 30, cum est stella in cardine infortunii, id est, conventu, tetragono sive oppositione. Sic enim existens, assimilatur pro adversis casibus seipsum excrucianti, que valde servanda precipimus. Sunt enim de intimis celestium secretis, ad iudiciorum *viam* magno opere *servanda*.

7. Abraham Ibn Ezra: xxx If a planet is at one of the cardines of a malefic, and it separates from aspect by one degree, it causes fear but ⟨its indication⟩ will not come true.

8. Henry Bate's translation: .30m. Si fuerit planeta in aliquo angulorum malivoli, et separetur ab aspectu *eius* per unum gradum, apparebit timor qui non perveniet (veniet Gl) ad opus, *nec erit*.

9. Pietro d'Abano: Si fuerit planeta fortuna cum angulo mali, separaturque ab eius aspectu uno gradu, apparebit et non perveniet ad effectum.

10. *Gloucester Text*: 5 Quicumque planeta in aliqua quatuor columnarum cum nocivo planeta fuerit, id est, in signo eodem orientali vel 4° vel 7° vel 10° in magna disceptatione et litigio est, ut a periculo vicinitatis planete nocivi liberetur. Hec autem durabit deceptatio et litigium quousque uno gradu ab eo removeatur. Abinde enim nocere non potest, potest tamen expavescere.

6

1.

الســــلام سر القمر أنما كان خالي السير لا يتصل بشيء، من الكواكب دل على العمر أع والبطالة والرجوع
من نلك الحالة وعلى فساد الحوائج

السادس القمر إذا كان خالي السير لا يتصل بشيء من الكواكب دل على الفراغ والبطالة
والرجوع من تلك الحالة (+ صفرا LD) وعلى فساد الحوائج (+ كلها LD).

2. The sixth. When the Moon is void of course, ⟨i.e.⟩, not joined with any of the planets, it indicates emptiness, futility, returning (+ empty LD) from this condition and harm of the matters.

3. John of Seville: Sextum (.4. M). Luna (planeta H) cum fuerit cursu (cursus MT) vacua et (**id est** HMSTpr) nulli planetarum iuncta, significat inanitionem et annullationem (+ **ac reversionem** HMSTpr) ab eadem causa (+ **et** HMSTpr) impedimentum *eiusdem causæ*.

4. EN-text: *Item*, solitudo Lune otii et inutilis negotii signum est.

5. *Liber trium iudicum*: Sextus, *quoniam* **solitudo** *Lune* otii *et* **inutilis negotii signum est.**

6. *Liber novem iudicum*: Secundus locus /V 11ra/ est solitudo, quoniam otii, inutilis (inutiles v) *etiam infructuosi* negotii signum est.

7. Abraham Ibn Ezra: ii If the Moon is in solitary motion, it signifies that everything the querent asks for is without substance and impossible.

8. Henry Bate's translation: .2m. est si Luna est solivaga; hoc significat super omnem rem vacuam, et quod nichil esse potest (poterit Gl) de omni re de qua querit querens *seu* (- querens seu Gl) *interrogator*.

9. Pietro d'Abano's translation: Si fuerit Luna solitaria *vel cursu vacua*, significat omne vacuum vel inane, et annullabitur omne quod querit quesitor.

10. *Gloucester Text*: 6 Quando Luna motu vacuo movetur, id est, quando nullus planeta eam respiciat, *hominis* otium designat, *id est, quod ab opere debeat cessare. Et si quid incipiat, non poterit finire.*

7

1.

فى ربيعة الكوكب القابل لتدبير القمر إن كان سعد نحير وإن كان نحس فشر.

السابع اتصال القمر يدل على ما يكون مما (وما LD) يرجى من الأمور على قدر طبيعة

الكوكب القابل لتدبير القمر إن كان سعد نحير وإن كان نحس فشر.

2. The seventh. The application of the Moon indicates what (+ will be and what LD) is hoped for from things according the nature of the planet receiving the management of the Moon: if it is a benefic, then good; if it is a malefic, then bad.

3. John of Seville: Septimum (.5. M). Coniunctio Lunæ (planete H) significat *quod futurum est et* quod speratur ex rebus secundum quantitatem naturæ [q.n.] naturam H) planetæ qui recipit dispositionem Lunæ (planete H), *id est*, si fuerit fortuna, bonum, et si fuerit malus, (+ id est S) malum.

4. EN-text: –

5. *Liber trium iudicum*: Septimus, lunaris applicatio. Gerit enim proventu⟨u⟩m ducatum ad morem earum quibus applicat—prosperum si benivolus, adversum si nocuus.

6. *Liber novem iudicum*: *Tertius est* lunaris applicatio. Gerit enim *in proventibus* ducatum ad morem *et naturam* earum quibus applicat—prosperum (prosperam v) si benivolus, adversum si nocuus.

7. Abraham Ibn Ezra: iii When a *planet* approaches conjunction *or some aspect* with the Moon, it signifies all future events and what the querent is hoping for—good fortune if the planet is a benefic, bad fortune if it is a malefic.

8. Henry Bate's translation: .3m. (+ est Gl) Coniunctio, qua Luna planete coniungitur aut aspicit eum, significat super omnem rem futuram et quidquid sperat interrogator vel expectare debet; si quidem planeta bonus fuerit, bonum, si malus, malum.

9. Pietro d'Abano's translation: Coniunctio Lune cum planeta aut aspectus significat omne quod futurum est et omne de quo quesitor sperat. Et si hic planeta fuerit fortuna (fortunatus pr), bonum, si autem malus, malum.

10. *Gloucester Text*: 7 Quando Luna alicui planete coniungitur ita quod sig-n⟨ific⟩at secundum naturam planete qui eam respicit, quia si planeta bonus fuerit, bonum significat, si malus, malum.

8

1.

الثامن انصراف القمر عن الكوكب يدل على ما (+ قد D) مضى من الأمور وذهب على
قدر طبيعة ذلك الكوكب المنصرف عنه القمر.

2. The eighth. The separation of the Moon from the planet indicates what things have passed and what has gone, according to the nature of that planet from which the Moon is separating.

3. John of Seville: Octavum (.6. M). Separatio Lunæ (planete H) a planeta significat quod præteritum est et quod iam recessit secundum quantitatem naturæ (q.n.] naturam H) planetæ illius (ipsius planetæ M, illius S, illius planete Tpr) a quo separatur Luna.

4. EN-text: *Item*, a quibuscumque stellis Luna *separatur*, secundum *harum* naturam et *statum* de eis que iam acciderunt (accidunt N) *iudicatur*.

5. *Liber trium iudicum*: Octavus, **Lune a quibus⟨cum⟩que stellis separatio** earumque **naturam** (*sic*) **et status de eis que iam acciderunt** diiudicat.

6. *Liber novem iudicum*: *Quartus*, Lune a quibuscumque stellis separatio. Earum *enim natura statusque proprietas* de *his* que iam acciderunt diiudicat.

7. Abraham Ibn Ezra: iv Separation by the Moon signifies past events. If it (the Moon) separates *from conjunction or aspect with a benefic planet*, they (the past events) were auspicious; and if from a malefic planet, they were inauspicious.

8. Henry Bate's translation: .4m. Separatio Lune super res significat preteritas; et si quidem separata fuerit a coniunctione aut ab aspectu planete boni, bonum fuerit (fuit Gl), si *vero* mali, malum (+ fuit Gl).

9. Pietro d'Abano's translation: Separatio Lune a planeta significat quod preteritum est, et si separetur a coniunctione vel aspectu fortune, affuit bonum, si vero mali, malum.

10. *Gloucester Text*: 8 Quando Luna ab aliquo planeta regreditur, significat rem que evasa est *vel que perdita est vel que preterita est* secundum naturam planete a quo egressa est.

9

1.

الـتّـاسِـع

إذا أكان يج هبوهله داعى الغدس والهم والبضينى

التاسع إذا كان في هبوطه دل على النحس والهم والضيق.

2. The ninth. When the planet is in its dejection, it indicates bad fortune, worry and distress.

3. John of Seville: Nonum (.7. M). Planeta cum (si H) fuerit in descensione sua, *id est* (-- id est HT), *in domo in* (- H) *qua cadit* (-- id est ... cadit MSpr), significat tristitiam, (+ et HSpr) carcerem (implying حبس for نحس) et angustiam.

4. EN-text: *Item*, stella in suo casu, perturbationis et angustie et adversitatis signum (+ est E).

5. *Liber trium iudicum*: Nonus, quoniam **stella in casu suo, perturbationis, angustie et adversitatis signum.**

6. *Liber novem iudicum*: 31, quoniam stella in casu suo, perturbationis, angustie et adversitatis signum.

7. Abraham Ibn Ezra: xxxi If the planet is in the house of its dejection, it signifies worry, hardship and distress.

8. Henry Bate's translation: .31m. Si fuerit planeta in casu suo, hoc significat tristitiam et anxietates atque angustias.

9. Pietro d'Abano's translation: Si fuerit planeta in eius dedecore, denotat dolorem ac angustiam (angustias Gl).

10. *Gloucester Text*: 9 Quando est in sua demissione, malum cogitationes, dolores, *homines etiam in arto existentes* significat.

10

1.

الـعَـاشُـرُ الكَوكب الرّابم يراعى إبعصيان وإنتقاض

والتردمِ يرودكا ختلا ه

العاشر الكوكب الراجع يدل على العصيان والانتقاض والترديد والاختلاف.

2. The tenth. The retrograding planet indicates disobedience, destruction, rejection and difference.

3. John of Seville: Decimum (.8. M). Planeta retrogradus significat inobedientiam (+ **et solutionem** H) et contradictionem (+ et involutionem

H, implying اختلاط) *et retractionem ac* (et MS) *reversionem* (- et r. ac r. T; ac reversionem et retractionem pr) et (ac M) diversitatem *seu discordiam.*

4. EN-text: Retrogradatio corruptionis, destructionis et contradictionis indicium est.

5. *Liber trium iudicum*: Decimus, *quod* **retrogradatio corruptionis, destructionis et contradictionis** *in via.*

6. *Liber novem iudicum*: 32, *quia* retrogradatio corruptionis, destructionis et contradictionis *marturia (?).*

7. Abraham Ibn Ezra: xxxii A retrograde planet signifies rebellion and destruction of everything that is planned.

8. Henry Bate's translation: .32m. Planeta retrogradus rebellionem significat et dissipationem eorum que cogitata sunt.

9. Pietro d'Abano's translation: Planeta retrogradus significat revolutionem (revelationem pr) et dissipationem omnis cogitati.

10. *Gloucester Text*: 10 Quando planeta retrogradus est, tristitiam, discordiam, desiderii diminutionem, *ut si terram optaret quis habere, medietatem vel eius aliquam partem haberet et huiusmodi alia significant.*

11

1.

الحادي عشر الكوكب المقيم يدل على التحمق (النحس D) والبلادة (التلذذ LD) وما كان
قد سكن.

2. The eleventh. The planet in stopping indicates folly (harm D) and stupidity (giving pleasure LD) and what has become quiet.

3. John of Seville: Undecimum (.9. M). Planeta in statione sua significat malum (= النحس; + **segnitiem** H) et quod iam quievit (q.i.q.] quietudinem *presentis rei* H)

4. EN-text: –

5. *Liber trium iudicum*: Undecimus, quod stelle statio dubitationem et rerum involucra significat.

6. *Liber novem iudicum*: 33, quod stelle statio dubitationem et rerum involucra significat.

7. Abraham Ibn Ezra: xxxiii A planet in its first station is like a man who does not know what to do and his end is unfortunate; in the second station, it is like a man who hopes and whose hope is not disappointed.[14]

8. Henry Bate's translation: .33m. Planeta existens in statione prima est sicut homo nesciens quid faciet et cuius finis ad malum est; in secunda *vero* existens statione est sicut homo qui sperat aliquantum (?) et non frustrabitur spes eius.

9. Pietro d'Abano's translation: planeta in statione prima est /S 92[va]/ sicut homo ignarus eius quid faciat, cuius adest finis malus. Et si fuerit in statione secunda, est velud sperans de re aliqua et nec frustrabitur spes ipsius.

10. *Gloucester Text*: 11 Quando vero stationarius est *ut retrogradiatur,* tunc incipit malum designare, quando vero stationarius est *ut recte velit progredi, quicquid stella illa terrenis ministrat, bonum est.*

12

1.

جَعَلَ الثَّانِي عَشَرَ والنحوس تراكِ على البسو والنكر في العمل

الثاني عشر و(- D) النحوس تدل على الفسق والنكد في العمل.

2. The twelfth. The malefics indicate depravity and hardship in the action.

3. John of Seville: Duodecimum (.10. M). Mali significant difficultatem et pressuram *et festinationem* (- **et festinationem** H) in opere.

4. EN-text: *Item, quod infortuna stella* promittit, laboriose et periculose solvit.

5. *Liber trium iudicum*: Duodecimus, quoniam **infortunia** id **quod** *promittunt* **laboriose atque periculose solvunt.**

6. *Liber novem iudicum*: 19, quoniam infortunia id quod promittunt laboriose atque periculose solvunt.

7. Abraham Ibn Ezra: –

8. Henry Bate's translation: –

9. Pietro d'Abano's translation: –

10. *Gloucester Text*: –

---

14   This is not very close to the Arabic.

13

1.

الثالث عشمّ الكوكب اذا كان بطيئا اخر عدته

عرته خير الوسترا وكـزله اخاكار في يوت زحاوالمش ونبه البروج الخعاب بجل

الثالث عشر الكوكب إذا كان بطيئا أخر عدته (+ ما وعد به L) خيرا (+ كان LD) أو شرا

وكذلك إذا كان في بيوت زحل والمشتري وفي البروج الخفاف يعجل (+ أي بروج السفلية

الزهرة وعطارد والقمر D).

2. The thirteenth. When the planet is slow it delays its promise, good or bad. And likewise when it is in the houses of Saturn and Jupiter, and it hurries in light signs (that is the lower signs (!) Venus, Mercury and the Moon).

3. John of Seville: Tredecimum (.11. M). Planeta cum fuerit tardus *et* (*id est* HMSTpr) *cum tarde* (*tardus* H) *ambulat*, postponit numerum (implying عِدَّة, dationem H implying هدية, rather than عدته; + sive **promissum** pr) suum (suam H), *id est, facit dilationem in numero* (donatione H, + sive **promisso** suo pr) tam in bono quam in malo. Similiter facit cum fuerit in domibus Saturni vel Iovis, et in domibus *planetarum* levium *festinat* (festinatur H).

4. EN-text: *Item*, stella *tarda in cursu*, tarde promittit, velox, velociter. *Similiter stella reperta* (separata N) *in domiciliis tardorum planetarum sicuti* Saturni, Iovis *etiam tarde promittit*, velocium *autem, velociter.*

5. *Liber trium iudicum*: Tertiusdecimus, **tardior stelle cursus** est, *scilicet minus suo aluuazat* (= الوسط) *incedit*, sicque quod **promittit tardat**. Eiusdem generis est cum **stella in domiciliis Saturni et Iovis** *invenitur*. Nam in domiciliis velocium promissa veloci consecutione parat, *eiusdemque est cum ipsa velocius incedit.*

6. *Liber novem iudicum*: 34, tardior stelle cursus est, scilicet minus suo *medio cursu* incedit, sic *enim* quod promittit tardat. Eiusdem generis est cum stella in domiciliis Saturni et Iovis *moratur*. In *domibus namque* velocium promissa veloci consecutione parat, eiusdemque est cum ipsa velocius incedit.

7. Abraham Ibn Ezra: xxxiv If a planet is slowing down, the event, whether good or evil, will be delayed. But if Jupiter and Saturn are *in the tropical signs* they hasten the event.

8. Henry Bate's translation: .34m. Si fuerit planeta tardus cursu, tardabit et res, sive bona sive mala (bonas sive malas Gl); et si fuerit Iupiter aut Saturnus in signis mobilibus (malivolis Gl),[15] festinabitur res.

9. Pietro d'Abano's translation: Si fuerit planeta tardus motu, tardabitur sive bonum sive malum. Et si fuerit Iupiter aut Saturnus (Venus S) in signis mobilibus, rem festinabunt.

10. *Gloucester Text*:12 Quando planete motu tardo moventur, quicquid significant, sive bonum sive malum sit, tarde continget. Set si veloci moveantur motu, quod designant velociter contingere verum est. Modus idem significationis est quando planeta in domo Saturni vel Iovis est. Si enim propitius in domo Saturni fuerit, bonus quod significat moratur. Si nocivus idem non moratur. Et similiter de domo Iovis, econverso iudicandum est.

14

1.

الرابع عشر إذا اتصل الكوكب بالقمر (القمر بكوكب LD) وتمّ اتصاله أعني إذا صار (كان DL) معه في دقيقة (+ واحدة DL) فانظر ما (فيما LD) يكون في تلك المسألة من الكوكب الذي (كواكب التي L) اتصل به القمر بعد ذلك.

2. The fourteenth. When the planet applies to the Moon and completes its application, i.e., when it happens to be with it in a (one DL) minute, look in regard to what is in that question at the planet to which the Moon applies after that.

3. John of Seville: Quartumdecimum (.12. M). Cum (Dum pr) iuncta (coniuncta Tpr) fuerit Luna (planeta H) alicui planetæ et perfecerit *suam coniunctionem*, id est, cum fuerit cum eo in (in eo cum M) uno minuto, aspice quod futurum est de ipsa interrogatione a planeta cum quo iungitur Luna (planeta H) post hæc.

---

15   'Signa mobilia' is the technical term for tropical signs, but 'mobilia' here must just mean 'moving', i.e. making swift progress and should apply to the fast-moving planets.

4. EN-text: *Item*, si hora questionis Luna reperiatur applicans *alicui* in eodem puncto, *tunc* ille planeta *recipit et* vendicat sibi totum *quidquid* attinet Lune de illa questione.

5. *Liber trium iudicum*: Quartusdecimus, **si in hora questionis Luna applicans reperiatur** cum **aliqua in eodem puncto**, sicque stella **recipiens**, *quantum* **Lune de** *questione* **pertinet**, totum sibi vendicat.

6. *Liber novem iudicum*: *Quintus*, si Luna *sub ipsius* hora questionis applicans reperiatur cum aliqua. *Sic enim* stella recipiens, quantum *ad Lunam* de questione *attinet*, totum sibi *vendicavit*.

7. Abraham Ibn Ezra: v If the planet to which the Moon gives its power is in its strength, then the thing will be done properly, but the opposite holds true if it was weak. vi The same holds true for any planet that pushes its power to another ⟨planet⟩; the event will occur according to the power of the receiver.[16]

8. Henry Bate's translation: .5m. (+ Et Gl) Si planeta cui Luna dat virtutem *vel fortitudinem* fuerit in fortitudine sua, tunc fiet res convenienter, et econtrario (econverso Gl) si fuerit debilis. 6m. Consimiliter planeta quilibet cum dat alii fortitudinem suam, secundum receptionis fortitudinem erit res illa.

9. Pietro d'Abano's translation: Si planeta cui Luna vim dederit est in sua fortitudine, tunc res (- S) decenter perficietur, contrarium vero si debilis extiterit. Similiter, in omni planeta dante vim alii (- S), secundum fortitudinem recipientis res existet.

10. *Gloucester Text*: 13 Quando Luna respectu aliquo planete alicui complicatur, secundum eius significationem perfecte iudicare non possumus donec /73ᵛ/ in eodem gradu cum planeta cui complicatur adveniat. *Quia prius quam in eodem gradu commoverunt, si alius intervenerit planeta, significatio Lune potest impediri.*

---

16   These two precepts in Abraham Ibn Ezra are not close to 14.

15

1.

الخامس عشر الكوكب إذا صار (كان L) في آخر درجة من البرج فقد تمت (ذهبت LD)
قوته من ذلك البرج وقوته في البرج الآخر وهو بمنزلة رجل وضع رجله في (على D) عتبة
الباب (+ وهم LD) بالخروج فإن سقط البيت لم يضره ذلك وإن (فإن LD) كان الكوكب
في درجة تسع (تسعة D) وعشرين فإن قوة ذلك الكوكب في ذلك البرج وذلك أن لكل
كوكب ثلاث درج تنتشر قوته في الدرجة التي هو فيها ودرجة خلفها ودرجة أمامه (أمامه
ودرجة خلفه LD).

In margin:

(Arabic margin text - two lines)

الخامس عشر الكوكب إذا صار (كان L) في آخر درجة من البرج فقد تمت (ذهبت LD)
قوته من ذلك البرج وقوته في البرج الآخر وهو بمنزلة رجل وضع رجله في (على D) عتبة
الباب (+ وهم LD) بالخروج فإن سقط البيت لم يضره ذلك وإن (فإن LD) كان الكوكب
في درجة تسع (تسعة D) وعشرين فإن قوة ذلك الكوكب في ذلك البرج وذلك أن لكل
كوكب ثلاث درج تنتشر قوته في الدرجة التي هو فيها ودرجة خلفها ودرجة أمامه (أمامه
ودرجة خلفه LD).

Margin:

انظر كيف هو لكل كوكب ... درج التي هو فيها والتي قبلها ... بعدها

2. The fifteenth. When it happens that the planet is in the last degree of the
sign, then its power has retreated from that sign and its power is in the
next sign, and it is like a man who places his foot in threshold of the door
for going out. Then, if the house falls down, it does not harm him. And if
the planet is in the 29th degree, then the power of that planet is in that
sign. And this is because the indications for every planet are three degree
to which its power extends: in the degree in which it is, and the degree
behind it and the degree in front of it.

3. John of Seville: Quintumdecimum (.13. M). Planeta cum fuerit in ul/P
p. 442b/timo gradu signi, iam recessit fortitu/H 24ᵛ/do eius ab ipso signo,
et erit fortitudo illius (eius MSTpr) in *alio* signo. Et est quasi (est quis T;
et quasi pr) vir qui posuit pedem suum super limen portæ, volens exire.

Quod si domus tunc ceciderit, non impediet (impediat T) eum. Si vero fuerit planeta in .xx.º .viiii.º (.27. M., .32. T) gradu, erit fortitudo illius planetæ (planeta eius pr) in eodem signo, quia (et S) sunt unicuique planetæ .iii. gradus in quibus expanditur virtus eius: gradus scilicet in quo est et gradus qui est ante eum et gradus qui est post eum (H,—e.g.q.e.p.e. P, **gradus qui est post eum et gradus qui est ante eum** MSTpr)

4. EN-text: *Item* (- N), stella in extremo /N 233ᵛᵃ/ signi *sicut circa .4ᵒʳ. gradus, non habet virtutem. Similiter* (- N), *stella ingrediens signum ante .5. gradus illius signi non habet virtutem.*[17]

5. *Liber trium iudicum*: Quintusdecimus, **stellam in extremo signi** reperiri. Generat enim id genus quandam circa stelle affectus tamquam in bivio detente variationem. *Sicque fit exitus de signo adverso non inutile. Cum enim* est stella in *.xxx.º* gradu, vires eius utrumque signum diripit. Habent etenim singule stelle proprie potentie ternos gradus dicatos, eos scilicet ipsos in quibus sunt et binos altrinsecus.

6. *Liber novem iudicum*: 36, est stellam in extremo signi reperiri. Generat enim id genus quandam circa stelle affectus tamquam in bivio variationem. Si⟨c⟩que *fiet* exitus de signo adverso non inutile. *Nam si* stella in 30 gradu *moratur*, vires eius utrumque signum diripit. Habent etenim singule stelle proprie potentie ternos gradus dicatos, eos scilicet ipsos in quibus sunt et binos altrinsecus.

7. Abraham Ibn Ezra: xxxv If a planet is at the end of the sign, its power from the first sign is exhausted and all its power is in the sign it is entering. If the planet is in the 29th degree of the sign, it still has the power of the sign where it is, because the planet has power in three degrees: in the degree it is in, in the previous degree, and in the next degree.

8. Henry Bate's translation: .35m. Planeta existens in fine signi, fortitudinem amisit signi precedentis et tota eius fortitudo in signo est in quod ingredietur; si *autem* fuerit planeta in .29. gradu signi, /Gl 62ʳ/ adhuc est eius fortitudo in signo illo in quo est; in tribus enim gradibus fortitudinem habet planeta: in gradu (+ scilicet Gl) in quo est planete virtus, et in gradu qui est (- Gl) ante ipsum, et in eo (- in eo Gl) qui post ipsum.

9. Pietro d'Abano's translation: Si fuerit planeta in fine signi, vis eius deperiit in illo signo (principio signo pr, primo signo?) et omnis vis eius est in si/pr ⟨X⟩xviiiʳᵃ/gno quod ingredietur. Et si fuerit in .29. gradu adhuc ipsius (- pr) vis existit in signo in quo manet, eo quod planete in tribus sit

---

17 'Similiter … non habet virtutem' corresponds to the opening of **44** below.

gradibus virtus, gradus scilicet in quo est et uno gradu ante ipsum et uno gradu (- gradu pr) post ipsum (eum pr).

10. *Gloucester Text*: 14 Quicumque planeta in ultimo gradu alicuius signi fuerit, quicquid significationis ab eodem signo contraxerit, amisit et abinde virtutem suam a sequenti signo incipit revirescere, ut in exeunte apparet. Cum enim a domo exiens pedem unum limini supponit, *tota exeuntis intentio extrinsecus est*. Si enim in 29 gradu fuerit, ab eodem signo virtutem adhuc habet.

16

1.

الشَّادِس مِنْ كَشَرَ الكوكب وربكون طالبا للاتصال
ثم إن ريطا لدّبه برج حتى يَنتقل الكوكب بسرعته وان زالمركه في برج آخر لم يتصل بغيره فحسنت الحاجة وان
اندم بغيره اذا انقل ثم اتصل بعد هذه تقض الحاجة كانه قد خالط نور كوكب غيره

السادس عشر الكوكب قد يكون طالبا للاتصال ثم لا يدرك ذلك في برج (برجه LD) حتى ينتقل الكوكب بسرعته فإن أدركه في برج آخر (+ و DL) لم يتصل بغيره (- LD) قضيت الحاجة وان اتصل بغيره (--) وان اتصل بغيره D) اذا (فإذا L) انتقل ثم اتصل بعد ذلك لم تقض الحاجة لأنه قد خالط نور كوكب غيره.

2. The sixteenth. It can happen that the planet seeks application, and then does not reach that in a sign (its sign LD) until the planet changes ⟨sign⟩ because of its speed; then, ⟨if⟩ it reaches it in the next sign but it does not apply with another, the matter is completed. And if the application is with another when it changes ⟨sign and⟩ then it applies after that, the matter is not completed because it mixes with the light of another planet.

3. John of Seville: Sextumdecimum (.14. M). Planeta petit (p(er)it T) *aliquando* coniunctionem, set non consequitur hanc in signo suo donec mutetur ipse planeta per festinationem suam, cumque insecutus fuerit (+ **eum** HSTpr, cum M) in alio signo et non fuerit iunctus alteri, perficietur (perficitur HSTpr) causa. Et si iunctus fuerit alteri *vel commixtus fuerit* (v.c.f.] **cum mutatus fuerit** HSTpr,—causa ... fuerit M), postea iunctus fuerit illi, non perficietur (perficitur HS) causa, quia iam commixtus est lumini planetæ alterius.

4. EN-text: –

5. *Liber trium iudicum*: Sextusdecimus, quando stella affectat applicare *cum alia*, nec sequi potest eam donec in sequenti signo. Si enim vel in alio

sequitur ut nullius alterius lumen interveniat, rerum proventus firmat. Nam si cum alia interveniente ante applicat quam cum illa (*supra*: superiori D), rem negat, *licet post ad illam perventura.*

6.   *Liber novem iudicum*: *37*, quando stella affectat applicare cum *altera*, nec *consequi* potest eam donec in sequenti signo. Si enim vel in alio *consequatur* ut nullius alterius lumen interveniat, rerum *firmavit* proventus. *Nam* si cum alia interveniente ante applicat quam cum illa, rem negat, licet post ad illam perventura.

7.   Abraham Ibn Ezra: xxxvi If a planet is about to conjoin a second ⟨planet⟩, but the second planet enters a different sign before they reach conjunction, and the first planet pursues it and catches up with it but does not conjoin it before it catches up with another planet, the object of the query will occur only after despair.

8.   Henry Bate's translation: .36m. Si fuerit planeta vadens ad coniunctionem alterius, et antequam coniungantur exeat alter ad signum sequens, primus *vero* sequatur hunc et attingat eum (ipsum Gl) ibidem, et antequam ipsum consequatur [non] coniungatur (iungatur Gl) ei alius planeta, perficietur utique res post desperationem.

9.   Pietro d'Abano's translation: Si petit planeta coniunctionem secundi et antequam sint iuncti transit secundus in signum secundum, fugatque ante seipsum primus planeta, ipsumque (et pr) attingit (attingat pr) illic (in loco illo pr) et non coniungitur (coniungatur pr) ei antequam alium attingat planetam, perficietur res quesita post desperationem.

10.   *Gloucester Text*: 15 Si planeta planetam voluerit respicere et antequam respiciat ab eo signo in quo debuerit respicere, recedat et tum ipsum expectet quousque respiciat, significat rem bene compleri debere. Set si planeta alius intervenerit quem ante alium respiciat, significat rem non debere compleri. Huiusmodi enim commixtione rerum perturbatur eventus.

17

1.

السابع عشر يريد الكوكب (الكوكب يريد LD) أن يجامع الكوكب في برج فلا يدركه في

ذلك البرج حتى يخرج إلى البرج الآخر فإن ادركه في البرج الآخر (- فإن ادركه في البرج

الآخر LD) فالحاجة مقضية (تنقضي D) إلا أن يجامع قبله غيره فإن اتصل بغيره لم يضره

ذلك لما وصفت لك أنّ الاتصال لا يبطل المجامعة والمجامعة تبطل الاتصال والنظر (فالنظر

L) لا يقطع النظر ويدفع الحاجة والاجتماع يقطع النظر (ويدفع الحاجة والاجتماع يقطع

النظر] فافهم LD).

2. The seventeenth. The planet wishes to combine with the planet in a sign,
then it does not reach it in that sign until it exits into the next sign. Then,
if it reaches it in the next sign, the matter is completed, unless it first combines with another. And if it combines with another, that does not harm
this, because of what I have described to you: that the application does
not negate the conjunction but the conjunction negates the application.
And the aspect does not cut the aspect and push away the matter, but the
conjunction cuts the aspect.

3. John of Seville: Septimumdecimum (.15. M). Planeta volens iungi planetæ
in uno signo, set (*corr. ex* si S) non *potest* eum consequi in eodem signo
donec egrediatur ad aliud signum, (+ **et si eum consequitur in alio signo
pr**) perficitur tunc causa **nisi** (ubi M) iungatur prius (p.i. MSTpr) alteri.
Set si alteri (-MT) iungitur (iungitur alteri Spr, + per aspectum pr), non
impedit eum hoc (hic MSTpr) propter quod dixi tibi, quod (quia HMSTpr)
coniunctio *quæ fit per aspectum* non annullat (+ eam M) coniunctionem
quæ fit per corpus in uno signo, et *huiusmodi* (huius pr) coniunctio annullat eam *quæ fit per aspectum*. Et aspectus non abscidit (abscindit pr)
aspectum set (**nec** H) prohibet causam. Set coniunctio *corporalis* abscidit
(abscidet M, abscindit pr) aspectum.

4. EN-text: –

5. *Liber trium iudicum*: Septimusdecimus, quando in eodem signo cupiens
convenire cum alia, eam illic non consequitur, si tamen eam in sequenti

comprehenderit, rem firmat, nisi ante *cum corpore* alterius iungatur. Licet enim applicet interim cum alia, non nocet, applicatio siquidem non solvit conventum. Conventus namque et applicationem et respectum (*supra*: solvit).

6. *Liber novem iudicum: 38,* quando in eodem signo cupiens *venire* cum alia, eam illic non consequitur, si tamen eam in sequenti comprehenderit, rem firmat, nisi ante cum corpore iungatur alterius. Licet enim applicet interim cum alia, non nocet, applicatio siquidem non conventum, conventus *autem* et applicationem et respectum *solvit.*

7. Abraham Ibn Ezra: xxxvii If a planet aspects a second planet, which moved from its position before a *light* planet reached it, it will not hurt it, because an aspect does not cancel out the ⟨power of the⟩ conjunction of the bodies.

8. Henry Bate's translation: .37m. Si aspexerit planeta planetam alterum qui motus est de loco suo ante consecutionem planete levis, non nocebit. Aspectus enim coniunctionem non deficiet (destruet Gl) corporalem.

9. Pietro d'Abano's translation: Si respicit planeta secundum planetam ex eius loco mutatum ante (+ idem pr) attingere planete levioris, non infortunabit (damnificabit pr), eo quod aspectus corporis coniunctionem non perturbat.

10. *Gloucester Text:* 16 Quando planeta voluerit coniungi alii planete in eodem signo, nec planetam nisi in altero signo possit expectare ut ei coniungatur, tunc significat rem bene completam, nisi hoc contingat quod alius planeta ei coniungatur prius. Set hec notandum est, quod si interim alium respiciat planetam, pro respectu virtus eius non impedietur. Respectus enim virtutem coniunctionis non impedit, set econverso, coniunctio virtutem respectus impedit. *Notandum iterum quod coniunctio coniunctionem non adnichilat, set aliquantulum rerum moratur eventum.*

18

1.

الثامن عشر النحس إذا كان شرقيا أعني إذا كان (- إذا كان DL) طالعا بالغدوات من المشرق في بيته أو شرفه ولم يتصل به نحس يفسده فهو أفضل من سعد راجع منكوس (منحوس D).

2. The eighteenth. When the malefic is oriental, i.e., when it is rising in the morning in the East, in its house or its exaltation, and a malefic which harms it does not apply to it, then this is better than a benefic that is retrograde ⟨and⟩ reversed (harmed D).

3. John of Seville: Octavumdecimum (.16. M). Malus planeta cum fuerit orientalis, id est, cum mane apparuerit in oriente, in domo sua aut in exaltatione sua (-- M), et non fuerit iunctus malo qui eum impediat, melior *ac dignior* est (e.a.d. pr) fortuna retrograda et impedita (= *manḥūs* منحوس).

4. EN-text: –

5. *Liber trium iudicum*: Octavusdecimus, infortunium orientale, in domicilio aut principatu suo, liberum ab alio, fortunata retrograda aut corrupta potius. Est autem orientalis mane in oriente, *occidentalis vespere et in occidente apparens*.

6. *Liber novem iudicum*: 22, quoniam infortunium orientale, in domicilio aut principatu suo, liberum ab alio, fortunata retrograda vel corrupta potius. Est autem orientale mane in oriente, occidentale vespere et in occidente apparens.

7. Abraham Ibn Ezra: xviii If a malefic is oriental of the Sun, *strong*, in a sign where it exerts lordship and is not aspected by another malefic, it is better than a benefic that is *burnt* or retrograde.

8. Henry Bate's translation: .18m. Si fuerit malivolus orientalis a Sole, in fortitudine sua, in signo (+ in Gl) quo dignitatem habet, et non aspexerit eum malivolus alter, (+ ipse Gl) melior est benivolo combusto vel retrogrado.

9. Pietro d'Abano's translation: Si fuerit malus orientalis a Sole *aut in eius .vi.* et in signo vigoris eiusdem, ac ipsum alius (- S) non aspiciat malus, melior est fortunata (fortuna pr) combusta vel retrograda.

10. *Gloucester Text*: 17 Planeta nocivus quando orientalis est, id est, quando mane in orienti ascendit, si in domo vel in honore suo fuerit ita quod non planeta illum impediat, prosperiorem significat eventum quam bonus planeta si fuerit retrogradus *vel si alius planetam illum impediat*.

19

1.

التاسع عشر النحوس إذا كانت أرباب الحوائج واتصل بها رب الطالع أو القمر من تربيع أو

مقابلة أعني من البرج الرابع أو السابع (والعاشر L) تكونت (نكدت LD) الحوائج وأفسدت

العاقبة (+ الا ان يكون بينهما قبول L) وتكون (فتكون LD) النحوس عند ذلك (+ إذا

كانت DL) هي الدافعة (الشاقية L، + أعني التي تتصل LD) خير من أن تكون هي قابلة

التدبير أعني يدفع إليها ويتصل بها.

2. The nineteenth. When the malefics are lords of the matters and the lord of
the ascendant or the Moon applies to them from quartile or opposition,
i.e., from the fourth or the seventh sign, they bring into being the matters
and destroy the result (+ unless there is reception in their own house L),
and ⟨that⟩ the malefics at that time are the pushers (i.e., that are applying
LD) ⟨is⟩ better than that they receive the management, i.e., it is pushed
on them or it applies to them.

3. John of Seville: Nonumdecimum (-- M). Mali cum fuerint domini causarum (rerum H) et iunctus fuerit eis dominus ascendentis aut Luna a
quarto aspectu aut (+ ab HMT) oppositione, id est, a quarto signo vel a
signo (- HMTpr, id est in .iiii°. signo aut S) .vii°. (+ disturbate H), faciunt
causam, set (et H) destruunt eam in fine (e.i.f.] finem H). Et *si* fuerint mali
illi (- S, illi mali T, mali fuerint illi pr) qui (quibus H) coniunguntur (+ bonis
pr), melius erit quam ut sint ipsi recipientes dispositionem, id est, ut ipsi
mali pulsent (pulsant MST) et iungantur eis.

4. EN-text: –

5. *Liber trium iudicum*: Nonusdecimus, quando infortunia questionum
dominia possederint, eisque dominus orientis aut Luna adversa figura
applicat, persolvent quidem quesita set laboriose. Unde melius *fortunatis*
applicare illicque ducatum contingere.

6. *Liber novem iudicum*: 20, quando infortunia dominia *possident in questione*, eisque dominus orientis aut Luna adversa figura applicet, persolvent quidem quesita set laboriose. Unde melius *est infortunia fortunis*
applicare illicque ducatum contingere.

7. Abraham Ibn Ezra: xix. If the lords of the object of the query are malefics,

the lord of the ascendant sign applies to them, and the Moon is in quartile or opposition, then, if the requested event takes place, its outcome will be inauspicious.

8. Henry Bate's translation: .19m. Si malivoli fuerint domini rei quesite, et coniungatur eis dominus ascendentis et Luna aspectu quarto vel opposito; etsi (si Gl) quidem evenerit res quesita, finis tamen eius malus erit.

9. Pietro d'Abano's translation: Si fuerint mali domini rei quesite, et eis dominus ascendentis coniungatur et Luna aspectu .4°. aut opposito, finis erit malus ques/pr xxvi^{vb}/iti.

10. *Gloucester Text*: 18 Nocivus planeta quando rerum *que queruntur ab homine* prefectus fuerit et dominus signi orientalis vel Luna illum respexerit quatuor angulis vel ab opposito, rerum adversatur eventui, nec bonum exitum eis largitur.

20

1.

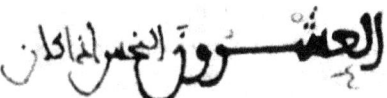

Fol. 48^v

العشرون النحس إذا كان في الطالع في (- الطالع في LD) بيته أو شرفه كفّ عن الشر إلا
أن (+ ان L) يكون راجعا في الطالع فإذا رجع اشتدت منحسته وكثر اختلاطه

2. The twentieth. When the malefic is in the ascendant (- in the ascendant LD) in its house or its exaltation, it is restrained from harm unless it is retrograding in the ascendant. When it retrogrades its harming is strengthened and its mixing is multiplied.

3. John of Seville: /P p. 443a/ Vicesimum (.17. M). Malus cum fuerit in ascendente in domo sua (i.d.s.i.a. H) aut (-- M) in exaltatione, refrenatur a malo, nisi ipse sit (s.i. MS) retrogradus in ascendente (- n.i.s.r.i.a. pr). Si autem (+ ipse sit pr) retrogradus fuerit (- fuerit pr) *in ascendente*, confortatur eius malum et multiplicatur eius diversitas *ac variatio* (varietas ac diversitas H; 'diversitas *ac variatio*' implies اختلافه rather than اختلاطه).

4. EN-text: –

5. *Liber trium iudicum*: Vigesimus, quoniam infortunium si in oriente fuerit idque domicilium aut principatus eius, sit mitius, nisi forte retrogradum fuerit, idque gravissimum perhibent.

6. *Liber novem iudicum*: 21, quoniam infortunium si in oriente fuerit idque domicilium aut principatus sit eius, *fit* mitius, nisi forte retrogradum fuerit, id *enim* gravissimum perhibent.

7. Abraham Ibn Ezra: xx If the malefic is in the sign of the ascendant and it has some lordship there, its harm is lessened, but if it is retrograde, the harm is redoubled.

8. Henry Bate's translation: .20m. Si fuerit malivolus in ascendente, et habuerit in eo dignitatem aliquam, alleviabitur eius malitia, sed si fuerit retrogradus, malum super malum addetur.

9. Pietro d'Abano's translation: Si fuerit in ascendente (aspectu pr) malus et in eo aliquam habeat dignitatem, minuetur de suo malo.

10. *Gloucester Text*: 19 Quando planeta nocivus in signo orientali fuerit et signum illud domus vel honos eius sit, planeta nocivus a mala significatione retrahitur, nisi retrogradus fuerit. Nocivus planeta quando retrogradatur, malum suum et adversitas augmentatur.

21

1.

الحادي وعشرون الكوكب إذا كان في شكله من البروج (البرج LD) فهو (+ له LD)
موافق أعني أن يكون زحل في بيته أو (+ في D) شرفه أو في برج (بارد L) بارد ويكون
المريخ يعني (على DL) ما وصفت (+ أو L) في برج حار فإذا كان على (في LD) خلاف
طبيعته فهو له (- D) رديء مثل الماء والزين (الزيت LD) الذي يخلط (يختلط DL) ولا
يمتزج وإذا كان في برج مشاكل له امتزج بمنزلة الماء واللبن.

2. The twenty-first. When the planet is in its form among the signs, then it is fitting (+ for it LD), i.e., when Saturn is in its house or its exaltation or in a cold sign, and Mars according to what I described in a hot sign. But when it is what is opposite to its nature, then it is bad for it, like water and oil which are combined and do not mix. If it is a sign of the same form as it, they mix like water and milk.

3. John of Seville: Vicesimumprimum (-- M). Planeta cum fuerit in suo *habitu ac* similitudine ex signis, erit ei conveniens, id est, si fuerit Saturnus in domo (+ sua M) aut in exaltatione sua aut in signo frigido, et fuerit Mars sicut predixi tibi, et (- H) in signo calido, erit bonum. Si vero fuerit in contrarietate suæ naturæ, erit ei malum, sicut aqua et oleum, que *non* commiscentur neque conplectuntur. Et si fuerit in signo (+ **sibi** HSpr) simili, commiscetur (-entur pr) *et complectitur* (complectetur HMS, complectuntur pr) sicut (sic pr) aqua et lac.

4. EN-text: –

5. *Liber trium iudicum*: Vigesimusprimus, quoniam stellam pro modo suo in signis consistere non parum iuvat, ut Saturnus in domicilio aut principatu suo sive in frigidis signis, Mars item in domicilio aut principatu suo, sive in signis calidis. Solent enim contraria nonnumquam nocere.

6. *Liber novem iudicum*: 39 est quod stellam *ad modum suum* in signis consistere non *modicum* iuvat, ut Saturnus in domicilio aut principatu suo sive in signis frigidis, Mars *vero itidem* in domicilio aut principatu suo, sive in signis calidis *commoretur*. Solent enim contraria *adversari* nonnumquam.

7. Abraham Ibn Ezra: xxxviii If a planet is in a sign that corresponds to its nature, its power is increased, but if its nature is opposed ⟨to the sign's nature⟩, it is weakened; e.g., Saturn in a sign that is cold and dry.

8. Henry Bate's translation: .38m. Si fuerit planeta in signo simili nature sue, augetur eius fortitudo; si vero in contrario nature eius, debilitatur, ut Saturnus in domo frigida et sicca.

9. Pietro d'Abano's translation: Planeta si fuerit cum eius natura, augmentabitur virtus eius. Si vero cum contrario, debilitabitur, sicut Saturnus in domo frigida et sicca.

10. *Gloucester Text*: 20 Quando planeta in signo sibi convenienti fuerit, ut si Saturnus fuerit in domo sua vel honore vel in signo frigido, vel si Mars in domo sua vel honore vel in signo calido fuerit, *tunc signum illud planete illi convenit*. Si vero in signis sue nature contrariis fuerint, nocivi sunt, veluti si aqua oleo commisceatur: utrum alii incommixtum in propria perseverat natura. Set si fuerint in signo sibi convenienti, sicut si aqua lacti adunetur (condunetur MS), commiscentur.

22

1. In text and margin:

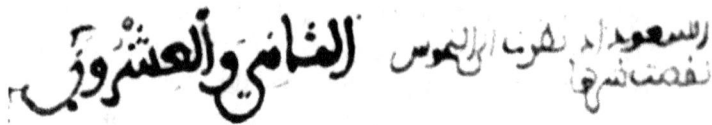

الثاني والعشرون السعود إذا نظرت إلى النحوس نقصت (+ من LD) شرها

2. The twenty-second. The benefics, when they aspect the malefics, decrease their harm.

3. John of Seville: /H 25ʳ/ Vicesimumsecundum (.18. M). Fortunæ quando aspiciunt malos minuunt eorum impedimentum.

4. EN-text: –

5. *Liber trium iudicum*: Vigesimussecundus, respectus benivolarum malivolas mitigant.

6. *Liber novem iudicum*: *9 vero est talis*: respectus benivolarum malivolas *mitigat*.

7. Abraham Ibn Ezra: xi If benefic planets aspect malefics, they diminish their harm.

8. Henry Bate's translation: .11m. Planete benevoli, si malivolos aspiciant, diminuetur eorum malitia.

9. Pietro d'Abano's translation: *Planeta denotans omne quod eventurum est in esse nisi aspiciat ascendens, non perficietur perfecte spes querentis.* Boni si aspexerunt malos minuunt eorum malitiam.

10. *Gloucester Text*: 21 Quando planeta propitius nocivum *a sex vel tribus angulis* respicit, adversitatem eius diminuit.

23

1. In marg.

المسلمات والعشرون

In text:

الثالث والعشرون النحوس إذا نظرت إلى السعود من تربيع أو مقابلة نقصت من سعادتها.

2.   The twenty-third. When the malefics aspect the benefics from quartile or opposition, they decrease their good fortune.

3.   John of Seville: Vicesimum .iii. (.19. (?) M). Mali quando aspiciunt fortunas a quarto aspectu vel ab oppositione, minuunt eorum fortunam.

4.   EN-text: –

5.   *Liber trium iudicum*: Vigesimustertius, *contra*. Quoniam infortuniorum respectus de adversa figura fortunatis nocent.

6.   *Liber novem iudicum*: 23, *quod* infortuniorum respectus de adversa figura fortunatis *nocet.*

7.   Abraham Ibn Ezra: xxi If a malefic aspects a benefic in quartile or opposition, it reduces its good fortune.

8.   Henry Bate's translation: .21m. Si aspexerit malivolum aspectu quarto, diminuetur de bono eius.

9.   Pietro d'Abano's translation: Si malus .4°. aspectu aspiciat, diminuetur ex eius bono.

10. *Gloucester Text*: 22 Quando planeta propitius *in aliquo quatuor locorum a quibus signum oriens non possit respicere*, fuerit ...

24

1.

الرابع والعشرون السعود إذا كانت ساقطة عن الطالع أو راجعة كانت فاسدة بمنزلة
النحوس.

2.   The twenty-fourth. When the benefics are falling from the ascendant, or retrograde, they are harmed, like the malefics.

3.   John of Seville: Vicesimum .iiii. (.20. M). Fortunæ cum fuerint cadentes ab ascendente aut retrogradæ, erunt impeditæ, similes malorum.

4.   EN-text: –

5.   *Liber trium iudicum*: Vigesimusquartus, quoniam fortunate /D 55ᵛ/ si averse fuerint et retrograde, equum fere est infortuniis.

6.   *Liber novem iudicum*: 17 est quoniam *benivole* si adverse fuerint et retrograde, equum fere est infortuniis.

7.   Abraham Ibn Ezra: –

8.   Henry Bate's translation: –

9.   Pietro d'Abano's translation: –

10. *Gloucester Text*: ... vel item si retrogradus fuerit, idem ac si nocivus fuerit significat.

25

1.

الخامس والعشرون الكوكب إذا كان مقبولا وكان سعدا كان أقوم له وإن كان نحسا
كان أقوى بضره (لضرره DL).

2. The twenty-fifth. When the planet is received and is a benefic, it is stronger for it. And if it is a malefic it is stronger in its harm.

3. John of Seville: Vicesimum .v. (.21. M). Planetæ cum fuerint recepti in domo alterius vel exaltatione (- **in d.a.v.e.** HMSTpr), et fuerint fortunæ, recepti (- **HMSTpr**), erit eis (post M, eorum bonum pr) fortius (fortis pr). Et si fuerint mali, erit fortius eorum impedimentum (f.e.i.] **eorum impedimentum minus** pr).

4. EN-text: –

5. *Liber trium iudicum*: Vigesimusquintus, quod (*corr. ex* quoniam) stella recepta si fortunata est, addit bono, si infortunium, malum minuit.

6. *Liber novem iudicum*: 10 *quidem* stella recepta si fortunata est, addit in bono, si *malivola*, **malum** *diminuit*.

7. Abraham Ibn Ezra: xxxix A planet that is received: if it is a benefic, its good fortune is increased, and if a malefic, **its misfortune is lessened**.

8. Henry Bate's translation: .39m. Planeta receptus, si est benivolus, augmentatur eius fortitudo, et si nocivus, alleviabitur malum eius.

9. Pietro d'Abano's translation: Planeta receptus, si fuerit fortuna, augmentabitur (augmentatur pr) fortitudo sua. Si vero malus, diminuetur ex malo suo (ex eius malo pr).

10. *Gloucester Text*: –

26

1.

السادس والعشرون النحوس إذا كانت في برج غريب أعني إذا لم تكن في بيتها ولا شرفها
ولا مثلثها (مثلها E) فإنها تزيد في الشر وتعظم منحستها وإن كانت في برج لها فيه شهادة
كفّت عن الشر و (ولكن LD) لا بد من مضرة.

2. The twenty-sixth. When the malefics are in an alien sign, i.e., when they are not in their house, their exaltation and their triplicity, they increase in badness, and their harm gets greater. If they are in a sign in which they have a testimony, they are averted from badness but some damage cannot be avoided.

3. John of Seville: Vicesimum .vi. (.22. M). Planetæ mali cum fuerint in signo peregrino, id est (i.e.] et pr), cum non (- P) fuerint in domibus suis nec in exaltatione nec in triplicitate, augent malum et magnificatur eorum impedimentum. Et cum fuerint in signis in quibus habent testimonium, refrenantur (refrenatur T) a malo et non (- HSpr) omnino (+ non pr) erit impedimentum.

4. EN-text: –

5. *Liber trium iudicum*: Vigesimussextus, infortunia in signis esse quorum prorsus sint experti⟨a⟩, mali augmentum. Si enim aliquam illic *dignitatem* obtinuerint, minus quidem adversum, non tamen penitus malorum sunt immunia.

6. *Liber novem iudicum*: *24 est quod* infortunia in signis esse quorum /V 11ʳᵇ/ prorsus sint *expertia*, mali est augmentum. Si enim aliquam dignitatem *ibi* obtinuerint, minus quidem adversum, non tamen penitus malorum sunt immunia.

7. Abraham Ibn Ezra: xxiii If the malefic is a stranger in its position, its misfortune is increased.

8. Henry Bate's translation: 23m.(22 Gl) Si malivolus peregrinus fuerit in loco in quo est, tunc multiplicabitur eius malitia.

9. Pietro d'Abano's translation: Si fuerit malus *extraneus vel* (- extraneus vel pr) peregrinus a loco suo (- a loco suo pr) augebitur (+ eius pr) malitia.

10. *Gloucester Text*: 23 Quando planeta nocivus in signo alieno fuerit, id est, in signo in quo nullam habet dignitatem, quod scilicet non sit domo, honore *vel gaudio vel visu* vel trinitate *vel diffinitione*, tunc malum et eius adversitas augmentatur. Quando /74ʳ/ vero in signo fuerit in quo aliquam habet dignitatem, adversitas sua minuitur.

27

1.

وهوته لله وهله

الســابع والعشرون ** والعشرون النحس إذا كان في بيته أو شرفه أو مثلثته أو حده وهو في (- L) الأوتاد
إ قونه لقول السعود بأمهم

أو ما يلي الأوتاد فإن قوته كقوة السعود فافهم (+ ما وصفت لك LD).

2. The twenty-seventh. When a malefic is in its house or its exaltation, its triplicity or its term, and it is in the cardines or what follows the cardines, its power is like the power of the benefics. And know this (**what I have told you** LD)!

3. John of Seville: Vicesimum .vii. (.23. M). Mali cum fuerint in domibus suis (- HMST) et fuerint domini rerum (- **et f.d.r.** HT) aut in exaltationibus (- a.i.e. T) aut in triplicitatibus (+ suis M) vel (aut HSTpr) in terminis suis, et in angulis (+ in quibus est M) vel in sequentibus angulorum, erit fortitudo eorum sicut fortitudo fortunarum. Intellige quod dixi (+ **tibi HMSTpr**).

4. EN-text: –

5. *Liber trium iudicum*: Vigesimusseptimus. Infortunia in quacumque dignitatum .v. ut simul in cardine sive post cardinem sint, *libera*, fortunatis fere equipara⟨n⟩t.

6. *Liber novem iudicum*: 25 quod infortunia in quacumque dignitatum, *sunt enim numero quinque*, simul in cardine *vel* post cardinem si fuerint, libera, fortunatis fere equiparant.

7. Abraham Ibn Ezra: xxii If a malefic is in a position where it exerts lordship and is in one of the cardines or succedent places, its power is considered to be like the power of the benefics.

8. Henry Bate's translation: .22m. Si fuerit malivolus in loco dignitatis sue, in aliquo angulorum aut succedentium, computanda est eius fortitudo quemadmodum fortitudo planete benevoli (Gl omits this precept).

9. Pietro d'Abano's translation: Si fuerit malus in loco sue dignitatis et fuerit in uno angulorum aut succedentium, *omnino* (- pr) numeratur eius fortitudo velud bonorum est (- pr) fortitudo.

10. *Gloucester Text*: 24 Quando nocivus planeta in domo vel in honore suo vel in aliqua suarum dignitatum est, et fuerit in aliqua quatuor columnarum, vel in aliqua quatuor secus columnas, malum et sua adversitas adnichilatur. Et idem acsi propitius esset significat.

28

1.

الثامن والعشرون السعود إذا كانت (إذا كانت السعود L) في برج ليس لها فيه شهادة (+
نقصت (+ من L) سعادتها وخيره وإذا كانت في برج لها فيه شهادة LD) أعني بيتا أو شرفا
أو مثلثة أو حدا تعظم سعادتها ويتمّ الأمر ويزيد الخير.

2. The twenty-eighth. When the benefics are in a sign in which they have no testimony, they decrease in their good fortune and goodness. And when they are in a sign in which they have a testimony, i.e., a house or an exaltation or a triplicity or a term, their good fortune is magnified, the matter is completed and the good increases.

3. John of Seville: Vicesimum.viii. (.24. M). Fortunæ cum fuerint in signo in quo non habent testimonium, minuitur eorum fortuna (f.e. S) ac (ad HM) bonum. Et cum fuerint in signo in quo est illis testimonium (testimonium est illis M), id est, in domibus vel (+ in MST) exaltationibus aut (vel M) triplicitatibus vel /P p. 443b/ terminis suis, magnificatur eorum (earum pr) fortuna et (ac pr) perficitur (+ eorum S) res atque augetur bonum.

4. EN-text: –

5. *Liber trium iudicum*: Vigesimusoctavus, fortunate in signis atque dignitatibus alienis minus potentes. Dignitas enim propria addit et corroborat.

6. *Liber novem iudicum*: 11 *quod* fortunate in signis *et* dignitatibus alienis minus potentes *sunt*. Dignitas *etenim* propria addit *atque* corroborat.

7. Abraham Ibn Ezra: –

8. Henry Bate's translation: –

9. Pietro d'Abano's translation: –

10. *Gloucester Text*: 25 Quando planeta propitius in aliquo signo fuerit in quo nullam virtutem habet, sue significationis virtus debilitatur. Quando vero bonum significaverit, non omnino illud, *vel si malum iterum non omino illud*.

29

1.

التاسع والعشرون إذا كانت النحوس والسعود (السعود والنحوس LD) في موضع رديء
أعني في أحد العيوب (البيوت L) التي وصفت (+ لك D) أو تحت الشعاع محترقة دلت
على أن الأمور صغيرة حقيرة (حقيرة صغيرة LD) ولم يستطع الكوكب (+ أن DL) يدل
على خير ولا شر لما هو فيه من الضعف لأن الكوكب إذا كان تحت الشعاع محترقا أو في

مقابلة الشمس فهو ضعيف لأن هذا المكان لا خير فيه للسعود ولا للنحوس لأن السعود

تدل على قلة الخير إذا كانت تحت الشعاع وكذلك النحوس إذا كانت تحت الشعاع كان

(كانت L) أقل لخيرها (لشرها DL).

2. The twenty-ninth. When the malefics and the benefics are in a bad place—i.e., in one of the defects (houses L) that I have described—or burnt under the rays, they indicate that the matters are small and paltry, and the planet is not able to indicate good and bad because of the weakness that is in it, because the planet, when it is burnt under the rays or in opposition to the Sun, is weak, because there is no good in this place for the benefics or the malefics, because the benefics indicate smallness of good when they are under the rays. And likewise for the malefics when they are under the rays, there is less of their harm.

3. John of Seville: Vicesimum .ix. (.25. M). Cum fuerint fortunæ et mali (f.e.m.f. M) in loco maligno—id est, in aliqua domorum (implying بيوت) quas prædixi—aut fuerint sub radiis combusti, significant (-cat M) res parvas et despicabiles, et non poterunt planetæ significare bonum vel malum præ debilitate (propter debilitatem Mpr) quæ est in eis, quia planeta cum fuerit (corr. ex fuerint H) sub radiis combustus aut in oppositione Solis, erit debilis, quia in hoc loco *nulla utilitas nec* aliquid boni est bonis planetis neque (+ aliquid mali Hpr) malis (- neque malis M), quia fortunæ significant modicum boni cum fuerint sub radiis, et mali similiter cum fuerint sub radiis, erit minus eorum impedimentum.

4. EN-text: –

5. *Liber trium iudicum*: Vigesimusnonus, quoniam tam fortunate quam infortunia pro locis adversis adversa, qualia sunt *signorum fines* et sub Sole locata. *Hic enim si ducatum obtinuerint,* humile rerum genus designant, neque ipse tam bonum malumve sic consum⟨m⟩are valebunt. Debilitat siquidem adustio, sicut et Solis oppositio, ut nec benivolarum affectus neque noxiarum ira prevaleat.

6. *Liber novem iudicum*: 12 quoniam tam fortunate quam infortunia pro locis adversis adversa *nuntiant*, qualia sunt *videlicet* signorum fines et Sub sole locata. Hic enim si ducatum obtinueri⟨n⟩t, humile rerum genus designant, neque ipse item bonum malumve sic consum⟨m⟩are valebunt. Debilitat siquidem adustio, sicut et Solis oppositio, ut nec benivolarum *effectus* neque noxiarum ira prevaleat.

7. Abraham Ibn Ezra: xvii If the benefics and the malefics are in an inauspicious position or are burnt, they signify an ignoble thing; because of their weakness, they will not cause good fortune or harm.

8. Henry Bate's translation: .17m. Cum fuerint planete boni et mali in locis malis vel combusti,⟨⟨...⟩⟩ necque bonum faciunt necque malum propter debilitatem.

9. Pietro d'Abano's translation: Fortune et mali, si fuerint in locis infortunatis aut combusti, nec bonum nec malum causant, propter eorum debilitatem.

10. *Gloucester Text*: –

30

1.

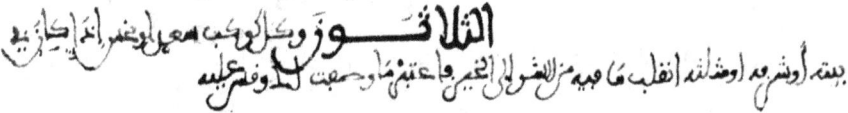

الثلاثون و(- D) كل كوكب سعد أو نحس إذا كان في بيته أو شرفه أو مثلثته انقلب ما

فيه من الشر إلى الخير فاعتبر ما (بما L) وصفت لك وقس عليه.

2. The thirtieth. And every benefic or malefic planet, when it is in its house or exaltation or triplicity, changes the bad that is in it to good. So, be warned of what I have described to you, and measure/make analogies according to it.

3. John of Seville: Tricesimum (.26. M). Et omnis planeta fortuna aut malus cum fuerit in domo sua aut in (- pr) exaltatione (+ sua MT) aut in triplicitate sua (-- M) *et cetera*, convertitur (**convertit** S, avertitur pr) quicquid in eis est ex malo in bonum. Ammirare (Admi- HS) ergo quod dixi tibi et ab eo accipe mensuram (+ iudicandi pr).

4. EN-text: –

5. *Liber trium iudicum*: Trigesimus (*corr. ex* tricesimus *passim*), super omnia servandum quotiens utrumque genus stellarum in domicilio aut principatu sive trigono suo fuerit, magnopere siquidem boni fert restaurationem.

6. *Liber novem iudicum*: 40, super omnia servandum quotiens utrumque genus stellarum *in domo aut regno seu* trigono fuerit, magno opere siquidem boni fert restaurationem.

7. Abraham Ibn Ezra: xxvii Every planet, whether benefic or malefic, always signifies good fortune if it is in its house or in the house of its exaltation.

8. Henry Bate's translation: –

9. Pietro d'Abano's translation: –

10. *Gloucester Text*: 26 Quislibet planeta sive bonus sive malus quando in

domo sua vel honore vel aliqua suarum dignitatum fuerit, si bonum significat, prosperitas eius augmentatur, si malum, adversitas eius minuitur.

31

1.

الحادي والثلاثون النحوس إذا كانت في (- L، ساقطة عن D) أوتاد الطالع و (أو DL) نحست من تربيع أو مقابلة فإنها رديئة قوية على الشر وهي أعظم ما يكون بينه (بلية L، بابه D) وبخاصّة (وخاصّة LD) إذا كانت قاهرة الكوكب (للكواكب DL) الذي يُحسها (التي منتحسه L، التي تُحسه D) أعني إذا (إن D) كانت أقوى من الكوكب فإذا (فأما إذا LD) انصرف (انصرفت LD) من تثليث أو تسديس كفّت عن الشر ونقصت من منحستها.

2. The thirty-first. When the malefics are in cardines of the ascendant and harm from quartile or opposition, then they are bad, strong to harm, and they are as great as possible in affliction, particularly when they are overcoming the planet (planets LD) which they harm, i.e., when they are more powerful than the planet. Then, when they separate from trine or sextile aspect, they are averted from harm and they decrease from harming.

3. John of Seville: Tricesimumprimum (.27. M). Mali cum fuerint in angulis ascendentis et impedierint a quarto *aspectu* vel ab (- H) oppositione, erunt mali, fortes ad nocendum, et maior (malorum T) erit eorum (eorum erit HSpr, – M) afflictio, *et maxime* ac proprie si fuerint fortiores planeta quem opprimunt (obp- M) *vel impediunt*, id est, si fuerint *in loco* fortiori (s.f.i.l.f.] si habuerint aliquam dignitatem pr). Set si aspexerint (-erit M; implying نظرت) a trino vel a sextili aspectu, refrenantur a malo et minuitur eorum impedimentum.

4. EN-text: –

5. *Liber trium iudicum*: Trigesimusprimus, infortunia in cardinibus posita, aut stellas in cardinibus sitas corrumpentia, *adversi* potentia, magisque si ipsa fuerint fortiora, non tamen de prospera figura adeo perniciosa.

6. *Liber novem iudicum*: 26, infortunia in cardinibus posita, aut stellas in cardinibus sitas corrumpentia, *diversi* potentia, magis si ipsa fuerint *fortunata*, non tamen de prospera figura adeo perniciosa sunt.

7.   Abraham Ibn Ezra: xxiv The malefic, if it is in one of the cardines or if it
     harms a planet from quartile or opposition, then its misfortune is abso-
     lute, particularly if it is stronger than the ⟨other⟩ planet; but in trine or
     sextile its misfortune is lessened.[18]

8.   Henry Bate's translation: .24m. Si fuerit malivolus in aliquo angulorum,
     damnificetque planetam aspectu quarto vel opposito, tunc perfecta erit
     eius malitia, et eo plus si fortior fuerit illo planeta; per aspectum aut
     trinum vel sextilem alleviabitur eius malitia.

9.   Pietro d'Abano's translation: Si fuerit planeta (- S) malus in aliquo angu-
     lorum aut infortunet planetam aspectu .4. vel opposito, perficietur tunc
     eius malitia, magis quoque si fuerit fortior planeta; aspectus tamen eius
     (- pr) sextilis (.8[us].21[us] S) aut trinus eius diminuit nocumentum.

10. *Gloucester Text*: 27 Quando novicus planeta in aliqua .4. columnarum celi
     fuerit vel quando nocivus planeta planetam quemlibet sive bonum sive
     malum respicit a quatuor angulis, vel ab opposito vel ei coniungitur, *id
     est, quod cum eo in eodem signo fuerit*, adversitate plenus est, et virtutem
     nimiam nocendi habet. Augmentatur eius adversitas si *planeta qui eum
     respicit eo fortior est*. Set si a tribus vel a sex angulis respiciatur, adversitas
     eius debilitatur.

32

1.

الثاني والثلاثون السعد (السعيد LD) لا يدل أبدا (أبدا لا يدل LD) إلا على السعادة

والنحس لا يدل أبدا (أبدا لا يدل LD) إلا على الشر لإفراطه في طبيعته وجور (جوّز

LD) امتزاجه فينبغي أن ينظر إلى موضع الكوكب أعني (+ إلى LD) موضعا من الطالع

والبرج الذي يكون فيه فإن الكوكب وإن كان نحسا وكان في حيزه (- حيزه D) وضوء

نفسه (+ أو في بيت نفسه أو شرفه L؛ + أي حيزه أي نهاري فوق الأفق أو ليلي تحت

الأفق أو في بيت شرفه D) أو مثلثته أو موضع جيد من الطالع دل على الخير.

---

18   Ibn Ezra's judgement xxv has no equivalent among the *50 Precepts*.

2. The thirty-second. The benefic never indicates other than good fortune, and the malefic does not indicate other than harm, because of its excess in its nature and the badness of its mixture. So it is necessary that one looks at the place of the planet, i.e., its place in relation to the ascendant, and to the sign in which it is, and that the planet, although it is a malefic, ⟨if it⟩ is in its domain (- domain D) and its own light, (+ or its own house or its exaltation L) or its triplicity or a good place from the ascendant, it indicates the good.

3. John of Seville: Tricesimum.ii. (.18. M). Fortuna non significat semper nisi (non T) fortunam, et ma/H 25ᵛ/lus non (nihil pr) significat semper nisi malum, propter superfluitatem naturæ illius et malignitatem eius complexionis. Oportet ergo aspicere loca planetarum, id est, loca eorum ab ascendente, et signa in quibus fuerint, quia licet sit planeta malus (+ tantum H), *tamen si* fuerit in similitudine sua vel in suo lumine aut in domo vel (aut M) exaltatione seu triplicitate sua aut in loco bono ab ascendente, significat bonum.

4. EN-text: –

5. *Liber trium iudicum*: .xxxiiᵘˢ., fortunate semper bonorum duces, infortunia malorum. *Non tamen simplex hec est sententie via*, set coniunctio quidem de eis orienti accedat, quidve de ipsis orienti attineat.

6. *Liber novem iudicum: 13 est quod* fortunate bonorum semper sunt duces, infortunia malorum. Non tamen simplex *haberi debet* hec via, si *hoc adiuncto* quod de *illis ad oriens* accedat, quidve *ipsis de oriente* attineat.

7. Abraham Ibn Ezra: xii The benefics always signify good fortune and the malefics harm; if the malefic is in its greatest strength it signifies good fortune, *but it will come with toil and sadness.*

8. Henry Bate's translation: 12m. Boni planete semper bonum significant, et mali planete (- Gl) malum; si *tamen* malus fuerit in fortitudine sua magna, significabit bonum, sed per laborem veniet et per (- Gl) tristitiam.

9. Pietro d'Abano's translation: Fortune semper bonum denotant, mali autem malum. Set si fuerit malus in sua grandi potestate, bonum denotabit, /S 92ʳᵇ/ erit tamen cum tribulatione et pena.

10. *Gloucester Text*: 28 Planeta propitius semper bonum significat, nocivus semper malum, quia cuiuslibet boni vel mali natura perfecta est. Notandum est quod locus planete semper considerandus est qualiter scilicet se habet ad oriens signum vel ad signum in quo est. Si enim planeta nocivus in bono signo fuerit, id est, in quo aliquam habet dignitatem vel a quo signum oriens bono respectu respiciatur, non significat malum. *Planeta propitius, quando in loco est in quo nullam habet dignitatem vel in alieno signo vel in signo quod malo respectu signum oriens respiciat, vel si sub*

*Solis claritate fuerit, non significat bonum, set malum sua pervertitur signi-
ficatio.*

33

1.

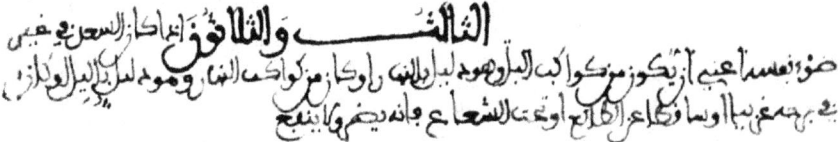

الثالث والثلاثون إذا (وإن L؛ إن D) كان السعد في غير ضوء (ضوء غير LD) نفسه أعني أن

يكون من كواكب الليل وهو دليل بالنهار أو كان (- LD) من كواكب النهار وهو دليل

بالليل أو كان في برجه غريبا (برج غريب LD) أو ساقطا عن الطالع أو تحت الشعاع فإنه

يضر ولا ينفع.

2. The thirty-third. When the benefic is not in its own light, i.e., if it is one
of the planets of the night and it is an indicator of the day, or it is one of
the planets of the day and it is an indicator of the night, or it is an alien
in its sign, or falling from the ascendant or under the rays, then it harms
and does not help.

3. John of Seville: Tricesimum.iii. (.29. M). Fortuna si non fuerit in lumine
suo, id est, si fuerit ex planetis noctis et fuerit significator in die aut fuerit
ex planetis diei et fuerit significator in (-- M) nocte, aut fuerit peregrinus
in (a pr) signo suo (- H) vel cadens ab ascendente aut sub radiis, impedit
et non proficit (perficit M).

4. EN-text: –

5. *Liber trium iudicum*: .xxxiii[us]., quoniam benivole si expertes fuerint *tam
dignitatum* quam naturalis lucis, aduste (*supra*: annoubarat[19] dicit), ut
diei diurne, noctis nocturne, simul et adverse vel, boni expertes.

6. *Liber novem iudicum*: *14 est* quoniam benivole si expertes fuerint tam dignitatum quam naturalis luminis, *quod annoubharat dicunt*, ut *videlicet*
diei diurne, noctis nocturne, simul *etiam* et adverse et aduste, boni *penitus* expertes.

---

19   The Arabic word is probably *al-nawba* ('the alternation (between day and night)'), but the
transliteration suggests a confusion with *al-nawbahrāt* ('the ninth parts (of a sign of the
zodiac))': al-Qabīṣī (Alcabitius), *Introduction to* Astrology, eds C. Burnett, K. Yamamoto
and M. Yano, London 2004, 4 [16].

7. Abraham Ibn Ezra: xiii If the benefics are opposite their similitude, or
    in the house of their dejection, or in the house of their detriment, or in
    cadent places that do not aspect each other or the ascendant sign, they
    are not beneficial at all.[20]

8. Henry Bate's translation: .13m. Si fuerint boni ⟨⟨...⟩⟩ in domo casus sui
    aut in domo odii vel in domibus cadentibus et non sit aspectus inter eos
    (ipsos Gl) et ascendens (ascensus Gl), non (nichil Gl) valebunt.

9. Pietro d'Abano's translation: Si fuerit fortuna in suo dedecore aut in
    occasu, *id est, in opposito sue domus* (-- i.e.i.o.s.d. pr) aut in cadenti domo
    (- pr) nec aspiciens (+ scilicet pr) ascendens, nullius erit valoris.

10. *Gloucester Text:* –

34

1.

الرابع وثلاثون السعد (السعد] والمشتري LD) إذا نظر إلى النحس حوّل طبيعته إلى الخير

و(ي و L) الزهرة لا تقدر (تقدم D) على (+ تحويل LD) الشيء العظيم إلا أن تناظر

(يناظرD) المشتري (+ المشتري يحل نحوسة زحل والمريخ، أما الزهرة فلا تقدر على تحويل

زحل لأنه أثقل منها إلا أن يتصل به المشتري كذلك D) والمشتري يحل ما يعقده زحل

أعني أن المشتري إذا اتصل بزحل كسر منحسته وفعله (وثقله LD) والزهرة تحل ما يعقد

المريخ.

2. The thirty-fourth. When a benefic (Jupiter LD) aspects a malefic it turns
    its nature into good. And Venus is not powerful over (+ changing LD) any-
    thing great unless it aspects Jupiter. (+ And Jupiter releases the badness
    of Saturn and Mars. As for Venus, it is not powerful over changing Sat-
    urn because it is heavier than her, unless Jupiter applies to it D). And (+
    in such a way D) Jupiter releases what Saturn has tied, i.e., that Jupiter,
    when it applies to Saturn, breaks its harm and its action (heaviness LD).
    And Venus releases what Mars has tied.

---

20 Ibn Ezra's judgements xiv and xv have no equivalent among the *50 Precepts*.

3. John of Seville: Tricesimum.iiii. (.30. M). Iupiter, cum aspex/P p. 444a/erit
    malum, vertit (mutat pr) naturam suam in bonum. Et Venus, non (si P)
    poterit (potest MSTpr) vertere (+ malum Saturni H) rem (- MT) magnam
    (rem magnam] in re magna H, + id est, malum Saturni prS *supra*) nisi
    aspiciat (aspiciant pr) Iovem. Iupiter enim solvit quod nodat (non dat
    MST) Saturnus, id est, si Iupiter iungitur Saturno, frangit eius (-- M, suam
    underscored T) malitiam (malitiam eius pr) et mutat eam (implying قبله),
    et Venus solvit quod nodat (non dat MT) Mars.

4. EN-text: –

5. *Liber trium iudicum*: xxxiiii[us]., Iupiter infortunium respiciens mitigat.
    Nam Venus nisi Iove adiuncta magnis (*corr. ex* magis) malorum viribus
    prevalet. Iupiter quippe si Saturno applicat, nodos illius solvit, sic Venus
    Martis.

6. *Liber novem iudicum*: *15 est quod* Iupiter infortunium respiciens miti-
    gat. Nam Venus nisi Iovi adiuncta magnis malorum viribus *non* prevalet.
    Iupiter quippe Saturno applicans, nodos illius *dissolvit, nam et* Venus Mar-
    tis.

7. Abraham Ibn Ezra: xvi If Jupiter aspects a malefic, it changes its nature
    for good, but Venus cannot change Saturn's nature without Jupiter's assis-
    tance. Jupiter removes Saturn's harm, but Venus removes Mars's harm
    more than Jupiter does.

8. Henry Bate's translation: 16m. Si aspexerit Iupiter aspicientem (ascenden-
    tem Gl), convertet naturam eius ad bonum; sed Venus auferre non potest
    malum Saturni nisi cum auxilio Iovis; Iupiter autem malum aufert Sat-
    urni, et Venus malum aufert Martis melius quam Iupiter.

9. Pietro d'Abano's translation: Si Iupiter aspiciat aspicientem (- pr), malum,
    convertet eius naturam in bonum *vel mutabit* (- vel mutabit pr). Venus
    autem non potest nocumentum removere Saturni, nisi adiuta (iuvata
    pr) sit a Iove. Set ipse removet nocumentum Saturni et Venus Martis
    meliusque Iove.

10. *Gloucester Text*: 29 Quando Iupiter nocivum respicit planetam amico
    respectu, de malo in bonum suam mutat naturam. Venus autem magnam
    nocivi planete adversitatem deprimere non potest. Iupiter solvet quod
    ligat Saturnus, id est, quando Iupiter amico respectu complicatur Saturno,
    adversitatem suam diminuit. Venus solvit quod ligat Mars.

35

1.

وهذا بابامزج هذه الأشياء،

Fol. 49ʳ:

لحاك ز نحم نيومہ الغمر وانہ يتحول غسافعل شرالال الشرولمذاكان ز سعدا بيومہ ان الغمر اجب بحرالجّمخشیّن

الخامس وثلاثون إذا كان نحس يدفع إلى نحس فإنه يتحوّل نحسا (- يتحوّل نحسا DL) نقل
(ينقل L) شرا (شر D) إلى شر (+ وإذا كان نحس يدفع إلى سعد فإنه يتحول من الشر إلى
الخير وإذا كان سعد يدفع إلى سعد فهو (- L) نقل خير إلى خير DL) وإذا كان سعد يدفع
إلى نحس أصاب بعد الخير شرا وهكذا فامزج (فامتزج L؛ فاشرح D) الأشياء.

2. The thirty-fifth. When a malefic pushes onto a malefic, it changes a harm
into a harm. (+ And when a malefic pushes onto a benefic, it changes from
bad to good. And when a benefic pushes onto a benefic, it changes good
to good DL). And when a benefic pushes to a malefic, it obtains bad after
the good. And mix the things accordingly!

3. John of Seville: Tricesimum.v. (.31. M). Cum malus pulsat, *id est, iungitur*
(-- i.e.i. H), malo (malum H), vertitur, *id est, mutatur*, malum in alium
(aliud HMSTpr) malum. Et si malus iungitur fortunæ (**pulsat fortunam**
H), convertitur malum in bonum. Si vero fortuna iungitur fortunæ (**pul-**
sat fortunam H), convertitur bonum in malum (**bonum HMTpr**). Et si
fortuna iungitur malo (**pulsat malum H**), conveniet (**veniet H, inveniet**
MTpr) post bonum malum. (+ et pr) Hoc modo commisce res (commis-
ceris MT).

4. EN-text: –

5. *Liber trium iudicum*: xxxvᵘˢ, quotiens infortunium fortunate confert, mali
in bonum fit translatio. Cum enim infortuniorum alterum alteri, de malo
in malum fit descensus. Contrario, similiter si omnium (*supra*: id est for-
tunatarum) alterum alteri (*supra*: fortune) confert, de bono in malum
fit progressio. Nam si benivola noxie bona (*sic*), malus expectatur finis.
Sic autem omnino miscenda sunt *in rerum diversitatibus diversa indicia*
celestium.

6. *Liber novem iudicum*: 27 Quotiens infortunium fortunate confert, mali in
    bonum *fiet* translatio. Cum enim infortuniorum alterum alteri, de malo
    in malum fit descensus. Contrario similiter *fortunatarum* alterum alteri
    conferat, de bono in *bonum* fit progressio. Nam si benivola noxie, malus
    expectatur finis. Si⟨c⟩ autem omnino miscenda sunt in rerum diversitat-
    ibus diversa celestium *indicia*.

7. Abraham Ibn Ezra: xxvi If a malefic gives power to a malefic, the misfor-
    tune is redoubled. If a benefic ⟨gives power⟩ to a benefic, the good fortune
    is redoubled. If a malefic ⟨gives power⟩ to a benefic, the fortune changes
    from evil to good. And if a benefic ⟨gives power⟩ to a malefic, the fortune
    changes from good to evil.

8. Henry Bate's translation: .26m. ... Si dederit malivolus malivolo forti-
    tudinem suam, addetur malum super malum; et si bonus bono, addetur
    bonum super bonum; et si malus bono, mutabitur res de malo in bonum;
    si *vero* econverso, erit econverso.

9. Pietro d'Abano's translation: Si malus vim tribuerit malo, malo malum
    adiungetur, et si bonus bono, bonum bono. Si vero malus bono, transmu-
    tatur (transmittatur pr) res de malo in bonum. Econverso (Econtrario pr)
    autem, contrarium.

10. *Gloucester Text*: 30 Quando nocivus planeta planete nocivo suum dirigit
    gubernaculum significatio sua de malo in peius augmentatur. Si vero
    planete propitio suum dirigat gubernaculum, natura sua de malo in
    bonum mutatur. Si propitius propitio suum dirigat gubernaculum, de
    bono in melius. Si propitius nocivo, natura sua de bono in malum mutatur.
    *Sciendum quod id quod hactenus dictum est secundum planetarum virtutes
    vel secundum eorum situs in signis diversos, cum iudiciis insisterimus*, sapi-
    enter contemperandum est.

36

1.

السادس وثلاثون القمر أو (و LD) رب الطالع إذا كان منحوسا من (في L) مقارنة أو
تربيع أو مقابلة وكانت السعود عند (ضد D) ذلك تتصل به من التربيع فإن الذي يصيب

الرجل من الشدة تحلله (يحلله LD) وتنجيه (وينجيه LD) منه وكذلك إذا اتصل بالنحس من

تربيع ونظرت إليه السعود من التثليث (بتليث LD) فإن ذلك الرجل يفلت (يقلت L) مما

لقي (بالتي D) من الشدة ويقع في شدة أخرى

2. The thirty-sixth. When the Moon or the lord of the ascendant are harmed from conjunction or quartile or opposition, and the benefics are at that time applying to it from quartile, then that distress which hits the man is released and he is rescued. Similarly, when a malefic hits from quartile and the benefics aspect it from trine, then that man escapes from the distress that hits him, and falls into a different distress.

3. John of Seville: Tricesimum.vi. (.32. M). Luna vel (et HMSTpr) dominus ascendentis cum fuerit impeditus a coniunctione vel (+ a HMTpr) quarto aspectu sive (+ ab HMTpr) oppositione *malorum*, si tunc fortunæ iungantur (iungatur T) ei a trino vel sextili (a t.v.s.] **quarto** HS, a quarto MTpr) *aspectu* (+ sive ab oppositione malorum si tunc fortunæ iungantur ei a quarto aspectu S *bis*), quicquid invenerit virum (vir T) ex **districtione** (distinctione MT, distructione pr), solvetur *a fortunis* et liberabitur ab eis. Similiter, si iuncti fuerint (f.i. MSTpr) malus (**malis** MTpr) a quarto aspectu et (-- i.f.a.m.a.e. H) aspexerint fortunæ a quarto (**trino** MSTpr) aspectu (si iuncti ... aspectu] si fortune aspexerint malo ex trino vel sextili aspectu H), evadet vir ille quod occurrit (occurrerit MT) ei ex districtione (distictione (*sic*) T, destructione pr) illa et cadet in alteram.

4. EN-text: –

5. *Liber trium iudicum*: xxxvi[us]., quotiens Lunam et orientis dominum adversa figura corrumpit sive conventus, si ad illas fortunate vel tetragono accedant, adversitati eripuit (*supra*: auferit aliquid) nisi infortuniis tetragono corrupti fuerint, licet enim fortunate vel trigono respiciant, liberant quidem a presenti difficultate, set sequentes arcere nequeunt.

6. *Liber novem iudicum*: 6 est quotiens Lunam et orientis dominum adversa figura corrumpit sive etiam conventus, *quod* si ad illas fortunate vel de *trigono* accedant, adversitati eripiunt nisi infortuniis tetragono corrupti fuerint, licet enim *benivole* vel trigono sic respiciant, liberant quidem a presenti difficultate, set sequentes arcere nequeunt.

7. Abraham Ibn Ezra: –

8. Henry Bate's translation: –

9. Pietro d'Abano: –

10. *Gloucester Text*: 31 Luna et dominus signi orientis quando alter eorum adversitatem a planeta nocivo recipit a quatuor angulis vel ab opposito vel a coniunctione, si alius planeta propitius eorum aliquem *a tribus vel*

sex angulis interim respexerit, adversitas illius in prosperitate mutata est. Item, si propitius planeta eorum aliquem a quatuor angulis respexerit, adversitatem suam relinquere et in aliam incidere eum cogit.

37

1.

السابع والثلاثون الكوكب اذا لم يكن في بيته و امر به واثلثته
وكابي حده وكا من برجه وكا نظ ايه وبان لم الاوتاد فان ذلك علا مة اخبر بها واخير بعده لذلك الكو كب

السابع وثلاثون الكوكب إذا لم يكن في بيته ولا (+ في LD) شرفه ولا مثلثته ولا في حده
ولا في فرحه (+ ولا وجهه LD) وكان ساقطا21عن الأوتاد فإن ذلك (تلك LD) علامة
رديئة (- D) لا خير فيها ولا خير(-A) في ذلك الكوكب.

2. The thirty-seventh. When the planet is not in its house, its exaltation, its triplicity nor its term, and not in its joy (+ and not its decan LD) and is falling from the cardines, then this is a bad sign without good in it, and there is no good in that planet.

3. John of Seville: Tricesimum.vii. (.33. M). Planeta cum non (- ST) fuerit in domo vel in exaltatione aut (vel S, + in M) triplicitate sua nec (vel pr) in termino vel in gaudio suo et fuerit cadens ab angulis, erit hoc signum (s.h. T) malum absque ulla utilitate et nichil boni est in ipso planeta (- planeta MT; in impedimento planete pr).

4. EN-text: –

5. *Liber trium iudicum*: .xxxvii[us]., quecumque stella penitus et dignitatum et gaudii expers ut pariter et a⟨d⟩versa, sit omnino *sine spe*.

6. *Liber novem iudicum*: 41, quecumque stella penitus et dignitatum et gaudii *de quo postmodum dicetur*, expers *fuerit*, ut pariter sit adversa, omnino sine spe.

7. Abraham Ibn Ezra: xl A planet is inauspicious if it is not in one of the places where it exerts lordship and *is in the sixth or twelfth place*.

8. Henry Bate's translation: .40m. Planeta non existens in aliqua dignitatum suarum, si fuerit in domo sexta vel duodecima, *hoc est bonum ei*.

9. Pietro d'Abano's translation: Planeta malus sive fuerit in locorum aliquo sue potestatis et ipse fuit in domo sexta aut duodecima, *bonum vel fortunabitur tunc illi inerit* (?)

---

21 Beginning of fragment in MS Arabic Istanbul University, A 6141 (A), fol. 35[r].

10. *Gloucester Text*: 32 Quando planeta aliquis nec in domicilio suo nec hon-
     ore nec aliqua suarum dignitatum fuerit, set in aliquo quatuor signorum
     /74ᵛ/ que non respiciunt signum oriens, adversitatem solam significat.

38

1.

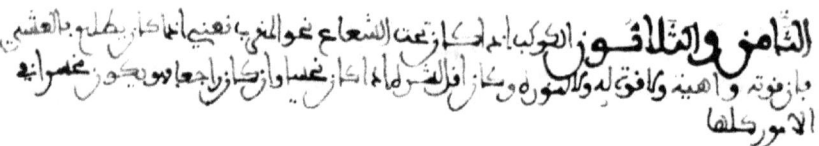

الثامن وثلاثون (الباب الثامن والثلاثين A) الكوكب إذا كان تحت الشعاع نحو المغرب

نعني (يعني LD) إذا كان يطلع بالعشي (بالعشاء D؛ - يعني إذا كان يطلع بالعشي A) فإن

(D -) قوته واهية (ذاهبة A) ولا قوة له ولا لنوره (لا ينوره L؛ بنوره D؛—ولا قوة له

ولا لنوره A) وكان أقل لشره إذا كان نحسا وإن كان راجعا فهو يكون مخسرا (شرا D) في

الأمور كلها.

2. The thirty-eighth. When the planet is under the rays in the direction of
    the West—we mean, when it rises in the evening—then its power is weak,
    and there is no power in it or in its light. It is less in its harm when it is a
    malefic. And if it is retrograde, it is causing damage in all matters.

3. John of Seville: Tricesimum.viii. (.34. M). Planeta cum fuerit sub radiis ver-
    sus occidentem, id est, quando oritur vespere, erit fortitudo eius debilis. (+
    Nulla (*supra*: ut) S, ut pr) *dictum est de superioribus* (-- d.e.d.s. MT). Nulla
    enim (tantum? H;—nulla enim S) fortitudo erit ei nec lumini (lumen S)
    eius. Et minus erit eius (eius erit T) impedimentum, si fuerit malus. Et si
    fuerit retrogradus, erit *tardus* in omnibus rebus.

4. EN-text: –

5. *Liber trium iudicum*: xxxviii.°, quoniam superiores stelle cum ex parte
    occidentis aduruntur, *aut* principio noctis oriuntur, minus potentes tam
    boni quam mali.

6. *Liber novem iudicum*: 42, quoniam superiores stelle cum ex parte *orientis*
    aduruntur, aut principio noctis oriuntur, minus potentes sunt tam boni
    quam mali.

7. Abraham Ibn Ezra: xli A planet has no power if it is under the ray (of the
    Sun) *and is one of the upper planets. The same holds true for the lower
    (planets), and if they are retrograde, nothing can be worse.*[22]

---

22   Ibn Ezra's judgements xlii and xliii have no equivalent among the *50 Precepts*.

8.   Henry Bate's translation: .41m. Planeta sub radiis existens, si fuerit de
     superioribus, nihil habet fortitudinis. Et consimiliter de inferioribus. Sed
     si sint retrogradi, nihil ita malum ut hoc est.

9.   Pietro d'Abano's translation: Planeta si fuerit sub radiis et fuerit (sit pr) de
     superioribus, omnino vigore caret. Et similiter in inferioribus. Nec adeo
     magnum ut hoc est infortunium retrogradationis (retrogradari pr).

10. *Gloucester Text*: 33 Quando planeta sub Sole fuerit in occidente, virtus eius
     cassa est *et vana*. Nec in eius virtute vel claritate eiusdem aliqua pros-
     peritatis virtus est. Item si planeta nocivus ibidem fuerit, eius potestas
     nocendi debilitatur. Si retrogradus ibidem, eius virtus penitus debilitata
     est.

39

1.

التاسع وثلاثون (الباب التاسع والثلاثين A) الكواكب إذا كانت تحت الشعاع كانت
ضعيفة في جميع (- D) الأمور وذلك (وكذلك LD) إذا كان بينها وبين الشمس أقل من
اثني عشرة (عشر LD) درجة في طلوعه بالغدوات (- في طلوعه بالغدوات LAD) إلا أن
يكون الكوكب في درجة الشمس (ه A) فإنه يكون قويا (+ الكوكب عندما يكون مع
الشمس في درجة واحدة نقول أنه في الصميم أو التصميم أو في قلب الشمس أي مقارنا
لها في نفس الدرجة وحينها يكون قويا وسعيدا D).

2.   The thirty-ninth. When the planets are under the rays, they are weak in
     all matters, and that is when between them and the Sun there are less
     than twelve degrees in its rising in the morning, unless the planet is in
     the degree of the Sun; then it is strong.

3.   John of Seville: Tricesimum .ix. (.35. M). Planetæ cum fuerint sub radiis
     erunt debiles in omnibus rebus. Hoc est, si fuerit (fuerint pr) inter eos et
     Solem minus .xii. gradibus, nisi sit planeta in gradu Solis, quia tunc erit
     fortis.

4.   EN-text: –

5.   *Liber trium iudicum*: .xxxix[us]., adustionis (*lacuna ca. 7 litterarum*) vis inter
     Solem et stellam minus .xii. gradibus.

6. *Liber novem iudicum*: 43, adustionis inter Solem et stellam minus 12 gradibus.
7. Abraham Ibn Ezra: –
8. Henry Bate's translation: –
9. Pietro d'Abano's translation: –
10. *Gloucester Text*: 34 Quando planeta sub Solis claritate fuerit, in omnibus que significat debilis est. Ita dico si minus quam 12 gradus eos interfuerint. Set si planeta *per diametrum* ei supponatur, non adeo debilis factus est.

40

1.

الموفي أربعين (الباب الأربعين A) الكوكب إذا تباعد من (تباعدت من A) الشمس اثنتا

عشرة (عشر LD) درجة (جزوءا A) في (من A) طلوعه بالغدوات من المشرق فإنه قوي

(- A) في كل ابتداء أو (و LD) عمل (+ نقول أنه خرج من الشعاع أو من تحت الشعاع

وبالفعل فالكواكب ذات القدر الأول أول ما ترى عند ابتعادها عن الشمس ب ١٢

درجة D). وإذا تباعد (+ عنها A) خمس عشرة درجة فإن الكوكب (فالكوكب LDA)

عند ذلك أقوى ما يكون و (+ انظر A)[23] إذا كان الكوكب أمام الشمس في ناحية المغرب

أعني أن يكون طالعا بالعشيات (بالعشاء D) في المغرب (- أعني ... المغرب A) وكان بينه

وبين الشمس من (- الشمس من A) سبع درجات (درج LDA) إلى خمس عشرة (عشر

L) درجة فإنه يبدأ بالضعف ومن سبع درجات (درج LDA) حتى يكون في قلب الشمس

(- حتى يكون في قلب الشمس A) يكون الكوكب (تكون الكواكب LD) أضعف ما

---

23 انظر appears in the margin of MS E, but only opposite *præceptum* 45, and the place of its insertion is unclear.

يكون (تكون L) وإذا كان في القلب كان قويا أعني بالقلب أنه كان (أن يكون DL، إذا

كان A) مع الشمس (A ه) في درجة (+ واحدة LD).

2. ⟨The number⟩ completing forty. When the planet is distant from the Sun by 12 degrees in its rising in the morning in the East, then it is powerful in every initiative or action. And when it is distant by 15 degrees, then the planet in this situation is as powerful as it can be. When the planet is in front of the Sun in the direction of the West—i.e., if it is rising in the evening in the West and between it and the Sun are seven to fifteen degrees—then it begins to be weak. And from seven degrees until it is in the heart of the Sun the planet is as weak as it can be. And when it is in the heart it is powerful—I mean by 'the heart' that it is with the Sun in one degree.

3. John of Seville: Quadragesimum (.36. M). Et (- HMTpr) planeta (planete H) cum fuerit longe a Sole per .xii. gradus in mane ab oriente, erit fortis in omni /H 26ʳ/ initio et in omni opere. Et cum promulgatur (**prolongatus** HMSTpr) et si (- **et si** HMSTpr) fuerit ab eo per (-- M) .xv. (.12. M, .axv.? T) gradus, tunc erit *fortior*, id est, tunc erit (+ **in** HMSTpr) maiori fortitudine quam debet esse. Et si fuerit planeta (+ **id est** T) ante Solem ex parte occidentis, id est, si oriatur /P p. 444b/ vespere in occidente et fuerit inter ipsum et Solem a (- MS) .xv. gradibus usque in .vii. (.15. M), tunc incipit debilitari; a .vii. (.axv. T) gradu (gradibus HMSpr) donec sit in corde Solis (+ **fit planeta debilior quam potest fieri. Et cum fuerit in corde** Solis HSTpr) erit debilis (**fortis** Hpr, **fortius** MST)—per cor Solis vult intelligi ut sit cum Sole (c.S.s. pr) in uno gradu.

4. EN-text: *Item*, quotiens stella .12. grad(ibus) a Sole elongatur, ut orientalis sit, rerum initiis viam prebet, magis magisque recedens. Si vero ex parte occidentis post Solem apparuerit, cum inter .15. et .7. ad Solem accesserit, debilitari incipit. A .7. *usque* in eodem gradu cum Sole conveniat, debilissima est.

5. *Liber trium iudicum*: .xl ᵘˢ., **quotiens stella .xii. gradibus elongatur a Sole, ut orientalis sit, rerum initiis viam prebet,** *magis magisque recedens.* **Si vero ex parte occidentis post Solem apparet, cum inter .xv. et .vii. ad Solem accesserit, debilitari incipit; a .vii. usquequo in eodem gradu cum Sole conveniat, debilissima est.** *Nam est zaminia* (= صيمي); *fuerit pro receptione quasi in clientela et de familia Solis libere fortis est.*

6. *Liber novem iudicum*: *44*, quotiens /V 11ᵛᵃ/ stella 12 gradibus elongatur a Sole, ut orientalis sit, rerum initiis viam prebet, magis magisque recedens. Si vero ex parte occidentis post Solem apparet, cum inter .15. et .7. ad Solem accesserit, debilitari incipiet. *Nam ad septem* usque in eodem

gradu cum Sole conveniat, debilissima est. Nam çaminia fuerint *in* receptione quasi in clientela et familia Solis libere fortis est, *nec vale[n]t esse felicior nec adustionis aliquam suscipiet lesionem dum vires Solis atque potentiam tunc demum perfecte suscipiet.*

7. Abraham Ibn Ezra: –
8. Henry Bate's translation: –
9. Pietro d'Abano's translation: –
10. *Gloucester Text*: 35 Quando planeta 12 gradus removetur a Sole et mane ascendit in orientem, tunc fortis est et quicquid significationis habet virtute non minima significat illud. Quando vero 15 gradu ab eo removetur, fortior est et potiorem in significandis virtutem habet. Item quando planeta ante Solem in occidente fuerit, si 15 gradu a Sole removetur quousque inter eos septem gradus sunt, incipit debilitari. A 7 gradu quousque in eodem conveniant gradu, debilis est. Quando in eodem fuerint gradu, virtutes suas iterum recolligit.

    41

1.

الحادي والاربعون (الباب الحادي والأربعين A) الكوكب إذا كان في بيته (غربة LD؛
غربة A) جيث (خبثت LD؛ حدّت A) نفسه و(- نفسه و A) طبيعته (+ الغربة أن
يكون الكوكب في برج لا حظ له فيه أي ليس بيته ولا شرفه ولا في مثلثته ولا في حده
وأخبث من ذلك أن يكون ساقطا أي في الثالث أو السادس أو التاسع أو الثاني عشر D)
وإذا كان في غير (- D؛ غربة A) بيته (بيت نفسه A؛—LD—A) أو (و A) شرفه مستقيم
السير في موضع جيد من الطالع أو وسط السماء أو الحادي عشر فهو جيد أيضا.

2. The forty-first. When the planet is in its alienation, its soul (itself) and its nature are malicious, and when it is not in its house or its exaltation but is direct in its course in a good place relative to the ascendant or medium cælum, or the eleventh, then it is good also.[24]

---

24   There seems to be some confusion here as to whether the sentence should be negative or positive. Note that MS D takes out the negative ('when it is in its house …').

3. John of Seville: Quadragesimum.i. (.37. M).[25] Planeta cum fuerit in pere-grinatione (+ id est, cum non fuerit in aliqua dignitatum suarum ut est exaltatio facies et cetera pr), fit animus eius calidus (*lege* callidus = خبيث) *et* eius natura. Et si non fuerit in domo sua aut in (- MSpr) exaltatione et fuerit directus et in loco bono ab ascendente, erit (**aut** HMTpr) in medio celi (-- M) vel in undecimo, erit bonus. (+ Si Luna iungitur alicui planete ille cui iungitur dicitur esse receptor dispositionis Lune et sic procedet receptio usque ad Saturnum, quia super Saturnum non est alius qui recip-iat dispositionem pr)

4. EN-text: –

5. *Liber trium iudicum*: .xli ᵘˢ., quoniam stella ext⟨ra⟩nea non est sue virtutis. Si tamen recta et bene orienti consistens, non expers boni /D 56ʳ/.

6. *Liber novem iudicum*: 45 *quod* stella extranea sue virtutis non est. Si tamen recta et *boni orientis* consistens, non *penitus* expers boni.

7. Abraham Ibn Ezra: –

8. Henry Bate's translation: –

9. Pietro d'Abano's translation: –

10. *Gloucester Text*: 36 Quando planeta est in loco alieno, virtus eius et natura admodum impedita est. Et si alicubi fuerit ubi nec domus nec honor suus sit, et tamen recte progrediatur et in loco signi prospero fuerit, id est, in 10 vel 11° ab orientali, bonum significat.

42

1.

الثاني والاربعون (الباب الثاني والأربعين A) قابل التدبير إذا كان غريبا (+ اعني LA) أمام الشمس (اماىره؟ A) كان ضعيفا منكسرا (منكسا D؛ منكرا A) لا يتمّ (ثم D) ما يقضى (يعطي A؛ + الكوكب الغربي هو الذي يغرب بعد الشمس ويشرق بعدها ونقول أمامها لأنه طوله أكبر من طول الشمس، أما الشرقي فهو الذي يشرق قبل الشمس ويغرب قبلها ونقول أنه خلفها لأن طوله أصغر من طول الشمس D) وإن (إذا LA) كان شرقيا كان قويا نشيطا (نشيطا قويا A) تامّ الفضيلة (الأطية A) لأن مثال النجم (الكوكب D؛

---

25 From here on H writes 'x' for 'xl', clearly copying from a manuscript which used the x *aspada*.

المنجم A) الفاسد مثل (مثال A) البناء إذا هدم و (فإذا DL) بني جاد وحسن (- و بني

جاد وحسن A).

2. The forty-second. The receiver of the management, when it is western, in front of the Sun, is weak, broken. What is judged is not completed (given A). And if it is eastern, it is strong and lively, and the virtue is complete (given A), because the example of the harming star is like the building which, when it is destroyed and ⟨re⟩built, becomes good and beautiful.

3. John of Seville: Quadragesimum.ii. (.38. M). Receptor dispositionis, cum fuerit occidentalis, *id est, ante Solem* (- ante Solem H, – i.d.a.S. MSTpr) *per .xii. gradus vel* (et HST) *infra* (+ ante Solem HTpr, + id est ante Solem M), erit debilis et confractus, (+ et pr) non perficitur (perficit H) quod iudicat (+ *quia planeta impeditus est similis edificio quod, cum cadit, numquam reedificatur* H). Et si fuerit occidentalis (**orientalis** HMSTpr), erit fortis et prudens (- e.p. A), perfectus (implying تام) in iudicio, quia planeta impeditus similis est (quia planeta ... est] et est similis H) edificio quod, cum cadit et (- cadit et H;—et S; q.c.c.e.] et cum ceciderit pr) reedificatur, (+ id est H) melioratur, et fit bonum (+ et est ei similis ortus H).

4. EN-text: –

5. *Liber trium iudicum*: .xlii ᵘˢ., quotiens superior stella occidentalis est infra predictos terminos, si questionis dux extiterit, non consumabit. Orientalis contra, fortis scilicet et perficiendi compos.

6. *Liber novem iudicum: 46*, quotiens superior stella occidentalis est infra predictos terminos, si questionis dux *extrahit, minime consum⟨m⟩are potest*. Orientalis contra, fortis scilicet et perficiendi compos.

7. Abraham Ibn Ezra: –

8. Henry Bate's translation: –

9. Pietro d'Abano's translation: –

10. *Gloucester Text*: 37 Planeta qui recipit gubernaculum quando fuerit occidentalis ante Solem debilis est, nec quod significat complere potest. Cum vero occidentalis post Solem fuerit, nichilominus virtute plenus suum complet significatum.

43

1.

اَلثَّالِثُ وَالْاَرْبَعُونَ الَّذِي ضَبَ أَخَأَ أَخَأَرَيْجَ الثَّامِنِ مِنَ الطَّالِعِ وَهُوَسَعْدُ بِقِسَمٍ خَيْرًا اَوْ شَرًّا وَالنُّجُوسُ

أَمَّا إِذَا كَانَتْ هُنَالِكَ يُفْطَمُ شَرُّهَا

الثالث والاربعون (الباب الثالث والأربعينA) الكوكب إذا كان في الثامن من الطالع
وهو سعد لم يقسم خيرا ولا شرا والنحوس إذا كانت هناك (كذلك A) يقطع (عظم LD؛
يعظم A) شرها.

2. The forty-third. When the planet is in the eighth from the ascendant and is a benefic, it does not distribute the good or the bad. And ⟨as for⟩ the malefics, if they are there, their harm is increased.

3. John of Seville: Quadragesimum.iii. (.39. M). Planeta cum fuerit in octavo ab ascendente et fuerit fortuna, non operatur bonum neque malum. Et mali cum fuerint ibidem (- MT), magnificatur eorum malum (malum] malitia semper in malum H).

4. EN-text: –

5. *Liber trium iudicum*: .xliii.us, fortunata in octavo ab oriente boni expers, nam infortunium mali compos et prepotens.

6. *Liber novem iudicum*: *16 est quod fortuna* in .8. ab oriente boni expers, infortunium *namque* mali compos et prepotens.

7. Abraham Ibn Ezra: xliv A benefic planet signifies neither good fortune nor misfortune if it is in the eighth place; but if it is one of the malefics, it signifies absolute misfortune.

8. Henry Bate's translation: .44m. Si fuerit planeta benivolus in octava domo, nec bonum nec malum (neque malum neque bonum Gl) significat; si *vero* malivolus (+ ibidem Gl) extiterit, malum significat perfectum (45 blank in Gl. 46 Si fortitudo duodenarie planete bono loco fuerit, addetur bonum super bonum Gl)

9. Pietro d'Abano's translation: Planeta fortuna in octava exstiterit domo, neque bonum neque malum denotat. Si autem *illic* malus fuerit, perfectum denotat malum.

10. *Gloucester Text*: 38 Quando planeta propitius in signo 8° ab oriente fuerit, nec bonum nec malum significat. Et si in eodem signo stella nocens fuerit, adversitas eius augmentatur.

44

1.

الرابع والاربعون (الباب الرابع والأربعين A) كل كوكب يكون في أول البرج (+ فهو A)
ضعيفا (- D) حتى يتمكن منه ويسير فيه خمس (- A) درج ولا يسقط الكوكب عن الوتد
إلا بعد خمس (- A) درج من خلفه (خلقه L) أعني إذا كان الوتد عشر درج من الحمل
(+ بعد في الوتد A) فإنه (فإن DL؛ و A) كل كوكب يكون في أقل من خمس درج الى
عشر درج (الى عشر درج] بينه وبين الوتد فإنه L) يعد في الوتد وكل كوكب يكون في
اقل (اكثر L) من خمس درج (- درج الي ... درج A) فإنه ساقط (- درج الي عشر ...
ساقط D؛—فإنه ساقط L) لا يعد في الوتد.

2. The forty-fourth. Every planet at the beginning of its sign is weak until it
gains strength from it and travels five degrees in it. And the planet is not
falling from the cardine except when more than five degrees back from
it—i.e., when the cardine is the 10th degree of Aries, every planet in less
than five degrees until ten degrees (until ten degrees] between it and the
cardine L) is reckoned ⟨as being⟩ 'in the cardine'. And every planet that
is distant by less (more L) than five degrees is falling, and is not reckoned
⟨as being⟩ in the cardine.

3. John of Seville: Quadragesimum.iiii. (.40. M). Planeta cum fuerit (+ in
HSTpr) initio signi erit debilis donec firmetur in eo et perambulet in eo (-
in eo H) .v. (sex pr) gradus (gradibus STpr). Et non cadit planeta ab angulis
nisi (non T) post .v. gradus. Verbi gratia, si fuerit angulus .x^us. gradus Arietis, omnis planeta qui fuerit (+ in HMST) minus (terminus pr) .v. gradibus
est cadens (+ versus primum H) et non putatur in angulo (+ **et si fuerit**
plus .v. gradibus versus .x., in angulo erit H).

4. EN-text:—[26]

5. *Liber trium iudicum*: .xliiii^us., nulla stella in principio signi usque ad .v.
gradus satis potens. Nam nec cadens est a cardine stella antequam .v.

---

26 But see 15 above where EN-Text gives this information, in different words.

gradus ipsum reliquerit, ut si cardo in .x. Arietis, quecumque supra .v. in Ariete fuerit in cardine est.

6. *Liber novem iudicum*: 47, nulla stella in principio signi usque ad quinque gradus satis potens. Nam nec cadens est a cardine stella antequam quinque gradus post ipsum reliquerit, ut si cardo *sit* in decimo Arietis, quecumque supra quinque in Ariete fuerit in cardine est.

7. Abraham Ibn Ezra: xxviii Every planet at the cusp of a sign is considered to be weak until it is 5 degrees past it. Likewise, if the planet is less than 5 degrees from the place, it is considered to be within the power of the place; but if it is more, it escapes the power of the place.

8. Henry Bate's translation: –

9. Pietro d'Abano's translation: –

10. *Gloucester Text*: 39 Quicumque planeta in principio alicuius signi fuerit, antequam ad 5 gradus eiusdem perveniat, ita debilis est quod nichil quod secundum illud debuerit designare significare potest ...

45

1.

الخامس والاربعون (الباب الخامس والأربعين A) كل (وكل LA) كوكب يكون (- D) من الوتد مما (فيما) يليه على خمس عشرة (وعشرين LD) درجة فهو بمنزلة من في الوتد وإن زاد فلا قوة له. ومثال ذلك أن يكون الوتد (- L) عشر درجات (درج LD) من الحمل (- مما ... الحمل A) فكل كوكب يكون من عشر درجات (- وكل كوكب يكون من عشر درجات LD) إلى خمس وعشرين درجة من الحمل (منه LD) فإنه في ذلك الوتد فإن (وإن LD) زاد على (عن D) خمس وعشرين درجة (- A) فلا.

2. The forty-fifth. Every planet being, with respect to the cardine, following it up to 15 degrees, is like being in the cardine. And if it exceeds this, it has no power. For example: if the cardine is 10 degrees of Aries and any planet is from ten degrees to 25 degrees in Aries then it is in this cardine; if it more than 25 degrees, then it is not.

3. John of Seville: Quadragesimum.v. (.41. M). *Et omnis planeta qui fuerit post angulum per .xv. gradus erit consimilis illi qui est in angulo, et si*

auxerit *gradus*, nulla erit fortitudo (f.e. HMTpr, fortitudo S) ei. Verbi gratia: si esset angulus .x^{us}. (in angulo .x. S) gradus *signi* Arietis, tunc omnis planeta qui fuerit ab eodem a (- **HMSTpr**) .x.º gradu usque in .xxv. gradus *eiusdem* Arietis *reputatur* (vir putatur pr) in eodem angulo. Quod si addiderit super (supra T) .xxv. (+ **gradus** MTpr), non erit in angulo. *Set Ptholomeus* (Pto- HMS, To- T) *dixit* (dicit HMSTpr) *quod* (qui P,—pr) *usque in .xxv. gradus post angulum erit planeta in angulo.*

4. EN-text: *Item*, omnis stella post cardinem usque ad .15. gradus *post cardinem* in cardine *est*, ut si .10us. *gradus Arietis in cardine*, quecumque a .5. usque ad .25. fuerit, in cardine est.

5. *Liber trium iudicum*: .xlv^{us}., **omnis stella post cardinem usque ad .xv. gradum in cardine, ut si item Aries in .x., quecumque a .v. usque ad .xxv. fuerit, in cardine est.**

6. *Liber novem iudicum: 48,* omnis stella post cardinem usque ad .xv. gradus in cardine, ut si fuerit Aries in .10., quecumque a quinque usque ad 25 fuerit, in cardine est.

7. Abraham Ibn Ezra: xxix From the beginning of a place until 15 degrees every planet has great power.

8. Henry Bate's translation: 29m. Omni planete qui fuerit (est Gl) in principio domus usque ad .15. gradus est fortitudo magna.

9. Pietro d'Abano's translation: Quilibet planeta (- S) existens a principio domus usque ad .15. gradus est fortis valde.

10. *Gloucester Text*: ... A 5 gradus quousque 20 transierit in maiori virtute quam possit habere, secundum signum illud perseverat. A 20 quousque 25 incipit debilitari. Set quando 25 transierit, virtute sua non aliter privatur ac si extra signum esse.

46

1.

الاسلام سروللاأزبعــوز الكواكب أنهااكانت به البروج الثابتة
له أنهعلى ثبــاتـ ت له امر الزيد يسأل عنه وأنه أكانت نتبره البروج منزلت الحسين عند تنضم الانتفاض
مره يعولخـر ونضمر الزلز الحاجنه حاجنه من ولر العينه أنو هرام وأنهأ كانت بع البروج النقليه لمت على
سرعه نرالانفكاب الز نحيراوشى

السادس والاربعون (الباب السادس والأربعين A) الكواكب إذا كانت في البروج الثابتة

دلت على ثبات (اثبات D) الأمر الذي يسأل عنه وإذا كانت في البروج ذوات الجسدين

دلت على الانتقاض (الانتقاص L) مرة بعد أخرى وتضم (ويضم LD) إلى تلك الحاجة

حاجة أخرى و (أو A) أمرا (امر LD) غير ذلك الأمر وإذا كانت في البروج المنقلبة دلت
على سرعة الانقلاب إلى خير أو (+ إلى LDA) شر.

2. The forty-sixth. When the planets are in the fixed signs, they indicate the fixedness of the thing which is enquired about. And when they are in bicorporeal signs, they indicate destruction one time after another, and they join another matter to this matter and another thing to this thing. When they are in tropical signs, they indicate swiftness of change to good or bad.

3. John of Seville: Quadragesimum.vi. (.42. M). Planetæ cum fuerint in signis fixis significant (significat ST) fixuram *id est, firmitatem* (infirmitatem pr) *et* (- firmitatem et H) *stabilitatem* rerum de quibus fit (sit H) interrogatio. Et cum fuerint in signis communibus, significant solutiones rerum ac restaurationes (**reiterationes** HMSTpr), et applicabitur illi rei altera vel aliquid (aliquod pr) aliud tale. Et cum fuerint in signis mobilibus, significant celeritatem conversionis *vel mutationis rerum* /P p. 445a/ in bonum vel malum.

4. EN-text: –

5. *Liber trium iudicum*: .xlvi^us., stella in signo firmo rem firmat. In bipertito hinc negat, hinc firmat, tamque rerum quam questionum duplicitatem figurat. Nam in conversivo statim bonum malumve sic mutat.

6. *Liber novem iudicum*: 49 stella in signo firmo firmat, in bipertito hinc firmat, hinc negat, tamque rerum quam questionum *duplicationem* prefigurat.

7. Abraham Ibn Ezra: xlvii If a planet is in a fixed sign, it signifies everything that persists and survives; if it is in a tropical sign, it signifies that the situation will be reversed; and if it is in a bicoporeal sign, it signifies that the event will occur in part or that it will occur twice.

8. Henry Bate's translation: .47m. Cum est planeta in signo fixo, significat omnem rem stabilem et firmam, et si in signo mobili, mutabitur et res; si *vero* (fuerit Gl) in signo bicorpore, significat quod pars rei firma erit aut (ac Gl) iterabitur res duabus vicibus.

9. Pietro d'Abano's translation: Si planeta fuerit in signo fixo, denotat omne fixum, stabile. Et si fuerit in mobili, transmutabitur illud. Et si fue/pr xxvii^rb/rit in communi *vel bicorporeo* (- vel bicorporeo pr) significat partim (statim S) rem stabilem partimque mutabilem.

10. *Gloucester Text*: 40 Quando planeta aliquis in aliquo signorum fixibilium fuerit, res quam significat fixibilis est. Quando vero in aliquo qualitatum duarum signo fuerit, res quam significant multimoda mutabilis est, *id est, quando creditur esse, non est, vel quando creditur non esse, est.* Quando

vero in signis mobilibus fuerit, quod significat cito contingere demonstrat sive bonum sive malum sit.

47

1.

Fol. 49ᵛ

السابع والاربعون (الباب السابع والأربعين A) البرج الثابت يدل على ثبات الأمر (الثبات للأمر A) الذي يسأل عنه وكل أمر ثابت وهو عون جيد للمسألة والبرج ذو الجسدين يدل على أمور غير واحدة (ذا حدة D) وكل أمر يكون له عودة (دعوة A) ثانية ويدل البرج المنقلب على سرعة انقلاب ذلك الشيء (الأمر DAL) إلى غيره.

2. The forty-seventh. The fixed sign indicates fixedness of the matter which is enquired about, and every fixed matter, and it is a good help for the question. The bicorporeal sign indicates matters which are more than one, and every matter that has a second return. The tropical signs indicate speed of change of that thing into something else.

3. John of Seville: Quadragesimum.vii. (.43. M). Signum fixum significat (- T) fixuram (figuram pr), *id est, firmitatem* interrogationum (+ et HMSpr) rerum de quibus fit (- interrogationum … fit T) interrogatio, et omnem rem fixam *et firmissimam atque stabilem* (+ et HMSTpr) est auxilium bonum interrogationibus (bone interrogationis pr). Et signa communia significant res *quæ* (quod res H,—*quæ* pr) *non possunt fieri* (possunt fieri] **fit una** H) et (+ significat H) omnes res (- res T,—omnes res pr) que secundo vertantur (**iterantur HMSTpr**). Et signum mobile significat (+ secundum H) celeritatem mutationis rei in aliud.

4. EN-text: *Item,* si signum firmum sit oriens, rem quesitam firmat, bipertitum vero duplicibus involvit, conversivum mutationem accelerat.

5. *Liber trium iudicum*: .xlvii^{us}., **signum firm**um, *si oriens extiterit*, item **quesita firmat**. Nam et questionem iuvat (*corr. ex* firmat). **Bipertitum vero bifidis et duplicibus involvit**. Nam **conversivum mutationem accelerat**.

6. *Liber novem iudicum*: *50* locus est quod signum firmum, si oriens extiterit, quesita *pariter affirmat*. Nam et questionem *etiam iuvabit*. Bipertitum vero bifidis et duplicibus involvit.

7. Abraham Ibn Ezra: –

8. Henry Bate's translation: –

9. Pietro d'Abano's translation: –

10. *Gloucester Text*: 41 Quando aliquis *a nobis* aliquid petierit, si signum oriens de fixibilibus fuerit, rem de qua quesierit veraciter contingere portendit. Si signum oriens de signis duarum qualitatum fuerit, rem de qua fit questio non unius generis set mixtam esse designat. *Significat etiam quod ad esse et ad non esse se habebit, quare de illa re vix a nobis verum potest fieri iudicium.* Si de signis mobilibus re de qua queritur de statu in quo est ad alium transire designat.

48

1.

الثامن والاربعون (الباب الثامن والأربعين A) الكوكب[27] إذا كان مقيما للرجوع دل على الانتقاض في تلك الحاجة (+ بغير عسر A) والعصيان وإذا كان (- مقيما للرجوع ...

اذا كان L) مقيما للاستقامة دل على (+ الاستقامة في تلك LA) الحاجة (- والعصيان وإذا

كان مقيما للاستقامة دل علي الحاجة D) بغير عسر وكل كوكب يكون دليلا وهو يريد

أن (--A) يستقيم يدل على صلاح الأمر وقوته واستقامته وإن كان مقيما للرجوع دل على

الفساد و (- الفساد و A) العسر (والعسرة LD) والانتقاض (الانتقاص L).

2. The forty-eighth. When the planet is stationary for retrogradation it indicates destruction in that matter and disobedience. When it is stationary

---

27 In this *præceptum* MS A puts the planets in the plural, with the corresponding plural verbs and adjectives, until وكل كوكب.

for direct movement it indicates directness in the thing, without difficulty. Every planet which is a signifier while seeking direct movement, indicates the soundness of the matter, its power and its directness. And if it is stationary for retrogradation it indicates harm, difficulty and destruction.

3. John of Seville: Quadragesimum.viii. (.44. M). Planeta cum steterit ad retrogradationem, *id est, cum fuerit in sua statione prima,* /H 26ᵛ/ significat solutionem causæ et inobedientiam (inobedientiæ M). Et cum steterit ad directionem, *id est, cum fuerit in sua* (- *in sua* T) *statione secunda,* significat *directionem* rei (- MSTpr) post tarditatem (+ rei HMSTpr) *vel duritiam.* Et omnis planeta qui fuerit significator et voluerit dirigi (d.v. H), *id est, si* (- ST) *fuerit in statione secunda,* significat renovationem (+ actionum pr) rerum *et earum* (eorum H) *aptationem* (aptionem HST, aptitionem M, actionem pr) ac fortitudinem seu directionem. Et si fuerit in statione *prima,* volens retrogradari, significat destructionem earum et (ac M) tarditatem ac dissolutionem.

4. EN-text: *Item,* prima statio stelle *negotium* negat, secunda cum labore promittit. *Retrogradatio negat. Directio bene promittit et dat.*

5. *Liber trium iudicum:* .xlviii°. **stelle prima statio rem negat, secunda** vero **cum labore promittit.** *Ad hunc itaque modum utraque inspecta negatio vel affirmatio in iudicium venit.*

6. *Liber novem iudicum: 35 est quod* stelle prima statio rem negat, secunda vero cum labore promittit. Ad hunc quoque modum utraque inspecta negatio vel affirmatio in iudicium veniet.

7. Abraham Ibn Ezra: xlv A planet signifies incompletion of the requested ⟨event⟩, difficulty and loss if it begins to be retrograde, and it signifies good fortune, power and moderation in the event, if it begins to be direct.[28]

8. Henry Bate's translation: –

9. Pietro d'Abano's translation: –

10. *Gloucester Text:* 42 Quando planeta in statu retrogradiendi est, rei de qua queritur diminutionem et eiusdem etiam non existentiam significat. Si in statu di/75ʳ/rectionis fuerit, rem de qua queritur bene compleri, et tamen priusquam completur impediri denuntiat. 43 Quicumque planeta prope directionem suam est, ita scilicet quod iam velit dirigi, rei de qua queritur, prosperitatem, virtutem et huiusmodi felicia designat. Quando vero prope retrogradationem, contrarium significat.

---

28 Ibn Ezra's judgements xlvi, xlviii, xlix and l have no equivalent among the *50 Precepts.*

49

1.

التاسع والاربعون (الباب التاسع والأربعين A) اعلم أن اليوم الذي يكون فيه القمر (القمر فيه A) منحوسا فكل من يسأل في ذلك اليوم (- A) منحوس إلا أن يكون الموضع (المواضع A) من الطالع يغير (بغير LD؛ —الطالع يغير A) ذلك في الزيادة والنقصان لأن النحس إذا أنحس القمر وهو ساقط عن (وهو ساقط عن] واسعد A) الطالع ادخل الروعات وإذا كان في الاوتاد ومواضع (- ساقط عن الطالع ... مواضع D) يليها (- A) أوقع الخوف بالبدن (بالبدن الخوف LDA).

2. The forty-ninth. Know that the day on which the Moon is harmed, every-thing which is asked for on that day is harmed, except that the place of the ascendant changes it in increase and decrease, because the malefic when it harms the Moon and is cadent from the ascendant, brings in fears. And when it is in the cardines and the places that follow them, it brings in dread in the body.

3. John of Seville: Quadragesimum.ix. (.45. M). Scito quod in die qua (quando H) fuerit Luna impedita, omne de quo (de quo] quod M) inter-rogatur in die illa (illo H) erit impedimentum (**impeditum** HSTpr), nisi (**locus ab ascendente mutet hoc augmentatione vel diminutione**, *id est ut* H) *malus* (in aliis P) *impediens eam sit cadens ab ascendente* (+ *et imped-itus ac* S) *et debilis et Luna tunc non habeat partem in* (ab M) *ascendente*, quia (+ *si* S *supra*) malus, cum (- MS) impedit eam (**Lunam** HSTpr), et ipse fuerit cadens ab ascendente, immittit timorem *et sollicitudinem*. Et cum fuerit in angulis vel in sequentibus angulorum ingerit corpori timorem (+ et H) *addit* (- MS).

4. EN-text: *Item, quidcumque eo die quo Luna corrupta fuerit, quesierit, sine dubio infortunatus habeatur, hoc solum adiecto, ut diligenter infortu-nium Lunam corrumpens deprehendas. Si illud in cardine aut post car-dinem fuerit, supremus malorum cumulus est. Nam a[d]versum et remo-tum non adeo prevalet.*

5. *Liber trium iudicum*: .xlix.us, **quidcumque eo die quo Lunam corrup-
    tam inveneris, quesierit, sine dubio infortunatum habeas, hoc solum
    adiecto, ut diligenter infortunium Lunam corrumpens deprehendas,
    sique id in cardine aut post cardinem fuerit, supremus malorum cumu-
    lus. Nam aversum et remotum non adeo prevalet.**

6. *Liber novem iudicum*: 7 *est quodcumque* eo die quo Lunam corruptam
    inveneris quesierit, *proculdubio* infortunatum *habeant*, hoc solum adi-
    ecto, ut diligenter infortunium Lunam corrumpens deprehendas. *Nam* si
    illum in cardine aut post cardinem fuerit, supremus malorum cumulus,
    adversum et remotum non adeo prevalet.

7. Abraham Ibn Ezra: vii On a day when the Moon is with malefics, every-
    thing the querent asks about will not occur fully and appropriately. If the
    planet is in the ascendant sign, if the Moon is in one of the cardines, it
    is more inauspicious, because it signifies fear *in the soul* and disease in
    the body. If it (the Moon) is in the cadent places it signifies fear *but not
    disease.*

8. Henry Bate's translation: .7m. (- Gl) In die qua Luna fuerit cum malivo-
    lis (malivola Gl), quidquid quesiverit quesitor *vel homo*, non perficietur
    convenienter. (+ 7 Gl) Et si planeta fuerit in ascendente et Luna similiter
    (fuerit Gl) in aliquo angulorum, tunc est hoc peius, quia hoc significat
    in anima timorem et egritudinem in corpore; si *vero* fuerit in domibus
    cadentibus, hoc significat timorem et non egritudinem.

9. Pietro d'Abano's translation: Die quoque si Luna fuerit cum malo (Die quo
    Luna fuerit cum malis pr), non perficietur aliquod quesitum decenter. Et
    si fuerit planeta in ascendente ac Luna in uno angulorum, est deterius.
    Hoc enim denotat timorem anime et corporis infirmitatem. Si vero fuerit
    in cadentibus, timorem significat et non morbum.

10. *Gloucester Text*: 44 Quocumque die Luna adversitatem receperit ab ali-
    qua stella, quicquid die illo ab aliquo queretur, infortunio replebitur, nisi
    in debili loco ab orienti planeta fuerit a quo Luna adversitatem recepit.
    Tunc enim tantum nocere non potest. Quod si in loco *prospero* ab orienti
    fuerit, *fortis et plenus virtute* adversitatis significatione replet Lunam.

50

1.

لِلسعودِ ... (Arabic handwritten lines)

الموفي خمسين (الباب الخمسون A) اعلم أن الكوكب الذي يتصل به القمر يدل على ما

يستقبل فإذا (فإن DL) اتصل بالسعود دل على الاستقبال للخير (بالخير LD؛ الخير A) وإن

اتصل بالنحوس دل على استقبال رديء (بالشر DL) واعلم أن صاحب (رب A) الطالع

أو (و A) القمر إذا كان في نظير (ضد A) بيته اعني (- نظر بينه اعني LD) السابع من بيته

كان (فإن A) صاحب المسألة (الحاجة LD) كارها للحاجة (كاره الحاجة A) التي يسأل

عنها (منها D) يثقل (ثقل L)، ويثقل (D) عليه (- ويثقل عليه A)

2. ⟨The number⟩ completing fifty. Know that the planet to which the Moon applies indicates what is to come, and when it applies to the benefics it indicates the future for the good and when it applies to the malefics it indicates a bad future. And know that, when the lord of the ascendant or the Moon is in the nadir of its house—i.e., the seventh from its house— the lord of the question is hating the matter which is questioned, and it will be a burden on him.

3. John of Seville: Quinquagesimum (.46. M). Scito quod planeta cum (cui HMSpr) iungitur Luna significat (significet T) quod futurum est *et proventum* (perventum M) *rerum* (rei MSTpr). Quæ si iungitur fortunis, significat proventum bonum, et si iungitur malo, significat proventum malum. Et scito quod dominus ascendentis aut Luna cum fuerit in oppositione domus suæ, id est, in .viii. (.vii.ᵐᵒ HS, septimo MTpr) domus suæ, erit dominus interrogationis horrens causam de qua interrogat. Gravis enim erit illi.

4. EN-text: *Item, quod* (corr. ex quando E) *stella cui Luna applicat, negotii finem indicat, prosperum si benivola, adversum si noxia. Item, quacumque hora questio datur, si orientis dominus aut Luna in exitio suo reperta fuerit, signum est querentem re quesita non modicum gravari.*

5. *Liber trium iudicum*: Quinquagesimus, quoniam **stella cui Luna applicat, ea negotii finem indicat, prosperum si benivola, adversum si noxia.** *His executis id tenaci memoria servandum est, quoniam* **quacumque hora questio datur,** *si orientis dominus aut Luna in exitio suo reperta fuerit,* **signum est querentem re quesita non** *parum* **gravari.**

6. *Liber novem iudicum*: *8*, quoniam stella cui Luna applicat, ea negotii finem indicat, prosperum *dico* si benivola, adversum si noxia. *50*, his executis id tenaci memoria servandum est, quoniam quacumque hora *quelibet data fuerit* questio, si orientis dominus aut Luna in *casu* suo reperta fuerit, querentem rem quesitam non parum gravari *insinuat*.

7. Abraham Ibn Ezra: –

8. Henry Bate's translation: –

9. Pietro d'Abano's translation: –

10. *Gloucester Text*: 45 Quicumque planeta a quo Luna virtutem recipiat, [Lunam respiciat] significat quod futurum est. Si planeta propitius fuerit, bonum, si nocivus, malum. 46 Sciendum est quod Luna vel dominus signi orientis quando in opposito sui domicilii fuerint, quicumque tunc temporis aliquam fecerit questionem, instabili corde et animo infido de questionis adventu non sollicitus quesivit.

Explicit

1.

تَمَّتْ نوادِرُ القضاءِ لِسَهْل بن بِشْر الاسرائيلي بحمد الله تعالى وحسن عونه وصل الله على سيدنا محمد وعلى آل[ه]

تمت نوادر القضاء لسهل بن بشر الاسرائيلي بحمد الله تعالى وحسن عونه وصلى الله على سيدنا محمد وعلى آله وسلم تسليما.

(- L؛ تم الرسالة النادرة A)

2. Here ends the Choice Nuggets of Judgement of Sahl ibn Bishr al-Isrāʾīlī, with praise to God the exalted, and his good help, and may God bless our lord, Muhammad and his family and grant [them] salvation.

3. John of Seville: Scito hoc totum (+ et intellige M).

4. EN-text: –

5. *Liber trium iudicum*: His igitur que de signorum proprietatibus et Lune impedimentis ab ipso Zæl (*supra*: h) sive alKindio (*corr. in* ?) proposita fuerant, dilucide pertractatis, ad ea que de interrogationibus firmandis et eligendo questionis duce et de .xii. domorum significatione Aomar docet Tyberias transeamus.

6. *Liber novem iudicum*: –

7. Abraham Ibn Ezra: –

8. Henry Bate's translation: –

9. Pietro d'Abano's translation: –
10. *Gloucester Text*: –

3 Commentary

The setting-out of the Arabic text, the four Latin versions and English translation of a Hebrew version in a synoptic way enables one to see the differences
between the versions and the influences of one on another. The first Latin
translation is part of the corpus of three translations (*Introduction, 50 Precepts*
and *Interrogations*) attributed in some manuscripts to John of Seville. It follows the Western manuscript of Sahl's text, Escorial 918 (written in maghrebi
script) very closely, including all the glosses in the Arabic manuscript, while
adding more of its own, or giving two translations for the same Arabic word
(doublets). The same astrological terminology is used as in the *Introduction
to Astrology* of al-Qabīṣī[29] and the *Great Introduction* of Abū Maʿshar,[30] which
are securely attributed to John of Seville. E.g. *fortuna* and *malus* are respectively a benefic and a malefic planet; *mobilis, fixus, communis* are the terms for
tropical, fixed and bicorporeal signs; *anguli* and *cadentes ab angulis* are the cardines and the cadent places. There is not complete consistency between these
texts, since the succedents to the cardines are called *succedentes* (*angulos*) in
al-Qabīṣī and Abū Maʿshar, but *sequentes* (*angulorum*) in Sahl, and the subject
matter of the astrological judgements—the *ḥāja*—is *res* ('thing') in al-Qabīṣī
and Abū Maʿshar, but usually *causa* (reflecting the vernacular *cosa*) in Sahl. But
also noticeable is that only the words in the gloss and second words in doublets
in the *50 Precepts* are typical of John of Seville: 18 'melior *ac dignior*' for *afḍal*;
35 'vertitur *id est mutatur*' for *taḥawwala*; 48 'renovationem ... et ... *aptationem*'
for *ṣalāḥ*.[31] Moreover, the version in British Library, Harley 5402 (H) appears to
privilege John's readings over the others, thus omitting 'excedentia' and keeping 'superfluitas' (John's word) in 2; adding a word (*involutionem*) which could

---

29 Al-Qabīṣī (Alcabitius), *Introduction to* Astrology, eds Charles Burnett, Keiji Yamamoto and
    Michio Yano, Warburg Institute, London 2004.
30 Abū Maʿšar, *The Great Introduction to Astrology*, eds Keiji Yamamoto and Charles Burnett,
    2 vols, Brill, Leiden 2019.
31 This situation is similar to what we find in John of Seville's translation of Thābit ibn Qurra's
    On Talismans, in which one of the two versions (and the second word in a doublet) of the
    same Latin translation from Arabic exhibits more of John's vocabulary than the other:
    Gideon Bohak and Charles Burnett, *Thābit ibn Qurra 'On Talismans' and Pseudo-Ptolemy
    'On Images 1–9' together with the 'Liber prestigiorum Thebidis' of Adelard of Bath*, Micrologo-
    gus Library, 106, SISMEL–Edizioni del Galluzzo, Florence, 2021, pp. 65–66.

be a misreading of اختلاف as اختلاط in 10;[32] in 19 H gives *rerum* (John's word) for 'causarum'; in 35 H misses out the gloss 'id est iungitur' to *pulsat* (John's word) and replaces subsequent *iungitur*'s with *pulsat*; in 46 H omits the non-Johnian term—*firmitas*—as an explanation of *fixura* and retains the Johnian *stabilitas*: *fixuram, id est firmitatem et* (- firmitatem et H) *stabilitatem*. H is often alone in giving readings which conform to the Arabic: 1, *deinde finitur* and *ei cui primum occurrit*; 10 + *et solutionem*; 12—*festinationem*; 35 *pulsat*; 40 *fortis*; 44 *et si fuerit plus ... in angulo erit*; 49 *locus ab ascendente ... diminutione*. But, in reading 'datio/donatio' in 13 instead of 'promissum', and 'planetæ' instead of 'Lunæ' in 6 and 7, H may be reading a different Arabic word in the original (هدية rather than عدته; كوكب rather than قر). We may, therefore, be in the presence of several hands involved with the translation, of which John of Seville's is only one.

The next stage in the full Latin translation is the version that appears in the *Liber trium iudicum*. Ironically, it is the very difference between this translation and that of John of Seville that might make one think that the former is a revision of the latter: a later scholar improved the flow and elegance of the Latin and imposed his own terminology. The differences, however, which include added phrases in 2, 4, 13, 14, and 40, seem to be too radical to allow this.[33] Moreover, the style and vocabulary suggest that the author of this version was Hermann of Carinthia (fl. 1138–1143), and Hermann clearly worked independently of John of Seville, as we can see from the fact that both scholars translated Abū Ma'shar's *Great Introduction* at about the same time (1133 and 1140 respectively). Hermann's style is characterized by succinctness; he also retains some Arabic words for effect, and enjoys using fancy Latin words.[34]

The version in the *Liber novem iudicum* gives every indication that it is a revision of the *Liber trium iudicum* by Hugo Sanctelliensis (fl. 1145). The whole of the *Liber novem iudicum* consists of translations of his own or his more or less

---

32   تخليط (another word from the root *kh-l-ṭ* = 'to mix') is equivalent to *involutio* in Abū Ma'shar's *De magnis coniunctionibus*, which also belongs to the circle of John of Seville: see glossaries to *Abū Ma'šar on Historical Astrology, The Book of Religions and Dynasties (On the Great Conjunctions)*, eds Keiji Yamamoto and Charles Burnett, 2 vols, Islamic Philosophy, Theology, and Science, 33–34 (Leiden: Brill, 2000), II, p. 387.

33   The addition of '(this applies to) superior planets' as a gloss in John of Seville, but in the text of the *Libri iudicum*, in 38 may suggest a connection, but is an isolated case and may be an independent addition of what was well known.

34   For the possibility that a partial version of Sahl's *Three Books* that was separate from the *Liber trium iudicum* and survives in two manuscript (the EN-text), was an earlier version of what became the text that was used in the *Liber trium iudicum*, see Appendix II below.

radical revisions of other scholars' works.[35] In the case of the *50 Precepts* Hugo
only lightly revises Hermann's work. Hugo's elaborate style is evident in *præceptum* 1 (already in the *Liber trium iudicum*), but most of the precepts are still
in the succinct style of Hermann. Words which appear as glosses in the *Liber
trium iudicum* are incorporated into the text of *Liber novem iudicum* in 17, 33,
35, but not *vice versa*, and one can see a few instances of Hugo substituting
his own terminology—e.g. *domus* for *domicilium* in 13, *in domo aut regno* for
in domicilio aut principatu to translate 'in house or exaltation' in 30,[36] 'casus' in
place of 'exitium' to translate 'fall/detriment' in 50[37]—and phrases that are typical of him, such as *ad hunc quoque modum* in 2 and 48 and *ut videlicet* in 33.[38]
His most radical revision is the changing of the order of the precepts, so that
those on the same subject are listed together: the first eight relate to the Moon
(*Luna*), nos. 9–17 relate to the benefics (*fortunate, benivole, Iupiter*), nos. 18–27
to the malefics (*infortunia*), nos. 28–50 to any planet (*stella*).

A very similar rearrangement of the precepts appears in chapter 8 of Abraham Ibn Ezra's *Reshit Ḥokhmah* (*Beginning of Wisdom*): 1–7 (Moon), 8 (planets
divided into benefics and malefics), 9–17 (benefics), 18–26 (malefics), 27 (introduction to 'every planet'), 28–50 (any planet). This work was written in Béziers
in 1148, where Hermann of Carinthia had completed his last dated work (the
cosmology *De essentiis*) in 1143. There are many connections between the interests and activities of Ibn Ezra, Hermann and Hugo Sanctelliensis and they may
well have studied the same Arabic manuscripts, if not each others' texts. Hugo

---

35   See Charles Burnett, 'The use of OCR for Establishing the Authorship of a Text: the case of
the *Liber novem iudicum*' (forthcoming).

36   Note, that Hermann was already aware of this difference of terminology for 'exaltation',
when he wrote in his translation of Abū Maʿshar's *Great Introduction*, bk. 5, ch. 5: 'Deinceps eam stellarum dignitatem quam nos principatum vocamus sive regnum alii' ('Then
that dignity of the planets which we call "principatus" or others "regnum"'): Albumasar,
Liber introductorii maioris ad scientiam judiciorum astrorum, ed. Richard Lemay, Istituto
Universitario Orientale, Naples, 1996–1997, vol. 8, p. 78.

37   Elsewhere in *50 Precepts* (9), both Hermann and Hugo have 'casus' for 'dejection' (the
opposite of 'exaltation'); here Hermann has 'exitium' (as he does in his translation of Sahl's
Introductorium) for 'detriment' (the opposite of the house), which, confusingly, is also
called 'casus' by Hugo.

38   For words and phrases exclusively belonging to one Arabic-Latin translator or another,
see Dag Nikolaus Hasse, 'Stylistic Evidence for Identifying John of Seville with the Translator of Some Twelfth-Century Astrological and Astronomical Texts from Arabic into Latin
on the Iberian Peninsula', in Charles Burnett, Pedro Mantas-España (eds), *Ex Oriente Lux.
Translating Words, Scripts and Styles in Medieval Mediterranean Society*, UCOPress, CNERU
/ The Warburg Institute: Córdoba / London: 2016, pp. 19–43. One may also note Hugo's use
of *morari* (13 and 15) for the position of a planet, and Hermann's use of *punctum* for a
'minute' (14), neither of which are typical of the other translator.

and Ibn Ezra's decisions to rearrange the order of the *50 Precepts* may not have arisen independently, and it is significant that both start the work with an appeal to the 'authority of the Ancients'.[39] Nevertheless, there are no sustained verbatim correspondences between the text of the *Liber novem iudicum* and Ibn Ezra's rewriting of the *50 Precepts*. These must be considered alongside his use of other works in Sahl's corpus. Ibn Ezra would have read these texts in Arabic, but it is worth considering whether a Hebrew translation of the corpus was also made, by him or under his instruction, and whether that also had an impact on the Latin tradition of the *50 Precepts*.[40]

At first one might have thought that one had discovered such a text. For in a manuscript from Gloucester Cathedral (no. 21), just after a copy of Abraham Ibn Ezra's *Beginning of Wisdom* in Henry Bate's Latin translation, there is a unique copy of a Latin translation of the *50 Precepts* (the '*Gloucester Text*'), in which 'honor' is used for 'exaltation'. The use of 'honor' (rather than 'exaltatio', or even 'principatus' or 'regnum') is a particular trait of Latin translations from Hebrew. It is found regularly in the Latin translations of Ibn Ezra's works that are contemporary with Ibn Ezra, as well as the late thirteenth-century translations of his works by Pietro d'Abano and Henry Bate. In the *Gloucester Text*, however, it is part of a whole repertoire of terms characteristic of this version—(*planeta*) *propitius* and (*planeta*) *nocivus* for benefic and malefic; *columna, secus columnas*, and *debilis locus ab orienti* for cardine, succedent and cadent places; *signa mobilia, signa fixibilia*, and *signa duarum qualitatum* for tropical, fixed and bicorporeal signs, *demissio* for 'dejection', and *complicare* for 'to apply'—and therefore to single it out as a calque on a Hebrew term is probably misguided.[41] The *Gloucester Text* shows no indebtedness or parallels to the previous translations, least of all to that of Abraham Ibn Ezra. It gives the impression of having been written by someone with a good knowledge of Latin and the original language, but less experience in astrological literature. The choice of technical terms suggests direct engagement with a Semitic language: in both Arabic and Hebrew the word for 'cardine' (*watad* Arabic, *yated* Hebrew), means 'tent peg/pole' which preserves a metaphor (the poles or columns holding up the sky) that is not present in *cardo* ('hinge') or *angulus* ('angle') but is close to the

---

39   Such an appeal is typical in the works of Ibn Ezra and, if anything, this would suggest an influence of Ibn Ezra on Hugo.

40   A Hebrew-Latin translation of Māshā'allāh's *On Interrogations* attributed to Ibn Ezra may provide a parallel to a translation of Sahl: see Sela, *Abraham Ibn Ezra's Introductions to Astrology*, p. 11n.

41   But note that 'nocivus' is also used for 'malefic' in the Hebrew-Latin translation of Henry Bate (see *præcepta* 1 and 25 above).

word 'columna' used in the *Gloucester Text*. The date and place of this version remains to be determined.

The Arabic-Hebrew-Latin tradition is evidently not influenced verbally by the Arabic-Latin tradition. Admittedly, it does not purport to be a translation; Abraham Ibn Ezra does not acknowledge that he is taking his information from Sahl ibn Bishr, and allows himself to be a bit more free in his retelling of Sahl's precepts. The precepts are transmitted to Latin via the French of Hagin the Jew, and Shlomo Sela has shown in detail how mistakes and misinterpretations in the French have passed into the Latin.[42] It is noticeable, however, that Pietro d'Abano uses much of the same terminology as John of Seville— *fortuna/malus, mobilis/fixus/communis, angulus/succedens/cadens*—which, of course, was widespread. Henry Bate is a little aberrant : *benivolus/malivolus* (*nocivus* in 1 and 25), *mobilis/fixus/bicorpor, angulus/succedens/cadens domus*. Ibn Ezra rigorously avoids referring to the individual dignities, and therefore, there are no instances of 'honor' in Henry or Pietro's translation,[43] but its antonym *dedecus* ('disgrace') does appear for the degree opposite the exaltation (the 'dejection') in Pietro in 9 and 33.

4   Appendix 1: The Introduction (or Link Passage) to the *50 Precepts* in the *Liber trium iudicum* (MS D, fol. 54ᵛ) and *Liber novem iudicum* (MS V, fol. 10ᵛ)

Both *Libri iudicum* link the *50 Precepts* to Sahl's *Introduction* which immediately precedes by means of a passage which is shorter in the *Liber trium iudicum* (= D), but expanded in the *Liber novem iudicum* (= V). In the following edition, the words shared by the two *Libri iudicum* are in roman type, while the additions in the *Liber novem iudicum* are in italics. For other variant readings D stands for Dublin, Trinity College, 368 (*Liber trium iudicum*) and V for Vatican. Vat.lat. 6766 (*Liber novem iudicum*).

1 Hactenus de circuli partitionibus stellisque (+ per eam celi regionem D) cum valido (valido cum D) rerum motu certaque proventuum significatione (significatio V) discurrentibus, *set etiam que et qualis sit earumdem tam per se quam cum aliis proprietas et significatio, satis commode et diligenter* discre-

42   Shlomo Sela, 'The Impact of Hagin le Juif's French Translations on Subsequent Latin Translations of Abraham Ibn Ezra's Astrological Writings', *Jewish Quarterly Review*, 111 (2021), pp. 55–82.

43   Ibn Ezra refers to 'exaltation' in *præceptum* 30, but this *præceptum* has not yet been identified in Henry or Pietro's translations.

tum est, *nichilominus quidem Solis et Lune atque ducis testimonia compendiose descripta.* 2 *Hec igitur ne diutius perscrutando,* (+ que ne si difficilius sequamur D), minus ad propositum attinentia atque appendentia (appenditia D) videantur, deinceps ⟨ad⟩ astronomie iudicia (astronomicis iudiciis D) ab hoc introitu certam *et congruam* ordinemus viam (v.o. D), *ac de multiplici suprascriptorum serie tamquam de preciosis optima quoque et necessaria eligentes, ne copia inopiam, prolixitas fastidium generet, quinquaginta preceptorum instituta ut que sufficere tamquam necessaria debeant, breviter supponamus.* 3 *Constructo* (corr. ex construtio v) *enim quolibet edificio, ut est Hermocratis a⟨u⟩ctoritas, si de collecto numero multa pretiosa atque profutura superesse videantur, et construentis largitas et opulentia, quod ad hoc ut nichil deesset et artificiis prudentie multiplicem daret materiam collegit, et opificis laudetur industria quod de tot et tantis non solum potiora verumtamen necessaria et que sufficerent segregare novit.* 4 Igitur inter principia iudiciorum primo quinquaginta (.L. primum D) loci disponuntur (d.l. D) e quibus certa iudicandi procedit ratio (rato v).

1 Thus far have been discerned *in a convenient and careful enough way*, the divisions of the sphere, and the planets running (+ through that region of the sky D) with strong movements of things and signification for things to come, *but also what and how is their property and significance both in themselves and with the others, and also the testimonies of the Sun and the Moon and the Leader,*[44] *summarily described.* 2 Lest, *by investigating these things any longer* (by investigating … longer] we follow ⟨these things⟩ with greater difficulty D), they might seem less relevant and pertinent to the purpose, let us next put in good order a definite *and fitting* path to the judgements of astronomy, *and from the multiple series of what has been written above, choosing, as it were, the best and also the necessary from the precious things, so that neither abundance generates helplessness, nor prolixity boredom, let us briefly lay down fifty teachings of precepts, as being the necessary things that ought to be sufficient.*

3 *For, on the authority of Hermocrates,*[45] *once a building has been built, if, from the number ⟨of things⟩ collected together, it appears that many precious and beneficial things are left over, both the generosity and wealth of the builder—because he has collected the various materials (for this) in a way that nothing would lack and that he can offer them to the skills of wisdom—and the hard work of the Creator should be praised—because he knew how to select from so many and great ⟨things⟩ not only the more important but also the necessary and sufficient.*

---

44   I.e., the force responsible for the *ducatus*, evidently used here for the *almubtaz* or *dominus rei*.

45   Hermocrates was one of the participants in Plato's dialogues *Timaeus* and *Critias*, but the source of the quotation here has not been found.

4 Therefore, among the principles of judgements, there first should be arranged 50 'places'[46] from which a dependable way of judging can proceed.

5 Appendix II: The Authorship of the Abbreviated Version of Sahl's *50 Precepts* (= EN-Text)

Two manuscripts, Munich, BSB, Clm 588 (= N) and Erfurt, Universitäts- und Forschungsbibliothek, 4⁰ 377 (= E), give a continuous text of the first three books of Sahl's *Iudicia*, in the order, *Introduction, On Interrogations*, and *50 Precepts* (henceforth, the 'EN-text').[47] In the *Liber trium iudicum* the books are split up: while the *Introduction* and *50 Precepts* follow each other without a break (judging from Dublin, Trinity College, 368 in which the *Introduction* occupies fols. 51ᵛ–56ʳ and the *50 Precepts*, 56ʳ⁻ᵛ), *On Interrogations* is separated from the *50 Precepts* by several chapters of ʿUmar ibn al-Farrukhān's *Iudicia* and is then divided through the twelve astrological places. Are there grounds for thinking that the continuous text in the EN-text is the original translation of Hermann of Carinthia? While this cannot properly be judged before the whole of Sahl's three books are surveyed, one can use the evidence of the *50 Precepts* for a preliminary assessment. First of all, the shibboleths of Hermann's translation are present: 'exitium' for 'detriment', 'negotium', as an alternative word for 'thing/subject matter' (*ḥāja*), and the general abbreviated nature of the text; in short, there is nothing in the language or style of this version that precludes Hermann's authorship.

The *50 Precepts* are headed 'ex .50. principalibus iudiciis' which already implies that a selection has been made.[48] And this is what we find: most of the first fifteen *præcepta* have been included, but then there is a break until *præceptum* 40, and then a jump to the last five *præcepta* (omitting 46). A passage at the end of 15 found in no other version of the *50 Precepts* bridges this break. The *præcepta* are not numbered. If we do propose that the EN-Text is the original version, we would have to presume that, having just made a selection, Hermann then completed the translation for the text that was included in the *Liber trium iudicum*. This is in keeping with the elaboration of the EN-text for

---

46   Note that, in Arabic, *mawāḍiʿ* = means both 'places' and 'subjects'; but 'locus' can also mean a 'topic' in Latin: cf. *locus communis* ('commonplace').

47   The first two of these books are described as the *Liber iudicialis Tholomei*.

48   This selection, however, may have been made by the scribe, for, on the next page (fol. 61ᵛ) there is the heading 'Ex Lupoldo de notificatione mortis' ('from Leopold (of Austria) on the indication of death').

the *Liber trium iudicum* (e.g. **47** 'bifidis et' added to 'duplicibus'). The further elaboration in the *Liber novem iudicum* shows that the EN-text is closer to Hermann than to Hugo: single words are expanded (*statum*] *statusque proprietas*) or supplemented: *inutilis* (+ *etiam infructuosi*) *negotii*. What one is looking for are instances where the EN-Text is closer to the original Arabic than the text in the *Liber trium iudicum*. There are five possible examples of this:

1. In 1 the EN-text gives the simple 'salva, salvantur res, et ea corrupta, corrumpuntur' corresponding to the Arabic: 'So its (the Moon's) soundness is the soundness of every thing and its harm is the harm of every thing', which appears in the *Liber trium iudicum* as 'si salva sit Luna, *spem atque fiduciam et securitatem promittat*, corrupta, *dubitandum incidet et metuendum*',

2. In 48 there is some repetition in the Arabic: 'When the planet is stationary for retrogradation it indicates destruction in that matter and disobedience. When it is stationary for direct movement it indicates directness in the thing, without difficulty. Every planet which is a signifier while seeking direct movement, indicates the soundness of the matter, its power and its directness. And if it is stationary for retrogradation it indicates harm, difficulty and destruction'. The consequences of being stationary for retrogradation and stationary for direct movement, are given twice, but in a different order: ABBA. In *Liber trium iudicum* this repetition is avoided and the whole process is set forth in simple terms: 'Stelle prima statio rem negat, secunda vero cum labore promittit'. This statement is given in the EN-text, but is followed by the repetition: 'prima statio stelle *negotium* negat, secunda cum labore promittit. *Retrogradatio negat. Directio bene promittit et dat*'. Admittedly, the order has been changed to ABAB, but the repetition is still there, and one can see why Hermann might have wanted to replace this repetition simply by the words: 'Ad hunc itaque modum utraque inspecta negatio vel affirmatio in iudicium venit' ('In this way, both (the two stations) having been inspected, negation or affirmation arrives in the judgement').

3. The passive 'habeatur' in **49** reflects the passive in the Arabic, which has been changed to a second person (*habeas*) in the *Libri iudicum*.

4. The preservation of the preposition (على *secundum*) in 8 also suggests a direct engagement with the Arabic text on the part of the EN-text.

5. Also in 8 the accusative 'naturam' in EN-text might have led the author of *Liber trium iudicum* to keep 'naturam' when the changed syntax requires 'natura'.

There is nothing in the EN-text that is not characteristic of Hermann. E.g., in his translation of the *Great Introduction* of Abū Maʿshar can be found the words *item, discursus, excipere, attinere* (more frequent than *pertinere*), and *ingredi*. Hermann was well known for abbreviating texts, and leaving out sections which he thought were redundant or repetitive (such as in his book on weatherforecasting (*Liber imbrium*) and his translation of the *Great Introduction* of Abū Maʿshar which, among other things, omits the whole of the sixth chapter of Book VIII, a summary of information on astrological lots given in the preceding chapters). Given these indications, I am inclined to consider the EN-text as being an early version of Hermann's translation of the three books of Sahl, which he elaborated for inclusion in the *Liber trium iudicum*.

Acknowledgements

I am grateful to David Juste and Emanuele Rovati for providing copies of manuscripts and digital sources, and correcting my text, for the advice of Aisha Alowais Alshamsi and Saba Alkuwari, and to Jean-Patrice Boudet for sharing his editions-in-preparation. We would like to thank the Escorial Library for allowing us to reproduce sections from MS Real Biblioteca del Monasterio de San Lorenzo, ar. 918, fols. 47ᵛ–49ᵛ.

CHAPTER 4

al-Ashraf ʿUmar's *Tabṣira*, Chapter xl.1

An election table as a tool for an astrologer?

Petra G. Schmidl

Abstract

This article assesses the suitability of an election table that allows to choose the appropriate time to begin an activity as a tool for an astrologer. It is found in chapter xl.1 of the *Kitāb al-Tabṣira fī ʿilm al-nujūm* ("Enlightenment in the science of the stars"). This treatise includes a wide range of topics, astronomical, astrological, mathematical, and geographical knowledge as well as calculating, prognostic, and magic practises written by al-Ashraf ʿUmar (d. 1296), who later in his life became the Rasūlid sultan and ruler over Yemen. In the first part, after shortly introducing the author, his oeuvre, and his treatise, this article describes the election table and its contents. Next, it compares it with further manifestations of this astrological practice in al-Ashraf ʿUmar's *Tabṣira*. As a criterion to classify them, their different methods in determining time are considered. This approach allows also to draw conclusions about the skills a practitioner needs to apply this election table and therefore to assess its suitability as a tool for an astrologer.

Keywords

al-Ashraf ʿUmar – *Kitāb al-Tabṣira fī ʿilm al-nujūm* – 13th century Yemen – elections – astrological tools & practices

1   The Tool and Its Background

1.1   *Author, Treatise, Chapter*

Shall we play chess today or plant a tree? One answer to this and comparable questions provides al-Malik al-Ashraf (Mumahhid al-Dīn) ʿUmar b. Yūsuf b. ʿUmar b. ʿAlī b. Rasūl (d. 1296) in the first part of chapter xl in his *Kitāb al-Tabṣira fī ʿilm al-nujūm* ("Enlightenment in the science of the stars").[1] Its author

---

1   This article belongs to a series by this author, all dealing with various aspects of the *Tabṣira*

was the third of the Rasūlid sultans in Yemen, who, most probably before his ascend to the throne after the death of his father al-Muẓaffar Yūsuf in 1295, engaged himself in making instruments and writing scholarly treatises about agriculture, animal studies, genealogy, astral sciences, and medicine.[2] His contribution to the science of the stars comprise at least six astrolabes, one still preserved,[3] and three treatises, of which two survived. While the contents of al-Ashraf ʿUmar's *Instrument Book* gives a consistent impression by dealing with the construction of astrolabes, sundials, water-clocks, and a magnetic compass for finding the direction towards Mecca, the *qibla*,[4] his *Tabṣira* is a mixed bag. It includes topics related to astronomy, astrology, prognostication, magic, calendars, timekeeping, mathematics, and geography.[5]

The *Tabṣira* is preserved in two manuscripts, one in Oxford (Bodleian Library, Huntington 233; henceforth: H) and one in Paris (Bibliothèque Nationale, arabe 2601.2; henceforth: P). Altogether, the Oxford copy, most probably from fourteenth-century Yemen and therefore quite close to the writing place and

---

and its author, al-Ashraf ʿUmar. They provide the basis of an edition, English translation, and study of the whole text; preprints of single chapters and further material informing on the contents and context of the treatise and its author are already published online via tabsira.hypotheses.org and will eventually be compiled into a printed volume.

2   Petra G. Schmidl, "al-Ashraf ʿUmar's Tabṣira: Chapter xxxiv: Rainbows, Shooting Stars, and Haloes as Signs of the Future," in *Dreams, Nature, and Practices as Signs of the Future in the Middle Ages*, eds. Klaus Herbers and Hans-Christian Lehner, Prognostication in History 10 (Leiden, Boston: Brill, 2022), 252–309, here 256–258, Petra G. Schmidl, "Rulers as Authors in 13th Century Yemen: al-Ashraf ʿUmar's Oeuvre," in *Rulers as Authors in the Islamic World: Knowledge, Authority and Legitimacy*, eds. Sonja Brentjes, Maribel Fierro, and Tilman Seidensticker, Islamic History and Civilization 213 (Leiden: Brill, 2024), 455–488; Petra G. Schmidl, "Ashraf," in *Biographical Encyclopedia of Astronomers*, 2 Volumes, eds. Thomas Hockey, Virgina Trimble, and Thomas R. Williams (New York: Springer, 2007), see also n. 1.

3   David A. King, *In Synchrony with the Heavens: Studies in Astronomical Timekeeping and Instrumentation in Medieval Islamic Civilization*. Volume Two: Instruments of Mass Calculation (Studies x–xviii), Islamic Philosophy, Theology and Science 55 (Leiden: Brill, 2005), 625–632; www.metmuseum.org/art/collection/search/444408 last accessed 2024-03-08.

4   King, *In Synchrony* 2, 632–639; Petra G. Schmidl, "Two Early Arabic Sources on the Magnetic Compass (Revised Translation of a Master Thesis, Johann Wolfgang Goethe-Universität Frankfurt 1994)," *Journal of Arabic and Islamic Studies* 1 (1997): 81–132, here 88–111.

5   For the table of contents Petra G. Schmidl, "al-Ashraf ʿUmar's *Tabṣira*: The Table of Contents. Supporting Sovereign Decision-making in 13th Century Yemen?" in *Unterstützung bei herrscherlichem Entscheiden: Experten und ihr Wissen in transkultureller und komparativer Perspektive*, ed. Michael Grünbart, Kulturen des Entscheidens Band 005 (Göttingen: Vandenhoeck & Ruprecht, 2021): 216–232, in particular 225–232 (Arabic text and English translation); for the chapters already studied tabsira.hypotheses.org and Petra G. Schmidl, "al-Ashraf ʿUmar's *Tabṣira*: The Preface. Announcing an Introductory Text?" *Zeitschrift für Geschichte der arabisch-islamischen Wissenschaften* 22 (2022): 163–196.

time of the *Tabṣira* in the 1270s,[6] is the more complete, the better organised, the more dependable, and the more neatly written of the two manuscripts. After the title follow preface,[7] table of contents,[8] and 50 numbered chapters. In the Paris copy the *Tabṣira* forms the second part of the manuscript, according to the script of an Eastern provenance and dated March 1626 (Muḥarram 1036). It also starts with the preface, but title and table of contents are omitted; the chapters not numbered.[9] Accordingly, this article relies on the Oxford copy, if not stated otherwise.

Chapter xl of the *Tabṣira* deals with two topics, elections that allow to choose the appropriate time to begin an activity, and incidents, sometimes also denoted as signs or omens.[10] Both parts present their information in double-argument tables. The second part, strikingly longer than the first, covers 25 pages and provides in its first column all together 300 incidents characterized by their unusual, random, occasional, spontaneous, and involuntary occur-

---

6   Taro Mimura and Petra G. Schmidl, "al-Ashraf ʿUmar's *Tabṣira*: Chapter ix (H, 22ᵇ, 3–25ᵃ, 8)—Lunar Nodes, Eclipses, Fortune and Misfortune of the Planets, Elections," published 2022-07-19 on tabsira.hypotheses.org, 8 with n. 24. tabsira.hypotheses.org/files/2022/07/Tabsira-22b-25a-Kap.-IX-2202.pdf

7   Schmidl, *al-Ashraf ʿUmar's Tabṣira: The Preface*, in particular 194–196 (Arabic text and English translation).

8   See n. 5.

9   See also n. 1 and Petra G. Schmidl, "Magic and Medicine in a 13th c. Treatise on the Science of the Stars," in *Herbal Medicine in Yemen: Traditional Knowledge and Practice, and their Value for Today's World*, eds. Hanne Schönig and Ingrid Hehmeyer with the collaboration of Anne Regourd, Islamic History and Civilization 96 (Leiden: Brill, 2012), 43–68, here 46–48.

10   For "sign—signs" often *dalīl—dalāʾil* is used, but also ʿalāma—ʿalāmāt, and, with a slightly different meaning, āya—āyāt, for "omen" faʾl, but also ʿiyāfa, ṭāʾir or ṭīra, and zajr, respectively and slightly different in meaning (e.g., Petra G. Schmidl, "Introductory Surveys: Medieval Traditions of Prognostication in the Islamic World," in *Prognostication in the Medieval World: A Handbook*, eds. Matthias Heiduk, Klaus Herbers, and Hans-Christian Lehner [Berlin: de Gruyter], 2021), 189–242, here 196, 213); a combination of elections and omens is also included in the ninth chapter of al-Bīrūnī's *Kitāb al-Āthār al-bāqiyya fī qurūn al-khāliyya* ("Book of the vestiges of the past", also known as "The chronology of the ancient nations"; C. Edward Sachau, *Chronologie Orientalischer Völker von Albêrūnī* [Leipzig: Brockhaus, 1878], repr. Islamic Mathematics and Astronomy 30 [Frankfurt: Institut für Geschichte der arabisch-islamischen Wissenschaften, 1998], 231–232 [Arabic text] and C. Edward Sachau, *The Chronology of Ancient Nations: An English Version of the Athār-Ul-Bākiya of Albīrūnī, or "Vestiges in the Past"* [London: W.H. Allen & Co., 1879], repr. Islamic Mathematics and Astronomy 31 [Frankfurt: Institut für Geschichte der arabisch-islamischen Wissenschaften, 1998], 218 [English translation]), namely a table presenting the سعد—"lucky", نحس—"unlucky", and وسط—"middling" days of the Persian calendar that includes a column informing about what the "appearance of a snake [...] signifies" at this day.

rence in everyday life. They include weather phenomena such as thunder and lightening, animal behaviours, particularly their sounds, all kind of encounters with humans and animals, bodily symptoms, e.g., sneezing, twitching, coughing, or hiccupping, and incidents due to human carelessness or clumsiness, particularly falling of items out of hand or things happening to clothes. In the double-argument table these incidents are related to the Moon's position in the zodiacal signs given in the first line. The single cells record the interpretations related to these two arguments and restrict themselves often to a single word or a short sentence such as "happiness", "voyage", "good will follow", or "it is spoken of him". The headings on the top of each spread comprising to opposite pages, attribute this incident table to the Indians, the Persians, and the (Eastern) Romans.[11]

1.2 *The Election Table*

The first part of chapter xlv presents an election table that relates activities to the Moon's position in the zodiac to get finally some advice, if it is appropriate, inappropriate or neither-nor to begin with an action. The table covers after the chapter heading at the end of one page (H, 121^a) the following two spreads (H, 121^b–123^a).[12] Its two headings stretch each from the *verso* to the opposite *recto* page and announce the topic of the tables. Below it in the first line of the table follow twice the zodiacal signs, one set on each page and two mirrored first columns of twelve lines listing the activities. The cells of this verbal double-argument table inform about the appropriateness to begin with an activity. On the first spread, they are written horizontally, vertically, and diagonally forming an outer octagon and an inner diamond reminding of 18 squeezed doughnuts. On the second double page, the design changes to hexagons resembling 36 lengthy easter eggs (see Figure 4.1). Rubrication is used for the headline and alternating in the first line and the first column to structure the zodiacal signs and the activities.

In the Paris copy (P, 170^a) only twelve activities have survived and are mixed with the incident table in the second part of chapter xl.[13] First line and first column are also written alternatingly in black and red ink. The strokes in the cells start nearly vertical in the beginning, nearly horizontal to the end.

Although the election table asks for the position of the Moon in the zodiacal signs, it does not include the necessary information to solve this problem; the

---

11   Tim Hertogh, Carine van Rhijn, Bruno Schalekamp, and Petra G. Schmidl, "Medieval Divination by Unexpected Incidents: The *Tabula Prenostica Salomonis*," *International Journal of Divination and Prognostication* 4 (2023): 81–103, in particular 96–98.

12   For Arabic text and English translation of chapter xl.1 of the *Tabṣira* see 4. Appendix.

13   In 4. Appendix the entries also preserved in the Paris manuscript are highlighted in grey.

FIGURE 4.1
The design elements of the election table (left: H, 121ᵇ–
122ᵃ; right: H, 122ᵇ–123ᵃ)

solution has to be found elsewhere.[14] Making an educated guess of what could
have been possible procedures in thirteenth century Yemen, although they are
not explicitly elaborated in the sources, three possibilities come to mind.

(1) Deducing the Moon's position.

Chapter xxii of the *Tabṣira* includes a double-argument table for deducing the Moon's position in the zodiacal signs by relating the days of the
lunar to the (Eastern) Roman months.[15] Placed in front is a short text
that explains in detail its use. Equally simple is the use of an ephemeris, a
yearbook, or annual calendar, that provides the positions of the Sun, the
Moon, and the planets for each day of one year,[16] often combined with
additional information, in particular elections.[17] Closest in time and place
comes to the *Tabṣira* the anonymous ephemeris made for Sanaa and the

---

14   In the Latin traditions, at least incident tables that also ask for the determination of the
      Moon's position in the zodiacal signs are accompanied by an auxiliary table that solves the
      problem (Hertogh, van Rhijn, Schalekamp, and Schmidl, *Unexpected Incidents, passim,* in
      particular 90).

15   Benno van Dalen and Petra G. Schmidl, "al-Ashraf ʿUmar's *Tabṣira*: Chapter xxii," to appear
      on tabsira.hypotheses.org; see also Schmidl, *al-Ashraf ʿUmar's Tabṣira: The Table of Con-
      tents,* 226 (Arabic text) and 230 (English translation); a similar table is found in a *majmūʿa*
      containing texts on geomancy, astronomy, and astrology that is now preserved in Leiden,
      Universiteitsbibliotheek, Or. 6638, fol. 157ᵇ (P. Voorhoeve, *Handlist of Arabic Manuscripts
      in the Library of the University of Leiden,* Codices Manuscripti 7 [Leiden: University Press,
      1957], 174–175, 244, 434).

16   E.g., Johannes Thomann, "Reverse Engineering Applied to Ephemerides: Analysis and Edi-
      tion of the Arabic Ephemeris of 1326/27 CE (MS Cairo, Dār Al-Kutub, Mīqāt 817)," in *Editing
      and Analysing Numerical Tables: Towards a Digital Information System for the History of
      Astral Sciences,* eds. Benno van Dalen, Matthieu Husson, and Clemency Montelle, Ptole-
      maeus Arabus et Latinus–Studies (PALS) 2 (Turnhout: Brepols Publishers, 2021), 469–510,
      here 470; also Michael Hofelich, "*Taḳwīm,*" in *The Encyclopaedia of Islam: New Edition,* 12
      Volumes and Indices (Leiden: Brill 1960–2009).

17   Johannes Thomann, "The Arabic Ephemeris for the Year 1149/1150 CE (P. Cambridge UL
      Inv. Michael. Chartae D 58) and the Arabic *baḥnīṭas,* Greek Παχνίτης and Coptic Παϣονϲ,"
      Chronique d'Egypte 90,179 (2015): 207–224, in particular 212–221 (Arabic text, facsimile, and
      English translation).

year 1327/28 preserved in Cairo.[18] Preceding the numeral tables, several prognostic practices are included, e.g., interpreting convulsions (*ikhtilāj*).

(2) Calculating the Moon's position.

Before al-Ashraf ʿUmar comes to the table in chapter xxii, he provides a rule of thumb for the determination of the Moon's position in the zodiac.[19] More difficult, and therefore rather for experts, is extracting the required data from a *zīj*, an astronomical-astrological handbook with tables,[20] such as the *Zīj al-kabīr al-Ḥākimī* by Ibn Yūnus (d. 1009) that was widely used in the Yemen,[21] and then calculating the lunar longitude.

(3) Observing the Moon's position.

One might gaze at the Moon at the moment in question and identify the constellation of its place because one's own familiarity with the starry sky, a task that might be simplified by using the depictions of the zodiacal signs in the *Kitāb al-Ṣuwar* ("Book of constellations") by ʿAbd al-Raḥmān al-Ṣūfī (903–986),[22] on a celestial globe,[23] or even on the rete of an astrolabe.[24]

---

18   David A. King, *A Catalogue of the Scientific Manuscripts in the Egyptian National Library* (in Arabic). 2 Volumes (Cairo: General Egyptian Book Organization, 1981/1986), vol. 2, 148, no. 2/3/2; David A. King, *Manuscripts in the Egyptian National Library* (Winona Lake, Indiana: Eisenbrauns, 1986), 132, no. E11; focussing on the numerical data Thomann, *Reverse Engineering*, in particular 493–507; investigating the *qibla* scheme Petra G. Schmidl, "al-Ashraf ʿUmar's *Tabṣira*: Chapter xxxvii.1: Qibla Schemes as Text-image Arrangements with an Example from 13th Century Yemen," in *Writing as Intermediary: Text-image Relations in Early Modern Islamic Cultures*, eds. Lorenz Korn and Berenike Metzler, Bamberger Orientstudien 16 (Bamberg: University of Bamberg Press, 2022), 65–96, here 88–89.

19   See n. 15.

20   For the use of *zīj*es for astrological purposes Margaret Gaida, "Zījes," in *Prognostication*, eds. Heiduk, Herbers, and Lehner, 999–1002.

21   David A. King, *Mathematical Astronomy in Medieval Yemen: A Biobibliographical Survey* (American Research Center in Egypt. Malibu: Udena Publications, 1983), 27, 30–32.

22   For further reading H.C.F.C. Schjellerup, *Description des étoiles fixes [...] par l'astronome Persan Abd-al-Rahman al-Sūfi [...]* (St. Petersburg: unknown, 1874); also Gotthard Strohmaier, *Die Sterne des Abd ar-Rahman as-Sufi* (Leipzig, Weimar: Gustav Kiepenheuer, 1984); for a list of the manuscripts, e.g., ismi.mpiwg-berlin.mpg.de/text/172144—last accessed 2024-03-09.

23   For a concise introduction Emilie Savage-Smith, "Globes," in *The Encyclopaedia of Islam: Three* (Leiden: Brill, 2007-to date); for further reading Emilie Savage-Smith, *Islamicate Celestial Globes: Their History, Construction, and Use*. With a Chapter on Iconography by Andrea P.A. Belloli, Smithsonian Studies in History and Technology 46 (Washington D.C: Smithsonian Institution, 1985).

24   For further reading and examples, e.g., Koenraad van Cleempoel, ed., *Astrolabes at Greenwich: A Catalogue of the Astrolabes in the National Maritime Museum* (Oxford, Greenwich: Oxford University Press, 2006).

This guess already conveys a first impression of the problems a practitioner faces when applying this table. It gives an idea of the skills and tools that are inevitable or helpful to mitigate them.

The activities listed in the election table cover from timeless and universal basic human needs related, e.g., to body care, to features depending strongly on time, place, and sociocultural settings, e.g., circumcision, many aspects of everyday life, some rather belonging to an elite surrounding, e.g., meeting kings, others to a more common, e.g., ablactation. They can be assigned to six spheres.

(1)   Social life including all kinds of games and amusement such as playing chess; also marrying belongs to it.

(2)   Politics and diplomacy, e.g., consulting ministers or sending a messenger. A subgroup forms activities related to warfare such as reviewing the troops, and those concerning meetings with persons such as commanders. Encounters, e.g., with humans possessing peculiar attributes or with animals at an unusual place, figure prominently in the incident table in the second part of chapter xl. So in particular the meeting with two snake-charmers (?) and with the old women (?) appear to be the odd two out. They rather seem to belong to incidental occurrences than to an election, an activity to begin at the appropriate time.

(3)   Trade and commerce, particularly all kinds of buying, from jewels and gold to animals and slaves.

(4)   Health and hygiene comprising, e.g., drinking a laxative, bloodletting, or bathing; two are explicitly related to nursery, engaging a wet nurse (?) and weaning.

(5)   Husbandry whose passage to commerce and trade is fluent and that includes planting trees or building.

(6)   Education and training such as apprenticing youths to the scribes.

Omitted in the election table in chapter xl.1 are all kinds of activities related to occult sciences, e.g., preparing amulets or making gold,[25] as found in other examples including chapter xxv and xlviii of the *Tabṣira*.[26]

Three terms given in the cells of the election table assess the moment in time. They restrict themselves to three ratings, depending on the Moon's posi-

---

25   Daniel Martin Varisco, "The Magical Significance of the Lunar Stations in the 13th Century Yemeni *Kitāb al-Tabṣira fī ʿilm al-nujūm* of al-Malik al-Ashraf," *Quaderni di Studi Arabi* 13 (1995): 19–40, here 26, 28–33; Michio Yano, ed., *Kūshyār ibn Labbān's Introduction to Astrology* (Tokio: Institute for the Study of Languages and Cultures of Asia and Africa [ILCAA], 1997), iv.2, 240–241, §3; see also n. 72.

26   See below p. 199f (chapter xxv) and p. 202ff (chapter xlviii).

tion in the zodiacal signs, if an activity is at this moment محمود—"appropriate",
مذموم—"inappropriate", or وسط—"neither-nor" to begin. This tripartite distinction appears for a moment unusual, since the relevant literature emphasis the
dichotomy by speaking of auspicious and inauspicious, or lucky and unlucky,
days.[27] It is, however, no isolated case; other elections also provide trefoils of
possible interpretations, e.g., in a treatise attributed to Jaʿfar al-Ṣādiq (d. 765),
"the imam, that both Imāmīs and Ismāʿīlīs, two Shīʿī branches, still recognize
and an authority [...] allegedly in mantic practices".[28] It bears the title *Maḥmū-
dāt al-ayyām wa-madhmūmātuhā wa-mutawassiṭātuhā fī aḥwāl min kull shahr*
("The appropriate days, the objectionable ones, and the indifferent in the affairs
of every month").[29] In another prognostic practice this triple also figures, when
rating the critical days, a pre- and early modern medical concept.[30] Ḥunayn
b. Isḥāq (d. 873), for instance, in his *Masāʾil fī ayyām al-buḥrān fī al-amrāḍ
al-ḥādda* ("Questions on the critical days in acute illnesses"), deriving from
the according treatise by Galen (2nd c.),[31] designates them either as محمود—

---

27   E.g., Toufic Fahd, "*Nudjūm, Aḥkām al-*," in *EI2*; David Pingree, "*Eḵtīārāt*," in *Encyclopaedia
      Iranica: Online edition* (www.iranicaonline.org last accessed 2024-03-16).

28   Schmidl, *Introductory Survey*, 200.

29   Ron Bluckley, "The Writings of Jaʿfar al-Ṣādiq," in *Books and Bibliophiles: Studies in Hon-
      our of Paul Auchterlonie on the Bio-bibliography of the Muslim World*, ed. Robert Gleave
      (Cambridge: Gibb Memorial Trust, 2014), 14–28, here 26, no. 26; further examples listed
      by Johannes Thomann, "From *katarchai* to *ikhtiyārāt*: The Emergence of a New Arabic
      Document Type Combining Ephemerides and Almanacs," in *Proceedings of the 28th Inter-
      national Congress of Papyrology* (Barcelona 1–6 August 2016), eds. Alberto Nodar and Sofía
      Torallas Tovar, Scripta orientalia 3 (Barcelona: Publicacions de l'Abadia de Monserrat, Uni-
      versitat Pompeu Fabra, 2019), primera edición, 342–354, here 342.

30   For a concise summary of the development of the critical days, e.g., Glen Michael Cooper,
      "Approaches to the Critical Days in Late Medieval and Renaissance Thinkers," *Early Sci-
      ence and Medicine* 18 (2013): 536–565, here 538–540; for Arabic text and English translation
      of Ḥunayn b. Isḥāq's Arabic version of Galen's treatise on the critical days Glen Michael
      Cooper, *Galen, De Diebus Decretoriis, from Greek into Arabic: A Critical Edition, with Trans-
      lation and Commentary, of Ḥunayn Ibn Isḥāq, Kitāb Ayyām al-buḥrān*, Medicine in the
      Medieval Mediterranean (London, New York: Routledge, Taylor & Francis Group, 2011);
      for Arabic and Hebrew text with English translations of the Alexandrian summaries of
      Galen's treatise on the critical days Gerrit Bos and Y. Tzvi. Langermann, *The Alexandrian
      Summaries of Galen's On Critical Days: Editions and Translations of the two Versions of the
      Jawāmiʿ*. With an Introduction and Notes, Islamic Philosophy, Theology and Science 92
      (Leiden: Brill, 2014).

31   Glen Michael Cooper, "Rational and Empirical Medicine in Ninth Century Baghdad: Qusṭā
      Ibn Lūqā's Questions on the Critical Days in Acute Illnesses," *Arabic Sciences and Philos-
      ophy* 24 (2014): 69–102, here 85 (English translation and commentary) and 100 (Arabic
      text).

"appropriate", مذموم—"inappropriate", or متوسّط—"intermediate", with only the
last word being slightly different in Arabic, though using the same root.[32]

2   The Method and Its Manifestations

2.1   *Elections*

After introducing the election table in chapter xl.1 and before comparing it with
further examples, it appears appropriate to turn first to the method in a more
general way. In the broader sense elections denote all methods that allow to
choose the appropriate time to begin an activity and contract various manifestations in the Afro-Eurasian *oikouménē* since pre- and early modern times,[33]

---

32   More farfetched is another trifold rating, Galen's assumption of an intermediate state
     between health and disease that is also reflected in ethics with its division into good,
     bad, and neutral things (Véronique Boudon, "Les définitions tripartites de la médecine
     chez Galien," in *Wissenschaften* [*Medizin und Biologie (Forts.)*], ed. Wolfgang Haase and
     Hildegard Temporini, Aufstieg und Niedergang der römischen Welt, Teil II, Bd. 37, Teilbd.
     2 [Berlin et al.: de Gruyter, 1994], 1468–1490; cf., e.g., Maaike van der Lugt, "Neither Ill
     nor Healthy: The Intermediate State Between Health and Disease in Medieval Medicine,"
     Quaderni storici, nuova serie 46,136 [2011]: 13–45, here 15–16 who reminds "of the antitheti-
     cal division, in Stoic ethics, of things into those that are good, bad, and 'neither' [*oudétera*]
     or 'indifferent' [*adiáfora*])."
33   For the term Matthew Melvin-Koushki, "Review Essay. Magic in Islam between Reli-
     gion and Science," *Magic, Ritual, and Witchcraft* 14 (2019): 255–287, here 272–273 with
     n. 32; for an overview, e.g., Rudolf, Stefanie, *Syrische Astrologie und das Syrische Medi-
     zinbuch*, Science, Technology, and Medicine in Ancient Cultures 7 (Berlin, Boston: de
     Gruyter, 2018), 132–136; Fabian Käs, "Astrologische Voraussagen über den Jagderfolg: Der
     Katarchen-Abschnitt des K. al-Qānūn al-Wāḍiḥ von Ibn Quštimur," in *Die Geheimnisse der
     oberen und der unteren Welt: Magie im Islam zwischen Glaube und Wissenschaft*, eds. Seba-
     stian Günther and Dorothee Pielow, Islamic History and Civilization 158 (Leiden: Brill,
     2018), 294–318, here 308–315; Pingree, *Eḵtīārāt*; Thomann, *From katarchai to ikhtiyārāt*,
     342–346; M.J.L. Young, "An Arabic Almanac of Favourable and Unfavourable Days," *Jour-
     nal of Semitic Studies* 27,2 (1982): 261–279, here 261–265; Toufic Fahd, *La divination arabe*
     (Leiden: Brill, 1966), 483–488; for treatises on electional astrology in Islamicate societies
     Toufic Fahd "Nudjūm, Aḥkām al-, ii. Hemerology and Menology," in *EI2*; Fahd, *Divination
     arabe*, 485–488; also Toufic Fahd, "Ikhtiyārāt," in *EI2*; for English translations of some of
     them, mainly relying on the Latin versions, Benjamin N. Dykes, *Choices and Inceptions:
     Traditional Electional Astrology* (Minneapolis, Minnesota: Cazimi Press, 2012); for individ-
     ual sources from the Islamicate societies see n. 50 and 2.3 Elections in the Tabṣira; for the
     Latin traditions, e.g., Philipp Nothaft, "Calendrical Calculations: Traditions and Practices
     in the Medieval Western Christian World," in *Prognostication*, eds. Heiduk, Herbers, and
     Lehner, 605–618; László Sándor Chardonnens, "Hemerology in Medieval Europe," in *Books
     of Fate and Popular Culture in Early China: The Daybook Manuscripts of the Warring States,
     Qin, and Han*, eds. by Donald J. Harper and Marc Kalinowski, Handbook of Oriental Stud-
     ies = Handbuch der Orientalistik, Section 4, China Volume 33 (Leiden, Boston: Brill, 2017),

already evidenced in Ancient Mesopotamian,[34] Ancient Egyptian,[35] Ancient Greek, and Roman sources.[36] This prognostic practice, however, does not necessarily involve astrological concepts or notions. Lucky and unlucky moments in time may be charged positively or negatively in other ways. Only in the narrower sense elections form one branch of astrology,[37] often classified with three others,[38] mundane astrology,[39] nativities,[40] and interrogations.[41]

373–407; also Charles Burnett, "Astral Sciences: Traditions and Practices in the Medieval Western Christian World," in *Prognostication*, eds. Heiduk, Herbers, and Lehner, 485–501, here 490, apparently only reflecting about complex elections (see n. 49); for the Latin sources Dykes, *Choices and Inceptions*; for a Hebrew example Shlomo/Shelomoh Sela, *Abraham Ibn Ezra on Elections, Interrogations, and Medical Astrology: A Parallel Hebrew-English Critical Edition of the Book of Elections (3 versions), the Book of Interrogations (3 versions), and the Book of the Luminaries*, Etudes sur le judaisme médiéval 50 (Leiden et al.: Brill, 2011).

34   For examples René Labat, *Un calendrier babylonien des travaux des signes et des mois: Séries Iqqur Îpuš*, Bibliothèque de l'École des Hautes Études 321 (Paris: Champion, 1965) and René Labat, *Hémérologies et ménologies d'Assur: Études d'assyriologie 1*, Doctoral thesis Paris: Université de Paris (Paris: Libr. d'Amérique et d'Orient, 1939); also Pingree, *Eḵtīārāt*; Daryn Lehoux, *Astronomy, Weather, and Calendars in the Ancient World: Parapegmata and Related Texts in Classical and Near-Eastern Societies* (Cambridge: Cambridge University Press, 2007), 113–114.

35   For examples Christian Leitz, *Tagewählerei: Das Buch ḥȝt nḥḥ pḥ.wy ḏt und verwandte Texte*. 1. Textband, 2. Tafelband (Wiesbaden: Harrassowitz, 1994); also, Lehoux, *Astronomy, Weather, and Calendars*, 129–130.

36   Kocku von Stuckrad, "Hemerology," in *New Pauly Online* (BrillOnline Reference Works. Leiden: Brill, 2005-to date).

37   Also known as "choices", "beginnings", "inceptions", or "initiatives", "elective", "electional" or "catarchic astrology", (e.g., Burnett, *Astral Sciences*; Anne-Laurence Caudano, "Astral Science: Traditions and Practices in the Medieval Eastern Christian World," in *Prognostication*, eds. Heiduk, Herbers, and Lehner, 502–515, here 505–506; Dorotheus Sidonius, *Carmen Astrologicum: The Umar al-Tabari Translation*, trans. and ed. Benjamin N. Dykes [Minneapolis, Minnesota: The Cazimi Press, 2017], 56–57); also in use is "hemerology" that, however, rather applies to elections in the broader sense (cf., e.g., Nothaft, *Calendrical Calcultions*, 606: "The ancient practice of distinguishing or identifying propitious days in a calendar is sometimes referred to as 'hemerology', [from the Greek *hémera*, 'day'], although this term has also been applied to the study of calendars more generally.").

38   E.g., Petra G. Schmidl, "Astral Sciences: Traditions and Practices in the Medieval Islamic World," in *Prognostication*, eds. Heiduk, Herbers, and Lehner, 532–550, here 543–545; Charles Burnett, "Astrology," in *EI3*; Dykes, *Choices and Inceptions*, 2; different Fahd, *Nudjūm, Aḥkām al-*.

39   Burnett, *Astrology* distinguishes additionally mundane astrology in general and anniversary astrology.

40   Nativities are also known as "genethlialogy" (e.g., Burnett, *Astrology*).

41   Interrogations are also called "questions" or "horary astrology" (e.g., Dykes, *Choices and Inceptions*, 2).

As to be expected, the closer one looks on such classifications the more the occurrence of overlaps and the lack of clarity catches the eye. One example forms the often careless to impossible attribution of a text to either elections or interrogations exacerbated by the similarity of topics dealt with in both practices.[42] Another concerns the inclusion of elections in chapter iv of the *Mujmal al-uṣūl fī aḥkām al-nujūm* ("The compendium of the principles in astrology") by Kūshyār b. Labbān (f. 1000),[43] a treatise that relies heavily on the *Tetrabiblos* by Ptolemy (2nd c.) being void of electional astrology,[44] and that is classified as introductory literature of astrology, a genre that focusses on background knowledge for nativities and interrogations.[45]

To compare the election table in chapter xl.1 included in al-Ashraf ʿUmar's *Tabṣira* with further examples of electional astrology faces two obstacles. First, the number of treatises dealing with this topic is enormous, even if one restricts oneself to recipe-like, procedural texts, lists, tables, schemes, and diagrams from pre- and early modern Islamicate texts and ignores all theoretical reflections; no comprehensive surveys or comparative studies exists so far.[46] To draw up a justifiable shortlist appears difficult to impossible. More promising looks to focus on one example with various manifestations of elections,[47] e.g., the

---

42   E.g., Burnett, *Astral Sciences*, 490; Dorotheus Sidonius (Dykes), *Carmen Astrologicum*, 57–58; Dykes, *Choices and Inceptions*, 3–9; Pingree, *Eḵtīārāt*; also the similarities of the activities listed in chapter xl.1 of the *Tabṣira* and the table of contents of al-Kindī's *Forty Chapters* in Benjamin N. Dykes, ed., *The Forty-Chapters of al-Kindī: Traditional Horary & Electional Astrology* (Minneapolis, Minnesota: The Cazimi Press, 2011; English translation mainly based on Hugo of Santalla's Latin version); also Nicholas Campion, *A History of Western Astrology. Vol. 1: The Ancient World. Vol. 2: The Medieval and Modern Times* (London, New York: Continuum, 2008/2009), vol. 1, 205–206.

43   Kūshyār b. Labbān (Yano), *Mujmal*, iv.1–2, 236–259.

44   *Ptolemy's Tetrabiblos in the Translation of William of Moerbeke: Claudii Ptolemaei Liber iudicialium*, eds. Gudrun Vuilllemin-Diem and Carlos Steel with the assistance of Pieter De Leemans, Ancient and Medieval Philosophy, De Wulf-Mansion Centre Series 1 19 (Leuven: Leuven University Press, 2015); Ptolemy, *Tetrabiblos*, trans. F.E. Robbins, Loeb Classical Library 435 (Cambridge, Mass., London: Harvard University Press, 1940), repr. Ann Arbor, Michigan, n. d.; for a concordance of the *Tetrabiblos* and the *Mujmal* by Kūshyār b. Labbān (Yano), *Mujmal*, vii, table 1.

45   Gaida, *Introductions to Astrology*; also Burnett, *Astrology*.

46   For overviews, see n. 33

47   For other examples including different manifestations of electional astrology, e.g., the anonymous ephemeris made for Sanaa and the year 1327/28 (see above p. 186f); the *Kitāb al-Bulhān* with its unclear textual history and greater parts apparently compiled by a certain ʿAbd al-Ḥasan b. Aḥmad b. ʿAlī b. al-Ḥasan al-Iṣfahānī for Ḥusayn al-Irbilī (manuscript Oxford, Bodleian Library, Or. 133 [Alexander Nicoll and Edward Bouverie Pusey, *Bibliothecae Bodleianae codicum manuscriptorum orientalium catalogi, partis secundae, volumen secundum, arabicos complectens* (Oxonii: Typographeo Academico, 1835), 270–

Tabṣira,[48] raising, however, a second issue; classifications introduced so far appear incomprehensible.[49]

2.2   *Organising Elections and the Role of Time*

One approach, however, looks promising, to organise elections according to their method of describing or determining time, better to understand when first reflecting about the role of time in prognostic practices in general, before presenting the examples found in the *Tabṣira*.

Time plays a crucial role in all kinds of prognostic practices,[50] be it in casting a geomantic tableau or in forecasting weather, regarding the four branches of astrology albeit epistemologically inverse in mundane astrology, nativities, and interrogations, and in elections. To put it simple, concerning the former trio, the moment in time is already known, while computations, interpretations, and prognostications based on it still will have to take place. The sky is reconstructed, particularly the positions of the Sun, the Moon, and the planets, for a specific place and moment in time,[51] and this reconstruction interpreted; a horoscope is casted.

---

277 and 541–544]; for the table of contents Stefano Carboni, *Il Kitāb al-bulhān di Oxford*, Eurasiatica 6 [1. ed., Torino: Editrice Tirrenia Stampatori, 1988], here 12–15; also Stefano Carboni, "The 'Book of Surprises' [Kitab al-Bulhan] of the Bodleian Library," *The La Trobe Journal* 91 [2013]: 22–34); the *Qabs al-anwār wa-bahjat al-asrār* copied in Jumādā I 960 (May 1553), though based on earlier material and, as it appears, incorrectly ascribed to Ibn al-ʿArabī (manuscript Leiden, Universiteitsbibliotheek, Or. 5; for the table of contents Jan Just Witkam, *Inventory of the Oriental Manuscripts of the Library of the University of Leiden: Volume 1: Manuscripts 0001–1000. Acquisitions in the Period between 1609 and 1665. Mainly the Collections of Jacobus Golius [1629], Josephus Justus Scaliger [1609] and Part of the Collection of Levinus Warner [1665]* [Leiden: Ter Lugt Press, 2007], 16–17); also Jan Just Witkam, "An Arabic Treatise on Hemerology Ascribed to Ǧaʿfar al-Sādiq," *Arabica* 26,1 (1979): 100–102, here 101–102 who shortly mentions a Persian example comprising various manifestations.

48   See n. 5.

49   Cf., e.g., Pingree, *Eḵtīārāt* who distinguishes "1. [...] hemerologies in which each of the thirty days of a month [...] is characterized as being good (*saʿd*) or bad (*naḥs*) for undertaking specified activities. 2. The goodness or badness of the time for activities depends on the lunar station (*manzel al-qamar*) occupied by the Moon. 3. The goodness or badness of the time for activities depends on the zodiacal sign occupied by the Moon. 4. The type of astrology usually denominated catarchic (*ḥokm al-nojūm*) [...].": Dykes 2012, *passim* speaks of incomplete and complete elections to denote, among the former zodiacal and lunar elections, among the latter complex elections.

50   Schmidl, *Introductory Surveys*, 203.

51   Cf. Charles Burnett and Keiji Yamamoto, *The Great Introduction to Astrology by Abū Maʿšar. With an Edition of the Greek Version by David Pingree* (Leiden: Brill, 2019), iii.2, 232–235:

The latter, elections, however, choose a point in time that is appropriate, inappropriate or neither-nor for beginning an activity already recorded,[52] a characteristic that can be conceived as prescribed predictions. Apparently, at least parts of the debate on the validity and legitimacy of elections lead in the sources start here.[53] This feature, however, also brings more flexibility in describing or determining time so that elections develop into different manifestations, which are again closely related to the skills of the practitioner who applies them. They allow to spotlight an astrologer at work.[54]

If-then clauses, which are typical in prognostic texts,[55] form another approach to conceiving of the different roles of time in mundane astrology, nativities, and interrogations, and in elections, respectively. Concerning the former trio, the conditional clause informs about the moment in time, in the latter the principal clause. From that point of view, one has, however, to admit that the election table stands between elections and interrogations. Different to a continuous text structured by protasis and apodosis, where the condition and the consequence are irreversibly defined, one can enter the double-argument table either by an activity one likes to begin, as suggested in the headline, but also by

وذلك لأنّ المنجّم العالم بأحكام النجوم ينظر في بعض الأوقات المعلومة في شيء من الأشياء فيقول

إنّ حركة الكواكب في هذا الوقت \ تدلّ على أنّ هذا الشيء في وقت الدلالة بعينه حاله كذا وكذا

وبعد هذا بسنة أو بوقت آخر محدود يكون حاله كذا وكذا فقد استدلّ من زمان معلوم على شيء في

وقته ذلك وفي زمان مستقبل

> That is because the astrologer who is knowledgeable in astrology examines something at a / specific time and says that the movement of the stars at this time indicates that the condition of this thing at the exact time of the indication is such and such, and in a year, or at another specified time after this, its condition will be such and such. So he has inferred from a specific time something ⟨occurring⟩ in that time or at some future time.

52   Fahd, *Nudjūm, Ahkām al-*, 107ᵃ locates the role of time in genethlialogy and *katarchai* differently: "[...] genethlialogy is concerned with the fate of individuals and permits the compilation of their horoscope, starting from the date of birth. The *ikhtiyārāt* (καταρχαί, choices) consist rather in establishing the calendar of the auspicious (*saʿd*) and of the inauspicious (*nahs*)."

53   Dykes, *Choices and Inceptions*, 15–17.

54   Shortly discussed in Schmidl, *Astral Sciences*, 544.

55   E.g., Francesca Rochberg, "'If P, then Q': Form and Reasoning in Babylonian Divination," in *Divination and Interpretation of Signs in the Ancient World*, ed. Amer Annus, Oriental Institute Seminars 6 (Chicago, Ill.: Oriental Institute of the Univ. of Chic., 2010), repr. in *In the Path of the Moon: Babylonian Celestial Divination and its Legacy*, ed. Francesca Rochberg, Studies in Ancient Magic and Divination 6 (Leiden: Brill, 2010), 399–410 and the examples in Heiduk, Herbers, and Lehner, eds., *Prognostication, passim*.

the Moon's position in the zodiac; if we want to play chess today, the Moon in Aries is appropriate, but not in Taurus etc. If the Moon is in Aries, playing chess is appropriate, but not playing ball with friends.[56]

2.3   Elections in the Tabṣira

Besides of the election table in chapter xl.1, the *Tabṣira* deals in five other chapters with electional astrology.[57] Apart of chapter xxxi, that is organised according to weekdays and hours, in all other examples the Moon plays a pivotal role, not surprising having, apart from the Sun, the most obvious influence on life on earth, a generally accepted view not only in pre- and early modern astrology, described, e.g., by Ptolemy in his *Tetrabiblos*, basis of the Islamicate and Christianate astrological traditions and beyond.[58] In chapter v and chapter xxv, it is, however, not considered alone, but in tandem with two reference systems, the zodiacal signs and the lunar mansions. They are again supplemented by additional features, in particular the houses and the planets, as in chapter xvi to become combined and complex elections, as in chapter xlviii. In the *Tabṣira*, the lunar phases do not figure in relation with elections, although this use is also attested as demonstrated, e.g., by a treatise bearing the title *Ikhtiyārāt ayyām al-shahr* ("Elections according to the days of the [lunar] month") attributed to Jaʿfar al-Ṣādiq.[59] They only occur in the second part of chapter xxxix where they specify the time when bloodletting causes an illnesses, and when it stops it.[60]

Chapter xxxi presents elections according to weekdays and hours; time is described independently of the Moon's position.[61] Instead, the planetary hours are used as reflected in its heading:

---

56   See 4. Appendix and in particular n. 110.

57   Further investigation deserves chapter xxxviii and xxxix of the *Tabṣira*, if the seasonal knowledge they provide also includes elections.

58   Ptolemy (Robbins), *Tetrabiblos*, i.2, 6–7; as a starting point to conceive Ptolemy's influence ptolemaeus.badw.de/start—last accessed 2024-03-11.

59   Bluckley, *Writings of Jaʿfar al-Ṣādiq*, 19–21 and 24–28; Ebied, R.Y., and M.J.L. Young, "A Treatise on Hemerology Ascribed to Ǧafar Al-Ṣadīq," *Arabica* 23:3 (1976): 296–307, in particular 297–298; *addenda et corrigenda* Witkam, *Hemerology*; both using the manuscript in Leiden, Universiteitsbibliotheek, Or. 7525 copied in 1891, a *majmūʿa* in Arabic and Javanese dealing with prognostic and magic practices (Voorhoeve, *Handlist*, 126).

60   Schmidl, *Magic and Medicine*, 58–60, see also p. 202 with n. 71.

61   For elections according to the weekdays independent of the concept of a planetary ruler Pingree, *Eḵtiārāt*; also the example from Ancient Egypt in Leitz, *Tagewählerei*; the table at the end of the chapter القول على ما في شهور الفرس من الأعياد—"On the festivals in the months of the Persians" by al-Bīrūnī (see n. 10); the Ottoman almanac for the year 1824–1825 investigated by Marlene Kurz, *Ein osmanischer Almanach für das Jahr 1239/1240 (1824/25)*, Islamkundliche Untersuchungen Bd. 276 (Berlin: Klaus Schwarz, 2007).

TABLE 4.1   The planetary hours at day according to al-Ashraf ʿUmar's *Tabṣira*

hour	Sunday	Monday	Tuesday	Wednesday	Thursday	Friday	Saturday
1	Sun	Moon	Mars	Mercury	Jupiter	Venus	Saturn
2	Venus	Saturn	Sun	Moon	Mars	Mercury	Jupiter
3	Mercury	Jupiter	Venus	Saturn	Sun	Moon	Mars
4	Moon	Mars	Mercury	Jupiter	Venus	Saturn	Sun
5	Saturn	Sun	Moon	Mars	Mercury	Jupiter	Venus
6	Jupiter	Venus	Saturn	Sun	Moon	Mars	Mercury
7	Mars	Mercury	Jupiter	Venus	Saturn	Sun	Moon
8	Sun	Moon	Mars	Mercury	Jupiter	Venus	Saturn
9	Venus	Saturn	Sun	Moon	Mars	Mercury	Jupiter
10	Mercury	Jupiter	Venus	Saturn	Sun	Moon	Mars
11	Moon	Mars	Mercury	Jupiter	Venus	Saturn	Sun
12	Saturn	Sun	Moon	Mars	Mercury	Jupiter	Venus

الباب الحادي والثلاثون في معرفة أرباب ساعات السبعة الأيّام ولياليها وما يحمد فيها [انت]ه[ى]

The thirty-first chapter on the knowledge of the lords of the hours of the
seven (week) days and nights, and what is appropriate in them—e(nd).[62]

The basic idea of this practice relates the lord of the day, or planetary ruler,
to the first diurnal hour, beginning at sunrise and using the unequal hours,
common in pre-modern and early modern times that subdivide the day from
sunrise to sunset into twelve hours, and the night, from sunset to sunrise, too.
The second hour is associated with the subsequent planet arranging them from
the outermost planet of pre- and early modern astronomy, Saturn, to the inner-
most, the Moon (see Table 4.1). The nocturnal hours follow the same rule (see
Table 4.2).[63]

After the heading a continuous text, starting with Sunday, lists for each week-
day the twelve hours of the day, the planet with which each is associated, and
the activities appropriate or inappropriate to begin at this time. Concerning the
twelve hours of night the text only informs about its first hour when mention-

---

62   Slightly different Schmidl, *al-Ashraf ʿUmar's Tabṣira: The Table of Contents*, 227 (Arabic
      text) and 231 (English translation).
63   For a brief introduction, e.g., Dykes, *Choices and Inceptions*, 47–50.

TABLE 4.2   The planetary hours at night according to al-Ashraf ʿUmar's *Tabṣira*

hour	Monday	Tuesday	Wednesday	Thursday	Friday	Saturday	Sunday
1	Jupiter	Venus	Saturn	Sun	Moon	Mars	Mercury
2	Mars	Mercury	Jupiter	Venus	Saturn	Sun	Moon
3	Sun	Moon	Mars	Mercury	Jupiter	Venus	Saturn
4	Venus	Saturn	Sun	Moon	Mars	Mercury	Jupiter
5	Mercury	Jupiter	Venus	Saturn	Sun	Moon	Mars
6	Moon	Mars	Mercury	Jupiter	Venus	Saturn	Sun
7	Saturn	Sun	Moon	Mars	Mercury	Jupiter	Venus
8	Jupiter	Venus	Saturn	Sun	Moon	Mars	Mercury
9	Mars	Mercury	Jupiter	Venus	Saturn	Sun	Moon
10	Sun	Moon	Mars	Mercury	Jupiter	Venus	Saturn
11	Venus	Saturn	Sun	Moon	Mars	Mercury	Jupiter
12	Mercury	Jupiter	Venus	Saturn	Sun	Moon	Mars

Please note: Only the planet for each first nocturnal hour is given.

ing the first diurnal hour.[64] Weekdays and hours are rubricated to structure the text.

While the activities mentioned closely resemble those included in the election table, the rating of the time is different, instead of three terms, "appropriate", "inappropriate", and "neither-nor", only the first category occurs, the verb يُحمَد فيه—"it is appropriate in (this hour)". Due to its presentation as continuous texts, chapter xxxi includes more activities, and describes them in more detail than the election table.

To apply these elections a practitioner needs to know how late it is in unequal hours. Again, making an educated guess, one could figure, e.g., reading a sundial or a water-clock, both described in al-Ashraf ʿUmar's *Instrument Book* and the easiest way,[65] using an astrolabe or a quadrant, or determining time by means of tables and texts, both more ambitious. Helpful for this task is at least chapter xlv of the *Tabṣira* that explains how to determine time in unequal hours by using an astrolabe.[66]

---

64   For three examples of elections according to the days, one focussing on illnesses, the other two, a shorter and a longer version, on more general topics Young, *Almanac*, 269–279.

65   See above n. 4.

66   Taro Mimura and Petra G. Schmidl, "al-Ashraf ʿUmar's *Tabṣira*: Chapter xlv (H, 146ᵇ, 16–

Chapter v, like the election table, deals with zodiacal elections;[67] the Moon's position in the zodiac defines the moment of time at which an activity is appropriate or inappropriate as announced in its heading:

الباب الخامس في معرفة حلول القمر في البروج الاثنى عشر وشرف الكواكب فيها وطبائعها

وما يحمد فيها وما يذمّ [انتا]هلى].

The fifth chapter on the knowledge of the halts of the Moon in the twelve zodiacal signs, the exaltation of the planets in them, their natures, and what is appropriate in them and what inappropriate—e(nd).[68]

Next follow twelve paragraphs corresponding to the zodiacal signs whose names are written in red to structure the text. Each of them informs first about their general characteristics and lists then activities that are rated either as يحمد فيه—"appropriate is (when the Moon is) in (this sign)" or as يذمّ فيه—"inappropriate is (when the Moon is) in (this sign)".[69] While the former information equals those given in the introductory literature into astrology,[70] the rating in comparison to the examples discussed so far differs again, in number and in wording, and suggests different origins for the zodiacal elections in chapter v and chapter xl.1. The presentation, in the former case as continuous text, in the latter as double-argument table, supports this suggestion, however, only for a moment. The *Tabṣira* itself provides a possible counterexample. In the second part of chapter xxxix the Oxford manuscript (H, 120ᵇ–121ᵃ) includes a list with two columns, the first, written in red, mentions the day in the lunar month, the second informs about illnesses caused by bloodletting when the Moon is waxing and stopped by it when waning,[71] while the Paris copy (P, 132ᵃ⁻ᵇ) presents the same information in a continuous text, again with the names of the days

---

152ᵃ, 13)—On the Use of the Astrolabe," published 2024-04-26 on tabsira.hypotheses.org, 8–11, §16–17, §19. tabsira.hypotheses.org/files/2024/05/Tabsira-146b-152a-Kap.-XLV-2402 .pdf

67   For an Ottoman example for the years 1740/41 Gerhard Behrens, *An Ottoman Calendar for 1740/41* (München: GRIN, 2017), 18 (facsimile) and 19 (English translation).

68   Schmidl, *al-Ashraf ʿUmar's Tabṣira: The Table of Contents*, 225 (Arabic text) and 229 (English translation).

69   In a few cases also the planets are brought into play, so that one might better speak of combined elections.

70   See n. 45.

71   For the table Schmidl, *Magic and Medicine*, 58–60 (Arabic text and English translation); for the chapter title Schmidl, *al-Ashraf ʿUmar's Tabṣira: The Table of Contents*, 227 (Arabic text) and 232 (English translation).

rubricated. While the aspects of everyday life addressed are alike, the divergent forms of representation allow to include different amounts of information regarding the activities.

Chapter xxv also draws on the Moon's position in the ecliptic belt, though not by using the zodiacal signs, but the lunar mansions. It includes lunar elections,[72] and as its heading announces, they only form its first part:[73]

الباب الخامس والعشرون في قسمة المنازل بين البروج الاثنى عشر وما ينسب إلى كلّ فصل
منها وما يحمد فيها من الأعمال ويذمّ عند حلول القمر في كلّ منزلة وصور المنازل والمعروف
فيها من الكواكب الثابتة وذكر سعود المنازل ونحوسها والممتزج :.

The twenty-fifth chapter on the division of the lunar mansions into the twelve zodiacal signs, and what is related to each season by them, what is appropriate of the activities in them, (what is) inappropriate during the halts of the Moon in each lunar mansion, (on) the depiction of the (fixed stars in the) lunar mansions, and the known of them of the fixed stars, and (on) the account of the benefic lunar mansions, the malefic, and the mixed :.[74]

The final part of chapter xxv also deals with lunar mansions, though not with elections. It comprises a paragraph attributed to Hermes and rating the lunar

---

72 For an earlier example from eleventh-century Hijaz, see Petra G. Schmidl, "Lunar Elections in Ibn Rahiq's Folk Astronomical Treatise," in *From Māshā Allāh to Kepler: Theory and Practice in Medieval and Renaissance Astrology*, eds. Charles Burnett and Dorian Gieseler Greenbaum (Ceredigion, Wales: Sophia Centre Press, 2015), 425–453, here, 450–453 (English translation); an example with a focus on talisman making is included in book 1, chapter 4 of the *Ghāyat al-ḥakīm*, also known as the *Picatrix* (Hellmut Ritter, ed., *Pseudo-Maǧrīṭī: Das Ziel des Weisen. 1.* Arabischer Text [Leipzig, Berlin: B.G. Teubner, 1933], 15–23; Martin Plessner and Hellmut Ritter, *Picatrix: Das Ziel der Weisen von Pseudo-Maǧrīṭī*. Translated into German from the Arabic, Studies of the Warburg Institute 27 [London: The Warburg Institute, 1962], 15–21 [German translation]; for the Latin version David Pingree, *Picatrix: The Latin Version of the Ghāyat al-Ḥakīm. Text, Appendices, Indices*, Studies of the Warburg Institute 56 [London: The Warburg Institute, 1986], 8–14); for an example in the Latin version of Ibn Abī l-Rijāl's *Kitāb al-Bāriʿ* Dykes, *Choices and Inceptions*, 61–75 (English translation); for on overview of the Christianate traditions Charles Burnett, "Lunar Astrology. The Varieties of Texts Using Lunar Mansions, with Emphasis on Jafar Indus," *Micrologus* 12 (2004): 43–133, here 48–51; an Indian origin of the lunar elections suggest Pingree, *Eḫtīārāt* and Alfonso Nallino, "Astrology," in *The Encyclopaedia of Islam, First Edition. 4 Volumes* (Leiden, London: Brill, 1913–1936), photomechanical repr. in 9 volumes (Leiden: Brill, 1987).

73 English translation in Varisco, *Magical Significance*, 28–33.

74 Schmidl, *al-Ashraf ʿUmar's Tabṣira: The Table of Contents*, 227 (Arabic text) and 230 (English translation).

mansions as سعد—"benefic", نحس—"malefic", and ممتزج—"mixed", general rules concerning activities in them, a list of merchandise associated with them, and a table with their depictions including another rating of them as صالحة—"good", فاسدة—"bad", and, again, ممتزج—"mixed".

The initial part directly after the heading mentions in a continuous text for each lunar mansion, whose names are emphasized in red, first the appendant zodiacal sign followed by a list of dos and don'ts. They include, different to the election table in chapter xl.1 also information related to the occult sciences such as making talismans.[75] Again, as in chapter v, the activities are only classified into two groups, this time addressed more directly by using the imperative and its negotiation. Apart from the different method of describing the moment in time, this linguistic difference constitutes another hint to, again, that this chapter relies on a fourth text different to that taken into consideration for the elections according to weekdays and hours in chapter xxxi, and for the zodiacal elections in chapter xl.1 and chapter v. Parallel to chapter xxxi and chapter v, it includes due to its presentation as continuous texts more, and more detailed, information.

What was said concerning deducing, calculating, and observing the Moon's position in the zodiacal signs,[76] applies in general also to its position in the lunar mansions. The *Tabṣira* itself provides two auxiliaries, that compensate, e.g., that the zodiacal signs figure more prominently on celestial globes and astrolabes than the lunar mansions. The third part of chapter xxvii provides two diagrams that allow easily to convert lunar mansions into zodiacal signs and *vice versa*.[77] The final part of chapter xxv presents a table with the depictions of the stars in each lunar mansion that help in identifying them.[78] So the necessary skills of a practitioner to apply these lunar elections are very much the same as those for the zodiacal signs.

Two further manifestations of electional astrology do not occur as standalone in the *Tabṣira*, the Moon's position in the astrological houses and its aspecting other planets. They are, however, known from other sources.[79]

---

75   See also below p. 202ff (chapter xlviii).

76   See above p. 185ff.

77   Petra G. Schmidl, "al-Ashraf ʿUmar's *Tabṣira*: Chapter xxvii.3. Introducing a Volvelle for Astronomical and Astrological Purposes?" to appear in the proceedings of the conference "Science and Craft: The Relations between the Theoretical and Practical Sides of the Occult and Esoteric Sciences in the Islamic World" organised by Godefroid de Callataÿ and Liana Saif, The Warburg Institute, London, 10–13 January 2023.

78   See above p. 199f (chapter xxv).

79   Although organised according to the astrological houses, as its title promises, Sahl b. al-Bishr's (d. ca. 854) *Kitāb al-Ikhtiyārāt ʿalā l-buyūt al-ithnā ʿashar* ("The book on elections

Chapter xvi, however, defines not only time by the Moon's position in one of the zodiacal signs, but takes also into consideration its aspects to one of the six other planets.[80] Zodiacal and planetary elections are combined as already its heading informs:

الباب السادس عشر في اختيارات الأعمال في اتّصال القمر بالكواكب من الأشكال الخمسة
من تثليث أو تسديس وتربيع ومقابلة ومقارنة مفضّلة على البروج الاثنى عشر ۰۰ ورمز في
الحساب.

The sixteenth chapter on the elections of the activities during the application of the Moon to the planets in relation to the five figures of trine or square, sextile, opposition, and conjunction, (and what is) preferable according to the twelve zodiacal signs ∴ And their symbol in astronomy (*al-ḥisāb*).[81]

Next follow on the twelve pages six lavishly arranged tables, each providing in the first column the twelve zodiacal signs denoting the Moon's position alternatingly written diagonally in red and black forming a zigzag line. Each spread is dedicated to one planet, beginning with Saturn, and continuing to Mercury. In their headings occur the aspects, on the *verso* page trine and sextile, which share one column, and quartile, on the opposite *recto* page opposition and con-

---

according to the twelve houses") comprises complex elections (Sahl b. Bišr al-Isrāʾīlī, *Kitāb al-Iḫtiyārāt ʿalā l-Buyūt al-Iṯnai ʿašar: With its Latin Translation De Electionibus*, ed. and trans. with introduction, annotations and glossaries, Carole Mary Crofts, Unpublished Doctoral Thesis [Glasgow: Department of Arabic and Islamic Studies and the Department of Humanity, 1985], 1–134 [Arabic and Latin text, English translation]; also Dykes, *Choices and Inceptions*, 91–133 [English translation based on Sahl b. al-Bishr (Crofts), *Ikhtiyārāt*]); despite of its title, Abū Yūsuf b. Yaʿqūb al-Kindī's *Ikhtiyārāt al-ayyām* ("The elections of the days") includes planetary elections (Leiden, Universiteitsbibliotheek, Or. 199.2 [Witkam, *Inventory*, 86]; Wiedemann, "Über einen astrologischen Traktat von al Kindî," *Archiv für die Geschichte der Naturwissenschaft und Technik* [1911], 224–226, repr. in *Gesammelte Schriften zur arabisch-islamischen Wissenschaftsgeschichte*, ed. Fuat Sezgin [Frankfurt: Institut für Geschichte der arabisch-islamischen Wissenschaften, 1984], vol. 2, 620–622, repr. in *Texts and Studies on Astrology: Selected and Reprinted*, ed. Fuat Sezgin [Frankfurt: Institut für Geschichte der arabisch-islamischen Wissenschaften, 2000], vol. 4, 214–216, here 224–226 [German translation]; Dykes, *Choices and Inceptions*, 59–60 [English translation based on Wiedemann, *al-Kindī*]).

80   For an earlier example made for 1149–1159 of this electional manifestation Thomann, *Ephemeris*, in particular 212 (Arabic text), 216 (figure), and 218–219 (English translation).

81   Schmidl, *Introductory Surveys*, 22 (Arabic text) and 229 (English translation) omitting in each case the half sentence at the end.

junction. The elections are given in the cells usually preceded by a broader spectrum of ratings as those in the other chapters of the *Tabṣira*, all, however, belonging to the three semantic fields discover so far, e.g., صالح—حمد "good", فيه—غير محمود "it is appropriate in (this zodiacal sign)", غير محمود—"not appropriate", or متوسط—"intermediate".[82]

Since the practitioner does not only have to determine the position of the Moon in the zodiacal signs,[83] but also its aspects to the planets, this example of combined elections asks for more advanced skills in astronomy and astrology as those introduced so far. Due to the use of these two parameters, the timekeeping element begins to be pushed in the background, the astrological component starts to come to the fore. Planets, zodiacal signs, and aspects have their own individual characteristics, responsibilities, associations, and correspondences often established by analogy as, e.g., concisely presented in the introductory literature to astrology.[84] It deserved further research, if, and how far, the elections relate to them.

This focal shift manifests even more in *chapter xlviii*; the elections become more complex. This fact is, however, not reflected in the heading:

الباب الثامن والأربعون في الاختيارات ليعقوب بن علي القرشي وسواه. واختيار تفصيل الخيم ودخولها. وبسط البسط وسائر الفروش :.

The forty-eighth chapter on the elections according to Yaʿqūb b. ʿAlī al-Qarshī and like it (?). And (on) the election for arranging the tents and entering them. And on (the election for) spreading out the carpets and arranging the thrones :.[85]

In the following, the *Tabṣira* lists in a continuous text more than 70 elections attributed to Dorotheos (fl. 1st c.),[86] Vettius Valens (fl. 2nd c.),[87] Abu l-

---

82   Similar in the hemerology attributed to Jaʿfar b. al-Ṣādiq (Ebied and Young, *Hemerology*, 299–307 [Arabic text and English translation]).

83   See above p. 185ff.

84   See n. 45.

85   Schmidl, *al-Ashraf ʿUmar's Tabṣira: The Table of Contents*, 228 (Arabic text) and 232 (English translation).

86   Fuat Sezgin, *Geschichte des arabischen Schrifttums*. 9 Volumes (Leiden: Brill, 1967–1984), vol. 7, 32–38; Manfred Ullmann, *Die Natur- und Geheimwissenschaften im Islam*, Handbuch der Orientalistik, Erste Abteilung Ergänzungsband VI, 2. Abschnitt (Leiden: Brill, 1972), 280–281; for the Arabic text (based on ʿUmar b. al-Farrukhān al-Ṭabarī's translation of a Pahlavi version) and the English translation of his astrological treatise in five books in David Pingree: *Dorothei Sidoni Carmen Astrologicum* (Leipzig: Teubner 1976); revised English translation Dorotheus Sidonius (Dykes), *Carmen Astrologicum*; also Viktor

ʿAnbas Muḥammad b. Isḥāq al-Ṣaymarī (d. 888),[88] Sinān b. al-Fatḥ al-Ḥarrānī,[89] Yaʿqūb b. ʿAlī al-Qarshī al-Qaṣrānī (fl. 2nd h. 9th c. [?]),[90] and Kūshyār b. Labbān.[91] After mentioning the actual activity, usually rubricated, a continuous text informs about the position of the Moon in the zodiacal signs, in the astrological houses, and in aspect to other planets, though not in a systematic and comprehensive way neither as in the elections according to weekdays and hours, nor in the zodiacal, lunar, and combined elections introduced so far.[92]

Stegemann, *Die Fragmente des Dorotheos von Sidon: 1. Lieferung*, Quellen und Studien zur Geschichte und Kultur des Altertums und des Mittelalters, Reihe D: Untersuchungen und Mitteilungen 1 (Heidelberg: Selbstverlag F. Bilabel, 1939); Viktor Stegemann, *Die Fragmente des Dorotheos von Sidon: 2. Lieferung*, Quellen und Studien zur Geschichte und Kultur des Altertums und des Mittelalters, Reihe D: Untersuchungen und Mitteilungen 1 (Heidelberg: Selbstverlag F. Bilabel, 1943).

87 Sezgin, *GAS*, vol. 7, 38–41 additionally mentioning an *Ikhtiyār al-ayyām* by Vettius Valens; Ullmann, *NGW*, 281–282; Greek text of his anthology in Vettius Valens, *Anthologiae*, ed. David Pingree, Bibliotheca scriptorum Graecorum et Romanorum Teubneriana (Leipzig: Teubner, 1986).

88 Sezgin, *GAS*, vol. 7, 152–153 with slightly varying titles of al-Ṣaymarī's *Kitāb Aṣl al-uṣūl* ("Book of the principle of the principles"); Ullmann, *NGW*, 325–326 doubts that the elections originally belonged to al-Ṣaymarī's treatise by relying on the manuscripts in Berlin, Staatsbiliothek Preußischer Kulturbesitz, Landberg 221 (W. Ahlwardt, *Die Handschriften-Verzeichnisse der Königlichen Bibliothek zu Berlin. 17. Band: Verzeichniss der Arabischen Handschriften. Band 5* [Berlin: A. Asher & Co., 1893], vol. xvii, 5, 181, no. 5711 and 297–298, no. 5898); also Ekmeleddin Ihsanoglu and Boris A. Rosenfeld, *Mathematicians, Astronomers and Other Scholars of Islamic Civilisation and Their Works (7th–19th C.)*, Series of Studies and Sources on History of Science 11 (Istanbul: Research Centre for Islamic History, Art and Culture [IRCICA], 2003), 45–46, no. 93; al-Ṣaymarī on *ISMI* (ismi.mpiwg-berlin.mpg.de/person/98260—last accessed 2024-03-02).

89 So far, no astrological treatise by Sinān b. al-Fatḥ is known (Sezgin, *GAS*, vol. 5, 301, vol. 6, 207, vol. 7, 406; Ihsanoglu and Rosenfeld, *Scholars*, 91–92, no. 231; also Sinān b. al-Fatḥ on *ISMI* [ismi.mpiwg-berlin.mpg.de/person/56642—last accessed 2024-03-02]).

90 Ullmann, *NGW*, 314–315; Ihsanoglu and Rosenfeld, *Scholars*, 46, no. 95; al-Qaṣrānī on *ISMI* (ismi.mpiwg-berlin.mpg.de/person/98080—last accessed 2024-03-02) only mentions his *Kitāb al-Masāʾil fī ʿilm aḥkām al-nujūm* ("Book of interrogations in astrology") that according to the table of contents in manuscript Berlin, Staatsbibliothek Preußischer Kulturbesitz, Landberg 70 (Ahlwardt, *Handschriften-Verzeichnisse*, 275–276, no. 5877; ismi.mpiwg-berlin.mpg.de/witness/200435—last accessed 2024-03-02) does not contain elections, one has, however, to keep in mind that given the close similarities of topics dealt with in elections and interrogations (see p. 191) this first search does not rule out that al-Qaṣrānī discusses here and there elections in his *Kitāb al-Masāʾil*, though not systematically; Sezgin, *GAS*, vol. 7, 138–139 additionally points out to a *Kitāb al-Mudkhal* ("Book of introduction [into astrology]") by al-Qaṣrānī that he mentions in his *Kitāb al-Masāʾil*.

91 See p. 191 with n. 43.

92 Ibn Qushtimur, a contemporary of al-Ashraf ʿUmar in Iraq, provides in his *al-Qānūn*

Although the element of timekeeping is still inherent, these instructions read as if one specifies for an activity the ideal lineup of the celestial objects in different reference systems and in relation to each other, e.g., the Moon in an earthy sign is benefic for buying land, in a watery sign for travelling on sea. This shift is also reflected in the diction even though due to the various sources the style varies. Not the time is rated as in the election table as "appropriate", "inappropriate", or "neither-nor", but the lineup in the sky for an activity. The Moon يُسْتَحَبّ—"is preferred" or فليكن—"shall be" in a specific position, in relation to the planets and to further notional reference points.

At least another two times, in chapter ix discussing the lunar nodes and in chapter xliv dealing with the signs straight and crooked in rising,[93] the *Tabṣira* also reflects about complex elections. In both cases, however, general rules are introduced, not individual activities listed, e.g., to begin with an activity at daytime, the ascendant and the Moon shall be in a diurnal sign.[94]

In the *Tabṣira*, the chapters dealing with electional astrology appear arbitrarily included. Only the elections according to weekdays and hours in chapter xxxi follow logically after chapter xxx dealing with timekeeping at night. Given their different levels of complexity and their arbitrarily inclusion in the *Tabṣira*, together with the differences in the presentation, and the linguistic and systematic variations, the suspicion arouses that the examples of elections in the *Tabṣira* are not only taken from different sources, but that al-Ashraf ʿUmar combines in his treatise different traditions strands of electional astrology, as he also does for other practices, e.g., the determination of the *qibla*, the direction towards Mecca, where he provides a geographical table and a *qibla* scheme.[95]

al-wāḍiḥ fī muʿālajāt al-jawāriḥ complex elections to find the appropriate moments for successful hunting (Käs, *Jagderfolg*, 299–305 [Arabic text and German translation]).

93 Mimura and Schmidl, *al-Ashraf ʿUmar's Tabṣira: Chapter ix*; Luís Ribeiro and Petra G. Schmidl, "al-Ashraf ʿUmar's *Tabṣira*: Chapter xliv (H, 144ᵃ, 6–146ᵇ, 16)—Signs Straight and Crooked in Rising," to be published on tabsira.hypotheses.org.

94 Mimura and Schmidl, *al-Ashraf ʿUmar's Tabṣira: Chapter ix*, 10–11, §10.

95 Petra G. Schmidl, "al-Ashraf ʿUmar's *Tabṣira*: Chapter xlvii (H, 153ᵇ, 1–154ᵃ, 7)—Mathematical Geography, Geographical Table," published 2020-10-01 on tabsira.hypotheses.org (geographical table in chapter xlvii) and Petra G. Schmidl, *al-Ashraf ʿUmar's Tabṣira: Chapter xxxvii.1*, 65–96 (*qibla* scheme in chapter xxxvii).tabsira.hypotheses.org/files/2020/10/Tabsira-153b-154a-Kap.-XLVII-2009.pdf

3   The Practice and Its Applicability

With this additional knowledge at hand one can start to assess the suitability of the election table in chapter xl.1 as a tool for an astrologer. When considering who might apply this practice of choosing the appropriate time to begin an activity, and in which context,[96] four issues are perceptible, already partially touched when describing the examples.

The first is related to the presentation; organisation and structure of knowledge influence its applicability and is related to its users or readers skills.[97] In the *Tabṣira*, information on electional astrology is either presented in double-argument tables or in continuous texts. Both presentations have their obvious advantages and disadvantages, in particular regarding their clarity and comprehensiveness. When considering the possible necessities of a practitioner and its client, one might ask when a table, when a continuous text is more advantageous. The one might fit in other contexts than the other and address other groups of practitioners and clients. Because, on the one hand, a table might be perceived, e.g., more scholarly, more intriguing, more attractive, and more secretive, and might therefore impress a client or a patron even more. On the other hand, the overwhelming wealth of words in a continuous text might awestruck a less literate audience. Further, different sociocultural settings, e.g., a practitioner-client-relationship or a teacher with its students might be in favour of one of the two presentations. Included in these considerations should be two further points, size of the book and its layout. Concerning the *Tabṣira*, it is handy, and therefore easy to transport, and neatly arranged reflecting the appreciation of its contents.[98]

These questions lead, second, to the different astronomical and astrological skills a practitioner needs for applying the varying manifestations of electional astrology. If one organises them in increasing order of required expertise, as in this article, the elections according to weekdays and hours are the simplest to apply, followed by zodiacal and lunar elections. Elections relying on the houses

---

96   For some suggestions Frederike-Wiebke Daub, *Formen und Funktionen des Layouts in arabischen Manuskripten anhand von Abschriften religiöser Texte: al-Būṣīrīs Burda, al-Ġazūlīs Dalāʾil und die Šifāʾ von Qāḍī ʿIyāḍ*, Arabische Studien Band 12 (Wiesbaden: Harrassowitz, 2016), 2.

97   Daub, *Formen*, 1.

98   E.g., Sonja Brentjes, "Textual Genres and Visual Representations in the Astral Sciences," in *Routledge Handbook on the Sciences in Islamicate Societies: Practices from the 2nd/8th to the 13th/19th Centuries*, ed. Sonja Brentjes (London, New York: Routledge, 2023), 447–460, here 447.

need more knowledge in astrology, planetary elections in astronomy. If one combines them and arrange them to complex elections, even the more.

Third, the activities mentioned in the examples obviously mean something to their audience, not only in thirteenth century Yemen. Their relation to politics and diplomacy, trade and commerce, health and hygiene, social life, education and training, husbandry, and occult sciences cover necessities of everyday life and seem in parts universal, though rather for an elite, educated, and courtly audience,[99] no matter where, and when, they live in the pre- and early modern Afro-Eurasian *oikouménē*. Although one can observe in the premodern astronomical literature in Islamicate societies, a clear fidelity to the sources,[100] texts on elections, but also on other prognostic practices, turn out to be fluid, easily crossing cultural, linguistic, religious, political, geographical, and temporal boundaries.[101] In cases, where they do not, as the omission of circumcision in the Chinese version in chapter iv dealing with electional astrology of Kūshyār b. Labbān's *Mujmal* demonstrates,[102] they can be easily adapted to new cultural settings, a feature that is also due to their compound, procedural structure.[103] This feature makes the election table in chapter xl.1. a more attractive tool, applicable and adoptable for varying situations, enforced by the looming aspect of failure and danger inherent to all the activities listed in elections, so that an aid for decision-making is welcome that also allows to

---

99   Cf., however, Thomann, *From katarchai to ikhtiyārāt*, 347: "A document described as astrological responses was found in room iv–6B. The house to which this room belongs is part of the worker's quarter. These houses are characterized by a lack of ornaments and highly unstable construction. Their inhabitants must have belonged to an underprivileged class of people in comparison to inhabitants of other quarters in al-Fustat. The fact that an astrological document was found at such a place indicates that astrology was not restricted to the elite or a bourgeois milieu but found its way to the houses of the proletarians."

100   E.g., Mohammad Karimi Zanjani Asl, Eva Orthmann, and Petra G. Schmidl, "The Sources and the Composition of the Dustūr al-munajjimīn," in *Science in the City of Fortune: The Dustūr al-munajjimīn and its World*, eds. Eva Orthmann and Petra G. Schmidl, Bonner Islamstudien Band 39 (Berlin: EBV, 2017), 35–113, here 50.

101   E.g., the modern Persian examples of elections mentioned by Witkam, *Hemerology*, 101 who states in n. 2: "There are many more editions, lithographed on cheap paper and for sale in the bazars of many towns in Iran, Afghanistan and the Indian subcontinent."; see also n. 33.

102   Kūshyār (Yano), *Mujmal*, iv.2, 249–249 with n. 4.

103   Cf. Witkam, *Hemerology*, 102, however focussing on the Islamicate traditions, that is just part of the story: "Texts like this hemerology can only fully be appreciated if one realizes that they are the product of the creativity of their compilers who use both written models and their traditional Islamic background, without caring much for a truthful, literal or reliable transmission. [...] we should consider this hemerology as representing a stage in a continuous tradition still very much alive."

delegate at least some of the responsibility, a feature common to prognostic practices.[104]

Fourth, the rating of the activities appears less informative than the three issues discussed so far when discussing the suitability of the election table in chapter xl.1 as a tool for an astrologer. The difference it makes for a practitioner or a client, if there are one, two, three or varying ratings related to an activity appear neglectable. In all examples, besides the complex elections, the wording emphasises the elections' quality to be on hand with advice.

Given the clear representation in a double-argument table, the rather simple method to describe time by the Moon's position in the zodiac, a list of activities that one might easily be affected with, and three keywords rating them, raises doubts if the election table in chapter xl.1 of the *Tabṣira* can be assessed as a tool for a professional astrologer. They rather appear to be a "'do-it-yourself'-prognostication".[105]

4   Appendix

Preliminary remarks: The following presents the Arabic text followed by the English translation of chapter xl.1 of al-Ashraf ʿUmar's *Kitāb al-Tabṣira fī ʿilm al-nujūm* (fol. 121ᵃ, 15–123ᵃ, after the table in manuscript Oxford, Bodleian Library, Huntington 233, hence: H; one fragment, fol. 170ᵃ, 1–12 in manuscript Paris, Bibliothèque Nationale, arabe 2601.2, hence: P; highlighted in grey in the Arabic and English text).

In the Arabic text, *hamza*, *madda*, *shadda*, and diacritical points have been silently added. Due to its fragmentary character, its overall condition, its age and its reliability, P is not taken into consideration for the critical apparatus, only consulted, when readings are difficult. Folios of H are provided in angular brackets ⟨ ⟩, paragraphs numbered in square brackets [ ]. In the English translation, parentheses ( ) have been inserted to assist the flow of the text. Emphases by bold face in the Arabic text and in italics in the English translation follow the rubrications in the manuscript and are also included in the English translation.

---

104   For examples, e.g., Heiduk, Herbers, and Lehner, eds., *Prognostication, passim*.

105   Matthias Heiduk, "Introductory Surveys: Medieval Traditions of Prognostication in the Western Christian World," in *Prognostication*, eds. Heiduk, Herbers, and Lehner, 109–151, here 125.

4.1 *Arabic Text and English Translation*

[1] الباب الأربعون في كرمة اختيارات قضاء الحوائج. وكرمة الزجر والحوادث.106

[2] ⟨H, 121b⟩ ابتدئ107 كرمة اختيارات قضاء الحوائج والأعمال108 على مسير القمر إلى البروج الاثنى عشر.108 [3]

الحوائج \ البروج	الحمل	الثور	الجوزاء	السرطان	الأسد	السنبلة	الميزان	العقرب	القوس	الجدي	الدلو	الحوت
جلوس الملوك على الأسرّة	محمود	وسط	مذموم	محمود	محمود	مذموم	محمود	محمود	وسط	محمود	مذموم	مذموم
طلب الصيد109	محمود	مذموم	محمود	محمود	مذموم	محمود (بالخيل)	محمود	محمود	محمود (بالخيل)	محمود (بالخيل)	محمود	محمود
ضرب الأكرة	محمود	مذموم	محمود	مذموم	محمود	مذموم	محمود	محمود	مذموم	محمود	مذموم	محمود
المصافّ للحرب	محمود	مذموم	مذموم	محمود	مذموم	مذموم	محمود	مذموم	محمود	محمود	محمود	محمود
عرض العسكر	محمود	مذموم	مذموم	مذموم	محمود	مذموم	مذموم	مذموم	مذموم	مذموم	مذموم	مذموم
الغارة وسباق الخيل	محمود	مذموم	وسط	مذموم	وسط	وسط	مذموم	وسط	وسط	مذموم	مذموم	وسط
عقد الذمم	محمود	محمود	وسط	مذموم	محمود	وسط	مذموم	وسط	محمود	مذموم	محمود	محمود
مكاتبة الملوك	وسط	مذموم	مذموم	مذموم	مذموم	محمود	وسط	محمود	مذموم	مذموم	وسط	محمود
لقاء الحواتين (؟)	وسط	محمود	مذموم	محمود	محمود	محمود	وسط	وسط	محمود	محمود	مذموم	وسط
لقاء الأمراء والحوائج منهم	مذموم	وسط	محمود	مذموم	وسط	محمود	مذموم	محمود	محمود	محمود	مذموم	وسط
لقاء القدماء النسن (؟)	مذموم	وسط	مذموم	مذموم	مذموم	وسط	محمود	وسط	محمود	محمود	محمود	وسط
عقد الولايات	مذموم	محمود	وسط	مذموم	محمود	محمود	وسط	محمود	مذموم	محمود	محمود	محمود

---

106 ... الا ... ماح الم ... follows diagonally in the corner of the page.

107 H writes ابتدي.

108 H continues on H, 122a.

109 H writes ـه (?) above the word.

⟨H, 122ᵃ⟩[110]

الحوت	الدلو	الجدي	القوس	العقرب	الميزان	السنبلة	الأسد	السرطان	الجوزاء	الثور	الحمل	البروج \ الحوائج
مذموم	محمود	مذموم	مذموم	محمود	وسط	وسط	مذموم	محمود	محمود	مذموم	محمود	حلّ عقد الولاية
مذموم	محمود	وسط	مذموم	وسط	محمود	وسط	وسط	محمود	وسط	مذموم	محمود	مراجعة الوزراء
وسط	وسط	محمود	مذموم	وسط	وسط	مذموم	وسط	محمود	مذموم	وسط	وسط	الركوب والرياضة
محمود	محمود	مذموم	وسط	محمود	مذموم	مذموم	مذموم	وسط	وسط	محمود	محمود	الانفراد بالندماء
مذموم	مذموم	وسط	محمود	مذموم	وسط	محمود	مذموم	وسط	مذموم	وسط	محمود	إلهاء كرة مع الأصدقاء
محمود	وسط	مذموم	محمود	مذموم	وسط	محمود	مذموم	وسط	محمود	مذموم	محمود	لعب النرد والشطرنج
محمود	وسط	مذموم	وسط	محمود	مذموم	وسط	محمود	مذموم	وسط	مذموم	محمود	السفر ولبس الثياب
وسط	مذموم	مذموم	محمود	مذموم	وسط	محمود	وسط	محمود	مذموم	محمود	محمود	تنفيس الدم
محمود	مذموم	مذموم	محمود	وسط	محمود	مذموم	وسط	محمود	مذموم	محمود	محمود	الاستحمام
مذموم	وسط	محمود	مذموم	محمود	محمود	مذموم	محمود	محمود	مذموم	وسط	محمود	قط(ع) الظفر
محمود	مذموم	مذموم	محمود	مذموم	محمود	مذموم	محمود	مذموم	محمود	محمود	محمود	التزويج
محمود	مذموم	وسط	مذموم	محمود	مذموم	مذموم	محمود	وسط	محمود	وسط	محمود	عقدة الأملاك

---

110   H writes سادسة عشرة in the upper left corner of the page.

[4] ⟨H, 122b⟩ تمام كرمة اختيارات قضاء الحوائج والأعمال والابتذأات[111] على مسير القمر إلى البروج الاثنى عشر[111]

الحوائج \ البروج	الحمل	الثور	الجوزاء	السرطان	الأسد	السنبلة	الميزان	العقرب	القوس	الجدي	الدلو	الحوت
شراء المماليك	مذموم	محمود	محمود	مذموم	محمود	وسط	مذموم	محمود	مذموم	محمود	مذموم	مذموم
شراء الدوابّ المركوبة	محمود	محمود	محمود	مذموم	محمود	محمود	محمود	مذموم	محمود	مذموم	وسط	محمود
شراء الجواهر	مذموم	محمود	محمود	مذموم	محمود	محمود	محمود	مذموم	محمود	مذموم	وسط	محمود
شراء الذهب	محمود	محمود	محمود	مذموم	محمود	محمود	محمود	مذموم	محمود	مذموم	مذموم	محمود
الختان وجضيء الخدّام	محمود	مذموم	وسط	مذموم	محمود	وسط	محمود	مذموم	وسط	مذموم	مذموم	محمود
شرب المسهل	محمود	مذموم	مذموم	محمود	محمود	مذموم	مذموم	محمود	مذموم	مذموم	وسط	محمود
إيفاد الرسل	محمود	وسط	محمود	محمود	وسط	محمود	وسط	مذموم	وسط	مذموم	وسط	وسط
توجيه الكتب	محمود	محمود	محمود	محمود	وسط	محمود	وسط	مذموم	وسط	مذموم	وسط	وسط
لقاء الملوك	محمود	مذموم	محمود	مذموم	مذموم	محمود	وسط	وسط	محمود	مذموم	مذموم	محمود
لقاء الكتّاب والتجّار	مذموم	وسط	محمود	وسط	وسط	محمود	وسط	وسط	مذموم	وسط	محمود	مذموم
الحوائج من الأشراف	محمود	وسط	مذموم	محمود	مذموم	مذموم	محمود	وسط	مذموم	محمود	وسط	محمود
طلب الحوائج من الغرّاب (؟)	مذموم	محمود	محمود	محمود	مذموم	مذموم	محمود	وسط	مذموم	محمود	وسط	محمود

---

111 H continues on H, 123a.

⟨H, 123ᵃ⟩

الحوت	الدلو	الجدي	القوس	العقرب	الميزان	السنبلة	الأسد	السرطان	الجوزاء	الثور	الحمل	البروج \ الحوائج
وسط	محمود	محمود	وسط	محمود	مذموم	مذموم	مذموم	وسط	محمود	وسط	محمود	لقاء الخدّام والحوائج منهم
وسط	مذموم	محمود	وسط	مذموم	وسط	محمود	مذموم	وسط	محمود	وسط	محمود	شراء الأر[ا]ضين
وسط	محمود	مذموم	وسط	محمود	مذموم	مذموم	محمود	وسط	مذموم	وسط	محمود	البناء (؟) والتقوّل (؟)
مذموم	محمود	مذموم	محمود	مذموم	محمود	وسط	مذموم	محمود	مذموم	مذموم	محمود	شراء الجواري والعبيد
وسط	وسط	محمود	مذموم	وسط	محمود	محمود	محمود	محمود	محمود	محمود (البقر)	محمود (الغنم)	شراء البقر والغنم
وسط	محمود	مذموم	وسط	محمود	مذموم	وسط	محمود	وسط	مذموم	وسط	محمود	غرس الشجر المأبّد
محمود	مذموم	مذموم	محمود	مذموم	مذموم	محمود	مذموم	مذموم	محمود	وسط	مذموم	مشاركة التجّار
مذموم	محمود	مذموم	محمود	مذموم	مذموم	محمود	مذموم	مذموم	محمود	مذموم	مذموم	تسليم الصغار للكتّاب
مذموم	مذموم	وسط	مذموم	محمود	محمود	مذموم	محمود	وسط	مذموم	محمود	مذموم	تعليم الصنع الدقيقة
محمود	مذموم	محمود	محمود	محمود	محمود	مذموم	مذموم	مذموم	مذموم	محمود	مذموم	الرضاع
محمود	وسط	مذموم	محمود	وسط	محمود	مذموم	محمود	مذموم	مذموم	محمود	وسط	تعليم السباحة
مذموم	مذموم	محمود	مذموم	محمود	مذموم	مذموم	مذموم	محمود	مذموم	مذموم	محمود	الفطام

concerns / sign	Aries	Taurus	Gemini	Cancer	Leo
The kings' ascending of the thrones	appropriate	inappropriate	neither-nor	appropriate	appropriate
Seeking out the hunting (ground) (?)	appropriate	inappropriate	appropriate	appropriate on horseback	appropriate
Hitting the ball[112]	appropriate	inappropriate	appropriate	inappropriate	inappropriate
Assembling for war	appropriate	inappropriate	inappropriate	inappropriate	appropriate
Reviewing the troops	appropriate	inappropriate	inappropriate	inappropriate	appropriate
The raid and the horse race	appropriate	inappropriate	neither-nor	neither-nor	neither-nor
Contracting protected persons (?)	appropriate	appropriate	neither-nor	inappropriate	appropriate
Correspondence with the kings	neither-nor	inappropriate	inappropriate	inappropriate	neither-nor
Meeting two snake charmers (?)	neither-nor	appropriate	inappropriate	neither-nor	appropriate
Meeting the commanders and their concerns (?)[113]	inappropriate	inappropriate	neither-nor	inappropriate	appropriate
Meeting old women (?)	inappropriate	neither-nor	inappropriate	inappropriate	inappropriate
Contracting the provinces (?)[114]	inappropriate	appropriate	neither-nor	inappropriate	appropriate

---

112 Most probably ضرب الأُكْرة—"hitting the ball" denotes the game of polo (cf. D. Ayalon, "Furūsiyya. In the Mamluk State," in *EI2*, 955ᵃ who mentions also the terms لعب الكرة—"playing the ball" and لعب الصولجان—"playing the (polo) stick").

113 Cf. Kūshyār b. Labbān (Yano), *Mujmal*, iv.2, 254–255: الحوائج—"needed person".

114 Cf. Kūshyār b. Labbān (Yano), *Mujmal*, iv.2, 254–255: عقد اللواء—"hoisting the flag", a lettering bearing a resemblance to عقد الولايات—"contracting provinces (?)".

Virgo	Libra	Scorpio	Sagittarius	Capricorn	Aquarius	Pisces
appropriate	inappropriate	appropriate	appropriate	neither-nor	inappropriate	inappropriate
appropriate	inappropriate	appropriate on horseback	appropriate on horseback	appropriate	appropriate	appropriate
appropriate	appropriate	inappropriate	appropriate	appropriate	inappropriate	appropriate
inappropriate	inappropriate	appropriate	appropriate	appropriate	appropriate	appropriate
appropriate	appropriate	inappropriate	inappropriate	inappropriate	inappropriate	inappropriate
inappropriate	neither-nor	inappropriate	neither-nor	neither-nor	inappropriate	neither-nor
neither-nor	inappropriate	appropriate	neither-nor	inappropriate	appropriate	appropriate
appropriate	appropriate	inappropriate	inappropriate	inappropriate	neither-nor	appropriate
appropriate	appropriate	inappropriate	neither-nor	appropriate	inappropriate	neither-nor
neither-nor	inappropriate	appropriate	appropriate	appropriate	inappropriate	neither-nor
neither-nor	appropriate	neither-nor	appropriate	appropriate	appropriate	neither-nor
neither-nor	appropriate	appropriate	appropriate	inappropriate	appropriate	appropriate

[1] *The fortieth chapter on the benefic elections for carrying out concerns, (on) the benefic omens, and (on) incidents.*

[2] ⟨121ᵇ⟩ *The beginning of the beneficent elections for carrying out concerns and works according to the course of the Moon in the twelve zodiacal signs.* [3]

Pisces	Aquarius	Capricorn	Sagittarius	Scorpio	Libra	Virgo
inappropriate	appropriate	inappropriate	appropriate	neither-nor	neither-nor	inappropriate
inappropriate	appropriate	neither-nor	inappropriate	neither-nor	appropriate	appropriate
neither-nor	neither-nor	appropriate	neither-nor	inappropriate	appropriate	neither-nor
appropriate	appropriate	appropriate	neither-nor	neither-nor	neither-nor	inappropriate
inappropriate	inappropriate	neither-nor	appropriate	inappropriate	neither-nor	inappropriate
appropriate	appropriate	neither-nor	inappropriate	appropriate	appropriate	neither-nor
appropriate	inappropriate	neither-nor	neither-nor	inappropriate	appropriate	neither-nor
neither-nor	inappropriate	inappropriate	appropriate	appropriate	neither-nor	inappropriate
appropriate	inappropriate	inappropriate	appropriate	appropriate	inappropriate	neither-nor
inappropriate	neither-nor	neither-nor	inappropriate	appropriate	appropriate	inappropriate
appropriate	appropriate	inappropriate	appropriate	appropriate	inappropriate	appropriate
appropriate	inappropriate	neither-nor	inappropriate	inappropriate	appropriate	neither-nor

..eo	Cancer	*Gemini*	Taurus	*Aries*	sign / concerns
appropriate	appropriate	neither-nor	inappropriate	inappropriate	*Cancelling the contract of the province (?)*
neither-nor	neither-nor	appropriate	neither-nor	inappropriate	Consulting the ministers
inappropriate	neither-nor	neither-nor	inappropriate	appropriate	*Riding and exercising*
inappropriate	appropriate	neither-nor	inappropriate	appropriate	Secluding from confidants
appropriate	neither-nor	inappropriate	appropriate	inappropriate	*Playing ball with friends*[115]
inappropriate	neither-nor	appropriate	inappropriate	appropriate	Playing backgammon and chess
inappropriate	appropriate	neither-nor	inappropriate	appropriate	*Travel and wearing (new) clothes*
appropriate	neither-nor	inappropriate	inappropriate	appropriate	Bloodletting
appropriate	appropriate	neither-nor	inappropriate	appropriate	*Bathing*
appropriate	appropriate	inappropriate	appropriate	appropriate	⟨C⟩utting nails
appropriate	inappropriate	appropriate	appropriate	inappropriate	*Marrying*
inappropriate	appropriate	neither-nor	neither-nor	appropriate	The contract of properties (?)

---

115 If ‏إلهاء كرة مع الأصدقاء‎—"playing ball with friends" also refers to the game of polo is uncertain (see n. 112).

concerns / sign	Aries	Taurus	Gemini	Cancer	Leo
Buying (military) slaves	inappropriate	appropriate	appropriate	inappropriate	neither-nor
Buying riding animals	appropriate	appropriate	inappropriate	appropriate	appropriate
Buying jewels	inappropriate	appropriate	appropriate	appropriate	appropriate
Buying gold	appropriate	appropriate	appropriate	inappropriate	appropriate
Circumcision and castrating servants	appropriate	inappropriate	neither-nor	appropriate	appropriate
Drinking a laxative	appropriate	inappropriate	inappropriate	appropriate	inappropriate
Sending the messengers	appropriate	neither-nor	appropriate	appropriate	neither-nor
Addressing books	appropriate	appropriate	appropriate	appropriate	appropriate
Meeting kings	appropriate	inappropriate	appropriate	neither-nor	appropriate
Meeting scribes and merchants	inappropriate	neither-nor	appropriate	neither-nor	neither-nor
Concerns of nobles[116]	appropriate	neither-nor	inappropriate	appropriate	appropriate
Looking after the concerns of strangers (?)[117]	inappropriate	appropriate	appropriate	appropriate	neither-nor

---

116   See also n. 113.
117   See also n. 113.

Virgo	Libra	Scorpio	Sagittarius	Capricorn	Aquarius	Pisces
appropriate	appropriate	inappropriate	appropriate	inappropriate	appropriate	inappropriate
appropriate	appropriate	inappropriate	appropriate	inappropriate	neither-nor	appropriate
appropriate	appropriate	inappropriate	appropriate	inappropriate	neither-nor	appropriate
appropriate	appropriate	inappropriate	appropriate	inappropriate	inappropriate	appropriate
neither-nor	inappropriate	inappropriate	neither-nor	inappropriate	inappropriate	appropriate
inappropriate	appropriate	appropriate	inappropriate	inappropriate	neither-nor	appropriate
appropriate	neither-nor	inappropriate	neither-nor	inappropriate	neither-nor	neither-nor
neither-nor	neither-nor	inappropriate	neither-nor	inappropriate	neither-nor	neither-nor
neither-nor	inappropriate	inappropriate	neither-nor	inappropriate	inappropriate	appropriate
appropriate	neither-nor	neither-nor	inappropriate	neither-nor	appropriate	inappropriate
inappropriate	neither-nor	inappropriate	appropriate	inappropriate	neither-nor	appropriate
inappropriate	appropriate	inappropriate	inappropriate	appropriate	neither-nor	appropriate

[4] ⟨H, 122ᵇ⟩ *The completion of the beneficent elections for carrying out concerns and works and the elections according to the course of the Moon in the twelve zodiacal signs.*

Pisces	*Aquarius*	Capricorn	*Sagittarius*	Scorpio	*Libra*	Virgo
neither-nor	appropriate	appropriate	appropriate	neither-nor	appropriate	neither-nor
neither-nor	appropriate	neither-nor	neither-nor	appropriate	neither-nor	appropriate
neither-nor	appropriate	inappropriate	neither-nor	neither-nor	inappropriate	neither-nor
inappropriate	appropriate	inappropriate	appropriate	inappropriate	appropriate	appropriate
neither-nor	neither-nor	appropriate	appropriate	inappropriate	neither-nor	appropriate
neither-nor	appropriate	inappropriate	neither-nor	appropriate	inappropriate	neither-nor
appropriate	inappropriate	inappropriate	appropriate	inappropriate	inappropriate	appropriate
inappropriate	appropriate	inappropriate	appropriate	inappropriate	appropriate	appropriate
inappropriate	inappropriate	appropriate	neither-nor	inappropriate	inappropriate	appropriate
appropriate	appropriate	inappropriate	appropriate	appropriate	inappropriate	appropriate
appropriate	neither-nor	inappropriate	appropriate	neither-nor	neither-nor	appropriate
appropriate	inappropriate	appropriate	appropriate	inappropriate	appropriate	inappropriate

...eo	Cancer	*Gemini*	Taurus	*Aries*	sign / concerns
...nappropriate	inappropriate	inappropriate	neither-nor	inappropriate	*Meeting servants and their concerns*[118]
...ppropriate	inappropriate	neither-nor	appropriate	inappropriate	Buying lands
...ppropriate	inappropriate	neither-nor	appropriate	inappropriate	*Building and spreading rumours*
...either-nor	inappropriate	appropriate	appropriate	inappropriate	Buying female and male slaves
...ppropriate	appropriate	appropriate	appropriate for cattle	appropriate for sheep (and goats)	*Buying cattle and sheep (and goats)*
...ppropriate	inappropriate	neither-nor	appropriate	inappropriate	Planting trees for the ages
...ppropriate	inappropriate	appropriate	neither-nor	inappropriate	*Partnership with the merchants*
...nappropriate	inappropriate	appropriate	inappropriate	inappropriate	Apprenticing youths to the scribes[119]
...ppropriate	neither-nor	inappropriate	appropriate	inappropriate	*Teaching how to make delicate things (?)*
...ppropriate	appropriate	inappropriate	inappropriate	inappropriate	Engaging a wet nurse (?)[120]
...nappropriate	appropriate	appropriate	inappropriate		*Training to swim*
...ppropriate	inappropriate	inappropriate	appropriate	inappropriate	The weaning

---

118 See also n. 113.

119 Cf. Kūshyār b. Labbān (Yano), *Mujmal*, iv.2, 246–247: تسليم الولد إلى التعليم—"putting a child to education".

120 Cf. Kūshyār b. Labbān (Yano), *Mujmal*, iv.2, 246–247: الرضاع—"foster relationship".

Acknowledgments

I particularly like to thank Luís Ribeiro, Lisbon, for his patience and the invitation to the ASTRA conference in Batalha where he established an eagerly awaited platform for exchange and discussions after a long pandemic-caused hibernation. Furthermore, I would like to express my gratitude to all colleagues who helped in improving and completing this paper, in particular Thony Christie, Erlangen for his careful copy-editing, Benno van Dalen, München, Nahyan Fancy, Exeter, David Juste, München, Sibel Mayuk, Erlangen, Berenike Metzler, Erlangen, Carine van Rhijn, Utrecht, Stephanie Rudolf, Berlin and Tübingen, Johannes Thomann, Zürich, and last but not least Martin M. Schmidl for his sympathy. The responsibility for the content falls entirely upon the author of this present text.

Bibliography

Manuscripts

ʿAbd al-Ḥasan al-Iṣfahānī (?). *Kitāb al-Bulhān*:

    Oxford, Bodleian Library, Or. 133 (digital.bodleian.ox.ac.uk/objects/5c9da286–6a02
–406c-b990–0896b8ddbbb0/surfaces/1da3c44e-ee32–4554-a755–10b074e8e1ac/—
last accessed 2024-03-16).

al-Ashraf ʿUmar. *Kitāb al-Tabṣira fī ʿilm al-nujūm*:

    Oxford, Bodleian Library, Huntington 233 (digital.bodleian.ox.ac.uk/objects/30f036
5b-326a-4552-a446–809f0adf5c5c/—last accessed 2024-03-16).

    Paris, Bibliothèque Nationale, arabe 2601.2 (gallica.bnf.fr/ark:/12148/btv1b100375751
/f189.item.r=Arabe%202601—last accessed 2024-03-16).

Anon. Ephemeris:

    Cairo, Dār al-kutub, Mīqāt 817.2.

Anon. *majmūʿāt*:

    Leiden, Universiteitsbibliotheek, Or. 6638 (hdl.handle.net/1887.1/item:2434912—
last accessed 2024-03-16).

    Leiden, Universiteitsbibliotheek, Or. 7525.

(Pseudo-) Ibn al-ʿArabī. *Qabs al-anwār wa-bahjat al-asrār*:

    Leiden, Universiteitsbibliotheek, Or. 5.

al-Kindī. *Ikhtiyārāt al-ayyām*:

    Leiden, Universiteitsbibliotheek, Or. 199.2 (hdl.handle.net/1887.1/item:3413382—
last accessed 2024-03-16).

al-Qaṣrānī. *Kitāb al-Masāʾil fī ʿilm aḥkām al-nujūm*:

    Berlin, Staatsbibliothek Preußischer Kulturbesitz, Landberg 70 (digital.staatsbibliot hek-berlin.de/werkansicht/?PPN=PPN746349211&PHYSID=PHYS_0003—last accessed 2024-03-16).

al-Ṣaymarī. *Kitāb Aṣl al-uṣūl*:

    Berlin, Staatsbibliothek Preußischer Kulturbesitz, Landberg 221 (digital.staatsbibliothek-berlin.de/werkansicht?PPN=PPN1743975759&PHYSID=PHYS_0016&DMD ID=DMDLOG_0001—last accessed 2024-03-01).

Literature

Abū Maʿshar (Burnett and Yamamoto), *Great Introduction* see Burnett and Yamamoto, *Abū Maʿshar's Great Introduction*.

Ahlwardt, W. *Die Handschriften-Verzeichnisse der Königlichen Bibliothek zu Berlin*. 17. Band: Verzeichniss der Arabischen Handschriften. Band 5. Berlin: A. Asher & Co, 1893.

BEA—Hockey, Thomas, Virgina Trimble, and Thomas R. Williams, eds. *Biographical Encyclopedia of Astronomers*. 2 Volumes. New York: Springer, 2007.

Behrens, Gerhard. *An Ottoman Calendar for 1740/41*. München: GRIN, 2017.

al-Bīrūnī (Sachau), *Chronology* see Sachau, *Chronology*.

al-Bīrūnī (Sachau), *Chronologie* see Sachau, *Chronologie*.

Bluckley, Ron. "The Writings of Jaʿfar al-Ṣādiq." In *Books and Bibliophiles: Studies in Honour of Paul Auchterlonie on the Bio-bibliography of the Muslim World*, edited by Robert Gleave, 14–28. Cambridge: Gibb Memorial Trust, 2014.

Bos, Gerrit, and Y. Tzvi. Langermann. *The Alexandrian Summaries of Galen's* On Critical Days: *Editions and Translations of the two Versions of the* Jawāmiʿ. With an Introduction and Notes. Islamic Philosophy, Theology and Science 92. Leiden: Brill, 2014.

Boudon, Véronique. "Les définitions tripartites de la médecine chez Galien." In *Wissenschaften* (Medizin und Biologie [Forts.]), edited by Wolfgang Haase and Hildegard Temporini, 1468–1490. Aufstieg und Niedergang der römischen Welt Teil II, Bd. 37, Teilbd. 2. Berlin et al.: de Gruyter, 1994.

Brentjes, Sonja. "Textual Genres and Visual Representations in the Astral Sciences." In *Routledge Handbook on the Sciences in Islamicate Societies: Practices from the 2nd/8th to the 13th/19th Centuries*, edited by Sonja Brentjes, 447–460. London, New York: Routledge, 2023.

Burnett, Charles. "Astral Sciences: Traditions and Practices in the Medieval Western Christian World." In *Prognostication*, eds. Heiduk, Herbers, and Lehner, 485–501.

Burnett, Charles and Keiji Yamamoto. *The Great Introduction to Astrology by Abū Maʿšar*. With an Edition of the Greek Version by David Pingree. Islamic Philosophy, Theology and Science 106. Leiden: Brill, 2019.

Burnett, Charles. "Lunar Astrology. The Varieties of Texts Using Lunar Mansions, with Emphasis on Jafar Indus." *Micrologus* 12 (2004): 43–133.

Campion, Nicholas. *A History of Western Astrology. Vol. 1: The Ancient World. Vol. 2: The Medieval and Modern Times.* London, New York: Continuum, 2008/2009.

Carboni, Stefano. "The 'Book of Surprises' (*Kitab al-Bulhan*) of the Bodleian Library." *The La Trobe Journal* 91 (2013): 22–34.

Carboni, Stefano. *Il Kitāb al-bulhān di Oxford.* 1. ed. Eurasiatica 6. Torino: Editrice Tirrenia Stampatori, 1988.

Caudano, Anne-Laurence. "Astral Science: Traditions and Practices in the Medieval Eastern Christian World." In *Prognostication*, eds. Heiduk, Herbers, and Lehner, 502–515.

Chardonnens, László Sándor. "Hemerology in Medieval Europe." In *Books of Fate and Popular Culture in Early China: The Daybook Manuscripts of the Warring States, Qin, and Han*, edited by Donald J. Harper and Marc Kalinowski, 373–407. Handbook of Oriental Studies = Handbuch der Orientalistik. Section 4, China Volume 33. Leiden, Boston: Brill, 2017.

van Cleempoel, Koenraad, ed. *Astrolabes at Greenwich: A Catalogue of the Astrolabes in the National Maritime Museum.* Oxford, Greenwich: Oxford University Press, 2006.

Cooper, Glen Michael. "Rational and Empirical Medicine in Ninth Century Baghdad: Qustā Ibn Lūqā's *Questions on the Critical Days in Acute Illnesses*." *Arabic Sciences and Philosophy* 24 (2014): 69–102.

Cooper, Glen Michael. "Approaches to the Critical Days in Late Medieval and Renaissance Thinkers." *Early Science and Medicine* 18 (2013): 536–565.

Cooper, Glen Michael. *Galen, De Diebus Decretoriis, from Greek into Arabic: A Critical Edition, with Translation and Commentary, of Ḥunayn Ibn Isḥāq, Kitāb Ayyām al-buḥrān.* Medicine in the Medieval Mediterranean. London, New York: Routledge, Taylor & Francis Group, 2011.

van Dalen, Benno and Petra G. Schmidl. "al-Ashraf ʿUmar's *Tabṣira*: Chapter xxii." To appear on tabsira.hypotheses.org.

Daub, Frederike-Wiebke. *Formen und Funktionen des Layouts in arabischenn Manuskripten anhand von Abschriften religiöser Texte: al-Būṣīrīs Burda, al-Ǧazūlīs Dalāʾil und die Šifāʾ von Qāḍī ʿIyāḍ.* Arabische Studien Band 12. Wiesbaden: Harrassowitz Verlag, 2016.

Dorotheus Sidonius. *Carmen Astrologicum: The Umar al-Tabari Translation.* Translated and edited by Benjamin N. Dykes. Minneapolis, Minnesota: The Cazimi Press, 2017.

Dorotheus (Pingree), *Carmen Astrologicum* see Pingree, *Dorothei Sidoni Carmen Astrologicum.*

Dykes, Benjamin N. *Choices and Inceptions: Traditional Electional Astrology.* Minneapolis, Minnesota: Cazimi Press, 2012.

Dykes, Benjamin N., ed. *The Forty-Chapters of al-Kindi: Traditional Horary & Electional Astrology.* Minneapolis, Minnesota: The Cazimi Press, 2011.

Dykes, Benjamin N., ed. *The Book of the Nine Judges: Traditional Horary Astrology*. Minneapolis, Minnesota: The Cazimi Press, 2011.

Ebied, R.Y., and M.J.L. Young. "A Treatise on Hemerology Ascribed to Ǧafar Al-Ṣadīq." *Arabica* 23:3 (1976): 296–307.

EI1—*The Encyclopaedia of Islam, First Edition*. 4 Volumes. Leiden, London: Brill, 1913–1936. Photomechanical Reprint in 9 Volumes. Leiden: Brill, 1987.

EI2—*The Encyclopaedia of Islam: New Edition*. 12 Volumes and Indices. Leiden: Brill, 1960–2009.

EI3—*The Encyclopaedia of Islam: Three*. Leiden: Brill, 2007-to date.

EIr—*Encyclopaedia Iranica: Online edition* (www.iranicaonline.org last accessed 2024-03-16).

Fahd, Toufic. *La divination arabe*. Leiden: Brill, 1966.

Gaida, Margaret. "Introductions to Astrology." In *Prognostication*, eds. Heiduk, Herbers, and Lehner, 814–817.

Gaida, Margaret. "Zījes." In *Prognostication*, eds. Heiduk, Herbers, and Lehner, 999–1002.

Galen (Bos and Langermann), *Alexandrian Summaries* see Bos and Langermann, *Alexandrian Summaries*.

Galen (Cooper), *De Diebus Decretoriis* see Cooper, *Galen's De Diebus Decretoriis*.

Heiduk, Matthias. "Introductory Surveys: Medieval Traditions of Prognostication in the Western Christian World." In *Prognostication*, eds. Heiduk, Herbers, and Lehner, 109–151.

Heiduk, Matthias, Klaus Herbers, and Hans-Christian Lehner, eds. *Prognostication in the Medieval World: A Handbook*. Berlin: de Gruyter, 2021.

Hertogh, Tim, Carine van Rhijn, Bruno Schalekamp, and Petra G. Schmidl. "Medieval Divination by Unexpected Incidents: The *Tabula Prenostica Salomonis*." *International Journal of Divination and Prognostication* 4 (2023): 81–103.

Ihsanoglu, Ekmeleddin, and Boris A. Rosenfeld. *Mathematicians, Astronomers and Other Scholars of Islamic Civilisation and Their Works (7th–19th C.)*. Series of Studies and Sources on History of Science 11. Istanbul: Research Centre for Islamic History, Art and Culture (IRCICA), 2003.

ISMI—Islamic Scientific Manuscripts Initiative (ismi.mpiwg-berlin.mpg.de/—last accessed 2024-03-02).

Käs, Fabian. "Astrologische Voraussagen über den Jagderfolg: Der Katarchen-Abschnitt des K. al-Qānūn al-Wāḍiḥ von Ibn Quštimur." In *Die Geheimnisse der oberen und der unteren Welt: Magie im Islam zwischen Glaube und Wissenschaft*, edited by Sebastian Günther and Dorothee Pielow, 294–318. Islamic History and Civilization 158. Leiden: Brill, 2018.

Karimi Zanjani Asl, Mohammad, Eva Orthmann, and Petra G. Schmidl. "The Sources and the Composition of the *Dustūr al-munajjimīn*." In *Science in the City of For-*

tune: *The Dustūr al-munajjimīn and its World*, edited by Eva Orthmann and Petra
G. Schmidl, 35–113. Bonner Islamstudien Band 39. Berlin: EBVerlag, 2017.

King, David A. *In Synchrony with the Heavens: Studies in Astronomical Timekeeping and
Instrumentation in Medieval Islamic Civilization.* Volume Two: Instruments of Mass
Calculation (Studies X–XVIII). Islamic Philosophy, Theology and Science 55. Leiden:
Brill, 2005.

King, David A. *A Survey of the Scientific Manuscripts in the Egyptian National Library.*
Winona Lake, Indiana: Eisenbrauns, 1986.

King, David A. *Mathematical Astronomy in Medieval Yemen: A Biobibliographical Survey.* American Research Center in Egypt. Malibu: Udena Publications, 1983.

King, David A. *A Catalogue of the Scientific Manuscripts in the Egyptian National Library*
(in Arabic). 2 Volumes. Cairo: General Egyptian Book Organization, 1981/1986.

Kurz, Marlene. *Ein osmanischer Almanach für das Jahr 1239/1240 (1824/25).* Islamkundliche Untersuchungen Bd. 276. Berlin: Klaus Schwarz, 2007.

Kūshyār b. Labbān (Yano), *Mujmal* see Yano, *Kūshyār ibn Labbān's* Introduction.

Labat, René. *Un calendrier babylonien des travaux des signes et des mois: Séries Iqqur
Îpuš.* Bibliothèque de l'École des Hautes Études 321. Paris: Champion, 1965.

Labat, René. Hémérologies et ménologies d'Assur: Études d'assyriologie 1. Paris: Libr.
d'Amérique et d'Orient. Doctoral thesis Paris: Université de Paris, 1939.

Langermann, Y. Tzvi. "The Astral Connections of Critical Days: Some Late Antique
Sources Preserved in Hebrew and Arabic." In *Astro-Medicine: Astrology and Medicine, East and West*, edited by Anna Akasoy, Charles Burnett, and Ronit Yoeli-Tlalim,
99–118. Firenze: SISMEL, 2008.

Lehoux, Daryn. *Astronomy, Weather, and Calendars in the Ancient World: Parapegmata
and Related Texts in Classical and Near-Eastern Societies.* Cambridge: Cambridge
University Press, 2007.

Leitz, Christian. *Tagewählerei: Das Buch ḥȝt nḥḥ pḥ.wy ḏt und verwandte Texte.* 2 Volumes. Wiesbaden: Harrassowitz, 1994. 1. Textband, 2. Tafelband.

van der Lugt, Maaike. "Neither Ill nor Healthy: The Intermediate State Between Health
and Disease in Medieval Medicine." *Quaderni storici, nuova serie* 46:136 (2011): 13–45.

Melvin-Koushki, Matthew. "Review Essay: Magic in Islam between Religion and Science." *Magic, Ritual, and Witchcraft* 14 (2019): 255–287.

Mimura, Taro, and Petra G. Schmidl. "al-Ashraf ʿUmar's *Tabṣira*: Chapter xl (H, 146ᵇ,
16–152ᵃ, 13)—On the Use of the Astrolabe." Published 2024-04-26 on tabsira.hypoth
eses.org.

Mimura, Taro, and Petra G. Schmidl. "al-Ashraf ʿUmar's *Tabṣira*: Chapter ix (H, 22ᵇ, 3–
25ᵃ, 8)—Lunar Nodes, Eclipses, Fortune and Misfortune of the Planets, Elections."
Published 2022-07-19 on tabsira.hypotheses.org.

Müller, Ute. *Deutsche Mondwahrsagetexte aus dem Spätmittelalter.* Doctoral Thesis
Berlin: Freie Universität Berlin, Fachbereich Germanistik, 1971.

New Pauly Online. BrillOnline Reference Works. Leiden: Brill, 2005-to date.

Nicoll, Alexander, and Edward Bouverie Pusey. *Bibliothecae Bodleianae codicum manuscriptorum orientalium catalogi,* partis secundae, volumen secundum, arabicos complectens. Oxonii: Typographeo Academico, 1835.

Nothaft, Philipp. "Calendrical Calculations: Traditions and Practices in the Medieval Western Christian World." In *Prognostication,* eds. Heiduk, Herbers, and Lehner, 605–618.

Pingree, David. *Picatrix: The Latin Version of the* Ghāyat al-Ḥakīm. *Text, Appendices, Indices.* Studies of the Warburg Institute 56. London: The Warburg Institute, 1986.

Pingree, David. *Dorothei Sidoni Carmen Astrologicum.* Leipzig: Teubner, 1976.

Plessner, Martin and Hellmut Ritter. *Picatrix: Das* Ziel der Weisen *von Pseudo-Maǧrīṭī.* Translated into German from the Arabic. Studies of the Warburg Institute 27. London: The Warburg Institute, 1962.

Ptolemy. *Ptolemy's* Tetrabiblos *in the Translation of William of Moerbeke:* Claudii Ptolemaei Liber iudicialium. Edited by Gudrun Vuilllemin-Diem and Carlos Steel with the Assistance of Pieter De Leemans. Ancient and Medieval Philosophy, De Wulf-Mansion Centre Series 1 19. Leuven: Leuven University Press, 2015.

Ptolemy. *Tetrabiblos*: Translated by F.E. Robbins. Loeb Classical Library 435. Cambridge, Mass., London: Harvard University Press, 1940. Repr. Ann Arbor, Michigan, n. d.

Ribeiro, Luís, and Petra G. Schmidl. "al-Ashraf ʿUmar's *Tabṣira*: Chapter xliv (H, 144ᵃ, 6–146ᵇ, 16)—Signs Straight and Crooked in Rising." To be published on tabsira.hypotheses.org.

Ritter, Hellmut, ed. *Pseudo-Maǧrīṭī: Das* Ziel des Weisen. 1. Arabischer Text. Leipzig, Berlin: B.G. Teubner, 1933.

Rochberg, Francesca. "'If P, then Q': Form and Reasoning in Babylonian Divination." In *Divination and Interpretation of Signs in the Ancient World,* edited by Amer Annus. Oriental Institute Seminars 6. Chicago, Ill.: Oriental Institute of the Univ. of Chic., 2010. Repr. in *In the Path of the Moon: Babylonian Celestial Divination and its Legacy,* edited by Francesca Rochberg, 399–410. Studies in Ancient Magic and Divination 6. Leiden: Brill, 2010.

Rudolf, Stefanie. *Syrische Astrologie und das Syrische Medizinbuch.* Science, Technology, and Medicine in Ancient Cultures 7. Berlin, Boston: de Gruyter, 2018. doi.org/10.1515/9783110565737.

Sachau, C. Edward. *The Chronology of Ancient Nations: An English Version of the* Athār-Ul-Bākiya *of Albīrūnī, or "Vestiges in the Past."* London: W.H. Allen & Co., 1879. Repr. in the series *Islamic Mathematics and Astronomy* 31. Frankfurt: Institut für Geschichte der arabisch-islamischen Wissenschaften, 1998.

Sachau, C. Edward. *Chronologie Orientalischer Völker von Albêrūnī.* Leipzig: Brockhaus, 1878. Repr. in the series *Islamic Mathematics and Astronomy.* 30. Frankfurt: Institut für Geschichte der arabisch-islamischen Wissenschaften, 1998.

Sahl b. Bišr al-Isrāʾīlī. *Kitāb al-Iḵtiyārāt ʿalā l-Buyūt al-Iṯnai ʿašar*: With its Latin Translation *De Electionibu*s. Edited and translated, with Introduction, Annotations and Glossaries by Carole Mary Crofts. Unpublished Doctoral Thesis Glasgow: Department of Arabic and Islamic Studies and the Department of Humanity, 1985.

Savage-Smith, Emilie. *Islamicate Celestial Globes. Their History, Construction, and Use*. With a Chapter on Iconography by Andrea P.A. Belloli. Smithsonian Studies in History and Technology 46. Washington D.C.: Smithsonian Institution, 1985.

Schjellerup, H.C.F.C. *Description des étoiles fixes* [...] *par l'astronome Persan Abd-al-Rahman al-Sūfī* [...]. St. Petersburg: (unknown), 1874.

Schmidl, Petra G. "Rulers as Authors in 13th Century Yemen: al-Ashraf ʿUmar's Oeuvre." In *Rulers as Authors in the Islamic World: Knowledge, Authority and Legitimacy*, edited by Sonja Brentjes, Maribel Fierro, and Tilman Seidensticker, 455–488. Islamic History and Civilization 213. Leiden: Brill, 2024.

Schmidl, Petra G. "al-Ashraf ʿUmar's *Tabṣira*: Chapter xxxiv: Rainbows, Shooting Stars, and Haloes as Signs of the Future." In *Dreams, Nature, and Practices as Signs of the Future in the Middle Ages*, edited by Klaus Herbers and Hans-Christian Lehner, 252–309. Prognostication in History 10. Leiden, Boston: Brill, 2022.

Schmidl, Petra G. "al-Ashraf ʿUmar's *Tabṣira*: Chapter xxxvii.1: Qibla Schemes as Text-image Arrangements with an Example from 13th Century Yemen." In *Writing as Intermediary: Text-image Relations in Early Modern Islamic Cultures*, edited by Lorenz Korn and Berenike Metzler, 65–96. Bamberger Orientstudien 16. Bamberg: University of Bamberg Press, 2022.

Schmidl, Petra G. "Introductory Surveys: Medieval Traditions of Prognostication in the Islamic World." In *Prognostication*, eds. Heiduk, Herbers, and Lehner, 189–242.

Schmidl, Petra G. "Astral Sciences: Traditions and Practices in the Medieval Islamic World." In *Prognostication*, eds. Heiduk, Herbers, and Lehner, 532–550.

Schmidl, Petra G. "al-Ashraf ʿUmar's *Tabṣira*: The Table of Contents: Supporting Sovereign Decision-making in 13th Century Yemen?" In *Unterstützung bei herrscherlichem Entscheiden: Experten und ihr Wissen in transkultureller und komparativer Perspektive*, edited by Michael Grünbart, 216–232. Kulturen des Entscheidens Band 005. Göttingen: Vandenhoeck & Ruprecht, 2021.

Schmidl, Petra G. "al-Ashraf ʿUmar's *Tabṣira*: The Preface. Announcing an Introductory Text?" *Zeitschrift für Geschichte der arabisch-islamischen Wissenschaften* 22 (2020): 163–196.

Schmidl, Petra G. "al-Ashraf ʿUmar's *Tabṣira*: Chapter xlvii (H, 153^b, 1–154^a, 7)—Mathematical Geography, Geographical Table." Published 2020-10-01 on tabsira.hypotheses.org.

Schmidl, Petra G. "Lunar Elections in Ibn Rahiq's Folk Astronomical Treatise." In *From Māshā Allāh to Kepler: Theory and Practice in Medieval and Renaissance Astrology*, edited by Charles Burnett and Dorian Gieseler Greenbaum, 425–453. Ceredigion, Wales: Sophia Centre Press, 2015.

Schmidl, Petra G. "Magic and Medicine in a 13th c. Treatise on the Science of the Stars." In *Herbal Medicine in Yemen: Traditional Knowledge and Practice, and their Value for Today's World*, edited by Hanne Schönig and Ingrid Hehmeyer. With the Collaboration of Anne Regourd, 43–68. Islamic History and Civilization 96. Leiden: Brill, 2012.

Schmidl, Petra G. "Two Early Arabic Sources on the Magnetic Compass (Revised Translation of a Master Thesis, Johann Wolfgang Goethe-Universität Frankfurt 1994)." *Journal of Arabic and Islamic Studies* 1 (1997): 81–132.

Schmidl, Petra G. "al-Ashraf ʿUmar's *Tabṣira*: Chapter xxvii.3. Introducing a Volvelle for Astronomical and Astrological Purposes?" To appear in the proceedings of the conference "Science and Craft: The Relations between the Theoretical and Practical Sides of the Occult and Esoteric Sciences in the Islamic World" organised by Godefroid the Callataÿ and Liana Saif, The Warburg Institute, London, 10–13 January 2023.

Sela, Shlomo/Shelomoh. *Abraham Ibn Ezra on Elections, Interrogations, and Medical Astrology: A Parallel Hebrew-English Critical Edition of the* Book of Elections (*3 versions*), the Book of Interrogations (*3 versions*), *and the* Book of the Luminaries. Etudes sur le judaisme médiéval 50. Leiden et al. Brill, 2011.

Sezgin, Fuat. *Geschichte des arabischen Schrifttums*. 9 Volumes. Leiden: Brill, 1967–1984.

Stegemann, Viktor. *Die Fragmente des Dorotheos von Sidon: 2. Lieferung*. Quellen und Studien zur Geschichte und Kultur des Altertums und des Mittelalters, Reihe D: Untersuchungen und Mitteilungen 1. Heidelberg: Selbstverlag F. Bilabel, 1943.

Stegemann, Viktor. *Die Fragmente des Dorotheos von Sidon: 1. Lieferung*. Quellen und Studien zur Geschichte und Kultur des Altertums und des Mittelalters, Reihe D: Untersuchungen und Mitteilungen 1. Heidelberg: Selbstverlag F. Bilabel, 1939.

Strohmaier, Gotthard. *Die Sterne des Abd ar-Rahman as-Sufi*. Leipzig, Weimar: Gustav Kiepenheuer, 1984.

Thomann, Johannes. "Reverse Engineering Applied to Ephemerides: Analysis and Edition of the Arabic Ephemeris of 1326/27 CE (MS Cairo, Dār Al-Kutub, Mīqāt 817)." In *Editing and Analysing Numerical Tables: Towards a Digital Information System for the History of Astral Sciences*, edited by Benno van Dalen, Matthieu Husson, and Clemency Montelle, 469–510. Ptolemaeus Arabus et Latinus–Studies (PALS) 2. Turnhout: Brepols Publishers, 2021.

Thomann, Johannes. "From *katarchai* to *ikhtiyārāt*: The Emergence of a New Arabic Document Type Combining Ephemerides and Almanacs." In *Proceedings of the 28th International Congress of Papyrology* (Barcelona 1–6 August 2016), edited by Alberto Nodar and Sofía Torallas Tovar. Primera edición, 342–354. Scripta orientalia 3. Barcelona: Publicacions de l'Abadia de Monserrat, Universitat Pompeu Fabra, 2019.

Thomann, Johannes. "The Arabic Ephemeris for the Year 1149/1150 CE (P. Cambridge

UL Inv. Michael. Chartae D 58) and the Arabic *baḥnīṭas*, Greek Παχνίτης and Coptic ПαϭοΝϲ." *Chronique d'Egypte* 90:179 (2015): 207–224.

Ullmann, Manfred. *Die Natur- und Geheimwissenschaften im Islam*. Handbuch der Orientalistik, Erste Abteilung Ergänzungsband VI, 2. Abschnitt. Leiden: Brill, 1972.

Vettius Valens. *Anthologiae*. Edidit Pingree, David. Bibliotheca scriptorum Graecorum et Romanorum Teubneriana. Leipzig: Teubner, 1986.

Varisco, Daniel Martin. "The Magical Significance of the Lunar Stations in the 13th Century Yemeni *Kitāb al-Tabṣira fī ʿilm al-nujūm* of al-Malik al-Ashraf." *Quaderni di Studi Arabi* 13 (1995): 19–40.

Varisco, Daniel Martin. *Medieval Agriculture and Islamic Science: The Almanac of a Yemeni Sultan*. Seattle, London: University of Washington Press, 1994.

Voorhoeve, P. *Handlist of Arabic Manuscripts in the Library of the University of Leiden*. Codices Manuscripti 7. Leiden: University Press, 1957.

Wiedemann, Eilhard. "Über einen astrologischen Traktat von al Kindî." *Archiv für die Geschichte der Naturwissenschaft und Technik* (1911): 224–226. Repr. in *Gesammelte Schriften zur arabisch-islamischen Wissenschaftsgeschichte*, edited by Fuat Sezgin, vol. 2, 620–622. Frankfurt: Institut für Geschichte der arabisch-islamischen Wissenschaften, 1984. Repr. in *Texts and Studies on Astrology: Selected and Reprinted*, edited by Fuat Sezgin, vol. 4, 214–216. Frankfurt: Institut für Geschichte der arabisch-islamischen Wissenschaften, 2000.

Witkam, Jan Just. *Inventory of the Oriental Manuscripts of the Library of the University of Leiden*: Volume 1: Manuscripts 0001–1000. Leiden: Ter Lugt Press, 2007. Acquisitions in the Period between 1609 and 1665. Mainly the Collections of Jacobus Golius (1629), Josephus Justus Scaliger (1609) and Part of the Collection of Levinus Warner (1665).

Witkam, Jan Just. 1979. "An Arabic Treatise on Hemerology Ascribed to Ǧaʿfar al- Sādiq." *Arabica* 26 (1): 100–102.

Yano, Michio, ed. *Kūshyār ibn Labbān's* Introduction to Astrology. Tokio: Institute for the Study of Languages and Cultures of Asia and Africa (ILCAA), 1997.

Young, M.J.L. "An Arabic Almanac of Favourable and Unfavourable Days." *Journal of Semitic Studies* 27:2 (1982): 261–279.

Techniques of a Japanese Buddhist Astrologer in the Twelfth Century: Notes on the *Sukuyō unmei kanroku* 宿曜運命勘録

Jeffrey Kotyk

Abstract

Foreign astrology came to China starting around the fourth century through Buddhist texts, but it was only in the eighth century when local Buddhists came to have a pressing need to seriously study it. In the mid-eighth century, the monk Amoghavajra compiled the first authoritative Buddhist manual of astrology in Chinese with which monks could use for timing rituals. The popularity of this text encouraged the translation of horoscopy into Chinese starting around the year 800, after which time the art became mainstream. In the tenth century, we see in Japan the emergence of a unique lineage of astrologer-monks called Sukuyōdō ("Way of the Asterisms and Planets"). These monks cast horoscopes and interpreted them using astrological lore derived from Chinese translations of what we can identify as Hellenistic astrology. Doctrines such as triplicity rulers, the twelve houses, domiciles, and annual profections are attested in medieval Japan. This paper is a study of a twelfth-century Japanese horoscope, showing the diverse concepts and doctrines that the astrologer used. It is demonstrated that Japanese horoscopy was not so different from what was practiced elsewhere in the world, in large part because of a common heritage.

Keywords

Japan – astrology – horoscopes – Sukuyōdō – astronomy – ephemerides

Starting from the fourth century, Chinese Buddhist translations mention forms of Indian astrology based on the *nakṣatra*s, but the first substantial attempt at translating and implementing foreign astrology in China only dates to the eighth century, when Amoghavajra (Bukong 不空; 705–774) produced a manual of astrology for Buddhist use. This was effectively just inserting Indian themes

and concepts over the traditional Chinese lunar calendar, in effect localiz-
ing the foreign content for immediate domestic use, but with the practical
astronomy dropped. Some decades after Amoghavajra, horoscopic astrology
was introduced, the impetus for which was perhaps the sudden Buddhist interest in astrology for not only the timing of rituals, but also as a means of analyzing an individual's fate. Chinese celestial omenology, which was reserved for
use by the court, concerned itself with matters of the state and ruler, hence individuals could not utilize it to predict their own fates. On the other hand, horoscopic astrology allowed an individual to evaluate their own fortunes based on
their nativity. So long as one knew the date and time of a birth, it was possible to produce a horoscopic chart displaying the positions of the planets at a
given hour in the past. Until the mid to late years of the Tang Dynasty (eighth
to ninth centuries), this practice was apparently unknown in China, but it evidently became quite popular: poets such as Han Yu 韓愈 (768–824) and Du
Mu 杜牧 (803–852) incorporated astrological themes in their literary works. Du
Guangting 杜光庭 (850–933), a Daoist adept, also demonstrated knowledge of
astrology in his writings.[1]

Horoscopic astrology in China was translated from diverse sources, but
material based on Dorotheus of Sidon became the primary (although certainly not exclusive) source with which astrologers in East Asia worked their
trade. The Chinese translation was presumably from a Middle Persian source,
although this cannot be definitively proven. The title *Duli yusi jing* 都利聿斯經
('Scripture of Dorotheus') is cited in a number of later sources, but the original
work is not extant.[2] The adaptation of horoscopy into a Chinese astronomical framework appears to have occurred around the year 800. For example,
rather than positioning the planets relative to zodiac signs and 360 degrees—
as we would expect from Hellenistic or Indian astrology—the available evidence instead shows that astrologers used the indigenous Chinese system of
coordinates comprised of 365.25 degrees based on twenty-eight lunar stations.

---

1   For a discussion of the historical introduction of foreign astrology into China, see Jeffrey
    Kotyk, 'Iranian Elements in Late-Tang Buddhist Astrology', *Asia Major* 30, no. 1 (2017): 25–58.
    See also Bill M. Mak, 'Indian Jyotiṣa Through the Lens of Chinese Buddhist Canon', *Journal
    of Oriental Studies* 48, no. 1 (2015): 1–19. On the use of astrology by poets in the late Tang, see
    Chan Man Sing 陳萬成, 'Du Mu yu xingming' 杜牧與星命, *Tang yanjiu* 唐研究 8 (2002):
    61–79.

2   Mak was the first to accurately make the connection between the fragments of this text and
    Dorotheus. See Bill M. Mak, '*Yusi Jing*—A treatise of 'Western' Astral Science in Chinese and
    its versified version *Xitian yusi jing*.' *SCIAMVS* 15 (2014): 105–169. See also an early study of
    the fragments of this text: Ishida Mikinosuke, 'Tori-isshi-kyō to sono itsubun', in *Tōyō ronsō:
    Haneda Hakushi shōju kinen* (Kyoto: Tōyōshi Kenkyūkai, 1950), 49–62.

Ephemerides were also made accessible around the same time. This meant that anyone with some basic training and knowhow could position the planets in a horoscope (in a table divided into twelve sections) without having to perform complex calculations or make observations of the heavens themselves. Buddhists and Daoists quickly adopted horoscopy; their roles as ritualists were only enhanced through practices of astral magic, much of which was also evidently imported from abroad.[3]

Japanese Buddhist monks brought back to Japan many of the books used in the Chinese system of astrology. In 806, Kūkai 空海 (774–835), for example, introduced the aforementioned manual of astrology by Amoghavajra to Japan. His later biographer insisted that the concept of Sunday—the seven-day week—had been first introduced to Japan by Kūkai, which may very well have been the case. In a subsequent generation, another Japanese monk, Shūei 宗叡 (809–884), returned to Japan from China in 865 with at least four separate texts on astrology, a total of eight fascicles, although his record expressly states that these were not Buddhist works.[4] None of the figures from the ninth century, however, were remembered as formal astrologers in later times. The title for 'astrologer' in Japanese is *sukuyōshi* 宿曜師 (literally, 'Master of the Asterisms and Planets'), but this word is only traced back to the late tenth century, without any obvious precedent in China. Although written in Chinese Characters, the term was created by the Japanese. Although Shūei brought astrology manuals to Japan and might even have understood how to cast a horoscope, documentation from the medieval period records a monk named Hōzō 法藏 (905–969) as the first *sukuyōshi*. The lineages of astrologers, in fact, were apparently all Buddhist monks, although we should not assume that Buddhism was ever strictly associated with astrology. The Japanese tradition of astrologer-monks was called Sukuyōdō 宿曜道, ('Way of the Asterisms and Planets'). In this context, the suffix -*dō* 道 ('way') is paralleled in some words familiar to modern Anglophones, such as Kendō 劍道 ('Way of the Sword'). Sukuyōdō was basically the 'Way of the Astrologers', but their tradition was contained within a Buddhist monastic environment. Another lineage of divination and ritual experts, the Onmyōdō 陰陽道 ('Way of Yin and Yang') also had their own prac-

---

3 On the Buddhist and Daoist adoption of astrology, see Jeffrey Kotyk, 'The Sinicization of Indo-Iranian Astrology in Medieval China', *Sino-Platonic Papers* 282 (2018): 1–95.

4 These include the Chinese translation of Dorotheus, plus the *Qiyao rangzai jue* 七曜禳災決 ('Secrets of the Seven-Planet Apotropaism'). The latter is extant. The other two texts appear to have been ephemerides for the seven planets. See the catalog of items brought back to Japan, recorded by Shūei himself. *Shin shosha shōrai hōmon tō mokuroku* 新書寫請來法門等目錄 ('Catalog of Dharma Items Brought Back') (Taishō 2174A, 55: 1111b20–1111c1).

tices of hemerology and astrology, but their systems did not evidently include horoscopy.[5]

Although horoscopy arrived in Japan after having passed through multiple languages and cultures, it is remarkable that the integrity of many core doctrines remained consistent over the centuries. In the present paper, I want to point out this fact, but I also believe that we must recognize some innovations and unique features of what we can call Sino-Japanese horoscopy (i.e., horoscopy practiced in Japan, but it was written in Chinese and based on Chinese manuals). Although there are differences, which I will discuss below, most (but not all) of the doctrines known to Japanese astrologers would have been immediately recognizable to their counterparts in the Islamic world, Europe, and India. This consistency of what were originally foreign astrological techniques in East Asia, I argue, demonstrates that horoscopy was a unique science in world history that—unlike religious doctrines and ritual practices—was better able to retain its core structure across multiple transmissions in diverse languages.

1   The Horoscope of 1113

There are two known extant horoscopes from Japan. The birthdates for these are 1113 and 1268 respectively (the horoscopes and analysis were drawn up decades later). There is also a horoscope from China that was rediscovered at Dunhuang in northwest China; it written by Kang Zun 康遵 and dated to 975 (Pelliot chinois 4071).[6] We are able to compare these three, but it is unfortunate that despite several astrological manuals in Chinese having survived until modernity, we only have three extant horoscopes written in Chinese from premodern times (Japanese authors often wrote in Classical Chinese throughout the medieval period). The horoscope of 1113 has been studied by Momo, Nakayama, Yano, and Kotyk, who will be cited below.

The document itself, which was clearly composed for the client to keep for himself after a personal consultation, is titled *Sukuyō unmei kanroku* 宿曜運命勘録 ('Report on Fate by the Asterisms and Planets'), although whether this

---

5   On these details, see the authoritative study by Yamashita Katsuaki, 'Sukuyōdō no keisei to tenkai', in *Kōki sekkan jidaishi no kenkyū* (Tokyo: Yoshikawa Kōbunkan, 1990), 481–527.

6   On the Dunhuang horoscope, see Isahaya Yoichi and Lin Jyuh Fuh, 'Entangled Representation of Heaven: A Chinese Divination Text from a Tenth-Century Dunhuang Fragment (P. 4071)', *Historia Scientiarum* 26, no. 3 (2017): 153–171. See also comments by Kotyk, 'The Sinicization of Indo-Iranian Astrology', 79–81.

was assigned by the astrologer himself or a later cataloger is uncertain.[7] The text itself was preserved as a handwritten manuscript as part of a larger collection of texts in Japan, which was included in a woodblock printed volume. Momo then made a typeset edition, but his reading of a number of characters is problematic. My citations below are based on the handwritten manuscript, but I also consulted Momo's edition.[8]

The date of birth of the native, a male, is given in the typical way based on the Chinese lunar calendar, but naturally the reign-era is given as a Japanese imperial year: year 3 of Ten'ei, in the twelfth lunar month, on the twenty-fifth day, at the hour of the ox (天永三年壬辰十二月廿五日戊申時丑誕生男). Yano converts this date to the Western date of January 15th, 1113.[9] The 'hour of the ox' is, strictly speaking, not an 'hour' in either the Greek sense (ὥρα) as a seasonal hour or a modern equinoctial hour. The Chinese divided the day and night together into twelve units of time (often translated as 'double hours'), which are indicated with the earthly branches (Chn. *dizhi* 地支). These are associated with twelve animals (colloquially called the 'Chinese zodiac', although this is a misnomer). This was only an approximate system that did not allow for exact measurements for the passage of time at a popular level. In this case, the minute of birth is not given, so an exact calculation of the rising degree at the Ascendant would not have been possible. Instead, we can only give an approximate time of 01:00–03:00 for the birth of the native, which is also noted to have fallen on a Wednesday. It appears that astrologers in East Asia did not calculate the Ascendant down to the degree (although Muslim and Indian astrologers resident in China would have presumably done this). This was technically not possible because they did not use a spherical-earth model and global latitude. Chinese Buddhist leaders even rejected the spherical earth in favor of the flat-earth worldview based on Mt. Sumeru and the Four Continents during the eighth century.[10] The Sun was simply positioned in the 'hour of birth', and from there the other details were filled in.

---

7   See Momo's early study on the Japanese horoscopes: Momo Hiroyuki, 'Sukuyōdō to sukuyō kanmon', *Risshō shigaku* 立正史學 39 (1975): 1–20.

8   Handwritten manuscript: *Zokugunshoruijū kyūhyakuhachi* 續羣書類從九百八 (宮内庁書陵部, マイクロ収集, 453・2; 20-146-1-848). https://doi.org/10.20730/100045263. Woodblock print: *Zoku gunshoruijū* 續羣書類從 (Hanawa Hokiichi 塙保己一, ed. Tokyo: Zoku Gunshoruijū Kanseikai, 1923–1943), vol. 31-31: 429–438. Momo's typeset edition: Momo Hiroyuki, 'Sukuyō kanmon shū', in *Momo Hiroyuki chosakushū*, vol. 8-2, Rekihō no kenkyū 暦法の研究, ed. Tsuchida Naoshige 土田直鎮 (Kyoto: Shibunkaku, 1990), 131–162.

9   Yano Michio, *Mikkyō senseijutsu: Sukuyōdō to Indo senseijutsu* (Tokyo: Tōyōshoin, 2013), 191–192.

10   On these issues, see Jeffrey Kotyk, 'Examining Amoghavajra's Flat-Earth Cosmology: Reli-

TABLE 5.1   Planetary positions in 1113 horoscope

九曜行度	Positional Degrees of the Nine Planets
太陽盈曆行女宿五度十九分	Sun, increasing in daylight, Nü 5.19
太陰遲曆行尾宿四度九十三分	Moon, slow, Wei 4.93
歲星後退行井宿廿一度三十分	Jupiter, below ecliptic, retrograde, Jing 21.30
熒惑前順遲行翼宿初九十三分	Mars, above ecliptic, forward, slow, Yi 1.93
鎮星後順行室宿九度三十二分	Saturn, below ecliptic, forward, Shi 9.32
太白後伏行女宿九度九十五分	Venus, below ecliptic, invisible, Nü 9.95
辰星前順續行危宿四度十分	Mercury, above ecliptic, forward, Wei 4.10
蝕神頭退行奎宿一度十四分	Eclipse-God Head, retrograde, Kui 1.14
蝕神尾順行軫宿九度四十四分	Eclipse-God Tail, forward, Zhen 9.44

Although this may have been an imprecise way of presenting the heavens at a given point in time, the positions of the planets were generally accurately calculated down to the degree using the Chinese system of coordinates, which are denominated using the classical twenty-eight stations or lodges (often called 'lunar stations' in English). These traditionally comprise 365.25 degrees, in contrast to the originally Mesopotamian value of 360 degrees.

Apart from the evident value of this document to the history of science in Japan, the first noticeable feature is that there are *nine* planets.[11] This number reflects the Indian model of the *navagraha* ('nine graspers'), yet the ordering of the five visible planets follows the Chinese model of the five elements/phases (*wuxing* 五行): Jupiter (wood), Mars (fire), Saturn (earth), Venus (metal), and Mercury (water). The two eclipse deities are otherwise called the Head and the Tail, which in Indian and some Chinese astrological sources are denominated as Rāhu and Ketu respectively. These are typically the ascending and descending nodes of the Moon. However, in this instance, the latter is *forward* in motion. In this instance, the Tail/Ketu *cannot* be the descending node of the Moon. Instead, the Tail/Ketu is the lunar apogee, a fact highlighted by Yano.[12] This is a unique feature of one tradition of astrology that is traced back

gious vs. Scientific Worldviews in Buddhist Astrology', *Studies in Chinese Religions* 8 (2021): 203–220.

11   The scientific value of the two Japanese horoscopes from the medieval period was recognized by Nakayama Shigeru, *A History of Japanese Astronomy: Chinese Background and Western Impact* (Cambridge, MA: Harvard University Press, 1969), 60.

12   Yano, *Mikkyō senseijutsu*, 193. For the identification of the apogee in Buddhist astrology in

to around the year 800, when a certain Cao Shiwei 曹士蔿 produced a set of ephemerides and evidently assigned the lunar apogee to Ketu.[13] The reasoning behind this was perhaps to preserve the orthodox model of nine planets, but at the same time to incorporate the lunar apogee. This system was adopted by Sukuyōdō in Japan, but the mainstream astrologers and Daoists in China used a system of eleven planets, in which a pseudo-planet called Yuebei/Yuebo 月孛/月勃 was used (apparently a translation or *candra-ucca* in Sanskrit or something comparable in another language; the 'apex of the Moon', which is akin to 'apogee' in Greek).[14] The first clear example of the lunar apogee in China is from the year 718, in which a Chinese translation of Sanskrit mathematical astronomy translates the term as 'high Moon' (*gao yue* 高月), but this term never became mainstream and the text in question was barely studied.[15]

The use of the lunar apogee as a pseudo-planet is only attested in East Asian astrology from around the year 800, but it was foreign in origin, although the parent tradition—which according to Chinese sources was in West India—is otherwise unknown in the extant documentation of ancient and medieval astrology.[16] Greek horoscopes show an awareness of the lunar apogee, but it is not treated as an astrological planet, as we see in P. Berl. 9825 from 319 CE, which was studied by Greenbaum and Jones.[17] My present speculation, based on the Chinese material, is that some astrologers from either Iran or Western India already treated the lunar nodes, Rāhu and Ketu, as pseudo-planets, and looked to the apogee as another invisible planet, which in turn could be regarded as malefic, in light of the fact that the Moon slows when approaching the apogee.

China, see Yano Michio, 'The Chi'yao jang-tsai-chueh and its Ephemerides', *Centaurus* 29, no. 1 (1986): 28–35.

13   On this figure, see Yabuuchi Kiyoshi 藪內清, 'Tō Sō Shii no *Futenreki* ni tsuite', *Biburia Tenri Toshokan* 78 (1982): 2–18.

14   Kotyk, 'The Sinicization of Indo-Iranian Astrology', 53–56, 75–78.

15   The text in Chinese is *Jiuzhi li* 九執曆 (**Navagraha-karaṇa*). Yabuuchi remarks that this text is primarily based on the *Pañcasiddhāntikā* (c. 550) by the Indian astronomer Varāhamihira, although it was clearly adapted to the Chinese environment. See Yabuuchi Kiyoshi, *Zuitō rekihō shi no kenkyū* (Rinsen Shoten, 1989), 12, 40. For recent comments on this text and partial translation, see Bill M. Mak, 'An 8th-Century CE Indian Astronomical Treatise in Chinese: The Nine Seizers Canon by Qutan Xida', in *Plurilingualism in Traditional Eurasian Scholarship*, eds. Glenn W. Most, Dagmar Schäfer, and Mårten Söderblom Saarela, (Leiden: Brill, 2023), 352–362.

16   The lunar apogee was introduced initially as the set of 'eleven planets' by Li Miqian 李彌乾 around the year 800 CE. See Kotyk, 'Iranian Elements in Late-Tang Buddhist Astrology', 35–36.

17   Dorian Greenbaum and Alexander Jones, 'P. Berl. 9825: An elaborate horoscope for 319 CE and its significance for Greek astronomical and astrological practice', *ISAW Papers* 12 (2017). http://hdl.handle.net/2451/49543

The apparent causal effect of the apogee on the Moon's orbit, during which time the Moon is weakened (in an astrological sense), would have been sufficient grounds to regard the apogee as a potent 'planet', not unlike Rāhu and Ketu, who are inherently connected with the eclipses of the Sun and Moon (regarded as ominous phenomena).

The above data reveals foreign influences, but the system of coordinates is entirely Chinese. Even if the apogee as a pseudo-planet was introduced from abroad, once its periodicity was understood, it was simple enough to track its movement in the same way as the lunar nodes. There was no need to adopt any foreign system of coordinates. Indeed, there is no reference to the degrees of the zodiac signs as positional coordinates in East Asian astrology, so far as I am aware. The value of 360 degrees for dividing the celestial sphere and ecliptic was certainly known in China from at least the year 718 when the *Navagraha-karaṇa* was translated into Chinese, but nobody in East Asia (apart from the Indian astronomers at the Chinese court) adopted this value until the early modern period at the earliest. The zodiac signs, as we will see below, are certainly a part of the horoscope, but they are connected with the twelve houses/places, rather than being used to indicate positions.

2   The Features of the Horoscope and Prose

The horoscope at hand provides a circular table, titled 'Illustration of the Twelve Signs Displayed' (*jūni kyū rissei no zu* 十二宮立成之圖). The term *jūni kyū* 十二宮 literally reads 'Twelve Palaces', but this actually indicates 'signs', although in an ambiguous manner: this technically can refer to both the twelve zodiac signs *and* twelve houses/places. The 'houses' can also be called 'places' in Sino-Japanese (Chn. *wei*, Jpn. *i* 位), which reflects the distant origin of the concept in Hellenistic astrology (τόποι). The East Asian system of astrological houses was always that of whole-sign configurations. A zodiac sign can occupy any one of the twelve houses, but there are no cusps. There is always a one-to-one correspondence between a zodiac sign and a house.

The twenty-eight lunar stations of Chinese astronomy are also indicated. These are interspersed across the zodiac signs and twelve houses. The lunar stations were not strictly divided across the twelve houses (e.g., dividing them into twelve separate divisions). The twelve houses are thematically labelled (the numbering I~XII added by me for clarity). Their individual names are each comprised of binomial Chinese terms followed by the suffix *-i* ('place'). These can be literally translated as follows:

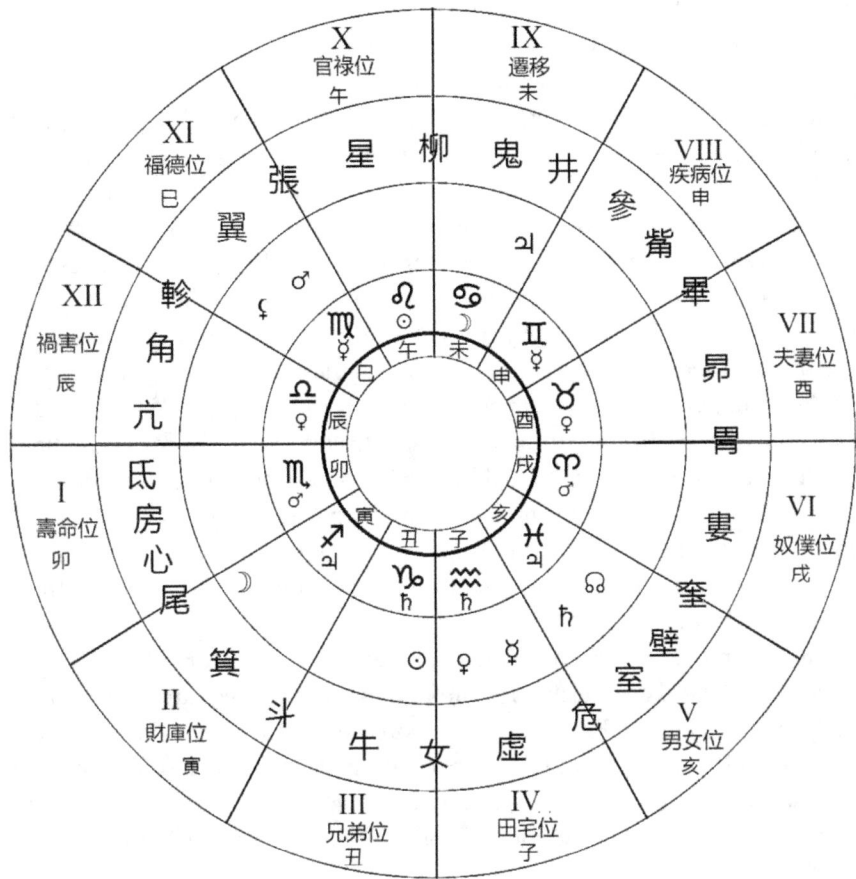

FIGURE 5.1   Reproduction of table in 1113 horoscope

I.   壽命位—Place of Longevity and Life
II.   財庫位—Place of Wealth and Repository
III. 兄弟位—Place of Elder and Younger Brothers
IV.   田宅位—Place of Fields and Houses
V.   男女位—Place of Sons and Daughters
VI.   奴僕位—Place of Slaves and Servants
VII. 夫妻位—Place of Husband and Wife
VIII. 疾病位—Place of Ailments and Illnesses
IX.   遷移位—Place of Moving and Mobility
X.   官禄位—Place of Office and Salary

XI.   福德位—Place of Fortune and Virtue

XII.   禍害位—Place of Disaster and Harm

These would have all been familiar to contemporary astrologers in West and South Asia, as well those in Europe, although the thematic designations had evolved since Hellenistic times.[18] The simple reason for this is that the heritage of East Asia horoscopy is ultimately traced back in large part to similar sources from Late Antiquity. In fact, a comparison between the astrological doctrines used by William Lilly (1602–1681) and Wan Minying 萬民英 (1521–1603) display many parallels. In one instance, however, there is one significant divergence between Wan Minying and Lilly in the house themes. Following earlier well-established precedents, Wan Minying refers to the twelfth house as the 'House of Characteristics and Appearance' (*xiang mao gong* 相貌宮). This theme for the twelfth house was the norm in Chinese astrology, but it is unseen elsewhere in the world. Normally, the twelfth house is assigned themes of misfortune.[19] The reasoning, we might imagine, was that it represents the formative years of the native immediately after the Ascendant (looking clockwise). The Sun follows the arc from there to the Descendant, which represents the period from birth until death.

The 1113 horoscope refers to the triplicity rulers. These are attested in an earlier astrological manual dating to around the late ninth century that was partially preserved in the Daoist canon.[20] Dorotheus utilizes the triplicity rulers to a great extent.[21] It was therefore natural that they would also be taken up in East Asian astrology, as material based on Dorotheus was foundational for horoscopy in China starting from around the year 800. The 1113 horoscope lists the triplicity rulers of three separate houses:

1.   'Triplicity rulers of the natal place: Mars, Venus, Moon', 本命位三方主: 火金月.

---

18   For information on the twelve places in Hellenistic astrology, see Dorian Gieseler Greenbaum, *The Daimon in Hellenistic Astrology: Origins and Influence* (Leiden: Brill, 2016), 400–402.

19   Jeffrey Kotyk, 'Chinese and English Horoscopy in the Sixteenth and Seventeenth Centuries: The Astrological Doctrines of the Twelve Houses and Lot of Fortune in *Xingxue dacheng* 星學大成 by Wan Minying 萬民英 (1521–1603) and *Christian Astrology* by William Lilly (1602–1681)', *International Journal of Divination & Prognostication* 1 (2019): 27–28.

20   *Lingtai jing* 靈臺經 ('Scripture of the Spiritual Terrace'). For information on this text and how it presents the triplicity rulers, see Kotyk, 'The Sinicization of Indo-Iranian Astrology', 16, 30–33.

21   See translation by Benjamin Dykes, *Dorotheus of Sidon: Carmen Astrologicum, The ʿUmar al-Tabarī Translation* (Minneapolis: The Cazimi Press, 2017), 61–62.

TABLE 5.2   Triplicity Rulers in *Lingtai jing*.[a]

Zodiac Sign	Diurnal	Nocturnal	Yin-Yang
寅・午・戌	日・木・土	木・日・土	
♐ ♌ ♈	☉・♃・♄	♃・☉・♄	Yang 陽 (diurnal)
申・子・辰	土・水・木	水・土・木	
♊ ♒ ♎	♄・☿・♃	☿・♄・♃	
亥・卯・未	金・火・月	火・金・月	
♓ ♏ ♋	♀・♂・☽	♂・♀・☾	Yin 陰 (nocturnal)
巳・酉・丑	金・月・火	月・金・火	
♍ ♉ ♑	♀・☾・♂	☾・♀・♂	

a   *Daozang* 288, 5: 22c.

2. 'Triplicity rulers of the place of prosperity and salary: Jupiter, Sun, Saturn', 榮祿位三方主: 木日土.

3. 'Triplicity rulers of the place of fortune and virtue: Moon, Venus, Mars', 福 德位三方主: 月金火.[22]

The following comment states that the client should make offerings to these planets. Based on the choice of domicile rulers, the native was evidently interested in their material well-being and career. We know that he was a Buddhist monk, but we need not expect ideals of renunciation and poverty. Social status and wealth were clearly strong concerns for the client.

The triplicity rulers in East Asia are identical to those of Hellenistic astrology, although they were indicated using indigenous terms. For example, diurnal and nocturnal were conceived of as Yang (diurnal) and Yin (nocturnal) respectively. The zodiac signs were also generally notated using the earthly branches, rather than by semantically derived names (e.g., Crab, Water Pot, etc.).

The astrologer offers some introductory prose before delving into a detailed analysis of the native's horoscope. There is a definite Buddhist character to his remarks. We can see this in the following excerpt:

> When people receive life, although social status and fortune are within the scope of karmic causes, the changes of misfortune and prosperity are also within the grasp of the *nakṣatras* and planets. Who of those born

22   Momo, 'Sukuyō kanmon shū', 134.

in the same year are without agreeable and disagreeable [experiences]? Those born with a favorable zodiac sign and planets have their support for fortune, while those under an unfavorable zodiac sign and planets bring about their own catastrophes. However, ordinary people are unaware of this.

人倫受生, 尊卑貧富寔, 雖業因之所, 災禍福榮囊裏, 猶是宿曜之所掌也. 生同行年, 誰無好惡. 生好宮好曜者, 自有福佐, 屬惡宮惡曜者, 自招禍殃, 然而凡人無識.[23]

The deterministic premise of astrology is technically at odds with a strict interpretation of the Buddhist concept of karma. Karma in its basic sense means 'action', but Buddhists *formally* regard karma in a doctrinal sense as *intentional* action, and it is from these actions in present and past lives that a fruit (*phalam*), i.e., a result, occurs. Harmful deeds result in suffering, whereas good deeds bring happiness. Indian Buddhism, however, generally displays a passive acceptance of astrology throughout the first millennium CE, apart from a few instances in which authors challenged the validity of astrology, but these instances are arguably exceptional and not normative. More generally the issue was monks earning a livelihood through practicing divination.[24] The Japanese astrologer who wrote the above prose offers a nod to the idea of karma, but he expresses a belief that fortune in life is also connected with the stars. The mechanism through which the stars affect human life is not a known topic of discussion in the extant literature from East Asia. Unlike discussions of the validity of astrology in monotheistic contexts, there was more of a loose or even enthusiastic acceptance of astrology in East Asia. In light of the fact that the stars were visually deified in various forms, and rituals were directed at them by the Japanese astrologers (Sukuyōshi) themselves, the stars were clearly understood to be divine intelligences.[25] This was unlike the materialist view of Ptolemy, who framed astrology as a natural science. Also, unlike in monotheistic cultures, Buddhist doctrines never curtailed the practice of astrology in any significant way in East Asia or India. The astrologer also presumably received

---

23   Momo, 'Sukuyō kanmon shū', 134. Translation from Kotyk, 'Japanese Buddhist Astrology and Astral Magic', 66.

24   See discussion of astrology in Indian Buddhism in by Jeffrey Kotyk 'Astrological Determinism in Indian Buddhism', *Journal of the International Association of Buddhist Studies* 41 (2018): 145–167.

25   On the rituals of Sukuyōdō, see Toda Yusuke, 'Sukuyō-dō saiki ni tsuite no ichi kōsatsu: hokuto hon haiku to hokuto hō', *Bukkyō Daigaku daigakuin kiyō* 36 (2008): 33–48.

some sort of compensation for casting a horoscope, even if monastic rules might have prohibited this. Monastic regulations (Vinaya), however, were not widely studied and upheld in East Asia for various reasons.[26]

3   The Astrologer's Analysis of the Chart

The astrologer divides his explanatory commentary of the horoscope into five sections. The first section discusses the inherent or inborn nature of the native (*ten shō* 天性). In the first line we read the following:

> The text states, 'Those born under the sign of Sagittarius are affluent and resolve problems. They receive the favor of rulers, and possess eminence. […]'

> 經云:「人馬宮坐人, 富相解事, 承君王愛寵, 有威德 […]」」.[27]

The title of the 'text' is not cited, but this is presumably the translation of Dorotheus, which is cited in the same section. In this instance, Sagittarius is positioned in the second house, so it is not the ruler of the Ascendant. Instead, we see the Moon in Sagittarius. The chart is nocturnal (the Sun is below the horizon), hence the astrologer looks to the position of the Moon to determine the zodiac sign in which the sect luminary is located. Sagittarius is designated as the 'Root Ruling Sign' 本主宮, whereas Scorpio at the Ascendant is called the 'Root Life Sign' 本命宮. The doctrine of sect and determining different rulers based on this is explained in the aforementioned manual of horoscopy in the Daoist canon:

> In regard to the above matter, in any diurnal birth, determine these [rulers] by looking at the sign in which the Sun is located. In a nocturnal birth, determine these by looking at the sign in which the Moon is located, and they are the rulers.

---

26   The issue of whether Buddhist monastics may practice astrology is taken up in Jeffrey Kotyk, 'Can Monks Practice Astrology? Astrology and the Vinaya in China', in *Rules of Engagement: Medieval Traditions of Buddhist Monastic Regulation*, eds. Susan Andrews, Jinhua Chen and Cuilan Liu (Bochum, Freiburg: Projekt Verlag, Numata Center for Buddhist Studies, 2017), 503–517.

27   See source text in Momo, 'Sukuyō kanmon shū', 135.

右件, 凡晝生, 看日所在之宮以定之. 夜生, 看月所在之宮以定之而為主
也.[28]

The fact that sect was utilized in this way in Japan only confirms that Japanese
astrologers maintained the integrity of what was originally a core doctrine in
Hellenistic astrology that had been transmitted through China. However, they
also freely utilized material from Indian sources. For example, the astrologer
cites the manual of Amoghavajra: 'The *Scripture of Mañjuśrī* states, "Those born
under [the *nakṣatra*] Mūla are cantankerous [...] By nature they relish flowers
and medicines"'. 文殊經云:「尾宿生人慳澀 [...] 性愛花藥」.[29]

A few other major horoscopic doctrines are mentioned in this section of the
commentary, which cites Dorotheus (*Yusi jing* 聿斯經). First instance, we see
the doctrine of conjunctions as follows: 'Venus and Mercury in the same zodiac
sign makes one benevolent, together possessing learning and craftsmanship,
producing writings', 金水同宮, 即令能仁, 兼有學藝, 作文章.[30] We also find
the decans: 'If Venus is in her root degrees, people will proclaim [the native's]
virtue. They shall gain the admiration of people', 金在本度, 衆人皆稱為賢德,
當得人欽仰.[31] Venus in the chart is in first third of Aquarius. It is therefore clear
this is a reference to decans. Finally, we also see the signification of a domicile
ruler (in this instance, Cancer): 'If Jupiter is in the sign of the Moon, they make
proclamations and speak of future things', 木在月宮, 有聲明, 解説未來之事.[32]
This predictions about the native are all in line with what we would expect
in Hellenistic astrology. For instance, that the native would engage in arts and
writing should Venus and Mercury be conjunct, or that they should be admired
by many if Venus is dignified.

The second section of the horoscopic commentary discusses 'prosperity and
fortune' (Jpn. *yō fuku* 榮福). This appears to be the topic in which the client was
particularly interested. At first, the astrologer cites a few Buddhist texts that
relate some information on *nakṣatra*s, before again citing Dorotheus and then

---

28   *Daozang* 288, 5: 22. See explanation in Jao Tsung-i 饒宗頤, 'Lun Qiyao Yu Shiyiyao' 論七
      曜與十一曜, in *Xuantang jilin* 選堂集林 (Taipei: Mingwen shuju, 1984), 579–580.

29   Momo reads 生 as 主, but the original source text clearly gives the former. See Wakita Bun-
      shō 脇田文紹, ed., *Sukuyō-kyō shukusatsu* 宿曜經縮刷 (Nagoya: Wakita Bunshō, 1897),
      22.

30   See translation in Kotyk, 'Japanese Buddhist Astrology and Astral Magic', 66.

31   Momo, 'Sukuyō kanmon shū', 135. Note that Classical Chinese, written by both Chinese and
      Japanese authors, is not gendered. However, Venus is depicted as a woman in the majority
      of iconographical examples from late antique and early medieval East Asia. I therefore use
      the feminine pronoun, even though in Chinese this is not explicitly indicated.

32   Momo, 'Sukuyō kanmon shū', 135.

discussing in detail a few of the planetary aspects of the chart (aspect is the doctrine in which the planets relate to one another based on their angles relative to each other). For instance, we read, 'They will be of an ennobled nature with a Saturn-Jupiter trine, for they both illuminate in high positions. [...]', 土木三合, 並居高處照見, 榮貴性 [...].[33] The word for 'trine' here might literally be translated as 'three angles' (Jpn. *san gō* 三合). In this instance, the 'high position' would presumably be Jupiter in Cancer (Cancer is the exaltation of Jupiter). At the same time, Saturn is in his own decan. The typical exaltations of the seven planets based on zodiacal degrees are given in a quite condensed and versified summary of Dorotheus, which was reproduced by Wan Minying in his large compendium of astrological material from the sixteenth century.[34] In the Japanese horoscope, however, the astrologer used a whole-sign system, rather than working with exaltations by degrees.

In this section, the astrologer again evokes the triplicity rulers:

As to fortunes, the fortunes of early, middle, and later years are all determined via the triplicity rulers. The triplicity rulers of the place of prosperity and salary are Jupiter, the Sun, and Saturn.

諸運, 皆以三方主定初中後年運. 榮祿位三方主者, 木日土也.[35]

Rather than focusing on the domicile ruler, the astrologer looks at all three triplicity rulers and their respective conditions in order to evaluate the long-term themes of 'prosperity and salary' (the tenth house). The condition of a planet can also be affected by Rāhu and Ketu: 'However, Saturn is in the same zodiac sign as Rāhu, and opposite to Ketu. When the time comes, there could be hindrances', 但件土星與羅睺星同宮, 與計都星對望. 臨期可妨也.[36] In this way, the states of the triplicity rulers, a Hellenistic concept, are considered also in relation to what were originally Indian pseudo-planets. This is paralleled in the integration of Rāhu and Ketu in Islamicate astrology, in which they are known

---

33   Momo, 136.
34   This versified text is written in an overly literary form, but the definitions follow the Hellenistic model except for the scribal error of Mercury = 10° Pisces (we would expect 15°). See *Xingxue dacheng* (sĸqs), 7.40ᵇ–41ᵃ. I consulted the digitized text on Kanripo (https://www.kanripo.org/). See discussion on this versified text by Mak, 'Yusi Jing', *passim*. The appended translation is problematic.
35   Momo, 'Sukuyō kanmon shū', 137.
36   See translation of these lines (slightly amended here) in Kotyk, 'Japanese Buddhist Astrology and Astral Magic', 67–68.

as the Head and the Tail of the Dragon. Abū Maʿšar (787–886), for example, treats the Head and the Tail.[37]

The third section addresses fate (Jpn. *unmei* 運命), which is an analysis of the longevity and eventual death of the native. This section commences with a quotation:

> The text states, 'Those born under the sign of Sagittarius live more than seventy-two. Those born under the lunar station of Wei [the *nakṣatra* Mūla] have a long lifespan',

經云:「人馬宮生人過上壽七十二, 尾宿生人長命.」

Again, quoting an unnamed source, the astrologer writes, 'The ruler of the sixth house is Mars. It will be either due to poisoning from medicines or vomiting blood from the belly that they will die from such distress as this, etc., etc.' 第六宮主火星. 因藥之中毒, 或腹病吐血, 依此厄死, 云々.[38] The theme of ejecting blood is certainly in line with Hellenistic conceptions of Mars as a planet.

The fourth section addresses 'various fortunes' (Jpn. *sho un* 諸運), in which the astrologer discusses the specific topics of disciples, servants, and friends. Again, we can imagine that these are the subjects in which the client had expressed most interest during the consultation. 'Disciples' are not normally one of the themes of the twelve houses, so the astrologer looks to the fifth house, which is normally related to sons and daughters. The client, however, was an ostensibly celibate monk, hence he would have taken on disciples, but not have had any biological children of his own (at least not officially). We read, 'If the ruler of the fifth house is an auspicious star, and is positioned in a good place, there will be abundant disciples', 第五宮主吉星, 在好處, 弟子昌盛也.[39] In this instance, the fifth house falls in Pisces, and Jupiter is in Cancer, thus it would be expected that the client ought to have many disciples. Normally, we would expect abundant children in such a configuration, but monastics clearly adapted the concepts to their monastic environment.

The fifth section deals with annual profections (Jpn. *gyōnen* 行年). The definition of this doctrine is already attested in earlier Chinese sources. The doctrine is defined in the aforementioned Daoist text:

---

37   See translation in Yamamoto Keiji and Charles Burnett, trans., *The Great Introduction to Astrology by Abū Maʿšar* (Leiden: Brill, 2019), 417.

38   Momo, 'Sukuyō kanmon shū', 137–138.

39   Momo, 138–139.

For each year of life [the profection] advances one sign, with the sign at the Ascendant reckoned as the beginning. [The profection] only moves signs after one's birthday has passed. Auspicious and inauspicious fortunes are always indicated by the ruler of the annual profection.

但以東出宮為首, 一歲一移宮, 直須過生日後, 方可移宮, 常以行年宮主, 言其吉凶.[40]

In this case, it is the domicile ruler and not the triplicity rulers who govern each year of life. This technique is identical to that of Hellenistic astrology, although in East Asia a different—ostensibly originally Indian system—existed, in which the first year of life is governed by Rāhu, followed by Saturn, Mercury, Venus, Sun, Mars, Ketu, Moon, and Jupiter in subsequent years.[41] This system is identically applied to everyone without regard to birth time or horoscope. These two systems are both attested in extant East Asian astrological texts, but we can imagine that the 'Indian' system (with Rāhu and Ketu) was more practical, since the time of birth was not considered. One need only now their current age to determine which planetary ruler governs their present year of life.

The astrologer paid great attention to the future profections of the client. He also examined planetary transits. For instance:

Saturn before 2/15 [i.e., day 15 of lunar month 2] will be in Cancer, and after 5/16, he will be in Leo. Rāhu throughout the year will be in Aquarius. [...].

土星二月十五日以前在未位, 五月十六日以後在午位. 羅睺星年內在子位. [...].

Finally, the astrologer makes comments about what to expect with each profection. For instance, he writes, 'In this year, your fate is under Saturn. Your profection year belongs to a malefic. As a result of this, there will be stagnation or perhaps distress from illness', 今年御運為土星, 御行年主配悪, 依是鈍滯, 或病事厄.[42] This highlights the fact that Saturn was regarded as a malefic, as was the case elsewhere in the world.

---

40   *Daozang* [Daoist Canon] 288, 5: 28ᵇ16–17. Kotyk, 'The Sinicization of Indo-Iranian Astrology', 34.

41   Kotyk, 'The Sinicization of Indo-Iranian Astrology', 37.

42   Momo, 'Sukuyō kanmon shū', 140. I read some of these lines differently from Momo based on the handwritten manuscript.

These transits appear to be accurately tracked for the year 1152, if we assume a tropical zodiac.[43] Japanese astrologers, like their counterparts in Tang China, appear to have technically calibrated Aries to the vernal equinox, but this was a projection atop the sidereal coordinate system of twenty-eight lunar stations. In practice, the 365.25 degrees of the ecliptic, as it was measured in the Chinese system, would not allow for an even distribution of degrees to the twelve zodiac signs, but one way around this was to define the zodiac signs based on the solar terms. The twenty-four solar terms (Chn. *jieqi* 節氣) are each comprised of fifteen days, hence the division of 360 days could easily allow for a conversion of zodiac signs into a familiar Chinese system.[44] The zodiac signs, in any case, were considered for their astrological significations and their connection with the twelve houses. In East Asia, the planetary coordinates did not depend on the zodiac signs in any way.

4   Conclusion

This paper has discussed the techniques used for casting and reading a horoscope by a Japanese Sukuyōshi in the twelfth century. The horoscope and its accompanying prose incorporate both Hellenistic and Indian doctrines, all translated into Classical Chinese. Meanwhile, the coordinate system for the planets is Chinese in origin. The Japanese faithfully reproduced a tradition of Sinicized astrology, which had originally come into form around the year 800. People were free to translate and practice horoscopy in East Asia, but the level of adaptation into a Chinese astronomical framework was arguably unprecedented from a global perspective. Latin, Arab, and Indian astrologers, for example, maintained the foundational Greek system of observational astronomy and the spherical earth with reference to latitude. East Asian horoscopy was done differently. The astrologer who we examined first cast a chart, but this was done without clear reference the degree of the Ascendant. The birthplace of the native is also left unmentioned. This resulted in only an approximately calculated natal chart, but the planetary positions were calculated with relative accuracy using Chinese astronomy with a few foreign elements (namely, the ascending node and the lunar apogee).

The astrologer in question relied heavily on direct citations of what were likely considered 'canonical' (infallible) astrological texts. My impression is

---

43   This is based on planetary positions generated by the software Astrolog.
44   See the diagram in Kotyk, 'The Sinicization of Indo-Iranian Astrology', 26.

that Japanese astrologers relied on these texts, not adding to them or creating 'apocryphal' texts of their own. The astrologer-monk in question also did not necessarily favor Buddhist texts over non-Buddhist texts if we examine at the quantity of citations of both types. The cited works can mostly be traced back to China, and the catalogs of texts brought back by Japanese monks in the ninth century account for their origins. I have not seen anything to indicate that astrologers in Japan wrote new treatises on horoscopy, which marks their tradition as different from many other lineages elsewhere in the world, where it was the norm to compose new literature. In this sense, Sukuyōdō leaned toward a conservative stance, rather than toward innovation. This is perhaps a reflection of Buddhist sensibilities; for instance, (at least in theory) nobody has the authority to write new sūtras. Similarly, the astrologers did not evidently write new manuals.

As a final observation, we should note that Japanese astrologers did not draw from the Islamicate tradition of astrology, based largely on Ptolemy's *Tetrabiblos*, which is first known to have been translated into Chinese in 1384. The *al-Madkhal* by Kūšyār ibn Labbān (late 10th cent.) offers a comprehensive introduction to natal and mundane systems of astrology, but whether this text was ever made available to Sukuyōdō is unlikely, simply because around the early fifteenth century, the Sukuyōshi vanish from history.[45] Ptolemaic ideas and concepts are not apparent in the Japanese materials available to me. Similarly, in premodern China, the *al-Madkhal* was not evidently popular, and treatises of earlier centuries show no ideas that could be directly connected with the *Tetrabiblos*. The situation only changes after the introduction of Latin astrology into East Asia during the early modern period, but this was long after the end of Sukuyōdō.[46]

Bibliography

Chan Man Sing 陳萬成. 'Du Mu yu xingming' 杜牧與星命 [Du Mu and Astrology]. *Tang yanjiu* 唐研究 8 (2002): 61–79.

---

45   On the demise of Sukuyōdō, see Kotyk, 'Japanese Buddhist Astrology and Astral Magic', 58–59. On the translation of Islamicate astrology into Chinese, see Yano Michio, *Kūšyār ibn Labbā's Introduction to Astrology* (Tokyo: Institute for the Study of Languages and Cultures of Asia and Africa, 1997).

46   On this, see Han Qi, 'From Adam Schall Von Bell to Jan Mikołaj Smogulecki: the Introduction of European Astrology in the Late Ming and Early Qing China', *Monumenta Serica* 59 (2011): 485–490.

Dykes, Benjamin N. *Dorotheus of Sidon: Carmen Astrologicum, The 'Umar al-Tabarī Translation*. Minneapolis: The Cazimi Press, 2017.

Greenbaum, Dorian Gieseler. *The Daimon in Hellenistic Astrology: Origins and Influence*. Leiden: Brill, 2016.

Greenbaum, Dorian, and Alexander Jones. 'P. Berl. 9825: An elaborate horoscope for 319 CE and its significance for Greek astronomical and astrological practice', *ISAW Papers* 12 (2017). http://hdl.handle.net/2451/49543.

Han Qi. 'From Adam Schall Von Bell to Jan Mikołaj Smogulecki: the Introduction of European Astrology in the Late Ming and Early Qing China', *Monumenta Serica* 59 (2011): 485–490.

Isahaya Yoichi and Lin Jyuh Fuh. 'Entangled Representation of Heaven: A Chinese Divination Text from a Tenth-Century Dunhuang Fragment (P. 4071)', *Historia Scientiarum* 26, no. 3 (2017): 153–171.

Ishida Mikinosuke 石田幹之助. 'Tori-isshi-kyō to sono itsubun', 都利聿斯經とその佚文 [The *Duli yusi jing* and its Fragments]. In *Tōyō ronsō: Haneda Hakushi shōju kinen* 東洋史論叢：羽田博士頌壽記念, 49–62. Kyoto: Tōyōshi Kenkyūkai, 1950.

Jao Tsung-i 饒宗頤. 'Lun Qiyao Yu Shiyiyao', 論七曜與十一曜 [On the Seven and Eleven Planets]. In *Xuantang jilin* 選堂集林, 771–793. Taipei: Mingwen shuju, 1984.

Kotyk, Jeffrey. 'Astrological Determinism in Indian Buddhism', *Journal of the International Association of Buddhist Studies* 41 (2018): 145–167.

Kotyk, Jeffrey. 'Can Monks Practice Astrology? Astrology and the Vinaya in China', In *Rules of Engagement: Medieval Traditions of Buddhist Monastic Regulation*, eds. Susan Andrews, Jinhua Chen and Cuilan Liu, 503–517. Bochum, Freiburg: Projekt Verlag, Numata Center for Buddhist Studies, 2017.

Kotyk, Jeffrey. 'Chinese and English Horoscopy in the Sixteenth and Seventeenth Centuries: The Astrological Doctrines of the Twelve Houses and Lot of Fortune in *Xingxue dacheng* 星學大成 by Wan Minying 萬民英 (1521–1603) and *Christian Astrology* by William Lilly (1602–1681)', *International Journal of Divination & Prognostication* 1 (2019): 3–35.

Kotyk, Jeffrey. 'Examining Amoghavajra's Flat-Earth Cosmology: Religious vs. Scientific Worldviews in Buddhist Astrology', *Studies in Chinese Religions* 8 (2021): 203–220.

Kotyk, Jeffrey. 'Iranian Elements in Late-Tang Buddhist Astrology', *Asia Major* 30, no. 1 (2017): 25–58.

Kotyk, Jeffrey. 'Japanese Buddhist Astrology and Astral Magic: Mikkyō and Sukuyōdō', *Japanese Journal of Religious Studies* 45, no. 1 (2018): 37–86.

Kotyk, Jeffrey. 'The Sinicization of Indo-Iranian Astrology in Medieval China', *Sino-Platonic Papers* 282 (2018): 1–95.

Mak, Bill M. 'An 8th-Century CE Indian Astronomical Treatise in Chinese: The Nine Seizers Canon by Qutan Xida', In *Plurilingualism in Traditional Eurasian Scholarship*, eds. Glenn W. Most, Dagmar Schäfer, and Mårten Söderblom Saarela, 352–362. Leiden: Brill, 2023.

Mak, Bill M. 'Indian Jyotiṣa Through the Lens of Chinese Buddhist Canon', *Journal of Oriental Studies* 48, no. 1 (2015): 1–19.

Mak, Bill M. 'Yusi Jing—A treatise of 'Western' Astral Science in Chinese and its versified version *Xitian yusi jing*', *SCIAMVS* 15 (2014): 105–169.

Momo Hiroyuki 桃裕行. 'Sukuyō kanmon shū' 宿曜勘文集 [Collected Horoscopes of Sukuyō]. In *Momo Hiroyuki chosakushū* 桃裕行著作集, vol. 8–2, *Rekihō no kenkyū* 曆法の研究, ed. Tsuchida Naoshige 土田直鎮. Kyoto: Shibunkaku, 1990.

Momo Hiroyuki 桃裕行. 'Sukuyōdō to sukuyō kanmon', 宿曜道と宿曜勘文 [Sukuyōdō and Sukuyō Horoscopes]. *Risshō shigaku* 立正史學 39 (1975): 1–20.

Nakayama Shigeru. A History of Japanese Astronomy: Chinese Background and Western Impact. Cambridge, MA: Harvard University Press, 1969.

Toda Yusuke 戸田雄介. 'Sukuyō-dō saiki ni tsuite no ichi kōsatsu: hokuto hon haiku to hokuto hō', 宿曜道祭祀についての一考察：北斗本拝供と北斗法 [On the Rituals of Sukuyōdō: Worship of the Northern Dipper and Northern Dipper Rites]. *Bukkyō Daigaku daigakuin kiyō* 佛教大學大學院紀要 36 (2008): 33–48.

Wakita Bunshō 脇田文紹, ed. *Sukuyō-kyō shukusatsu* 宿曜經縮刷 [Typeset Edition of the *Xiuyao jing*]. 2 vols. Nagoya: Wakita Bunshō, 1897.

Yabuuchi Kiyoshi 藪內清. 'Tō Sō Shii no *Futenreki* ni tsuite', 唐曹士蔿の符天暦につい て [On the *Futian Calendar* of Cao Shiwei in the Tang]. *Biburia Tenri Toshokan hō* ビ ブリア 天理圖書館報 78 (1982): 2–18.

Yabuuchi Kiyoshi 藪內清. *Zuitō rekihō shi no kenkyū* 隋唐暦法史の研究 [Research on the Calendrical Science of the Sui-Tang Period]. Kyōto: Rinsen Shoten, 1989.

Yano Michio. *Kūšyār ibn Labbā's Introduction to Astrology*. Tokyo: Institute for the Study of Languages and Cultures of Asia and Africa, 1997.

Yano Michio. *Mikkyō senseijutsu: Sukuyōdō to Indo senseijutsu* 密教占星術: 宿曜道とイ ンド 占星術 [Esoteric Buddhist Astrology: Sukuyōdō and Indian Astrology]. Tokyo: Tōyōshoin, 2013.

Yano Michio. 'The *Chi'yao jang-tsai-chueh* and its Ephemerides'. *Centaurus* 29, no. 1 (1986): 28–35.

Yamamoto, Keiji and Charles Burnett, trans. *The Great Introduction to Astrology by Abū Maʿšar*. Leiden: Brill, 2019.

Yamashita Katsuaki 山下克明. 'Sukuyōdō no keisei to tenkai', 宿曜道の形成と展開 [The Formation and Development of Sukuyōdō]. In *Kōki sekkan jidaishi no kenkyū* 後期 攝關時代史の研究, 481–527. Tokyo: Yoshikawa Kōbunkan, 1990.

Some Features of Astrology in Light of the Inceptions of the Emperor Zeno's Anonymous Astrologer

Levente László

Abstract

Based on an analysis of ten real-life horoscopes from late 5th-century Byzantium, several key features of Hellenistic astrological practice emerge. These include using astrology not only for prediction but also for confirming known facts; employing advanced tools strategically; and exploiting the fact that a single astrological factor has multiple possible interpretations and *vice versa*. It is argued that every terrestrial phenomenon was rendered astrologically verifiable and thus unfalsifiable, reflecting astrology's fundamental aim of offering an all-encompassing explanatory framework.

Keywords

Hellenistic astrology – Byzantine horoscopes – inceptions – astrological predictions – unfalsifiability

Authors of astrological treatises often illustrate their teachings with horoscopic examples, typically real-life horoscopes from their casebooks or elsewhere. Hellenistic astrology[1] is no exception: from at least the mid-first century CE onwards, its authors exemplified their material with varying numbers of horoscopes.[2] The vast majority of these happen to be *nativities* (γενέσεις), horo-

---

1   Since this type of astrology, developed in the Hellenistic milieu in the second and first century BCE, continued to flourish without external stimuli well beyond the Hellenistic and even the Greco-Roman period, the adoption of the descriptor used in Alan C. Bowen and Francesca Rochberg, *Hellenistic Astronomy: The Science and Its Contexts* (Leiden: Brill, 2020), xiii seems justifiable.

2   The two nativities excerpted from the now-lost treatise of Ti. Claudius Balbillus (fl. between ca. 40 and 80 CE) are the earliest known literary horoscopes; see Otto Neugebauer and

scopes cast for the birth location and time of an individual to provide information about various aspects of this person's life. However, scattered in Byzantine Greek manuscripts and an Arabic astrological compendium, the *Book of Astrological Inquiries* (*Kitāb masā'il fī 'ilm aḥkām al-nujūm*) of al-Qaṣrānī (fl. around 900), ten horoscopes cast between 474 and 487 are found, which are not nativities but the only surviving real-life Hellenistic *inceptions* (καταρχαί), horoscopes related to specific events rather than the lives of individuals.[3] Despite their different provenances, the numerous similarities—most prominently, the fact that many of them were analysed from the perspective of a supporter of the emperor Zeno (474–491)—strongly suggest that these casebook inceptions were recorded by the same person, an anonymous Roman astrologer.[4]

The horoscopes, numbered in their reconstructible order, may be summarised as follows.

I. The letter (*5 September, 487*). A letter arrived, which the astrologer initially believed contained favourable news, but the case turned out to be the opposite. The astrologer explains the reasons for his error as his overlooking of some crucial factors in the horoscope. Nothing is said about the message or the person of the receiver, however, but the letter may have been sent to Zeno in relation to the siege of Constantinople by the Ostrogothic king Theoderic (ca. 471–526) in 487.

II. The theft (*29 August, 478*). The astrologer identifies the perpetrator for stealing a handmaid's old clothing.

III. The lion cub (*8 July, 483*). A small lion was sent from Upper Egypt (probably from Alexandria) by a designated consul (undoubtedly Theoderic) to a person bearing or having borne consulship (most probably to Zeno himself) as a gift. The astrologer predicts that the lion will be successfully brought up

---

H.B. van Hoesen, *Greek Horoscopes* (Philadelphia: The American Philosophical Society, 1959), 76–78. For the most comprehensive catalogue of Hellenistic horoscopes, including the ones discussed in the present article, see Stephan Heilen, *'Hadriani genitura'—Die astrologischen Fragmente des Antigonos von Nikaia* (Berlin: De Gruyter, 2015), 213–313, 314, and 316–331.

3   For catarchic or inceptional astrology in general and the subtypes of the inceptions in particular, see Dorian Gieseler Greenbaum, 'The Hellenistic Horoscope', in Bowen and Rochberg, *Hellenistic Astronomy*, 448–450, as well as her contribution to the present volume. For a slightly different classification, see Levente László, 'The Inceptions of the Emperor Zeno's Anonymous Astrologer' (PhD diss., Eötvös Loránd University, 2022), 18–19 and 28–32, https://dx.doi.org/10.15476/ELTE.2022.188.

4   For a new edition, translation, and commentary of the cases, see László, 'The Inceptions', 77–197, where the previous editions and translations are also listed. The present article, where the references are keyed to this edition (G designating the Greek and A the Arabic versions), summarises and expands on some significant findings laid out in the commentary.

and tamed and alludes obliquely to the fact that this lavish gift will facilitate an agreement between the two politicians.

IV. *Basiliscus's coronation* (*12 January, 475*). A usurper (obviously Basiliscus [475–476], the brother of the legitimate emperor Zeno's mother-in-law) was crowned Roman emperor in Constantinople. The astrologer predicts his imminent downfall from the horoscope allegedly cast by Basiliscus's advisors.

V. *Leontius's coronation* (*18 July, 484*). Another usurper (evidently Leontius [484–488]) was proclaimed emperor. The astrologer claims that the time had been chosen by two experts of the usurper, but he criticises their professionalism, drawing attention to some classic indications of failure and even violent death.

VI. *An unidentified coronation* (*9 April, 483*). An unnamed person, who has not been identified convincingly, is said to have been crowned.[5] The astrologer emphasises the astrological factors that made his rule righteous at the beginning, eventually caused his removal from office.

VII. *Theodorus's entrance* (*17 March, 486*). The augustalian prefect Theodorus entered Alexandria, and using the corresponding horoscope, the astrologer concludes that, although the beginning of his rule will be righteous, and the populace will respect him, his stubbornness and impudence will lead to his untimely removal and punishment.

VIII. *The voyage* (*1 October, 474*). An unnamed person's (perhaps the astrologer's own) adventures during his voyage from Caesarea (most probably Caesarea Maritima in Palestine) via Abydus to Constantinople are recorded together with the corresponding astrological indications.

IX. *The ship expected in Athens* (*16 July, 475*). Auspicious predictions are given to a client who worries about the fate of a boat that is expected but has not yet arrived in Athens. The astrologer claims that despite all the dangers and losses, the ship will come with its cargo when the Moon reaches Sagittarius or Pisces, and it is told that the earlier timing, corresponding to 29 July, was proved right.

X. *The ship expected in Smyrna* (*14 July, 479*). A similar case about a vessel destined for Smyrna. The astrologer reveals that the cargo had to be moved onto another ship due to some damages caused by a storm. He also foretells that the goods will arrive when the Moon is in Aquarius or Pisces, and we are informed that the ship did arrive on the eighth day, when the Moon was in Aquarius.

---

5   David Pingree, 'Political Horoscopes from the Reign of Zeno', *Dumbarton Oaks Papers* 30 (1976): 143 identifies the event as investing Theoderic with the title *magister militum praesentialis* and appointing him for the consulship of the following year, but see my objections in László, 'The Inceptions', 160–161.

1   The Information That Astrology Provides

The primary motivation for astrologers to present their cases should be, obviously, to demonstrate that astrological analysis as taught provides reliable and valuable information for its audience. Although it is reasonable to assume that the actual value of the information derived from a horoscope lies in the fact that it is difficult or even impossible to obtain from other sources, our anonymous astrologer would have disagreed with such simplistic views, for instead of confining himself to recording his novel discoveries, he devotes not a few words to identifying well-known facts.

For instance, in the case of the theft, he tells which astrological factors indicate that the inception is about the disappearance of a slave woman's old and worn-out cloth, identifying each element—the theft, the victim, and the stolen item—one by one (II §§ 2ᵃ and 3). Also, half of the astrological indications interpreted for the case of the lion cub say nothing more than the subject is an animal, specifically a lion, which will be transported on a ship (III §§ 2 and 4), a hardly surprising way of delivering goods from Alexandria to Constantinople. Finally, he demonstrates the reliability of the inherited teachings—and, as will be discussed below, his resourcefulness in adapting them to the context—by guessing what goods the ships are carrying (IX §§ 5–7, and X G§ 5 and A§§ 7–8) and then showing how accurate his conjectures are (IX ibid. and X G§ 7). Reading these examples, one should raise the question: why did he find it necessary to treat several predictabilities astrologically?

One notable technique used in these four cases to reveal what is already known involves the so-called 'Lot of Fortune' (κλῆρος τῆς τύχης), an artificial horoscopic factor computed from the positions of the Sun, the Moon, and the ascendant. The procedure probably originates from Dorotheus of Sidon, a first-century author, whose influential didactic poem is now lost, but the relevant chapter is extant in a prosaic paraphrase.[6] Here, it is stated that by falling into a specific horoscopic place (or 'house' in modern terminology), the Lot of Fortune shows the topic the client will ask about. In other words, the original use of the technique was mapping the client's concerns before hearing them said.

But what are the advantages of predicting what one will reveal within a moment? One possible answer is that if the prediction is successful, it should impress the client so much that the astrologer will earn their trust immediately.

---

6   It was edited in Carlo Oreste Zuretti, ed., *Catalogus Codicum Astrologorum Graecorum, Tomus XI. Codices Hispanienses, Pars 1* (Brussels: Maurice Lamertin, 1932), 202–203. For the arguments of the Dorothean origin or adoption of the technique, see László, 'The Inceptions', 54–56.

Alternatively, if the client's question is too vaguely worded or some unspecified general guidance is being sought, the technique may help to find focus. However, even if these benefits were anticipated when the present inceptions were originally cast and interpreted, they are not enough to adequately explain why the astrologer felt compelled to include such an amount of known information obtained by this and other techniques in his published examples.

If we examine the broader picture, we will soon realise that it was not the anonymous astrologer's unique practice to address information already known, either. In natal astrology, there existed procedures to investigate not only the social standing of the native's parents and the elder siblings but also whether the native is a boy or a girl and whether he or she is a twin or not, physically able or not, and so forth, even though these matters should have been known either before or at least shortly after birth. Still, the abundant attestation of methods aimed at finding this information strongly suggests that Hellenistic astrologers universally thought astrology was a venture of not only exploring the unknown but also confirming the known. It is also likely that identifying in the horoscopes what was already known considerably helped in the detective work that a successful exploration of the unknown required.

Yet another possible explanation for the existence of such practices is that by checking the astrological indications against known reality, the astrologer could verify the horoscope's time. Verification must have been vital in natal astrology but even more so in inceptional practice, for if the time of the event was unknown—for example, the time a slave ran away from the master— astrologers had to rely on horoscopes cast for the discovery of the occurrence or, ultimately, for the consultation of the client (which is evidently the case for the ship horoscopes, for which there was no other available location and time) but the validity of such horoscopes could always be questioned. Therefore, it must have also been a safety measure to match astrological indications to the known circumstances, which makes plausible the assumption that our astrologer's inclusion of such details was at least partly motivated by the aim of demonstrating the validity of his inceptions.

2   Basic and Advanced Astrological Tools

To demonstrate how astrological factors indicate the known circumstances as much as the actual outcomes, the astrologer relies on a vast array of tools. These include utilising general astrological precepts, such as the benefic and the malefic planets in prominent positions indicating propitious and unpropitious outcomes, respectively. On the other hand, he also uses inherited subject-specific teachings, provided such exist; for example, while theft was an oft-treated subject in the manuals, thus providing blueprints for those treating such a case, taming lions was obviously not, which required him to appeal to astrological basics only. He explicitly suggests that thorough familiarity with the tradition is a prerequisite when he quotes Dorotheus's otherwise lost verses verbatim to ridicule Leontius's unprofessional astrologers (v G§ 6; cf. A§ 6), who ignored such a classic. Elsewhere (IX § 9), he also states that specific doctrines unrelated to the issue at hand may be sources of inspiration and demonstrates this claim in the cases of the ships by successfully using Dorotheus's precepts on knowing what the lost item is for ascertaining what some carried goods are.[7]

However, beyond leveraging the well-established astrological toolkit in every possible way, he also turns to unusual or advanced tools that are attested only sporadically in the theoretical literature or represent a single author's view. Four types may be distinguished: uncommon concepts, idiosyncratic conditions, alternative placements, and auxiliary horoscopes. Let us see a few examples of each.

1. Uncommon concepts. Whilst based on their polygonal relationships, the signs are commonly divided into two (diurnal/masculine and nocturnal/feminine), three (movable, fixed, and common), and four (corresponding to the cardinal directions and the four classical elements) groups, there are numerous further classifications, differently defined from author to author but ultimately based on the perceived qualities of the eponymous zodiacal constellations.[8] Our astrologer refers to four of these uncommon classifications—aquatic (κάθυγρος), terrestrial (χερσαῖος), quadrupedal (τετράπους), and winged (πτερωτός) signs—in four of his examples[9] but always seeks for other indications to confirm his interpretations.

He does not do so, however, for another unusual tool, the so-called *paranatellonta*, the extra-zodiacal constellations co-rising with the signs. Although he argues that both the constellation Argo (a ship) co-rising with the Lot of Fortune's sign, Sagittarius, and the lot's lord, Jupiter, being in an aquatic sign

---

7 This type of creative reinterpretation has always played a significant role in the development of astrology; see Jeffrey Kotyk's contribution in this volume for how 'children', the primary meaning of the fifth place, are reinterpreted as 'disciples' of dharma families.

8 These classifications together with the more common ones are almost exhaustively surveyed in Wolfgang Hübner, *Die Eigenschaften der Tierkreiszeichen in der Antike: Ihre Darstellung und Verwendung unter besonderer Berücksichtigung des Manilius* (Wiesbaden: Franz Steiner Verlag, 1982).

9 These are the cases of the lion, the voyage, and both ships; see László, 'The Inceptions', 141–142.

(Aquarius) show that the inquiry made in Smyrna concerns a ship (x G§ 3 and A§ 5), his single argument for predicting that ship was carrying, among others, some medical equipment is the constellation Ophiuchus—interpreted as a depiction of the Greek god of medicine, Asclepius—co-rising with the Moon's sign, Scorpio (x G§§ 5 and 7; cf. A§ 8ᶜ).

2. *Idiosyncratic conditions.* Explaining away his error in interpreting the letter's contents, the astrologer invokes the conditions of 'enclosure' (ἐμπερίοχή) and 'intervention' (μεσεμβολή)—perhaps subtly referring to Constantinople's siege and Zeno's barring from command—as understood by Antigonus and Dorotheus, respectively (I §§ 6–8). (He will appeal again to Dorothean intervention for Leontius's inability to rule [V G§ 4ᵃ].) Broadly speaking, enclosure involves two benefics or malefics surrounding and thus helping or hindering a third planet, whereas intervention is caused by a planet's unwelcome interposition between a ruler and the ruled, but the precise definitions vary amongst the authors treating them,[10] and therefore it is crucial to refer to the authorities by name. Had he used, for example, the definitions of Antiochus of Athens, the conditions would not have applied here, yet the existence of competing understandings of these evocative conditions enabled the astrologer to choose those fit for his purposes.

3. *Alternative placements.* In the cases of the letter (I § 4), the lion (III § 2), and the ship of Smyrna (x G§ 2), the astrologer makes use of the 'twelfth-parts' (δωδεκατημόρια). They are the results of dividing each sign into twelve 2° 30' segments, which are understood to possess the same qualities as the signs. The first segment of each sign always corresponds to the sign itself; that is to say, the first segment of Aries is thought to be virtually identical to Aries, its second segment to Taurus, and so forth until the last segment is identified with Pisces. The twelfth-parts constitute, so the theory goes, alternative zodiacal placements for any planet, angle, or lot, which doubles the astrological factors by adding virtual counterparts, which will thus provide further indications.

Although the astrologer uses twelfth-parts only to confirm other indications, it remains unclear what the reasons behind his choices are: in the case of the letter, only the virtual version of the 'lady of the inception', Venus, is examined, and he considers merely the virtual Moon for the ship, but in the case of the lion, he investigates the twelfth-parts of the ascendant, the Sun, the Moon, and, for reasons unclear, Mars, all falling in quadrupedal signs, to conclude that the inception concerns an animal.

---

10   László, 'The Inceptions', 117–123.

Another unexplained instance of his creating alternative placements is switching between his usual routine of taking the horoscopic places as entire signs—in short, using 'whole-sign places'—and as divisions based on the degrees of the ascendant and midheaven, all without notice.[11] Be it as it may, the use of degree-based places for *some* planets in the cases of Basiliscus, Leontius, and Theodorus is the only possible explanation for his occasional deviations from what one would expect by using whole-sign places. For example, in the Basiliscus horoscope, where late Aquarius is ascending,[12] Venus at 29 Sagittarius and Mercury at 10 Aquarius are said to be in the tenth place and the twelfth, respectively (IV §§ 2 and 5), even though they are in the eleventh sign from the ascendant and in the ascending sign; consequently, these claims are valid only in so far as a degree-based division is employed. More surprising is that in the same horoscope, the Sun at 22 Capricorn, Saturn at 26 Cancer, and the Moon at 5 Virgo are stated to be in the twelfth, sixth, and eighth places, respectively (IV §§ 3–5). However, despite the uncertainties with the precise degree of the ascendant, none will be possible in a division by any degree-based method as they are bound to fall in the eleventh, fifth, and seventh places according to each, yet they are apparently in the twelfth, sixth, and eighth signs from the ascendant, implying the use of whole-sign places here. In other words, even within a single horoscope, the astrologer has no misgivings about exploiting the possibility that the planets strong by being in prominent angles in one system are cadent and thus weak in another and vice versa. This way, unwelcome indicators are dismissed while hitherto insignificant factors are brought into the limelight.

4. Auxiliary horoscopes. Several sources recommend examining the Moon's position on the third, seventh, and fortieth days after a birth or inception.[13] (These days are counted inclusively, corresponding to the second, sixth, and thirty-ninth days as we now understand them.) In this way, up to three auxiliary horoscopes can be created, since not only the Moon is progressed by 30, 90, and 510 degrees, respectively, but also the other planets in accordance with their actual speed. These are not horoscopes in the strict sense, however, as the angles are not calculated for them.

Although the various sources assign different interpretations to these progressions, the three resulting configurations are broadly associated with youth, middle age, and the end of life, respectively. In respect of the present collection,

---

11   László, 'The Inceptions', 145–150.

12   The manuscripts assign different values (20, 25, or 30) to the ascendant's degree, of which
       30 is the most likely; see László, 'The Inceptions', 114.

13   For an exhaustive survey, see Heilen, *Hadriani genitura*, 895–972.

the astrologer progresses the Moon and a few other planets to the third day for
the letter (I §4), to the seventh for the ship of Smyrna (x G§2), and to both
for the lion (III §3), but the rationale behind his choices is not always clear. In
the case of the lion, one might argue that the technique is fitting to the examination of whether the cub will survive the transport and reach adulthood, yet
there is no ready explanation for the reasons why the letter's contents should
be associated with the third day and the rescue of the ship with the seventh,
especially if the technique has not been employed in the case of the other vessel.

On the other hand, in one or two political cases, the use of synastry, a
comparison of two different horoscopes, is implied. Concerning Theodorus's
entrance into Alexandria, a cryptic statement is made twice, saying that Jupiter
and Venus 'of the city' are in the second place from the ascendant (VII §§3
and 4[d]). In fact, no planet is in the second place in this horoscope, but Jupiter
and Venus are situated in Taurus in Alexandria's foundation horoscope extant
elsewhere.[14] Now, while Taurus is the tenth whole-sign place of Alexandria's
horoscope, it is indeed the second in this inception, which suggests that the
astrologer compared the horoscopes of the city and its governor. The reference
to Pisces as the sign of the city—perhaps Constantinople—may also be related
to the use of synastry in the unidentified person's coronation horoscope (VI
§4[b]), but confirming evidence is lacking.[15] Nevertheless, it is evident that the
astrologer not only progressed his inceptions but also made comparisons with
other relevant horoscopes whenever he deemed it right.

3   Indications and Inferences

Since its Mesopotamian origins, the basic model of astrological inferences has
been the formula 'if *celestial sign S* is perceived, it indicates *terrestrial outcome
O*', However, things are rarely so straightforward: several possible outcomes
may and are often associated with a particular sign in Hellenistic theoretical
literature, and conversely, different signs may converge in indicating one and
the same outcome; we can call these features *polysemy* and *synonymy*, respectively.[16] We have seen a few examples of how the astrologer confirms his infer-

---

14   It is Hor. gr. -329.IV.16 in Heilen's catalogue (*Hadriani genitura*, 213).
15   László, 'The Inceptions', 161.
16   For a proposed model of astrological indication with investigations in general and specific
     inceptional contexts, see László, 'The Inceptions', 19–20 and 33–47.

ences by synonymous indications, but it is the two cases of ships that offer us an excellent opportunity to see how he would have most extensively harnessed these two features in his astrological detective work.

In the case of the ship of Athens, the astrologer, utilising the abovementioned technique, first turns to the Lot of Fortune, which he finds in the twelfth place in an aquatic sign, Cancer (IX G§§ 2 and 4ᵃ, and A§ 1–2). To paraphrase Dorotheus, whose precepts are inserted in G§ 3 and A§ 1, this placement indicates not only fear, danger, and damage or injury but also wanderers, slaves, and four-footed animals; in short, we find rich polysemy. Wandering is also implied by the lords of the ascendant and the Moon (the Sun and Mercury) being cadent in the twelfth place (G§ 4ᵇ and A§ 2ᵇ). Combining these synonymous indications with the lot's aquatic sign, the astrologer could confirm the inquiry is about a delayed ship. The malefic Mars and Saturn in the most prominent place, the ascendant, show danger and damage, another instance of synonymy (G§§ 4ᵇ and A§ 3). Finally, the ascendant in a quadrupedal sign (Leo) confirmed that four-footed animals—as it turns out, dromedaries—were being carried (§ 5).

In the horoscope of the other ship, the Lot of Fortune falls in the fourth place in Sagittarius. According to Dorotheus, the fourth place should suggest ancestors, a land or things on it or under it—such as buildings or treasures—and even a change of location, but the astrologer refers to none of these indications; probably, he did not find them applicable. But he notices that Argo co-rises with the lot's sign, Sagittarius, which is winged and common, and then goes on to confirm the interpretations—that the inquiry involves a ship, which carries birds, but which will have to be left behind for another boat—with further synonymous indications (X G§§ 3–5 and A§§ 5–7ᵃ).

These examples illustrate that the astrologer could reduce polysemy by eliminating the interpretations that were impossible or implausible in the given context and then by preferring those confirmed by synonymous indications. Not infrequently, however, his judgements are based on single factors; for instance, as we have seen above, on Ophiuchus's involvement in the present case. Without corroborating evidence, predicting that medical appliances were carried would have been a gamble, so we are entitled to question whether it was predicted as claimed and not added only in hindsight.

In the case of the voyage, it is beyond doubt that we read subsequent judgements. The story goes (VIII G§ 2 and A§§ 1–4) that the protagonist—probably the astrologer himself—departs from Caesarea Maritima, but after some delay, a storm damages the steering oars, and fights break out among the passengers. Fortunately, the man stays safe and sound, but eventually, the ship runs ashore on an island. While it is being repaired, he has a love affair with a local woman, but then he sails away, leaving her behind, and after changing to a small coaster in Abydus, he arrives in the capital.

What the astrologer wishes to demonstrate is that each event is identifiable with various astrological indications involving the ascendant and, except for the Sun, every planet. For example, the lord of the ascendant (Jupiter) in the midheaven signifies that the person avoids the fights (§ 2ᵇ), but by being in a common sign (Virgo)—just like the ascendant being in another common sign (Sagittarius)—the change of ships is also explained (G§ 2ᶠ and A§ 4). We also learn that Venus is in a terrestrial sign (Leo), and if we add her trine configuration with Mars, we will have the explanation for the ship running ashore (G§ 2ᶜ). Also, if we consider her square configuration with the Moon—which happens to be in another terrestrial sign (Scorpio)—we must understand what made him begin an affair with a woman (G§ 2ᵈ). However, even if these and the other identifications are valid from an astrological perspective, it remains unexplained—because it is, in fact, not explicable—why the events should follow each other in this temporal sequence.

Whereas the astrologer triumphantly demonstrates that virtually each and every moment of the cases is verifiable by astrological means, especially using advanced tools and taking full advantage of the synonymous indications so proliferated, quite inadvertently, he also makes evident that there was no room for falsifiability in his astrological practice. We have already seen how particular indications may be suppressed in favour of others by employing alternative divisions of the places, but they can be ignored as well, which is what the astrologer seems to do sometimes.[17] And, as the case of the letter and the coronations of the two usurpers suggest, even if the eventual outcome blatantly refutes what has been predicted, failure may always be explained by the astrologer's short-sightedness, leaving the infallibility of astrology uncontested.

This discomforting feature is most conspicuous when judgements are based on flawed astronomical data. This is the case in the horoscope of the lion: although the astrologer assumes that the Moon was at 10 Aquarius (III §1), a re-computation with Ptolemy's parameters, which the astrologer also used, reveals that it was, in fact, at 13 Aquarius. Only the erroneous longitude allows him to claim that the Moon's twelfth-part falls in a quadrupedal sign (Taurus) and the Lot of Fortune is in the seventh place in an aquatic sign (Aquarius), yet these are the indications interpreted as an animal's involvement and its transportation on a ship (§§ 2 and 4). Supposing that the astrologer had been confronted with the astronomical facts that the Moon's twelfth-part will fall

---

17   See the examples in László, 'The Inceptions', 163, 171, and 195.

in Cancer, not a quadrupedal sign, and the Lot of Fortune will be found in another aquatic sign (Pisces) but in the eighth place, how could he have saved his conclusions? Presumably, without any difficulty: there still remain four indications for the nature of the subject, and even if the Lot of Fortune cannot show the voyage, the Moon in the seventh place in Aquarius undoubtedly can.

4   Conclusion

The anonymous author's collection, evidently revised in retrospection, reveals much about the features of Hellenistic—and we might conjecture, every kind of—astrological practice. These include that the indications may be multiplied by appealing to advanced tools, and the inherent polysemy of celestial signs may be reduced by preferring interpretations confirmed by synonymous indications. Incidentally, the cases also demonstrate the unfalsifiability of astrology: that everything can be verified even if such confirmation requires ignoring or downplaying undesirable indications tacitly or in an astrologically sanctioned manner—such as by employing alternative divisions of the places—and that even invalid interpretations based on wrong astronomical data may be counterweighed by valid others. However, no matter whether one might consequently doubt the reliability of predictions achieved by the present astrologer or others, it must be admitted that astrology was designed to be capable of explaining everything, which, as the evidence of horoscopic examples, including the present ones, suggests, has been one of its major goals.

Bibliography

Bowen, Alan C., and Francesca Rochberg, eds. *Hellenistic Astronomy: The Science and Its Contexts*. Leiden: Brill, 2020.

Greenbaum, Dorial Gieseler. 'The Hellenistic Horoscope', In *Hellenistic Astronomy*, edited by Bowen and Rochberg. Leiden: Brill, 2020.

Heilen, Stephan. *'Hadriani genitura'—Die astrologischen Fragmente des Antigonos von Nikaia*. Berlin: De Gruyter, 2015.

Hübner, Wolfgang. *Die Eigenschaften der Tierkreiszeichen in der Antike: Ihre Darstellung und Verwendung unter besonderer Berücksichtung des Manilius*. Sudhoffs Archiv, Beiheft 22. Wiesbaden: Franz Steiner Verlag, 1982.

László, Levente. 'The Inceptions of the Emperor Zeno's Anonymous Astrologer', PhD diss., Eötvös Loránd University, 2022. https://dx.doi.org/10.15476/ELTE.2022.188.

Neugebauer, Otto, and H.B. van Hoesen. *Greek Horoscopes*. Philadelphia: The American Philosophical Society, 1959.

Pingree, David. 'Political Horoscopes from the Reign of Zeno', *Dumbarton Oaks Papers* 30 (1976): 133–150.

Zuretti, Carolus Orestes [Carlo Oreste], ed. *Catalogus Codicum Astrologorum Graecorum, Tomus XI. Codices Hispanienses, Pars 1*. Bruxellae [Brussels]: Mauritius [Maurice] Lamertin, 1932.

CHAPTER 7

The Astrology of Nativities in Richard de Fournival's *Nativitas* and in the *Speculum Astronomiae*

Jean-Patrice Boudet and Christopher Lucken

Abstract

Following on from the studies by Bruno Roy and Charles Burnett, this study revisits the possible attribution of the *Speculum astronomiae* to Richard de Fournival. In addition to the comparisons already noted between this treatise and Richard's *Biblionomia*, it highlights a number of elements in common with its *Nativitas*, concerning in particular the technical vocabulary of birth horoscope astrology. They tend to strengthen the hypothesis of its authorship.

Keywords

Astrology of nativities – *Biblionomia* – *Nativitas* – Richard de Fournival – *Speculum astronomiae*

1 Introduction

Richard de Fournival (1201–1260) was the son of Roger, physician of the king of France, Philip Augustus. Canon of the Cathedral of Amiens, he became its chancellor around 1240, at a time when his half-brother Arnoul de La Pierre was its bishop (from 1236 to 1247), after having been chaplain of the cardinal Robert of Somercote in Rome. He is better known for being the author of two important texts:

- the *Bestiaire d'Amours* (*Bestiary of Love*, c. 1250?), in medieval French, supposed to be the last message of a lover to his lady, preserved in at least 23 copies;[1]

---

1 Richard de Fournival, *Le Bestiaire d'Amour et la Response du Bestiaire*, ed. Gabriel Biancotto

- the *Biblionomia* (after 1244), in Latin, an analytic but partial catalogue of his own library, describing more than 162 manuscripts that he wanted to make available to the students of Amiens. The *Biblionomia* is preserved in a unique codex of the fourteenth century: Paris, Bibliothèque universitaire de la Sorbonne, MS 636.[2]

Also attributed to Richard de Fournival (perhaps wrongly) has been the *De vetula*,[3] an apocryphal poem in three books preserved in about fifty copies, in which Ovid relates his conversion from love to Christianity. To him is also attributed a treatise on alchemy preserved in eleven *codices* and written under the name 'Arturus', an 'author' identified with Richard by the explicit of its oldest manuscript (Firenze, Biblioteca Medicea Laurenziana, Plut. 30.29): 'Arturus qui est Ricardus de Furnivalle',[4]

This manuscript containing the treatise on alchemy attributed to Richard, probably copied in Paris around 1270–1275, is also the oldest copy of a work which was initially anonymous and untitled, but which was attributed since the 1320s onwards to Albertus Magnus, first under the title of *Tractatus Alberti de continencia librorum astronomicorum et differencia eorum qui sint noxii et qui non* (title given in the thematic repertory of the *libraria communis* of the

---

(Paris: Champion Classique, 2009). Cf. Christopher Lucken, 'Le *contreescrit* de l'amant lettré. Le *Bestiaire d'Amours* de Richard de Fournival', in *La lettre-miroir dans l'Occident latin et vernaculaire du Ve au XVe s.*, eds. Dominique Demartini, Sumi Shimahara, Christiane Veyrard-Cosme (Turnhout: Brepols, 2018), 145–171.

2   Léopold Delisle, ed., 'La *Biblionomie* de Richard de Fournival', in Id., *Le cabinet des manuscrits de la Bibliothèque impériale puis nationale* (Paris: Imprimerie impériale, 1868–1881), II, 518–535 (new edition in preparation by Christopher Lucken). Cf. Christopher Lucken, 'La *Biblionomia* et la bibliothèque de Richard de Fournival: un idéal du savoir et sa traduction manuscrite', in *Les Livres des maîtres. Histoire et rayonnement du collège de Sorbonne et de ses bibliothèques du XIIIe siècle à la Renaissance*, eds. Claire Angotti, Gilbert Fournier and Donatella Nebbiai (Paris: Publications de la Sorbonne, 2017, 63–96).

3   Roger Bacon or one of his relatives could be a better candidate for the authorship of this text, according to Charles Burnett, 'The Astrological Categorization of Religions in Abū Ma'shar, the *De vetula* and Roger Bacon', in *Language of Religion, Language of the People: Medieval Judaism, Christianity and Islam*, ed. Ernst Bremer and al. (Munich: 2006), 127–138, and more recently Cecilia Panti, 'An Astrological Path to Wisdom: Richard de Fournival, Roger Bacon and the Attribution of the Pseudo-Ovidian *De vetula*', in *Richard de Fournival et les sciences au XIIIe siècle*, eds. Joëlle Ducos and Christopher Lucken (Florence: SISMEL-Edizioni del Galluzzo, 2018), 363–400, and John Haynes, 'Roger Bacon and the Pseudo-Ovidian *De vetula*', *The Journal of Medieval Latin* 32 (2022), 21–63.

4   Antoine Calvet, 'Le *De arte alchemica* (inc.: Dixit Arturus explicator huius operis) est-il une œuvre authentique de Richard de Fournival?', in *Richard de Fournival et les sciences*, 243–282.

Sorbonne College, c. 1321–1338),[5] then under the title of *Speculum astronomiae*, and preserved in more than 60 *codices*.[6]

There are many similarities between the astronomical manuscripts described in the *Biblionomia* (nos. 53–60) and the astronomical treatises listed in the *Speculum* (chapter 2). Hence the hypothesis formulated by David Pingree and Paola Zambelli, who were both convinced that the *Speculum* was written by Albertus Magnus or a close associate of his, and that Albert had access to the library of Richard de Fournival.[7] Since the codicological survey published in 2001 by Agostino Paravicini Bagliani, the attribution of the *Speculum* to Albert seems no longer possible.[8] But a series of convincing arguments put forward in 2000 by Bruno Roy and more recently by Charles Burnett invite us to ascribe the *Speculum* to Richard de Fournival.[9] We shall reconsider this hypothesis on the

5 Agostino Paravicini Bagliani, *Le Speculum astronomiae: une énigme? Enquête sur les manu-scrits* (Florence: SISMEL-Edizioni del Galluzzo, 2001), 119–122. This copy was a part of the *liber minor de astronomia* (numbered as B.b in the catalogue of the *libraria communis*) that belonged to Pierre de Limoges, a fragment of which survives in MS Vatican, BAV, Reg. lat. 1191. See Laure Miolo, 'Un manuscrit de Pierre de Limoges à la British Library: à propos du codex London, BL, Additional MS 38688', *Scriptorium*, 74 (2020), 79–111 (99 and 110–111). Cf. also the reference to the *Speculum astronomiae* under the title *Libellus de omnibus libris astronomicis* in a marginal note by Pierre de Limoges in MS Paris, BnF, lat. 16658, f. 115ʳ (edited by Laure Miolo, *Le fonds scientifique d'un collège de théologie: le cas de la bibliothèque de Sorbonne, 1257–1500*, thèse de l'Univ. de Lyon II dir. by L. Moulinier-Brogi, 2017, vol. I, 433; vol. II, 171). Pierre refers in this manuscript to the year 1267 in the past tense and to an almanac for the year 1283 (ff. 38ᵛ and 115ʳᵃ). Detailed notice of this codex in Miolo, *Le fonds scientifique*, vol. II, 168–171. The *Speculum* is attributed to Albertus Magnus in a letter from John of Jandun dated 28 October 1321, but the latter refers to this text only by its incipit, without giving a title: see C.P.E. Nothaft, 'Glorious Science or "Dead Dog"? Jean de Jandun and the Quarrel over Astrology in Fourteenth Century Paris', *Vivarium* 57 (2019): 51–101 (59 and 100).

6 Cf. Alberto Magno, *Speculum Astronomiae*, ed. Paola Zambelli et al. (Pisa, 1977); Paola Zambelli and al., *The* Speculum Astronomiae *and its Enigma. Astrology, Theology and Science in Albertus Magnus and his Contemporaries* (Dordrecht: Kluwer Academic Publisher, 1992), with an introduction, an edition and an English translation.

7 David Pingree, 'The Diffusion of Arabic Magic Texts in Western Europe', in *La diffusione delle scienze islamiche nel Medio Evo europeo*, ed. B. Scarcia Amoretti (Roma: Academia nazionale dei Lincei, 1987), 57–102 (here 99–100); Zambelli and al., *The* Speculum Astronomiae *and its Enigma*, 105–111 and 189–191.

8 Paravicini Bagliani, *Le Speculum astronomiae*: une énigme?; Id., 'Un nuovo codice dello *Speculum Astronomiae* (Siena, Biblioteca Comunale degli Intronati, L III 11)', in *Riflessioni codico-logiche, in Vedere nell'ombra. Studi su natura, spiritualità e scienze operative offerti a Michela Pereira*, a cura di Cecilia Panti e Nicola Polloni (Florence: SISMEL-Edizioni del Galluzzo, 2018), 251–264.

9 Bruno Roy, 'Richard de Fournival, auteur du Speculum astronomie?', *Archives d'histoire doc-trinale et littéraire du Moyen Âge*, 67 (2000), 159–180; Charles Burnett, 'Richard de Fournival and the *Speculum Astronomiae*', in *Richard de Fournival et les sciences au XIIIᵉ siècle*, 339–

basis of a comparison between the *Speculum*, especially chapter 8 on the nativities, and a small text yet unpublished and in all likelihood written by Richard, the *Nativitas*.

2   The *Nativitas*

As was demonstrated a long time ago by Aleksander Birkenmajer, Richard can be considered as the author of what seems to be (even if this very short text is restricted to technical preliminaries) the oldest astrological autobiography in the history of the medieval West, a *Nativitas* composed before 1239, preserved in four manuscripts and commented thirty years later (presumably before 1273) by the theologian and astronomer Pierre de Limoges.[10] In his famous paper published in 1949, Birkenmajer retraces his research from his first discovery of the *Nativitas* in 1912 to the publication of this study, more than thirty years later, offering his 'eventual successor [...] all the elements necessary to bring to a successful conclusion the work [he has] left unfinished', Finishing that work is what we are trying to do.[11] But it is not an easy task ... Our edition of the *Nativitas* with the commentary of Pierre de Limoges is still in preparation, and we shall refer here to a simple transcription of the *Nativitas* according to the oldest and best copy, Vatican, BAV, Reg. lat. 1261, ff. 59^r–60^v (sigla: $V_{1'}$), which

---

348. B. Roy proposes (p. 171) that the *Speculum astronomiae* be considered as the 'catalogue raisonné' of the *libri secretorum* of the library described in the *Biblionomia*, which is globally confirmed by Burnett. Concerning the discussion of the authorship of the *Speculum astronomiae*, see also H Darrel Rutkin, 'Astrology and Magic', in *A Companion to Albert the Great*, ed. I.M. Resnick (Leiden, 2013), 451–505; Jeremiah Hackett, 'Albert the Great and the *Speculum astronomiae*: The State of Research at the Beginning of the 21st Century', 437–449; Nicolas Weill-Parot, 'La *Biblionomia* de Richard de Fournival, le *Speculum astronomiae* et le secret', in *Richard de Fournival et les sciences au XIIIe siècle*, 323–338.

10   Aleksander Birkenmajer, 'Pierre de Limoges, commentateur de Richard de Fournival', *Isis*, 40 (1949), 18–31, article reprinted in his *Études d'histoire des sciences et de philosophie du Moyen Âge* (Wroclaw-Warsaw-Cracow: Studia Copernicana I, 1970), 222–235. The *terminus a quo* of Pierre de Limoges' commentary is the date of composition of Leopold of Austria's *Compilatio de astrorum scientia*, which refers to 13 March 1271 (ed. Augsbourg, E. Ratdolt, 1489, f. d6^r) and is mentioned by Pierre in the margin of the MS Vatican, Reg. lat. 1261, f. 60^v. Its *terminus ad quem* is linked to the fact that, at the time of writing, he was unaware of the work of Abraham ibn Ezra, which he later came to know through the French translations of Hagin the Jew, including the *Beginning of Wisdom*, dated December 1273.

11   See Jean-Patrice Boudet and Christopher Lucken, 'In Quest of an Astrological Identity Chart: Richard de Fournival's *Nativitas*', in *Richard de Fournival et les sciences au XIIIe siècle*, 283–322.

was annotated and possessed by Pierre de Limoges after Richard's death (1260), c. 1271–1273 (see the appendix).

At the beginning of the first paragraph, Richard says: 'I want to assert that my nativity took place under the ascendant ⟨sign⟩ of Virgo, after midnight, on the eve of Saint Denis, and that the day which was arising was that of Mercury. I consider therefore that my nativity took place after 1200 years of the Lord, 7 months from March and 9 days fully accomplished', Counting the years *in annis perfectis* that have elapsed since the beginning of the Christian era, the months from March, considered to be the first month of the year in the adaptations of the Toledan tables to the Christian calendar in the thirteenth century, and the number of days, we can assume that Richard was born on Wednesday, October 10, 1201, on the day following the feast of Saint Denis (which occurs on the 9th), between midnight and sunrise.

But at what time exactly? Although his father Roger was a doctor and an astrologer, he may not have been present at the birth of his son Richard in October 1201; and although Richard seems convinced from the outset that his birth ascendant was in Virgo, he does not know precisely what time it was. This is why, if he wants to find it, he has to resort to an astrological method known as *animodar* or *annimodar* (from the Arabic *an-namūdār*, coming itself from a Persian word meaning 'that what shows'), a term that is defined as *investigatio gradus ascendentis alicuius nativitatis* in the fourth chapter of Alcabitius' *Liber introductorius* (translated from Arabic circa or before 1135).[12] This indicator designates the planet which, at the moment of the conjunction or opposition of the Sun and the Moon which precedes the birth, is the lord of the degree of the zodiac where this conjunction or opposition took place.

The commentary of 'Hali' (i.e. Abū Jaʿfar Ahmad ibn Yūsuf) to the 34th proposition of the *Centiloquium* of the pseudo-Ptolemy, accompanying the *Mundanorum* version in MS BnF, lat. 16204,[13] calls this indicator *animodar Ptholomei* and asserts that it is an unavoidable technique for the determination

---

12   Al-Qabīṣī (Alcabitius), *The Introduction of Astrology. Editions of the Arabic and Latin Texts and an English Translation*, eds. Charles Burnett, Keiji Yamamoto and Michio Yano (London-Torino: The Warburg Institute-Nino Aragno Editore, 2004), IV, 3, 316. The date of the Latin translation can be deduced from the date (c. 1135–1141) of the annotations in the oldest manuscript, Chartres, BM 213, destroyed during the Second World War Cf. https://www.manuscrits-de-chartres.fr/fr/manuscrits/chartres-bm-ms-213

13   This volume is a famous anthology of astrological texts mainly translated from Arabic into Latin by John of Seville, which was originally thought to have been copied for Richard de Fournival, but it seems to have been copied after his death in 1260, perhaps from one or more manuscripts that belonged to him. See the last version of the record of this manuscript made by David Juste and the bibliography (partly unpublished) to which he

of the nativity of a human being. Once the *animodar* has been established, it is possible to know the degree of the ascendant. According to the 34th proposition of the *Centiloquium* to which a gloss of Pierre de Limoges refers in the margin of the *Nativitas*, 'the lord of the place of conjunction will be in the same degree angle as that of the angles of the nativities of men born during such a conjunction',[14]

In the second paragraph of his *Nativitas*, Richard asserts that his nativity was *coniunctionalis*,[15] which means that the knowledge of the exact moment of his birth depends on the conjunction of the two luminaries that preceded it. In order to seek the degree of the ascendant in Virgo through the *animodar*, one must begin by situating the conjunction, or new Moon, which precedes the birth. Richard says that this conjunction took place after 1200 years, 6 months, 28 days, 12 hours and 28 minutes after noon of the previous day, i.e. on September 29 at 0:28, in the sign of Libra, the Sun finding itself at $12;16.57°$ and the Moon at $12;16.49°$.[16] One needs subsequently to determine the lord of this conjunction. According to Richard, 'the degree of the conjunction [12° Libra] was in the domicile (*domus*) of Venus, the exaltation of Saturn, the term of Mercury, the face of Saturn and the triplicity of Mercury',[17] The different rulers who govern the five dignities of the degree of conjunction indicate therefore that the *animodar* can be either Venus, Saturn or Mercury. In the following paragraphs (IV to VI), each of these three possibilities is carefully examined in order to determine the planet which, having the most power, will be chosen to fulfil this function.

---

refers: '*MS Paris, Bibliothèque nationale de France, lat. 16204*' (update: 11.12.2023), *Ptolemaeus Arabus et Latinus. Manuscripts*, URL = http://ptolemaeus.badw.de/ms/194.

14   *Centiloquium, Mundanorum* version, MS Paris, BnF, lat. 16204, p. 564[b], with corrections from MS Vienna, ÖNB 2388, ff. 13ra–13rb: 'Verbum 34. Dominus gradus coniunctionis erit tot gradibus alicuius angulorum nativitatum hominum qui nascuntur in ipsa coniunctione. [Comm.] Dixit Ptholomeus: Dominus gradus, etc. Omnis homo qui natus fuerit sub imperio planete qui maiorem dignitatem habuit in gradus coniunctionis seu preventionis habebit aliquem ex IIII angulis in hora nativitatis eius similem gradui et minuto eiusdem planete. Hoc est animodar Ptholomei quem semper aspexi et nunquam deceptus fui. [...]'

15   Cf. Al-Qabīṣī (Alcabitius), *The Introduction of Astrology*, IV, 3, 317.

16   According to the Toledan tables, from which the Toulouse tables used by Richard were derived (see below), this conjunction of the Sun and Moon at around 12° Libra actually took place on the 28th of September c. 12h *post meridiem*.

17   The sign of Libra is in fact the nocturnal domicile of Venus, Saturn is in exaltation at 21° Libra. Libra belongs to the third triplicity which is dominated at night by Mercury, the second term of Libra (between 6° and 14°) is also dominated by Mercury, and finally the second face (or decan) of Libra is dominated by Saturn. Cf. Al-Qabīṣī (Alcabitius), *The Introduction of Astrology*, I, 14, 230–232 and 236–238.

After examining these three possible *animodars*, Richard finds—in the seventh paragraph—that Venus, who has her domicile in the place of the conjunction of the luminaries preceding the hour of birth (12° Libra), has 5 powers (*fortitudines*);[18] but Saturn, who has his exaltation and his face, has also 5 powers; and Mercury, which has its triplicity and its term, has also 5 powers. These three planets are therefore equal in power and dignity, except that Mercury aspects the degree of conjunction and that one must take into account the part of power that this aspect possesses. Furthermore, according to the nature of the places in which they are at the moment of the birth, Saturn and Venus, being, respectively, in Pisces and Scorpio, would be in places in which they have no power: neither of these two planets would be situated in his domicile, his exaltation, his triplicity, his decan or his term. As is specified, Venus is here peregrine, which means that this planet is neither in its domicile nor in its exaltation. Saturn is retrograde. On the other hand, Mercury, which is in Libra (therefore in its triplicity), is considered by Richard as *zamon* or *zamin*: placed in the 'heart of the Sun', Mercury appears for him at its maximum strength.[19] Richard concludes that Mercury seems to be the most powerful planet. Therefore, it will be the *animodar*, knowing moreover that the ascendant sign of

---

18   Al-Qabīṣī, I, 22, 239–240: 'Nam dominus domus habet quinque fortitudines, et dominus exaltationis .iv., et dominus triplicitatis .iii., et dominus termini duas, et dominus faciei unam. Intellige ergo ex hoc numero fortitudines planetarum; qui enim magis habundat in numero, magis habundat in fortitudine.'

19   'Mercurius zamon in corde Solis forcior quam esse possit' (*V1*, f. 59ᵛ). *Zamon* or *zamin* (*zamim*) comes from an Arabic expression meaning 'in the heart' (ṣamīm). Translated in Latin by 'in corde Solis' or 'unitus', it designates the position of a planet located up to 16' of arc on either side of the Sun. This position is considered as very favorable in astrology, whereas the *combustio* or *adustio* of a planet by the Sun (between 16' and 6° of arc) is considered on the contrary as harmful. Cf. Abū Maʿshar al-Balkhi (Albumasar), *Liber introductorii maioris ad scientiam iudiciorum astrorum*, ed. R. Lemay (Naples: Istituto Universitario Orientale, 1995–1996), vol. v, *Traduction latine de Jean de Séville*, VII, 2, 276–277: 'Primum quidem est coniunctio planete cum Sole in uno minuto. Et cum fuerit planeta ante veritatem coniunctionis vel post illam per XVI [XVI *corr. interl. of* VI] minuta, tunc dicitur zamim. Et ideo posita sunt eis hec minuta quia minor quantitas circuli Solis est XXXII minuta fere, positumque est hoc per duas medietates, et plus quod pervenit quantitas circuli Solis prope XXXIIII minuta. Cumque fuerit inter planetam et Solem ex minutis infra quantitatem dimidii circuli huius aut similis eius, id est in eius minuto, in aliqua partium, est zamim significans fortunam.' See also *The Great Introduction to Astrology by Abū Maʿšar*, eds. Keiji Yamamoto, Charles Burnett (Leiden-Boston: Brill, 2019), vol. I, 725: 'When a planet is 16 minutes before or after the very moment of the conjunction [with the Sun], it is called "in the heart". But in the *figura celi*, with the Sun at 23;23° Libra and Mercury at 23;6°, Mercury is actually located at a distance of 17' from the Sun, not at a distance of 16': Mercury is therefore not 'in the heart of the Sun' (*zamin*) but burned (*combustus*) by the Sun. There seems here to be an incoherence!

Richard's birth is the sign of Virgo, where Mercury is both in domicile and in exaltation.

The importance that Richard de Fournival ascribes to Mercury in his celestial configuration, and to Virgo as his ascendant, is highly significant. Indeed, Richard states at the beginning of his *Biblionomia* that 'a man among the sons of Amiens, exercised in the mathematical sciences (or astrology) (*exercitatus in mathematicis*), was able to establish, with God's help but not without difficulty, that the ascending sign at the time of his birth (*signum ascendens sue nativitatis*) was similar to the ascendant of the first foundation of this city [i.e. Amiens]. He wished therefore, as much as he could but all the more viscerally as their celestial configuration were similar (*similior in figure*), that the situation of his city be elevated',[20] Richard seems to refer in the *Biblionomia* to the search for his birth ascendant that he carried out in the *Nativitas*. He was also informed about the date of the foundation of Amiens by a note contained in a manuscript of astronomy and astrology which belonged to his father Roger, also born in this city: 'Anno ab Urbe condita .dccc°.lxvii°., refundata est civitas Ambianensis ubi natus est' (MS Paris, BnF, lat. 16208, f. 136ʳ). The birth ascendant of Amiens, in 114 CE, is hence implicitly placed by Richard in the sign of Virgo, in which Mercury exerts the greatest power, accordingly to his own birth horoscope.

Richard himself was born on the day of Mercury (*dies Mercurii*), i.e. on a Wednesday. The *animodar* selected to determine the precise degree of his ascendant is Mercury. Located at 23;6° in Libra, this planet is in a dominant position in its triplicity (constituted by the signs of Gemini, Libra and Aquarius). We will see that Mercury is also considered by him as the *alquoquodeu* or *alkocoden*, i.e. the *dator annorum*, which makes it possible to determine the length of life.

Richard is now able to complete the information he had previously given for a birth whose ascendant was fixed at 23.6° in Virgo (in the third face of Virgo, ruled by Mercury). He can also draw the astrological chart (*figura celi*) corresponding to the exact degree of his ascendant. The date of birth indicated at the beginning of the *Nativitas* is repeated in the middle of this diagram (§10), but in a slightly different way (mentioning this time the hours corresponding to

---

20   MS Paris, Bibliothèque de la Sorbonne, 636, f. 1ᵛ: 'Ex cuius [i.e. Amiens] filiis vir unus, exercitatus in mathematicis, ex dono Dei nec sine labore, potuit adipisci quod signum ascendens sue nativitatis simile fuerat ascendenti fundacionis primarie civitatis eiusdem. Quare tanto viscerosius statum eius desiderabat pro suo modulo sublimari, quanto similior in figura.' Cf. Delisle, 'La *Biblionomie* de Richard de Fournival', 520.

the degree of the ascendant and from the beginning of January). It is now stated that the author of this *Nativitas* was born 1200 years after God, 9 months from January, 15 hours and 26 minutes counting from noon, in astronomical days (i.e. 3 hours and 26 minutes in the morning of the 10th day, counting from midnight), which corresponds, adds Richard, if one takes into account the equation of time (i.e. the difference between the true position and the mean position of the Sun), at 15 hours, 56 minutes and 32 seconds in equal hours, and at 15 hours and approximately 30 minutes in unequal hours.

The calculation of the position of the stars at a given moment, as well as the knowledge of the different data needed to establish a map of the sky, are based on astronomical tables. As indicated in a gloss by Pierre de Limoges in the margin of MS Vatican, BAV, Reg. lat. 1261, f. 59ʳ, Richard seems to have used the Toulouse tables, a version of the Toledan tables adapted to the Christian calendar and to the Toulouse meridian, frequently used by Parisian astronomers in the thirteenth and early fourteenth centuries because of the proximity in longitude between Toulouse and Paris.[21] But the copy used by Richard of the Toulouse tables does not seem to have survived, and the MS BnF, lat. 16209, which belonged to Richard, contains the Toledan tables and not those of Toulouse.

The data provided by the *Deviations* software developed by Raymond Mercier and those provided by *Astromodels* developed by Lars Gislén,[22] confirm the accuracy of Richard de Fournival's calculations and their overall conformity (except for Saturn, whose position shows an abnormal deviation of nearly 2° of longitude)[23] to the planetary positions that he could have found using, if not the Toulouse tables, at least the Toledan ones (TT Dev for *Deviations*; TT Astr. for *Astromodels*):

---

21   Emmanuel Poulle, 'Un témoin de l'astronomie latine du XIIIᵉ siècle. Les tables de Toulouse', in *Comprendre et maîtriser la nature au Moyen Âge. Mélanges d'histoire des sciences offerts à Guy Beaujouan* (Genève-Paris: Droz-Champion, 1994), 55–81, reprinted in Id., *Astronomie planétaire au Moyen Age latin* (Variorum: 1996), text I; Fritz S. Pedersen, 'The Toulouse Tables. A List of Manuscripts', *Cahiers de l'Institut du Moyen Age grec et latin*, 68 (1998), 3–12. Richard was familiar with the Toulouse tables, of which he owned at least one copy (*Biblionomia*, no. 60, ed. Delisle, 'La *Biblionomie* de Richard de Fournival', 528). It should be noted that the Toulouse tables were also known by the author of the *Speculum astronomiae* (Zambelli and al., *The* Speculum Astronomiae *and its Enigma*, 216–219).

22   See https://www.raymondm.co.uk/ and https://www.particle-nuclear.lu.se/lars-gislen/downloads

23   Poulle, 'Un témoin de l'astronomie latine du XIIIᵉ siècle', 62, notes that in the Toulouse tables, those of Saturn 'are invariably about one and a half degrees ahead of their Toledan respondent'.

Planets:	Saturn	Jupiter	Mars	Sun	Venus	Mercury	Moon
Fournival:	355;14°	264;33°	201;04°	203;23°	236;56°	203;06°	334;53°
TT Dev:	353;18°	264;49°	201;05°	203;27°	236;44°	202;54°	334;21°
TT Astr:	353;03°	264;38°	200;56°	203;11°	236;44°	202;54°	336;08°

The main astronomical substratum on which the *Nativitas* is based seems to be rather solid, at least as far as the position of the planets is concerned. As for the position of the celestial houses, it clearly corresponds to the most common system of domification in the medieval West, described as 'standard' by John North.[24]

Once the *figura celi* has been generated, it is possible to concentrate on its astrological interpretation. The only real 'judgment' Richard draws from his *figura celi* concerns the length of his life. According to the main Arabic-Latin translation of Ptolemy's *Quadripartitum* available in Medieval Europe since 1138, that of Plato of Tivoli, 'the method which over all others is more in accordance with natural reason is that which is derived from the place of the *hyleg*, from the planets which have power over the *hyleg*, and with the places of the destructive stars',[25] According to the manuscripts we have been able to identify as his, Richard does not seem to have owned a copy of this translation of the *Quadripartitum* when he wrote the *Nativitas*. But it is still possible he had one. Anyway, we have seen that he relied on other sources, in particular on Alcabitius' *Liber introductorius*, where the *hyleg* (Arabic *hay-lāğ*, a word meaning the principal aphetic or prorogative place), or *dator vite*, gives the initial impulse to the life of the subject and is associated to the *alquo-quodeu* or *alkocoden/alcochoden*, synonym of *significator vite* or *dator anno-rum*, a word which comes from the Arabic *al-kadkhudāh*, coming itself from the Greek *oikodespotès* and indicating the planet which is the 'master of the

---

24   John D. North, *Horoscopes and History* (London: The Warburg Institute, 1986), 46 and sq.

25   Ptholomeus, *Quadripartitum* (Venice: B. Locatello, 1493), III, 10, *In spacio vite*, f. 65rb: 'Modus autem qui secundum nostrum existimationem pervenit et qui naturalem viam imitatur, est ut enarrabimus. Hec autem observatio ex loco alhileg et eorum qui super alhileg potestatem habuerint necnon et stellarum interficientium locis consideratur.' Cf. Ptolemy, *Tetrabiblos*, ed. and transl. F.E. Robbins (Cambridge [Mass.]-London: 1971), 270–271: 'The method most pleasing to us and, besides, in harmony with nature is the following. For it depends entirely upon the determination of the prorogative places and the stars that rule the prorogation, and upon the determination of the destructive places or stars.'

geniture' (or master of the horoscope), dispenser of the years of life that allows us to measure the amount of the life to which a first impulse has been given.[26]

The choice of the *hyleg* depends on the moment of birth. For a nocturnal nativity, Alcabitius, following the example of Ptolemy and most Arab and Persian astrologers, recommends to take first into account the position of the Moon and, if this is not suitable because the Moon is in an unfavourable situation, the position of the Sun. Richard follows this recommendation in paragraph XII:

> To know the hyleg of this nocturnal nativity, it should be noted that the masters of nourishment (*domini nutritionis*) seem safe and free and that the native should enjoy a long life, God willing. The Moon cannot serve as a *hyleg* (*hyles* MS), for she is cadent from the angle (*cadens ab angulo*).[27] On the contrary, the Sun is useful as a *hyleg*, since he is succedent from the angle and in mutual aspect of conjunction with Mercury, who is ruler of its triplicity. Therefore, Mercury is the *alkocoden* (*alquoquodeu* MS) and gives the native his middle years, according to God's command, which are 48, and because he is *zamin* and succedent from the angle. Moreover, Jupiter is fortunate, looks at Mercury with a sextile aspect and is in an angle, which increases his lesser years which are 12. Mars, who is unfortunate, close to Mercury by a distance smaller than the half-orbit of either of them,[28] and succedent from the angle, diminishes the months of life of the native according to the number of his lesser years, which are 15. Moreover, the Sun, who is unfortunate because of its corporal conjunction [with Mercury], diminishes his months of life according to the number of his lesser years, which are 19. The lifespan of the native should therefore be 57 years and 2 months, if the Lord wills, or close to it, because of the directions of the significators to the places of the interruption ⟨of life⟩ (*loca concisionis*).

Richard's main source on his lifespan given by the *alkocoden* and other planets is obviously the *De nativitatibus* of Albohali (Abū ʿAlī al-Khayyat), chapter 4,

---

26 Al-Qabīṣī (Alcabitius), *The Introduction of Astrology*, IV, 4, 319–324. See also Paul Kunitzsch, *Mittelalterliche astronomisch-astrologische Glossare mit arabischen Fachausdrücken* (Munich: Verlag der Bayerischen Akademie der Wissenschaften, 1977), 12, 31, 36–37, 49–50.

27 Indeed, at 4.53° Pisces, in the 6th house, the Moon is cadent, even though it appears in the 7th house on the *figura celi*, where each house corresponds to a sign of the zodiac.

28 Mars is at 21.6° Libra, just 2° longitude from Mercury at 23.6° Libra.

	angulo maiores	succedente medii	cadente minores
Saturnus	57	43 ½	30
Jupiter	79	45 ½	12
Mars	66	40 ½	15
Sol	120	69 ½	19
Venus	82	45	8
Mercurius	76	48	20
Luna	108	66 ½	25[29]

which was contained originally in MS BnF, lat. 16204, since he knows that the beneficent stars add some years or months and the maleficent subtract:

Anni quos singuli planete cum alcochoden sunt, decernunt in

Mercury, as *alkocoden*, gives to Richard 'his middle years' of life expectancy (48). Jupiter, says Richard, is beneficent: at 24;33° in Sagittarius, this planet is in sextile aspect with Mercury and in a house located in the angle (house IV). It increases, therefore, the life of the individual for at least the number of years allotted to it, which is 12. That makes 60 years. However, Mars is maleficent: at 21;6° in Libra, he is close to Mercury from a distance smaller than the half-sphere of each of these planets and is succedent from the angle (in house II). It reduces therefore the life of the individual by a number of months corresponding at least to the number of years allotted to it, which is 15. That makes 58 years and 9 months. Furthermore, the Sun is maleficent here because of its conjunction with Mercury, and it diminishes the life of the individual by a number of

---

29   Albohali, *De iudiciis nativitatum*, Nuremberg 1546, f. ci^v (We have put in bold font the numbers to which Richard refers in paragraph XII of *Nativitas*). If MS BnF, lat. 16204 does not contain anymore the *De nativitatibus* of Albohali and the *De nativitatibus* of Aomar, they were originally included in this collection of astrological texts, as evidenced by the catalogue of eleven 'librorum ab Arabis scriptorum quos forsan transtulerat Iohannes Hispalensis in Latinum' given by MS Oxford, Corpus Christi College, 248, f. 82^r: cf. Lynn Thorndike, 'Notes on Some Astronomical, Astrological and Mathematical Manuscripts of the Bibliothèque Nationale, Paris', *Journal of the Warburg and Courtauld Institutes*, 20 (1957), 112–172 (150–151); Juste, 'MS Paris, Bibliothèque nationale de France, lat. 16204'. On Albohali's treatise, translated twice in the twelfth century and preserved in at least 35 *codices*, see David Juste, 'The Impact of Arabic Sources on European Astrology: Some Facts and Numbers', *Micrologus*, XXIV (2016), *The Impact of Arabic Sciences in Europe and Asia*, 173–194 (178 and 191).

months corresponding at least to the number of years allotted to it, which is 19. Therefore, the subject will live 57 years and 2 months, God willing. This brings us to December 10, 1258.

Since Richard, according to the obituary of Amiens Cathedral, seems to have died on March 1, 1260, this prediction may be too accurate to be authentic, and one might wonder if the *Nativitas* was not completed after the death of its author. But we do not think this is the case. The four manuscripts of the *Nativitas* that have come down to us do not mention any proper names, and their medieval readers—including its commentator, Pierre de Limoges, who seems to be unaware that the *Nativitas* he is annotating and commenting on is that of Richard de Fournival—[30] had no way of verifying the validity of the assumptions of the individual referred to. It is therefore unlikely that Richard's name has disappeared from the text of the *Nativitas* and that it can be considered as an apology for the accuracy of an astrologer's prediction *post eventum*. It is more reasonable to think that the author of this text composed it for himself and that he had no intention to diffuse it. He must not have felt the need to sign it or to specify the identity of the person concerned within the astrological square, as is often the case.

Having calculated his probable length of life, Richard de Fournival mentions a certain number of events of his preceding life, dating them in an astrological way so he can validate the celestial configuration drawn from the degree of his ascendant obtained by *animodar*. He employs to this end (§ XIII) two profections of the ascendant and nine different directions.[31] They consist in measuring on an astrological chart established for the hour of birth the distance between a particular point, such as the ascendant, the midheaven, the place of the Lot of Fortune or one of the seven planets (especially the *hyleg*), and another point chosen according to the event in question. The distance covered in degrees will be translated into time, which, in turn, will be used to determine the date of the event considered: for a profection, a zodiac sign of 30° corresponds to a period of one year for the native, whereas for a direction,

---

30   In his extensive and didactic commentary on the *Nativitas* (cf. *supra*, n. 10), Pierre de Limoges refers only to an 'actor nativitatis que est ante *Geometriam*' (MS Oxford, Hertford College 4, f. 161ʳ), which corresponds to the order of copying of the texts in MS Vatican, Reg. lat. 1261, where the *Nativitas* (ff. 59ʳ–60ᵛ) precedes Euclid's *Elementa* translated by Campanus of Novara (ff. 61ʳ–197ᵛ). Pierre de Limoges' commentary on the *Nativitas*, probably composed between 1271 and 1273, is preserved in three manuscripts: Oxford, Hertford College 4, ff. 160ᵛ–166ʳ, Vatican, BAV, Pal. lat. 1443, ff. 211ʳ–222ᵛ, and Pal. lat. 1380, ff. 184ʳ–187ʳ.

31   Al-Qabīṣī (Alcabitius), *The Introduction of Astrology*, IV, 8, 326 (for profections), and IV, 11–14, 331–338 (for directions).

it is generally the oblique or right ascensions of the points considered that are taken into account.

The death of his father, Roger de Fournival, took place in the year when the profection of the ascendant reached the Lot of the Death of the Father (this lot is absent in Richard's horoscope but mentioned in §VIII, where it is located at 23;47° Sagittarius). According to this profection, his father seems to have died in 1222.[32] This death would also have corresponded to the direction of the Lot of Fortune at the point where the sign of Aries passed into that of Pisces.[33] According to the obituary of the cathedral of Amiens, Roger de Fournival died on July 12. He would therefore have died on July 12, 1222. If we accept that a note about a birth in MS BnF lat. 16208, f. 136^r, is indeed in Roger's hand and that he was born on May 6, 1179, he would have died at the age of 43.

Concerning the death of his mother and her lot (the Lot of the Mother is at 15;7° Cancer in Richard's horoscope),[34] Richard refers to the direction of this lot at the point where the sign of Taurus passed into that of Aries. According to the direction of Venus at the sextile of Mars and the direction of the midheaven at the square of Mars, she would have died in 1233, at the moment determined by the direction of the mother's lot at the point where the sign of Taurus passed into that of Aries.[35] According to the obituary of the cathedral of Amiens, Elis-

---

32   According to Abū Maʿšar, *Great Introduction to Astrology*, VIII, 4.15, the *pars mortis patrum* must be calculated, for a nocturnal nativity, by adding to the longitude of the ascendant the angular distance between Jupiter and Saturn. See *The Great Introduction to Astrology by Abū Maʿšar*, 863, and Abū Maʿshar al-Balkhī (Albumasar), *Liber Introductorii Maioris*, vol. V, *Traduction latine de Jean de Séville*, 341: 'Pars mortis patrum accipitur in die a Saturno in Iovem et in nocte econverso, et proicitur ab ascendente. Et hec pars significat causam mortis patrum. Et quotienscumque pervenerit perfectio [*sic, for* profectio] anni ad hanc partem vel ad dominum eius, significat periculum patri. Et similiter cum pervenerit aliquis eorum ad significatores patris.' But in fact, Richard acted as if his birth had been diurnal and therefore added the angular difference between Saturn and Jupiter to the longitude of the ascendant. In 1222, the profection of the ascendant fell to 23;6° Gemini, in square aspect with the ascendant, while the profection of the father's death fell to 13;47° Virgo, in the 12th house of the birth chart, that of enemies.

33   The direction of the Lot of Fortune at 0° Aries falls to 21.7°, i.e. just over 21 years, which corresponds to 1222, but not to 7 July 1222 (the presumed date of Roger's death), rather to around 1 December 1222: a period of infamy which, according to Richard, followed his father's death.

34   Cf. Abū Maʿshar, *Great Introduction to Astrology*, VIII, 4.70, 901, and Abū Maʿshar al-Balkhī (Albumasar), *Liber Introductorii Maioris*, vol. V, *Traduction latine de Jean de Séville*, 360: 'Hec pars [matris] accipitur in die a Venere in Lunam et in nocte econverso et proiicitur ab ascendente. Et hec pars significat esse matrum. Ideo autem posuimus partem matris in signo decimo quia signum decimum significat esse matrum, eo quod opponatur domui patrum.'

35   According to the tables of oblique ascensions for the 7th climate of the Toledan tables, the

abeth de la Pierre died on January 19. If we combine these two texts as above, she would have died on January 19, 1233.

The third autobiographical event mentioned by the author of the *Nativitas* is a quartan fever he has suffered at the time determined by the direction of the Moon at the opposite aspect of Mars, that is, around November 15, 1223, at the age of 22 years and 36 days.

The last past event mentioned by the *Nativitas* is a serious injury its author has received from an Atrebate, i.e. an inhabitant of Arras or its region, in the same year that he has lost his father, i.e. at the end of 1222, an event determined by the direction of the Lot of Fortune at the point where the sign of Aries passed into that of Pisces, which would be in accordance with the profection of the ascendant to the Lot of Death, which was in the ninth house, at the end of Taurus or in Gemini, in Richard's horoscope.[36]

Richard completes his *Nativitas* by indicating three specific moments of which he must be wary in the future (§XIII). The first one, an event whose nature is not specified, is to be feared at the moment determined by the

---

ascension of the *pars matris* at 15;7° Gemini is 46;38°: see Fritz S. Pedersen, *The Toledan Tables. A Review of the Manuscripts and Textual Versions with an Edition* (Copenhagen: Kongelige Danske Videnskabernes Selskab, 2002), 1067. The oblique ascension of 0° Taurus is 14;33°. 46;38° minus 14;33° = 32;5°. 1201 + 32 = 1233. The right ascension of the midheaven for 21° Gemini is 170;12°: see Pedersen, *The Toledan Tables*, 973. The direction of the midheaven in 1233 is 170;12° + 32 = 202;12°, in conjunction with the right ascension of the square of Mars.

36 According to the Latin translation of Alcabitius's *Liber introductorius* in Al-Qabīṣī (Alcabitius), *The Introduction of Astrology*, V, 11, 355, 'pars mortis accipitur in die ac nocte a Luna in gradum et minutum domus octave, et additur desuper quod ambulaverit.' See also Abū Maʿshar al-Balkhī (Albumasar), *Liber Introductorii Maioris*, vol. V, *Traduction latine de Jean de Séville*, VIII, 8, 351–352: 'Cum esset Luna significatrix corporum, et domus octava esset significatrix mortis et perditionis, essetque Saturnus significator finis et destructionis, angustie quoque et tristitie, planctus et lamentationis et meroris, posuit Hermes his tribus significatoribus significationem super mortem et dixit: pars mortis accipitur in die et nocte a gradu Lune in gradum (domini) domus VIII per gradus equales et augetur desuper quo perambulaverit Saturnus in signo in quo fuerit et proicitur ab inicio eiusdem signi, et quo pervenerit, ibidem erit hec pars ...' But there is a discrepancy between the location of the Lot of Death between the 8th paragraph of the text, where the Lot of Death is located at 12;25° Scorpio, and the *figura celi*, where the Lot of Death is placed in the 9th house, at the end of Taurus or in Gemini. However, it seems that the second hypothesis, the one proposed by the horoscope, is the right one: The Moon is at 4.53° Pisces. The cusp of the 8th house is at 25° Aries. Saturn is at 25;14° Pisces. In 1222, the profection of the part of death seems to fall at 10;21° Pisces, in the 7th house, that of adversaries, and in conjunction with the Moon of the birth sky. This could be linked to the wound received by Richard from the Atrebate.

direction of the ascendant (i.e. the *algerbuthar*, according to Alcabitius,[37] but Richard does not use the term) to Mars: i.e., without going into further details, after the age of 38 years and 12 days, or from the 22nd of October 1239—date before which the *Nativitas* was probably composed. The second one is an event to be feared at the moment determined by the direction of the ascendant at the Sun, that is, after the age of 41 years and 2 and a half months, or from December 25, 1242. The last one is taken from the direction of the degree of the *hyleg* to the square of the Moon and from the direction of the Lot of the *Hyleg* to the tail of the Dragon, which both seem to indicate that the native has to fear his death after 56 years and 10 months, i.e. after the 10th of August 1258, which coincides with its life expectancy calculated from *alkocoden* and the other planets, as indicated in paragraph XII.[38]

Such is the fate of this son of Amiens. As for his city, Richard seems to be convinced that his birth ascendant was in the sign of Virgo, which, for a Christian scholar of the thirteenth century, has necessarily an apologetic meaning: just think of the chapter 12 of the *Speculum astronomiae*, which, interpreting a famous passage of the *Introductorius maius* of Albumasar, situated the ascendant of Christ's birth in the first decan of Virgo.[39] This is perhaps the reason why Richard de Fournival wanted to contribute to the splendour of his city by founding his library—and by writing the *Biblionomia* that accompanies it. The *libri secreti*, however, are not described in it. Those *libri secreti*[40] included, among other books, treatises on astrology, whereas astronomical texts are clearly mentioned in the *Biblionomia*.[41]

---

37   Al-Qabīṣī (Alcabitius), *The Introduction of Astrology*, IV, 14, 337–338.

38   On the Lot of the *Hyleg*, see Abū Ma'shar, *The Great Introduction to Astrology*, VIII, 5.2ᵃ, 911, and Abū Ma'shar al-Balkhī (Albumasar), *Liber Introductorii Maioris*, vol. V, *Traduction latine de Jean de Séville*, VIII, 5, 365: 'In parte hyles aspice nativitatem. Que si fuerit coniunctionalis, accipe a gradu atque minute coniunctionis que fuerit ante nativitatem, usque Lunam.' The Lot of the Hyleg is at 15;42° Pisces in Richard's horoscope.

39   Zambelli and al., *The* Speculum Astronomiae *and its Enigma*, 254–255.

40   Richard de Fournival calls *libri secreti* (or *tractati secreti*) the manuscripts of his library which are not accessible to everyone because of their *profunditas*, and which, therefore, are not described in its catalogue (Delisle, 'La *Biblionomie* de Richard de Fournival', 521, 523).

41   See also Albohali, *De nativitatibus*, chapter 44, *De Mercurio in suis ac aliorum planetae domibus*, f. 04ᵛ: 'Quod [Mercurius] si in domo sua permanserit, significant omnes scientias trivii et quadrivii, et prophetie, maxime si in Virgine fuerit', a passage translated as follows by Benjamin Dykes, *Persian Nativities*, vol. I, *Māshā'allāh and Abū 'Ali* (Minneaopolis: The Cazimi Press, 2009), 315: 'Which (should be corrected to: But if) he [Mercury] persisted in his own domicile, it signifies all sciences of the *trivium* and *quadrivium*, and of prophecy, and especially if he were in Virgo.'

3   The *Speculum astronomiae*

Let us now have a look at the chapter 8 of the *Speculum astronomiae*, devoted to nativities. We have checked Paola Zambelli's editions[42] against the oldest surviving manuscript of the *Speculum*, Firenze, Biblioteca Medicea Laurenziana, Plut. 30.29, ff. 81va–81vb, a codex containing the alchemical treatise attribute to Richard de Fournival and probably copied in Paris, which may derive indirectly from Richard or his circle:[43]

Caput Octavum

Nativitatum vero pars docet in nativitatibus, quorum significatores nutritionis liberi fuerint, eligere locum hyles ex luminaribus et parte fortune, ex gradu quoque ascendentis et gradu coniunctionis seu preventionis que fuerit ante nativitatem; eligere quoque alquoquodeu ex dominis .4. dignitatum ipsius loci hyles, que sunt domus, exaltatio, terminus, triplicitas, aspicientis scilicet et eius precipue qui fuerit aspectus propior; et per directionem gradus hyles ad loca concisionis, donationem quoque annorum alquoquodeu cum augmento et diminutione ex aspectu planetarum ad eum, iudicare quantitatem vite nati, non quantum scilicet ipsum oporteat vivere de necessitate, sed ultra quod vita eius non protenditur ex natura; et cum hoc dirigere gradum ascendentis et gradum Lune ad eventus corporis ex infirmitate et sanitate, gradum vero medii celi et gradum Solis ad esse eius regno, et gradum partis fortune ad acquisitionem divitiarum, patri quoque aspicere ex Sole et domino quarti, matri autem ex Luna et domino medii celi, partem etiam hyles dirigere sicut dirigitur locus hiles, nisi quia dirigitur retrorsum. Amplius scire modos directionis ex divisore qui est algebutam [algerubram MS], et ex domino radiorum et ex recipientibus dispositiones ipsorum. Docet etiam revolvere annos nati ex signo profectionis ad maiora esse et ex ascendente revolutionis ad minora, et demum [decr. eorum MS] iudicare dignitates nati et eius accidentia per commixtionem almubtez super ascendens, cum almubtez autem super quedam loca ex circulo et ex .14. modis, qui significant effectum et destructionem jussu Dei, quorum fit mentio in 3^a parte libri Ptholomei, qui *Quadripartitus* inscribitur,[44] et de quibus ple-

---

42   Alberto Magno, *Speculum Astronomiae*, 22–23; Zambelli and al.; *The* Speculum Astronomiae *and its Enigma*, 232–235.

43   See David Juste's notice on the PAL website, https://ptolemaeus.badw.de/ms/186.

44   Cf. Ptholomeus, *Quadripartitum*, transl. Plato of Tivoli, III, 10, *In spacio vite* (Venice: 1493), ff. 64vb–71va. However, in chapter 6 (Zambelli and al., *The* Speculum Astronomiae *and its*

nius agitur in libro Aomar Tyberiadis, qui sic incipit: 'Scito quod diffini-
tiones nativitatum, etc'.[45] Et in libro Albohali, qui sic incipit: 'Iste est liber
in quo exposui, etc.'[46] Et in libro Joannis Hispalensis, qui dicitur Secunda
pars artis, et sic incipit: 'Primum est considerandum, etc.'[47]

Here is the English translation of this chapter provided by Paola Zambelli and
her team, with some minor corrections:

> The part on nativities teaches us about nativities of those for whom there
> are signifiers of the growth of a child. [It teaches us how] [1] to select the
> place of the hyleg from amongst the luminaries and the Lot of Fortune,
> and also from the degree of the ascendant and the degree of the conjunc-
> tion or opposition [of the Sun and Moon], which preceded the birth; [2]
> also to choose [the place of] the alkocoden, [which is] from amongst the
> lords of the four dignities of the place of the hyleg (which are [its] house,
> exaltation, term and triplicity), that is, the one which aspects [the hyleg],
> and especially that one whose aspect is more appropriate; [3] and to judge
> the length of life of the native by means of the direction of the degree of
> the hyleg to the place of the cutting off [and] also by means of the gift of
> years of the alkocoden together with the increase and decrease [result-
> ing] from the planets' aspect to it, not certainly how long he must live by
> necessity, but [the time] beyond which his life is not extended by nature,
> and [4] together with this [a] to direct the degree of the ascendant and
> the degree of the Moon for the occurrences of disease and of health in the
> body, but [b] the degree of midheaven and the degree of the Sun for his
> being in rulership, and [c] the degree of the Lot of Fortune for his acqui-
> sition of riches, [and] also [d] for [his] father to look from the Sun and
> the lord of the fourth place, but for his mother from the Moon and the
> lord of the midheaven, [and] also [5] to direct the Lot of the Hyleg just
> as the place of the hyleg is directed, except that it is directed retrogres-

---

Enigma, 226–227), the author of the *Speculum* refers not to this version of the *Quadripartitum* but to that of Hugo Sanctelliensis (incipit 'Iuxta providam philosophorum asser-
tionem, etc.'), transcribed by Maria Sorokina and available on the PAL project website: PAL:
Ms/243/351/Text/1 (badw.de)

45   Aomar Tiberiadis ('Umar ibn al-Farrukhān al-Tabarī, d. c. 815), *De nativitatibus*, transl.
      Johannes Hispalensis (Venice: 1503).

46   Albohali Alchaiat (Abū ʿAli al-Khayyāt, d. 835), *De iudiciis nativitatum*, transl. Plato of
      Tivoli, 1136; transl. John of Toledo, 1153 (Nuremberg: 1546).

47   Pseudo-Johannes Hispalensis; *Epitome totius astrologiae* (*Quadripartitum*), 1142, Pars sec-
      unda (Nuremberg, 1548), ff. H3r–N2v.

sively, [and] [6] in addition, to know the modes of the direction from the 'divider', that is, the algebutar, and from the lord of the rays and from the recipients of their dispositions. It also teaches [one how] to revolve [i.e., to calculate the revolution of] the years of the native from the sign of the profection [for determining] the more important events [in the life of the native] and from the ascendant of the revolution for the less important events; and, finally, to judge the dignities of the native and his accidents by means of mixing together the almubtez and the ascendant; and with the almubtez, however, in certain places on the circle of the fourteen [different] ways which indicate [good] effect or destruction by the command of God. These subjects are mentioned in the third part of Ptolemy's book entitled the *Quadripartitus* (The four parts); a fuller discussion appears in the book of Omar Tiberiadis which begins thus: 'Scito quod definitiones nativitatum, etc.' ('Know that the definitions of the nativities, etc.'); and in Albohali's book, which begins in this manner: 'Iste est liber in quo exposui, etc.' ('This is the book in which I have explained, etc.'); and in the book by John of Seville called *Secunda pars artis* (The second part of the art), and [which] begins thus: 'Primum est considerandum, etc.' ('First is to be considered, etc.').

We can now compare the astrological vocabulary of the *Nativitas* with that of the *Speculum astronomiae*, particularly in chapter 8:

Terminology of astrology, esp. on nativities, in the *Nativitas* and in the *Speculum astronomiae* (chap. 8)

Nativitas	Speculum
ascendens; gradus ascendens	ascendens; gradus ascendens
nativitas	nativitas
nativitas coniunctionalis	/
nativitas nocturna	/
coniunctio	coniunctio; preventio
zamon/zamin	(chap. 5) zamin[48]
animodar	(chap. 9) animodar[49]
fortitudines	(chap. 5) fortitudine[50]
dignitas	dignitas

---

48   Zambelli and al.; *The* Speculum Astronomiae *and its Enigma*, 224.
49   Zambelli and al., 234.
50   Zambelli and al., 222.

domus	domus
exaltacio	exaltatio
terminus	terminus
facies	(chap. 5) facies[51]
triplicitas	triplicitas
aspicere/aspectus	aspicere/aspectus
medium celum	medium celum
angulus terre, angulus 7[i]	/
cadere/cadens ab angulo	(chap. 5) anguli,
in succedenti angulum	(chap. 5) succedentia angulorum[52]
acmar[53]	/
hyles	hyles
alquoquodeu	donatio annorum/alquoquodeu
pars hyles	pars hyles
pars mortis	/
pars matris	/
pars vite	/
pars contencionum[54]	/
geuzaar	/
Cauda [Draconis]	(chap. 7) Cauda [Draconis][55]
domini nutritionis	significatores nutritionis
directiones significatorum ad loca concisionis	directio gradus hyles ad loca concisionis
directio ascendentis	dirigere gradum ascendentis
directio Veneris	/
directio medii celi	dirigere gradum vero medii celi
directio gradus Lune	dirigere gradum Lune

---

51   Zambelli and al., 224.

52   Zambelli and al., 224.

53   Transliteration of the Arabic *al-qamar*, meaning the position of the Moon. Cf. *Nativitas*, §XI: 'Motus Lune in hora 34;57', et proficiscitur a suo cursu medio ad cursum suum maiorem, ut in principio tercii acmar ex universorum sentencia.' (Transl.: 'Movement of the Moon in one hour: 34;57', and it increases between its middle and greatest course, as is the case at the beginning of the third phase of the Moon, according to the opinion of all scholars.').

54   We only took into account the *partes* located on the *figura celi*, and not all those mentioned at the end of paragraph VIII of the *Nativitas*. The *pars contencionum* is the Lot of Quarrels and Adversaries: cf. Abū Maʿshar, *The Great Introduction to Astrology*, VIII, 8, 4.46, 883, and Abū Maʿshar al-Balkhī (Albumasar), *Liber Introductorii Maioris*, vol. V, *Traduction latine de Jean de Séville*, 351: *pars contendentium et contentionum*; MS BnF, lat. 16204, p. 168ᵃ.

55   Zambelli and al., *The* Speculum Astronomiae *and its Enigma*, 230.

directio partis fortune	dirigere gradum partis fortune
directio gradus hyles	dirigitur locus hiles
directio partis hyle	partem etiam hyles dirigere
profectio ascendentis	revolvere annos nati ex signo pro-
	fectionis ad maiora esse et ex ascen-
	dente revolutionis ad minora
/	divisor qui est algebutam
/	commixtio almubtez super ascendens

If we are correct, 25 terms or polylexical units of technical meaning used in the *Nativitas* are found in the chapter 8 of the *Speculum*, the most remarkable being the transliterations *hyles* and *alquoquodeu* and the expression *directio ... ad loca concisionis*, i.e. 'direction to the places of cutting', an expression that we have found only in the *Nativitas* and the *Speculum*. Three terms among the most significant are not mentioned in this chapter, but can be found in other chapters of the *Speculum*: *animodar* (*animodar* is in chapter 9 on interrogations: 'cum almutam super ipsum gradum coniunctionis seu preventionis ipsius, qui est animodar in nativitatibus'),[56] *fortitudines* (but *fortitudine* is in chapter 5 of the *Speculum* dedicated to the *principia iudiciorum*), and *facies* (*facies* is found in chapters 5, 10 and 12 of the *Speculum* but not in chapter 8, although it is one of the five essential dignities of the planets, according to Alcabitius: chapter 8 speaks of only four dignities and omits the fifth).

At the same time, two equally significant terms used in the *Speculum* are absent in the *Nativitas*: *divisor qui est algebutam* (*algebubtar*),[57] and *almubtez*.[58]

In total, if we take into account chapters 5, 7, 8 and 9 of the *Speculum*, 29 terms or polylexical units of the *Nativitas* out of 39 are found in the text of the *Speculum*. Of course, this common terminology is mostly due to common sources, in particular Alcabitius' *Liber introductorius*, Albumasar's *Introductorius maior* (for *zamin* and the lots) and the two *De nativitatibus* by Albohali—which is one of the major sources of the *Nativitas* and of chapter 8 of the

---

56   Zambelli and al., 234.

57   *Algebubtar* comes from the Arabic *al-jārbukhtār*, 'giver of life'. The *divisor* is the planet dominating the place of the direction of the ascendant of a nativity which is likely to indicate the lifetime of the subject. Cf. Al-Qabīṣī (Alcabitius), *The Introduction to Astrology*, IV, 14, 337–338.

58   *Almubtez* is a transliteration form the Arabic *al-mubtazz*, 'who reigns', 'who dominates'. In a horoscope of birth, it is the dominant planet because it enjoys the greatest number of essential and accidental dignities. Cf. Al-Qabīṣī (Alcabitius), *The Introduction to Astrology*, IV, 7, 325–326.

Speculum—and by Aomar Tiberiadis, which is a secondary source of the *Nativ-itas* (the expressions *domini nutritionis* and *scientia hyleg* may be found in Aomar's *De nativitatibus*)[59] and is mentioned at the end of chapter 8 of the *Speculum*.

Undeniably, the word *animodar*, so crucial in Richard's *Nativitas* and so important when the precise time of the subject's birth is unknown, which is generally the case in the thirteenth century, is missing in the chapter 8 of the *Speculum*, devoted to the nativities; but it is present and properly contextualized in the next chapter of the *Speculum*. On the other hand, the *Magister Speculi* evokes in chapter 8 other notions such as the *divisor qui est algebutam* and the *almubtez*, which are absent in the *Nativitas*. But these differences in vocabulary can at least partly be explained by different contexts (practical for the *Nativitas* and theoretical for the *Speculum*) and they are very much in minority. Qualitatively, the polylexical unit *directio ad loca concisionis*, that we have encountered nowhere else but in the *Nativitas* and the *Speculum*, seems highly significant. As for the fact that the chapter 8 of the *Speculum* mentions only four essential dignities of the planets and leaves out the decans, this may be explained by the authority of Ptolemy's *Quadripartitum*, which is invoked in chapter 8 of the *Speculum* and which ignores the decans: we have seen that Richard de Fournival based himself on the typology of Alcabitius in the *Nativitas*, but he may have changed his mind later on by consulting the *Quadri-partitum*, as the *magister Speculi* did.

Finally, on the terminological level, and contrary to what we have previously said,[60] the *Nativitas* and the *Speculum* offer a rather coherent system, which constitutes an additional argument in favour of the attribution of the *Speculum* to Richard de Fournival. And one must recall that, like the *Nativitas*, written by a *servus Dei gloriosi*, the *Speculum* is first and foremost an anonymous work, written by a *quidam vir* and a *zelator fidei* who obviously did not want to reveal his identity: proof not only of the relativity of the notion of author in the thirteenth century, but also of the limits of intellectual freedom at that time, when one tackles heated and controversial topics, on the boundaries of the religious norm, such as astrology.

---

59   Aomar Tiberiadis, *De nativitatibus* (Venice: J.B. Sessa, 1503), I, 3 and 4, f. 3ʳ: 'Quarta autem diffinitio est eorum quibus fuerit hylech et alcochoden et liberi fuerit domini nutritionis quos diximus in primo capitulo si Deus voluerit. / Scientia hylech aspicies in nativitatibus diei ad Solem ...'

60   Boudet and Lucken, 'In Quest of an Astrological Identity Chart: Richard de Fournival's *Nativitas*', 320–321.

4   Appendix: Richard de Fournival's *Nativitas*, MS Vatican, Reg. lat. 1261, fol. 59ʳ–60ᵛ

[I] In nomine Patris et Filii et Spiritus Sancti. Volo supponere quod nativitas mea fuerit sub ascendente Virginis, post mediam noctem que sequitur diem sancti Dyonisii et quod dies crastina fuerit dies Mercurii. Ex hoc arguo nativitatem fuisse annis Domini 1200, mensibus a martio 7 et diebus 9 perfectis.

[II] Fuit autem nativitas coniunctionalis. Unde ad investigandum gradum ascendentem ex Virgine per animodar erat aspicienda coniunctio. Porro anno Domini 1200, 6 [mens.], 28 [d.], 12 [h.], 28 [min.], medius cursus Solis 6.5;35.⁶¹ 40°, medius Lune 6.4;27.47°, porcio 0.10;0.36°, equacio motus 8 spere 8;35.41°, locus Solis cum illa Libre 12;16.49°, locus Lune Libre 12;16.57°, ascensiones⁶² gradus Solis 281;17°, ascensiones horarum equatarum 193;58°, ascensiones medii celi 115;15.5°, medium celum Arietis 27°, ascendens Leonis 13°; gradus coniunctionis domus Veneris, exaltacio Saturni, terminus Mercurii, facies Saturni, triplicitas Mercurii hora coniunctionis. Hora vero nativitatis sub ascendente primorum 5 graduum Virginis, triplicitas Saturni; sub ascendente autem Virginis ex 5 gradibus usque ad explecionem 18 graduum fere, triplicitas Iovis; et sub ascendente residui Virginis, triplicitas Mercurii. Animodar quoque aut Venus /ᵛᵢ 59ᵛ/ aut Mercurius aut Saturnus.

[III] Si Venus animodar, cum ipsa esset propior angulo terre, fuit medium celum simile loco Veneris hora nativitatis; et hoc potuit esse sub ascendente Virginis et de Geminis et de Tauro. Si de Tauro, erant hore post mediam diem 13;42, medius Solis 6.16;29.13°, locus eius 6.23;18.41°, porcio Veneris 5.12;12.38°, locus illius 7.26;55.55°, ascensiones gradus Solis 291;32°, equacio dierum 7;38°, ascensiones horarum 205;30°, ascensiones medii celi 144;40°, et ita ascendens Virginis 4;10° fere, medium celum Tauri 27°. Sed tunc est hora noctis diversa octava et gradus coniunctionis triplicitas Saturni, ut dictum est; ergo cum multiplicaverit dignitatem ex exaltacione, triplicitate et facie, non potuit esse Venus animodar hora illa.

[IV] Si vero medium celum fuerit de Geminis simile loco Veneris, erant hore post mediam diem quasi 15;50, medius Solis 6.16;34.28°, locus eius 6.23;24.2°, porcio Veneris 5.12;15.55°, locus eius 7.26;57.6°, ascensiones gradus Solis 291;38°, equacio dierum sicut prius, ascensiones horarum 237;30°, ascensiones medii celi 176;46°, et ita ascendens Virginis 27;37°, medium celum Geminorum 27° fere; et tunc est Mercurius dominus triplicitatis gradus coniunctionis, ut dictum est.

---

61   5 corr. supral. of 4.
62   ascensiones corr. by Pierre de Limoges of ascendens.

[v] Similiter si Saturnus animodar, cum ipse esset propior angulo 7^i, hora nativitatis fuit ascendens simile loco Saturni. Erant hore post mediam diem quasi 15;38, medius Solis 6.16;33.58°, locus eius 6.23;23.32°, ascensiones[63] illius 291;37°, equacio dierum sicut prius, ascensiones horarum 234;30°, ascensiones medii celi 173;45°, medium celum Geminorum 24°, ascendens Virginis 25;24°, medius Saturni 11.25;49.43°, locus eius 11.25;13.20°, retrogradus; et tunc etiam Mercurius dominus triplicitatis gradus coniunctionis.

[vi] Ita quoque si Mercurius animodar, cum ipse esset propior ascendenti, fuit ascendens simile loco Mercurii. Erant hore post mediam diem 15;26, medius Solis 6.16;33.14°, locus eius 6.23;22.47°, porcio Mercurii 11.21;30.52°, locus eius 6.23;5.40°, ascensiones gradus Solis 291;36°, equacio dierum sicut prius, ascensiones horarum 239;8°, ascensiones medii celi 170;44°, medium celum Geminorum 21;24°, ascendens Virginis 23;6°; nam et tunc Mercurius dominus triplicitatis gradus coniunctionis.

[vii] Facta ergo collatione dictorum trium, scilicet Veneris, Saturni et Mercurii, Venus habet ex domo 5 fortitudines, Saturnus ex exaltacione et facie 5, Mercurius ex triplicitate et termino similiter 5. Itaque equales in fortitudine, nisi quia Mercurius aspicit gradum coniunctionis, ceteri non aspiciunt et ponendus est aspectus pars fortitudinis. Ex natura autem locorum in quibus sunt, Saturnus et Venus sunt in locis in quibus nulla est eis dignitas, sed est Venus peregrina, Mercurius est in triplicitate sua. Ex domibus vero circuli, Saturnus est in loco forcior, Venus et Mercurius equales fere, quia secundum licet non aspiciat ascendens, tamen succedit angulum, tertium licet cadat ab angulo, tamen aspicit ascendens. Quantum est autem de esse a Sole, Saturnus est retrogradus, Venus prope stacionem primam retrogressura, Mercurius zamon in corde Solis forcior quam esse possit. Visis omnibus Mercurius apparet forcior.

[viii] Posito itaque ipso animodar ad horas ultimo dictas, medius Solis et locus eius ut ibidem dictum est, similiter porcio Mercurii et locus eius ut ibidem, medius Lune 11.1;1.56°, porcio eius 4.27;20.26°, locus Lune 11.4;53.4°, porcio Veneris 5.12;15.18°, locus eius 7.26;56.53°, medius Martis 6.20;47.54°, locus eius 6.21;4.10°, medius Iovis 9.0;38.31°, locus eius 8.24;32.31°, medius Saturni 11.25;49.42°, locus eius ut prius, medius geuzaar 9.15;32.1°, locus eius 2.14;28°, locus caude in eius nadair; domus 11^a Cancri 20°, domus 12^a Leonis 21°, domus secunda Libre 25°, domus 3^a Scorpionis 24°, et cetera loca eis opposita. /V_1 60^r/ Pars fortune Tauri 11;36°, pars futurorum Aquarii 4;36°, pars hyles Aquarii 15;42°, pars vite Geminorum 12;26°, pars mortis Scorpionis 12;25°, pars planete

---

63   ascensiones *corr. by Pierre de Limoges of* ascendens.

interficientis Tauri 11;19°, pars anni in quo timetur nato mors et ipsa est pars finis rerum Tauri 24;49°, pars loci ponderosi Piscium 27;15°, pars contencionum Cancri 19;37°, pars exaltacionis nati Capricorni 2;8°, pars nobilitatis Sagittarii 21;31°, pars amoris Cancri 0;6°, pars mortis patris Sagittarii 23;47°.

[IX] Ascensiones ascendentis	170;44°
Ascensiones gradus Solis	211;57° (in declivi, sed in directo 291;37°)[64]
Ascensiones gradus Lune	347;54°
Ascensiones partis fortune	21;7°
Ascensiones partis hyles	337;15°
Ascensiones partis patris	10;0°
Ascensiones partis matris	45;41°
Ascensiones corporis Saturni	357;49°
Ascensiones oppositionis eiusdem	173;46°
Ascensiones quadrati eius dextri	55;40°
Ascensiones quadrati eius sinistri	294;12°
Ascensiones corporis Martis	208;46°
Ascensiones oppositionis eiusdem	10;0°
Ascensiones quadrati eius dextri	319;43°
Ascensiones quadrati eius sinistri	85;57°
Ascensiones corporis Iovis	293;14°
Ascensiones trini eius dextri	11;45°
Ascensiones trini eius sinistri	131;21°
Ascensiones sextilis eius dextri	342;26°
Ascensiones sextilis eius sinistri	213;34°
Ascensiones corporis Veneris	257;7°
Ascensiones trini eius dextri	358;32°
Ascensiones trini eius sinistri	93;40°
Ascensiones sextilis eius dextri	324;25°
Ascensiones sextilis eius sinistri	175;40°
Ascensiones capitis	45;5°
[Ascensiones] caude	281;5°

[X] [In medio figure:] Annis Domini 1200, 9 [mensibus] a Ianuario, 9 [diebus], 15 [horis], 26 [minutis] ad dies medios, ad equatos autem 15 [h.], 56 [m.], 32 [secundis] de horis equalibus, de diversis vero 15 [h.], 30 [m.] fere, ad medium diem civitatis Ambianis, cuius longitudo est graduum 40, minutorum 30 ab

---

64   Cf. Pedersen, *The Toledan Tables*, 975 (table of right ascensions) and 1069 (table of ascensions for the 7th climate).

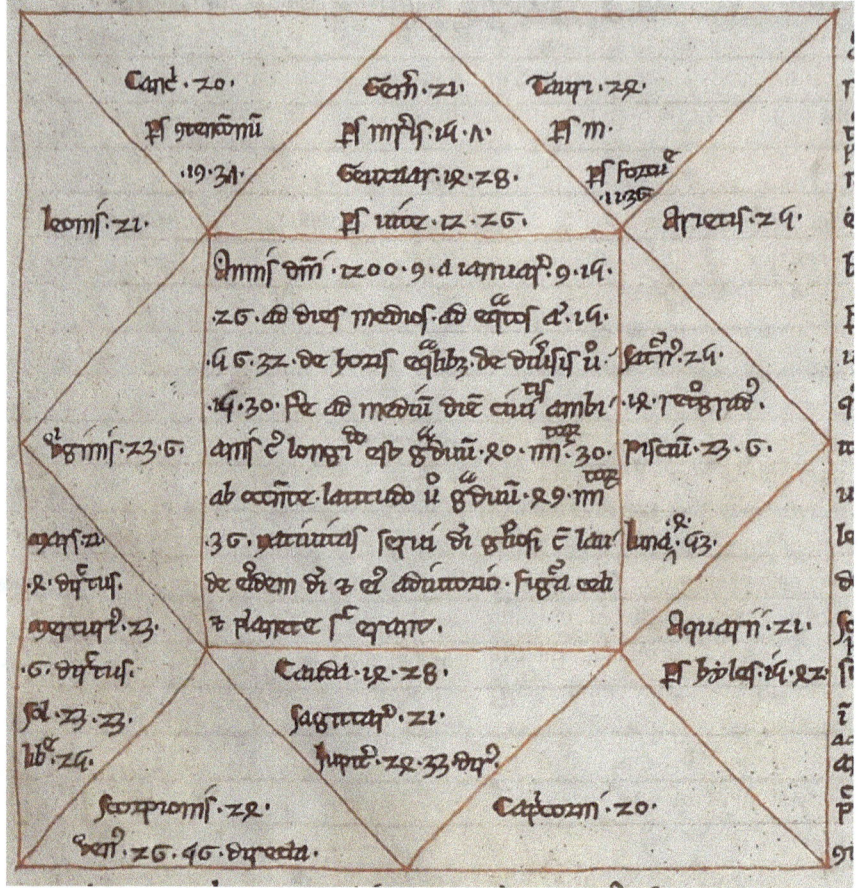

FIGURE 7.1   Nativity figure of Richard of Fournival (MS Vatican, Reg. lat. 1261, fol. 60ʳ)

Occidente, latitudo vero graduum 49, minutorum 36, nativitas servi Dei gloriosi, cum laude eiusdem Dei et eius adiutorio, figura celi et planete sic erant.

[Domus I. Ascendant:] Virginis 23;6°

[Domus II:] Libre 25°; Mars 21;6° [Libre], directus; Mercurius 23;6° [Libre],
directus; Sol 23;23° [Libre]

[Domus III]: Scorpionis 24°; Venus 26;56°[Scorpionis], directa

[Domus IV:] Sagitarii 21°; Jupiter 24;33° [Sagittarii], directus; Cauda 14;28°
[Sagitarii]

[Domus V:] Capricorni 20°

[Domus VI:] Aquarii 21°; pars hyles 15;42° [Aquarii]

[Domus VII:] Piscium 23;6°; Luna 4;53° [Piscium]; Saturnus 25;14° [Piscium],
retrogradus

[Domus VIII:] Arietis 25°

[Domus IX:] Tauri 24°; pars m[ortis]; pars fortune 11;36° [Tauri]

[Domus X:] Geminorum 21°; pars matris 15;7° [Geminorum]; geuzaar 14;28° [Geminorum]; pars vite 12;26° [Geminorum]

[Domus XI :] Cancri 20°; pars contencionum 19;37° [Cancri]

[Domus XII:] Leonis 21°.

[XI] Motus Lune in hora 34;57', et proficiscitur a suo cursu medio ad cursum suum maiorem, ut in principio tercii acmar ex universorum sentencia.

[XII] Scientia hyles huius nativitatis nocturne, eo quod domini nutricionis apparent salvi et liberi et quod natus perveniat ad vitam longinquam, si Deus voluerit. Luna non est utilis ut sit hyles, eo quod sit cadens ab angulo. Sol est utilis ut sit hyles, quia est in succedenti angulum in aspectu mutuo coniunctione Mercurii, qui est dominus triplicitatis ipsius. Et est idem Mercurius alquoquodeu et dat annos suos medios, iussu Dei, qui sunt 48, eo quod ipse sit zamin in succedenti angulum. Jupiter /^V_I 60^v/ autem, qui est fortuna et aspicit eum sextili aspectu et est in angulo, auget annos suos minores, qui sunt anni 12. Mars, qui est infortuna et est prope eum minus quantitate dimidii orbis utriusque eorum et est in succedenti angulum, minuit menses iuxta numerum annorum suorum minorum, qui sunt 15. Sol similiter, qui est infortuna per coniunctionem corporalem, minuit menses iuxta numerum annorum suorum minorum, qui sunt 19. Vita itaque nati anni 57, menses 2, si Dominus voluerit, aut forte prope hoc propter directiones significatorum ad loca concisionis.

[XIII] Pervenit profectio ascendentis ad partem mortis patris ex anno quo pater mortuus est.

Pervenit directio Veneris ad sextilem Martis aspectum ex anno quo mater mortua est.

Pervenit directio medii celi per ascensiones circuli directi ad quadratum Martis aspectum eodem anno.

Ex directione gradus Lune ad oppositum Martis sui quartanarius.

Ex directione partis fortune a mutacione ab Ariete in Pisces amisi patrem et eodem anno infamiam.

Ex directione partis matris ad mutacionem a Tauro ad Arietem amisi matrem.

Ex profectione ascendentis ad partem mortis infirmatus sum Attrebati graviter.

Ex directione ascendentis ad Martem timendum nato post annos 38, 12.

Ex directione ascendentis ad Solem timendum nato post annos 41, 2 et dimidium.

Ex directione gradus hyles ad quadratos Lune timenda mors post annos 56, 10.

Ex directione partis hyles ad caudam similiter timenda mors post annos 56, 10.

Et eodem anno perfecti erunt anni alquoquodeu cum augmento fere.

4.1   *Translation of the* Nativitas

[I] In the name of the Father, the Son and the Holy Spirit. I want to assert that my nativity took place under the ascendant ⟨sign⟩ of Virgo, after midnight, on the eve of Saint Denis, and that the day which was arising was that of Mercury. I consider therefore that my nativity took place after 1200 years of the Lord, 7 months from March and 9 days fully accomplished.

[II] This nativity was conjunctional. We must therefore examine the conjunction ⟨preceding this birth⟩, so we can find by animodar the ascendant degree located in Virgo. This conjunction took place after the completion of 1200 year of our Lord, 6 months, 12 hours and 28 minutes, when the mean motion of the Sun was at 6.5;35.40°, the mean motion of the Moon was at 6.4;27.47°, the argument ⟨of the Moon⟩ was at 0.10;0.36°, and the equation of motion of the 8th sphere was at 8;35.41°. The ⟨true⟩ locus of the Sun was in company of the Moon at 12;16.49° in Libra, the ⟨true⟩ locus of the Moon was at 12;16.57° in Libra, the degrees of ascensions of the Sun were at 281;17°, the ascensions in equal hours were at 193;58°, the midheaven ascensions were at 115;15.5°. The midheaven was at 27° in Aries, the ascendant was at 13° in Leo. At the time of this conjunction, the degree of the conjunction was in the domicile of Venus, the exaltation of Saturn, the term of Mercury, the face of Saturn and the triplicity of Mercury. When the hour of nativity is placed under the ascendant of the first 5 degrees of Virgo, it is in the triplicity of Saturn; when the hour of nativity is placed under the ascendant of the degrees between the end of the 5th degree and the end of the 18th degree of Virgo, it is in the triplicity of Jupiter; and when the hour of nativity is placed under the ascendant of the last degrees of Virgo, it is in the triplicity of Mercury. The animodar is therefore Venus, Mercury or Saturn.

[III] If Venus is the animodar, since she was closer to the angle of the Earth, it implies that, at the time of this nativity, the midheaven was in the same place as Venus; and this place could have been under the ascendant of Virgo, Gemini and Taurus. If it was Taurus, the time was 13;42 after noon, the Sun's mean motion was at 6.16;29.13°, its ⟨true⟩ locus was at 6.23;18.41°, Venus' argument was at 5.12;12.38°, its ⟨true⟩ locus at 7.26;55.55°. The degrees of ascensions of the Sun were at 291;32°, the day's equation was at 7;38°, the hour ascensions were at 205;30°, the midheaven ascensions at 144;40°, and so the ascendant was at about 4;10° in Virgo, the midheaven at 27° in Taurus. But, at this moment, it was the unequal eighth hour of the night and, as has been said, the degree of the conjunction corresponded to the triplicity of Saturn; since its dignity was multiplied, due to its exaltation, triplicity and face, Venus couldn't be at that time the animodar.

[IV] If the midheaven was in Gemini, like Venus' locus, the hours would have been nearly 15;50 after noon, the Sun's mean motion would have been at 6.16;34.28°, its ⟨true⟩ locus would have been at 6.23;24.2°, Venus' argument would have been at 5.12;15.55°, its ⟨true⟩ locus would have been at 7. 26;57.6°, the ascensions of the degree of the Sun being at 291;38°, the equation of the Sun as stated above, the ascensions of hours at 237;30°, the ascensions of the midheaven at 176;46°, and so the ascendant would have been at 27;37° in Virgo and the midheaven at about 27° in Gemini. At this time, as has been said, Mercury was the lord of the triplicity of the degree of conjunction.

[V] If Saturn is the animodar, since he was closer to the angle of the seventh house, it implies that, at the time of this nativity, the ascendant would have been in the same place as Saturn. The hours would have been almost 15;38 after noon, the Sun's mean motion would have been at 6.16;33.58°, its ⟨real⟩ locus would have been at 6.23;23. 32°, his ascensions would have been at 291;37°, the Sun's equation as stated above, the hourly ascensions at 234;30°, the midheaven ascensions at 173;45°, the midheaven at 24° in Gemini, the ascendant at 25;24° in Virgo, Saturn's mean motion at 11.25;49.43°, his ⟨true⟩ locus at 11.25;13.20°, retrograde. And again, at this time, Mercury was the lord of the triplicity of the degree of conjunction.

[VI] If Mercury is the animodar, since he was closer to the ascendant, the ascendant would have been in the same place as Mercury. The hours would have been 15;26 after noon, the mean motion of the Sun would have been at 6.16;33.14°, his ⟨true⟩ locus at 6.23;22.47°, Mercury's argument would have been at 11.21;30.52°, its ⟨true⟩ locus would have been at 6.23;5. 40°, the ascensions of the degree of the Sun would have been at 291;36°, the equation of the Sun as said above, the ascensions of hours at 239;8°, the ascensions of the midheaven at 170;44°, the midheaven would have been at 21;24° in Gemini, the ascendant at 23;6° in Virgo, Mercury being at this time the lord of the triplicity of the degree of conjunction.

[VII] When we compare these three planets, namely Venus, Saturn and Mercury, we can notice that Venus has 5 powers because of her domicile, Saturn has 5 powers because of his exaltation and face, and Mercury has also 5 powers because of its triplicity and term. These three planets are therefore of an equal strength, except that Mercury aspects the degree of conjunction while the others do not, and one has to take into account the fact that the aspect confers an additional element of power. As for the nature of the places where these planets are located, Saturn and Venus are in places where they have no dignity, while

Venus is peregrine and Mercury is in its triplicity. From the point of view of their location in the houses of the ⟨celestial⟩ circle, Saturn is in the strongest place, while Venus and Mercury are more or less equal, because ⟨Mercury⟩ does not aspect the ascendant but is succeedent from the angle and ⟨Venus⟩ falls from the angle while aspecting the ascendant. As for their position in relation to the Sun, Saturn is retrograde, Venus is approaching her second station regressively, while Mercury is zamin in the heart of the Sun, in the strongest possible position. Considering all these element, it appears that Mercury is the strongest planet.

[VIII] The animodar being established as we have just said, the mean motion of the Sun and his ⟨true⟩ place as mentioned above, as well as the argument of Mercury and its ⟨true⟩ place, the mean motion of the Moon was at 11.1;1.56°, her argument at 4.27;20.26°, the ⟨true⟩ locus of the Moon was at 11.4;53.4°, the argument of Venus was at 5.12;15.18°, her ⟨true⟩ locus at 7.26;56. 53°, the mean motion of Mars was at 6.20;47.54°, his ⟨true⟩ locus at 6.21;4.10°, the mean motion of Jupiter was at 9.0;38.31°, his ⟨true⟩ locus at 8.24;32.31°, the mean motion of Saturn was at 11. 25;49.42°, his ⟨true⟩ locus being as above stated, the mean motion of the Dragon's head was at 9.15;32.1°, its ⟨true⟩ locus being at 2.14;28°, that of the Dragon's tail at its nadir. The cusp of the 11th house was at 20° in Cancer, the cusp of the 12th house at 21° in Leo, the cusp of the second house at 25° in Libra, the cusp of the third house at 24° in Scorpio, and the cusps of the other houses at the opposite places in the sky. The Lot of Fortune was at 11;36° in Taurus, the Lot of the Future at 4;36° in Aquarius, the Lot of Hyleg at 15;42° in Aquarius, the Lot of Life at 12;26° in Gemini, the Lot of Death at 12;25° in Scorpio, the Lot of the Planet which Kills at 11;19° in Taurus, the Lot of the Year in which the Native Must Fear Death, that is to say, the Lot of the End of Things, was at 24;49° in Taurus, the Lot of the Weighty Place at 27;15° in Pisces, the Lot of Quarrels at 19;37° in Cancer, the Lot of the Native's Exaltation at 2;8° in Capricorn, the Lot of Nobility at 21;31° in Sagittarius, the Lot of Love at 0;6° in Cancer and the Lot of the Father's Death at 23;47° in Sagittarius.

[IX] Ascensions of the ascendant	170;44
Ascensions of the degree of the Sun	211;57° (in oblique ascension, but in right ascension 291;37°)
Ascensions of the degree of the Moon	347;54
Ascensions of the Lot of Fortune	21;7
Ascensions of the Lot of the Hyleg	337;15
Ascensions of the Lot of the Father	10;0
Ascensions of the Lot of the Mother	45;41

Ascensions of the body of Saturn	357;49
Ascensions of his opposition	173;46
Ascensions of his right square	55;40
Ascensions of his left square	294;12
Ascensions of the body of Mars	208;46
Ascensions of his opposition	10;0
Ascensions of his right square	319;43
Ascensions of his left square	85;57
Ascensions of the body of Jupiter	293;14
Ascensions of his right trine	11;45
Ascensions of his left trine	131;21
Ascensions of his right sextile	342;26
Ascensions of his left sextile	213;34
Ascensions of Venus' body	257;7
Ascensions of her right trine	358;32
Ascensions of her left trine	93;40
Ascensions of her right sextile	324;25
Ascensions of her left sextile	175;40
Ascensions of the Dragon's head	45;5
[Ascensions] of the Dragon's tail	281;5°.

[x] [In the central square:] After 1200 years of the Lord, 9 months from January, and 9 days, 15 hours and 26 minutes in average days, that is to say 15 hours, 56 minutes and 32 seconds in equal hours, and 15 hours and about 30 minutes in unequal hours, at the meridian of Amiens, whose longitude is 40 degrees and 30 minutes from the West and whose latitude is 49 degrees and 36 minutes, the nativity of the Servant of God in glory took place, to the praise of God and with his help, the figure of the sky and that of the planets were thus.

[House I. Ascendant:] Virgo 23;6°

[House II:] Libra 25°; Mars 21;6° [Libra], direct; Mercury 23;6° [Libra], direct; Sun 23;23° [Libra]

[House III]: Scorpio 24°; Venus 26;56°[Scorpio], direct

[House IV:] Sagittarius 21°; Jupiter 24;33° [Sagittarius], direct; Tail [of the Dragon] 14;28° [Sagittarius]

[House V:] Capricorn 20°

[House VI:] Aquarius 21°; Lot of Hyleg 15;42° [Aquarius]

[House VII:] Pisces 23;6°; Moon 4;53° [Pisces]; Saturn 25;14° [Pisces], retro- grade

[House VIII:] Aries 25°

[House IX:] Taurus 24°; Lot of Death; Lot of Fortune 11;26° [Taurus]

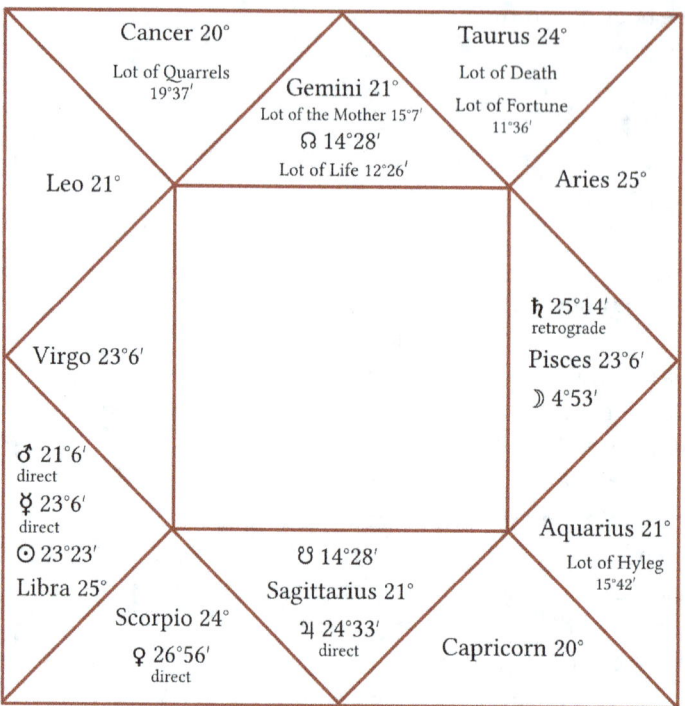

FIGURE 7.2 Nativity figure of Richard of Fournival (translation)

[House X:] Gemini 21°; Lot of the Mother 15;7° [Gemini]; Head [of the Dragon] 14;28° [Gemini]; Lot of Life 12;26° [Gemini]

[House XI :] Cancer 20°; Lot of Quarrels 19;37° [Cancer]

[House XII:] Leo 21°.

[XI] The movement of the Moon during one hour is 34;57', and it increases between its middle course and its greatest course, as is the case at the beginning of its third phase, according to the opinion of all scholars.

[XII] Considering the hyleg of this nocturnal nativity, it appears that the masters of nourishment seem safe and free and that the native should enjoy a long life, God willing. The Moon is not as useful as the hyleg, for she is cadent from the angle. On the contrary, the Sun is as useful as the hyleg, since he is succedent from the angle and in mutual aspect of conjunction with Mercury, which is the ruler of its triplicity. Mercury is the alkocoden and gives the native his middle years, according to God's command, which are 48, and because he is zamin and succedent from the angle. Moreover, Jupiter is fortunate, looks at Mercury with a sextile aspect and is in an angle, which increases his lesser years which are 12. Mars, who is unfortunate, close to Mercury by a distance smaller than the half-orbit of either of them, and who is succedent from the angle, diminishes the months of life of the native according to the number of his lesser years, which are 15. The Sun, who is unfortunate because of its corporal conjunction [with Mercury], diminishes also the months of life according to the number of his lesser years, which are 19. The life span of the native should therefore be 57 years and 2 months, if the Lord wills, or something close to it, because of the directions of the significators to the places of the interruption ⟨of life⟩.

[XIII] The profection of the ascendant has reached the Lot of the Father's Death the year the father died.

The direction of Venus has reached the sextile aspect of Mars the year the mother died.

The direction of the midheaven by the right circle ascensions reached the square aspect of Mars the same year.

According to the direction of the degree of the Moon at the opposition of Mars, the native suffered a quartan fever.

According to the direction of the Lot of Fortune at the point where the sign of Aries passed into that of Pisces, I've lost my father and, this same year, had to suffer a shameful event.

According to the direction of the Lot of the Mother at the point where the sign of Taurus passed into that of Aries, I've lost my mother.

According to the profection of the ascendant to the Lot of Death, I've been badly wounded by an Attrebate.

According to the direction of the ascendant to the position of Mars, the native must fear something after 38 years and 12 days.

According to the direction of the ascendant to the position of the Sun, the native must fear something after 41 years and 2 months and a half.

According to the direction of the degree of the hyleg to the square of the Moon, the native must fear death after 56 years and 10 months.

According to the direction of the Lot of the Hyleg to the tail of the Dragon, the native must again fear death after 56 years and 10 months.

And in this same year, the years conferred by the alkocoden will be completed, with maybe some extra.

Acknowledgments

We would like to thank Laure Miolo and David Juste for their helpful comments on earlier drafts of this paper. We would also like to thank Levente László for his suggestion, during the Astra Project conference, concerning the absence of the decans in Ptolemy's *Tetrabiblos/Quadripartitum* and the probable influence of this omission in the choice to exclude the decans among the essential dignities of the planets in chapter 8 of the *Speculum astronomiae*.

Bibliography

Primary Sources
Manuscripts

Firenze, Biblioteca Medicea Laurenziana, Plut. 30.29.

Oxford, Corpus Christi College, 248.

Oxford, Hertford College 4.

Paris, BnF, lat. 16204.

Paris, BnF, lat. 16208.

Paris, Bibliothèque de la Sorbonne, 636.

Vatican, BAV, Pal. lat. 1380.

Vatican, BAV, Pal. lat. 1443.

Vatican, BAV, Reg. lat. 1261.

Vienna, ÖNB 2388.

Editions

Abū Maʿshar al-Balkhi (Albumasar), *Liber introductorii maioris ad scientiam iudiciorum astrorum*, 8 vols., edited by R. Lemay. Naples: Istituto Universitario Orientale, 1995–1996.

The Great Introduction to Astrology by Abū Maʿšar, 2 vols., edited by Keiji Yamamoto and Charles Burnett. Leiden-Boston: Brill, 2019.

Alberto Magno. *Speculum Astronomiae*, edited by Paola Zambelli and al. Pisa: 1977.

Albohali Alchaiat. *De iudiciis nativitatum*, translated by John of Toledo, 1153. Nuremberg: 1546.

Al-Qabīṣī (Alcabitius). *The Introduction of Astrology. Editions of the Arabic and Latin Texts and an English Translation*, edited by. Charles Burnett, Keiji Yamamoto and Michio Yano. London-Torino: The Warburg Institute-Nino Aragno Editore, 2004.

Aomar Tiberiadis. *De nativitatibus*, translated by Johannes Hispalensis. Venice: 1503.

Léopold Delisle, ed., 'La *Biblionomie* de Richard de Fournival', In Id., *Le cabinet des manuscrits de la Bibliothèque impériale puis nationale*. Paris: Imprimerie impériale, 1868–1881, II.

Benjamin Dykes. *Persian Nativities*, 2 vols. Minneaopolis: The Cazimi Press, 2009.

[Pseudo-] Johannes Hispalensis. *Epitome totius astrologiae (Quadripartitum)*. Nuremberg: 1548.

Leopold of Austria. *Compilatio de astrorum scientia*. Augsbourg: E. Ratdolt, 1489.

Ptolemy, *Tetrabiblos*, edited and translated by F.E. Robbins. Cambridge [Mass.]-London: 1971.

Ptolemy Ptholomeus. *Quadripartitum*, translated by Plato of Tivoli. Venice: B. Locatello, 1493.

Ptolemy. *Quadripartitum*, translated by Hugo Sanctelliensis, transcribed by Maria Sorokina, PAL: Ms/243/351/Text/1 (badw.de)

Richard de Fournival. *Le Bestiaire d'Amour et la Response du Bestiaire*, edited by Gabriel Biancotto. Paris: Champion Classique, 2009.

Secondary Sources

Birkenmajer, Aleksander. 'Pierre de Limoges, commentateur de Richard de Fournival'. *Isis*, 40 (1949), 18–31, article reprinted in his *Études d'histoire des sciences et de philosophie du Moyen Âge*. Wroclaw-Warsaw-Cracow: Studia Copernicana I, 1970.

Boudet, Jean-Patrice, and Lucken, Christopher. 'In Quest of an Astrological Identity Chart: Richard de Fournival's *Nativitas*'. In *Richard de Fournival et les sciences au XIIIᵉ siècle*, edited by Joëlle Ducos and Christopher Lucken. Florence: SISMEL-Edizioni del Galluzzo, 2018.

Burnett, Charles. 'The Astrological Categorization of Religions in Abū Ma'shar, the *De vetula* and Roger Bacon'. In *Language of Religion, Language of the People: Medieval Judaism, Christianity and Islam*, edited by Ernst Bremer and al. Munich: 2006.

Calvet, Antoine. 'Le *De arte alchemica* (inc.: Dixit Arturus explicator huius operis) est-il une œuvre authentique de Richard de Fournival?'. In *Richard de Fournival et les sciences au XIIIᵉ siècle*, edited by Joëlle Ducos and Christopher Lucken. Florence: SISMEL-Edizioni del Galluzzo, 2018.

Ducos, Joëlle, and Lucken, Christopher, eds. *Richard de Fournival et les sciences au XIIIᵉ siècle*. Florence: SISMEL-Edizioni del Galluzzo, 2018.

Hackett, Jeremiah. 'Albert the Great and the *Speculum astronomiae*: The State of Research at the Beginning of the 21st Century'. In *A Companion to Albert the Great* ed. I.M. Resnick. Leiden: Brill, 2013.

Haynes, John. 'Roger Bacon and the Pseudo-Ovidian *De vetula*'. *The Journal of Medieval Latin* 32 (2022): 21–63.

Juste, David. 'The Impact of Arabic Sources on European Astrology: Some Facts and Numbers'. *Micrologus*, XXIV (2016), *The Impact of Arabic Sciences in Europe and Asia*: 173–194.

Juste, David. 'MS Florence, Biblioteca Medicea Laurenziana, Plut. 30.29 (update: 06.06. 2023)' *Ptolemaeus Arabus et Latinus. Manuscripts*. URL = http://ptolemaeus.badw.d e/ms/186.

Juste, David. 'MS Paris, Bibliothèque nationale de France, lat. 16204 (update: 11.12.2023)'. *Ptolemaeus Arabus et Latinus. Manuscripts*. URL = http://ptolemaeus.badw.de/ms/ 194.

Kunitzsch, Paul. *Mittelalterliche astronomisch-astrologische Glossare mit arabischen Fachausdrücken*. Munich: Verlag der Bayerischen Akademie der Wissenschaften, 1977.

Lucken, Christopher. Les portes de la mémoire. Richard de Fournival et l'Arriereban d'Amours, Genève: Droz, 2024.

Lucken, Christopher. 'Le *contreescrit* de l'amant lettré. Le *Bestiaire d'Amours* de Richard de Fournival'. In *La lettre-miroir dans l'Occident latin et vernaculaire du Vᵉ au XVᵉ s.*, edited by Dominique Demartini, Sumi Shimahara, Christiane Veyrard-Cosme. Turnhout: Brepols, 2018.

Lucken, Christopher. 'La Biblionomia et la bibliothèque de Richard de Fournival: un idéal du savoir et sa traduction manuscrite'. In *Les Livres des maîtres. Histoire et rayonnement du collège de Sorbonne et de ses bibliothèques du XIIIᵉ siècle à la Renaissance*, edited by Claire Angotti, Gilbert Fournier and Donatella Nebbiai. Paris: Publications de la Sorbonne, 2017.

Miolo, Laure. 'Le fonds scientifique d'un collège de théologie: le cas de la bibliothèque de Sorbonne, 1257–1500', 2 vols. Thèse de l'Univ. de Lyon II dir. by L. Moulinier-Brogi, 2017.

Miolo, Laure. 'Un manuscrit de Pierre de Limoges à la British Library: à propos du codex London, BL, Additional MS 38688'. *Scriptorium*, 74 (2020): 79–111.

North, John D. *Horoscopes and History*. London: The Warburg Institute, 1986.

Nothaft, C. Philipp E. 'Glorious Science or "Dead Dog"? Jean de Jandun and the Quarrel over Astrology in Fourteenth Century Paris'. *Vivarium* 57 (2019): 51–101.

Panti, Cecilia. 'An Astrological Path to Wisdom: Richard de Fournival, Roger Bacon and the Attribution of the Pseudo-Ovidian *De vetula*'. In *Richard de Fournival et les sciences au XIIIᵉ siècle*, edited by Joëlle Ducos and Christopher Lucken. Florence: SISMEL-Edizioni del Galluzzo, 2018.

Paravicini Bagliani, Agostino. *Le Speculum astronomiae: une énigme? Enquête sur les manuscrits*. Florence: SISMEL-Edizioni del Galluzzo, 2001.

Paravicini Bagliani, Agostino. 'Un nuovo codice dello Speculum Astronomiae (Siena, Biblioteca Comunale degli Intronati, L III 11)'. In *Riflessioni codicologiche, in Vedere nell'ombra. Studi su natura, spiritualità e scienze operative offerti a Michela Pereira*, a cura di Cecilia Panti e Nicola Polloni. Florence: SISMEL-Edizioni del Galluzzo, 2018.

Pedersen, Fritz S. 'The Toulouse Tables. A List of Manuscripts'. *Cahiers de l'Institut du Moyen Age grec et latin*, 68 (1998): 3–12.

Pedersen, Fritz S. *The Toledan Tables. A Review of the Manuscripts and Textual Versions with an Edition*, 4 vols., (Copenhagen: Kongelige Danske Videnskabernes Selskab, 2002).

Pingree, David. 'The Diffusion of Arabic Magic Texts in Western Europe'. In *La diffusione delle scienze islamiche nel Medio Evo europeo*, edited by B. Scarcia Amoretti. Roma: Academia nazionale dei Lincei, 1987.

Poulle, Emmanuel. 'Un témoin de l'astronomie latine du XIIIᵉ siècle. Les tables de Toulouse'. In *Comprendre et maîtriser la nature au Moyen Âge. Mélanges d'histoire des sciences offerts à Guy Beaujouan*. Genève-Paris: Droz-Champion, 1994, reprinted in Id., *Astronomie planétaire au Moyen Age latin* (Variorum: 1996), text I.

Resnick, Irven M., ed. *A Companion to Albert the Great*. Leiden, 2013.

Roy, Bruno. 'Richard de Fournival, auteur du Speculum astronomie?'. *Archives d'histoire doctrinale et littéraire du Moyen Âge*, 67 (2000): 159–180.

Rutkin, H. Darrel. 'Astrology and Magic'. In *A Companion to Albert the Great*, edited by I.M. Resnick. Leiden: Brill, 2013.

Thorndike, Lynn. 'Notes on Some Astronomical, Astrological and Mathematical Manuscripts of the Bibliothèque Nationale, Paris'. *Journal of the Warburg and Courtauld Institutes*, 20 (1957): 112–172.

Weill-Parot, Nicolas. 'La Biblionomia de Richard de Fournival, le Speculum astronomiae et le secret' In *Richard de Fournival et les sciences au XIIIe siècle*. Firenze, Sismel-Edizioni del Galluzzo, 2018.

Zambelli, Paola, and al. *The* Speculum Astronomiae *and its Enigma. Astrology, Theology and Science in Albertus Magnus and his Contemporarie*s. Dordrecht: Kluwer Academic Publisher, 1992.

CHAPTER 8

John of Lübeck's Antichrist-Prediction (1474): A Unique Astrological Practice

Stephan Heilen

Abstract

In 1474, John of Lübeck wrote a 'prognostication regarding the coming of Antichrist and the Messiah of the Jews', predicting that the conjunction of Saturn and Jupiter in 1504 would bring about the birth of the widely feared Antichrist on 14 September 1506 at about 5 a.m. In addition, John manages to provide detailed astrological explanations, all based on the same conjunction horoscope, of a series of canonical details of Antichrist's 'biography'. He thus bolsters the credibility of the one and crucial hitherto unknown date, namely that of the birth of Antichrist. The present article examines John's astrological technique.

Keywords

Abū Maʿšar (*Albumasar*) – Adso of Montier-en-Der – al-Qabīṣī (*Alcabitius*) – Antichrist – Emperor Frederic III – historical astrology – John of Glogau – John of Lübeck – Pseudo-Ovid *De vetula* – Roger Bacon

1 Introduction

John of Lübeck is an extremely shadowy figure.[1] All we know about his biography is that he traveled Italy extensively and that he wrote his 'prognostication regarding the coming of Antichrist and the Messiah of the Jews' (*Pronosticum*

---

1 What follows is a much shortened version (enriched by some new observations) of select passages of Stephan Heilen, *Konjunktionsprognostik in der Frühen Neuzeit, Band 1: Die Antichrist-Prognose des Johannes von Lübeck (1474) zur Saturn-Jupiter-Konjunktion von 1504 und ihre frühneuzeitliche Rezeption* (Baden-Baden: Koerner, 2020). John's Latin text will here be quoted as edited (in Heilen, 228–270), i.e., without discussion of textual variants, for which see the commentary ibid.

Ioannis de Lubec Almani super antechristi aduentu Iudeorumque messiae) in
Padua, where he probably lived for a longer time, in April 1474. According to
John of Glogau, who was professor at the university of Cracow, John of Lübeck
dedicated his prediction of the future to emperor Frederic III.[2] It was printed
in 1474 or soon afterwards without dedication to the emperor, and no less than
eighteen copies of that incunabulum are extant (besides three manuscripts,
but no autograph).[3] This clearly structured and very original prediction had
been almost totally neglected by modern research until the present author's
recent attempt (2020) to elucidate it.

John's prediction is based on conjunction astrology (also called: historical
astrology) which was of Perso-Arabic origin. The most authoritative and complex (yet by no means the only) version of this doctrine was Abū Maʿšar's
Book of religions and dynasties. Once Latin translations of this and other Arabic manuals of conjunction astrology became available in the West, the Oriental doctrine was adapted to the Christian faith by the anonymous author
of the Pseudo-Ovidian *De vetula*, by Roger Bacon, and by Pierre d'Ailly.[4] The
major consequence of this adaptation was that the Perso-Arabic theory's cycli-
cal concept of history was replaced by a linear concept in compliance with the
Christian view of world history and eschatology. Hence, the Western adepts
of conjunction astrology did no longer assume an unlimited number of possible religions; instead, they were convinced that besides five world religions
which had already originated in the past only one was still to come, the pseudo-
religion of Antichrist (see table 8.1).

John's text is original in three respects. Firstly, there had been astrological
predictions of the coming of Antichrist before John's, and others would be
made after his lifetime, all of them inspired by the wide-spread late medieval
belief that the end of the world was near, but John's prediction is unique insofar as it almost totally avoids the traditional prophetic elements of earlier,
purely religious predictions of Antichrist.[5] While such prophetic elements had

---

2 John of Glogau's testimony dates from around 1500. On John of Lübeck's life and work as well
   as his dedication to the emperor cf. Heilen, *Konjunktionsprognostik*, 50–59, 186–188, and 426–
   427.

3 On all these textual witnesses see Heilen, *Konjunktionsprognostik*, 196–217. The incunabulum
   comprises twenty-four pages of which the first sixteen are the prediction proper and the last
   eight John's vehement polemic against the detractors of astrology.

4 The author was probably Richard de Fournival (1201–1260). See Heilen, *Konjunktionsprognostik*, 72 with n. 216. See chapter 7 on Fournival's astrology by Jean-Patrice Boudet and Christopher Lucken.

5 See Heilen, *Konjunktionsprognostik*, 24, for the definition of religiously inspired prophecy as

TABLE 8.1   The sixfold typology of religions according to Abū Maʿšar compared to the modified Western tradition[a]

The 'mixing' of Jupiter with ...	... results in the following religions:	
	Abū Maʿšar (cyclical concept)	Ps.-Ovid and Roger Bacon (linear concept)
1 Saturn	Judaism	Judaism
2 Mars	Mazdaism	the religion of the 'Chaldeans'
3 Sun	(*no historical example given*)	the religion of the Egyptians
4 Venus	e.g. (!) Islam	Islam
5 Mercury	e.g. (!) Christianity	Christianity
6 Moon	(*no historical example given*)	the pseudo-religion of Antichrist

a   Sources: Abū Maʿšar's *Book of religions and dynasties* 1.4.3–4 (ed. Keiji Yamamoto and Charles
Burnett, *Abū Maʿšar, On Historical Astrology. The Book of Religions and Dynasties [On the
Great Conjunctions]*, Edited and Translated, 2 vols. [Leiden: Brill, 2000], vol. I, 44–45, Latin
trans., vol. II, 28–29), Ps.-Ovid *De vetula* 3.522–575 (ed. Paul Klopsch, *Pseudo-Ovidius De Vetula.
Untersuchungen und Text* [Leiden: Brill, 1967], 269–270), and Roger Bacon, *Opus maius* pars
IV (ed. John Henry Bridges, *The 'Opus maius' of Roger Bacon*, vol. 1 [Oxford: Clarendon Press,
1897], 256–257).

loomed large in astrological predictions of Antichrist before John's, he focuses
on a distinctly technical discussion.

Secondly, he found a solution to the technical problem that from his own
time through the end of the sixteenth century no-one of the relevant conjunctions of Saturn and Jupiter—i.e., in 1484 (♏︎), 1504 (♋︎), 1524 (♓︎), 1544 (♏︎),
1563 (♋︎), and 1583 (♓︎)—would entail a 'shift of triplicity' and thus fulfil one
of several indispensable prerequisites for the prediction of a 'new prophet'.
John overcame this problem by interpreting one of these conjunctions, that
of 1504, in a shrewd argumentation based on a combination of select tenets of
revered authorities such as Māšāʾallāh and Abū Maʿšar as signifying the coming
of Antichrist.[6] No-one of the available manuals of these authorities would have
allowed this interpretation if taken alone.

---

essentially different from prediction of the future based on astrological technique. See also
the analysis (p. 89) of the meager presence of prophetic elements in John's text.

6   Māšāʾallāh died about 815 CE. Abū Maʿšar lived 787–886 CE. As to the latter, cf. S. Heilen,
The debt to Abū Maʿšar's astrological works in the historical predictions by John of Lübeck
and Paul of Middelburg, forthcoming in a volume on Abū Maʿšar edited by Charles Burnett.

Thirdly, John's text is original with regard to the manner how he employs the tenets of historical astrology. Half a millennium before his own time the abbot Adso of Montier-en-Der had assembled all relevant passages from the Bible and the Church Fathers' writings into a short 'biography' of Antichrist[7] that could easily be memorized and was indeed common knowledge at John's time. All details of this biography are either parallels or contrasts regarding the life of Jesus Christ. The only biographical detail of Antichrist that John's contemporaries did not already 'know', or believe to know, was arguably the most important one, namely when exactly the eschatological opponent of Christ would come into the world, that is, when Antichrist would be born. Hence, John could have focused exclusively on this tantalizing question, and predicted the precise date. What he does, instead, looks superfluous at first sight but serves a clever purpose: for the first time ever, and based on the chart of the conjunction of Saturn and Jupiter in 1504, he provides systematic astrological explanations of most of the canonical, well-known details of the 'biography' of Antichrist, thus bolstering the credibility of his one and only prediction of a still unknown detail, namely that of Antichrist's date of birth. Most of his predecessors who had predicted the date of the coming of Antichrist by means of prophecy or astrology, or a mix of both, had already been proven wrong by history because the predicted time had passed but Antichrist had not come. Therefore it is easy to imagine that late medieval readers were both curious and sceptical regarding new predictions.

John's strong emphasis on a thorough technical discussion of the eschatological event in question appears to have impressed more than a few of his contemporaries, as is clear from the wide reception of his text, not surprisingly: an expert who was able to explain the other, long 'known' details of Antichrist's 'biography' so convincingly from a single chart, drawing systematically on the doctrine of historical astrology, was probably right in his calculation of the still unknown date and time of Antichrist's birth based on the same chart and the same doctrine, more precisely, on the computational method taught by the foremost authority, Abū Maʿšar.

It goes without saying that it is not an easy self-chosen task to provide convincing astrological explanation of a whole set of given 'biographical' data. By accepting this challenge, John tackles in principle the same kind of problem

---

7 *Epistola de ortu et tempore Antichristi* (c. 950 CE), ed. Ernst Sackur, *Sibyllinische Texte und Forschungen. Pseudomethodius, Adso und die Tiburtinische Sibylle* (Halle: Niemeyer, 1898, repr. Turin: Bottega d'Erasmo, 1976), 104–113, and Daniel Verhelst, ed., *Adso Dervensis, De ortu et tempore Antichristi necnon et tractatus qui ab eo dependunt* (Turnhout: Brepols, 1976), 20–30.

tackled by many earlier astrologers who had tried to explain the life of this or
that already deceased individual, mostly for the sake of illustrating astrological
manuals with striking analyses of nativities of historical figures whose major
biographical details were well known to the readers and had, therefore, to be
both respected and accounted for. John's case, however, is unique in that it actually concerns a future life whose details were universally acknowledged to be
known *a priori*.

2   The Conjunction Horoscope

As usual at that time, John computed his chart (see figure 8.1) with the Alfonsine Tables. What his contemporaries were unaware of is that he rectified the
chart[8] and, more importantly, that some of his data (the astronomical longitudes of Mars and Venus[9] as well as four details in quotations from Arabic
authorities) are erroneous, mutilated, distorted, or arbitrarily expanded. Since
these are gross mistakes and each one of them would, once corrected, make the
whole prediction collapse, there is hardly any room left for reasonable objections to the conclusion that they are a result of intentional manipulation. Since
this conclusion has already been argued in detail elsewhere,[10] it will here be
taken for granted—and readily dismissed because the purpose of the present
contribution is not to examine the honesty of John of Lübeck but rather the
technical details of his astrological prediction on the basis of the given chart
which we shall accept in the same manner as John's contemporaries accepted
it.

Let us now review the eleven relevant passages of John's text in the same
chronological order of Antichrist's 'biography' as presented in John's text. I shall

---

8   This technique was alien to conjunction astrology but common in genethlialogy when an
      adult individual's exact time of birth was unknown; then the hour and minute was cho-
      sen so as to match the native's already available biographical data as closely as possible.
      In the present case rectification may have seemed pardonable because the conjunction
      horoscope signified the birth of a native (Antichrist) whose biography was already avail-
      able.

9   On the given date of the conjunction of Saturn and Jupiter, Mars and Venus would, as cor-
      rectly predicted by the *Alfonsine Tables*, not be in Cancer, as the text makes the readers
      believe, but in Taurus (Venus) and Leo (Mars).

10   See Heilen, *Konjunktionsprognostik*, chapters IV.D and XII, and the English summary (with
      some new details) in S. Heilen, 'Doctoring the Data in John of Lübeck's Astrological Predic-
      tion of the Birth of Antichrist', *Cahiers de Recherches Médiévales et Humanistes* 47 (2024),
      475–495.

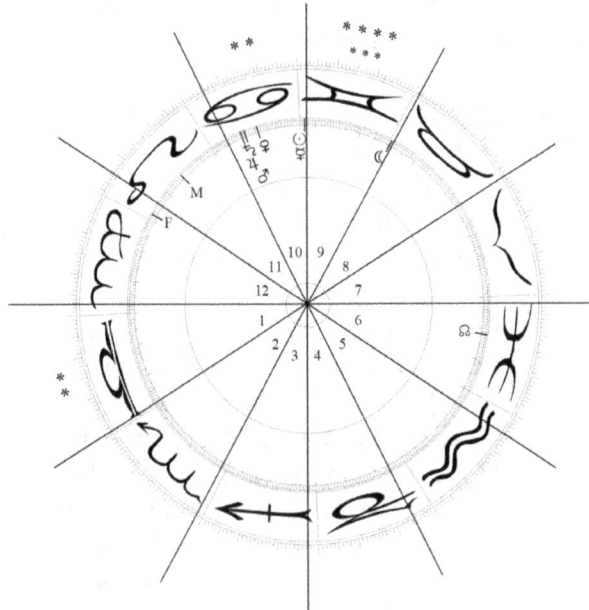

FIGURE 8.1
John's data of the conjunction horoscope cast for 10 June 1504, 11:54:48 a.m.

F = *PARS FORTUNE* = LOT OF FORTUNE,
M = *PARS MATRIS* = LOT OF THE MOTHER

introduce each passage with a header specifying the question at issue. Since nine of these passages give astrological explanations why this or that well-known biographical detail must come about, these nine headers begin with 'why'. Only passages v and xi are about hitherto unknown dates; hence, their headers will begin with 'when'. However, only the answer to question v was entirely unknown from the perspective of John's readers, while that to question xi was agreed to be 3½ years after the date inquired by question v (more on this below in the commentary *ad locum*). Each header will be followed by a brief reference to the respective parallel or contrast in the life of Jesus Christ. The English translations will be elucidated in two complementary manners: while brief clarifications of detail will, whenever possible, be interspersed in parentheses, explanations of more complex issues will be given in the following commentaries.[11]

---

11   It will be taken for granted that the reader is basically familiar with the astrological doctrine. For the major planetary dignities see Heilen, *Konjunktionsprognostik*, 46 (tab. 3). Explanatory references to astronomical data will be based on Heilen, 135 (tab. 7) and 143 (tab. 9) where all data regarding the longitudes of house cusps, planets, luminaries, lots, etc., are gathered from John of Lübeck's text. For in-depth commentaries on the same questions, the reader may wish to consult the respective sections in Heilen, *Konjunktionsprognostik*.

2.1 Why Antichrist's Mother Will Be of Jewish Ancestry (§§ 97–100)
Parallel with Jesus Christ: his mother, Mary, is Jewish.

[97] *Visoque cognito Iudeorum messiæ Lunarisque prophetæ aduentu perscrutandum est de natione et conditione concipientis ipsumque parientis.* [98] *In hac coniunctione cuspis decimæ domus matres significantis est terminus Saturni, in quo Mercurius dominus ascendentis et decimæ in propria domo ibi situatus,* [99] *parsque matris in tridecimum gradum cadens Leonis etiam terminum Saturni.* [100] *Et quia Saturnus Iudeorum significator, concluditur, quod ista concipiensque pariens erit nationis Iudaicæ.*

[97] Having seen and recognized the arrival of the Messiah of the Jews and (astrologically speaking) a lunar prophet, we must examine the nation and (social) condition of (her who will) conceive him and give birth to him. [98] In this conjunction the cusp of the tenth house (27° 19′ ♊), which (house) signifies mothers, is a term of Saturn (24°–30° ♊), in which Mercury (stands, at 28° 37′ ♊), the lord of the ascending (sign, namely Virgo, the ASC being 27° 34′ ♍) and of the tenth (house, namely Gemini, the MC being 27° 19′ ♊), who is placed there (in the tenth house) in his own house, [99] and the Lot of the Mother falls in the thirteenth degree of Leo (more precisely, 13° 4′ ♌), another term of Saturn (11°–18° ♌). [100] And since Saturn is the (astrological) signifier of the Jews, it is to be concluded that this (person) conceiving and giving birth (to Antichrist) will belong to the Jewish nation.

The four central arguments on which this reasoning is based are probably all derived from the writings of Abū Maʿšar whom John of Lübeck had mentioned three times in earlier passages of his prediction (§§ 61, 85, 88; all three passages refer to *De coniunctionibus*,[12] the Latin translation of Abū Maʿšar's *Book of religions and dynasties*):

1. While the chart's tenth house is usually associated with career and social rank, John's association of this house with mothers is justified by Abū Maʿšar's *Great Introduction* 6.26.14 which states: 'The tenth place is called that of authority and it indicates high rank, kingship, authority, the ruler, the judge, nobility, renown, fame, skills, actions, and mothers'.[13] John's next step is to focus on this

---

12 Either this or *Liber coniunctionum* is, for the reasons given in Heilen, *Konjunktionsprognostik*, 25, the work's correct title, not *De magnis coniunctionibus*.

13 Keiji Yamamoto and Charles Burnett, eds., *Abū Maʿšar, The Great Introduction to Astrology, Edited and Translated, with an Edition of the Greek Version by David Pingree*, 2 vols. (Lei-

house's cusp (i.e., on the exact zodiacal longitude where it begins), and to examine the planetary term to which this cusp belongs: it is a term of Saturn (on whose religious interpretation see below, point 4).

Whenever John mentions planetary terms, he is—as to be expected—tacitly referring to the canonical 'Egyptian' system of terms (tabularized by Ptol. *Tetr.* 1.21.9–10), not the Ptolemaic one (*Tetr.* 1.21.28–29). This preference is not obvious in the present instance because the cusp's longitude 27° 19′ ♊ falls in Saturn's term according to both frames of reference ('Egyptian': 24°–30° ♊; Ptolemaic: 26°–30° ♊), but it becomes clear in instances where the two systems disagree among each other and John complies with the 'Egyptian' system alone, as is the case in the present text's second instance where the Lot of the Mother's longitude (13° 4′ ♌) matches the 'Egyptian' definition of Saturn's term (11°–18° ♌) but not the Ptolemaic one (0°–6° ♌).

2. In Saturn's term 24°–30° ♊ John finds not only the cusp of the tenth house (27° 19′ ♊) but also Mercury (28° 37′ ♊) who happens to be, in the present chart, lord of the two most important cardinal houses (I and X), and is therefore strong. Although John mentions the ascending first house, too, we may assume that he is focusing especially on Mercury's lordship over the tenth house which signifies the mother. The fact that Mercury rules this house and is located not only in it but right in the aforementioned term of Saturn, where the cusp falls, appears to strengthen the religious signification of the planetary term of the cusp of the house of mothers. This interpretation is supported by the observation that John does not mention the second celestial body located in that term, namely the Sun, presumably because the Sun is not lord of the tenth house nor does it hold any other planetary dignity in this chart.

At least the author could have mentioned, if he had wanted to, that the Sun rules Leo, the sign (not the house) of the mother's lot, and is itself in the tenth house, which signifies motherhood; that he refrains from doing so is probably due to the fact that these details weigh less than what has been said about Mercury, that the mother's lot has not yet been mentioned (making remarks on the

---

den: Brill, 2019), vol. I, 685. Whichever of the two Latin translations John of Lübeck used, he would find there the same reference to mothers. John of Seville translates (ed. Richard Lemay, *Abū Maʿšar al-Balḫī* [*Albumasar*]. *Liber introductorii maioris ad scientiam judiciorum astrorum. Édition critique*, 9 vols [Naples: Istituto Universitario Orientale, 1995–1996], vol. V, 259, lin. 1593–1596): *Decima dicitur domus* REGIA, *et hec significat sublimitatem et regnum atque imperium, eum quoque qui preest et iudicem, nobilitatem etiam* [*et gloriam*] *et memoriam ac vocis auditionem, magisteria quoque et opera ac matres.* Hermann of Carinthia translates (Lemay, vol. VIII, 122, lin. 987–989): *Decimi* [scil. *domicilii*] *sunt dignitates, regna principatus dominia potestas iudices eloquentia voces artificia opera, matres, conventus cum regibus.* For further details, cf. Heilen, *Konjunktionsprognostik*, 386–387.

Sun after mentioning this lot would make the sentence rather long and complicated), and perhaps also because the youthful planetary god Mercury more
often symbolizes the son, grandson, or younger brother in astrology[14] and is
thus more suitable for association with mother-child relationships than the sun
god, who is already an adult and stands outside the genealogy of the Olympian
gods.

Hence, in the present argument Mercury seems to count primarily (maybe
even exclusively) with regard to his accidental strength and energy in this specific chart, and far less (maybe not at all) with regard to his permanent astrological characteristics and associations.[15]

3. In a later passage of his *Great Introduction*, Abū Maʿšar addresses the Lot
of the Mother and explains both how it is calculated and why it belongs to the
tenth place: 'The twelfth is the Lot of the Mother. It is taken by day from Venus
to the Moon and by night the opposite, and it is cast out from the ascendant.
This lot indicates the conditions of mothers. We have put the Lot of the Mother
in the tenth sign because the tenth sign indicates the conditions of mothers
because it is opposite the place of the fathers', The formula given by Abū Maʿšar
for the Lot of the Mother (λ_M) is identical with the only extant Greco-Roman
text that gives its formula, namely Firmicus Maternus, *Mathesis* 6.32.21.[16] In
mathematical notation, it can be expressed thus:

$$\lambda_M = \lambda_{ASC} + \begin{cases} \lambda_{\mathrm{☽}} - \lambda_{\mathrm{♀}} \text{ (day)} \\ \lambda_{\mathrm{♀}} - \lambda_{\mathrm{☽}} \text{ (night)} \end{cases}$$

In the present case it leads to 27° 34′ ♍ + 29° 22′ ♉ - 13° 52′ ♋ = 177° 34′ + 59°
22′ - 103° 52′ = 133° 4′ = 13° 4′ ♌.

4. The association of Saturn with the Jewish religion is central to conjunction
astrology (cf. tab. 1 above). Abū Maʿšar's key sentence in this respect is this: 'If
it [*i.e., Jupiter, the general signifier of religion*] is mixed with Saturn, it indicates
that the faith of the people of that religion is Judaism which is similar to the
essence of Saturn […]',[17]

---

14   Cf. Stephan Heilen, *Hadriani genitura. Die astrologischen Fragmente des Antigonos von
Nikaia* (Berlin: De Gruyter, 2015, repr. 2017), vol. II, 870–871 and 1206–1207.
15   A similar function appears to underlie John's reference to Jupiter in text III (see the commentary below) and John's reference to the precise number of fixed stars of first and
second magnitude in the first, ninth, and tenth houses (§§ 76–78, not discussed in the
present contribution).
16   Cf. Heilen, *Konjunktionsprognostik*, 145. In the extant texts from Greco-Roman antiquity,
the Lot of the Mother had further been mentioned without its formula by Dorotheus,
Valens, Rhetorius, and Olympiodorus.
17   *The book of religions and dynasties* 1.4.4 (ed. and trans. Yamamoto and Burnett, *On Histor-*

In sum, John has, based on his conjunction chart, explained the canonical Jewish origin of the mother of Antichrist in a manner that must have appeared convincing to his late medieval readers.

2.2 Why the Conception Will Take Place Entirely in Secret (§ 113)

Parallel with Jesus Christ: only Mary is present at the angel's annunciation (Luke 1:26–38), also called *conceptio Christi* in the Latin tradition.

[113] *Haec conceptio et impregnatio erit multum occulta propter Mercurium dominum ascendentis coniunctionis et decimæ in domo propria sub radio solari occultum.*	[113] This conception and impregnation will take place entirely in secret, because Mercury, the lord of the ascendant of the conjunction (♍) and of the tenth (house, ♌), is hidden in his own house (♌) under the rays of the Sun.

John is here referring to a concept inherited from Greco-Roman astrology: when a planet is 'under the rays of the Sun', i.e. within a maximum elongation of 15°[18] from the glaring luminary and thus invisible, the action signified by that planet will take place in secret or go unnoticed. In the present horoscope, Mercury (28° 37′ ♊) is the only planet within that distance from the Sun (28° 22′ ♊). Actually, the distance is tiny (15′). Moreover, Mercury seems particularly suitable for this kind of argument because John had, in text I above, emphasized Mercury's strong signification regarding Antichrist's mother, and motherhood is closely related to conception.

2.3 Why Antichrist's Mother Will Be of Noble Lineage (§ 114)

Parallel with Jesus Christ: Jesus is (legally speaking, not biologically) son of Joseph, a descendant of the house of king David (Matthew 1:1; 1:6; 1:16; Luke 1:32; 2:4).

[114] *Hæc concipiens in sua secta erit magnæ progeniei propter Iouem dominum septimæ in angulo decimæ in sua exaltatione.*	[114] This (woman) getting pregnant will be of eminent lineage in her community of faith because of Jupiter, the lord of the seventh (house, ♓, who stands) in the cardine of the tenth (house) in his own exaltation (♋).

---

ical Astrology, vol. I, 44–45); Latin trans. (vol. II, 28): *Si enim fuerit* [scil. *Iupiter*] *complexus Saturno, significabit quod fides civium eiusdem secte sit iudaismus qui congruit substantie Saturni* [...].

18 This figure is, in astrology, valid for all planets regardless of the fact that their astronomical elongations at first/last visibility vary slightly from one planet to another.

Within the tenth house, whose relevance for Antichrist's mother had been made clear in §98 (see text I above), we find Jupiter (19° 42′ ♋), symbol of kingship. Hence, the mother will be of noble lineage, all the more so because Jupiter is particularly strong in this chart because the tenth house happens to be his zodiacal exaltation (♋) and also because Jupiter is lord of one cardinal house, namely the seventh (♓).[19] It seems that in the present argumentation the seventh house is not of interest in its own right (as signifying women and marriage)[20] but only insofar as its zodiacal rulership strengthens Jupiter in the tenth.[21]

Since Jupiter happens to be ruler of the fourth house (♐), too (cf. §127 in text VI below with comm. ad loc.), one may conjecture that the Latin text originally read ⟨quartæ et⟩ septimæ ('of the fourth and the seventh houses').[22] This conjecture gains plausibility from the fact that the extant text is clearly incomplete in four other instances due to scribal omissions.[23] Moreover, we have circumstantial evidence that John had at least occasionally (maybe even systematically) employed Roman numerals in his original text, with the consequence that a *saut du même au même* can even more easily be imagined if John wrote *IVᵉ et VIIᵉ*.[24] A third argument is that John had mentioned both cardinal houses ruled by Mercury in text I although Mercury's rule over the ascending sign seemed to serve no other purpose than to emphasize Mercury's overall strength; therefore mentioning both cardinal houses of Jupiter in the present text III would analogously strengthen Jupiter's signification.

2.4   Why Antichrist's Mother Will Be Lewd (§§115–116)[25]
Contrast with Jesus Christ: his mother is the pure and chaste virgin Mary (Matthew 1:25 and Luke 1:34).

---

19 It is here called *angulus*. On this terminology cf. Heilen, *Konjunktionsprognostik*, 313, ad §45.
20 Cf. e.g. Abū Ma'šar, *Great Introduction* 6.26.11 (ed. & trans. Yamamoto and Burnett, *The Great Introduction*, vol. I, 684–685; Latin trans.: ed. Lemay, *Abū Ma'šar*, vol. V, 259, lin. 1582–1584) or Alcab. *Intr.* 1.63 (ed. Charles Burnett, Keiji Yamamoto, and Michio Yano, *Al-Qabīṣī (Alcabitius): The Introduction to Astrology. Editions of the Arabic and Latin texts and an English translation* [London: The Warburg Institute, 2004], 53; Latin trans., 258).
21 Cf. the similar explanation regarding Mercury in text I (see esp. n. 15 above).
22 This conjecture is new compared to Heilen, *Konjunktionsprognostik*.
23 See Heilen, *Konjunktionsprognostik*, 217–218, 224 (stemma), and notes 840, 860, 1079, and 1084 to the following edition of the Latin text.
24 Cf. Heilen, *Konjunktionsprognostik*, 225.
25 According to various popular works of the 13th century she will even be a prostitute. Cf. Heilen, *Konjunktionsprognostik*, 388, ad §100 *erit nationis Iudaicæ*.

[115] *Etiam erit luxuriosa* | [115] Furthermore, she will be lewd[26]
propter Venerem dominam | because Venus, the ruler of the ninth (house)
nonæ et triplicitatis ascendentis | and the triplicity of the ascendant (♉, ♍, ♑)
et exaltationis et triplicitatis | and the exaltation (♓) and triplicity (♋, ♏,
septimæ tribus superioribus | ♓) of the seventh (house, ♓), is in conjunc-
per medium orbem sui lumi- | tion with the three upper (planets) within
nis coniunctam [116] *et propter* | half of her orb (14°) [116] and because the
Lunam almutaz coniunctionis | Moon, the ruler of the conjunction (of Sat-
in cuspide nonæ in sua exalta- | urn and Jupiter), in the cusp of the ninth
tione ascendens trigono radio | (house) in her own exaltation (♉) illumi-
illustrantem Saturnumque | nates the rising (sign, ♍) with a trigonal ray
Iouem ex sextili aspectu per | and receives Saturn and Jupiter, aspecting
medium orbem sui luminis in | them from sextile, within her orb in her own
domo sua recipientem. | house (♋).

John's explanation is twofold, dealing first with Venus (§ 115) and then with the Moon (§ 116).

1. the argument from Venus: the cusp of the ninth house is 29° 8′ ♉; Taurus is ruled by Venus. The day ruler of the triplicity of the earth signs ♉, ♍, and ♑, to which the present ascendant (♍) belongs, as well as that of the water signs (♋, ♏, ♓), to which the present descendant (♓) belongs, is Venus, and the present chart is indeed a diurnal chart. Moreover, the cusp of the seventh house (27° 34′ ♓) matches the exaltation of Venus (27° ♓) not only in the usual sense, i.e. with precision to full signs, but almost exactly. Hence, all details regarding Venus as mentioned by John in this passage are correct. One may presume that they all deserve attention, even if John does not explicitly say so, because they emphasize the strength of Venus in the present chart. Moreover, since Venus is located in the tenth house, which signifies Antichrist's mother (cf. text I above), Venus' astrological qualities, especially fondness of sexual pleasures, are projected on the mother of Antichrist as were those of Jupiter (namely kingship) in text III above.[27]

---

26   The semantic range of *luxuriosa* is not limited to sexuality, but the meaning intended here is clear because John continues (§§ 117–118) emphasizing twice that she will feign virginity and chastity while indulging in the opposite.

27   John does not explicitly mention Venus' position in the tenth house in § 115, but he must have taken this detail for granted thanks to his emphasis, in the same sentence, on Venus' conjunction with the three upper planets (which are all in the tenth house). As the text of § 115 stands, its argument could also have been employed to predict lewdness in Antichrist himself, but that would have been pointless because lewdness was not part of Antichrist's biography.

Instead of saying this, John focuses explicitly on another tenet, namely the canonical astrological orb of Venus which measures 14°, i.e., 7° (= *medium*, one half of it) on either side.[28] Since Venus is located at 13° 52' ♋,[29] Jupiter and Saturn (19° 42' ♋) as well as Mars (18° 22' ♋) are within Venus' orb, and therefore in conjunction with her, not only loosely (by full zodiacal signs) but strictly speaking. Hence, John's argument seems to be this: the historical conjunction of the three superior planets (especially Jupiter and Saturn) in 1504 in Cancer will lead to the conception of Antichrist in the aforementioned Jewish woman; since Venus will be in close conjunction with the superior planets, her typical qualities, in particular fondness of sexual pleasures, will be reflected in the mother of the prophet who is indicated by the conjunct planets, namely Antichrist.

2. the argument from the Moon: for John it goes without saying that its position (29° 22' ♉) falls in one of the four signs classified as 'lecherous' (♈, ♉, ♑, ♓) both in the ancient Greco-Roman tradition and by Abū Maʿšar (*Great Introduction* 6.14.2).[30] The Moon is, in the present chart, particularly strong (and therefore particularly capable of causing lecherousness) for a variety of reasons: she[31] is *almutaz*, the ruler of the entire conjunction chart;[32] she is located in her exaltation (♉); her position coincides almost exactly with the cusp of the ninth house (29° 8' ♉) which signifies religion and is thus particularly relevant to the eschatological figure of Antichrist; she is in an almost perfect trine aspect with the most important cardinal point (ASC, = 27° 34' ♍), and she entertains a similarly favorable, well-defined sextile aspect with Saturn and Jupiter who are in conjunction in the Moon's zodiacal house (♋). More precisely, the Moon casts an exact sextile aspect on 29° 22' ♋; the angular distance between that point and the conjunction (19° 42' ♋) is 9° 40'; this is less than one half (12°) of the canonical orb of the Moon (24°).[33]

---

28 The different canonical orbs of all seven planets are given by Abū Maʿšar, *Great Introduction* 7.3.2 (ed. & trans. Yamamoto—Burnett, *The Great Introduction*, vol. I, 738–739; Latin trans. ed. Lemay, *Abū Maʿšar*, vol. v, 281, lin. 333–339). For further details, cf. Heilen, *Konjunktionsprognostik*, 398–399.

29 This longitude is preferable to the textual variant 19° 52' ♋ (cf. Heilen, *Konjunktionsprognostik*, 145), but John's reasoning is mathematically correct with either reading.

30 Ed. & trans. Yamamoto and Burnett, *The Great Introduction*, vol. I, 654–655; Latin trans. ed. Lemay, *Abū Maʿšar*, vol. v, 253, lin. 1387. Note that Abū Maʿšar (loc. cit.) counts Leo, too, among the lewd signs, as did already two Greek sources. Cf. Wolfgang Hübner, *Die Eigenschaften der Tierkreiszeichen in der Antike. Ihre Darstellung und Verwendung unter besonderer Berücksichtigung des Manilius* (Wiesbaden: Steiner, 1982), 215.

31 I.e., the lunar planetary goddess (while the sun god is male).

32 On this term and its application by John of Lübeck cf. Heilen, *Konjunktionsprognostik*, 284–288.

33 See n. 28 above.

2.5   *When Antichrist Will Be Born (§§ 121–123)*

[121] *Ab hora superiorum coniunc-* [121] From the hour of the conjunction of
tionis ad dicti Lunaris prophetæ the superior (planets) to the appearance
apparitionem erunt anni duo, dies of the said lunar prophet it will be two
nonaginta quinque, horæ decem years, ninety-five days, (and) seventeen
et septem. [122] *Erit ergo tempus* hours. [122] Therefore, the time of his
suæ natiuitatis anno millesimo birth will be during the year 1506, on the
quingentesimo sexto currente die thirteenth day of September, seventeen
tredecima Septembris post meri- hours after noon [*i.e., on 14 Sept. 1506 at*
diem horis decem et septem. [123] *5 a.m.*].[34] [123] It will surely be then, as
Certe tunc nascetur dæmonis filius demonstrated by the stars, that the son of
astrorum persuasione, ... the daemon will be born, ...

John makes his prediction of the time-span between the conjunction itself
and the event signified by it without methodological explanation. As to be
expected, he is following Abū Maʿšar's *Book of religions and dynasties* (1.3.9)
which defines criteria for measuring either (a) the distance from the ascendant to the conjunction or—as is here the case—(b) from the conjunction to
the ascendant. What follows is a quotation of Yamamoto's and Burnett's English
translation of the Arabic original with some interspersed clarifications of my
own in square brackets and italics: 'As for how to know the time at which they
[*i.e., prophets*] appear, it is discovered from the ascendant of the conjunction
and the position of the conjunction indicating their coming out. If [*case a*] the
ascendant is one of the houses of the superior planets [*i.e.*, ♏, ♐, ♑, ♒, ♓, *or*
♈] or the exaltation of Jupiter and the house of the Moon [*i.e.*, ♋], and Saturn
is in a cardine by number or by equation, the prorogation is from the ascendant of the conjunction to the position of the conjunction, ⟨giving to⟩ each
sign one year. If [*case b*] the ascendant is not one of those we have described,
the prorogation is from ⟨the position of⟩ the conjunction to the ascendant of
the conjunction, ⟨giving to⟩ each sign one year, except if the sign [*of the conjunction*] is ⟨bi⟩corporeal [*i.e.*, ♊, ♍, ♐, *or* ♓]. For this indicates [...]',[35]

---

34   John counts the hours, in compliance with late medieval astronomical practice, from
      noon, not (as we do) from midnight.

35   Yamamoto and Burnett, *On Historical Astrology*, vol. I, 41. The Latin translation (vol. II, 25)
      reads thus: *Scientia quoque temporis, quo apparebunt* [scil. *prophete*], *accipitur ab ascen-
      dente coniunctionis et a loco coniunctionis, que significat apparitionem eorum. Et si fuerit
      ascendens aliqua domorum planetarum altiorum vel exaltatio Iovis et domus Lune et si fuerit
      Saturnus in angulo per numerum vel per equationem, erit directio ab ascendente coniunc-
      tionis in locum coniunctionis, ad unumquodque signum annum unum. Si vero non fuerit*

Since the ascendant of our chart is Virgo, case b applies; and since the sign of the conjunction is Cancer, the exception regarding bicorporeal signs does not apply. Hence, the application of Abū Maʿšar's rule runs as follows: the time-span in question (henceforth: *ts*) results from the zodiacal distance between the conjunction (19° 42′ ♋) and the ascendant (27° 34′ ♍), which amounts to 67° 52′. Now Abū Maʿšar wants one full sign to be equated with one full year. Hence, 67° 52′ are equivalent to two full years (60°) and a remainder of 7° 52′ (= 472′) whose relation to one full zodiacal sign (30° or 1800′) is the same as that of the time-span *ts* to one full year. Hence, $ts = {}^{472}/_{1800} \times 365 = 95{,}7111 = 95$ days, 17 hours, and 4 minutes. John's calculation complies with the authoritative instruction by Abū Maʿšar and is mathematically correct.

In the next step, we must add the time-span *ts* to the previously established exact date and time of the conjunction, namely 10 June 1504, 11:54:48 a.m.[36] This leads to 14 September 1506 at 4:58:48 a.m., as correctly stated by John of Lübeck who rounded the result to full hours and expressed it with the usual noon epoch of the previous day.

2.6 Why He Will Be Born in Babylon (§§ 124–125)[37]

Contrast with Jesus Christ: he was born in Bethlehem (Matthew 2:1 and Luke 2:4–11)[38]

[124] ... *et nascetur in partibus meridionalibus propter locum coniunctionis in angulo medij celi, in terra uersus orientem situata, Cancro subiecta, Luna ibi dominante,* [125] *et credo, quod erit in prouincia Eradie, in qua est terra Babiloniæ.*	[124] ... and he will be born in southern parts (of the world) because of the conjunction place in the cardinal place of the midheaven, in a land that lies to the east and is subjected to Cancer (the sign of the conjunction), where the Moon rules, [125] and I believe that it will be in the area of Iraq, in which lies the land of Babylonia.

---

ascendens unum eorum, que diximus, erit directio a coniunctione in ascendens coniunctio-nis, ad unumquodque signum annum unum, nisi (scil. *signum coniunctionis*, as the gloss mentioned by Yamamoto und Burnett in their apparatus correctly explains) *sit signum commune* (etc.). For bicorporeal signs, cf. Hübner, *Eigenschaften*, 74–75.

36   John expresses this as 9 June, 23h 54m 48s p.m. (§ 64); cf. n. 34 above.

37   The most important sources for this belief (esp. Hieronymus and Adso of Montier-en-Der) are quoted by Heilen, *Konjunktionsprognostik*, 408–409. Cf. Richard Kenneth Emmerson, *Antichrist in the Middle Ages. A Study of Medieval Apocalypticism, Art, and Literature* (Manchester: Manchester University Press, 1981), 80: 'Because of the numerous apocalyptic condemnations of Babylon and its symbolic representation of evil, Babylon is often chosen as Antichrist's birthplace.' With a view to text IV, one is especially reminded of the Biblical 'whore of Babylon' (Revelation 17–18).

38   Note that both toponyms begin with B- and comprise three syllables.

John is once more following Abū Maʿšar's *Book of religions and dynasties* 1.3.9 (cf. text V above). That paragraph continues saying about new prophets that 'their coming out is from cities belonging to the sign in which the conjunction occurs'.[39] John's reference to Iraq is probably based on an anonymous, spurious appendix to Abū Maʿšar's treatise; it reads: 'Cancer: the countries belonging to it are the land of Babylon, Ifriqiya, Libya, which is in the land of the Byzantine Empire, Francia, al-Arbaʿa(?), and wadis'.[40] Abū Maʿšar's authentic work on historical astrology contains the same information split in two halves.[41] One also finds the association of Cancer with *Eradia* in the Latin translation of Abraham Ibn Ezra's work on conjunction astrology.[42]

Before we move on, let us return to the previous paragraph's quotation from Abū Maʿšar's paragraph 1.3.9. The immediately following words there (they are still part of 1.3.9) read thus: 'their activities are in cities belonging to the signs quartile to the ascendant of the conjunction; the days of their periods in their rule are according to the small years of the lord of the sign dominating the city in which their activities appear',[43] It seems impossible that John did not take notice of these two sentences, and they both must have caused serious problems to his purpose.

The first sentence is about the signs quartile to the ascendant, and since our chart's ascendant is Virgo, the quartile signs are Gemini and Sagittarius. Hence, Antichrist's activities must be in cities ruled either by Gemini or by Sagittarius. In contrast to this, the medieval 'biography' of Antichrist takes it

39   Trans. Yamamoto and Burnett, *On Historical Astrology*, vol. I, 41; Latin trans., vol. II, 26: *Et erunt exitus eorum* [scil. *prophetarum*] *de civitate signi, in quo ceciderit coniunctio.*

40   *On Historical Astrology*, bk. 4, app. 1.6 (trans. Yamamoto and Burnett, *On Historical Astrology*, vol. I, 515); Latin. trans., vol. II, 142): *Cancer habet ex regionibus terram Babilonie et Africam et Luchiam, que est in terra Grecorum, et Franciam et Areniam.*

41   *On Historical Astrology*, 2.4.4 and 2.8.3 (trans. Yamamoto and Burnett, *On Historical Astrology*, vol. I, 67 and 123; Latin trans., vol. II, 46 and 80–81). These passages are quoted in full by Heilen, *Konjunktionsprognostik*, 407–408.

42   *Abrahe Auenare* [i.e. Abraham ibn Esra, 12th c. CE] *De planetarum coniunctionibus et annorum reuolutionibus, qui dicitur de mundo uel seculo,* in: *Abrahe Auenaris Iudei astrologi peritissimi in re iudiciali opera ab excellentissimo philosopho Petro de Abano post accuratam castigationem in Latinum traducta,* Venice: Peter Liechtenstein, 1507 [EDIT16 CNCE 35576], ff. LXXVI^r–LXXXV^r, here: f. LXXXIII^va–b: *Dicit Enoch primus quod Iupiter cum Cancro significat super Alaerat idest Eradie et iam rememoratus est Euemmassar quod signum Alaerat est in termino Iouis in signo Cancri qui est in 21 grad. signi.*

43   Trans. Yamamoto and Burnett, *On Historical Astrology*, vol. I, 41; Latin trans., vol. II, 26: *actus quoque eorum* [scil. *prophetarum*] *erunt in civitatibus signorum que sunt in quadrante ascendentis coniunctionis, eruntque dies spatii regni eorum secundum quantitatem minorum annorum domini signi civitatis in qua apparebunt actus eorum.*

for granted that he will take his seat in Jerusalem and terrorize the world from there.[44] Jerusalem belongs to Palestine, more precisely: to Judea, which is ruled by Aries according to Ptolemy's astrological geography[45] and also according to the aforementioned spurious appendix to Abū Maʿšar's *Book of religions and dynasties* which John followed for the association of Babylonia with Cancer.[46] We must, therefore, assume that John found Jerusalem to be ruled by Aries, and since Aries is neither Gemini nor Sagittarius, it is no surprise that John passes in silence over the city in which Antichrist will be active.

Abū Maʿšar's second sentence ('the days … appear') entails a bigger problem: it instructs the reader to calculate the time-span of the prophet's rule by converting the small years of the lord of the sign dominating the city in which their activities appear into days. Now the Christian tradition unanimously states that Antichrist will rule '42 months' (Revelation 11:2 and 13:5), that is '1260 days' (11:3); that is '3½ years' in the authoritative words of Adso of Montier-en-Der: *Haec autem tam terribilis et timenda tribulatio tribus annis manebit in toto mundo et dimidio.*[47] The astrological small years of the planets, however, vary between far smaller numbers, regardless of which planetary ruler of which geographical area we take (see table 8.2).

In the case of the Moon, which John mentions correctly in the same sentence as the planetary ruler of Cancer, this tenet would lead to only 25 days of Antichrist's rule. Not even the greatest numbers in tab. 2 would have provided any satisfactory match for John's purpose. Not surprisingly, then, he prefers to pass in silence over the fact that the Christian eschatology is in this respect incompatible with astrological doctrine (see also text XI below).

One may wonder, however: even if John's remark that Cancer is subject to the Moon was probably prompted by Abū Maʿšar's second sentence above ('the days … appear'), why did John make this remark at all, although it has no apparent function in text VI? Maybe he did so because he was either himself prone

---

44   Cf. Adso epist., ed. Sackur, *Sibyllinische Texte*, 107, = Verhelst, *Adso Dervensis*, 24.
45   Cf. Ptol. apotel. 2.3.31 and 2.4.2 as well as the map of Ptolemy's geography in Stephan Heilen, 'The Star of Bethlehem and Greco-Roman Astrology, Especially Astrological Geography', in *The Star of Bethlehem and the Magi. Interdisciplinary Perspectives from Experts on the Ancient Near East, the Greco-Roman World, and Modern Astronomy*, edited by Peter D. Barthel and George H. van Kooten (Leiden: Brill, 2015), 297–357, here: 324. The same article shows that there were other ancient systems of astrological geography which assigned Judea to signs other than Aries, but they do not seem to have influenced the Arabic tradition, in particular Abū Maʿšar.
46   Bk. 4 app. 1.6 (trans. Yamamoto and Burnett, *On Historical Astrology*, vol. I, 515; Latin. trans., vol. II, 141).
47   Adso epist., ed. Sackur, *Sibyllinische Texte*, 109, = Verhelst, *Adso Dervensis*, 25.

TABLE 8.2   The planetary years according to Abū Ma'šar, *Great Introduction* 7.8.3a–b

Planet	Greatest Years	Great Years	Middle Years	Small Years
Saturn	265	57	43½	30
Jupiter	427	79	45½	12
Mars	284	66	40½	15
Venus	1151	82	45	8
Mercury	480	76	48	20
Sun	1461	120	69½	19
Moon	520	108	66½	25

to see this or lure his readers into seeing this as further confirmation (without Abū Ma'šar's support) that the historical figure signified by the conjunction of 1504 would be a 'lunar prophet' according to the scheme tabularized above (tab. 1).

2.7   *Why He Will Be Eloquent (§ 126)*[48]
Parallel with Jesus Christ: see e.g. Mark 5:1–7:29 (the Sermon on the Mount), 12:15–17, or John 18:33–37

[126] *Hic pseudopropheta erit eloquens propter Mercurium, ...*	[126] This false prophet will be eloquent because of Mercury, ...

Eloquence is a typical influence of Mercury in genethlialogy, and Mercury is strong in the present chart, as John himself had explained earlier (§§ 98 and 113, see texts I and II above): he rules the two most important cardines (ASC and MC) and is himself located in the midheaven where the conjunction takes place. However, being placed in the immediate proximity of the Sun, Mercury is also 'burned',[49] an important weakening factor[50] that John prefers to pass over in silence on the present occasion.

---

48   Cf. Revelation 13:11–14.

49   Cf. §113 in text II above as well as Hieronymus Vitali, *Lexicon Mathematicum Astronomicum Geometricum* [...], Paris: Louis Billaine, 1668 (repr. edited by Giuseppe Bezza, with a preface by Ornella Pompeo Faracovi, La Spezia: Agorà Edizioni, 2003), 117–118 s.v. *combustus*.

50   Cf. e.g. Alcab. *Intr.* 3.28 and Vitali, *Lexicon*, 118: *planeta combustus semper debilis est.*

2.8   *Why He Will Be Powerful (§ 126)*
Contrast with Jesus Christ: his kingdom is not of this world (John 18:36)

[126] ... *potens et magnus propter Solem cum cæteris quinque planetis in medio cæli in domo regia.*	[126] ... powerful and important because of the Sun (located) in the midheaven in the royal house with the other five planets.

The Sun is by far the brightest celestial body and therefore, since Greco-Roman antiquity, 'cosmocrator', i.e., 'ruler of the cosmos', and astrologically associated with human beings wielding highest power, such as Roman emperors.[51] The five planets reinforce the influence of the Sun without, however, being aligned in the present chart as the Sun's 'spear-bearers'.[52] It is standard practice in ancient and medieval astrology to speak of the tenth house as the 'royal house' (cf. e.g. n. 13 above).

2.9   *Why He Will Be Rich (§§ 127–128)*
Contrast with Jesus Christ: he appears to own nothing but the clothes he is wearing.

[127] *Omnes thesauri absconditi in sua erunt potestate propter Iouem dominum quartæ in medio cæli coniunctum Saturno significanti thesauros et res sub terra absconditas.* [128] *Aurum et argentum in mari perditum sui patres sibi apportabunt.*	[127] All hidden treasures will be in his power because Jupiter, the lord of the fourth house, is in the midheaven in conjunction with Saturn who signifies treasures and things hidden under the earth's surface. [128] Gold and silver lost on the sea will be brought to him by his fathers.

Antichrist's 'fathers' are daemons called *succubi* and *incubi* who had, as described in §§ 104–112, engendered Antichrist in the course of a 'génération extraordinaire'.[53] While Antichrist's material wealth is in contrast with the

---

51   Cf. Heilen, *Hadriani genitura*, 734–736.

52   On this astrological sociomorphic metaphor see Susanne Denningmann, *Die astrologische Lehre der Doryphorie. Eine soziomorphe Metapher in der antiken Planetenastrologie* (Munich: Saur, 2005), and Stephan Heilen, 'Greek and Roman Astrology', in *The Oxford Handbook of Ancient Astronomy*, ed. John Steele (Oxford: Oxford University Press, forthcoming), section v (end).

53   See, in general, Maaike van der Lugt, *Le ver, le démon et la vierge. Les théories médiévales de la génération extraordinaire. Une étude sur les rapports entre théologie, philosophie*

poverty of Jesus, the daemons who bring gold and silver to Antichrist are here predicted as a perversion of the biblical tale of the magi (Matthew 2:1–11).

To explain Antichrist's treasures, John draws on common astrological symbols. As to the fourth house, cf. e.g. Abū Maʿšar who says (*Great Introduction* 6.26.8): 'The fourth place is called that of fathers and it indicates the conditions of fathers, roots, race, lands, villages, towns, buildings, and waters, everything hidden and secret, and what is under the earth, and treasures, [...]',[54] And al-Qabīṣī's introduction to astrology, whose Latin translation was a mandatory reading in various late medieval universities,[55] reads thus (*Introductorius* 1.60): 'The fourth is the place of fathers, landed properties, outcomes, treasures, and every matter which is covered over and hidden'.[56]

Treasures are also signified by Saturn, but most of the ancient Greek evidence is unlikely to have been available to John of Lübeck. See, however, Ptol. apotel. 3.14.11 in the Latin translation by William of Moerbeke which says that Saturn produces human souls amassing treasures (*thesaurizatiuas*).[57]

2.10 Why He Will Perpetrate His Deeds Quickly (§ 129)

Parallel with Jesus Christ: he started preaching at about age 30 (Luke 3:23) and died about three years later.

---

naturelle et médecine (Paris: Les belles lettres, 2004), and more specifically—i.e., with regard to the scandalous demonic impregnation of Antichrist's mother and its origins in medieval natural philosophy (while it is alien to Perso-Arabic conjunction astrology)— Heilen, *Konjunktionsprognostik*, 95–121.

54 Trans. Yamamoto and Burnett, *The Great Introduction*, vol. I, 683; Latin trans. (ed. Lemay, *Abū Maʿšar*, vol. V, 259, lin. 1567–1570): *Quarta dicitur domus* PATRUM, *et hec significat esse patrum et progeniei et ⟨carceres⟩, terras quoque ac rura, civitates et edificia atque aquas, et omnem rem ⟨tectam⟩ atque occultam, vel quicquid fuerit sub terra, et thesauros [...].*

55 See Dag Nikolaus Hasse, *Success and Suppression. Arabic Sciences and Philosophy in the Renaissance* (Cambridge/Mass.: Harvard University Press, 2016), 329. No less than 211 Latin manuscripts of this introduction are extant, more than of any other Latin astrological manual; see David Juste, 'The Impact of Arabic Sources on European Astrology: Some Facts and Numbers', in: *The Impact of Arabic Sciences in Europe and Asia*, edited by Agostino Paravicini Bagliani (Florence: SISMEL. Edizioni del Galluzzo, 2016), 173–194, here: 177, tab. 1, no. 1.

56 Trans. (from the Arabic original) Burnett, Yamamoto, and Yano, *Al-Qabīṣī*, 51; Latin trans., 257: *Quarta, domus patrum et hereditatum et finis rerum et thesaurorum et omnium absconditorum atque occultorum.*

57 Gudrun Vuillemin-Diem and Carlos Steel, with the assistance of Pieter De Leemans, eds., *Ptolemy's Tetrabiblos in the Translation of William of Moerbeke. Claudii Ptolemaei Liber Iudicialium* (Leuven: Leuven University Press, 2015), 267. See further the ancient Greek attestations collected by Heilen, *Hadriani genitura*, 1082.

[129] *Sua facta cito monstra-*
bit propter Lunam almutaz
coniunctionis, quæ est uelocis
cursus pre ceteris planetis.

[129] He will show his deeds quickly because
of the Moon, the ruling planet of the conjunction, whose course is faster than that of
the other planets.

While the swift lunar motion is a well-known astronomical fact, John's astrological source is far less obvious: he is probably drawing on a hitherto unedited
work on historical astrology that was highly esteemed by no less a critic than
Regiomontanus but has fallen into oblivion ever since, namely Antonio da
Montolmo's (late fourteenth century) treatise on historical astrology (presumably titled *De revolutionibus annorum mundi*), ch. 2.1, where Antonio writes
regarding the conjunction that will bring about the eschatological lunar
prophet (i.e., Antichrist): 'From it a faith will result that will supplant every
other faith [...] and will corrupt every religion because the Moon is the closest planet (to earth), strongly influencing, and faster than the other planets,
and this faith will not last long because the Moon moves quickly and changes
(constantly) with regard to its light and completes its course quickly',[58]

2.11   When Will Antichrist—and With Him the Church and the Entire World—End? (§135)

[135] *Heu Petri nauicula tunc*
fluctuabit multorumque pompa
misere cessabit anno millesimo
quingentesimo quadragesimo.

[135] Woe, the boat of (St.) Peter will be
tossed about on the waves and will perish
miserably through the vain arrogance of
many in the year 1540.

It has been shown above, in the commentary to text VI, that Abū Maʿšar's relevant tenet in the *Book of religions and dynasties* 1.3.9 is not suitable to explain
the time-span of Antichrist's reign astrologically. Therefore John makes this
final calculation basing it exclusively on the Christian tradition. The year 1540[59]
results from the addition of 30 and 3½ years to Antichrist's birthdate as pre-

---

58   *Vnde resultabit fides, que tollet omnem aliam fidem [...] et corrumpet omnem legem, quia*
      Luna est planeta propinquior, fortiter influens, et uelocior quam sint alij planete, et hec fides
      non diu durabit, quia Luna cito mouetur et mutatur lumine et suum cito perficit cursum. My
      quotation is from MS Nürnberg, Stadtbibliothek, Cent. V 68, f. 11ᵛ. On Antonio's work cf.
      Heilen, *Konjunktionsprognostik*, 302–308.
59   This figure is a necessary emendation of various corruptions in the incunabulum and in
      the manuscripts. For details, see Heilen, *Konjunktionsprognostik*, 252 with n. 957, and 422–
      424.

dicted in text V above (namely 14 September 1506): 30 years for the time from Antichrist's birth until he would first appear in public, seize power, and start terrorizing the world, in analogy with the life of Jesus who first appeared in public and started preaching at about age 30 (Luke 3:23); and then 3½ years until his distruction and the final Judgement, as predicted by the *Apocalypse* and later authorities such as Adso of Montier-en-Der (for details, see above on text VI); this last time-span is once more about the same as that of Jesus' public activity until his crucifixion.

3   Conclusions

John of Lübeck manages to provide a whole series of astrologically plausible, partly striking explanations of given 'biographical' data regarding the life of Antichrist. His explanations are firmly rooted in the tradition of historical astrology, especially in the writings of Abū Maʿšar. It is the same source that he follows in his determination of the only still unknown detail, namely the date of Antichrist's birth (text V). In view of the paramount importance of this detail, one may wonder why John did not explain his mathematically correct application of Abū Maʿšar's respective tenet, while he does provide explanations of many other, less important details. It deserves attention, however, that John predicts one other date, namely that of Antichrist's distruction and the end of the world (text XI), and again the underlying calculation is left unexplained. In this second case John could safely assume his readers' knowledge of Antichrist's alleged life-span which simply had to be added to his birthdate predicted earlier (text V). Did John, in the first case, analogously count on expert readers' familiarity with Abū Maʿšar's *Book of religions and dynasties*, or at least with its most prominent sections, including § 1.3.9 where the relevant instruction is found? If so, did he not provide a technical explanation in the hope that such readers would find his given result confirmed by their own calculations and, being impressed with his competence and accuracy, not bother critically to examine other details of seemingly minor importance, including those he had actually doctored? Or did he not explain the calculation of Antichrist's birthday because he feared its mathematical difficulty might deter non-experts from reading on? Or because the explanation would simply have cost too much space? We do not know.

What we can, instead, assert is that when this specific astrologer passes in silence over an explanation or a discussion we might have expected, it is impossible to know *a priori* whether our own analysis will bring to light an impeccable astrological procedure or a problem the author preferred to cover up. More-

over, we can assert that he does not hesitate to employ, in his discussion of a
conjunction horoscope, which pertains to historical astrology, tenets derived
from genethlialogy, such as the Lot of the Mother and the tenth place signifying the native's mother (text 1). He probably found this legitimous because
in his interpretation the conjunction signified a birth, but critical minds may
rightly object that Antichrist's birth will, according to John's prediction, take
place more than a full year after the conjunction and have its own, profoundly
different horoscope.

With regard to future research opportunities, the present case study shows
that critical examinations of historical horoscope interpretations require reliable editions of the respective authoritative manuals. Although much progress
has been made, in this respect, in recent decades (suffice it gratefully to admit
that the present case study would have been impossible without the various
recent editions of Abū Maʿšar's works),[60] other important works still lack critical editions, such as Antonio da Montolmo's much acclaimed *De reuolutionibus
annorum mundi* which John of Lübeck quotes three times (§§ 31, 62, and 84),
i.e., as often as he quotes Abū Maʿšar (§§ 61, 85, 88). It is to be hoped that the
ASTRA conference will inspire further editorial and analytical work on such
texts.

Bibliography

Bridges, John Henry, ed. *The 'Opus maius' of Roger Bacon*, vol. 1. Oxford: Clarendon Press,
1897.

Burnett, Charles, Keiji Yamamoto, and Michio Yano, eds. *Al-Qabīṣī (Alcabitius): The
Introduction to Astrology. Editions of the Arabic and Latin texts and an English translation.* London: The Warburg Institute, 2004.

Denningmann, Susanne. *Die astrologische Lehre der Doryphorie. Eine soziomorphe
Metapher in der antiken Planetenastrologie.* Munich: Saur, 2005.

Emmerson, Richard Kenneth. *Antichrist in the Middle Ages. A Study of Medieval Apocalypticism, Art, and Literature.* Manchester: Manchester University Press, 1981.

Nikolaus Hasse, Dag. *Success and Suppression. Arabic Sciences and Philosophy in the
Renaissance.* Cambridge/Mass.: Harvard University Press, 2016.

Heilen, Stephan, Hadriani genitura. *Die astrologischen Fragmente des Antigonos von
Nikaia*, 2 vols. Berlin: De Gruyter, 2015 (repr. 2017).

---

60   Lemay, *Abū Maʿšar*; Yamamoto and Burnett, *On Historical Astrology*; and Yamamoto and
Burnett, *The Great Introduction.*

Heilen, Stephan. 'The Star of Bethlehem and Greco-Roman Astrology, Especially Astrological Geography'. In *The Star of Bethlehem and the Magi. Interdisciplinary Perspectives from Experts on the Ancient Near East, the Greco-Roman World, and Modern Astronomy*, edited by Peter D. Barthel and George H. van Kooten, 297–357. Leiden: Brill, 2015.

Heilen, Stephan. *Konjunktionsprognostik in der Frühen Neuzeit, Band 1: Die Antichrist-Prognose des Johannes von Lübeck (1474) zur Saturn-Jupiter-Konjunktion von 1504 und ihre frühneuzeitliche Rezeption*. Baden-Baden: Koerner, 2020.

Heilen, Stephan. 'Doctoring the Data in John of Lübeck's Astrological Prediction of the Birth of Antichrist', *Cahiers de Recherches Médiévales et Humanistes* 47 (2024), 475–495.

Heilen, Stephan. 'Greek and Roman Astrology'. In *The Oxford Handbook of Ancient Astronomy*, edited by John Steele. Oxford: Oxford University Press (forthcoming).

Hübner, Wolfgang. *Die Eigenschaften der Tierkreiszeichen in der Antike. Ihre Darstellung und Verwendung unter besonderer Berücksichtigung des Manilius*. Wiesbaden: Steiner, 1982.

Juste, David. 'The Impact of Arabic Sources on European Astrology: Some Facts and Numbers'. In *The Impact of Arabic Sciences in Europe and Asia*, edited by Agostino Paravicini Bagliani. Florence: SISMEL. Edizioni del Galluzzo, 2016.

Klopsch, Paul, ed. *Pseudo-Ovidius De Vetula. Untersuchungen und Text*. Leiden: Brill, 1967.

Lemay, Richard, ed. *Abū Ma'šar al-Balḫī [Albumasar]. Liber introductorii maioris ad scientiam judiciorum astrorum. Édition critique*. 9 vols. Naples: Istituto Universitario Orientale, 1995–1996.

Sackur, Ernst. *Sibyllinische Texte und Forschungen. Pseudomethodius, Adso und die Tiburtinische Sibylle*. Halle: Niemeyer, 1898 (repr. Turin: Bottega d'Erasmo, 1976).

van der Lugt, Maaike. *Le ver, le démon et la vierge. Les théories médiévales de la génération extraordinaire. Une étude sur les rapports entre théologie, philosophie naturelle et médecine*. Paris: Les belles lettres, 2004.

Verhelst, Daniel, ed. *Adso Dervensis, De ortu et tempore Antichristi necnon et tractatus qui ab eo dependunt*. Turnhout: Brepols, 1976.

Vitali, Hieronymus. *Lexicon Mathematicum Astronomicum Geometricum [...]*. Paris: Louis Billaine, 1668 (repr. edited by Giuseppe Bezza, with a preface by Ornella Pompeo Faracovi, La Spezia: Agorà Edizioni, 2003).

Vuillemin-Diem, Gudrun, and Carlos Steel, with the assistance of Pieter De Leemans, eds. *Ptolemy's Tetrabiblos in the Translation of William of Moerbeke. Claudii Ptolemaei Liber Iudicialium*. Leuven: Leuven University Press, 2015.

Yamamoto, Keiji, and Charles Burnett, eds. *Abū Ma'šar, On Historical Astrology. The Book of Religions and Dynasties (On the Great Conjunctions), Edited and Translated*. 2 vols. Leiden: Brill, 2000.

Yamamoto, Keiji, and Charles Burnett, eds. *Abū Maʿšar, The Great Introduction to Astrology, Edited and Translated, with an Edition of the Greek Version by David Pingree.* 2 vols. Leiden: Brill, 2019.

CHAPTER 9

Marsilio Ficino's Early Astrological Practices (ca. 1469–1489): A Preliminary Survey

H Darrel Rutkin

Abstract

The brief of this chapter is straightforward: to gather together, describe and analyze an instructive and suggestive but by no means comprehensive selection of the reasonably extensive evidence for Marsilio Ficino's astrological practices in his earlier period (ca. 1469–1489) that—perhaps surprisingly—has never been fully marshalled. This includes the valuable evidence in his pre-*De vita* (1489) works for nativities, revolutions and elections, three of the four canonical types of practical astrology. There are apparently no interrogations—the fourth and most controversial type of astrological practice—nor do we have any manuscript horoscopes of any sort in his own hand, nor any notes or calculations related thereto. Although these surely may exist, they have not yet been identified, despite Ficino's hand being quite well known, and there having been a great deal of scholarship in the last century on Ficino's manuscript Nachlaß, as well as on a broad range of Latin astrological manuscripts.

Regardless, there are numerous traces of practical astrology in Ficino's extensive writings—mostly published—which have never been properly gathered together and treated as such. Focusing almost exclusively on Ficino's extensive correspondence, this is the main contribution I intend to make in this chapter, although it will certainly not be exhaustive, and it will only treat the earlier part of Ficino's engagement with astrology (ca. 1469–1489), and even at that it will not be comprehensive. Further evidence may then be co-ordinated with this partial but I hope useful treatment in an eventually comprehensive study that should be closely co-ordinated with the full range of Ficino's writings and within the context of his biography and career, for which this is a preliminary contribution.

Keywords

Marsilio Ficino – astrological practices – early modern astrology – nativities – revolutions – elections

1   Introduction

Marsilio Ficino (1433–1499) was born on Oct. 19, 1433 with a famously Saturnine nativity or birth horoscope, in which the Sun was in Scorpio, the Moon
in Capricorn and Aquarius rising, with Saturn, which rules both Aquarius and
Capricorn, in Aquarius in Ficino's first house, as he himself tells us in at least
three letters. I will discuss these letters and others below.[1] Furthermore, and as
a strikingly potent image—and perhaps as a portent as well—throughout all
of that very October, a comet was seen over Florence and elsewhere that was
systematically observed by Paolo dal Pozzo Toscanelli (1397–1482), the famous
Florentine astronomer, astrologer, mathematician and physician, who traced
the path of this comet in a manuscript that still exists, and has been studied
by Jane L. Jervis.[2] This comet—together with his particularly Saturnine natal
configuration—thus set the celestial stage for the birth of an extraordinary and
influential thinker and author, some of whose early astrological practices and
related writings I will explore in this essay.

The brief of this chapter is straightforward: to gather together, describe and
analyze an instructive and suggestive but by no means comprehensive selection of the reasonably extensive evidence for Ficino's astrological practices in
his earlier period (ca. 1469–1489)[3] that—perhaps surprisingly—has never been

---

1   I use existing English translations where I can, but I also modify them where necessary. Since
    this essay is focused almost entirely on discussions in Ficino's correspondence, I use the
    valuable translations in *The Letters of Marsilio Ficino*, tr. by [the unnamed] members of the
    Language Department of the School of Economic Science, London, in 11 volumes, London:
    Shepheard-Walwyn, 1975-<2020> (hereafter *SES*). Because they chose to skip Book 11 with its
    philosophical treatises, the numeration for the *SES* volumes in relation to the Books of Ficino's
    Epistolae are somewhat confusing, with *SES* vol. 1 = Ficino Book 1, but then *SES* vol. 2 = Book 111,
    with the rest of Ficino's Books being vol. n + 1. For my purposes here, I will refer to the letters
    as such: *SES* 2 [111].22 (p. 30) = *SES* vol. 2 [*Epistolae*, Book 111]. Letter 22 (page 30). I apologize
    in advance for the cumbersome nature of such a reference, which, I hope, is at least function-
    ally if not perfectly clear. This essay, focused on Ficino's correspondence, is complementary to
    and only minimally overlaps with Chap. 4 of my soon-to-be-forthcoming volume 11 on astrol-
    ogy and magic in the Renaissance (proper reference below), which treats most of the other
    texts regarding Ficino's early views on astrology.
2   Jane L. Jervis, *Cometary Theory in Fifteenth-Century Europe*, (Wroclaw: Ossolineum, 1985), 43–
    85, esp. 56–58. In the rich introduction to his overall introduction to Ficino's correspondence,
    Sebastiano Gentile points to this comet appearing at the time of Ficino's birth, which brought
    it to my attention; Marsilio Ficino, *Lettere* 1, Epistolarum familiarum liber 1, ed. S. Gentile (Flo-
    rence: Olschki, 1990), xxxvii–viii. I do not know if Ficino himself ever mentioned it; I presume
    that he knew about it, at least from Paolo Toscanelli, but I do not have any evidence for this.
3   I call this Ficino's 'early period' for simplicity's sake. Our first evidence for Ficino's knowledge
    and discussion of astrology comes from the first iteration of his *De amore* (1469); the second

fully marshalled. This includes the valuable evidence in his pre-*De vita* (1489) works for nativities, revolutions and elections, three of the four canonical types of practical astrology.[4] There are apparently no interrogations—the fourth and most controversial type of astrological practice—nor do we have any manuscript horoscopes of any sort in his own hand, nor any notes or calculations related thereto. Although these surely may exist, they have not yet been identified, despite Ficino's hand being quite well known, and there having been a great deal of scholarship in the last century on Ficino's manuscript Nachlaß, as well as on a broad range of Latin astrological manuscripts.[5]

---

piece of evidence comes from 1474 with *De amore*'s second iteration with seven astrological additions, and his letter to Marescalchi mentioned just below. That is all I know of. Ficino was born in 1433; he studied at the University of Florence from 1451–1462, and our first example of his philosophical writing, which naturally was deeply scholastic, comes from 1454. Since his first mention of astrology seems to come from 1469, fully fifteen years after his first philosophical writing, perhaps I should better call this his 'middle period', which could be said to go from 1469–1489, ending with the publication of *De vita* in December 1489. Then the early period of his writings would be from 1454 to 1469, when he was 21 to 36 years of age. 1469–1489 is still the earliest period of his astrological writings, which is how I will use 'early' here. I sketch out Ficino's early life and education in Chap. 4 of my vol. II, as well as the astrological dimension of his *De amore* in both its first and second iterations.

4 For these astrological practices, see Charles S.F. Burnett, 'Astrology', in *Medieval Latin: An Introduction and Bibliographical Guide*, ed. F.A.C. Mantello and A.G. Rigg (Washington, D.C.: Catholic University of America Press, 1996), 369–382, and the excursus to my volume I, *Sapientia Astrologica: Astrology, Magic and Natural Knowledge, ca. 1250–1800* (Cham, SW: Springer), 3 vols. Volume I, 'Medieval Structures (1250–1500): Conceptual, Institutional, Socio-Political, Theologico-Religious and Cultural', 2019. Volume II will be entitled 'Renaissance Structures (1450–1500): Continuities and Transformations.'

5 I do not know of any astrological notes, calculations or horoscopes in Ficino's vast manuscript Nachlaß. None are mentioned by Paul Oskar Kristeller in his foundational *Supplementum Ficinianum*, 2 vols (Florence: Olschki, 1937) [hereafter *SF*], nor in David Juste's catalogues of Latin astrological manuscripts, of which two volumes have appeared so far: *Catalogus Codicum Astrologorum Latinorum* I: *Les manuscrits astrologiques latins conservés à la Bayerische Staatsbibliothek de Munich*, ed. David Juste, Documents, Études et Répertoires Publiés par l'Institut de Recherche et d'Histoire des Textes 81 (Paris: CNRS Éditions, 2011); volume II is for the Bibliothèque National de France in Paris (84, 2015); nor have any been mentioned to me by Christopher Celenza, Denis J.-J. Robichaud or Daniele Conti, who all know Ficino's manuscripts far better than I do. In particular, we do not seem to possess his potentially annotated copy of Regiomontanus's self-published *Ephemerides* for 1475–1506 (Nuremberg, 1474 [ISTC: ir00104500]), a book published precisely when Ficino's astrological writings started to expand, and which could have been—and, I believe, most likely was—profoundly useful to him for easily, quickly and accurately tracking planetary motions and aspects, and eclipses of the luminaries, for what turned out to be the rest of his life. I use the electronic facsimile from the Bayerische Staatsbibliothek, Munich. I should note here also, that, based on the evidence presented in this essay, Richard Kremer informs me that he does not believe that Ficino used Regiomontanus's *Ephemerides*. Otherwise, he contends, Ficino would have prob-

Regardless, there are numerous traces of practical astrology in Ficino's extensive writings—mostly published—which have never been properly gathered together and treated as such.[6] Focusing almost exclusively on Ficino's extensive correspondence, this is the main contribution I intend to make in this chapter, although it will certainly not be exhaustive, and it will only treat the earlier part of Ficino's engagement with astrology (ca. 1469–1489), and even at that it will not be comprehensive.[7] Further evidence may then be co-ordinated with this partial but I hope useful treatment in an eventually comprehensive

---

ably been more numerically oriented in his astrological practices than he actually is, which is absolutely minimal. For the period before 1475, however, Ficino would probably have used the Parisian Alfonsine Tables, including for calculating the astrological circumstances of his own birth in 1433. It is unclear if Ficino made his own calculations of planetary locations, or whether he had someone more skilled than he was do so. At any rate, it is impossible to tell which tables he might have used, in part because he never lists the degrees of the zodiacal signs in which the planets are located in any of the descriptions of the horoscopes that we have for him, whether of his own nativity, or for someone else's, or for an event, as we will see. As Richard Kremer also informed me, tables with formats like Regiomontanus's *Ephemerides*, or the almanac for 1468–1480 compiled by Simon Belle, as published and described in Helena Avelar's important study, were very rare indeed, due to the time-intensive nature of the calculations necessary to compile them, on the one hand, and then again for copying them, on the other; see e.g. Helena Avelar de Carvalho, *An Astrologer at Work in Late Medieval France: The Notebooks of S. Belle* (Leiden: Brill, 2021). Printing here proved to be a game-changer, although printing too, needless to say, is also not perfect. With specific reference to Regiomontanus's *Ephemerides*, see Richard L. Kremer, 'Controlling Errors in the First Printed Book of Astronomical Tables: Regiomontanus's *Ephemerides* (Nuremberg, 1474)', in *Printing and Misprinting: A Companion to Mistakes and In-House Corrections in Renaissance Europe (1450–1650)*, ed. G. della Rocca de Candal, A. Grafton and P. Sachet (Oxford: Oxford University Press, 2023), 295–324. Regarding Ficino's hand, there are many examples in the many plates included in the invaluable *Marsilio Ficino e il ritorno di Platone: Manoscritti stampe e documenti*, ed. S. Gentile, S. Niccoli and P. Viti (Florence: Le Lettere, 1984) (hereafter, Gentile, *Catologo*).

6   There is no such essay mentioned in David Juste's virtually comprehensive bibliography on the history of astrology on the Ptolemaeus Arabus et Latinus website, https://ptolemaeus .badw.de/astrobibl/start (last checked 8 Feb 2024). The two compilations that I know of (both partial), are Ornella Pompeo Faracovi's translation into Italian, *Marsilio Ficino, Scritti sull'astrologia* (Milan: BUR, 1999), and Angela Voss's collection of texts regarding astrology in her volume, *Marsilio Ficino* (Berkeley: North Atlantic, 2006); both have extensive introductions. The great contribution of Faracovi's *Scritti* is to present an integral annotated translation into Italian of Ficino's unpublished 1477 *Disputatio contra iudicium astrologorum* (49–174), about which she also devotes most of her valuable introduction. Unfortunately, she does not also offer an integral Latin text. This and an annotated English translation are a desideratum. I will discuss the *Disputatio* in greater detail in Chap. 4 of my vol. II.

7   I focus primarily on the later period in my volume II, and especially on the *De vita* (1489).

study that should be closely co-ordinated with the full range of Ficino's writings and within the context of his biography and career, for which this is a preliminary contribution.[8]

I also believe that Ficino himself embodied and effected the transition from medieval to Renaissance in the realms of astrology and talismanic or image magic in the *De vita* of 1489, but I do not argue for this here.[9] In fact, as we will see, the lion's share of Ficino's early astrological practices are perfectly traditional—i.e. medieval—with only astrology's cosmological, metaphysical and theological foundations having ultimately been transformed in a Renaissance direction. Nevertheless, Ficino seems to have also offered a new astrologico-religious practice in his justly famous *De vita*, Book III—*De vita coelitus comparanda*—which I have come to call a theurgical astrology.[10] I argue for this Renaissance transformation much more fully in Part 2 of my volume II, to which this chapter is complementary.

In this chapter, I will present and analyse most of the evidence that we have for the range of astrological practices in Ficino's early writings, the lion's share of which come from his correspondence. I will focus here on the four canonical types of astrological practice: [1] nativities or birth horoscopes; [2] revolutions or general astrology; [3] elections, the choosing of astrologically propitious times, and [4] interrogations, which respond to a broad range of questions by constructing a horoscope for the time the question was asked. Evidence for interrogations seems to be wholly lacking within Ficino's writings, unlike for the other three, which were oriented towards both medical and other ends.

By exploring this evidence, we can begin to build up a more accurate picture of Ficino's early relationship to astrology by focusing on his various prac-

---

8   This essay is complementary to chapter 4 of my volume II, which also treats Ficino's early writings on astrology ca. 1469–1489, but primarily in his more literary works, including the unpublished *Disputatio* (1477). There is, consequently, little overlap with the material treated here.

9   There is also a vast historiography on Ficino and magic that I will avoid here, but will treat in my volume II, since I believe that it is vitally important to treat astrology and magic together in an author's thought to both understand it accurately and to provide the proper basis for comparisons, as I also strove to do in my volume I.

10   See my 'Dancing with the Stars: A Preliminary Exploration as to Whether the Astrology in Ficino's *De vita* is Theurgical', in *Marsilio Ficino's Cosmology: Sources and Reception*, ed. H Darrel Rutkin and Denis J.-J. Robichaud, *Bruniana & Campanelliana* 26 (2020/2): 403–419. I would also like to note that there is now a very recent posthumous publication by Faracovi of her translation with annotations of *De vita*, Book III; Marsilio Ficino, *Come attingere vita dal cielo*, introduzione, traduzione e note by Ornella Pompeo Faracovi (Sarzana: Agorà & Co., 2024).

tices, on the one hand, and by removing by essentially ignoring several layers of outdated historiographical overlays, accretions and/or incrustations, on the other.[11] Let us begin simply by asking the relevant questions: What evidence do we have for Marsilio Ficino's practice of astrology ca. 1469–1489, and how does this reflect his understanding thereof? How does it relate to his broader world view(s)? What are his views in the *Disputatio* of 1477? What are those in *De vita* of 1489? What are those in his commentary on Plotinus (1492), especially on *Enneads* II.3 and III.1? And what are those in his *De sole et lumine* (1493)? I will mainly focus on the first two questions here.

Furthermore, since we now understand the history of astrology better as well, we can also better assess Ficino's relationship thereto by asking, for example, if he is wholly a traditional (i.e. medieval), or also an innovative practitioner and/or theoretician? In particular, regarding the self-analysis revealed in discussing his own nativity, Ficino's few scattered references to it, and especially to its Saturnine nature, are positively paltry in comparison with Henry Bate's richly detailed and insightful analysis of his own nativity, ca. 1280/81, that we can now compare in detail.[12] As ever, it is more fruitful to ask foundational questions and attempt to answer them on the basis of the actual evidence we possess, than to simply assume their answers beforehand—or, even worse, to rely on outdated and partial and/or ideologically overburdened scholarship to answer them without engaging the primary sources directly, to which I will now turn.

2   Nativities

2.1   *Ficino's Own Nativity*

A study of practical astrology in Marsilio Ficino's early astrological writings should reasonably begin with his analysis of his own nativity or birth horo-

---

11   I explore this mainly in chapter 4 of my volume II, including on questions of Ficino's so-called vacillations regarding his views on astrology over the course of his career. I will also discuss the influential older work of (e.g.) Ernst Cassirer and Eugenio Garin.

12   See *The Astrological Autobiography of a Medieval Philosopher: Henry Bate's* Nativitas *(1280–1281)*, ed. Carlos Steel, Steven vanden Broecke, David Juste and Shlomo Sela (Leuven: Leuven University Press, 2018). See also David Juste, 'Reading Birth Horoscopes in the Middle Ages: Latin Judgements on Nativities, 1100–1450', in *Le Moyen Âge et les sciences*, ed. D. Jacquart et A. Paravicini Bagliani (Florence: SISMEL–Galluzzo, 2021), 549–593, who presents all of the evidence we have for the practice of nativities in the Middle Ages. Avelar also valuably treats Belle's practice of nativities in his extant manuscripts.

scope. The limited details derived from Ficino's few discussions of his own nativity can help to inform us about both his own knowledge about and practice of astrology, and also, at least to some extent, about his own broader views thereon, as we can see primarily in his letter to Johannes Pannonius (1484/85), discussed below.[13] This is also one of the great historiographic cruxes concerning Ficino's astrology, namely, his own inner, self-directed, reflective and deeply psychological views about astrology as related to his own profoundly Saturnine nativity, which is discussed insightfully by Melissa M. Bullard, and always includes discussions of his own melancholic nature.[14] In fact, Kaske and Clark begin their valuable section on Ficino's nativity (19–21) thus (19): 'Ficino had a very bad horoscope'.[15]

Ruth Clydesdale (2011) offers the most recent treatment of Ficino's nativity (123–126) and of his use of astrology in the correspondence, but it seems to be more the work of an astrologer with psychological and historical interests than of a scholar per se.[16] It is useful, to be sure, but very general, and oddly includes the printout of a horoscope in a modern circular format that also shows the modern outer planets—Uranus, Neptune and Pluto—that Ficino could only have known as mythological figures, not as actual planets.[17] Nonetheless, Clydesdale points to some significant evidence. Bullard's 'Inward Zodiac' from 1990, although twenty years older, is much more valuable, especially because her knowledge of Ficino and his historical circumstances is profound. Thus, her argument to read Ficino's interest in and views about astrology in a developmental manner within his own personal and historical context is insightful and should be further developed.

---

13   I discuss it very briefly here, but will treat it and especially its broader philosophical context more fully in my vol. II.

14   Bullard's discussion of Ficino's psychological turn is explicitly informed by James Hillman and Thomas Moore's more overtly psychological analyses; 'The Inward Zodiac: A Development in Ficino's Thoughts on Astrology', *Renaissance Quarterly* 43 (1990): 687–708. For a more psychological and less historical approach, see Thomas Moore, *The Planets Within: The Astrological Psychology of Marsilio Ficino*, 2nd revised edition (Great Barrington, MA: Lindisfarne Books, 1989).

15   Marsilio Ficino, *Three Books on Life*, ed. Carol V. Kaske and John R. Clark (Tempe, AZ: MRTS, 1989).

16   Ruth Clydesdale, '"Jupiter Tames Saturn": Astrology in Ficino's *Epistolae*', in Laus Platonici Philosophi: *Marsilio Ficino and his Influence* (Leiden: Brill, 2011), 117–131.

17   Voss (2006), page 27, does so too, but Faracovi (1999) does not (*Scritti*, 255). Clydesdale also provides a graph (at p. 119) that purports to represent the number of letters in each book of the correspondence in which Ficino discusses astrology, but she does not discuss her methodology at all, nor mention the individual letters in which astrology occurs. Such a detailed list would be very useful indeed.

Bullard also quite rightly wishes to place more emphasis on the importance of the *Disputatio* (690 f. and 693 f.) in a broader interpretation of Ficino's views about astrology, especially as it was composed so soon after the discussion with Cavalcanti about his own nativity that I will discuss just below. Nevertheless, using the *Disputatio* to better understand Ficino's own personal views about astrology can be tricky, as I discuss more fully in my vol. II.[18] Although Bullard discusses Ficino's nativity with insight (694), her knowledge about astrology could be sharper, as we can see with this comment on p. 699 as she moves to discuss the *De vita*: 'Quite obviously in the *De vita* Ficino is no longer concerned with horoscopes and judgments. Elections is (*sic*) the only branch of traditional astrology that shares anything in common with the treatise'. Besides being factually incorrect—i.e. Ficino does discuss 'horoscopes' in the *De vita*, by which she means 'nativities', which he treats more fully at *De vita* III.23–24 and elsewhere—Ficino also discusses revolutions in *De vita*, both of the year writ large (*revolutio annorum mundi* [= *revolutio mundi*]) and regarding their nativities on a person's birthday (*revolutio annorum nati* [= *revolutio nati*]),[19] both of which, like nativities proper and elections, all require the use of horoscopes or astrological figures to make a proper interpretation.

In their rightly classic and tremendously influential *Saturn and Melancholy* (1964), Raymond Klibansky, Ernst Panofsky and Fritz Saxl very briefly discuss Ficino's nativity at 256–258, relying only on Ficino's letter to Cavalcanti from 1476–1477.[20] They also provide the references for some of Ficino's other discussions thereof in the correspondence together with some of the relevant texts in

---

18   In two ground-breaking articles from 2015, Maria Sorokina has profoundly revised our understanding thereof: 'Une source inconnue de la *Disputatio contra iudicium astrologorum* de Marsile Ficin: la *Summa de astris* de Gérard de Feltre', *Bruniana e Campanelliana* 21 (2015): 169–189; and her 'Un tournant dans le critique de l'astrologie? La *Summa de astris* de Gerard de Feltre', *Philosophical Readings* 7 (2015): 71–92.

19   My thanks to David Juste for helping me to sharpen my usage here.

20   They date the letter to between 1470 and 1480 (p. 256 f.), which points to one of the main problems with their still widely cited text. Although the English first edition was published in 1964, none of its references for Ficino date to after 1930, due to the complex and highly vexed circumstances of its composition, which they describe in the Preface (v–vi). Thus, there are no references to any scholarship on Ficino after 1930 in the text, and therefore not even to Kristeller's foundational *Supplementum Ficinianum* of 1937, with (among many other things) its authoritative dating of the books of Ficino's correspondence. The somewhat revised German translation of 1992 (*Saturn und Melancholie: Studien zur Geschichte der Naturphilosophie und Medizin, der Religion und der Kunst*, Frankfurt: Suhrkamp), although adding nothing to its treatment of Ficino (367–394), does include a selective bibliographical contribution (573–584) by the sole surviving author (Klibansky), which brings the bibliography at least somewhat up to date, primarily for studies of Dürer, but remains profoundly inadequate and out-of-date. Despite still being the reference point

Latin and in a loose translation. M.J.B. Allen also discusses Ficino's nativity valuably but briefly on p. 15 f. of his insightful essay on Saturn in Ficino. Although
he does not focus much on Saturn in relation to normal astrology, what he has
to say is very interesting indeed (13–16), and, together with his discussion in
Chap. 4 of *Nuptial Arithmetic*, these are the fullest treatments of Ficino's astrology that I know of in his extensive and foundational scholarship.[21] To my lights
Kaske and Clark treat Ficino's nativity most satisfactorily on pp. 19–21 of their
introduction to his *De vita* along with Faracovi (2000), and it is to his nativity
that I now turn.

2.1.1   The Three Main Texts for Ficino's Nativity

I begin here by focusing on the evidence presented by Ornella Pompeo Faracovi in her valuable article from 2000, 'L'oroscopo di Ficino e le sue varianti',[22]
namely, two of Ficino's letters that discuss the basic features of his own nativity, which I will provide with English translations. Then I will briefly discuss
her interpretation of—and possible explanations for—certain curious inconsistencies in the planetary locations for Venus and Jupiter between the two
letters.[23] Finally, I will discuss a third letter of 1484/85 to Johannes Pannonius,
in which Ficino briefly discusses his own nativity. Allen usefully discusses this
letter in the first chapter of his *Synoptic Art*, but not with respect to Ficino's
nativity.[24]

First, however, there is an earlier mention of his nativity in a letter from
Ficino to Francesco Marescalchi, which is dated to 6 Sep 1474. This is the earliest
reference I know of to Ficino discussing his own nativity: 'I have not yet finished
my book *On the Christian Religion*, Francesco, because during August, while I
was still correcting it, I caught a fever and diarrhoea. Perhaps this year Saturn
threatened me with this, since at the time of my birth, it was in the ascend-

---

for most such studies, *Saturn and Melancholy* is in dire need of updating and revision,
especially in its section on Ficino, which is utterly central for its overall argument.

21   See Michael J.B. Allen, 'Marsilio Ficino on Saturn, the Plotinian Mind, and the Monster of
Averroes', *Bruniana e Campanelliana* 16 (2010): 11–29, and his *Nuptial Arithmetic: Marsilio
Ficino's Commentary on the Fatal Number in Book VIII of Plato's* Republic, Berkeley: Uni-
versity of California Press, 1994, Chap. 4 (106–142), which is entitled, 'Jupiter, the Stars and
Golden Age.'

22   Ornella Pompeo Faracovi, 'L'oroscopo di Ficino e le sue varianti', *Bruniana e Campanelliana* 6 (2000): 611–617.

23   Kaske and Clark, *Three Books*, also usefully discuss this on p. 21 in the introduction to their
edition of *De vita*.

24   Michael J.B. Allen, *Synoptic Art: Marsilio Ficino on the History of Platonic Interpretation*,
Florence: Olschki, 1998, 1–49.

ing sign of Aquarius and just recently was in Cancer, my sixth house'.[25] Here
we have both a reference to a very limited number of basic features of Ficino's
nativity—with a focus on Saturn—and to a *revolutio nati* (in the loose sense
to be discussed below) regarding his health. There is not much detail here: he
refers primarily to his natal Saturn being in Aquarius, which was ascending at
the time of his birth, with the further contemporary information that Saturn
was recently in Cancer in his own sixth house, which is concerned with health.
This astronomical data was not in Regiomontanus's *Ephemerides* because it
began in 1475.

2.1.2   Letter to Giovanni Cavalcanti (between August 1476 and May 1477)
Our first reasonably detailed evidence for Ficino's nativity comes from a let-
ter to his younger contemporary and uniquely dear friend—his *'unicus'*—
Giovanni di Niccolò Cavalcanti (1444–1495), in Book III of the correspondence.
This letter is undated, but should be dated to at some point between Aug 1476
and May 1477, as Kristeller has shown.[26] Here is the relevant passage, in which
Ficino describes his own nativity:[27]

> Saturn seems to have impressed it [sc. the seal of melancholy] on me from
> the beginning; set, as it is, almost in the middle of Aquarius, my ascen-
> dant,[28] and receiving Mars, also in the same [sc. zodiacal sign] Aquarius.
> The Moon was in Capricorn, and aspecting in a square the Sun and Mer-
> cury in Scorpio, which occupy the ninth house of heaven (*nonam coeli
> plagam*). To this, perhaps, Venus in Libra and Jupiter in Cancer resist in
> some measure [sc. my] melancholy nature.[29]

---

25   The Latin is from Gentile's ed. of *Lettere* I, n. 80, p. 140: 'Librum *De Christiana religione*
      nondum absolvi, Francisce, quia dum emendarem hoc Augusto in febrem incidi atque
      diarriam. Minabitur id forte mihi Saturnus hoc anno, qui et in mee nativitatis ascendente
      Aquario ab initio fuerat et his temporibus est in Cancro, domo mee nativitatis sexta.' The
      English translation for this letter is SES 1 [I].80 (p. 94).
26   SF, IC. The editors of the English translation of Ficino's letters provide a useful biographi-
      cal section in each volume to identify Ficino's correspondents.
27   SES 2 [III].24 (pp. 33–34). Letters 22 and 23 provide further relevant information on Ficino's
      view of Saturn, which are hardly all negative, just challenging in various but ultimately
      valuable ways. Two of the positive dimensions are the desire to explore recondite topics
      and a powerful memory.
28   According to Richard Kremer: 'From the Parisian Alfonsine Tables, I compute Saturn at 12
      Aquarius on 19 Oct 1433.'
29   'Quam mihi ab initio videtur impressisse Saturnus in medio ferme Aquario ascendente
      meo constitutus, et in Aquario eodem recipiens Martem, et Lunam in Capricorno, atque
      aspiciens ex quadratura Solem Mercuriumque in Scorpio, nonam coeli plagam occu-

Ficino mentions all seven planets in their zodiacal signs here: Sun in Scorpio, Moon in Capricorn, Mercury in Scorpio, Venus in Libra, Mars in Aquarius, Jupiter in Cancer and Saturn in Aquarius, but he does not provide any of their degrees.[30]

We also get a little further information from his description, including the identification of his ascendant or rising sign—Aquarius, which Saturn rules, along with Capricorn—and one explicit reference to one of the terrestrial houses,[31] namely, the ninth, where his Sun and Mercury are in Scorpio. Saturn is certainly Ficino's ruling planet, i.e. the lord of his geniture, due to its overwhelming strength deriving in part from its dignities:[32] Saturn is in its *domus* (Aquarius), and Ficino's ascendant is also in one of Saturn's celestial houses (= zodiacal signs) that it also rules, namely, Aquarius. The planet that rules his Sun sign, Scorpio, namely Mars, is also in Aquarius, and his Moon is in Capricorn, which Saturn also rules, resulting in quite a Saturnine astrological profile, as he is painfully but also perhaps somewhat boastfully aware.[33]

Regardless, Ficino does not offer much in the way of either detail or interpretation: He mentions all of the planets in their zodiacal signs, plus the sign of the ascendant, and that two of the planets in the ninth terrestrial house—Sun

---

pantes. Huic forte nonnihil ad naturam melancholiam restiterunt Venus in Libra, Jupiterque in Cancro.' The Latin is on pp. 732–733 in the 1576 edition of Ficino's *Opera omnia*, but the numeration here is deeply problematic, especially from 730–736, which runs as follows: 730, 631 (= 731), 732, 733, 736 (= 734), 635 (= 735), 736, whence it straightens out, at least for a while. The lion's share of my references to Ficino's Latin are to this standard edition, which I usually refer to as OO.

30   Kaske and Clark note at p. 77 (n. 9) that David Pingree computed the details of Ficino's nativity for them, thereby providing the degrees for his natal planets that Ficino himself never once supplied, namely: Saturn at 12° of Aquarius, Mars at 0° Aquarius, Jupiter at 19° Leo and Venus at 21° Virgo, which are the only planets they mention.

31   Celestial houses = zodiacal signs, whereas terrestrial houses = the houses from one to twelve, counting counter-clockwise, beginning with the ascendant as the first house cusp. I discuss this in the excursus to my volume I: lix–lxxix; the terminology can be confusing. I try to be consistent between [zodiacal] signs and [terrestrial] houses.

32   In my volume II, I discuss the broader importance of discovering the lord of the geniture in Ficino's understanding of astrology, including for identifying one's personal daemon in one's nativity. Specifying the locations of the planets at specific degrees of zodiacal signs is also relevant for determining at least some of the astrological dignities—e.g. the terms and decans or faces—although these are not the most important ones.

33   In addition, Venus rules Libra, which is its '*domus*', and Jupiter is exalted in Cancer, both of which offer dignities for their respective planets, which thereby, at least to some extent, serve to counterbalance Ficino's strongly Saturnine nativity. As it turns out, Ficino offers different placements for Venus and Jupiter in the description of his nativity in a later letter to Uranio that I will discuss next.

and Mercury in Scorpio—are in a squared aspect with his Moon in Capricorn. But he provides no degrees at all for any of the planets in their signs, nor for his Aquarius ascendant. His description is thus sound but elementary and overly general—and besides the phrase 'the seal of melancholy' just above, there is only the hint of an interpretation.[34]

2.1.3   Letter to Martinus Uranius Prenninger (29 Aug 1489)

The other letter with relatively extensive information about Ficino's nativity that Faracovi discusses is one to Martinus Uranius Prenninger,[35] which is dated precisely to 29 August 1489, i.e. when Ficino had just completed composing *De vita* Books II and III, and soon before he composed its pre-emptive *Apologiae* in September; it issued from the press on 3 December 1489.[36] This letter provides additional detailed information about the date and time of Ficino's birth:

> My birth (*natalis*) was on the 19th day of October, in the 1433rd year from Our Salvation, but the hour of the day was not written down by my father, Ficino, even though he was a physician (*medicus*). Nevertheless, I [sc. the royal we] have conjectured (*coniecimus*) from his and my mother's words that it was in the 21st [sc. hour]. I believe that Aquarius was then rising (*ascendisse*) almost in the middle [so, ca. 15° Aquarius] together with Pisces.[37] Saturn in Aquarius then held the Eastern angle [sc. it was in the first house near the cusp of his ascendant]. Mars in the same [sc. zodiacal sign, Aquarius] held the twelfth [sc. house], prison (*carcer*). The Sun and Mercury in Scorpio were in the ninth house (*domus*),[38] and the Moon was in Capricorn. Jupiter in Leo was in the seventh [house], and Venus in Virgo was in the same place [sc. the seventh house], and [sc. the lot/part of] Fortune was in Aries.[39]

---

34   He also says just above that because he has a strongly Saturnine nativity, which is an eternal gift from God, he does not have a strong desire for mortal goods; also, without the sweetness from frequently playing his lyre, he would tend towards bitterness.

35   For more on Uranius, see Wolfgang Zeller, *Der Jurist und Humanist Martin Prenninger gen. Uranius, 1450–1501* (Tübingen: Franz Steiner Verlag, 1973).

36   See Kaske and Clark, *Three Books*, 7, and Gentile, *Catalogo*, nn. 102–105.

37   I.e. the other zodiacal sign rising in his nativity, since Pisces follows Aquarius in the zodiac. They are both thus in his first house. Also, Ficino describes his ascendant as '*ascendisse tunc Aquarium ferme medium*' here, and as '*in medio ferme Aquario ascendente*' in the earlier letter to Cavalcanti, and thus with strikingly similar phrasing.

38   As opposed to '*plaga*' in the letter to Cavalcanti, an insignificant terminological *variatio*.

39   'Nonus ergo supra decimum Octobris dies mihi natalis fuit, anno videlicet a salute nostra Millesimo quadringentesimo ⟨trigesimo[?]⟩ tertio, hora vero diei, quamvis a Patre Ficino medico, descripta non fuerit, eius tamen Matrisque verbis coniecimus fuisse unam supra

Here Ficino provides a somewhat more detailed treatment of his nativity, but it is not much fuller. He provides more information about the house structure of his nativity, but, once again, nothing by way of interpretation. In addition to the information supporting the Saturnine nature of his natal astrological makeup—Aquarius rising together with Saturn in Aquarius on his ascendant, with Mars also in Aquarius and the Moon in Capricorn, both in signs ruled by Saturn—Ficino also, curiously, presents significantly different placements for Venus and Jupiter. That is, he locates them in different zodiacal signs altogether (still without degrees) than in the letter to Cavalcanti twelve years before.[40] There is also a further different set in a later edition, which Kaske and Clark, and especially Faracovi attempt to explain, as I discuss below.

Even though his father was a physician, Ficino informs us in this letter that his father had not recorded Marsilio's time of birth, and his baptismal records are not known.[41] Thus, Ficino relied on his father and mother's recollections to make a conjecture—i.e. a rectification—about his time of birth, and thus his ascendant.[42] Although Ficino does not provide any proper interpretation

---

vigesimam, ascendisse tunc Aquarium ferme medium, una cum Piscibus, arbitror. Saturnus in Aquario tunc Orientis angulum tenuisse, Martem in eodem, Carcerem duodecima tenuisse, in Scorpione Solem, atque Mercurium in domo nona, Lunam in Capricorno. In Leone Iovem in septima. Ibidem in Virgine Venerem, in Ariete, Fortunam (901).' This is my translation. There is also a translation at SES 8 [IX].18 (pp. 25–26).

40   Venus is in Virgo here vs. in Libra in the letter to Cavalcanti, and Jupiter is in Leo here vs. in Cancer there. I will discuss this further below.

41   Gentile discusses Ficino's date of birth and the lack of documentary evidence for it in his *Catalogo*, n. 133. According to Mary Quinlan-McGrath, 'The Villa Farnesina: Time-Telling Conventions and Renaissance Astrological Practice', *Journal of the Warburg and Courtauld Institute* 58 (1995): 52–71, 60: 'Although fathers were individually responsible for entering the information about their own children, we find that they normally wrote only the date of baptism; much less frequently they added the date of birth. In only a few cases was a specific time recorded, and it is altogether exceptional to find the portion of the hour given', citing a recent study by Nicholas Mann 'of almost a thousand entries for the years 1460–1470 in Siena.' This is in reference to Agostino Chigi's father Mariano unusually, she persuasively argues, entering the precise time for his son's birth in 1466 in the baptismal registry in Siena; hence the emphasis in Ficino's statement here, assuming the same practice in Florence a generation earlier.

42   Here is David Juste's note to this text which I have lightly edited: According to Solar Fire Gold, Ficino was born between 13:06 and 13:41 (Florence) if we are to meet the conditions described here, especially AS Aquarius + Saturn in the first house (before 13:06 AS was Capricorn and after 13:41 Saturn entered the 12th house). Of course, this is modern calculation, but medieval calculation would not be drastically different, and since early afternoon cannot be equated with the 21st hour by any reckoning, either there is a serious mistake or his nativity was rectified.

of his nativity beyond that it was severely Saturnine—in the texts discussed here or anywhere else, as far as I know—we know from *De vita* III, composed at exactly the same time, that he had a much fuller knowledge of astrology than that represented here. This is also apparent in *De vita*, Book I, composed in 1480, which famously presents a much richer and deeply influential astrologico-physiological analysis of the Saturnine-Melancholic temperament and character at *De vita* 1.3–6. Book 1.7–8 also includes Ficino's astrologically-informed medical advice to students about how to optimize their study habits. I will discuss this further in my volume II.

I will now briefly discuss the disparity between the placements of Venus and Jupiter in their respective zodiacal signs in these two letters that are twelve years apart, as Ficino does not mention either Venus or Jupiter in letter [3] to Pannonius, nor does Faracovi (2000) discuss this letter. In the letter to Cavalcanti, Venus is in Libra and Jupiter in Cancer, whereas in the later letter to Uranio, Venus is in Virgo and Jupiter in Leo. As it turns out, the new position in their adjacent zodiacal signs is accurate for both Venus and Jupiter in the letter to Uranio, with Kaske and Clark reporting in n. 9 (p. 77) that David Pingree had computed Venus at 21° Virgo and Jupiter at 19° Leo. Kaske and Clark do not report the minutes if in fact Pingree had provided them.[43]

On the other hand, Faracovi derives the data for Venus and Jupiter from a computer (without indicating the program used), providing very similar but more precise data to what Pingree had offered: Venus at 20° 06′ Virgo, and Jupiter at 18° 26′ Leo. Ficino himself, of course, only provides the zodiacal signs, but no degrees whatsoever. Regarding their placement in the terrestrial houses, Ficino does not mention this in the letter to Cavalcanti, but in the letter to Uranio, Jupiter in Leo and Venus in Virgo are both now located in the seventh house, which is itself ruled by Venus. Faracovi does not take this into account in her interpretation of the disparity.

Here is how Kaske and Clark and Faracovi attempt to account for the differences—and we do not know how Ficino got to the new data. Perhaps his computational skills had improved over the intervening twelve years, or someone more skillful had calculated them for him.[44] Or, as Faracovi suggests (615 f.),

---

43 According to Richard Kremer: 'Assuming Florence is 1;30hr east of Toledo, I compute for 19;30 hrs past noon, 19 Oct 1433: Sun 6 Sco, Moon 22 Cap, Sat 12 Aqu, Jup 18 Leo, Mar 3 Aqu, Ven 20 Vir, Mer 26 Sco.'

44 On p. 21 of *Three Books*, Kaske and Clark, suggest that Jupiter in Leo would oppose and thus counterbalance Saturn in Aquarius, and that Venus in Virgo is 'vocationally favorable' for Ficino, as it indicates one who could be a physician.

perhaps Ficino deliberately misrepresented his nativity in the earlier letter so that Venus and Jupiter—both with dignities—could more effectively counteract the role of Saturn in his nativity. Faracovi also notes a further difference in the first publication of a translation into Italian of Ficino's Letters by Felice Figliucci (1546), where, in the translation of the letter to Cavalcanti, Jupiter goes back to Cancer and Venus moves into Scorpio, returning neither to Virgo or Libra, its previous homes. To this switch, she attributes the striking similarities between the normal glyphs for Virgo and Scorpio which thereby confused the typographer (616–617).

2.1.4 Letter to Johannes Pannonius (1484/85)

I will now discuss a third description of his own nativity by Ficino in a letter of 1484/85 to Johannes Pannonius.[45] In an insightful article, Michael J.B. Allen discusses in detail the material in this letter concerning Ficino's response to John's range of penetrating questions critical of what was implied in and/or could be read into or interpreted from one of Ficino's letters sent to Francesco Bandini, also in Buda, that he had read. Allen does not, however, discuss its astrological content. Although this article makes a significant contribution to our knowledge—as he did so very often—I believe that Allen also misses an important philosophical background structure to which Ficino implicitly but clearly refers. Ficino also discusses it elsewhere, which is how I was able to identify and amplify it here.[46]

Before discussing Ficino's response, though, I would first like to present further evidence of Ficino's knowledge of astrology from Johannes's initial letter to Ficino with its probing questions:[47]

> Besides, some time ago, when I had gone to Italy and was being taught Latin and Greek in Florence, I remember hearing from two of your astrologers (*a duobus vestrorum Astrologis*) that you were going to revive the ancient philosophical teaching (*te* [...] *antiquas renovaturum Philosophorum sententias*) in accordance with a particular configuration of the stars

---

45 This letter was translated and analyzed by Michael J.B. Allen in 'Golden Wits, Zoroaster and the Revival of Plato', the first chapter of his *Synoptic Art*, 14–16. I use his translation here. SES also translate it: 7 [VIII].19 (pp. 21–24); Ficino's nativity is on p. 23. Allen dates it to 'in 1484 or 1485' (p. 1), whereas Hankins, *PIR*, 302 dates it more generally to 'before 1488.' Neither of them discuss the criteria they use for dating it. Regardless, Hankins explicitly associates it with the great conjunction of 1484 (303). Kristeller dates the letters in Book VIII to between Summer 1484 and October 1488; *SF*, CII.

46 I only discuss this briefly here. I will develop it more fully in Chap. 4 of my vol. II.

47 SES 7 [VIII].18 (pp. 20–21).

(*ex quadam syderum positione*). Now although I was told of this configuration of the stars, I do not recall it clearly, but I believe that you remem-
ber it; indeed, that you discovered it by yourself. In support of their own
interpretation (*ad suum iudicium confirmandum*) those astrologers (*illi
Astrologi*) also declared that at the appointed time (*fatali quodam tempore*) you had restored to light the ancient sound of the lyre, as well as the
ancient style of singing and the Orphic hymns which had previously been
consigned to oblivion (20–21).[48]

Given Allen's dating of this letter to 1484/85, this 'particular configuration of the
stars' seems like it could well refer to the great conjunction of Jupiter and Saturn in Scorpio in 1484 (as Hankins also believes), but it is impossible to tell for
sure without a more precise dating of the letter or more specific terminology
within the letter.

We should now turn to Ficino's response, which can also help us to understand his views on astrology more fully, especially in the 1484/85 period, that
is, around the time that he published his Plato translation in late 1484 to correspond precisely with the portentous great conjunction then.[49] Here is part of
Ficino's response to Pannonius:

> But why did you mention my nativity (*genesis*) when you wished to assign
> the cause of my work to fate (*fatum*)? I do not deny that in this planetary
> arrangement (*in hac ipsa figura*)—that is, Saturn ascending in Aquar-
> ius with the Sun and Mercury in the ninth house (*plaga*) of heaven, and
> with the other planets in aspect to this ninth house—it signifies (*signifi-
> care*) that a man will be a renewer of the ancient mysteries (*hominem
> rerum antiquarum innovatorem*).[50] But I do deny that this arrangement

---

48 [P]raeterea memini cum olim in Italiam profectus latinis, et Graecis erudirer Florentiae,
    me a duobus vestrorum Astrologis audivisse, te ex quadam syderum positione antiquas
    renovaturum Philosophorum sententias. Quam quidem positionem syderum et si audi-
    verim non satis recolo, sed te arbitror meminisse, imo et per te invenisse. Adduxerunt item
    illi Astrologi ad suum iudicium confirmandum quod fatali quodam tempore antiquum
    cytharae sonum, et cantum, at carmina Orphica oblivioni prius tradita luci restituisses
    (871)[.]
49 I discuss why the timing of the Plato publication to 1484 is significant in Chap. 4 of my
    vol. II as an example of astrological revolutions.
50 'Ancient mysteries' seems to be an overtranslation of '*res antiquae*' which simply means
    'ancient matters.' This may certainly include ancient mysteries, but surely need not refer
    only to them.

causes (sed efficere nego) the renewal.[51] You too, if you read most diligently [1] my letter on the Star of the Magi, and [2] the related argument in my [sc. *Platonic*] *Theology*, and likewise [3] the books of Plotinus which deal with such matters [i.e. fate in relation to astrology, and in particular, *Ennead* III.1 *On Fate*] (which I have also translated), will plainly understand, first, that the offices and care of the public good which pertain to souls principally depend [1] as if from their common and prime causes (*a communibus primisque causis*), on the supernal minds who are the ministers of the highest God (*a supernis mentibus Dei summi ministris*); second [2] that they also derive in a way, as if from their particular and immediate causes (*a causis propriis atque ultimis*), from the counsels of men when men accommodate themselves to these supernal minds; and third [3] that they are merely *signified* by the celestial figures and motions (*significari autem a figuris motibusque caelestibus*), the latter being like the instruments of the divine minds (*velut divinarum mentium instrumentis*), [sc. which divine minds are thus their true causes]. You will also learn that fate, which is the series of celestial causes (*fatum, id est, caelestium seriem causarum*), serves divine providence (*providentiae divinae servire*); but that our souls are thought to be most free when they accord (*consentiunt*) with the divine will (15).[52]

Although we do not learn more about the details of Ficino's nativity here, we do get significant clues about his own interpretation of his nativity, namely, that it signifies but does not effect, cause or make him a renewer of ancient matters, which is surely how he actually understood himself and his vocation. Rather, he came to see that it was God's providential plan for him—by interpreting the celestial configurations and motions in his nativity (and perhaps also with

---

51   I discuss the significant issue of signs vs. causes in greater detail in Chap. 4 of my volume II.

52   Quod vero tu nostri huius operis causam in fatum referre volens de nostra genesi attigisti? Non inficior equidem in hac ipsa figura—Saturnum in Aquario ascendentem et Solem Mercuriumque in nona caeli plaga aspectumque reliquorum planetarum ad ipsam nonam—significare hominem rerum antiquarum innovatorem, sed efficere nego. Tu quoque, si epistolam nostram de Magorum stella et similem in *Theologia* nostra disputationem, item Plotini libros hac ipsa de re tractantes, quos et traduximus, diligentissime legeris, plane intelliges officia publici boni ad animos pertinentia dependere quidem praecipua, velut a communibus primisque causis, a supernis mentibus Dei summi ministris; proficisci etiam quodammodo, tanquam a causis propriis atque ultimis, ab humanis consiliis ubi se supernis accommodant; significari autem a figuris motibusque caelestibus velut divinarum mentium instrumentis. Disces praeterea fatum, id est, caelestium seriem causarum, providentiae divinae servire; animos vero nostros tunc maxime liberos iudicari quando maxime cum divina voluntate consentiunt (n. 27, pp. 16–17 [*oo*, 871–872]).

the comet that appeared at his birth)[53]—and thus he accommodated his own actions and desires to be in harmony with the divine will, especially with a portentous great conjunction appearing recently in his own ninth house in Scorpio, where his natal Sun and Mercury were. This is also similar to his advice in *De vita* III.23 on how a person should work with his or her own nativity, but there he couched it in terms of engaging constructively with one's guardian daemon as identifiable in one's own nativity, as I discuss in detail in my volume II.

We also find out more in this letter about Ficino's broader vision of astrology's role within the essentially medieval theological framework embracing divine providence and fate. This can then be further articulated on the basis of a unique addition to Ficino's translation of and commentary on Plotinus's *Enneads* (1492) that was originally composed in 1477 in the *Disputatio*, but which remained unpublished until 1492. In particular, I refer to the singular addition to his treatment of Plotinus's *Ennead* III.1, *On Fate*—which I believe is the central text to which Ficino refers in this letter to Pannonius.[54] In it, Ficino added a description of how he understands a deeply astrological and non-deterministic fate, in order to complement both his translation of Plotinus from Greek into Latin and his formal commentary thereon. Ficino thus explicitly articulated his own deeply astrological understanding of fate.

In this unique addition to the commentary, which is called *Summa Marsiliana* there, Ficino explicitly tells Lorenzo de' Medici that he will here inform Lorenzo about his own views on fate, which I believe he does at least partially to distance them from Plotinus's views. I will discuss this more fully in my volume II.[55] These basic themes of fate in relation to astrology have been discussed extensively in the scholarship regarding Ficino's views about astrology, but to my lights they have not yet been fully understood, in large measure

---

53   Gentile discusses the comets of 1433 and 1456 as significant signs that inspired Cosimo to choose Ficino to be the *Restaurator Platonicarum rerum*; *Lettere* I: XXXVII–XL.

54   I call this a unique and singular addition to Ficino's commentary because, with all of the other *Enneads*, Ficino only provides his translation and a commentary on what he thinks Plotinus means, whereas here only Ficino adds an additional text to explain his own views on the subject at question, namely fate.

55   I have learned a great deal from Stephen Gersh's edition and translation of Ficino's translation of and commentary on Plotinus's *Enneads* III and IV in the I Tatti Renaissance Library, with their extensive analytic introductions; Marsilio Ficino, *Commentary on Plotinus*, Vol. 4: *Ennead III*, Part 1; Vol. 5, *Ennead III*, Part 2 and *Ennead IV* (Cambridge, MA: Harvard University Press, 2017 and 2018 respectively). The text in question appears in vol. 4, pp. 56–79.

because Ficino's views need to be explicated in terms of medieval structures that have never been properly brought to bear on his views on fate. Thus, the older interpretations normally distort our understanding by viewing both fate and nativities through an essentially Stoic lens, therefore understanding both as deterministic, whereas for Ficino neither of them were.[56]

Unfortunately, Allen misses this dimension of Ficino's response to Pannonius regarding his own nativity for two main reasons, it seems to me: [1] Allen does not focus on but only minimally treats the astrological dimension, and [2] he focuses more generally on the Neoplatonic and Patristic backgrounds and not the medieval one, to which Ficino seems to me clearly to refer here. This framework is also relevant for fully grasping Ficino's broader understanding of nativities (including his own), and also and perhaps moreso for revolutions. Furthermore, like Albertus Magnus as discussed in my volume I, Ficino seems much more interested in theology and natural philosophy than in practical astrology *per se*; but for both him and Albert, astrology seems to have played an important role in informing that broader conceptual framework. In fact, it seems as though he drew directly on Albert here, whose work Ficino had known since his earliest philosophical studies in the 1450s.[57]

---

56 I discuss these background views from Albertus Magnus and Thomas Aquinas in relation to Boethius's deeply influential *Consolatio philosophiae*, Books IV and V much more fully in Chap. 5 of my volume I.

57 For Ficino's early knowledge of Albert's commentary on Aristotle's *Physica*, see Edward Mahony, 'Albert the Great and the *Studio Patavino* in the Late Fifteenth and Early Sixteenth Centuries', in *Albertus Magnus and the Sciences*, ed. James A. Weisheipl, O.P. (Toronto: Pontifical Institute of Mediaeval Studies, 1980), 527–563, 542 with references (in n. 11) to Kristeller, *Studies in Renaissance Thought and Letters* (Rome: Edizioni di Storia e Letteratura, 1969), 149 with his remark at 143. Here is what Mahoney has to say: 'In an early letter of 1454, Marsilio Ficino cites Albert's commentary on the *Physics* and states that he is not afraid to put him in second place among the Latin philosophers (*Latinorum philosophorum secondo loco*), apparently intending to rank him just after Thomas Aquinas.' Kristeller's invaluable article that Mahoney refers to was first published as: 'The Scholastic Background of Marsilio Ficino with an Edition of Unpublished Texts', *Traditio* 2 (1944): 257–318. We also know that Ficino knew Albert's conceptually related but later *De fato* (which he refers to explicitly at *De vita* III.18.148–151). He thought that it was written by Thomas Aquinas, however, which gave it an even greater authority. Ficino also knew the 13th-century *Speculum astronomiae* that also discusses astrology in relation to divine providence, which he thinks is by Albert (also in *De vita* III.18.127–129). Ficino also knew Boethius's *Consolatio Philosophiae*, since it was a ubiquitous school text in Italy at this time; see Robert Black and Gabriella Pomaro, *Boethius's* Consolation of Philosophy *in Italian Medieval and Renaissance Education* (Florence: SISMEL—Galluzzo, 2000), and also Gentile, *Catalogo*, n. 4. Thus, Ficino knew all of the main texts in this tradition that I reconstructed in Chap. 5 of my vol. I as well as Thomas's *Summa contra gentiles*, which we know that Ficino knew well from Kristeller's foundational study, 'Thomism and the Italian Thought of the Renais-

In my understanding, these views are central to Ficino's broader understanding of God, divine providence and fate, and they have a marvelously sound and authoritative Christian pedigree, with Albertus Magnus articulating and astrologizing central Boethian concepts from the profoundly influential *Consolatio Philosophiae*, Books IV and V, within an overall Thomist view of divine providence. Here the broader philosophico-religious context is essential to fully understanding Ficino's position, which is only adumbrated in my treatment here, but, when filled in by Albert, can be articulated in detail. I reconstruct Albert's position much more fully in Chap. 5 of my vol. I.[58] This is the conceptual nexus to which much 20th-century scholarship referred, but without fully understanding it, as I will also show more fully in my vol. II.

I can now draw some limited conclusions about Ficino's astrological knowledge and practice concerning his own nativity, which are essentially sound but elementary. As we have seen, Ficino really only mentions the planets in their zodiacal signs and in their terrestrial houses, but without ever mentioning any degrees, and with only a very general statement that his ascendant is in the middle of Aquarius, once again without an indication of degrees. He also adds a few aspects, primarily of his Sun and Mercury in Scorpio in the ninth house of philosophy and religion—which he does not explicitly describe, but about which I presume he was well aware—that are squared to his Saturn, Mars and ascendant, all in Aquarius. There are virtually no interpretations beyond that he is melancholic, due to Saturn's deep influence on his nativity—and that he will be a renewer of ancient matters. Especially in the letter to Pannonius, however, Ficino's discussion of his own nativity also explicitly points towards a deeper philosophical structure that is central, I believe, to understanding Ficino's essentially medieval world view at this time that is alluded to and partially articulated here.[59] As it turns out, practical astrology functions precisely

---

sance', in his *Medieval Aspects of Renaissance Learning*, ed. E. Mahoney (Durham, N.C: Duke University Press, 1974) (2nd ed, Columbia University Press, 1992), 29–91; he treats Ficino in particular and in detail at pp. 73–79. On the scg in particular, see p. 73. All of this emphasizes the importance of understanding Ficino's use of medieval structures to be able to fully assess his own originality and contributions in relation to the sources that he often draws deeply on but does not always explicitly identify.

58   Allen's interpretation is extremely learned, as ever, but does not engage the fundamental features of the interpretation that I think is at the heart of Ficino's thinking regarding astrology in relation to divine providence, fate and free will, including practical astrology. It focuses rather—and valuably—on Zoroaster. Hence my discussion will ultimately make a contribution to filling in a further dimension of Allen's analysis.

59   Ficino also held a very different Neoplatonic world view a few years later in the *De vita*

within this broader philosophical context: especially of nativities within the broader context of revolutions *mundi* and *nati*, but also for using elections to operate in and on the world, as we will see.

2.2 *Ficino on Other Peoples' Nativities*

2.2.1 Ficino on Plato's Nativity as Found in Firmicus Maternus

Ficino discusses Plato's nativity in his letter to Francesco Bandini within a letter expounding Plato's life and philosophy, entitled '*De vita Platonis*'.[60] The previous letter (18) to Francesco Ippoliti, count of Gazoldo, is an essay about the nature, institution and action of Plato's philosophy.[61] [**Image** of Plato's horoscope in both editions of the Letters] The horoscope printed there (as also in the 1495 first edition of the Letters [on f. LXXXVIIIʳ]),[62] which is in the very first section of the extensive letter on Plato's birth, offers all of Plato's planets within the grid of the signs and houses, but with no degrees indicated at all, either for the planets or for the house cusps, which we can now see is Ficino's normal procedure. This is similar, of course, to how Ficino discusses his own nativity. In fact, this is the only horoscope—or diagram for that matter—printed in the 1495 *princeps* of Ficino's *Epistolae* as well as in the 1576 *Opera Omnia* version, at least regarding the *Letters*. The letter that follows Bandini's in Book IV to Bernardo Bembo is about how the astrologers' lie. Ficino disparages astrologers here with a play on words in the title of the letter: 'As much as the astronomers measure, so much do the astrologers lie' (*Quantum Astronomi metiuntur, tantum Astrologi mentiuntur*, 771 [SES 3 [IV].20 (pp. 48–49)]).

Here is Ficino's discussion of Plato's nativity. On the side of the figure in both editions is printed: 'Julius Firmicus [Maternus] asserts that this nativity (*genesis*)[63] signifies a man who is esteemed to have wondrous eloquence, and

---

(1489), especially in Book III, which I reconstruct in detail in Part 2 of my volume II. I will argue there that Ficino held both world views simultaneously, at least from the end of 1489 onward, and that he did so without any fundamental conflicts or tensions. This may sound strange to us, but I cannot discuss it further here.

60 SES 3 [IV].19 (pp. 32–37 [00, 763–770]), with the horoscope at pp. 32–33; the dates for the letters in Book IV are between 1 March and 1 August 1477 (SF, IC).

61 This Ippoliti is the same person who also received Ficino's letter with the Proem to the *Disputatio*, which I discuss in Chap. 4 of my vol. II.

62 In the 1495 first edition, the planets and the signs are written out in full, whereas in the 1576 *Opera omnia*, only the characters for the planets and the signs are given, along with the grid of the houses in the horoscope.

63 This is the same term for a nativity that Ficino uses in his response to Pannonius's letter.

who approaches all the secrets of divinity with a heavenly intelligence'.[64] After discussing Plato's date of birth and his family's genealogy, Ficino discusses the nativity itself, but only briefly. This is all he has to say:

> Plato was born either in Athens or on Aegina 756 years after the capture of Troy, 333 years after the founding of Rome and 423 years before the coming of Christ. In my book *De amore* [sc. in 1469], I described the position of the planets at Plato's birth, as I heard of them in my youth [Ficino was 36 years old at that point].[65] But now I shall draw your attention to their position as described by Julius Firmicus, the astrologer (*astronomus*), whose opinion on this matter I consider to be more correct. And it is as follows: Mars, Mercury and Venus are in Aquarius, which is in the ascendant. In the second house the Sun is in Pisces; in the fifth the Moon is in Gemini; in the seventh Jupiter is in Leo, and in the ninth Saturn is in Libra (*SES* 3 [IV].19 [pp. 32–33]).[66]

---

64 'Hanc Genesim Iulius Firmi⟨c⟩us asserit significare virum, qui mirabili eloquentia polleat. Coelestique ingenio ad omnia secreta divinitatis accedat.' This is my translation. SES 3 [IV].19 has a translation on p. 33. The passage in Firmicus is VI.30.24 (full reference below).

65 This is a significant overstatement in that Ficino only gives Plato's date of birth, not the other planets in his nativity. In *De amore* Ficino states explicitly that Nov. 7th is Plato's birthday and thus that his Sun, like Ficino's, is in Scorpio. In fact this is all he says in the very first sentence of Speech I (in Jayne's translation): 'Plato, the father of philosophers, died at the age of eighty-one, on November 7, which was his birthday, reclining at a banquet, after the feast had been cleared away (35; Marsilio Ficino, *Commentary on Plato's* Symposium *on Love*, tr. Sears Jayne, 2nd completely revised edition, Dallas, TX: Spring Publications, 1985 [orig. 1944]).' (*Plato philosophorum pater annos unum et octuaginta etatis natus, septimo Novembris die, quo ortus fuerat, discumbens in convivio remotis dapibus expiravit*; Marsile Ficin, *Commentaire sur le Banquet de Platon*, ed. Raymond Marcel (Paris: Les Belles Lettres, 1956, 37)). In fact, it was this same Bandini, the addressee of this letter, who had initially arranged the banquet fictionally reconstructed in the *De amore*. On this and much more, see Sebastiano Gentile on the textual tradition of the *De amore*, 'Per la storia del testo del "Commentarium in Convivium" di Marsilio Ficino', *Rinascimento* Ser. 2, 21 (1982): 3–27.

66 'Nascitur Athenis vel in Egina, a Troiae captivitate 756. ab urbe condita trecentesimo XXXIII. Ante Christi adventum quadringentessimo. XXIII. Platonis genesim qualem adolescens audiveram in libro de Amore significavi. Sed nunc adducam, qualem Iulius Firmicus Astronomus describit, cuius opinionem hac in re existimo veriorem. Est autem eiusmodi. In Ascendente Aquario, [Mars], [Mercury], [Venus]. In secunda Sol in Piscibus. In quinta Luna in Geminis. In Septima Iuppiter in Leone. In nona Saturnus in Libra (763).' As noted earlier, the dates for the letters in Book IV are between 1 March 1477 and 1 August 1477; this letter was originally composed earlier, as per Allen, *Philebus Commentary*, p. 8.

That is all Ficino has to say about Plato's nativity.

Here is the entire text in Firmicus (VI.30.24):

> If the ascendant (*horoscopus*) is in Aquarius, and Mars, Mercury, and Venus are located equally in that part of the ascendant; Jupiter is on the descendant in Leo; the Sun is on the anaphora of the ascendant in Pisces; the Moon is in the fifth house in Gemini, in trine to the ascendant; and Saturn is in the ninth house in Libra, this chart produces an interpreter of divine and celestial matters (*divinarum et caelestium institutionum* [...] *interpretem*). He possesses a combination of learned speech and divine intelligence and is trained by some kind of heavenly power to give true expression to all secrets of divinity. This geniture is said to have been that of Plato.[67]

As usual, Ficino only mentions the most basic planetary data with no degrees whatsoever, precisely as Firmicus did as well; only planets in signs and houses, and nothing even approaching a proper interpretation, although Firmicus offers a limited interpretation towards that end. Plato thus also seems to be Saturnine. Ficino himself, of course, also has Aquarius rising, just like Plato does here, as well as Mars in Aquarius. Saturn itself is also in Libra, where it is exalted, another of its dignities, which also points in that same Saturnine direction. Unfortunately for Marsilio, however, and unlike in the *De amore*, Plato no longer has both the Sun in Scorpio together with Aquarius rising, precisely as Ficino himself has, which I presume he would have found profoundly disappointing. Furthermore, Ficino does not discuss why he thinks that this Piscean birthday from Firmicus is better and/or more accurate than the Scorpionic one that he had first presented in the *De amore*.

---

67 'Si horoscopus in Aquario fuerit inventus, et in parte horoscopi Mars et Mercurius et Venus sint pariter collocati, in occasu vero Iuppiter positus Leonis habeat signum, et in anaphora horoscopi Sol constitutus signum Piscium teneat, Luna vero in Geminis collocata, et in quinto geniturae loco constituta, horoscopum trigonica radiatione respiciat, et Saturnus nonum ab horoscopo ⟨locum⟩ tenens in Librae sit signo constitutus, haec genitura divinarum et caelestium institutionum reddit interpretem, qui docili sermone et divini ingenii potestate compositus, ⟨et⟩ caelesti quodammodo institutione formatus, vera disputationum licentia ad omnia secreta divinitatis accedat. Haec genitura Platonis fuisse suggeritur (80, 82).' I take the Latin text from Firmicus Maternus, *Mathesis*, Tome III, Livres VI–VIII, ed. P. Monat, Paris: Les Belles Lettres, 2003. The English translation is taken from *Ancient Astrology, Theory and Practice*: Matheseos Libri VIII, by Firmicus Maternus, tr. by Jean Rhys Bram (Park Ridge, N.J: Noyes Press, 1975), 209. Benjamin N. Dykes also offers a translation with very strange terminology in Julius Firmicus Maternus, *Mathêsis*, tr. Dykes (Minneapolis: Cazimi Press, 2023) at VI.30.46 (p. 432).

2.2.2   Nativity of Lorenzo di Pierfrancesco de' Medici (1477/78)

In a famous letter to Lorenzo di Pierfrancesco de' Medici (1463–1503 [= Lorenzo Minor]) from 1477/78, Ficino describes a generic horoscope of the Moon in aspect to the other planets, but without any planet being particularized even by its zodiacal sign, as Ficino usually does. Here he discusses only their planetary natures. In a justly famous article, Ernst H. Gombrich argued that the Venusian painting discussed in the letter, which Ficino calls his gift to Lorenzo Minor, is none other than Botticelli's 'Primavera', Because the discussion is both so generic and also so well known, I will only mention it here and skip over it. The interested reader can refer to a valuable translation and discussion in Gombrich, 'Botticelli's Mythologies: A Study in the Neoplatonic Symbolism of His Circle', *Journal of the Warburg and Courtauld Institutes* 8 (1945): 7–60, 16. There is also a translation in SES 4 [v].46 (pp. 61–63).

2.2.3   Letter to Johannes, Cardinal of Aragon

In this peculiar letter,[68] Ficino included the very partial nativities of the dead Alfonso I the Magnanimous, king of Aragon and Naples (24 February 1396–1458),[69] and of his son Ferdinand (Ferrante) of Aragon, king of Naples (2 June 1424–1494),[70] which were sent to Johannes (Giovanni), cardinal of Aragon (25 June 1456–1485), as a part of the prophecy that Ficino says he translated into Latin from the language of the angels. In it, Ficino encouraged the cardinal to communicate this partially astrological prophecy to Ferrante the king, his father, in the interest of promoting peace between the king and Florence. After discussing divine providence and fate, Ficino turns to astrology, on which I will focus. There is also a section on divination as well.

The letter is divided into two parts: [1] the letter proper from Ficino to Cardinal Giovanni, which is dated to 28 Feb 1479, and thus very much in the thick of the military aftermath to the Pazzi conspiracy.[71] [2] The second part is the prophecy that Ficino sent to Giovanni for him to then communicate to his father Ferrante, the current king of Naples. The nature of the astrological dis-

---

68   From SES 5 [VI].13 (pp. 23–31); OO, 816–820.

69   He is called Alfonso V of Aragon, king of Sicily and king of Naples in the DBI article from 1960 by Ruggero Moscati, who says that he was born, presumably in 1396, and that he died on 27 June 1458.

70   These dates do not seem to correspond to Ficino's astrological discussion; there are no dates for Alfonso in his DBI article. The date given above for Ferrante comes from Alan Ryder's 1996 DBI article. In SES 5, p. 101 (from 1994) they note that no exact birth dates have been found for Alfonso or Ferrante.

71   For this infamous conspiracy against the Medici, see (e.g.) Lauro Martines, *April Blood: Florence and the Plot against the Medici* (London: Jonathan Cape, 2003).

course in this letter is quite limited. Here is a taste from a section entitled, 'The Nature of Saturn and Mars':

> Two of the planets in particular continuously devise perils for men: Mars and Saturn. However, each of these, as experience teaches you, usually spares those under him: Saturn, I mean, generally does not injure those [sc. born] under Saturn, nor Mars those under Mars. Certainly I was once a companion of Saturn; whenever I showed compassion to my own people, that is those under Saturn, Saturn favored me. But whenever I did not show them compassion, Saturn never favored me at all. Therefore, my Ferdinand, companion of fiery Mars, if you wish your reign to prosper, spare your own people. Of all peoples those who are especially your own are shown to you by that fiery quality of Aries with whom both Leo and Sagittarius are in accord. So treat all the sons of Aries, Leo and Sagittarius as your brothers. Go beyond this: cherish, serve my people also, if you will. But do you want to know who my people are? Why, they are those ruled by Capricorn or Aquarius, the abodes of Saturn (28).[72]

After discussing the natures of Mars and Saturn, 'Alfonso' then mentions the fiery triplicity and the abodes or domiciles of Saturn. Ficino enumerates all of these astrological dignities, namely, the domiciles and the elemental triplicities in *De vita* III.9. This is all very general, needless to say. I will not go any further into this example of astrologico-political propaganda.

We can see from this limited but consistent evidence concerning Ficino's treatment of his own and of others' nativities that his level of astrological analysis and expertise only includes planets in their signs and in some of their houses and aspects. He also indicates his own and Plato's Aquarius ascendants, but no degrees for any of the planets or house cusps whatsoever (beyond that his own Aquarian ascendant is 'in the middle' of Aquarius), thus indicating a very basic

---

72   Duo potissimum inter Planetas hominibus assidue pericula machinantur, Mars videlicet et Saturnus. Uterque tamen, sicut vos docet experientia, plerunque parcit suis, Saturniis inquam Saturnus, Mars similiter Martiis, ut plurimum nescit obesse. Ego certe olim Saturni comes quotiens peperci meis, hoc est, Saturniis, totiens favit mihi Saturnus. Contra vero nihil unquam favit. Ergo Ferdinande mi, Martis comes ardentis, (si feliciter regnare cupis) parce tuis. Qui vero sint inter omnes praecipui tui, ostendit tibi ignea illa qualitas Arietis, qui cum et Leo Sagittariusque consentiunt. Omnes igitur Arietis, Leonis, Sagittarii filios ipse tanquam fratres habeto. Praeterea, ignosce, indulge, obsequrer, (si placet) et meis. Qui nam mei sint maxime quaeris? Qui videlicet vel Capricorno, vel Aquario sedibus Saturni reguntur (819).

and elementary level of astrological practice with almost no interpretation whatsoever. He does, however, seem to allude also to a psychological under-standing of astrology as well as to his broader philosophico-religious views regarding how astrology works in relation to divine providence, fate and free will. To be sure, offering planets in their zodiacal signs without degrees in these letters could surely indicate that Ficino is summarizing and simplifying a much more detailed horoscope and not ignorance or disinterest on his part, but there is absolutely no countervailing evidence that I know of to support this claim in any of the letters or elsewhere in his early writings on astrology.

3   Revolutions

> *For, in these things which God does by means of the heavens, the significa-tion of the heavens is nothing other than divine providence.*[73]

I would now like to discuss a few examples of Ficino's practice of astrologi-cal revolutions, which also function within this same broader medieval natural philosophical and theological framework of divine providence and fate. In this structure, fate is precisely the unfolding configuration of the celestial bodies over time,[74] which is exactly what revolutions are, with the unfolding of the stars precisely expressing and thereby also signifying divine providence. In fact, in the deeply influential *Speculum astronomiae*, the deliberately anonymous author, whom Ficino thought was Albertus Magnus, stated this view clearly and directly, and in plain Latin, as we can see in the epigram to this section.

Revolutions concern the unfolding motion of the planets over time, and they fall into two main categories: those dealing with broad effects in the world in general, and those related to individuals. The most precise form of the first is called a '*revolutio mundi*' and employs the construction of a horoscope for a par-

---

73   [N]am in his quae operatur Dominus per caelum, nihil aliud est caeli significatio quam divina providentia (*Speculum astronomiae*, XIV.84–85).

74   As Ficino said explicitly in his response to Pannonius that we saw just above: *fatum, id est, caelestium series causarum.* It is striking to note in relation to the issue of signs vs. causes that Ficino explicitly calls the planets the series of celestial *causes*, which is, I believe, Ficino's view, as I discuss further in Chap. 4 of my vol. II. In short, the plan-ets provide the efficient causes, and divine providence in the mind of God provides the ultimate—including the formal and final—causes, which then use the physical planets as His embodied instruments, precisely as I reconstructed in detail in Chaps. 1, 2 and 5 of my vol. I. Ficino ultimately both embraces and Platonizes this structure by bringing the universe to life and ensouling the planets, but I will also treat this further in volume II.

ticular locality when the Sun enters Aries (its ingress) at the beginning of the astrological year. This can also apply more generally to when the Sun enters each of the three other seasons at the beginning of Cancer (Summer), Libra (Autumn) and Capricorn (Winter) respectively. Otherwise, at any other times of the year, it is simply more of a general revolution, but we can still call it a *'revolutio mundi'* in a loose sense. Likewise, for the second type, a *'revolutio nati'* properly speaking is a horoscope made for an individual on their birthday when the Sun returns to where it was in the zodiac when they were born. We can also call any revolution that concerns an individual and their nativity, even if it is not on their actual birthday, a *'revolutio nati'* in a loose sense. This at least will be my usage here.

The proper *revolutiones mundi* provided the basis for annual prognostications, which were required of some university professors of mathematics, astronomy and astrology, at least in Italy at Ficino's time, as we can see in the 1405 statutes of the University of Bologna.[75] They were also published together with annual almanacs that started to appear with increasing frequency precisely at this time, i.e. in the mid-1470s.[76] Splendid examples of such annual prognostications during the 1480s and '90s (with a rich introduction), may be found in a collection of such texts by Domenico Maria da Novara (1454–1504), professor of mathematics, astronomy and astrology at the University of Bologna, and Copernicus's master there.[77]

Revolutions or general astrology are general and for everyone, whereas nativities are for particular individuals, which then have their own revolutions. They are thus complementary astrological practices—with nativities expressing a particular 'quantum' of the heavens at a particular time vis-à-vis a particular place—and they are both *'iudiciaria'*, i.e. knowledge oriented. Revolutions in particular can provide insight into the broader patterns of divine providence, which the revolutions of the heavens over time embody and represent. These are then supplemented with elections, which are an astrological practice for acting in and on the world, and are thus *'operativa'*, many examples of which occur in *De vita*, Book III, as I will discuss in detail in my vol. II, and very briefly in the next section [4] of this chapter.

---

75   I discuss this in detail in my volume I: 391–395.

76   For this important topic, see Alexandre Tur, *'Hora introitus solis in Arietem*: Les predictions astrologiques annuelles latines dans l'Europe du XVe siècle (1405–1484)'*, PhD thesis, Université d'Orléans, 2018, and Elide Casali, *Le spie del cielo: Oroscopi, lunari e almanacchi nell'Italia moderna* (Turin: Einaudi, 2003); and my vol. I: 391–400.

77   *I pronostici di Domenico Maria da Novara*, ed. F. Bònoli, G. Bezza, S. De Meis, and C. Colavita (Florence: Olschki, 2012).

3.1   *Letter to Giovanni Cavalcanti*

For our first example of a revolution in this section, we have another letter from Ficino to his dear friend Cavalcanti, in which Ficino explains that his father, a physician, will not let him visit his friend due to fears about the plague. In this light, Marsilio offers the astrological circumstances, which I will quote here in full:

> But I am writing this letter to you when [1] the Moon is in opposition to the Sun [i.e. at full Moon] and [2] in some degree [sc. of opposition] to Mercury and Saturn, and furthermore, [3] Mars is square to both the Sun and the Moon [sc. thus making a 't-square']. According to the astrologers (*apud astronomos*), this could hardly be a more inauspicious time. Nevertheless, I know that it is most propitious for me to write. For we have been united in friendship from early years not just by the influence of the stars, but by the decree of God, who commands the stars (11).[78]

In this example of a revolution, Ficino explains that, although the current astrological circumstances are difficult, nevertheless it is a good time for him to write. Unfortunately, Ficino only mentions the aspects between some of the planets—primarily the maleficent Mars and Saturn—but without indicating what zodiacal signs they are in, let alone their degrees, making it virtually impossible to date them.[79] Since this letter is from Book III, and so is the next one, they are both to be dated to at some point between August 1476 and May 1477.

3.2   *Letter to Rinaldo Orsini, Archbishop of Florence*

Our next example of a revolution is in Ficino's letter to Rinaldo Orsini, Archbishop of Florence, and Lorenzo de' Medici's brother-in-law. It too is also at

---

78   'Ego autem hanc ad te epistolam sub oppositione Lunae ad Solem, quodammodo etiam ad Mercurium et Saturnum, ac etiam sub Martis ad Solem Lunamque quadratura scribe, quo tempore nihil ferme apud Astronomos infoelicius. Nihilominus scio foelicissime me scripturum. Non enim conducentibus astris solum, verum et decemente Deo astrorum duce (714).' SES 2 [III].4 (p. 11).

79   I could not find any configurations in Regiomontanus's *Ephemerides* for the date range of this letter (Aug. 1476-May 1477) with Mars in t-square to a full Moon, and also more or less in opposition to Mercury and Saturn. According to Richard Kremer's calculations: '[1] On 7 June 1476, Moon-Sun was 178°, Mars-Sun was 86°, Moon-Sat was 137° (does not match the letter), Moon-Mer was 200°. Three of the 4 aspects match the letter! [2] Or better, on 19 Dec 1477, Moon-Sun was 190°, Mars-Sun was 88°, Moon-Sat was 69° (bad), Moon-Mer was 178°, better match to letter.'

least in part an astrological excuse for why Ficino could not visit his correspondent, a repeated theme in these letters. Furthermore—and as with the previous letter—I presume that all of this astrological information was read directly out of Regiomontanus's *Ephemerides*.[80] This letter concerns Ficino's patronage within the Church, and also a bump along that path. There are numerous letters to Archbishop Orsini in Ficino's correspondence:[81]

Then, when I wished to thank you personally for the favor granted at your behest, ill health detained me for many days. At last I determined to make the attempt the day before yesterday, but my breath so failed me in mid-journey that I was scarcely able to walk back home. Soon it was reported to me that your favor had been suspended. I was utterly astonished. When I looked most carefully for the cause of this reversal, I could not find it on earth (*in terra*); but at last I discovered it in the heavens (*in coelo*). [...] So I observed what had recently prevented my coming to you, and found that it was a malign aspect of Saturn, which was square to the Moon (*inveni quadratum malignumque Saturni ad Lunam aspectum*). Whence I concluded that your favor to me had been intercepted by the wiles of a certain Saturnine man. [Ficino's astrological interpretation] At first, I abandoned almost all hope of remedy, for I considered that perhaps Saturn was the most powerful, as well as the highest, of the planets. But then I recalled what the ancient sages say, and not without good reason, in their fables about Saturn and Jupiter, Mars and Venus; they say that Mars is bound by Venus, and Saturn by Jupiter. This simply means that the benignity of Jupiter and Venus holds in check the malignity of Saturn and Mars. I believe, therefore, that an injury inflicted by a Saturnine man may be effectively cured by one of a Jovial disposition. Now, in whom do I see the full reflection of Jupiter, his power and gifts? At present I find no one in Florence except you. People will perhaps laugh at a priest who heeds astronomical matters (*sacerdotem astronomica observantem*). But I, relying on the authority of the Persians, Egyptians and Chaldeans, considered that while earthly matters (*terrena*) were indeed the concern of

---

80   Richard Kremer who was kind enough to read an earlier draft of this chapter does not agree with my assessment. Rather, he does not think that Ficino even had access to a copy of Regiomontanus's *Ephemerides*, and that if he did, he most likely would have embraced a more numerically robust approach to astrology. I respectfully disagree, although he may well be correct. Unfortunately, there is no clear evidence to support either position.

81   SES 2 [III].10 (pp. 15–16).

others, heavenly matters (*coelestia*) in truth were the sole concern of the priest (16)[.][82]

In fact, the astrological dimension here, once again, is quite general, namely, that Saturn was in a malign squared aspect to the Moon resulting in Ficino's imminent return due to ill health and his professional injury due to a hypothetical malign Saturnine individual. Ficino then provides even more general adages, namely, that Jupiter tempers Saturn and Venus, Mars. Once again, Ficino only mentions a very few planets in aspect, but without any zodiacal signs or degrees.[83] He does, however, offer an interpretation, pointed but limited in scope. The end of this passage also seems to foreshadow Ficino's preemptive *Apologia* to his *De vita* (ll. 29–54).

3.3   *Letter to Sixtus IV (25 December 1478)*

Ficino's letter to Pope Sixtus IV (1414–1484)[84] is easily the richest astrological letter in Ficino's correspondence, and it is addressed to a very esteemed person indeed—and the most powerful enemy of Florence and the Medici during the Pazzi Conspiracy and its aftermath![85] Astrology only occurs on the first page of

---

82   Volentem deinde me tibi coram gratias agere ob beneficium tua causa designatum, plures dies adversa valetudo detinuit, denique nudius tertius obnixius id tentantem, spiritus in medio itinere usque adeo defecit, ut vix domum pedibus redire potuerim. Mox mihi nunciatum est, munus id tuum interturbatum fuisse. Miratus sum mirum in modum, ac diligentissime turbationis causam perscrutatus, quum eam in terra invenire non possem, in coelo denique reperi. Miraris hoc venerande pater. Nonne Thales Milesius in terra lapsus, surrexit in coelo, ut quae non viderat hic, illic inspiceret. Observavi igitur quid nuper meum ad te adventum impediverit, inveni quadratum malignumque Saturni ad Lunam aspectum id fecisse. Unde conclusi, Saturni cuiusdam hominis insidiis fuisse mihi beneficium interceptum. Primum quidem pene omnium remedii spem amisi, quum cogitarem Saturnum forte ita Planetarum potentissimum esse, ut altissimum. Sed deinde in mentem rediit, quod antiqui sapientes non absque summa ratione de Saturno et Iove, Marteque et Venere fabulantur. Martem videlicet a Venere, Saturnum ab Iove ligari. Hoc autem nihil aliud significat, quam quod Saturni Martisque malignitatem, benignitas Iovis Venerisque coercet. Opinor igitur vulnus, quod forsitan a Saturnio aliquo illatum est, ab Iovio quodam maxime posses curare. In quo autem omnem Iovis effigiem, vim, dotes, agnoscam, praeter te in praesentia Florentiae invenio neminem. Deridebit hic fortasse quispiam sacerdotem astronomica observantem. At ego Persarum, Aegyptiorum, Chaldaeorum authoritate fretus, putabam ad caeteros quidem terrena, ad sacerdotem vero solum coelestia pertinere (726)[.]

83   According to Richard Kremer: 'But we do not expect to find such detail. Your analysis is revealing a Ficino well versed in astrological doctrines but working at a general rather than a mathematical level in his day-to-day activities.'

84   SES 5 [VI].9 (pp. 15–19); 00, 813–815.

85   Bullard, 'Inward Zodiac', 694 ff. describes Ficino's increasingly bleak mood at this point.

the letter and it indicates Ficino's knowledge about revolutions to predict what will take place in the near future. In this dramatic letter, Ficino first discusses prophecy and then the 'astrologica'. Given that this letter is so different from all the others, in particular for the richness of its astrological content and detail, it is worth asking: how much of it was actually composed by Ficino himself? In fact, Ficino states explicitly that he explored this astrological material with three other philosopher-astrologers who are named in the margin of Letter 7 in MS M9. They are Francesco Berlinghieri (1440–1501),[86] Pietro da Rimini and Giorgio Ciprio, as SES indicates in their n. 3 to this letter on p. 97. Perhaps it was written by one of these collaborators, or, more probably, it was a collective endeavor.

Once again, Ficino and his collaborators could read all of this information directly out of Regiomontanus's *Ephemerides* for the period around December 1478. I will focus here only on the astrological part of this extensive letter, which begins thus: 'Marsilio Ficino of Florence and all of his fellow philosophers proclaim a celestial victory for the blessed Pope Sixtus'.[87] After an introduction beseeching the pope to listen to them, Ficino begins in earnest:

> Last year, most blessed Father, on the very birthday of all-powerful Christ [i.e., 25 December 1477], certain relics of the apostle Peter, found in the town of Volterra, produced in a single month twelve great miracles for all to see. And so, stirred by these new signs (*novis commoti signis*), we four philosophers (*conphilosophi quatuor*), equally devoted to both prophecy and astrology (*et prophetiae et Astrologiae pariter studiosi*), met together. First, by examining hidden prophecies (*propheticorum examinatio mysteriorum*) we agreed that those miracles connected with the relics of Peter portended that Sixtus, the successor to Peter, would at some time perform miracles which would become known to all peoples and nations (22).[88]

---

86 There is a *DBI* article on him from 1967 by Angela Codazzi, in which he is called a humanist geographer, who, among other things, worked on Ptolemy's *Geography*. I did not find anything on the other two figures mentioned here.

87 Sixto Pontifici Marsilius Ficinus Florentinus atque una omnes Conphilosophi sui, coelestem victoriam dicunt (813).

88 Anno superiore, beatissime pater, in ipso omnipotentis Christi natali, reliquiae quaedam Apostoli Petri urbe Volaterrana, miracula duodecim mense uno ingentia ostenderunt, omni populo manifesta. His ergo novis commoti signis convenimus una conphilosophi quatuor, et prophetiae et Astrologiae pariter studiosi. Primum quidem Propheticorum examinatione mysteriorum consensimus, ex illis reliquiarum Petri miraculis portendi, Sixtum successorrum Petri effecturum quandoque miracula cunctis populis Gentibusque notissima (813).

Thus Ficino *et alii* set the stage for the interesting discussion to follow.

The four co-philosophers continue by examining the relevant astrological phenomena:

> Secondly, applying ourselves to astrological matters (*nos ad Astrologica conferentes*), we carefully considered [1] the last conjunction of Saturn and Mars in Virgo, and the next one. We also considered [2] the next entrance of the Sun into Aries, and the beginnings of the quarters of the whole year. In addition, we considered [3] the eclipses of the Moon in Aquarius, as well as [4] the future eclipses of the Sun in Leo, and [5] other eclipses of the following year. Finally, we considered [6] the discordant combination of Mars and Jupiter, besides much else (22).[89]

Here is my brief discussion of these astrological phenomena that Ficino and his collaborators explored, which are keyed to the numbers I added to the text:

[1]   That last and the next conjunctions of Saturn and Mars, the two great malefics, in Virgo. According to Regiomontanus, the first took place on 13 Oct 1477 at 3° Virgo; the next one will be on 2 Nov 1479 at 20° Virgo.[90]

[2]   The next *Revolutio mundi*, and those for each of the other three seasons, namely, the next approach (entry = ingress) of the Sun into Aries, and also the beginnings of the three other quarters of the year, which were also relevant for annual prognostications.

[3]   Eclipse (lunar): The eclipses of the Moon in Aquarius. There are no eclipses indicated for 1477 in Regiomontanus's *Ephemerides*, nor are there any for 1478.

---

89   Deinde nos ad Astrologica conferentes, consideravimus diligenter:
       [1] praeteritam illam rursusque futuram coniunctionem Saturni ac Martis in Virgine.
       [2] Iterum proximum Solis accessum ad Arietem, quartarum quoque anni totius initia.
       [3] Eclypses praeterea Lunae quidem in Aquario.
       [4] Solis autem in Leone futuras.
       [5] Aliquasque rursus anni sequentis Eclypses.
       [6] Martis denique dissonam cum Iove permixtionem, caeteraque quam plurima (813).

90   In their notes to this letter (SES 5, p. 97, n. 5), they give different dates for the conjunctions, namely 19 Oct 1477 and 30 Oct 1479, but they do not say where they got this information. The conjunctions for the dates I give are clearly marked as such ad loc. in Regiomontanus's *Ephemerides*. SES has this to say about the eclipses: 'The eclipse of the Moon in Aquarius was in February 1479, and that of the Sun in Leo on 19th July, 1479.' They also note that 'Mars and Jupiter were conjunct two weeks after this[,]' but this is not mentioned in the letter, nor does any of it correspond with the accurate and contemporary information in Regiomontanus's *Ephemerides*.

[4]   Eclipse (solar): The future eclipses of the Sun in Leo. There is a solar eclipse listed for 1478 at 13° Leo on 29 July, but this would not be in the future at the time the letter was written in late 1478.[91]

[5]   Next year's eclipses: The other eclipses of the following year. Three eclipses are listed for 1479: Two lunar eclipses, at 14° Capricorn on July 3, and at 12° Cancer on 28 December. The solar eclipse is noted for 23° Sagittarius on 12 December.

[6]   Finally, the dissonant mixture [= bad aspect] of Mars with Jupiter, and many other things.

These are the range of astrological factors that Ficino and his collaborators consider, and this is all before the plague of 1479 had struck so virulently, which only served to amplify the bleakness of Ficino's already bleak mood.

Here is their apocalyptic interpretation:

We have concluded (*conclusimus*)[92] from all this that the next two years will be so miserable that it will commonly be believed that the utter destruction of the world is imminent, a universal and final calamity overwhelming the human race by war, pestilence and famine. Many leaders from every nation will be overthrown, and then a new heresy under a false prophet will arise.[93] The mind shudders to narrate what follows: soon, God forbid, the bark of Peter will be all but swamped by the waves of the Tiber. In the end, the Barbarians will lay waste Italy (15–16).[94]

No one could deny that their concluding imagery here is extremely apocalyptic.[95]

---

91   According to Richard Kremer: 'I checked all the solar and lunar eclipses in 1476–1479; none had the Moon in Aquarius.'

92   Not the 'royal we' this time!

93   This was also thought to be the case regarding the upcoming Great Conjunction of 1484. See (e.g.) my 'Teaching Astrology in the 16th Century: Giuliano Ristori and Filippo Fantoni on Pseudo-Prophets and Other Effects of Great Conjunctions.' SES 5, p. 98 n. 6 describes what they consider to be the historical fulfilment of these prophecies.

94   Inde conclusimus, proximum biennium fore adeo miserabile, (ut vulgo putetur) supremum illud mundi exitium imminere, commune scilicet et extremam generis humani calamitatem, bello, peste, fame, praementem. Principum cuiusque generis interitum plurimorum. Novam deinde sub falso Propheta haeresim surrecturam. Horret hic animus narrare quod sequitur, mox Tyberinis undis, (quod absit) Petri naviculam nataturam. Barbaros demum Italiam vastaturos (813).

95   In addition to eloquently describing Ficino's bleak mood here, Bullard also quotes from Ficino's *Consilio against the Plague*, which I will discuss more fully in my vol. II; 'Inward Zodiac', 694 ff.

The four philosophers continue by discussing Mars and Saturn in particular:

> Since in all these configurations of the heavens which we have discussed,
> Mars, the bringer of war, is more powerful than Saturn, the author of dis-
> ease, famine, treachery and heresy, we are agreed that it is from the strife
> in heaven that all the other evils will come. And so, at this point we said
> to each other in amazement: Where then are those life-saving miracles of
> Sixtus? What was the meaning for us of those miracles of Peter, if, in our
> judgment and in the considered opinion of astrologers the world over, so
> terrible a disaster, under the pontificate of Sixtus, is to afflict the Church,
> princes and citizens far and wide (16)?[96]

Surely Pope Sixtus with his miracles could and should have allayed these apocalyptic eventualities.

Our philosophers then draw their conclusions:

> After long and thorough reasoning, our discussion led us at last to these
> conclusions, which we have now set forth. [After citing several opportu-
> nities for Sixtus to prove his worth, they state:] [A]nd that he may tame
> fierce Mars and stern Saturn by his marvelous benevolence. And that Six-
> tus will shortly do this, not only the oracles of the prophets, but also
> certain celestial signs (*coelestia quaedam signa*) manifestly demonstrate
> (16).[97]

In the astrologically-informed eyes of these deeply interested interpreters,
then, Pope Sixtus will soon resolve all of these frightening predictions. This is
by far the most complex and sophisticated astrological discussion that we have
seen so far. And here there are both astrological data and interpretations, something we do not see very often in Ficino's other writings, even though there are
still no zodiacal degrees for any of the planets.[98]

---

96   Quoniam vero Mars illi dux, Saturnum pestis, famis proditionis, haeresis, authorem, in
      omnibus illis quas narravimus coeli dispositionibus, superabat, convenimus ex ipso bello
      reliqua mala omnia eventura. Hic ergo admirabundi invicem dicebamus. Ubi nam igitur
      salubria illa Sixta miracula? Quae ex illis Petri miraculis nobis portendebantur, si, ut et nos
      iudicamus, et caeteri deinde Astrologi totius orbis existimant, tam dira sub eius Pontifi-
      catu clades privatos passim et principes ecclesiamque vexabit (813).
97   In hanc tandem, (quam narravimus) sententiam disceptatio nos longa certa ratione per-
      duxit. [...] [M]irifica benignitate sua domet saevum Martem rigidumque Saturnum. Atque
      id quidem Sixtum brevi facturum non solum oracula Prophetarum, verumtamen coelestia
      quaedam signa manifeste demonstrant (813).
98   For more on the broader context of this letter (including on the relationship between

3.4   *Letter to Lorenzo de' Medici (26 September 1480)*

Our next example of a revolution is found in one of Ficino's letters to Lorenzo de' Medici, which was also written in the aftermath of the Pazzi Conspiracy.[99] This is another letter explaining the astrological reasons for why Ficino was unable to visit his correspondent, but wrote instead on 26 Sep. 1480. This is essentially a revolution in relation to Lorenzo's nativity, and thus a *revolutio nati*:

> Lorenzo, today and also tomorrow, be on your guard; for [1] Mars, passing into Capricorn, your ascendant, is seen [2] to look with square aspect, today [a] at Saturn and tomorrow [b] at the Sun. Besides this, [3] Saturn himself, the lord of your ascendant, has still not quite passed through the rays of the Sun [i.e. it is thus combust]. For this last reason, I, too, should take care [i.e. since Ficino himself also has Aquarius rising, which Saturn rules, just like Capricorn, Lorenzo's ascendant].[100]

According to Regiomontanus's *Ephemerides*, [1] Mars entered Capricorn on 7 September, 1480 and was thus [2a] squared Saturn at 5° Libra (today, i.e. on Sep 26th), and is [2b] squared the Sun tomorrow (27 Sep): Mars at 12° Capricorn was exactly squared the Sun at 12° Libra. Saturn conjoined the Sun on 18 Sep at 4° Libra, and was then within five degrees of the Sun, and thus combust through 23 Sep. Saturn went beyond five degrees of separation from the Sun on 24 September, with the Sun at 10° Libra and Saturn at 4° Libra.[101]

---

astrology and prophecy, a vast topic in its own right), see Donald Weinstein, *Savonarola and Florence: Prophecy and Patriotism in the Renaissance* (Princeton: Princeton University Press, 1970). For the Pazzi conspiracy in particular, in which Pope Sixtus was a central anti-Medicean player, in addition to Martines, *April Blood*, see SES's 'historical note', which discusses Sixtus's role as well as that of Federigo da Montefeltro and Ferrante, King of Naples: vol. 5, pp. 86–91. See also John M. Najemy, *A History of Florence, 1200–1575* (Oxford: Blackwell, 2006–2009), 352–361. As it turns out, Ficino corresponded with three of the main combatants against Lorenzo and the Medici faction, and all of these letters have astrological material: directly with Pope Sixtus himself and with Federigo da Montefeltro, duke of Urbino, and indirectly with Ferrante of Aragon, king of Naples, via his son Giovanni, the cardinal, as we saw.

99   SES 5 [VI].37 (pp. 59–60).

100   Hodie Laurenti atque cras caveto tibi, Mars enim sub Capricorno tuo ascendente percurrens quadrato aspectu hodie quidem Saturnum, cras vero Solem videtur aspicere. Praeterea Saturnus ipse ascendentis tui Dominus nondum Solis radios prorsus evasit. Ob hanc ultimam rationem mihi quoque est cavendum (831)[.]

101   The numbers here do not correspond precisely to Regiomontanus's *Ephemerides* for September 1480, but they are close.

Ficino continues:

> I was coming to you the other day to tell you all this, but on the way it
> occurred to me that it would be better to wait until now (i.e. 26 Sep), so as
> not to burden you with fear and unease any longer than necessary. For by
> our predictions we often anticipate evils (*mala*) that are in the far distant
> future, or sometimes imagine evils that will never come to pass. While all
> who at any time are subject to fear are considered wretched, those are
> certainly less wretched who are troubled by fear for a shorter time. I cer-
> tainly trust, and my faith is not unfounded, that the one ruler of the stars
> and of men, who has till now miraculously saved you time and again from
> the threats of the stars and from the heinous hands of men,[102] will of his
> mercy likewise save you in the future. 26 September 1480.[103]

Among other things, Ficino reflects here on some of the ethical concerns that
arise with making astrological predictions. And we should note that Ficino
here seems to represent himself as Lorenzo's astrologer, in which capacity he
discusses current transits of Lorenzo's Capricorn ascendant in a reasonably
detailed and sophisticated treatment, at least in comparison to what we have
seen so far.[104]

---

102   This is a reference to the attempt on Lorenzo's life during the Pazzi Conspiracy.

103   [V]eniebam superioribus diebus ad te, eadem praedicturus, sed obiter succurret, praestare
       ut in hanc horam usque differrem, ne diuturniore te metu et molestia praemerem. Sole-
       mus enim saepe praedictionibus nostris mala vel procul futura anticipare diu, vel inter-
       dum fingere non futura. Cum vero miseri censeantur omnes, quibus aliquando sit timen-
       dum, illi certe minus miseri, qui breviore metu sollicitantur. Spero equidem, neque vana
       fides, eundem syderum hominumque regem, qui te hactenus et a syderum minis, et
       ab immanibus hominum minibus mirifice saepe servavit, in posterum quoque pro sua
       clementia similiter servaturum. xxvi. Septembris. M. cccc. lxxx (831).

104   Claudia Rousseau discusses Lorenzo's horoscope in rich detail in her 1983 PhD thesis,
       which also reconstructs more of the relevant cultural context of astrology in Medicean
       Florence; 'Cosimo i de' Medici and Astrology: The Symbolism of Prophecy', PhD thesis,
       Columbia University, 1983, 132 ff.

3.5   *Letter to Federigo da Montefeltro, Duke of Urbino* (*6 Jan 1482*), *and*
        [6] the Related Sermon on the Star of the Magi (De stella magorum
        [*ca. 1484–1494*])[105]

Two more texts with Ficino's discussion and use of practical astrology in his
early writings occur in this sermon on the Star of the Magi (ca. 1484–1494),[106]
and in a related letter to Federico da Montefeltro, duke of Urbino, from 6 Jan
1482,[107] in which Ficino also discusses Christ's birth. The comet that led the
Magi to the Christ child can be treated on its own as a particular type of irregular astronomico-celestial phenomenon that inspired strong and characteristic types of predictions—mainly negative—with a rich history going back
to Antiquity.[108] This included by interpreting the comet partially in terms of
where it appears in the heavens vis-à-vis the zodiac and the other planets,
which is why I include it within revolutions. Of course, comets could not be
accurately predicted until Newton provided a successful model for understand-

---

105   I will not treat Ficino's *De stella magorum* here, despite its interest, primarily because it
      has already received some valuable scholarship, and it is translated in both Faracovi and
      Voss, as well as in the interest of space. For more on Ficino's sermon, see Stephen M. Büh-
      ler, 'Marsilio Ficino's *De stella magorum* and Renaissance Views of the Magi', *Renaissance*
      Quarterly 43 (1990): 348–371, and Ornella Pompeo Faracovi, *Gli oroscopo di Cristo*, 107–
      122. See now also Denis J.-J. Robichaud, 'The Star of the Magi or the Afterlife of Chaldean
      Angels in Iamblichus, Proclus, Psellos, Pletho, and Ficino', in *Inventer les Anges del'Antiq-
      uité à Byzance: Conception, Représentation, Perception*, ed. Delphine Lauritzen (Paris: Amis
      du Centre d'Histoire et Civilisation de Byzance, 2021), 763–808. Robichaud's article is
      based in part on the recent edition with a rich introduction on Ficino's sermons by Daniele
      Conti, *Marsilii Ficini Florentini Predicationes* (Turin: Aragno, 2014). I will treat the *De stella*
      magorum with Robichaud's analysis and Conti's introduction in greater depth in chapter 4
      of my vol. II.
106   In his edition, Conti dates *De stella magorum* broadly to between 1484 and 1494 (CIXff.).
      Faracovi dates it to 1482 at *Gli oroscopi*, 115, and *Scritti*, 175, n. 1. Robichaud follows Conti
      on the dating. Conti also makes clear that much of the *De stella magorum* is dependent
      on the 1482 letter to Federigo da Montefeltro.
107   Federigo was also one of Florence and the Medici's enemies in the wake of the Pazzi Con-
      spiracy, which had by now been resolved. He died on 10 Sep 1482 soon after receiving this
      letter. For more on the rich astrological culture of the Urbino court, see (e.g.) Stephan
      Heilen, 'Astrology at the Court of Urbino under Federico and Guidobaldo da Montefeltro',
      in *De Fréderic II à Rodolphe II: Astrologie, divination et magie dans les cours* (*XIIIe–XVIIe*
      siècle), ed. J.-P. Boudet, M. Ostorero and A. Paravicini Bagliani (Sismel: Galluzzo, 2017),
      313–368.
108   See (e.g.) Sarah J. Schechner, *Comets, Popular Culture, and the Birth of Modern Cosmology*
      (Princeton: Princeton University Press, 1999). There is a rich scholarship on comets that
      I will not rehearse here. Robichaud (2021) argues strongly in his first section that Ficino
      interpreted the Star of the Magi as the Angel Gabriel in the guise of a comet, which is a
      striking part of his fascinating interpretation.

ing their motion in his *Principia* of 1687,[109] before which they were considered to be an expression of God's absolute power, i.e., not of his ordered or ordained power, as were the normal and predictable motions of the planets and luminaries within the zodiac in their diurnal and annual motions.[110]

I will only briefly mention comets here in the interest of space, and also because they were surely dear to Ficino's heart, given that he too—like Christ—had been born during the appearance of a comet, thereby indicating a providentially significant life. Instead, I will focus all-too-briefly on Ficino's letter to Federigo, in which I will simply indicate some of the practical astrological themes that Ficino raises there that we have not yet seen, but without going into proper detail, which I will do in chap. 4 of my vol. II. In fact, this letter is more of a critical philosophical treatment of astrologically-related issues than a discussion of practical astrology *per se*, although there is some of this too, especially concerning revolutions, but also nativities.

In this rich letter, Ficino discusses the relationship between astrology and religion more generally, and Christianity in particular, including God's governance of the world and of the human beings living here (84).[111] In this process, Ficino refers to the astrology of religions in relation to the great conjunction cycles of 20, 240 and 960 years, thus referring explicitly to Albumasar, and implicitly to Roger Bacon and the more recently published Pierre d'Ailly. Ficino thus refers to a particularly significant type of astrological revolutions regarding the broader patterns of history, including the appearance and longevity of religions, their coming-into-being and passing away.[112] Ficino also raises the themes of divine providence and fate within this context, and he claims that the Christian martyrs were educated in astrology (85).

109   See (e.g.) Simon Schaffer, 'Newton's Comets and the Transformation of Astrology', in *Astrology, Science and Society: Historical Essays*, ed. Patrick Curry (Woodbridge: Boydell Press, 1987), 219–243.

110   On this fundamental medieval distinction, see (e.g.) Francis Oakley, 'The Absolute and Ordained Power of God in Sixteenth- and Seventeenth-Century Theology', *Journal of the History of Ideas* 59 (1998): 437–461; especially 440–449, with much additional bibliography.

111   The page references here are to the translation in Voss (2006), pp. 83–94, who takes it from SES 6 [VII].17. The page numbers in Ficino's OO are 849–853.

112   For these, see (e.g.) Laura A. Smoller, *History, Prophecy and the Stars: The Christian Astrology of Pierre d'Ailly, 1350–1420* (Princeton: Princeton University Press, 1994), and my volume I: 254–261. D'Ailly's relevant works had just been printed for the first time in Louvain, ca. 1480–1482 (ISTC: ia00477000), although Smoller thinks it is 1483. This also relates to the great significance Ficino gave to publishing his Plato *Opera omnia* in late 1484 to correspond with the great conjunction of Jupiter and Saturn in Scorpio then. I also treat this great conjunction more fully in chap. 4 of my vol. II.

For our concerns, one of the most interesting features of Ficino's discussion here is that he repeatedly raises and to some extent articulates the well-defined causal structures that I discussed earlier in relation to the slightly later letter to Johannes Pannonius, which here treat providence and fate together with the souls of the spheres, thereby identifying Ficino's construction here as deeply Platonic, and showing, at least in part, how he augmented the medieval astrologizing-Boethian system by explicitly Platonizing it (85). Perhaps it also indicates a development in Ficino's thought. Regardless, the celestial bodies are instruments here and thus are efficient causes, but not the ultimate cause, which continues to be divine providence.[113] There is much more to this letter and the sermon on the Star of the Magi, but I cannot treat them further here.[114]

3.6 Letter to Nicholas Bathory, Bishop of Vác

Our final example of an astrological revolution is in Ficino's letter to Nicholas Bathory, Bishop of Vác, regarding King Matthias's invitation for Ficino to come to Hungary.[115] Here Ficino explains why he cannot visit his correspondent, which is, as we have seen, a regular astrological theme in his letters:

> It would be a wonder for me to leave the home of my birth, for either the move will be prevented by Saturn, rising for me in Aquarius, as perhaps an astrologer might think, or it will be forbidden by one of those spirits (a *genius* [= daemon]) of Saturn, as a Magus might believe (*seu vetet aliquis eiusmodi genius, quod Magus forsitan opinabitur*). [...] Now I have put forward several possible causes for this situation. For the Platonists think that human events are indeed sometimes signified by the stars (*humanos eventus a stellis quidem interdum significari*), but are frequently set in motion by daemons attending upon the stars (*incitari vero frequenter a daemonibus stellarum quasi pedissequis*), and are finally brought to completion (*peragi*) by us human beings, according to our earthly circumstances (55).[116]

---

113   Ficino discusses these causal structures in some detail on pp. 85, 87, 89 and 93.
114   I intend to treat this material more fully in chapter 4 of my vol. II as it points to a significant nexus in Ficino's early views about astrology within its broader providential framework.
115   SES 7 [VIII].48, p. 55. Since it is in Book VIII, it should be dated to between Summer 1484 and October 1488.
116   '[M]e vero patrias mutare sedes mirum fuerit, sive mutationem prohibeat Saturnus in Aquario nobis ascendens, quod forte iudicabit Astrologus, seu vetet aliquis eiusmodi genius, quod Magus forsitan opinabitur, sive corpusculum ineptum laboribus impediat iter, seu mens contemplationi semper intenta quiescere iubeat. Ambiguas equidem hac de re causas assignavi. Nam Platonici putant humanos eventus a stellis quidem interdum

In this letter, Ficino refers to Saturn, but also to the *daemones* attendant upon each planet as well.[117] The mention of these Platonic views on astrology is also very similar to what we find in the important passages of *De vita* III.14 that are dependent on Proclus's fragmentary *De sacrificio et magia*, as Brian P. Copenhaver has clearly shown.[118] This material is thus unlike anything we have seen so far, which has been, for the very most part, normal traditional medieval astrologizing Aristotelianism.[119] This passage also thus points forward directly to the Renaissance Neoplatonic world view of the *De Vita*.[120]

4   Elections

I would now like to briefly discuss Ficino's use of the third type of practical astrology—elections—the choosing of astrologically propitious times to begin any sort of venture. This is the main astrological practice that Ficino employs, for which we have abundant evidence, mainly in the *De vita*, including for both the theory and practice of making medicaments and talismans, many of which I will discuss in volume II.

4.1   *Cornerstone for Palazzo Strozzi*
Our first example of an election is of Ficino consulting with Filippo Strozzi to lay the cornerstone of his palazzo on 16 Aug 1489.[121] In his *Vita di Filippo*

---

significari, incitari vero frequenter a daemonibus stellarum quasi pedissequis [these are the same terms that Ficino used in *De vita* III.20.21–24], peragi denique ab hominibus, pro conditione rerum nobis propinquarum. Vale (884).' In this letter, Ficino also refers to the letter to the same Johannes Pannonius as well, whom Bathory seems to know, which is also in Book VIII (p. 871).

117   There are more *daemones* in the long letter in SES 7 [VIII].29 (pp. 33–39; OO, p. 876) and it has magic too; this is derived from Ficino's translation of Porphyry's *De abstinentia*.

118   'Hermes Trismegistus, Proclus, and the Question of a Philosophy of Magic in the Renaissance', in *Hermeticism and the Renaissance: Intellectual History and the Occult in Early Modern Europe, ed.* Ingrid Merkel and Allen G. Debus, London: Associated University Presses, 1988, 79–110.

119   This talk of *daemones* also occurs in both the 1469 and 1474 iterations of the *De amore* in a cosmological context in Book VI, Chaps. 3 and 4, which I will discuss more fully in my vol. II.

120   I discuss '*daemones*' in relation to nativities and for their use regarding Neoplatonic 'epistrophe' or 'return to the divine' in my volume II.

121   Bullard mentions this; 'Inward Zodiac', 692, and n. 18. This was also the case with Giuliano Ristori fifty years later as part of the commission to determine the same with the Fortezza da Basso in Florence; see John R. Hale, 'The End of Florentine Liberty: The Fortezza da Basso', in his *Renaissance War Studies* (London: Hambledon Press, 1983), 31–62. Although

Strozzi,[122] Lorenzo Strozzi noted that Ficino, along with Benedetto Biliotti, Maestro Nicolò and Maestro Antonio Benivieni, had agreed on 16 August 1489 as a propitious day for the cornerstone to be placed.[123]

4.2 *Letter to Pico regarding De vita,* Book II (23 August 1489)

In a letter to Pico in Book VIII dated precisely to 23 August 1489—which is just before the letter to Uranio describing his own nativity that I treated above, and contemporary with the election just discussed concerning the Palazzo Strozzi—Ficino discusses in detail the astrological circumstances prevailing for his undertaking *De vita*, Book II (*De vita longa*), including its relationship to his own nativity.[124] Since it is about the astrological timing of beginnings, I consider it to be an election, although this could probably be debated, as it is also, at least in part, about Ficino's own and also Pico's *revolutio nati*, and thus two revolution horoscopes. The letter is entitled: *Astronomicum auspicium pro libro de vita longa*. The previous letter to Pierleone da Spoleto also has astrological symbolism, and it mentions Ficino's translation of Proclus.

Ficino begins thus:

---

this evidence does not come from Ficino's correspondence, I include it here due to the very limited nature of the pre-*De vita* evidence that I know of for Ficino's use of elections.

122 Marsilio Ficino, *Vita di Filippo Strozzi*, ed. G. Bini and P. Bigazzi (Florence: Casa di Correzione, 1851), 70. Also see Kristeller, *SF*, II: 307.

123 In this edition, on p. 70 are 'documenti aggiunti', of which this is: 'Da un libro di debitori e creditori di Filippo si toglie a carte 170 il seguente Ricordo, di sua mano' from 1489: 'A di 16 d'Agosto, appunto su l'uscire del Sole da' monti, in nome di Dio, e di buon principio per me e mia discendenti, e di qualunque se ne travaglierà, gettai la prima pietra ne' fondamenti. E a questa medesima ora feci cantare una Messa dello Spirito Santo da' frati di S. Marco, e una dale Donne delle Murate, e una all mia S. Maria di Licceto, e una da' frati di S. Maria di Licceto, tutti mia divoti, con pregare Iddio, che sia in buon principio per me, e per mia discendenti, e per tutti quelli, che in dettta muraglia daranno favore. // Ebbi tal punto dal soprannominato Benedetto Biliotti, e Maestro Niccolò, e Maestro Antonio Benivienti medici, el Vescovo de' Pagagnotti, e M. Marsilio; tutti lo approvono per buono.' In his article on related issues with the architect Filarete, Berthold Hub also mentions this foundation for the Palazzo Strozzi, where he dates it to 6 August 1489; 'Founding an Ideal City in Filarete's *Libro Architettonico*', in *Foundation, Dedication and Consecration Ritual in Early Modern Culture, ed.* M. Schraven and M. Delbeke (Leiden: Brill, 2011), 17–57, 34. He discusses astrology more generally in this context on pp. 23–25. In discussing the Palazzo Strozzi, the website 'sgira.org' also gives the date as 6 August 1489; https://www.sgira.org/palaces7.htm (last accessed 26 July 2024).

124 SES 7 [VIII].17 (pp. 24–25).

Astrological Auspices for the Book *De vita longa*

But since I realized that I was undertaking a task beyond my earthly powers, I began this important work by heeding the celestial powers [sc. with an election]. [First, though, his nativity] At the time of my birth, Jupiter, occupying Cancer in the sixth house and from there aspecting Venus, the Sun, Mercury, and the Moon, promised a wholesome combination of medicines.[125]

Ficino emphasizes Jupiter, and Jupiter here is in Cancer in his sixth house, which is the same sign placement as in the 1476/77 letter to Cavalcanti, but it is different from that in the very next letter to Uranio. And Jupiter here aspects Venus, the Sun, Mercury and the Moon, with Venus in Libra (so squared Jupiter), the Sun and Mercury in Scorpio (so trine Jupiter), and the Moon in Capricorn (so opposite Jupiter). Although he does not mention any of the placements here in either their signs or houses, because he explicitly states that Jupiter is in Cancer, it justifies me using the configuration discussed in the earlier letter to Cavalcanti, especially Venus in Libra, although Venus in Virgo would also aspect Jupiter in a sextile. It does, however, seem exceedingly strange that Ficino would revert to the old and incorrect configuration with Jupiter in Cancer from twelve years before, when he provided the correct information in the very next letter to Uranio!

After discussing some of the structure of his nativity—and in a somewhat different way than he had discussed it in Part 2 above—Ficino then treats the celestial circumstances in play when he began *De vita*, Book II:

[However, so that Jupiter's promises might one day be fulfilled to greater effect,] I again took the auspices (*auspicatus sum*) for the present work from those who dwell in heaven: [Planets in signs, as usual] [1] Mercury was favourably pursuing a direct course in his own sign of Virgo [sc. its dignity: house]; [2] the Moon was entering Taurus [sc. where it is exalted, another dignity] and [3] coming into conjunction with Jupiter [sc. a great benefic] in that sign [sc. Taurus]; and from there [4] the Moon was aspecting the Sun in a trine, as well as Venus and Mercury.[126]

---

125   'Quoniam vero rem supra terrenas vires moliri me noveram, a coelestibus opusculum tantum auspicatus sum. Et si Iupiter me nascente, cancrum in sexta tenens: atque inde: Venerem et Apollinem, et Mercurium Dianamque conspiciens salutarem medicinarum confectionem est pollicitus (901)[.]' The text after 'auspicatus sum' is neither in the 1495 *Princeps* nor in the 1576 *OO*. In n. 4 on p. 71, SES says that they provide the 'Latin text missing from the printed edition(s)' on p. 104, which I have included here.

126   [A] Mercurio quidem rectum iter sub Virgine sua feliciter prosequente, a Luna rursum,

Thus, according to Regiomontanus, as Ficino was beginning to compose *De vita*, Book II, the Sun entered Virgo on 14 August. At this time, [1] Mercury was direct in Virgo from 29 July through 18 August, in direct motion and with a dignity. [2] The Moon entered Taurus on 17–18 August, with the Moon exalted in Taurus; and [3] the Moon approached conjunction with Jupiter in Taurus, since Jupiter entered Taurus on 20 July 1489. Finally, [4] the Moon is trine the Sun, Venus and Mercury.[127] In addition to being an election, this configuration is also a *revolutio mundi* in the loose sense for this time—a revolution of the moment—which may have also persuaded Ficino to begin then. Choosing this moment in advance is precisely what makes it an election.

In my understanding, for Ficino 'taking the auspices' would mean simply to look at his copy of Regiomontanus's *Ephemerides* and see what the celestial circumstances were or will be, and to locate a beneficial celestial configuration for him and his work both in itself and in relation to his own nativity. Together with the letter to Sixtus IV and that to Lorenzo de' Medici of 26 Sep 1480, this is the most detailed astrological description in Ficino's early writings that I know of, and Ficino seems to have written this one by himself. Once again, although he discusses planets in signs and in aspect to each other, Ficino still provides no planetary degrees whatsoever.

After discussing these astrological circumstances at the onset of composing Book II, Ficino then relates it to Pico's nativity, knowledge of which he indicates here:

> My purpose was that my work, born under life-giving planets, with Mercury dominant (*regnante Mercurio*),[128] might bestow longer life on those studying philosophy, and especially on you, my dearest Pico, of all students of philosophy, the one most worthy of life. So that our attentive efforts might be of the greatest benefit at least to you, I for my part watched the Sun playing with Taurus [sc. trining, as above], a situation you yourself were fortunate enough to meet with at the time of your birth.[129]

Taurum subeunte, atque ibidem coeunte cum Iove, et illinc Phoebum suspiciente per Trigonum et Venerem similiter, atque Mercurium (901)[.]

127 Venus was in Virgo from 4 July, going retrograde on 21 July at 4 degrees Virgo, leaving Virgo for Leo on 7 August, and not re-entering Virgo until 28 September. So the window with Venus in Virgo is small, but Ficino only says here that it is trine the Sun, not that it is also in Virgo.

128 I.e. with Mercury in Virgo together with the Sun.

129 [U]t compositio nostra vitalibus nata Planetis, regnante Mercurio, Philosophantibus conferret ad vitam, tibi praesertim dilectissime Pice philosophantium omnium vita dignis-

In fact, there is a sextile aspect between Pico's Sun at 4° Pisces and his Moon at 25° Taurus.[130]

After discussing the beginning of *De vita*, Book II in relation to one feature of Pico's nativity, Ficino turns to the celestial situation upon completion of his text, and thus to the revolution at that time. This section is also, at least in part, related to Pico's nativity:

> Finally, today I have come to an end [sc. of composing *De vita*, Book II]. Diana [sc. the Moon] is coming into trine with Saturn and will thus care for lofty Saturn's son, Pico, before all others, especially because victorious Saturn is seated at this time in Capricorn [sc. which it rules], holding the huge head of the Dragon in his right hand and gazing in splendor upon the Sun with the trine rays of his eyes (*trinis oculorum radiis*).[131] He [sc. Saturn] will confirm the promises of the heavenly ones to his own people with an utterly unshakeable covenant, if only, as is to be hoped, Jupiter the most high shows favour to the worshipers of Minerva with a nod of that very head from which he gave birth to Minerva. 23 Aug 1489.[132]

Singing Saturn's and Jupiter's praises, this letter brings us up to the moment that Ficino completed the second book of his *De vita libri tres*, *De vita longa*. In this richly informative letter, Ficino makes an integrated use of different astrological practices: primarily elections and revolutions, but also nativities, including

---

simo. Cui sane ut maxime diligenti nostra prodesset, Phoebum cum Tauro ludentem, qualem ipse nascens feliciter nactus es (901)[.]

130   According to David Juste in his comments to my earlier version ad loc: 'Ancient and medieval astrologers, with very few exceptions, considered aspects to be relationships between signs, regardless of the degree and/or the orb, so that 4° Pisces is actually sextile to 25° Taurus (likewise two planets at 29° Aries and 1° Taurus are not in conjunction). But, admittedly, that does not tell you why Ficino speaks of a trine between the Sun and the Moon.'

131   Saturn is conjunct the North Node in Capricorn for all of August, 1489, but Saturn is trine the Sun precisely only on Aug 23rd, i.e. when the letter was dated. In fact, in *De vita*, Book III, Ficino calls the planets 'the eyes of the world', whose extramitted radiation is alive, as I discuss in Part 2 of my volume II.

132   [E]quidem observavi hodie, postremo peragi ad Saturni trigonum veniente Diana, ita Picum sublimis Saturni filium prae caeteris curatura. Praesertim quoniam Saturnus interea victor insidet Capricorno, caputque Draconis ingens destra tenet, et gloriabundus, trinis oculorum radiis Apollinem intuetur, hoc statim aspectu suis promissa coelestium stabili prorsus foedere firmaturus, si modo, quod sperandum est, Iuppiter ille summus, Capite quo Minervam genuit, Minervae cultoribus annuat. XXIII. Augusti. M. CCCC. LXXXIX (901).

his and Pico's. This is a much fuller use of astrology than anything we have seen so far, with the exception of the 1478 letter to Sixtus IV, which Ficino explicitly did not compose on his own. Nevertheless, he still does not offer any degrees for any of the planets, which we can now see is his normal practical astrological *modus operandi*.

4.3 De vita, *Book III (a Teaser)*

This discussion of the astrological origins and circumstances of *De vita*, Book II, takes us right up to the doorstep, as it were, of *De vita*, Book III, the famous *De vita coelitus comparanda*. In Book III, Ficino uses elections primarily for designing and manufacturing medicines and talismans, with his analysis of compound medicaments providing the precise model for making talismans (III.12), as I will argue in detail in my volume II. Here astrological theory is oriented towards practice, including his discussion of numerous practical examples with the astrologically-informed ingredients for both medicaments and talismans—sc. the material dimension—with astrology thus operating at several levels of his analysis (III.13–22). Furthermore, in III.25, Ficino explicitly defends elections from a zealous prelate with numerous examples but little detail, which is thus similar to his defense of talismans at III.18. I will treat both features and much more in my volume II.

In lieu of treating them in detail here, I would now like to at least indicate some of the astrological dimensions of Ficino's *De vita*, Book III. *De vita* III.9–12 present an integrated astrologico-medical primer: Chapters 9 and 10 discuss medical astrology in relation to the body, including a detailed treatment of the astrological dignities in III.9. Chapter 11 treats the astrological physiology of human spirit (as based on and developing *De vita* I.2). Chapter 12 provides a detailed model of how to design and make astrological medicines as strong as possible in order to treat individuals within the integrated understanding of III.9–11. Then, in III.13–22, after saying that he will devote one chapter to talismans, Ficino provides an intensive mini-treatise on talismans, and thus a horse of a very different but related color to that of medicaments. Although it too is deeply astrological, including towards practice, a much fuller treatment must be left to my volume II. Thus, Ficino focuses on astrological medicine in III.9–12, and on astrological magic and theurgy in III.13–22, including the design and manufacture of talismans. His main astrological practice there is elections, but not only, as he also discusses both nativities and revolutions, both *mundi* and *nati*.

Ficino's system in *De vita* possesses a deeply astrological core in practical, natural philosophical, cosmological and metaphysical respects, including his extensive treatment of talismans, but I will only mention the practical astrological features of the medical dimensions here.[133] First are his usage of practical astrology (including dignities, houses and aspects) towards a medical end; he also transforms their metaphysical, cosmological and natural philosophical foundations in a Platonic direction (including by adding cosmic *spiritus* and stellar rays), and by bringing the entire system to life by (i.a.) ensouling the planets. Ficino discusses this ultimately in relation to making and using medicines and talismans. I believe that this is Ficino's properly 'Renaissance' contribution: [1] to add Neoplatonic metaphysics, cosmology, theology and theurgy to normative medieval astrologizing-Aristotelian natural knowledge and practice, and then [2] to expand and deepen the astrological dimensions of this integrated system throughout every level of its structure.[134]

5 Conclusion

From the examples I have offered in this chapter, we can now see that the overwhelming number of Ficino's practice of nativities, revolutions and elections in his early (ca. 1469–1489) writings that treat astrology were mostly utterly normal traditional medieval practices, but this changes dramatically in the *De vita*—and especially in its Book III—with his offering of a theurgical astrology together with a radically transformed Platonic world view, replete with a living universe, although he still continues to employ traditional astrological practices as well in the *De vita*, even in Book III. In this, we can see Ficino himself transform from a medieval into a Renaissance conception and practice of both astrology and talismans, and thus both its *iudiciaria* and *operativa* domains.[135]

Finally, we can see that in most of his early astrological writings and especially those in the correspondence, Marsilio Ficino seems to have been a solid but not very sophisticated practitioner of traditional, i.e. medieval astrology, at least until when he composed *De vita*, Books II and III.[136] When we look

---

133 I treat the talismanic and other dimensions of *De vita* III in Part 2 of my vol. II.
134 I provide a preliminary account in my 'Dancing with the Stars'. I treat this all much more fully in my volume II.
135 For this distinction in Roger Bacon, see my vol. I:119–120. I will develop this assertion much more fully in my volume II.
136 David Juste thinks that my interpretation is too strict. Here is his comment: 'I find your interpretation of Ficino's letters too strict. You repeatedly point out the absence of degrees as some sort of defect or shortcoming on Ficino's part, but why would Ficino need to specify degrees in those letters, where astrology is not even the subject? After reading your account of those letters, I can't see why they would indicate "a very basic and elementary

more widely, however, astrology seems to have been very important to Ficino's broader world view, but I can only mention this here, saving a much fuller treatment for my volume II. Finally, practical astrology also appears in works later than the *De vita*, including in his commentary on Plotinus's *Ennead* II.3 (1492) and in the *De sole et lumine* (1493), as well as in other famous letters (including the one to Poliziano from 1494), but these will all need to wait for my volume II, although they will not all be treated fully there either. Ultimately, all of these texts should be analyzed in a comprehensive treatment of astrology within Ficino's life and works, for which this chapter has been a preliminary sounding.

We will also have noticed, perhaps surprisingly, that Ficino shows exceedingly little interest in predictions of any sort, except in the joint letter to Sixtus IV, and retrospectively in the letter to Lorenzo de' Medici (II.5 above). By contrast, Ficino's letters and related texts concerning practical astrology mainly concern diagnosis, explanation or analysis of a situation, including why he could not visit his correspondents. This continues to be very much the case in *De vita* as well, as I will discuss in much greater detail in my volume II. Finally, it is also the case that the overwhelming emphasis in all of this evidence is on the planet Saturn and its related zodiacal signs, Capricorn and Aquarius. I suppose that this will come as no surprise to anyone who knows even the slightest amount about Ficino and his Saturnine obsessions.

Acknowledgments

This essay was undertaken as an opportunity to write something about Ficino's actual astrological practices to honour the memory of Helena Avelar, whom I sadly never met in person, only virtually on Zoom. I also dedicate this to the memory of Michael J.B. Allen who taught us all so much about Ficino and his writings, and to that of Ornella Pompeo Faracovi, who did the same with Ficino's astrology in particular. I would also like to acknowledge Richard Kremer and David Juste for reading a later stage of this essay and making many

---

level of astrological practice" or that Ficino was "not a very sophisticated practitioner". I am not saying that they indicate the opposite, but just that we cannot assess Ficino's level of astrological practice from those letters'. Richard Kremer also essentially agrees with Juste's position: 'Is this "simplistic and elementary" or rather "barely mathematical"? He could have made sophisticated astrological readings of horoscopes with planets located only in houses'. Perhaps, although I would like to see more detail and interpretation to agree with these assessments, I do not disagree lightly.

valuable comments (some of which I include here), and to Angela Dressen for a range of timely scans. Finally, I would like to acknowledge my Research Fellowship at CAS-e of the FAU Erlangen-Nuremberg, where this essay was substantially written. It took on a life of its own soon after it began, and I learned a great deal writing it.

Bibliography

Allen, Michael J.B. *Nuptial Arithmetic: Marsilio Ficino's Commentary on the Fatal Number in Book VIII of Plato's Republic*. Berkeley: University of California Press, 1994.

Allen, Michael J.B. *Synoptic Art: Marsilio Ficino on the History of Platonic Interpretation*. Florence: Olschki, 1998.

Allen, Michael J.B. 'Marsilio Ficino on Saturn, the Plotinian Mind, and the Monster of Averroes'. *Bruniana e Campanelliana* 16 (2010): 11–29.

Avelar de Carvalho, Helena. *An Astrologer at Work in Late Medieval France: The Notebooks of S. Belle*. Leiden: Brill, 2021.

Bate, Henry. *The Astrological Autobiography of a Medieval Philosopher: Henry Bate's Nativitas (1280–1281)*, edited by Carlos Steel, Steven vanden Broecke, David Juste and Shlomo Sela. Leuven: Leuven University Press, 2018.

Black, Robert, and Gabriella Pomaro. *Boethius's* Consolation of Philosophy *in Italian Medieval and Renaissance Education*. Florence: Sismel–Galluzzo, 2000.

Bühler, Stephen M. 'Marsilio Ficino's *De stella magorum* and Renaissance Views of the Magi'. *Renaissance Quarterly* 43 (1990): 348–371.

Bullard, Melissa M. 'The Inward Zodiac: A Development in Ficino's Thoughts on Astrology'. *Renaissance Quarterly* 43 (1990): 687–708.

Burnett, Charles S.F. 'Astrology'. In *Medieval Latin: An Introduction and Bibliographical Guide*, edited by F.A.C. Mantello and A.G. Rigg. Washington, D.C.: Catholic University of America Press, 1996.

Casali, Elide. *Le spie del cielo: Oroscopi, lunari e almanacchi nell'Italia moderna*. Turin: Einaudi, 2003.

Catalogus Codicum Astrologorum Latinorum I: Les manuscrits astrologiques latins conservés à la Bayerische Staatsbibliothek de Munich, edited by David Juste, (Documents, Études et Répertoires Publiés par l'Institut de Recherche et d'Histoire des Textes 81; Paris: CNRS Éditions, 2011); volume II is for the Bibliothèque National de France in Paris (84, 2015).

Clydesdale, Ruth. '"Jupiter Tames Saturn": Astrology in Ficino's *Epistolae*'. In Laus Platonici Philosophi: *Marsilio Ficino and his Influence*. Leiden: Brill, 2011, 117–131.

Copenhaver, Brian C. 'Hermes Trismegistus, Proclus, and the Question of a Philosophy of Magic in the Renaissance'. In *Hermeticism and the Renaissance: Intellectual*

History and the Occult in Early Modern Europe, edited by Ingrid Merkel and Allen G. Debus. London: Associated University Presses, 1988, 79–110.

Domenico Maria da Novara. *I pronostici di Domenico Maria da Novara*, ed. F. Bònoli, G. Bezza, S. De Meis, C. Colavita. Florence: Olschki, 2012.

Ficin, Marsile. *Commentaire sur le Banquet de Platon*, ed. Raymond Marcel. Paris: Les Belles Lettres, 1956.

Ficino, Marsilio. *Commentary on Plato's* Symposium *on Love*, tr. Sears Jayne, 2nd completely revised edition. Dallas, TX: Spring Publications, 1985 [orig. 1944]

Ficino, Marsilio. *Come attingere vita dal cielo*, introduzione, traduzione e note by Ornella Pompeo Faracovi. Sarzana: Agorà & Co., 2024.

Ficino, Marsilio. *Commentary on Plotinus*, Vol. 4: *Ennead III*, Part 1; Vol. 5: *Ennead III*, Part 2 and *Ennead IV*, ed. and tr. Stephen Gersh (with extensive commentary). Cambridge, MA: Harvard University Press, 2017 and 2018 respectively.

Ficino, Marsilio. *Lettere* I, Epistolarum familiarum liber I, ed. S. Gentile. Florence: Olschki, 1990.

Ficino, Marsilio. *The Letters of Marsilio Ficino*, tr. by [the unnamed] members of the Language Department of the School of Economic Science, London, in 11 volumes. London: Shepheard-Walwyn, 1975-<2020>.

Ficino, Marsilio. *Marsilii Ficini Florentini Predicationes*, ed. Daniele Conti. Turin: Aragno, 2014.

Ficino, Marsilio. *Marsilio Ficino, Scritti sull'astrologia*, ed. Ornella Pompeo Faracovi. Milan: BUR, 1999.

Ficino, Marsilio. *Marsilio Ficino*, ed. Angela Voss. Berkeley: North Atlantic, 2006.

Ficino, Marsilio. *Opera omnia*, 2 vols., Basel, 1576.

Ficino, Marsilio. *Three Books on Life*, edited by Carol V. Kaske and John R. Clark. Tempe, AZ: MRTS, 1989.

Gentile, Sebastiano. 'Per la storia del testo del "Commentarium in Convivium" di Marsilio Ficino'. *Rinascimento* Ser. 2, 21 (1982): 3–27.

Heilen, Stephan. 'Astrology at the Court of Urbino under Federico and Guidobaldo da Montefeltro'. In *De Fréderic II à Rodolphe II: Astrologie, divination et magie dans les cours (XIIIe–XVIIe siècle)*, edited by J.-P. Boudet, M. Ostorero and A. Paravicini Bagliani. Sismel: Galluzzo, 2017, 313–368.

Hub, Berthold. 'Founding an Ideal City in Filarete's *Libro Architettonico*'. In *Foundation, Dedication and Consecration Ritual in Early Modern Culture, edited by* M. Schraven, & M. Delbeke. Leiden: Brill, 2011, 17–57.

Jervis, Jane L. *Cometary Theory in Fifteenth-Century Europe*. Wroclaw: Ossolineum, 1985.

Juste, David. 'Reading Birth Horoscopes in the Middle Ages: Latin Judgements on Nativities, 1100–1450'. In *Le Moyen Âge et les sciences*, edited by D. Jacquart et A. Paravicini Bagliani. Florence: Sismel–Galluzzo, 2021.

Klibansky, Raymond, Ernst Panofsky and Fritz Saxl. *Saturn and Melancholy*. London:

Thomas Nelson and Sons Ltd., 1964. Revised edition translated into German: *Saturn und Melancholie: Studien zur Geschichte der Naturphilosophie und Medizin, der Religion und der Kunst*. Frankfurt: Suhrkamp, 1992.

Kremer, Richard L. 'Controlling Errors in the First Printed Book of Astronomical Tables: Regiomontanus's *Ephemerides* (Nuremberg, 1474)'. In *Printing and Misprinting: A Companion to Mistakes and In-House Corrections in Renaissance Europe (1450–1650)*, edited by G. della Rocca de Candal, A. Grafton and P. Sachet. Oxford: Oxford University Press, 2023.

Kristeller, Paul Oskar. 'Thomism and the Italian Thought of the Renaissance'. In *Medieval Aspects of Renaissance Learning*, edited by E. Mahoney. Durham, N.C: Duke University Press, 1974 (2nd ed, Columbia University Press, 1992), 29–91.

Kristeller, Paul Oskar. *Supplementum Ficinianum*, 2 vols. Florence: Olschki, 1937.

Kristeller, Paul Oskar. 'The Scholastic Background of Marsilio Ficino with an Edition of Unpublished Texts'. *Traditio* 2 (1944): 257–318.

Mahony, Edward. 'Albert the Great and the *Studio Patavino* in the Late Fifteenth and Early Sixteenth Centuries'. In *Albertus Magnus and the Sciences*, edited by James A. Weisheipl, O.P. Toronto: Pontifical Institute of Mediaeval Studies, 1980, 527–563.

Marsilio Ficino e il ritorno di Platone: Manoscritti stampe e documenti, edited by S. Gentile, S. Niccoli and P. Viti. Florence: Le Lettere, 1984.

Martines, Lauro. *April Blood: Florence and the Plot against the Medici*. London: Jonathan Cape, 2003.

Maternus, Firmicus. *Mathesis*, Tome III, Livres VI–VIII, edited by P. Monat. Paris: Les Belles Lettres, 2003.

Maternus, Julius Firmicus. *Mathêsis*, translated by Benjamin N. Dykes. Minneapolis: Cazimi Press, 2023.

Maternus, Firmicus. *Ancient Astrology, Theory and Practice*: Matheseos Libri VIII, translated by Jean Rhys Bram. Park Ridge, N.J: Noyes Press, 1975.

Moore, Thomas. *The Planets Within: The Astrological Psychology of Marsilio Ficino*, 2nd revised edition. Great Barrington, MA: Lindisfarne Books, 1989.

Najemy, John M. *A History of Florence, 1200–1575*. Oxford: Blackwell, 2006.

Oakley, Francis. 'The Absolute and Ordained Power of God in Sixteenth- and Seventeenth-Century Theology'. *Journal of the History of Ideas* 59 (1998): 437–461.

Plato. *Platonis opera omnia*, translated by Marsilio Ficino, 1484.

Pompeo Faracovi, Ornella. *Gli oroscopo di Cristo*. Venice: Marsilio, 1999.

Pompeo Faracovi, Ornella. 'L'oroscopo di Ficino e le sue varianti'. *Bruniana e Campanelliana* 6 (2000): 611–617.

Quinlan-McGrath, Mary. 'The Villa Farnesina: Time-Telling Conventions and Renaissance Astrological Practice'. *Journal of the Warburg and Courtauld Institute* 58 (1995): 52–71.

Regiomontanus. *Ephemerides* (1475–1506). Nuremberg, 1474.

Robichaud, Denis J.-J. 'The Star of the Magi or the Afterlife of Chaldean Angels in Iamblichus, Proclus, Psellos, Pletho, and Ficino'. In *Inventer les Anges del'Antiquité à Byzance: Conception, Représentation, Perception*, edited by Delphine Lauritzen. Paris: Amis du Centre d'Histoire et Civilisation de Byzance, 2021, 763–808.

Rousseau, Claudia, 'Cosimo I de' Medici and Astrology: The Symbolism of Prophecy', PhD thesis, Columbia University, 1983.

Rutkin, H Darrel. *Sapientia Astrologica: Astrology, Magic and Natural Knowledge, ca. 1250–1800*. Cham, SW: Springer, 3 vols. Volume I, 'Medieval Structures (1250–1500): Conceptual, Institutional, Socio-Political, Theologico-Religious and Cultural', 2019. Volume II will be entitled 'Renaissance Structures (1450–1500): Continuities and Transformations',

Rutkin, H Darrel. 'Dancing with the Stars: A Preliminary Exploration as to Whether the Astrology in Ficino's *De vita* is Theurgical'. In *Marsilio Ficino's Cosmology: Sources and Reception*, edited by H Darrel Rutkin and Denis J.-J. Robichaud, *Bruniana & Campanelliana* 26 (2020/2): 403–419.

Schaffer, Simon. 'Newton's Comets and the Transformation of Astrology'. In *Astrology, Science and Society: Historical Essays*, edited by Patrick Curry. Woodbridge: Boydell Press, 1987, 219–243.

Schechner, Sarah J. *Comets, Popular Culture, and the Birth of Modern Cosmology*. Princeton: Princeton University Press, 1999.

Smoller, Laura A. *History, Prophecy and the Stars: The Christian Astrology of Pierre d'Ailly, 1350–1420*. Princeton: Princeton University Press, 1994.

Sorokina, Maria. 'Une source inconnue de la *Disputatio contra iudicium astrologorum* de Marsile Ficin: la *Summa de astris* de Gérard de Feltre'. *Bruniana e Campanelliana* 21 (2015): 169–189.

Sorokina, Maria. 'Un tournant dans le critique de l'astrologie? La *Summa de astris* de Gerard de Feltre'. *Philosophical Readings* 7 (2015): 71–92.

Strozzi, Lorenzo. *Vita di Filippo Strozzi*, edited by G. Bini and P. Bigazzi. Florence: Casa di Correzione, 1851.

Tur, Alexandre. '*Hora introitus solis in Arietem*: Les predictions astrologiques annuelles latines dans l'Europe du XVe siècle (1405–1484)'. PhD thesis, Université d'Orléans, 2018.

Weinstein, Donald. *Savonarola and Florence: Prophecy and Patriotism in the Renaissance*. Princeton: Princeton University Press, 1970.

Zeller, Wolfgang. *Der Jurist und Humanist Martin Prenninger gen. Uranius, 1450–1501*. Tübingen: Franz Steiner Verlag, 1973.

CHAPTER 10

The Changing Meaning of Astrological Elections: Ficino and the Astrologers

Steven Vanden Broecke

Abstract

This chapter re-evaluates Marsilio Ficino's shifting engagement with astrological elections by moving beyond the binary of 'for' or 'against' astrology. It argues that Ficino's *Disputatio contra iudicium astrologorum* (1477) should not only be read as a wholesale rejection of astrology but as a text that simultaneously articulates the specific kind of astrological agency Ficino sought to develop. While late medieval astrologers viewed elections as a means of negotiating fortune, Ficino's critique redefined the very meaning of celestial influence and human agency. His later *De vita* (1489) appears to endorse electional techniques, but this continuity is ambivalent: rather than adopting traditional astrology's concern with managing fortune, Ficino transforms elections into a method for refining sublunary substances and accommodating human spirit to celestial forces. This shift, traced through Ficino's reinterpretation of *Centiloquium* 22, reveals how he strategically repurposed astrological practice, retaining its techniques while fundamentally altering their focus, agency, and end.

Keywords

Renaissance astrology – astrological technique – fortune – Marsilio Ficino – Gerard of Feltre

1   Introduction

In 1477, Marsilio Ficino wrote a *Disputation against the Judgment of Astrologers*. Its unfinished text remained largely unknown until Hans Baron discovered and edited the sole extant manuscript in 1925.[1] As Baron already observed, Ficino's

---

[1] Baron's edition was subsequently published in Kristeller, *Supplementum*, 11–76. See Ficino, *Scritti*, 7n3.

Disputatio has two main parts.[2] The first offers a systematic critique of the concept of astrological fate. The second, by contrast, is unfinished and comprises various critical notes and reflections on astrology's aetiological, technical, epistemological and religious problems. In the opening section of the latter part of the *Disputatio*, Ficino distinguished four types of effects considered in astral science. The first type is necessary and 'cannot not be or come about differently'. The second type is contingent but its 'causes incline the effect one way rather than another'. The third kind of effect is an act of will, which can swing either way and has no determined cause. Finally, there is a fourth type of effect that cannot be reduced to either elemental or volitional causes, and which happens through luck or a multiplicity of diverse causes. Alongside 'becoming a king, having an unfaithful wife, dying from poison', Ficino here gives the example of one 'who shall become ill because he donned new clothes in a specific hour'.[3]

Students of pre-modern astrology will immediately recognize Ficino's reference to the pseudo-Ptolemaic *Centiloquium*, a collection of one hundred astrological aphorisms, probably written in Cairo in the early tenth century CE. Aphorism 22 of this collection, in the seventeenth-century English translation by Henry Coley, runs as follows:

> Neither cut out, or first put on a new garment whilst the Moon is in the sign Leo: if she then be unfortunate, it's so much the worse.[4]

The aphorism puts us squarely in the astrological domain of elections. The art of astrological elections revolved around the practice of selecting astrologically propitious times for specific practices: building new houses, marrying a wife, investing rulers, or indeed donning new garments. In theory, birth charts and natal astrology constituted the methodological backbone of late medieval astrological practice. But there is good evidence that more specific issues involving the resolution or timing of everyday affairs were at least as central to late medieval astrological practice. A large proportion of the astrological predictions in the notebook of the London astrologer Richard Trewythian (b. 1393), for instance, concerned the closely related practice of interrogations.[5] An astrological vademecum for a French courtier, written in the same period

---

2 Baron, 'Willensfreiheit', 164–165.
3 Kristeller, *Supplementum*, 27–28; Ficino, *Scritti*, 95–97.
4 Coley, *Clavis*, 318.
5 Page, 'Richard Trewythian', 204–207.

by Conrad Heingarter, contained extensive individualized rules for astrological electing, which were arguably more useful than the natal information offered at the beginning of the compendium.

Ficino's *Disputatio*, however, summarily dismissed the astrologer's habit of electing a propitious time for changing clothes:

> It is ridiculous to say that a new fate is donned by new clothes, as if through clothes celestial things change one's fate in body and soul.[6]

Twelve years later, Ficino published *De vita* (1489), his medico-magical compendium on how to extend and optimize life through the skilled manipulation of natural causes. After reading the *Disputatio*, one may be in for a surprise when consulting chapter III.25. Here is Ficino defending the astrological tradition of elections, including the very practice of astrological vestiture that he criticized in 1477:

> And since we happened to mention clothing here, will you forbid a person, pious Father, when making a garment or first wearing it, to take care to catch a little of Venus's breath by which the garment, becoming as it were Venereal, may likewise imbue the body and spirit with a beneficial quality?[7]

Ficino's wavering relation to astrology is a well-known issue in Ficino scholarship. No one really doubts that astral influx played an important role in Ficino's natural philosophy, and that his personal mastery of the astrological tradition was exemplary. But there are also several texts and testimonies, ranging between 1477 and 1494, in which Ficino is seen to adopt a deeply critical and dismissive attitude towards astrology.[8] In the past decade, the issue has become even more complicated by Maria Sorokina's discovery that the second aforementioned part of Ficino's *Disputatio* largely paraphrased a thirteenth-century critique of astrology in *Summa de astris*, authored by the Dominican friar Gerard of Feltre.[9]

---

6 Kristeller, *Supplementum*, 28.
7 Ficino, *Three Books*, III.25.41–44 (trans. Kaske and Clark, 383).
8 See Baron, 'Willensfreiheit', 148–156; Kaske, 'Ficino's Shifting Attitude', 372–376; Faracovi, 'Destino e fato', 3–11.
9 Sorokina, 'Une source inconnue'. For an initial study of Gerard of Feltre's *Summa de astris*, see Sorokina, 'Un tournant'.

Instead of seeing the *Disputatio* in somewhat anachronistic categories (e.g. 'for' or 'against' astrology), several scholars have tried to situate the text against Ficino's broader trajectory vis-à-vis astrology. Charles Trinkaus identified Ficino's philosophical emphasis on human autonomy and dominance over the stars as a major source of continuity between the earlier *Disputatio* and the later *De vita*.[10] According to Melissa Meriam Bullard, it was the *Disputatio* that put Ficino on track towards the notion of a manageable 'inward zodiac' in man, which in turn allowed him to retool astrological techniques in *De vita*.[11] Ornella Faracovi too approached the *Disputatio* as part of Ficino's lifelong search for a different, more psychological form of astrology. Unlike Bullard, she diagnosed its Plotinian campaign against astral fatalism as untimely, and its extreme criticism of astrological practice as a (temporary) dead end.[12]

Useful as these claims are, they paint the role of Ficino's *Disputatio* in broad terms at best. One major reason for this is that we are not sure what continuities to look for vis-à-vis astrology. Ficino's *Disputatio* presented much of what the astrologers did as a nefarious practice of philosophical fatalism. Although Ornella Faracovi was right to question the accuracy of this portrait, she only countered it by pointing out that the late medieval Latin astrology which Ficino knew so well had made ample room for human free will.[13] Likewise, Darrel Rutkin and Anthony Grafton were right to point out that Ficino's *De vita* endowed astrological practice with deep potential for human self-transformation.[14] But it is unclear how this compares to the aspirations for human agency embedded in the astrological traditions that Ficino knew so well.

This is where the case of Ficino's volte-face on *Centiloquium* 22 becomes significant and instructive. Commonly attributed to Ptolemy, *Centiloquium* was a quintessential reference for late medieval Latin astrologers wishing to understand the kind of agency that astrology could bring, or seeking guidance on astrological electing (and much more). Especially in university contexts, *Centiloquium* was also the object of much commentary.[15] Through this, we can first build a plausible reconstruction of the kind of human agency that late medieval

---

10   Trinkaus, 'Ficino and the Ideal of Human Autonomy', 200–205.

11   Meriam Bullard, 'The Inward Zodiac', 698–699.

12   Faracovi, 'Destino e fato', 16–19, 21.

13   Pompeo Farakovi, 'Destino e fato', 17–18.

14   Rutkin, 'Dancing with the Stars'; Grafton, *Magus*, 100–103. Also compare Garin, 'Le "elezioni"', p. 27.

15   For Latin commentaries on *Centiloquium*, see now the 'Latin works' section of Bayerische Akademie der Wissenschaften's website on 'Ptolemaeus Arabus et Latinus'.

Latin astrologers sought to impart through astrological practice, as well as of the meaning they gave to *Centiloquium* 22. Secondly, this gives us a suitable point of departure against which to assess Ficino's criticism in the *Disputatio*. Here, we will try to heed Maria Sorokina's important observation that Ficino's selective note taking from Gerard of Feltre's text is not necessarily passive, but can also be interpreted as the active taking up of a position.[16] Moreover, even if he largely compiles materials from Gerard's *Summa*, Ficino's *Disputatio* does occasionally add original notes and comments. Finally, we can use our comparison of the interpretation of astrological practice by the astrologers and by Ficino's *Disputatio*, respectively, as a baseline against which to triangulate Ficino's take on astrological elections in the later *De vita*.

2   Agency and Elections in the Late Middle Ages

At least since Ernst Cassirer's *Individuum und Kosmos* (1927), scholars have often approached Ficino as a philosophical modernizer who operated from within the very frameworks that he sought to overcome. His attitude to astrology is a case in point. According to Cassirer, Ficino managed to stake out a forceful assertion of freedom from *within* a deterministic astrological worldview.[17] Cassirer sketches Ficino's notion of freedom as follows:

> A man is born under a certain star and has to conduct his life under its dominion; but it is nevertheless up to him to decide which of the powers and possibilities contained by this star he will develop and bring to full maturity in himself. Indeed, according to the intellectual tendencies and aspirations that he allows to flourish and nourishes within him, he can place himself now under the influence of one star, now under the influence of another.[18]

In 1960, Eugenio Garin deepened Cassirer's suggestion by arguing that medieval authorities on astrological elections already celebrated its value as a technique of human self-determination vis-à-vis the stars. 'If the stars choose man in genitures', Garin wrote, 'man chooses the stars through science in elections'.[19] If

---

16   Sorokina, 'Une source inconnue', 183.
17   Cassirer, *Individual*, 112.
18   Cassirer, *Individual*, 113–114.
19   Garin, 'Le "elezioni"', 32.

nothing else, elections practiced the ideal of free self-fashioning by 'conquering the stars'.[20]

However, there is reason to question Garin's take on the medieval interpretation of elections. Although the author of the *Speculum astronomiae* considered it inconsiderate haste of the will, not freedom, to disregard astrological elections, Latin astrology also disagreed whether elections could bring something into being whose possibility was not promised by a person's nativity or (in the absence of precise birth data) by the star's answer to a specific question about the future (a so-called interrogation).[21] On the one hand, there was the authority of aphorism 6 of ps.-Ptolemy's *Centiloquium*, or of Haly Embrani's *De electionibus horarum*, which voiced considerable skepticism about the usefulness of an election countering indications in someone's nativity.[22] On the other hand, there were many authors who, like Guido Bonatti's influential *Tractatus astrologiae*, hinted at the idea that a good election could positively overturn a pre-signified evil.[23]

But even in the latter case, it was generally assumed that hopes should be tempered. Consider Lucio Bellanti's *De astrologica veritate* (1498) q14a12, where the Siennese astrologer discussed 'whether through elections, not only can future evil be diminished and good increased, but also future evil can be entirely removed, and good not promised by the roots can be granted?' Bellanti hesitatingly determined the question in the affirmative: '(...) through elections, not only can the effects of the roots be increased and diminished, but some-

---

20 Garin, 'Le "elezioni"', 35. Taking his cue from Garin, Nicolas Weill-Parot also argued that astrological elections were interpreted as techniques for conferring specific celestial virtues on sublunary objects, such as sick bodies or buildings, with the astrologer acting as the artful medium. See Weill Parot, 'Causalité astrale', 229–230, 232–234.

21 Zambelli, *The* Speculum astronomiae, xv:3–5 (p. 266).

22 Ps. Ptolemy, *Centiloquium*, sig. 107va: 'Tunc electiones proficiunt, cum fortitudo temporis vel electionis maior fuerit quam superfluitas quae inter duos receptores erit. Si vero minor fuerit, eius proficuum non tantum apparebit, licet aliquantulum proficiat' (trans. Plato of Tivoli, see: https://ptolemaeus.badw.de/work/309). Also compare Sahl bin Bishr, *De electionibus*, sig. 138[va]: '(...) cave igitur eligere ei cuius radix nativitatis vel interrogationis significaverit aliquid horribile, ad quod cum pervenerit si posueris omnes fortunas in angulis, et cadere feceris omnes malos ab eo, nihil proficiet ei'. For Haly Embrani's position, see: Dykes, *Choices*, 19.

23 Bonatti, *De astronomia*, col. 389: 'Vitantes enim electiones quae non fiunt super nativitatibus vel super interrogationibus, non videntur mihi ex toto sapientes, quia si non possunt habere id boni quod volunt, non debent tamen spernere id boni quod habere possunt'; Bonatti, col. 416: '(...) fuit intentio pilosophorum quod mala quae significantur per nativitatem vel per questionem, possent tolli per bonam electionem, et si non tollantur ex toto, possunt multum diminui et alleviari'.

times they can be entirely removed, and good not promised can be produced'. Even so, he ended by stressing the message of *Centiloquium* aphorism 6: '(…) if the nativity is contrary to the election, it will rarely lead to the intended result, and even then with difficulty'.[24]

Leading astrologers like Bonatti or Bellanti would have been unwilling to subscribe to Garin's claim that they promoted astrological election as a means for conquering the stars. What kind of agency were they practicing then? To answer this question, consider the commentary on *Centiloquium* by the Neapolitan astrologer Giovanni Pontano (1429–1503). Pontano translated and commented on the *Centiloquium* between 1474/5 and 1479, and the text is therefore contemporaneous with Ficino's *Disputatio*.[25] Pontano's commentary on the aforementioned aphorism 6 of *Centiloquium*, which discussed the utility of elections vis-à-vis innate astral dispositions, was particularly clear. According to Pontano, birth charts were 'the root of all events that will happen to the person in the years to come, as if someone were to unwind a tangled rope'.[26] Accordingly, elections could only work if the astrologer had previously assessed which life events were possible at all (on the basis of a birth chart), as well as their approximate time of manifestation (on the basis of annual revolutions).[27] There was no point, Pontano asserted, in seeking out a favourable hour and day for a wedding 'if the configuration of the natal heavens portends ugly and unfortunate marriages'.[28] Likewise, a favourable election was useless 'if the time appointed by the heavens has not yet arrived'.[29] Astrological elections served to time and capture the celestial favours and opportunities indicated in one's nativity. They did not allow one to turn a promised evil into a good.

---

24 Bellanti, *De astrologica veritate*, 135: 'An electionibus possit non solum malum futurum minui, & bonum augeri, sed etiam malum futurum in totum auferri, & bonum non futurum radicibus tribui. Articulus duodecimus (…) respondeo dicendo, quod per electiones non solum augeri & minui possunt radicum effectus, sed etiam quandoque in totum auferri, & bonum non promissum produci (…) concedendo quod si natiuitas contraria sit electioni, raro ad intentum perducet, & illud etiam cum difficultate fiet'.

25 See Bayerische Akademie der Wissenschaften, 'Ptolemaeus Arabus et Latinus', https://ptolemaeus.badw.de/work/114

26 Pontano, *Opera*, vol. 3, 13: '(…) [primus coelestis constitutionis ac figurae locus] principum & tanquam radix est omnium quae nato uoluendis annis sint euentura, ut si quis complicatum funem explicet'.

27 Pontano, 14.

28 Pontano, 15: '(…) si turpes atque infelices nuptias natalis coeli constitutio portenderit, frustra horam & diem eligi, frustra felices stellarum aspectus quaeri, frustra planetarum amicas coniunctiones expectari'.

29 Pontano, 16: 'Itaque si tempus à coelo praestitutum nondum aduenit, nihil profuerit felicem electionem fecisse'.

Clearly, astrological agency was cast in the mode of negotiation rather than resistance. This brings up the broader question of what was meant by the 'wisdom' that astrological practice, according to the well-known maxim 'the wise man will rule the stars' (*sapiens dominabitur astris*), conferred.[30] Aphorism 5 of *Centiloquium*, the classic reference for premodern astrologers seeking to articulate the benefits of their art in relation to celestially induced misfortune, helps us better understand this. In Pontano's own translation from the Greek, this aphorism read: 'A person who is knowledgeable can avert many of the effects of the stars when they know their nature and prepare themselves before those effects occur'.[31] Like many astrologers, Pontano here took humoral medicine as his model for conceptualizing human agency. A 'prudent physician', Pontano pointed out, 'can temper a dry and cold bodily complexion through measured application of humid and hot substances', thus making the native less prone to Saturnian melancholy. The humoral medical analogy encouraged astrologers to conceptualize human agency as a tactic of evasion and compensation, not as proactive insulation from cosmic forces. This led Pontano to emphasize that if nefarious events could not always be 'evaded', they could at least be 'alleviated' or 'mitigated'. Mitigating celestially induced misfortune was a matter of altering the quality of recipient bodies; changing their location; donning the artful compensation of a breastplate.[32]

The classic reference for the converse topic—astrology's usefulness in relation to celestial fortune—was aphorism 8 of *Centiloquium*: 'A wise soul contributes to celestial operations, just as the best farmer contributes to nature by plowing and weeding'.[33] Pontano first positioned astrology as an art that cultivates the supreme virtue of prudence (by assisting the natural desire to avoid evil and pursuit good).[34] In this regard, another part of its brief was to identify future goods decreed by the stars and to 'open the way for them as they arrive; and after they have arrived, to bring them firmness'.[35] As was often the case, Pontano compared this to agriculture:

---

30   On the history of this maxim, see Boudet, 'Ptolémée dans l'Occident medieval'; Niermeyer-Dohoney, 'Sapiens dominabitur astris'; Sorokina, *Les sphères*, vol. 1, 340–342, 458–459; Vanden Broecke, 'Astrological Self-Government', 60.

31   Pontano, Opera, vol. 3, 12 'Potest qui sciens est, multos stellarum effectus auertere, quando naturam earum nouerit, ac seipsum ante illorum euentum praeparare'.

32   Pontano, 12: '(...) adhibita diligenti opera corporum nostrorum qualitates (...) temperare'.

33   Pontano, 19: 'Sapiens anima confert coelesti operationi, quemadmodum optimus agricola arando, expurgandoque confert naturae'.

34   Pontano, 19.

35   Pontano, 19–20: '(...) [sapiens uir] uiam aduentantibus illis aperiet: & postquam peruenerint, firmitatem quoque afferent'.

For just as the crops expected from the earth and from well-sown seeds are usually fuller and more abundant if the diligence and care of the farmer is applied according to the nature of each, so the goods bestowed by the stars, if wise counsel and prudent effort are added, will flow as if from a more inclined stream.[36]

There is a clear symmetry in Pontano's prescriptions on what it means to avoid evils and pursue goods through astrological knowledge. In both cases, the central project is one of negotiating celestially induced changes and events. Celestial influx is never understood as a repository of natural forces that humans can tap into and exploit at will. In both cases, such negotiation also comes down to a qualitative change in the sublunary subject of celestial influx. To mitigate coming evils, one alters one's bodily complexion or place. To actualize future goods, one cultivates the virtue of prudence in oneself. To 'perfect' the natural flow of evils and goods was to assist such change through medical and moral art.[37]

This was also Pontano's basic interpretation of aphorism 22, the object of Ficino's volte-face between 1477 and 1489. In Pontano's own translation, the aphorism read:

Do not put on or cut a garment for the first time when the Moon is positioned in Leo. It is even worse if the Moon is in a malefic state.[38]

Pontano's commentary explained this through Leo's status as a so-called fixed zodiacal sign. Clothes that were cut or put on under such a sign would be unusually durable, but would also probably outlast the person for whom they were tailored. When this happens, Pontano explained:

(...) the garments themselves will appear to last longer, but there is [also] an indication of a future cause of illness or other evils, so that we may not

36 Pontano, 20: 'Etenim ut prouenturus è terra satisque seminibus fructus plenior atque uberior esse solet, si agricolae diligentia cultusque pro natura cuiusque accesserit: sic conferenda quoque à stellis bona, si sapiens consilium prudensque adiuncta sit opera, ea tanquam procliuiore defluent riuo'.

37 Pontano, 20: 'Nam & ars naturalibus etiam bonis magno praesidio esse solet (...) bonisque homini à natura datis, nisi diligens adiuncti sit institutio, non est cur perfectum aliquid suo in genere possis dicere'.

38 Pontano, *Opera*, vol. 3, 37: 'Vestem nec primùm induas, nec incidas, ubi Luna fuerit in Leone collocata. Est autem peius, si eadem malè affecta fuerit'.

be able to use them, or at least they will be set aside and kept in a chest, not being used for any purpose of their owner's body.[39]

The older Arabic commentary by Abū Jaʿfar Aḥmad, in the widespread Latin translation by Plato of Tivoli, also interpreted aphorism 22 as a broader warning against instituting significant change while the Moon is in the fixed sign of Leo.[40] In the *Tractatus astronomiae*, Guido Bonatti offered a few possible exceptions, but went out of his way to defend the soundness of the aphorism.[41] Ficino's friend Lorenzo Bonincontri (1410–c. 1491), who taught astrology (including *Centiloquium*) at the University of Florence from 1475 to 1478, offered largely the same explanation as Pontano, agreeing that 'fixed signs (...) are to be feared in all matters where we desire change and alteration'.[42]

We are now in a position to better evaluate the judgment of aphorism 22 by Gerard of Feltre, which Ficino's *Disputatio* later borrowed:

> There are also certain other things that astrologers try to predict which do not pertain to the body's temperament but come from external sources, such as predicting that someone will have a contentious wife, or that they are destined to be a king—because many seek honours but never attain a kingdom—or that they will end their life by poison, hanging, or beheading, even though not all who receive a death sentence are of the same temperament. Or predicting that someone has incurred fortune or misfortune because they put on or cut new clothes at a certain hour, as if celestial bodies exerted influence over our bodies or souls through the mediation of clothing.[43]

---

39   Pontano, 38: 'Quod ubi contigerit, uestes ipsae quum diutius perennaturae [sic] appareant, fit significatio, aut morbos, aut alia mala, causam futuram, ne illis uti possimus, aut saltem ut sepositae atque in arca conseruatae ad nullos corporis domini usus comparatae sint (...)'.

40   Ps.-Ptolemy, *Centiloquium*, sig. 108vb.

41   Bonatti, *De astronomia*, cols. 444–445.

42   Bonincontri, *Commentum*, fol. 78^{r}: 'Signa inquam fixa timenda in omnibus rebus quarum alterationem et mutationem desideramus' (see https://ptolemaeus.badw.de/work/113).

43   Gerard of Feltre, *Summa de astris*, ed. Sorokina (forthcoming), dist. 2: 'Sunt et quedam alia, que astrologi conantur predicere, ad corporis complexionem non pertinentia, sed extrinsecus advenientia, scilicet quod iste habiturus sit uxorem contentiosam, vel quod debeat esse rex, quia multi honores appetunt qui nunquam ad regnum perveniunt, vel quod debeat veneno aut suspendio vel capitis obtruncatione vitam finire, cum tamen non omnes sint eiusdem complexionis qui capitalem accipiunt sententiam, vel quod iste for-

Notice Gerard's double assumption that astrological predictions aim to capture the effects of medical 'temperament' (*complexio*), and that they claim knowledge of easily verifiable particular effects (marital strife, kingship, etc) rather than more subterranean inclinations, possibilities, and risks. Neither assumption would have been readily shared by the aforementioned astrologers, thus reminding us of the perspectival nature of astrological debates. More interesting for our purposes, however, is Gerard's subsequent criticism of the claim that the astral qualities of clothing can in turn shape the wearer's fortunes in body or soul. This criticism serves as a helpful heuristic for astrologers' interpretations of aphorism 22, which we previously discussed.

Unlike Gerard, none of these astrologers understood this text to be about the celestially induced qualities of an artificial thing (in this case, clothing). The Latinized Abū Ja'far, Bonincontri, and Pontano all made sense of the aphorism as a practical rule on how to optimize the auspiciousness of a practical change in life (in this case, donning new clothes). In a culture where clothing was largely seen in terms of 'an individual's patrimony and investment for one's heirs', one can readily understand how new clothes could simultaneously evoke issues of personal finitude and mortality.[44] This agrees with the broader fact that astrological elections, as we have seen, were centrally about negotiating a celestial space for human action. To that extent, Gerard's claim about elections seeking to 'change the fate of your nativity' were also a less than accurate description.[45] More specifically, it overlooked the way in which late medieval Latin astrology foregrounded, in typically Aristotelian fashion, the qualitative appropriation of celestial influx.

3   **Happiness and Astrological Critique: Ficino's *Disputatio***

In his reworking of the forementioned passage from Gerard of Feltre's *Summa*, dist. 2, Ficino's *Disputatio* added a few original comments:

> (...) astrologers try to predict that (...) this person will die by poison, or fall ill because he put on new clothes at this hour. Such effects do not

---

tunium vel infortunium incurrerit, quia tali hora incidi fecit vel induit vestes novas, ac si mediante veste super corpora nostra vel animas influerent celestia corpora'.

44   Rosenthal, 'Cultures of Clothing', 460.

45   Gerard of Feltre, *Summa*, ed. Sorokina (forthcoming), dist. 25: '(...) tu potes mutare fatum nativitatis tue'.

follow from complexion, because they can happen to any complexion. Likewise, they do not follow from intention, because they often happen beyond intention. Nor do the elements cause these things. How then will the most remote and most general heavens cause these things without a proximate and specific cause? Therefore, these things happen either by chance or occasion, that is, by many and diverse causes coming together. Since such a concurrence of causes cannot be comprehended, they certainly cannot be predicted. Besides, it is ridiculous to say that new fate is assumed because of new clothes, as if celestial bodies would change fate in the body and soul through clothes.[46]

Most medieval critics of astrology emphasized the structural uncertainty of astrological prediction that followed from how sublunary causes locally changed the quality of celestial influx. However, Ficino's reprisal of this theme took things a little further. We see this more clearly in a later section of the *Disputatio* that compiled materials found in distinction 25 of the *Summa* (where Gerard of Feltre treated the issue of elections more fully). The following table juxtaposes both passages, with Ficino's addition marked in italics.

Gerard of Feltre, *Summa de astris*, dist. 25	Marsilio Ficino, *Disputatio*
'Likewise, the first cause is said to influence its effect more than the second cause, as stated at the beginning of *On Causes*. The reason is that its effect is more intimate and permanent in the	'Likewise, although the first cause acts more principally in a work than the second cause, in that its influence is more internal and stable, the second cause has greater power in ensuring that the effect is of a certain type and specific constitution

---

46 Kristeller, *Supplementum*, 28: '(...) astrologi conantur predicere, scilicet hunc regem fore vel uxorem habiturum incontinentem aut veneno periturum aut egrotaturum, quia novas vestes hac induit hora. Effectus eiusmodi complexionem non secuntur, quia cuilibet eveniunt complexioni. Rursus non secuntur consilium, quia sepe preter intentionem eveniunt. Sed neque elementa hec faciunt. Quomodo ergo celum remotissimum et communissimum ista faciet absque proxima et propria causa? Ergo vel casu vel occasione, idest multis et diversis causis concurrentibus ista fiunt. Cum vero tot causarum concursus comprehendi non possit, certe predici non possunt. Mitto quod ridiculum est dicere ob novas vestes novum indui fatum. perinde ac si per vestes celestia in corpus animamque sortem mutant'. Ficino, *Saggi*, 97.

(cont.)

Gerard of Feltre, *Summa de astris*, dist. 25	Marsilio Ficino, *Disputatio*
effect than the effect of the second cause. Nevertheless, it [the effect] resembles the second cause more, because it somehow determines the act of the first cause to this effect. Therefore, it sometimes does not seem to be an effect of the first cause, which it does not resemble as much as it resembles the second. Again, an effect does not follow from the first cause except when combined with the second cause'.[47]	of the individual. (...) *For the most general influence of the most distant cause is determined through the subsequent causes. However, actions and such passions follow individual and specific principles rather than the most general ones, especially when these are equivocal and of vastly different kinds, as is the case with celestial bodies.* Therefore, effects are similar to the proximate causes, not the remote ones. An effect does not follow from the first cause except as it is combined with the second cause [my italics]'.[48]

On the one hand, the comparison highlights Ficino's proximity to the *Summa*, to which Maria Sorokina called attention. On the other hand, Ficino's addition (marked in italics) also alters the message of Gerard's text in small but meaningful ways. The point of Gerard of Feltre's original text was to distinguish, in modern terms, between the force and the quality of a natural effect.

---

47 Gerard of Feltre, *Summa*, ed. Sorokina (forthcoming), dist. 25: 'Item, causa prima plus dicitur influere in causatum cause secunde quam etiam causa secunda, ut dicitur in principio *De causis*. Ratio huius est, quia eius effectus est intimior et permanentior in causato quam effectus cause secunde. Tamen magis similatur cause secunde, quia per eam determinatur quodammodo actus prime cause ad hunc effectum. Ideoque non videtur aliquando esse effectus cause prime, cui non ita similatur ut secunde. Rursum, effectus non sequitur ex causa prima, nisi composita cum secunda'.

48 Kristeller, *Supplementum*, 62: 'Item quamvis causa prima principalius agat in opere quam secunda quantum ad hoc quod influxus eius est interior et stabilior, tamen causa secunda plus valet ad hoc quod effectus sit in certa specie et certa complexione individui. (...) *Generalissimus enim influxus cause remotissime per causas sequentes determinatur. Actiones autem et passions tales vel tales sequuntur potius principia individualia et specialia quam communissima, presertim quando sunt equivoca et in genere diversissima ut celestia,* unde effectus similes sunt causis proximis non remotis. Effectus non sequitur ex causa prima nisi prout componitur cum secunda [my italics]'.

On this basis, he granted the primacy of astral causes in terms of force, while asserting the primacy of sublunary causes in terms of qualities. But Gerard next used this to explain why we sometimes do not recognize the presence of first astral causes ('therefore, it sometimes does not *seem* to be an effect of the first cause [my italics]'). Clearly, maintaining a role for first causes was key to his project.

Ficino initially copied Gerard's argument, but then became far less interested in striking a balance between first and secondary causes in the explanation of sublunary effects. His addition referred to the first, astral cause as 'most general and most remote'. Also, he rephrased Gerard's next sentence in such a way that it no longer stated that sublunary effects sometimes do not *seem* to be similar to first causes. Instead, it now made the bolder claim that such effects *are* similar to proximate causes, not remote ones.

This squares with a point that Ficino had already made in the original first part of the *Disputatio*, in a long section later published as part of his commentary on Plotinus' *Enneads* under the title 'That not all things come about from fatal necessity'.[49] Having defended the reality of universal divine government and providence, as well as of human free will, in the preceding sections, Ficino now sought to account for the reality of sublunary contingency. Here, he took the position that contingency is an effect of the diminishing generative virtue of the heavens as it descends down the degrees of being.[50] Although the overall natural order and regularity is preserved at all times, Ficino in fact argued that sublunary proximate causes were always more efficacious than remote celestial ones:

> Now, it is clear that individual effects are more similar to their proximate causes than to distant ones. Thus, plants and animals, for example, are not judged to be as similar to the celestial bodies as they are to their own parents and the seeds from which they arise. From this, it is evident that effects of this kind follow the nature and destiny of their seeds rather than that of the celestial bodies, and that they occur in a changeable manner

---

49 See Ficino, *Opera*, vol. 2, 1679–1681 (*Summa Marsiliana*, 'Quod non omnia fatali necessitate proueniant'). Kristeller, *Supplementum*, 16–21. Ficino, *Scritti*, 66–75.

50 Ficino, *Opera*, vol. 2, 1679: 'Cum enim per plurimos deinceps agentium gradus & uirtus efficax minuatur,& complurima tandem repugnantium formarum confluat multitudo, nimirum sequitur, ut propria quæque natura ab officio sepe deficiat, dum paulatim dcbilitata uirtus diuersorum occursu facilius impeditur [corrections added from Kristeller, *Supplementum*, 17]'.

according to the condition of familiar causes, which is entirely mutable, rather than necessarily according to the condition of the celestial bodies, and rightly so, since the nature of the celestial bodies does not necessarily retain its existence but can fall away from it, and thus their power does not necessarily act, but sometimes fails to act.[51]

This was the very point that Ficino also embedded in his forementioned re-workings of Gerard of Feltre's critique of astrological elections. Although the second part of the *Disputatio* largely paraphrased Gerard of Feltre's *Summa*, it is clear that Ficino was simultaneously mindful of internal coherence with the original first part of the *Disputatio*. More importantly, it is also clear that whatever else Ficino might think about astrological elections (and astral influx in general), the efficacious primacy of proximate causes was a key issue for him.

We can better understand why by turning to the final sections of the first part of the *Disputatio*, which returned to the topic of divine government and human free will (often on the basis of materials from Ficino's *Platonic Theology*). There, Ficino made the interesting argument that unlike plants or animals, humans are governed by their perfectly free own intellect, rather than by the divine mind. This, Ficino continued, explained a greater degree of erring in comparison with other living sublunary beings, despite humans being more perfect instruments of divine government in principle.[52] As early as 1927, Hans Baron argued that Renaissance humanists sought to strike a balance between accessing natural power through astrological knowledge, and defending the credibility of human free will against astral fatalism.[53] Even by the standards of the anti-astrological debate, Ficino came out unusually strongly on the side

---

51   Ficino, *Opera*, vol. 2, 1680: 'Iam uero manifestum est affectus singulos causis proximis similiores euadere quam remotis. Sic plantae et animalia quaelibet, non tam coelestibus similia iudicantur, quam proprijs genitoribus et seminibus unde nascuntur, ex quo patet, effectus eiusmodi natura sortemque suorum seminum sequi, potius quam coelestium, ac pro conditione familiarium causarum, quae omnino mutabilis est, mutabiliter euenire, non necessario pro conditione coelestium, et merito, quorum natura non necessario suum retinet esse, sed ab eo deficere potest, eorundem quoque virtus non necessario agit, sed interdum cadit ab actione [corrections added from Kristeller, *Supplementum*, 17]'.

52   Ficino, *Opera*, vol. 1, 207: 'Vnde enim contingere id putamus, quod arbores bestiaeque in suis quibusdam motibus, artibus, electionibusque nunquam aberrant, homo uero saepissimę? Non quidem ex eo quod intellectus insit illis perfectior, quibus nec intellectus quidem inest ullus, sed quia ab intellectu diuino nunquam errante trahuntur, homo uero a suo, qui errare potest, dicitur'. Kristeller, *Supplementum*, 24; Ficino, *Scritti*, 82.

53   Baron, 'Willensfreiheit', 146, 150, 153.

of human freedom, which might very well explain his prior insistence on the priority of sublunary causes.[54]

Also consider the following passage from *Platonic Theology* IX.4, which Ficino inserted at the end of the first part of the *Disputatio*:

> Nor should anyone dare to say that the minds of humans are moved by the higher minds through the heavens as if through some instrument or medium. For minds are more in harmony with minds than with bodies; therefore, the heavens are not placed between those minds and ours, but rather, our minds occupy the middle ground between those minds and the heavens. And for this reason, it would be more fitting for the heavens to be moved by divine beings through the minds of humans than for our minds to be moved by the heavens.[55]

Ficino's final quip about heavens ruled by human minds is reminiscent of the metaphor of the 'inward zodiac', which Ficino also used in two letters from late 1477 and early 1478, only months after he wrote the *Disputatio*.[56] In both of these letters, Ficino used the metaphor to draw a contrast between an astrological heaven of planetary forces, invoked to anticipate fortune and prosperity, and an inward heaven of virtues, invoked to prepare true happiness.[57] Although historians have often taken Ficino's metaphor as evidence for his cultivating a new form of psychological astrology, it was actually invoked to authorize a triple distinction: between 'the astrologers' and philosophers like himself; between the pursuit of fortune and the pursuit of happiness; between astral influx and human virtue. This would also help explain why Ficino, in the opening sentences of the *Disputatio*, immediately came out against the astrologers in the name of human freedom *and tranquillity*.[58]

---

54   Compare Sorokina, *Les sphères*, vol. 1, 231–244, 427–433.
55   Ficino, *Opera*, vol. 1, 210: 'Neque audeat quisquam dicere, mentes hominum a supernis mentibus moueri per coelum tanquam per instrumentum aliquod, atque medium. Magis enim conueniunt mentes cum mentibus quam cum corporibus, ideo inter illas mentes ac nostras coelum non interponitur, sed potius inter mentes illas, ac coelum nostrae mentes medium obtinent. Proptereaque coeli a numinibus per mentes hominum mouendi essent potius, quam nostrae inde per coelos'. Kristeller, *Supplementum*, 25; Ficino, *Scritti*, 91–92.
56   Bullard, 'Inward Zodiac', 698–699.
57   Ficino, *Opera*, vol. 1, 805: 'Prospera in fato fortuna, uera in uirtute felicitas'; Ficino, 806: 'Caelum pollicetur bona, uirtus praestat'. Translated in: Ficino, *Letters*, vol. 4, 61–63.
58   Ficino, *Opera*, vol. 1, 781: 'Hominibus denique qui non minus quam bestiae, ut illis uidetur, huc et illuc impelluntur, auferunt libertate, omnique priuant tranquillitate [corrections added from Kristeller, *Supplementum*, 11]'. Ficino, *Scritti*, 49.

4   Ficino's *De vita* vs. the Astrologers

Ficino was not shy to present *De vita* as closely wedded to the astrological tradition. He often recruited astrological knowledge to authorize his own claims, but also invoked the astrologers as a suitable foil against which to distinguish his own medical enterprise.[59] Moreover, the complementary *Apology* identified 'astronomy' as an essential component of the ancient priestly medicine that Ficino sought to recover.[60] Even so, it has often been said that of the classical branches of astrology, *De vita* retained only election astrology and astrological image making.[61] Melissa Bullard writes:

> Quite obviously in the *De vita* Ficino is no longer concerned with horoscopes and judgments. Elections is the only branch of traditional astrology that shares anything in common with the treatise.[62]

Likewise, Giancarlo Zanier states:

> *De vita coelitus comparanda* is presented as a treatise on 'elections' based on a causal astrological theory.[63]

There is much to say for this view. Throughout book III of *De vita*, Ficino draws amply upon the resources of astrological elections in shaping and theorizing his own version of astral medicine. Moreover, these resources were used more broadly than for the astrological talismans that were the focus of chapters 13 through 22. Ficino also drew on the techniques of electing to fine-tune the precise time when to gird oneself with substances attracting specific planetary properties (III.2.37–42, 82–85). As often happened in electing, he sought out favourable aspects between Sun and Jupiter to purify the subject's spirit (III.3.61), and privileged Moon and Mercury as signifiers of celestial gifts (III.5.7 sqq., III.6.56 sqq.). In chapter 25, he invoked the standard repertoire of astrological electing as an argument in favour of his own procedures (III.25.9–20), including the preparation of meals (III.25.27–28).

---

59   Authorizing: Ficino, *On Life*, 104:37; 228:41; 232:15–20; 236:22; 240:26; 250:14; 254:89, 256:23, 260:55, 264:8, 270:95, 276:1, 286:26, 298:24, 304:115, 306:24, 310:32, 320:103, 330:26, 338:92. Distinguishing: Ficino, *On Life*, 166:10; 232:24–28; 262:8, 296:135, 306:33, 318:93, 334:35.
60   Ficino, *On Life*, 'Apologia' 29–40 (trans. Kaske and Clark, 397).
61   Also see Ficino, *On Life*, 37, 58.
62   Bullard, 'Inward Zodiac', 699.
63   Zanier, *La medicina astrologica*, 32.

In light of what we discovered in the previous two sections, however, this can only be a point of departure for understanding Ficino's astrological project. As we have seen, astrological elections were a philosophically sophisticated tradition in their own right, which embedded astrological rules and aphorisms in articulate conceptions of human agency.

In this respect, Section 2 already highlighted important discrepancies between late medieval Latin election theory and the interpretation thereof by modern scholars like Eugenio Garin. As a result, the supposed continuity between the tradition of astrological electing and Ficino's *De vita* must be handled with caution. This is where the critique of the *Disputatio* becomes useful, since it alerts us to the specific concerns and attitudes that Ficino brought to this tradition. In the previous section, we found Ficino laying strong emphasis on the primacy of sublunary, proximate causes (with human free will at the pinnacle), rejecting the astrologers' focus on the pursuit of fortune in favour of a more overtly moral program of cultivating happiness, and suggesting that through personal virtues, the human soul could positively transcend the heavens' astral influx. How did this inflect Ficino's reworking of the tradition of astrological elections in *De vita*?

4.1   *The Matter of Elections*
One could argue that the astrologers and Ficino shared a central goal for their art: to procure a long life. At the end of book II of *De vita*, however, Ficino already staked out a major difference on what this meant:

> Do not be ashamed to listen often to those who seem to have arrived at a prosperous old age not so much by fortune as by vigor [*virtute*].[64]

'Fortune' was arguably the key matter that late medieval Latin astrologers sought to negotiate.[65] As we saw in the previous section, it was usually specified as the favourable or unfavourable quality of specific life events or actions. Hence also the astrologers' emphasis on birth charts, from which events were assumed to follow 'as if someone were to unwind a tangled rope', as a quintessential reference point for astrological agency.[66]

The techniques described in book III of *De vita*, however, mostly targeted a different kind of object: substances, not events or actions. As is well known,

---

64   Ficino, *On Life*, II.20.30–31: 'Neque pudeat saepe illos auscultare, qui non tam fortuna quam virtute senectutem prosperam consecuti videntur' (trans. Kaske and Clark, 233).

65   See Vanden Broecke. 'Astrological Self-Government', 45–47.

66   Pontano, *Opera*, vol. 3, 13: '(...) ut si quis complicatum funem explicet'.

Ficino thought that human spirits (subtle physiological vapours that permit
different life functions) became infected and depleted by the material conditions to which sublunary life inevitably commits them. *De vita* offered techniques for purging and replenishing these spirits through the intermediary
of substances that were particularly rich in them—including metals, animals,
plants, or air. These sublunary material substances, however, were also defined
as embedded in a cosmic chain of being that has the seven planets on top, and
through which each planet (and its associated substances) impart a different
kind of virtue to the spirit.[67]

Although many of the basic techniques of astrological electing reappeared
in the procedures that Ficino describes in book III, their meaning was very
different. Here, the heavens were no longer the principle of a life narrative of
misfortunes and/or graces that one could negotiate, as the astrologers assumed,
but a natural reservoir for the empowerment of sublunary substances which
Ficino taught his readers to tap at will. As we saw in the previous section, the
letter that Ficino wrote to Lorenzo I de' Medici (1449–1492) after finishing the
Disputatio, had already promoted the moral virtues (*virtutes*) as a source of
eudaimonic empowerment, superior to what the astrologers had to offer. There,
Ficino already deployed the metaphor of an inward heaven to denote this alternative source of empowerment:

> For these celestial bodies are not to be sought by us outside in some other
> place; for the heavens in their entirety are within us, in whom the light
> of life and the origin of heaven dwell. (...) what else does the Moon in
> us signify other than that continuous movement of our mind and body?
> Next Mars signifies swiftness, and Saturn tardiness; the Sun signifies God;
> Jupiter, law; Mercury, reason; Venus, human nature.[68]

In book III of *De vita*, Ficino's Platonizing medical natural philosophy allowed
him to expand this basic metaphor beyond virtue ethics and into medico-
magical terrain, and to turn the inward heaven into the basis for a different kind
of engagement with the astrologers' outward heaven. In *De vita*, the terms *vis*

---

67   Walker, *Spiritual and Demonic Magic*, 3–35; Ficino, *On Life*, 42–49.
68   Ficino, *Opera*, vol. 1, p. 805: 'Non enim sunt haec alicubi nobis extra quaerenda, nempe
      totum in nobis est coelum, quibus igneus uigor inest et coelestis origo.~~Principio.~~ Luna
      quidnam in nobis significat aliud praeter nostram illam continuam animi et corporis
      motionem; Mars deinde celeritatem, tarditatem uero Saturnus. Proinde Sol Deum, Iupiter
      legem, Mercurius rationem, Venus humanitatem'.

and *virtus* were omnipresent to denote the planetary forces that Ficino sought to channel, and helped support the new focus on the vigour of substances and their spirits.[69] This was not unique to Ficino. Anthony Parel showed how Machiavelli—the most famous Renaissance exponent of these shifting meanings of *virtus*—also drew on medical resources to theorize this concept.[70]

Ficino's reorientation of elections (from events and actions to substances) can also be discerned in other ways. Like the elections on which they were often based, many medico-magical techniques in book III required careful calibration against specific astrological conditions for their success. However, individual birth charts are surprisingly absent from this repertoire of relevant astral conditions in *De vita*. At best, they now served as a heuristic tool for selecting which astral power to access, or as an object to be engraved on an astronomical image.[71] Given that birth charts were key to verifying the possibility of elected events, their relative absence in book III's is also an indication of Ficino's turn away from events and actions as key objects of astrological agency.

4.2   The Agency of Elections

To describe the kind of agency carried out by his election techniques in book III of *De vita*, Ficino often used the verb 'to accommodate' (*accommodare*). 'Our bodies, rightly accommodated to the body and spirit of the world', we hear, 'can drink in the life of the world'.[72] Likewise, the human species can increase the gifts it receives from Sun, Mercury, and Jupiter 'if it will accommodate itself daily more and more' to them.[73] 'The spirit is exposed [and] accommodated to the [heavenly] Graces' through the qualities of touch (III.12.3), and so on.[74] At first sight, 'accommodating' appears to be a synonym of the verb that

---

69   Ficino, *On Life*, III.6.1sqq. (trans. Kaske and Clark, 265).

70   Parel, *The Machiavellian Cosmos*, 101–112.

71   Heuristic tool: *De vita* III.2.82–83 (trans. Kaske and Clark, 255); III.10.54 (trans. Kaske and Clark 287); III.14.22 (trans. Kaske and Clark, 311); III.23.8sqq. (trans. Kaske and Clark, 371); III.24.13 (trans Kaske and Clark 379). Engraving of astronomical image: *De vita* III.18.86–91 (trans. Kaske and Clark 339).

72   Ficino, *On Life*, III.1.88–90 (trans. Kaske and Clark, 247): '(...) corpora nostra rite accommodata corpori spirituique mundano, videlicet per res mundanas et per nostrum spiritum, hauriunt ex vita mundana quam plurimum'.

73   Ficino, *On Life*, III.2.25 (trans. Kaske and Clark, 251): '(...) si per Solaria Mercurialiaque et Iovia se ipsam eis magis indies atque magis accommodabit'.

74   Other examples: Through preparation, one accommodates oneself to receiving celestial gifts (III.2.11); The world soul is accommodated to the body of the world (III.3.4); The influx of Jupiter is most accommodated to man (III.5 and III.6.81); A temper verging toward heat and moisture allows spirit and body to be accommodated to celestial things (III.12.27); The

the astrologers often used in describing the operation of elections: 'to adapt'
(*aptare*). There is an important difference, however, that may explain Ficino's
change of terminology.

As we saw in section 2, astrologers like Giovanni Pontano approached elections as a technique for negotiating celestially induced changes and events. In
line with their Aristotelian-medical training, they conceptualized such astrological agency in terms of pre-emptive qualitative change in the sublunary
subject of celestial influx. By doing so, the unfortunate quality of a coming
change could be mitigated or, in the best scenario, annulled; potential fortunate changes, on the other hand, could be assisted in their actualization.

Ficino's techniques worked differently. In chapter III.1, he sketched a hierarchy of being with Intellect and Body, the 'divine' and the 'transient', at the
extremes. These are so unlike each other that only the World Soul, an intermediate agent bearing some likeness to both, can mediate. The soul possesses
'seminal reasons' of each species in her bosom, which mediate by enabling the
eternal ideas in the divine Intellect to be instantiated in the matter of Body. This
mediated relation hinged on love, since seminal reasons operate as 'baits' (*esca*)
for the World Soul.[75] On this basis, *De vita* was a manual for the artful exploita-
tion of cosmic seduction. By combining substances and stars with the same
privileged relation to a specific Idea, 'like a piece of wood treated with sulphur
for a flame that is present everywhere', humans could create their own 'lures'
(*illices*) for the World Soul.[76] This process in turn seduces the Soul to infuse
'gifts' and 'graces' specific to that Idea into the depleted spirits of humans—
gifts carried down from daemons and planets.

The astrologers operated in a world of body, where the visible heavens were
defined as God's intermediaries for the government of sublunary embodied
things.[77] Such government was guaranteed, and the astrologer's task was to
help deploy man's intellectual soul in such a way that possible fortunes and
actions could be optimized. By comparison, Ficino operated in a world of
extremes where the gifts of divine and celestial government were not similarly

---

Sun is accommodated to generation (III.19.22); One accommodates colours to mothers
(III.19.33–34); One accommodates fumigations to the stars (III.20.42); One accommodates
oneself to the stars' natural influx; to receiving the Sun's light and heat: one accommo-
dates human song to the stars (III.21.58–62); One accommodates oneself to celestial things
(Ch. III.22); One accommodates planets and stars towards the effecting of some work
(III.23.77–78).

75   Ficino, *On Life*, III.1.26.
76   Ficino, *On Life*, III.1.38–39 (trans. Kaske and Clark, 245): '(...) velut lignum per sulphur
      paratum ad flammam ubique praesentem'.
77   See the authoritative treatment by Thomas Aquinas, *Summa contra gentiles*, III.82.2.

guaranteed to embodied humans. As a result, human agency hinged far more on the artful manipulation of sublunary substances to make them more celestial. For the astrologers, agency in relation to the stars revolved around what we would call 'appropriation': altering the quality of celestial influx through the artful manipulation of the sublunary bodies and souls that received it. For Ficino, human agency was a matter of 'accommodation': turning sublunary bodies and souls into substances more attuned to celestial gifts of one's own choosing.

The difference is particularly clear in how the astrologers and Ficino approached aphorism 8 of *Centiloquium*, which Pontano translated as follows: 'A wise soul contributes to celestial operations, just as the best farmer contributes to nature by plowing and weeding' (cf. section 2). Interestingly, Pontano's commentary also used Ficino's preferred language of seduction:

> (...) why should not also the goods that are decreed by the stars, being recognized in advance, be attracted [*allectari*] by industry and counsel before they arrive?[78]

But this is where the similarity ended. Pontano, much like Ficino's friend Bonincontri, interpreted the farmer analogy around the activity of qualitatively improving the recipient body of celestial influx: plowing, weeding, burning, using manure, etc.[79] Ficino, on the other hand, interpreted the analogy on the model of bringing fresh [celestial] grafts into old [bodily] stock:

> With this in mind, agriculture prepares the field and the seed for celestial gifts and by grafting prolongs the life of the shoot and refashions it into another and better species. (...) The philosopher who knows about natural objects and stars, whom we rightly are accustomed to call a Magus, does the very same things: he seasonably introduces the celestial into the earthly by particular lures just as the farmer interested in grafting brings the fresh graft into the old stock. Ptolemy also strongly argues this, affirming that a wise man of this sort can help the work of the stars just as the farmer does the power of the earth.[80]

---

78 Pontano, *Opera*, vol. 3, 19: '(...) cur non et bona quae ab illis decernantur, ante etiam cognita, industria consilioque poterunt tanquam allectari prius quam eueniant?'.

79 Compare Bonincontri, *Commentum*, fol. 68ʳ: 'Et sic faciet ut bonus agricola adiuvat fortitudines naturales terre quam serere vult aut fimo, aut cultura, aut adustione lupinorum et similium, quibus campus feracior redditur'.

80 Ficino, *On Life*, III.26.49–58. (trans. Kaske and Clark, 387).

4.3   *The End of Elections*

This brings us to a third difference: the end of these techniques. As we saw in section 2, elections sought to negotiate celestial influx so as to fashion a more fortunate life: to mitigate coming misfortunes, and to avoid human action that might spoil a promised good. As Guido Bonatti put it in his *Tractatus astronomiae*:

> Election is counsel for the appetite of the client. For, choosing is an intellectual appetite that stems from an act of free will. (...) Through elections, we can apprehend many good things and similarly avoid many evils that will come from the stars. I do not claim that an election makes a thing but that it removes it, so that an event does not occur.[81]

In the prefatory letter to the reader of book III, Ficino immediately set out a different end:

> This shop of ours displays various antidotes, drugs, fomentations, ointments, and remedies (...). At least do not neglect medicines which have been strengthened by some sort of heavenly aid, unless perhaps you would neglect life itself. For I have found by long and repeated experience that medicines of this kind are as different from other medicines made without astrological election as wine is from water.[82]

Ficino not only re-oriented the object of elections towards sublunary substances (cf. section 4.1): he also described the end of those operations in distinctly preternatural terms. If the astrologers, for instance, used elections to optimize the medical action of administering a natural drug, Ficino instead set out to make celestial designer drugs.

Much has been written on the transformative goals of Ficino's magical medicine, particularly in the context of his not-so-covert flirtations with late antique Neoplatonic theurgy.[83] In a recent paper, Darrel Rutkin also argued that

---

81   Bonatti, *De astronomia*, col. 385: 'Est autem electio, prae consiliati appetitu [the text has appetitus] consilium. Eligere autem, est appetitus intellectus resultans ex actu liberi arbitrij. (...) Per electiones enim apprehendere possumus multa bona, similiter et multa mala possumus evitare, quae secundum stellas ventura sunt. Non tamen dico quod electio faciat rem, sed removet, prohibens ne res fiat'. On this passage, also see Vanden Broecke, 'Astrological Self-Government', 36–37.

82   Ficino, *On Life*, 'Ad lectorem', 17–26 (trans. Kaske and Clark, 239–241).

83   For basic orientation, see Celenza, 'Late Antiquity'; Robichaud, 'Ficino on Force'; Giglioni, 'Theurgy and Philosophy'; Giglioni, 'Healing Rituals'.

De vita's famous chapters on astrological image making (chs. III.13–22) sought to disclose rituals for effecting a theurgical union with the ensouled planets.[84] Without going into the specific issue of Ficino's theurgical ambitions, it does appear that Ficino's elections aimed for the 'the heavens to be moved by divine beings through the minds of humans', as he had put it in the *Disputatio* (cf. section 3).

Consider chapter III.22 of *De vita*, where Ficino extensively discussed the dangers and challenges of Saturn—the ominous planet that occupied the ascendant of Ficino's own birth chart.[85] According to Ficino, there were only two effective ways of negotiating Saturn: either to 'flee to Jupiter', or to whole-heartedly embrace the life of divine contemplation that Saturn uniquely favoured. The former route could be taken by seeking out Jupiter's 'natural qual-ity' (presumably through elections), Jovial foodstuffs, drugs, and talismans, and by leading the kind of public life that Jupiter favoured.[86] The latter route was even more promising, according to Ficino, since the 'Chaldeans, Egyptians, and Platonists' all confirmed that this allowed one to access gifts from the angelic intelligences above the heavens and to 'avoid the malice of fate'.[87]

For Ficino, it really was possible for human minds to take control over the planets. The astrologers, too, had claimed for centuries that 'the wise man will rule the stars' (*sapiens dominabitur astris*). But at least in the Latin astrological tradition of the late Middle Ages, this referred to ways of appropriating cosmic government from within, not as ways of distancing or transcending astral influ-ence.[88] For Ficino, astrology did offer the possibility of transcending the stars by purifying spirit and soul.

5   Conclusion

Astrologers in the late Middle Ages approached astrological elections as a tool to identify propitious times for specific actions, such as marriage or starting a business. Their practice was deeply rooted in the belief that celestial influ-ences could shape human affairs, and by carefully selecting favorable moments, astrologers believed they could mitigate future misfortunes or enhance prom-

---

84   Rutkin, 'Dancing With the Stars'.
85   Klibansky, *Saturn and Melancholy*, 256.
86   Ficino, *On Life*, III.22.78–81.
87   Ficino, *On Life*, III.22.82–90.
88   Vanden Broecke, 'Astrological Self-Government', 61.

ised goods. In the unpublished *Disputatio* of 1477, Ficino came out strongly against this tradition of astrological electing, as we saw in his complaint about aphorism 22 of the influential *Centiloquium*. In the published *De vita* of 1489, however, Ficino recommended election techniques for celestially improving the quality of a new garment.

This volte-face offers an attractive entry point into the scholarly conundrum of Ficino's wavering position on the legitimacy of astrology. On the one hand, it allows us to abandon the classic but crude 'for or against astrology'-question, in favour of a historically sensitive focus on the kind of astrology that Ficino preferred. On the other hand, it allows us to answer the latter question through a more fine-grained comparison between the elections practiced by Ficino's astrological peers and the version of election astrology that he offered in *De vita*.

Contrary to Eugenio Garin's interpretation of astrological electing as an art of conquering the stars and changing fate, late medieval practitioners described astrological agency as a matter of negotiating the (un-)fortunate effects of cosmic influences. More specifically, they sought practical ways to effect a pre-emptive qualitative change in the sublunary subject of celestial influxes. We see this, for instance, in the commentaries on *Centiloquium* by Ficino's contemporaries Giovanni Pontano and Lorenzo Bonincontri. To mitigate coming evils, one sought to alter one's bodily complexion or place. To actualize future goods, one cultivated the virtue of prudence in oneself. To 'perfect' the cosmic flow of evils and goods, then, was to assist such change through practices that took the farmer's assistance of natural processes as their basic model. Likewise, aphorism 22 was seen to discuss the cosmic auspiciousness of an event like donning new clothes, not the celestially induced qualities of clothes.

Both in his subtle rephrasings of medieval sources and in the original sections of the *Disputatio* of 1477, Ficino can be seen bringing specific concerns and attitudes to this tradition. First, he placed strong emphasis on the primacy of sublunary, proximate causes (with human free will at the pinnacle). Second, he rejected the astrologers' focus on the pursuit of fortune in favour of a more overtly moral program of cultivating happiness. Third, he suggested that through an 'inner zodiac' of personal virtues, the human soul could positively transcend the outer zodiac's astral influx. Such differences in Ficino's account of celestial influx and human agency in turn helped alter the meaning of the practice of electing in *De vita*.

There, the matter or object of elections changed decisively. For Ficino's astrological peers, 'fortune' (the favourable or unfavourable quality of specific life events or actions) was the key matter to be negotiated.[89] The techniques of book III of *De vita*, however, mostly targeted substances (including human spirit), not events or actions. The agency ascribed to elections changed as well. For astrologers like Pontano, the favour of the stars was a given, to be facilitated through qualitative optimization of sublunary recipient bodies. Agency in relation to the stars accordingly revolved around what we called 'appropriation'. For Ficino, the favour of the stars was something that one actively seduced or conjured. Human agency was a matter of what he called 'accommodation': the artful refashioning of sublunary bodies and souls into substances attuned to celestial gifts of one's own choosing.

Finally, the end of elections changed too. The astrologers ultimately sought to optimize the embodied nature of man: to make life more fortunate, the lower soul less passionate, and the intellectual soul more prudent. Ficino's elections, however, sought to tap into the hidden preternatural virtues of sublunary substances. Significantly, the age-old analogy between astrologer and farmer was now based on the latter's skill in grafting new plants. This included, as Ficino put it, 'the planting of man' (III.25.21). By the patient conjuring of cosmic virtues, Ficino was adamant that humans really could transcend the stars.

Acknowledgments

The author wishes to express his deep gratitude to Dr. Maria Sorokina (Institut de recherche et d'histoire des textes, CNRS) for generously sharing relevant parts of her forthcoming edition of Gerard of Feltre's *Summa*, and for her helpful remarks on an earlier version of this paper. Many thanks are also due to the organizers, speakers, and participants of the Astra Project Conference 'The Tools of the Art', whose comments were vital in bringing the basic ideas of this paper to fruition.

Bibliography

Baron, Hans. 'Willensfreiheit und Astrologie bei Marsilio Ficino und Pico della Mirandola'. *Kultur- und Universalgeschichte: Walter Goetz zu seinem 60. Geburtstage.* Leipzig, B.G. Teubner, 1927. 145–170.

---

89   See Vanden Broecke. 'Astrological Self-Government', 45–47.

Bayerische Akademie der Wissenschaften. 'Ptolemaeus Arabus et Latinus', Accessed
    16 August, 2024. https://ptolemaeus.badw.de/start

Bellanti, Lucio. *De astrologica veritate liber quaestionum. Astrologiae defensio contra
    Ioannem Picum Mirandulanum*. Basel, Jacobus Parcus, 1554.

Bonatti, Guido. *De astronomia tractatus x*. Basel, [Jacobus Parcus,] 1550.

Bonincontri, Lorenzo. *Commentum super Centiloquio Ptholomei*. Vatican, BAV, Vat. lat.
    3379, fols. 62^r–114^r.

Boudet, Jean-Patrice. 'Ptolémée dans l'Occident médiéval: roi, savant et philosophe',
    The Medieval Legends of Philosophers and Scholars. Ed. Agostino Paravicini Bagliani.
    Florence, SISMEL, 2013. Pp. 193–217.

Cassirer, Ernst. *The Individual and the Cosmos in Renaissance Philosophy*. Trans. Mario
    Domandi. New York, Harper and Row, 1964 [1927].

Celenza, Christopher S. 'Late Antiquity and Florentine Platonism: The 'Post-Ploti-
    nian' Ficino', *Marsilio Ficino: His Theology, His Philosophy, His Legacy*. Eds. Michael
    J.B. Allen, Valery Rees and Martin Davies. Leiden, Brill, 2002. Pp. 71–97.

Coley, Henry. *Clavis astrologiae elimata, or a key to the whole art of astrology new filed
    and polished*. 2nd ed. London, Benjamin Tooke, 1676.

Dykes, Benjamin N. *Choices and Inceptions. Traditional Electional Astrology*. Minneapo-
    lis MN, Cazimi Press, 2012.

Ficino, Marsilio. *Opera omnia*. 2 vols. Basel: Heinrich Petri, 1576.

Ficino, Marsilio. *Letters*. Trans. Members of the Language department of the School of
    economic science. 11 vols. London, Shepheard-Walwyn, 1975–2020.

Ficino, Marsilio. *Three Books on Life*, ed./trans. Carol V. Kaske and John R. Clark. Tempe
    AZ, Medieval and Renaissance Texts and Studies, 1998.

Ficino, Marsilio. *Scritti sull'astrologia*. Trans. Ornella Pompeo Faracovi. Milano, RCS
    Libri, 1999.

Garin, Eugenio. 'Le 'elezioni' e il problema dell'astrologia', *Umanesimo e esoterismo*, ed.
    Eugenio Garin. Padova, CEDAM, 1960. Pp. 17–38.

Gerard of Feltre. *Summa de astris*. Ed. Maria Sorokina (forthcoming).

Giglioni, Guido. 'Theurgy and Philosophy in Marsilio Ficino's Paraphrase of Iambli-
    chus's *De Mysteriis Aegyptiorum*', *Rinascimento*, 2nd series, 52 (2012): 3–36.

Giglioni, Guido. 'Healing rituals and their philosophical significance in Marsilio Ficino's
    Philosophy', *Platonism: Ficino to Foucault*. Eds. Valery Rees, Anna Corrias, Francesca
    Maria Crasta, Laura Follesa and Guido Giglioni. Boston: Brill, 2020. Pp. 55–77.

Grafton, Anthony. *Magus. The Art of Magic from Faustus to Agrippa*. Cambridge MA,
    Belknap Press, 2023.

Kaske, Carol. 'Ficino's shifting attitude towards astrology in the *De vita coelitus com-
    paranda*, the Letter to Poliziano, and the *Apologia* to the Cardinals', *Marsilio Ficino
    e il ritorno di Platone. Studi e documenti*, ed. Gian Carlo Garfagnini. 2 vols. Firenze,
    Leo S. Olschki, 1986. Vol. 2, 371–382.

Klibansky, Raymond, Erwin Panofsky, and Fritz Saxl. *Saturn and Melancholy: Studies in the History of Natural Philosophy, Religion, and Art*. London, Nelson, 1964.

Kristeller, Paul O. *Supplementum Ficinianum*. Firenze, Leo S. Olschki, 1937.

Meriam Bullard, Melissa. 'The Inward Zodiac: A Development in Ficino's Thought on Astrology', *Renaissance Quarterly*, 43 4 (1990):687–708.

Niermeier-Dohoney, Justin. 'Sapiens Dominabitur Astris: A Diachonic Survey of a Ubiquitous Astrological Phrase', *Humanities*, 10 4 (2021), 117. https://doi.org/10.3390/h100 40117

Page, Sophie. 'Richard Trewythian and the Uses of Astrology', *Journal of the Warburg and Courtauld Institutes*, 64 (2001): 193–228.

Parel, Anthony J. *The Machiavellian Cosmos*. New Haven/London, Yale University Press, 1992.

Pompeo Faracovi, Ornella. 'Destino e fato nelle pagine astrologiche di Marsilio Ficino', *Nella luce degli astri. L'astrologia nella cultura del Rinascimento*, ed. Ornella Pompeo Faracovi. Sarzana, Agorà, 2004, 1–24.

Pontano, Giovanni. *Opera omnia*. Basel, Andreas Cratander, 1538–1540.

Ps.-Ptolemy. *Centiloquium*. Trans. Plato of Tivoli. Venice, Bonetus Locatellis, 1493, sig. 107^r–116^v.

Robichaud, Denis J.-J. 'Ficino on Force, Magic, and Prayers: Neoplatonic and Hermetic Influences in Ficino's *Three Books on Life*', *Renaissance Quarterly*, 70 1 (2017):44–87.

Rosenthal, Margaret F. 'Cultures of Clothing in Later Medieval and Early Modern Europe', *Journal of Medieval and Early Modern Studies* 39 (2009):459–481.

Rutkin, Darrel H 'Dancing with the Stars: a Preliminary Exploration as to whether the Astrology in Marsilio Ficino's De vita is Theurgical', *Bruniana & Campanelliana* 26 (2020):403–419.

Sahl bin Bishr [Zael]. *De electionibus*. Venice, Bonetus Locatellis, 1493, sig. 138^v–141^v.

Sorokina, Maria. 'Une source inconnue de la *Disputatio contra iudicium astrologorum* de Marsile Ficin: la *Summa de astris* de Gérard de Feltre', *Bruniana e Campanelliana*, 21 1 (2015):169–189.

Sorokina, Maria. 'Un tournant dans la critique de l'astrologie? La *Summa de astris* de Gérard de Feltre', *Philosophical Readings*, 7 (2015):71–92.

Sorokina, Maria. *Les sphères, les astres et les théologiens. L'influence céleste entre science et foi dans les commentaires des Sentences (v. 1220–v. 1340)*. 2 vols. Turnhout, Brepols, 2021.

Trinkaus, Charles. 'Marsilio Ficino and the Ideal of Human Autonomy', *Marsilio Ficino e il ritorno di Platone. Studi e documenti*, ed. Gian Carlo Garfagnini. 2 vols. Firenze, Leo S. Olschki, 1986. Vol. 1, 197–210.

Vanden Broecke, Steven. 'Astrological Self-Government at the Fifteenth-Century Court of Bourbon', *Early Science and Medicine* 28 (2023):34–62.

Walker, Daniel Pickering. *Spiritual and Demonic Magic from Ficino to Campanella*. London, The Warburg Institute, 1958.

Weill Parot, Nicolas. 'Causalité astrale et "science des images" au Moyen Age: éléments de réflexion', *Revue d'histoire des sciences*, 52 2 (1999): 207–240.

Zambelli, Paola. The Speculum Astronomiae and its Enigma: Astrology, Theology and Science in Albertus Magnus and his Contemporaries. Dordrecht, Kluwer, 1992.

Zanier, Giancarlo. *La medicina astrologica e la sua teoria: Marsilio Ficino e i suoi critici contemporanei.* Roma, Edizioni dell'Ateneo & Bizzarri, 1977.

CHAPTER 11

Ignorance, Pitfalls and Scribal Errors: On the Proper Assessment of Historical Horoscopes of the Early Modern Period

Günther Oestmann

Abstract

Historical Horoscopes are a very special type of source material and can be read as depositories of unique mathematical and biographical information and contemporary anecdotes (and sometimes gossip) about famous or lesser-known characters, as well as a form of reception. Indeed, a horoscope always tends to collect, explain and contextualize pieces of information and biographical data about the person or event in question. But the examination of a horoscope must begin with its astronomical and mathematical contents, and the researcher must be well aware of the parameters he uses. Methodical approaches, as well as pitfalls, will be demonstrated by means of two exemplary nativities of the sixteenth and seventeenth centuries and the famous horoscope for Wallenstein, cast by Johannes Kepler.

Keywords

Historical horoscopes – geniture collections – astrology of the early modern period – planetary tables – house systems

1 Introduction

The history of science in the Early Modern Period remains incomprehensible to a large extent without taking astrology into consideration. The antiquarian and biographer John Aubrey (1626–1697), one of the early members of the Royal Society and deeply convinced of astrology, put it this way: 'For we are governed by the planets, as the wheeles & weights move the Index of the clock'.[1] Astrology

---

[1] Letter from Aubrey to Anthony Wood (May 14th, 1673; Oxford, Bodleian Library: Ms. Wood F.39, fol. 206ʳ).

was the most popular of the divinatory arts in the Middle Ages and remained so in the Renaissance and Early Modern Period. But the postulated existence of a connection between celestial bodies and events in the sky and on earth was shattered in the so-called 'Age of Scientific Revolution' and saw a rapid decline in the course of the seventeenth century (which is a problem in itself). Astrology was increasingly marginalized as a practice that belonged to the realm of superstition and had no legitimacy in contemporary scientific discourses. It is not my aim to present a comprehensive history of research here—suffice it to say that the history of astrology as an important element of western science and culture is now recognized and has received much scholarly attention in recent decades. But one still encounters problems and prejudices.

The researcher usually faces two camps. On the one hand, there are academic historians of science, who are concerned with the history of their respective discipline, and on the other hand, there are ardent believers and supporters of astrology, which is still very much alive and flourishing today. Therefore, often a decided discomfort among historians and natural scientists (especially astronomers) can be perceived when dealing with astrological matters. Studies in the history of astrology are often undertaken by professional astrologers, who seek to legitimize their craft through historical research. Many academics are suspicious of these studies and regard them as unscientific. Even when historians of science work on such allegedly despicable objects of research, they may receive harsh comments from their colleagues, which evolves into debates between 'believers' and 'non-believers'. Communication can be difficult on both sides, and the literature produced by astrologers is too often ignored by the academic community. However, interpreting and validating astrology in terms of 'true' or 'false' is an inappropriate approach from a historical perspective.

2   Computation Parameters

The examination of the astronomical and mathematical contents of a horoscope must start with an adequate recalculation, applying the same methods and means as the historical calculator had at his disposal. In former days, this was an extremely cumbersome procedure; it is now greatly facilitated by the use of computer programmes. Some of these incorporate even the most intricate 'classical' approaches, e.g., doctrines of Hellenistic astrology. But the results of such programmes depend on correct input, and one has to be careful to handle the material with appropriate parameters. Moreover, historical horoscopes often contain calculation and/or scribal errors.

The following six parameters must be taken into account:

2.1   Date

Is the date given according to the Julian or Gregorian calendar? Here, the very different (i.e., delayed) dates of introduction of the new calendar in Protestant, as well as Catholic, territories must be considered.[2]

2.2   Time

Usually, true local solar time is used, unless the chimes of a mechanical clock are mentioned explicitly. Time indications in minutes and even seconds are not the result of measurements, however. These refer to specific astrological calculations (methods of rectification), but a detailed discussion of these procedures is beyond the scope of this article.

Ephemerides are always calculated in mean time. According to the solar longitude, i.e. the season of the year, the equation of time ranges from -14 to +16 minutes approximately, thereby affecting the houses to some degrees and lunar longitude to several minutes of arc.

2.3   Epoch of Day

The type of day division must be taken into account: In astronomy, the date change takes place at 12.00 noon, and the hours are counted from there to 24. But in civil usage, sunrise or sunset was usually the beginning of the day. The midnight epoch, which was already used by the Romans for legal purposes, became established with the increasing spread of mechanical clocks in the late Middle Ages, whereby the counting is usually done in 2 x 12 hours (halbe Uhr).[3] E.g., the civil time of 10 February 8.30 would read 9 February 20.30 for astronomical use.

There are four traditions concerning where to start the hours from:
– Noon p.m. (*post meridiem*)
– Sunset p.o. (*post occasum solis*)
– Midnight a.m. (*ante meridiem*)
– Sunrise p.s. (*post solis ortum*)
These are the epochs of day, which are different from the civil epoch of date which indicates at what time of day the date changes along with the day of the week. This is not linked with the first hour necessarily, e.g. in Italy the date changed at sunset.

---

2   For details see Friedrich Karl Ginzel, *Handbuch der mathematischen und technischen Chronologie*. repr. Leipzig: Deutscher Buch-Export und -Import GmbH, 1958, vol. 3, 266–277, and (enormously comprehensive) Dirk Steinmetz: *Die Gregorianische Kalenderreform von 1582: Korrektur der christlichen Zeitrechnung in der Frühen Neuzeit*, Oftersheim: Dirk Steinmetz, 2011 (PhD thesis, Heidelberg 2010).

3   On local methods of counting the hours, see Ginzel, Handbuch, 3:94–6.

2.4   Geographical Coordinates

The geographical position given in the source must be used, or in the absence
of coordinates, contemporary sources need to be consulted, as these may differ
significantly from modern values. The history of the transmission of geographical coordinates is still largely unexplored. Apart from topographical indices
in planetary tables, the lists published by Johann Schöner (*Luculentissima
quaedam terrae totius descriptio*, Nuremberg, 1515) and Peter Apian's *Cosmography* (first edition Landshut, 1524)[4] are convenient to use when dealing with
horoscopes of the Early Modern Period.

The choice of a prime meridian is arbitrary and depends on customs, historical and even political reasons.[5] In planetary tables of the Early Modern Period
the following prime meridians are used:

Table	Meridian	Longitude to Greenwich	Latitude
Alfonsine Tables	Toledo	−3°59'	39°52'
[Copernicus]	Frauenburg	19°41'	54°21'
Prutenic Tables	Königsberg	20°30'	54°43'
Modern	Greenwich	−	51°29'

Horoscopes for southern latitudes first appeared in the final stages of the col-
onization of South America at the beginning of the seventeenth century.[6]

---

4 Apian's cosmography was edited and expanded from 1529 by the Frisian cosmographer and
   instrument maker Rainer Gemma Frisius (Jemme Reinerszoon, 1508–1555). The book was
   widely distributed and appeared in 44 editions by 1609, including Flemish/Dutch, French and
   Spanish translations; see Fernand van Ortroy, 'Bibliographie de l'oeuvre de Pierre Apian', in
   Le Bibliographe Moderne: Courrier International des Archives et des Bibliothèques 5 (1901),
   113–156; id., Bibliographie de Gemma Frisius fondateur de l'école Belge de geographie de son
   fils Corneille et de ses neveux les Arsenius, Brussels: Hayez, 1920, 165–189.

5 Heinrich Haag, Die Geschichte des Nullmeridians, Gießen: Otto Wigand, 1913; Charles W.J.
   Withers, Zero Degrees: Geographies of the Prime Meridian, Cambridge, MA/London: Harvard University Press, 2017.

6 John David North, 'Georg Markgraf: An Astronomer in the New World', in *Johan Maurits van
   Nassau-Siegen, 1604–1679: Essays on the occasion of the tercentenary of his death*, ed. by E.
   van den Boogaart, H.R. Hoetink and P.J.P. Whitehead, The Hague: Johan Maurits van Nassau
   Stichting, 394–423.

2.5   *Planetary Positions*

Contemporary parameters must be used to recalculate and reexamine planetary positions. Astronomers and astrologers either used tables containing planetary positions for a certain time interval in advance (ephemerides) or tables that allowed the calculation of planetary positions for any desired time.

Only a very concise survey can be given here—suffice it to say that until the sixteenth century—the Alfonsine Tables, based on the planetary models of Ptolemy, were used for the main part. In 1551, the Prutenic Tables were published for the first time. These were based on the parameters in Copernicus's *De revolutionibus*. Most of the remaining ephemerides of the second half of the sixteenth century were derivatives of the Prutenic Tables.[7]

The prediction of planetary positions according to various planetary tables and ephemerides yielded discrepancies that could provoke conflicting astrological interpretations. This problem was repeatedly discussed in the sixteenth century.[8] The Prutenic Tables had a periodic error of the Sun's longitude of only 16', but for Mars deviations between about +3° and -2° occurred. Moreover, the position of Mercury could be erroneous up to 10° and Venus of -4° at worst. The error for Mars and Jupiter was 30–40', and the error for the Moon's mean motion was about +/- 40', because variation (first discovered by Tycho Brahe) was not considered.[9]

Kepler's discovery of the laws of planetary motion marks a turning point in celestial mechanics and in the attainment of accuracy in predicting planetary positions. Deviations between Kepler's parameters and modern calculations are marginal and can be ignored for historical recalculations.[10]

---

7   Günther Oestmann, 'Ephemeridenwerke des 16. Jahrhunderts, eine wichtige Arbeitsgrundlage für Astronomen und Astrologen', *Gemeinnützige Mathematik: Adam Ries und seine Folgen* (Acta Academiae Scientiarum, 8), ed. by Jürgen Kiefer and Karin Reich, Erfurt: Akademie gemeinnütziger Wissenschaften zu Erfurt, 2003, 149–164.

8   Jürgen Hamel, 'Die Rezeption des mathematisch-astronomischen Teils des mathematisch-astronomischen Teils des Werkes von Nicolaus Copernicus in der astronomisch-astrologischen Kleinliteratur um 1600', in *Cosmographica et Geographica: Festschrift für Heribert M. Nobis zum 70. Geburtstag*, ed. by Bernhard Fritscher and Gerhard Brey, München: Institut für Geschichte der Naturwissenschaften, 1994, vol. 1, 315–335; Andreas Lerch, *Scientia astrologiae: Der Diskurs über die Wissenschaftlichkeit der Astrologie und die lateinischen Lehrbücher 1470–1610* (= Acta Historica Astronomiae, 56), Leipzig: Leipziger Universitätsverlag, 2015, 158–187, as well as the chapter 'Beyond Computation: Copernican Ephemerists on Hypotheses, Astrology and Natural Philosophy' in Pietro Omodeo, *Copernicus in the Cultural Debates of the Renaissance: Reception, Legacy, Transformation* (= History of Science and Medicine Library, 45), Leiden/Boston: Brill, 2014, 124–157.

9   Owen Gingerich, 'Early Copernican Ephemerides', in Science and History: Studies in Honor of Edward Rosen (= Studia Copernicana, 16), Wrocław/Kraków/Gdańsk: Polish Academy of Sciences Press, 1978, 407–408.

10   Owen Gingerich, 'A Study of Kepler's "Rudolphine Tables"' in *Actes du XIe Congrès Inter*

2.6   *Houses (Domification)*

This is a purely astrological concept, a division of the zodiac into twelve fields formed by six great circles in the form of spherical triangles. Specific meanings have been ascribed to the twelve houses.[11] The signs and planets all move through these in varying periods of time, and each house provides information on different areas of human life.

The first house begins at the ascendant and the others are numbered counterclockwise from that point (the first six houses are therefore below the horizon, and the other six are above). Their positions remain fixed according to the place and time of the native.

There are manifold methods of house division,[12] but discussing these in detail and delineating their very complex history would be clearly beyond the scope of this paper, so only short comments shall be given.

Generally, methods of house division can be classified into three groups:[13]
- Ecliptical methods: The division of the ecliptic is used.
- Space systems: The conceptual foundation is the celestial sphere without reference to the ecliptic. By partitioning the space into sections by trigonometrical methods the houses are formed, and then the location of the ecliptic is considered.
- Time systems: These refer to the diurnal rotation of the celestial sphere. In contrast to other systems, neither the ecliptic nor the heavens are used for house division, but time units.

Most likely the following methods are being encountered in historical sources (some contemporary attributions are spurious, but these have been retained to avoid confusion, and the discussion on Whole Sign Houses shall not be addressed here).
- Firmicus (Equal houses): The ecliptic is divided into equal segments of 30 degrees each starting from the degree of the ascendant.
- Porphyry: This is the oldest system of quadrant style house division. Each quadrant of the ecliptic is divided into three equal parts between the four angles (ascendant, midheaven, descendant and lower heaven).

---

national d'Histoire des Sciences, 1965, Wrocław/Kraków/Gdańsk: Ossolineum, 1968, vol. 3, 36.

11   Deborah Houlding, *The Houses: Temples of the Sky*, Bournemouth: The Wessex Astrologer, ²2006.

12   Dona Marie Lorenz, Tools of Astrology—Houses, Topanga, CA: Eomega Grove Press, 1973; Ralph William Holden, *The Elements of House Division*, London: The Faculty of Astrological Studies/The Urania Trust, 1977; John David North, *Horoscopes and History* (= Warburg Institute: Surveys and Texts, 13), London: The Warburg Institute/University of London, 1986.

13   Holden, The Elements of House Division, 60–61.

- Alcabitius: One trisects the diurnal and nocturnal semiarcs equally and projects the parts onto the ecliptic with circles of declination. This house system was disseminated widely before the introduction of the Regiomontanus system, and it is not without reason that John North coined for it the definition 'standard method' of the Middle Ages.
- Campanus: One trisects the quadrants of the prime vertical equally and projects the parts onto the ecliptic with circles of position joining in the north and south points of the horizon.
- Regiomontanus: One trisects the quadrants of the equator equally and projects the parts onto the ecliptic with circles of position joining in the north and south points of the horizon. This method was commonly used and became standard in the sixteenth and the seventeenth century.
- Placidus: One trisects the ecliptic between meridian and horizon proportionally. The diurnal and nocturnal semiarcs are divided in the same proportion as the corresponding points on the equator divide their own right ascensions. Placidus became the most commonly used house system from the second half of the seventeenth-century onwards and remains the most popular system among English-speaking astrologers.

3 Historical Examples

Four examples shall illustrate the correct examination of historical horoscopes.

3.1 Schöner's Nativity

The nativity of the astronomer Johannes Schöner (1477–1547), published first in his *Opera mathematica* (Nuremberg 1551) (Fig. 11.1), is present in different horoscope collections, albeit with slightly different birth times.[14]

According to Schöner's own statement, the latitude of his birthplace Karlstadt is 50°N (the actual value is 49°57′N). In his *Luculentissima quaedam terrae totius descriptio* (Nuremberg 1515) Schöner gives 50°5′ and a longitude of 26°54′ east of the chosen prime meridian on the island of Porto Santo near Madeira.

Schöner most likely used the Alfonsine Tables for calculating the planetary positions. The reference meridian is Toledo (9°4′ east of Porto Santo). Karlstadt is therefore 17°50′ east of Toledo.

---

14 Paris, Bibliothèque nationale de France: ms. lat. 7395, fol. 327ʳ: Jan. 16th, 1477, 10:53 P.M.; Leipzig, Universitätsbibliothek: Rep. IV, 87, fol. 110ʳ (124ʳ): Jan. 16th, 1477, 10:55 [p.m.]; Munich, Bayerische Staatsbibliothek, Clm 27003, fol. 26ᵛ: Jan. 16th, 1477, 10:53 P.M.; Wolfenbüttel, Herzog August Bibliothek: 35.2 Astron. 4°, fol. 248ᵛ: Jan. 16th, 1477, 11:00 P.M.; Hamburg, Lehrerbibliothek des Christianeums, R 31/3, 180: Jan. 16th, 1477 10:53 [P.M.];

For January 16th, 1477, 11:00 P.M. the following positions result (degrees; minutes; sign; on the left the values given in Schöner's *Opera mathematica*):[15]

Sun	6°00' Aq	6°39' Aq
Moon	16°00' Aq	27°00' Aq
Saturn	20°00' Le retrograde	20°32' Le
Jupiter	19°00' Pi	18°57' Pi
Mars	18°00' Aq	28°37' Aq
Venus	9°00' Sa	19°46' Sa
Mercury	20°00' Cp	9°57' Cp

The ecliptical longitudes are rendered in full degrees. It is obvious that the positions of the Moon, as well as Mars, Venus, and Mercury are deviating considerably. The ecliptical longitudes of Mars, Venus and Mercury are obviously misprints (it should read 28°, 19° and 10° respectively). For the Moon no explanation can be offered, however.

Regarding the houses it is notable that the cardinal houses (i.e., Ascendant, Midheaven, Descendant, Imum coeli) have been given precisely in degrees and minutes, whereas Schöner contented himself with full degrees only for intermediate houses. Schöner has used Regiomontanus's method of domification.[16] Here is the result of the recalculation (on the left the original values):

	10:00 p.m.		11:25 p.m.
	Source	Recalculation	
X	28°16' Ca	22°15' Ca	28°12' Ca
XI	4°00' Vi	29°04' Le	4°25' Vi
XII	0°00' Li	25°31' Vi	0°14' Li

Francesco Giuntini, *Speculum astrologiae*, Lyon: Philippe Tinghi, 1581, 512: Jan. 6th, 1476 11:00 P.M.

15 All calculations for this paper have been executed with a well-conceived and very convenient, albeit now outdated MS-DOS program especially created for the needs of historians by the late Peter Schiller (*Geschichte der Himmelskunde*, Wilnsdorf: Clio, 2001), which regrettably has not found the distribution it deserves. Thanks to the efforts of George Borski and his colleagues (Stichting De Rebus, Almere) it is available online here: http://www.derebus.nl/schiller.aspx

16 In some copies of the *Opera mathematica* (e.g., Zürich, ETH Library, Rar 3870) the horoscope shows Equal Houses.

(*cont.*)

	10:00 p.m.		11:25 p.m.
	Source	Recalculation	
I	21°42' Li	17°15' Li	21°43' Li
II	15°00' Sc	10°26' Sc	15°06' Sc
III	17°00' Sa	11°30' Sa	16°54' Sa

At first glance, it can be seen that there must be something wrong: A time of 11:25 (on the right) gives the best approximation. This is a puzzling result as Schöner was a very competent and knowledgeable astronomer, astrologer, and geographer. But the horoscope seems to have been handed down in a somewhat garbled form. There is also a manuscript version extant in Schöner's estate preserved in Vienna in the Austrian National Library (Cod. Vin. 5280, fol. 55ᵛ) (Fig. 11.2).

The celestial configuration for January 16th, 1477, 10:53 P.M., Latitude 50°N, Longitude 17°50' east of Toledo is as follows (again the values given in the original source are on the left):

Sun	6°36' Aq	6°38' Aq
Moon	26°41' Aq	26°56' Aq
Saturn	20°32' Le retrograde	20°32' Le
Jupiter	18°57' Pi	18°57' Pi
Mars	28°33' Aq	28°36' Aq
Venus	19°44' Sa	19°46' Sa
Mercury	10°02' Cp	9°56' Cp
Asc. Node	9°04' Vi	9°05' Vi

Houses (Regiomontanus)

X	20°32' Ca	20°36' Ca
XI	28°00' Le	27°35' Le
XII	25°00' Vi	24°12' Vi
I	15°56' Li	15°59' Li
II	10°00' Sc	9°08' Sc

(*cont.*)

| III | 11°00' Sa | 10°00' Sa |
| Lot of Fortune | 6°10' Sc | 6°17' Sc |

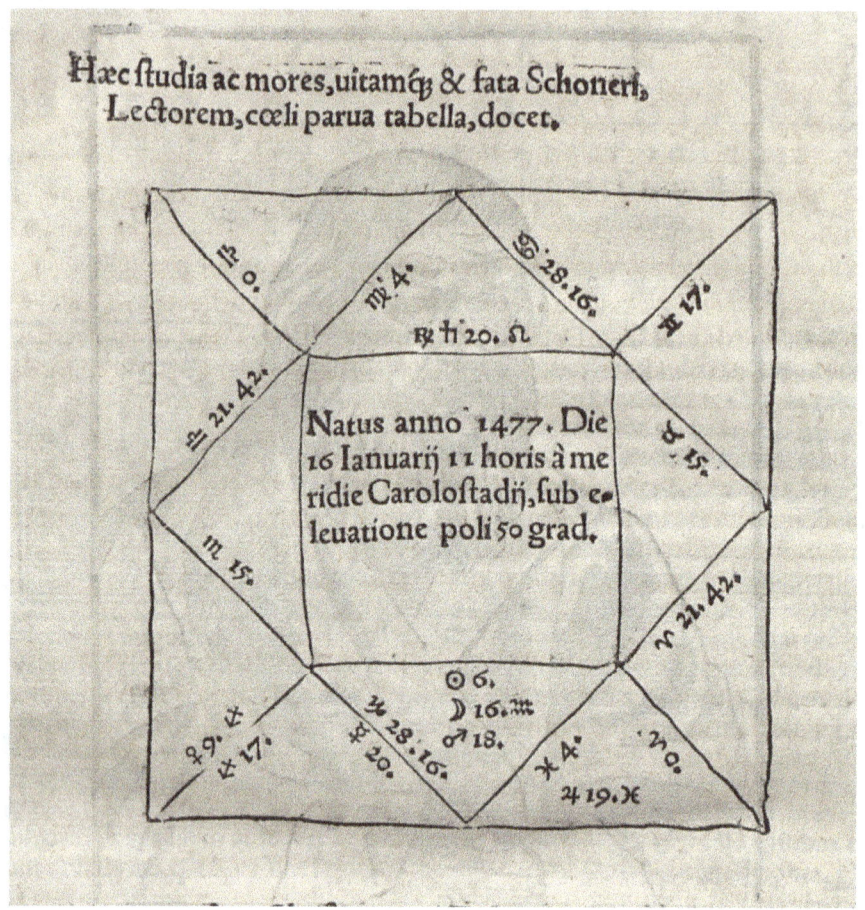

FIGURE 11.1 Johannes Schöner, Geniture (*Opera mathematica*, Nuremberg 1551: Johannes Berg
and Ulrich Neuber, after the preface by Philipp Melanchthon)

Apart from a slight difference (cusp of the 3rd house), everything is correct
(including the Lot of Fortune, i.e. the difference between the ecliptical longitudes of the Sun and Moon added to the ascendant). This should be expected
from a competent astronomer.

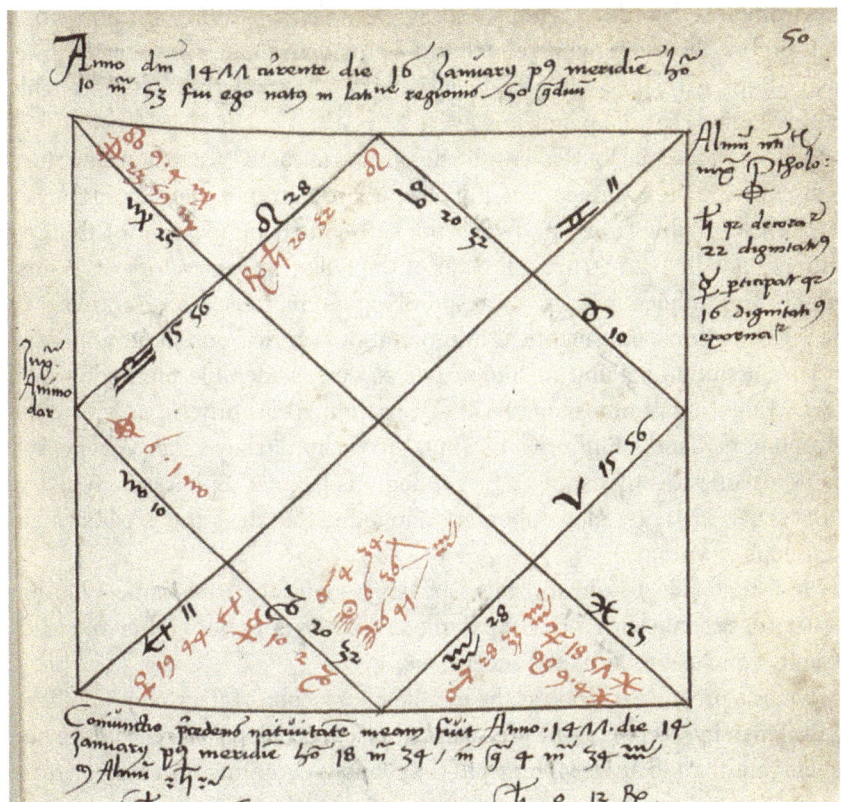

FIGURE 11.2 Johannes Schöner, Geniture (Vienna, Austrian National Library, Cod. Vin. 5280, fol. 55ᵛ)

3.2 *Wallenstein's Horoscope*

(11) Johannes Kepler amassed a comprehensive collection of horoscopes of about 350 pages and for approximately 800 individuals, which was published in 2009.[17] His collection also contains the famous horoscope for Wallenstein (Fig. 11.3).[18] The story surrounding it is well known. In 1608, Gerhard v. Taxis, a nobleman in the service of Wallenstein, acted as an intermediary and approached Kepler via a physician named Stromaier. He requested a horoscope for himself, as well as for a certain 'Bohemian gentleman'. Kepler cast the two horoscopes but corrected (rectified) the birth time of his anonymous client, as can be

---

17   Johannes Kepler, *Gesammelte Werke*, ed. Max Caspar et. al., Munich: C.H. Beck, 1938–2017, vol. XXI, 2.2, 5–492 (2019).

18   Kepler, *Gesammelte Werke*, 445–455.

seen from the crossed-out figures. Later in 1625, Kepler rectified the horoscope again and—albeit somewhat reluctantly—provided detailed astrological prognostications, garnished with skeptical remarks (analyzing this text thoroughly would require a special paper, however).

Kepler's horoscope for Wallenstein has always attracted great attention since its discovery in the nineteenth century by the Dresden grammar school teacher Karl Gustav Helbig (1808–1875) and the subsequent publication of the first edition made by Otto Struve (Director of the Pulkovo Observatory, St. Petersburg).[19] The publications are correspondingly numerous. However, many of the recalculations and historical interpretations carried out so far are based on false assumptions and in some cases show considerable methodological flaws. Wallenstein's horoscope has been examined recently (in 2005) by the astronomers Klaudia Einhorn and Günther Wuchterl. They state: 'We checked the horoscope with Redshift 32 [...] ephemeris [...] and Ephemeris Tool 4.53 with VSOP87 high precision ephemeris and found that the famous Wallenstein horoscope is wrong'.[20]

Now, this fact is—historically speaking—entirely irrelevant. Whether Kepler's data agree with modern parameters or not, does not matter and leads to faulty conclusions and misconceptions.

Here is a preliminary look at the rectified horoscope of 1625:

Wallenstein was born on September 14th, 1583 (Old Style) in Heřmanice nad Labem (Hermanitz an der Elbe), and the modern coordinates of the town are $50°23'$ N, $15°55'$ east of Greenwich. The recalculation shows that Kepler used the Prutenic Tables with the reference meridian of Königsberg.

According to Apian's *Cosmographicus liber* of 1533 Kutná Hora (Kuttenberg), which is a little west of Heřmanice nad Labem, lies $32°45'$ east of the island of Porto Santo near Madeira, and Königsberg is $42°16'$ east. This is a difference of longitude of $9°27'$ and nearly twice the modern amount ($5°13'$). On the other hand, Erasmus Reinhold, in his *Tabulae Prutenicae*, published in 1551, places Prague only $0°40'$ west of Königsberg! This example illustrates clearly how imprecise geographical coordinates (especially longitudes) could be in the sixteenth century.

19   Otto Struve, 'Beitrag zur Feststellung des Verhältnisses von Keppler zu Wallenstein', Mémoires de l'Académie impériale des sciences de St. Petersbourg, sér. 7, vol. 2, nr. 4, 1860.

20   Klaudia Einhorn and Günther Wuchterl, 'Kepler's Wallenstein-Horoscopes', in *Astronomy in and around Prague: Colloquium of the Working Group of the History of Astronomy, Prague, September 20, 2004* (= Acta Universitatis Carolinae Mathematica et Physica, 46, Supplement), Prag: Univerzita Karlova, 2005, 103.

In the following recalculation, a longitude of 9° west of Königsberg has been assumed (the value is important for the Moon's position only; the figures given in the original source are on the left, the recalculated figures on the right):

14.9.1583 (Julian Calendar), 4:01:30 P.M., 51° N, 9° W (Königsberg)

Sun	0°45' Li	0°39' Li
Moon	7°03' Cp	6°49' Cp
Saturn	19°00' Pi	19°10' Pi
Jupiter	22°43' Pi	22°14' Pi
Mars	27°59' Li	28°21' Li
Venus	16°50' Sc	16°03' Sc
Mercury	22°35' Vi	21°59' Vi
Asc. Node	16°07' Sa	16°00' Sa

Houses (Regiomontanus)

			[4:23]
X	8°00 Sa	2°54' Sa	8°07' Sa
XI	22°00 Sa	16°55' Sa	21°44' Sa
XII	8°00 Cp	2°58' Cp	8°20' Cp
I	10°00 Aq	2°24' Aq	10°59' Aq
II	13°00 Le	1°43' Ar	12°50' Ar
III	20°00 Ta	13°26' Sa	20°16' Ta

When we look at the house cusps, it is clearly discernible that the horoscope cannot be calculated for 4:01 P.M., but rather 4:23 P.M. Such inconsistencies, of course, affect all subsequent calculations of directions.

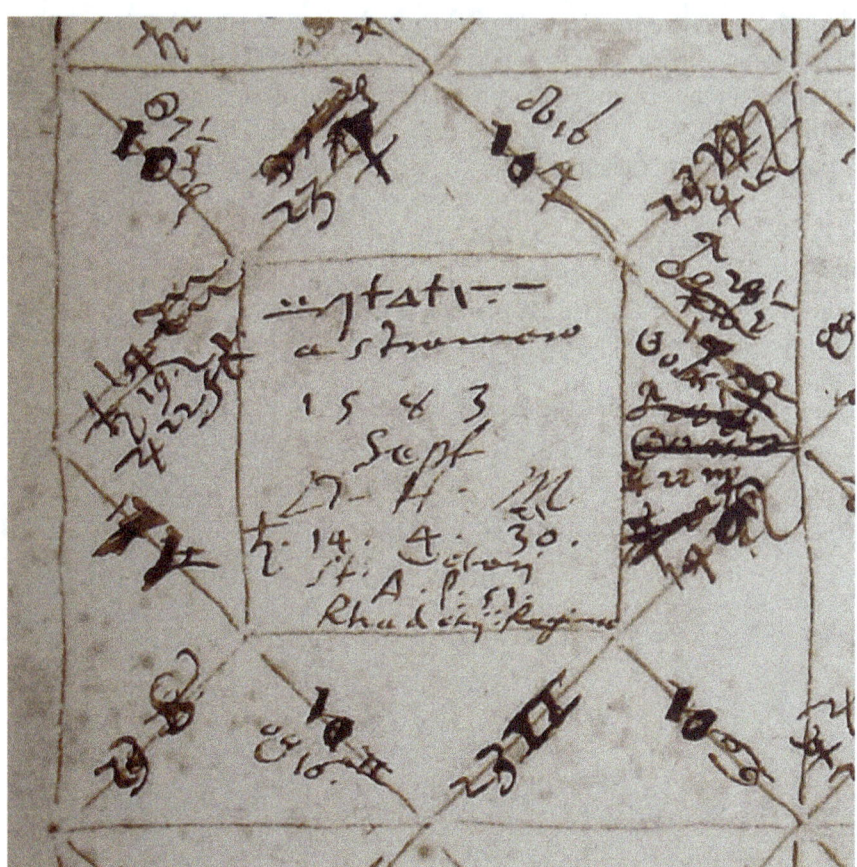

FIGURE 11.3 Kepler's Horoscope for Wallenstein (St. Petersburg, Russian Academy of Sciences:
P XVIII, fol. 250ᵛ: Institute for the Study of Cosmology and Astronomy in History,
Philosophy and Culture, reproduced from Karine Dilanian, *The Kepler Project:
Kepler's Astrology, Phase 2. Astrological Manuscripts of Johannes Kepler*, Moscow
2017, 123)

3.3   *Wilhelm IV's Solar Return*

The third example is a solar return chart (i.e., solar revolution) for the 59th year
of Duke Wilhelm IV of Saxe-Weimar, cast by Erhard Weigel (1625–1699), professor of philosophy and mathematics in Jena, accompanied by interpretations
for the year to come.[21]

This type of horoscope is erected when the Sun is returning to its ecliptical
longitude at birth and is set in relation to the birth horoscope (radix).[22] From

---

21   Berlin, Staatsbibliothek Preußischer Kulturbesitz: Ms. germ. qu. 2168, with a circular dia-
      gram on fol. 1ᵛ; most likely Weigel's autograph.
22   Jean-Baptiste Morin (1583–1656), on the other hand, departed from this tradition and

this, it was assumed that the course of events in the following year could be discerned, whereby the transits of the planets via certain horoscope factors (such as the house cusps) allowed a sharper chronological determination. The significance of a solar return lay in the fact that one could infer the effect of directions in the year of life in question.

Usually, for casting a solar return chart the latitude of the birthplace was used. This also the case with the present horoscope, in which we find the circular diagram popularly used in the sixteenth and seventeenth centuries, which could be easily constructed using a compass (Fig. 11.4).

The date is given according to the Julian calendar, and the day epoch corresponds to astronomical usage (date change at 12:00 noon). As usual, the true solar time is given. Altenburg is located about 40 km south of Leipzig.

The geographical coordinates of the town are rendered in 1669 by the Saxon astronomer and *art chamberlain* of the Saxon electors, Tobias Beutel (c. 1627–1690) as latitude 51° North and longitude 35°58' East, with the reference meridian presumably passing through the island of Ferro.[23] London lies at 20°30', resulting in a difference in longitude between Altenburg and London of 15°28' (for comparison, the modern coordinates are 50°59' N, 12°26' east of Greenwich). Again, this example clearly shows how uncertain longitudes could be in the seventeenth century. However, deviations in longitude only lead to significant errors in the case of the rapid movement of the Moon, and the positions of the other planets are hardly affected by this. On the other hand, the use of an incorrect latitude distorts the ascendant and the house cusps considerably.

In his *Disputatio de Eclipsibus* of 1654, Weigel mentions that he based his calculations on Kepler's Rudolphine Tables published in 1627.[24] It can be assumed

used to erect revolutionary horoscopes for the respective location of the native, see his *Astrologia gallica principiis et rationibus propriis stabilita atque in xxvi libros distributa*, The Hague: Adrian Vlacq, 1661, bk. XXIII, ch. IV, 600–601.

23   Tobias Beutel, *Arboretum Mathematicum, Darinnen zu befinden: Himmels-Figuren Und Geburts-Stunden / Hoher Häupter / Auch außgerechnete Finsternüsse / Sonnen- Mond- und Sternen-Uhren / Astrologia, Themata, und richtig calculirte Longitudines und Latitudines Der Städte des Churfürstenthums Sachsen / und benachbarter Lande*, Dresden 1669, 503. In 1634, the French chose the western edge of Ferro, the westernmost island of the Canary Islands, as the prime meridian; see Haag, *Die Geschichte des Nullmeridians*, 54–60.

24   Klaus-Dieter Herbst, 'Erhard Weigel's Disputation anlässlich der Sonnenfinsternis vom 2./12. August 1654', in id., *Erhard Weigel (1625–1699) und die Wissenschaften*, Frankfurt/M.: Peter Lang, 2013, 89.

that Weigel also used these tables to calculate the present horoscope. If we look at the planetary positions (the ecliptical longitudes are given in degrees and minutes), it is noticeable that he has given the longitudes of the Sun and Moon down to arc seconds. This is unusual, as using only full degrees in horoscopes was a more common practice.

The recalculation shows slight deviations only:

10.4.1656 (Julian Calendar), 9:25 P.M., Altenburg

	Source	Recalculation
Sun	1°26'03" Ta	1°19' Ta
Moon	17°38'38"	Pi 17°28" Pi
Saturn	17°07' Vi	16°37' Vi
Jupiter	10°08' Ta	10°14' Ta
Mars	12°03' Ge	12°03' Ge
Venus	24°08' Pi	24°11' Pi
Merkur	7°20' Ar	7°48' Ar
Asc. Node	23°03' Cp	22°30' Cp

As far as Weigel's preferred house division is concerned, it can be assumed that he used the 'rational manner' associated with the name of Johannes Regiomontanus. The recalculation clearly confirms this assumption:

Houses (Regiomontanus) for latitude 51;00

	Source	Recalculation
X	19°45' Vi	19°34' Vi
XI	17°30' Li	17°30' Li
XII	7°30' Sc	7°19' Sc
I	26°50' Sc	26°49' Sc
II	23°28' Sa	23°32' Sa
III	6°00' Aq	5°52' Aq

'The most important fixed stars are also taken into account [...] which reveal much about the inclinations and destinies of man', as Johann Georg Job put it,[25]

---

25   'Es kommen auch die vornehmsten Fix-Sterne [...] in Consideration, und offenbahren ein

and a special feature of Weigel's horoscope is the presence of four fixed stars of first magnitude and the star cluster of the Pleiades (6 stars visible to the naked eye in Taurus):

- Ophiuchus (α Ophiuchi, Ras Alhague) and Cor Scorpionis (α Scorpii, Antares) in I.
- Cor Leonis (α Leonis, Regulus) in IX.
- Spica (α Virginis, Azimech) in XI.
- Pleiades in VII.

It is not known which aspects were decisive in this selection. The astrological influences of the stars mentioned are partly quite problematic; for example, Antares in the first house brings honour and generosity, but also many dangers and misfortunes, malice, destructiveness, evil forebodings, and danger of death. On the other hand, it is an important star for military personnel and is said to convey mental alertness, strategic skill and courage, and to make daredevils.[26] Regulus, on the other hand, conveys royal qualities, noble spirit, openness and courage, bringing success, lofty ideals and strength of mind, but also violence, destructiveness, military honours of short duration, imprisonment and violent death. With Saturn, he provides, among other things, friends among the clergy, success in the church or in law, wealth, speculative gains, high position, and good health.[27]

Spica rising provides unlimited luck, wealth, unexpected honour or advancement beyond the hopes or abilities of the born, as well as love of art and science.[28] The Pleiades with Mars, on the other hand, have a decidedly negative effect, promising lust, ambition, unrest, and a violent death.[29] Finally,

---

vieles von des Menschen Inclination und Fatis'; Johann Georg Job, Anleitung zu denen curiösen Wissenschafften [...], Frankfurt a. M., Leipzig: Nikolai, 1717, 220.

26 'Cor Scorpii denotiret Großmüthigkeit, Gewalt, Verwegenheit, Kühnheit, Grausamkeit, Raub, Begierigkeit: wenn Merkur dabey stehet, machet es greuliche Schläger und Mörder'; Job, Anleitung, 221. See also Vivian Erwood Robson, The Fixed Stars and Constellations in Astrology, London: Cecil Palmer, 1923 (repr. New York: Samuel Weiser/Aquarian Press, 1969), 136–137.

27 'Cor Leonis stellet vor, einen braven, tapffern, gravitätischen, großmüthigen und genereusen Menschen, der über andere zu herrschen trachtet'; Job, Anleitung, 221, Robson, The Fixed Stars, 195.

28 'Spica Virginis, erwecket grossen Fleiß in Erlernung guter Künste, Sprachen und Wissenschafften, absonderlich wenn Merkur darzu kommt: Ein solcher Mensch ist honnet und gravitätisch, und doch dabey auch freundlich; Ist aber Saturn dabey, so deutet er, an statt der Freundlichkeit, auf Unfreundlichkeit, Baurenstolz und Jalousie: Kommt aber Mars darzu, so ist der Mensch importun, zornig und gar zu ernsthafftig'; Job, Anleitung, 221. Mars with the Pleiades indicates a violent death in a tumult; Robson, The Fixed Stars, 211.

29 'Die Plejades, machen geile und zur Wollust geneigte, ehrgeitzige und unruhige Leute'; Job, Anleitung, 220.

FIGURE 11.4
Erhard Weigel, Solar
return chart for Duke
Wilhelm IV of Saxe-
Weimar (Berlin, Staats-
bibliothek Preußischer
Kulturbesitz, Ms. germ.
qu. 2168, fol. 1ᵛ)

Ophiuchus brings misfortune through women, perverted tastes, and spiritual depravity.[30]

Weigel divided his interpretation of the configuration of the heavens into four sections: 1. Of the state of the body; 2. Of the state of the mind; 3. Of the state of happiness; 4. Of obnoxiousness. He concluded his remarks with the following words:

> Finally, I wish from God Almighty that He would graciously avert all that is unpleasant, but fatherly bestow the good, and grant Your Princely Grace a blissful, healthy, peaceful and joyful new year, and countless years of life following with continuous happiness.[31]

---

30   According to Ptolemy Ras Alhague (Ophiuchus) is of the nature of Saturn and Venus; Rob-
      son, *The Fixed Stars*, 193.

31   '*Schließlich wünsche ich von Gott dem Allmächtigen, daß Er alles widerwertige gnediglich
      abwenden, das gute aber väterlich bescheren, vnd Ihrer Fürstlichen Gnaden ein glück-
      seliges, gesundes, fried und freudenreiches neues Jahr, vnd vnzehlich viel mit continuirlichem
      Glückes nachfolgende Lebens Jahre verleihe wollte*'; Berlin, StB PK, Ms. germ. qu. 2168,
      fol. 19ᵛ.

3.4   *Rheticus's Horoscope*

(IV) Finally, a collection of manuscripts by Nicolaus Gugler (1521–1577)[32] has been preserved in the Bibliothèque national de France, which also contains several horoscopes, including that of the mathematician and astronomer Georg Joachim Rheticus (1514–1574). Gugler studied astronomy and medicine in Wittenberg from 1536 to 1538 and accompanied Rheticus on a trip to Nuremberg, Ingolstadt and Tübingen in the autumn of 1538. The horoscope has repeatedly been the subject of discussion in scholarship on Rheticus.[33]

Gugler has erected Rheticus' nativity for 15 February 1514 (Old Style), 15:26 p.m and latitude of 47°.[34] (Fig. 11.5)

According to Apian, Feldkirch lies at 47°00' north latitude and 27°42' east of the island of Porto Santo, Apian's prime meridian.[35] Toledo (reference meridian of the Alfonsine Tables) is 9°04' east of Porto Santo, and therefore, the difference in longitude to Feldkirch is 18°38'.

These values result in the following planetary positions (the ascending lunar node at 11°51' Vi and the Lot of Fortune at 29°00' Vi are also entered in the chart):

	Source	Recalculation
Sun	7°07' Pi	7°08' Pi
Moon	0°45' Sa	2°01' Sa
Saturn	25°21' Sc	25°19' Sc
Jupiter	7°07' Ta	7°04' Ta

---

32 Biographical information on Gugler in Laurence Moulinier-Brogi, 'Un médecin et son image au XVIe siècle? Nicolaus Gugler, de Nuremberg', *Sudhoffs Archiv: Zeitschrift für Wissenschaftsgeschichte* 89 (2005) 23–38; Karl Heinz Burmeister, *Magister Rheticus und seine Schulgesellen: Das Ringen um Kenntnis und Durchsetzung des heliozentrischen Weltsystems um 1540/50* (= Forschungen zur Geschichte Vorarlbergs, n. s., 11). Constance and Munich: UVK Verlagsgesellschaft, 2015.

33 Karl Heinz Burmeister, *Georg Joachim Rheticus 1514–1574: Eine Bio-Bibliographie*, Wiesbaden: Guido Pressler, 1967, vol. 1, 5–7; Jesse Kraai, *Rheticus' Heliocentric Providence: A Study concerning the Astrology, Astronomy of the Sixteenth Century*, PhD thesis, Heidelberg 2003 (URN: urn:nbn:de:bsz:16-opus-32541; URL: http://www.ub.uni-heidelberg.d e/archiv/3254/), 50–55. The horoscope was already analysed by Christian-Paul Berger in 1992—'Georg Joachim Rhetikus' Geburtshoroskop aus astronomisch-chronologischer Sicht', *Montfort: Vierteljahresschrift für Geschichte und Gegenwart* 44 (1992), 144–150. However, his publication contains a whole series of errors and fundamental methodological flaws, which will not be addressed here.

34 Paris, Bibliothèque Nationale de France: Ms. lat. 7395, fol. 326v.

35 Peter Apian, *Cosmographicus liber*, Antwerp 1533: Arnold Birckman, fol. 36ᵛ.

(*cont.*)

	Source	Recalculation
Mars	25°07 Sa	25°07' Sa
Venus	11°08' Aq	11°09' Aq
Merkur	27°26' Aq	27°18' Aq

With the exception of the position of the Moon, everything is accurate, but the houses (apparently Regiomontan) are rather imprecise. Only full degrees are given, which indicates the use of a house table.

Houses (Regiomontanus) for latitude 47°00'

	Source	Recalculation
X	4°00' Sc	2°34' Sc
XI	24°00' Sc	22°29' Sc
XII	12°00' Sa	9°58' Sa
I	6°00' Cp	2°23' Cp
II	14°00' Aq	10°47' Aq
III	2°00' Ar	0°30' Ar

Another birth time (16 February 1514, 1:51) is entered in the margin of the chart. Whether this might be a correction on the part of Rheticus is purely speculative, however. A horoscope with this time (but for 15 February) is preserved in a horoscope collection in the Bavarian State Library (Fig. 11.6).[36]

The chart in Gugler's manuscript was included in the extensive horoscope collection of Johannes Garcaeus (Gartze) and labelled '*Georg Velcurio, Physicus*' (Fig. 11.7).[37] He obviously did not realise that this was the astronomer born in Feldkirch (Velcuria), because the book also contains a horoscope for

---

36   München, Bayerische Staatsbibliothek, Clm 27003, fol. 31ᵛ.

37   Johannes Garcaeus (Gartze), *Astrologiae methodus*, Basel: Heinrich Petri, 1576, 153. In Wittenberg, several Feldkirch students were labelled *Velcurio* according to their origin. Rheticus was apparently also given this name; see Karl Heinz Burmeister, 'Georg Joachim Rheticus, Varianten und Herkunft seines Namens', *Bludenzer Geschichtsblätter* 108 (2014), 62.

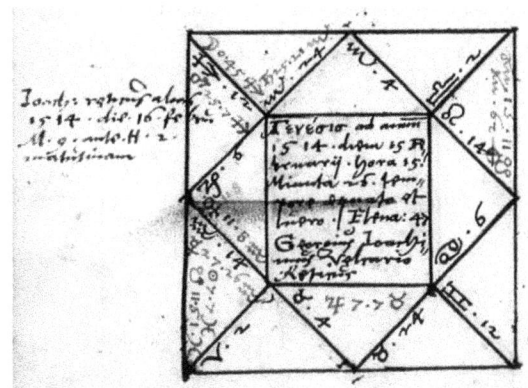

FIGURE 11.5
Nicolaus Gugler, Horoscope for
Georg Joachim Rheticus (Paris,
Bibliothèque nationale de
France, ms. lat. 7395, fol. 326ᵛ)

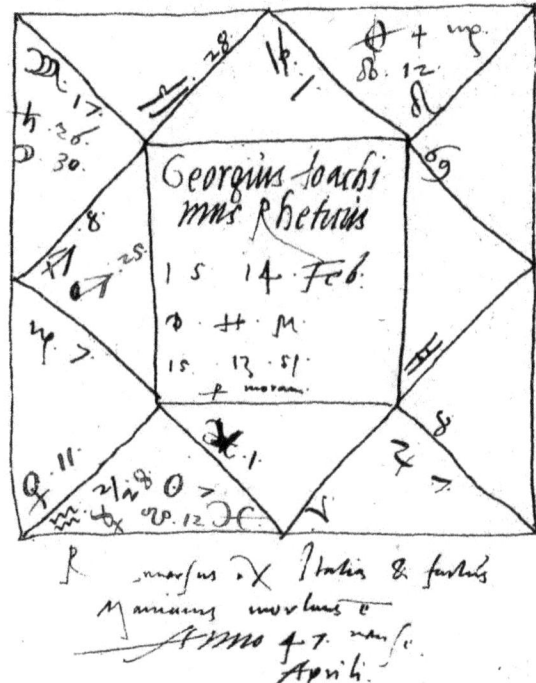

FIGURE 11.6
Horoscope for Georg
Joachim Rheticus (Munich,
Bavarian State Library, Clm
27003, fol. 31ᵛ)

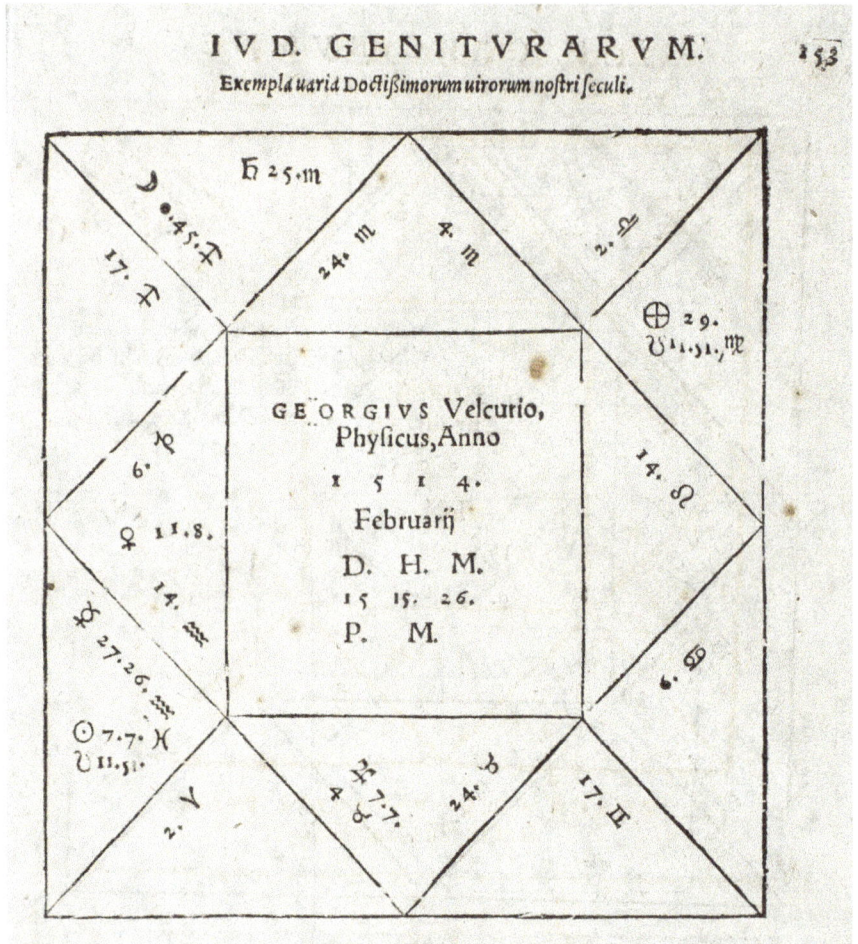

FIGURE 11.7 Horoscope for a certain *'Georg Velcurio, Physicus'* (Johannes Garcaeus, *Astrologiae methodus*, Basel: Heinrich Petri, 1576, 153)

'Ioachimus Reticus, Mathematicus', but with the birth time 13:30 (Fig. 11.8).[38] This variant can also be found in three other horoscope collections.[39]

From this rather cursory survey it is clear that the question of Georg Joachim Rheticus' actual time of birth is not easy to answer. This proves how carefully the data of historical horoscopes must be handled in order to avoid serious mistakes.

---

38   Garcaeus, *Astrologiae methodus*, 341.

39   Leipzig, Universitätsbibliothek, Rep. IV, 87, fol. 109ᵛ (123ᵛ); Wolfenbüttel, Herzog August Bibliothek, 35.2 Astron. 4°, fol. 217ᵛ; Hamburg, Lehrerbibliothek des Christianeums, R 31/3, 207.

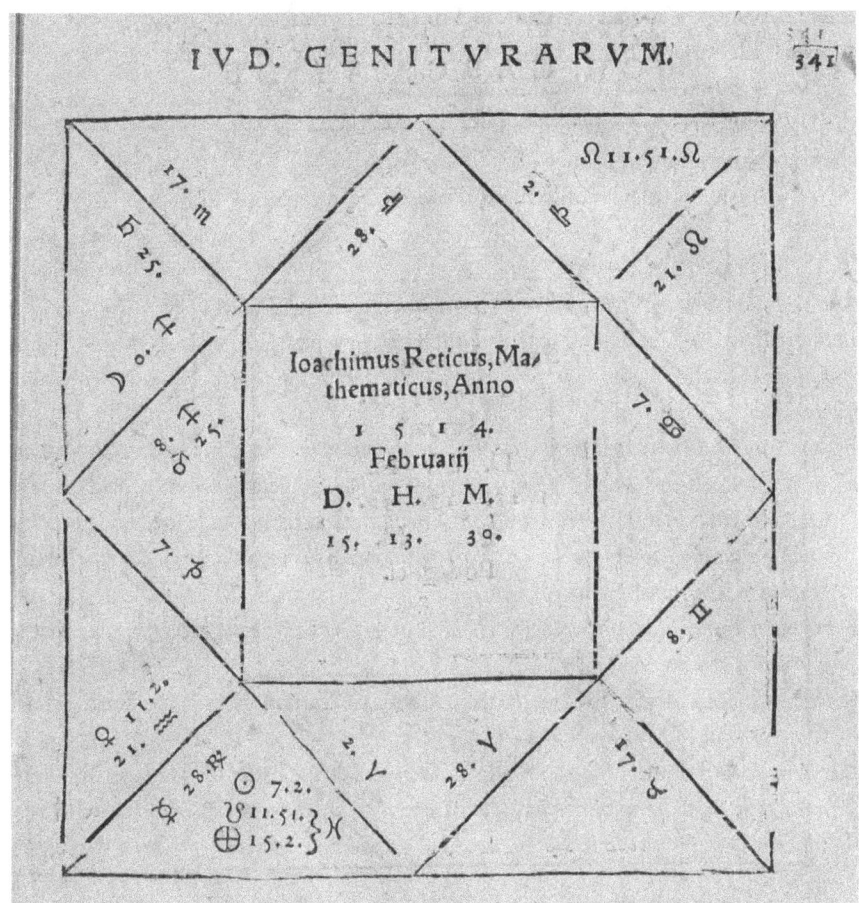

FIGURE 11.8 Horoscope for Georg Joachim Rheticus (Johannes Garcaeus, *Astrologiae metho-dus*, Basel: Heinrich Petri, 1576, 341)

Acknowledgements

In addition to the memory of Helena Avelar, I would also like to dedicate this paper to the memory of my friend and colleague Peter Schiller, who passed away in 2013.

Bibliography

Archival Sources

Paris, Bibliothèque nationale de France, Ms. lat. 7395
Oxford, Bodleian Library, Ms. Wood F.39

OESTMANN

Vienna, Austrian National Library, Cod. Vin. 5280
Leipzig, Universitätsbibliothek, Rep. IV, 87
Munich, Bavarian State Library, Clm 27003
Wolfenbüttel, Herzog August Bibliothek, 35.2 Astron. 4°
Hamburg, Lehrerbibliothek des Christianeums, R 31/3
Berlin, Staatsbibliothek Preußischer Kulturbesitz, Ms. germ. qu. 2168

Apian, Peter. *Cosmographicus liber*: Arnold Birckman, Antwerp 1533

Berger, Christian-Paul. 'Georg Joachim Rhetikus' Geburtshoroskop aus astronomisch-chronologischer Sicht'. *Montfort: Vierteljahresschrift für Geschichte und Gegenwart* 44 (1992), 144–150

Beutel, Tobias. *Arboretum Mathematicum, Darinnen zu befinden: Himmels-Figuren Und Geburts-Stunden / Hoher Häupter / Auch außgerechnete Finsternüsse / Sonnen- Mond- und Sternen-Uhren / Astrologia, Themata, und richtig calculirte Longitudines und Latitudines Der Städte des Churfürstenthums Sachsen / und benachbarter Lande*, Dresden: Melchior Bergens Witwe, 1669

Burmeister, Karl Heinz. *Georg Joachim Rhetikus 1514–1574: Eine Bio-Bibliographie*. Wiesbaden: Guido Pressler, 1967

Burmeister, Karl Heinz. 'Georg Joachim Rheticus, Varianten und Herkunft seines Namens'. *Bludenzer Geschichtsblätter* 108 (2014), 55–63

Burmeister, Karl Heinz. *Magister Rheticus und seine Schulgesellen: Das Ringen um Kenntnis und Durchsetzung des heliozentrischen Weltsystems um 1540/50* (= Forschungen zur Geschichte Vorarlbergs, n. s., 11). Constance and Munich: UVK Verlagsgesellschaft, 2015

Einhorn, Klaudia, and Günther Wuchterl. 'Kepler's Wallenstein-Horoscopes', in *Astronomy in and around Prague: Colloquium of the Working Group of the History of Astronomy, Prague, September 20, 2004* (= Acta Universitatis Carolinae Mathematica et Physica, 46, Supplement), Prague: Univerzita Karlova, 2005, 101–114

Garcaeus (Gartze), Johannes. *Astrologiae methodus*. Basel: Heinrich Petri, 1576

Gingerich, Owen. 'A Study of Kepler's "Rudolphine Tables" in *Actes du XIe Congrès International d'Histoire des Sciences, 1965*, Wrocław/Kraków/Gdańsk: Ossolineum, 1968, vol. 3, 31–36

Gingerich, Owen. 'Early Copernican Ephemerides'. *Science and History: Studies in Honor of Edward Rosen* (= Studia Copernicana, 16), Wrocław/Kraków/Gdańsk: Polish Academy of Sciences Press, 1978, 403–417

Ginzel, Friedrich Karl. *Handbuch der mathematischen und technischen Chronologie*. repr. Leipzig: Deutscher Buch-Export und -Import GmbH, 1958

Giuntini, Francesco. *Speculum astrologiae: comprehendens commentaria in theoricas planetarum, et in Sphaeram Ioannis de Sacro Bosco: Vná cum tabulis de Eclipsi-*

bus Georgii Purbachii, et supputationibus motuum Planetarum, secundum decreta Alphonsii Regis Hispaniae: et Nicolai Copernici, cum diversis aliis tractatibus Astrologicis. Lyon: Philippe Tinghi, 1581

Haag, Heinrich. *Die Geschichte des Nullmeridians*. Gießen: Otto Wigand, 1913

Hamel, Jürgen. 'Die Rezeption des mathematisch-astronomischen Teils des mathematisch-astronomischen Teils des Werkes von Nicolaus Copernicus in der astronomisch-astrologischen Kleinliteratur um 1600', in *Cosmographica et Geographica: Festschrift für Heribert M. Nobis zum 70. Geburtstag*, ed. by Bernhard Fritscher and Gerhard Brey, München: Institut für Geschichte der Naturwissenschaften, 1994, vol. 1, 315–335

Helbig, Carl Gustav. *Der Kaiser Ferdinand und der Herzog von Friedland während des Winters 1633–1634: Nach handschriftlichen Quellen des Königlich Sächsischen Haupt-Staats-Archivs und mit kritischer Berücksichtigung der gedruckten Berichte dargestellt*. Dresden: Adler und Dietze, 1852

Herbst, Klaus-Dieter. 'Erhard Weigels Disputation anlässlich der Sonnenfinsternis vom 2./12. August 1654', in id., *Erhard Weigel (1625–1699) und die Wissenschaften*. Frankfurt a. M.: Peter Lang, 2013, 71–95

Holden, Ralph William. *The Elements of House Division*. London: The Faculty of Astrological Studies/The Urania Trust, 1977

Houlding, Deborah. *The Houses: Temples of the Sky*. Bournemouth: The Wessex Astrologer, [2]2006

Johann Georg Job. *Anleitung zu denen curiösen Wissenschafften [...] Worinnen denen Curiösen Gemüthern aufs deut- und gründlichste gezeiget wird, wie man aus des Menschen Gesichte, Händen und Geburths-Stunden, nach der Sonnen, Mond- und Sterne-Lauf, item Punctiren, Träumen, Nahmen und erscheinenden Wunder-Zeichen Ein Prognosticon und Nativität von seinem bevorstehenden Glück und Unglück stellen könne*. Frankfurt a. M., Leipzig: Nikolai, 1717

Kepler, Johannes. *Gesammelte Werke*, ed. Max Caspar et. al. Munich: C.H. Beck, 1938–2017

Kraai, Jesse. 'Rheticus' Heliocentric Providence: A Study concerning the Astrology, Astronomy of the Sixteenth Century'. PhD thesis, Heidelberg 2003. URN: urn:nbn:de:bsz:16-opus-32541. URL: http://www.ub.uni-heidelberg.de/archiv/3254/

Lerch, Andreas. *Scientia astrologiae: Der Diskurs über die Wissenschaftlichkeit der Astrologie und die lateinischen Lehrbücher 1470–1610* (= Acta Historica Astronomiae, 56). Leipzig: Leipziger Universitätsverlag, 2015

Lorenz, Dona Marie. *Tools of Astrology—Houses*. Topanga, CA: Eomega Grove Press, 1973

Moulinier-Brogi, Laurence. 'Un médecin et son image au XVIe siècle? Nicolaus Gugler, de Nuremberg'. *Sudhoffs Archiv: Zeitschrift für Wissenschaftsgeschichte* 89 (2005) 23–38

North, John David. 'Georg Markgraf: An Astronomer in the New World', in *Johan Maurits van Nassau-Siegen, 1604–1679: Essays on the occasion of the tercentenary of his death*, ed. by E. van den Boogaart, H.R. Hoetink and P.J.P. Whitehead. The Hague: Johan Maurits van Nassau Stichting, 394–423

North, John David. *Horoscopes and History* (= Warburg Institute: Surveys and Texts, 13). London: The Warburg Institute/University of London, 1986

Oestmann, Günther. 'Ephemeridenwerke des 16. Jahrhunderts, eine wichtige Arbeitsgrundlage für Astronomen und Astrologen', *Gemeinnützige Mathematik: Adam Ries und seine Folgen* (Acta Academiae Scientiarum, 8), ed. by Jürgen Kiefer and Karin Reich, Erfurt: Akademie gemeinnütziger Wissenschaften zu Erfurt, 2003, 149–164

Omodeo, Pietro. *Copernicus in the Cultural Debates of the Renaissance: Reception, Legacy, Transformation* (= History of Science and Medicine Library, 45). Leiden/Boston: Brill, 2014

Ortroy, Fernand van. 'Bibliographie de l'oeuvre de Pierre Apian'. *Le Bibliographe Moderne: Courrier International des Archives et des Bibliothèques* 5 (1901) 89–156, 284–333

Ortroy, Fernand van. *Bibliographie de Gemma Frisius fondateur de l'école Belge de geographie de son fils Corneille et de ses neveux les Arsenius*. Brüssel: Hayez, 1920

Morin, Jean-Baptiste Morin. *Astrologia gallica principiis et rationibus propriis stabilita atque in XXVI libros distributa*. The Hague: Adrian Vlacq, 1661

Robson, Vivian Erwood. *The Fixed Stars and Constellations in Astrology*. London: Cecil Palmer, 1923 (repr. New York: Samuel Weiser/Aquarian Press, 1969)

Schiller, Peter. *Geschichte der Himmelskunde* [CD-ROM with accompanying booklet]. Wilnsdorf: Clio, 2001

Schöner, Johannes. *Luculentissima quaedam terrae totius descriptio: cum multis utilissimis Cosmographiae iniciis. Novaque et quae ante fuit verior Europae nostrae formatio. Praeterea, Fluviorum: montium: provintiarum: Urbium: et gentium quae plurimorum vetustissima nomina recentioribus admixta vocabulis. Multa etiam quae diligens lector nova usuique futura inveniet*. Nuremberg: Stuchs, 1515

Schöner, Johannes. *Opera mathematica*. Nuremberg: Johannes Berg and Ulrich Neuber, 1551

Steinmetz, Dirk. 'Die Gregorianische Kalenderreform von 1582: Korrektur der christlichen Zeitrechnung in der Frühen Neuzeit'. Oftersheim: Dirk Steinmetz, 2011 (PhD thesis, Heidelberg 2010)

Struve, Otto. 'Beitrag zur Feststellung des Verhältnisses von Keppler zu Wallenstein'. *Mémoires de l'Académie impériale des sciences de St. Petersbourg*, sér. 7, vol. 2, nr. 4, 1860

Withers, Charles W.J. *Zero Degrees: Geographies of the Prime Meridian*. Cambridge, MA/London: Harvard University Press, 2017

CHAPTER 12

Astrology by Numbers: Early Modern Quantification of Planetary Power

Luís Campos Ribeiro

Abstract

During the sixteenth century, the scoring system applied to the essential dignities of the planets was extended to the accidental conditions, becoming a standard method by the seventeenth century. The first example of this scoring appears in print in 1539 in the *Opusculum astrologicum* by Johannes Schöner. In the following decades, the table was replicated, modified, and expanded by several authors. The most relevant of these was Cyprián Lvovický, who disseminated one of the two main variants of the table and extended the scoring to lots and house cusps. This paper explores the rationale, origin, and transmission of this scoring system as one of the examples of the search for mathematical precision that characterises early modern astrology.

Keywords

Planetary strengths and debilities – lord of the geniture – Cyprián Lvovický – Antonio of Montulmo – Johannes Schöner

1 Introduction

Since antiquity, astrology, together with astronomy, was part of the so-called mathematical sciences. What are currently two very separate fields of knowledge were, for most of history, part of the same branch of mathematics. In premodern literature, astrologers were frequently designated as mathematicians (*mathematici*), as the practice of astrology required mathematical expertise for its calculations. This term appears frequently in astrological literature, utilized by its proponents, like Marcus Manilius (fl. 1st century), as well as its detractors, such as Isidore of Seville (c. 590–636).[1]

---

1 Marcus Manilius, *Astronomica*, trans. George Patrick Goold (Cambridge, Mass: Harvard

In the early modern period, the inclusion of astrology under the broader umbrella of mathematics was still evident in many mathematical treatises.[2] Here, astrology is often defined as the practical half of astronomy, as it provided a concrete application for astronomical data. However, by the mid-seventeenth century, the inclusion of astrology within mathematics began to be questioned, and gradually astronomical computation became an entirely separate field of knowledge, giving rise to modern astronomy. Astrological interpretation (i.e., judgement) was progressively marginalized from accepted scientific knowledge and removed from astronomy and mathematics.[3]

This distinction between the observation and computation of planetary movements as separate from the interpretation doctrines of astrology is not unprecedented. Early in its history, astronomy-astrology, often referred to as the science of the stars, was divided into two parts: a theoretical aspect, namely astronomy, and a practical or applied aspect, namely astrology. Claudius Ptolemy (2nd century) makes this division in the *Tetrabiblos*, organising the science of the stars into a part 'whereby we apprehend the aspects of the movements of Sun, Moon, and stars in relation to each other and to the earth' (i.e., astronomy) and another 'in which by means of the natural character of these aspects themselves we investigate the changes which they bring about in that which they surround' (i.e., astrology).[4] This is also the case with Arabic authors, such as Albiruni (Abu Rayhan Muhammad ibn Ahmad al-Biruni, 973–c. 1050).[5] Nonetheless, even with the awareness of these divisions within the discipline, the terms astrology and astronomy were used interchangeably during the premodern period. In the early modern period, this division was known as speculative astrology or astronomy, referring to astronomy proper, and judicial or

---

University Press, 1977); Isidore, *The etymologies of Isidore of Seville*, ed. Stephen A. Barney (Cambridge, UK; New York: Cambridge University Press, 2006).

2   For example in the works of Jesuit scholars, Chistopher Clavius and Hugh Sempill. See, Christophorus Clavius, *In Sphaeram Ioannis de Sacro Bosco commentarius* (Roma: ex officina Dominici Basae, 1585), 7; Hugh Sempill, *De mathematicis disciplinis Libri duodecim* (Antwerp: Balthasar Moreti, 1635). On these autors, see Luís Campos Ribeiro, *Jesuit Astrology: Prognostication and Science in Early Modern Culture* (Leiden; Boston: Brill, 2023), 106–128, 144–152.

3   On this topic see the collection of papers on Rienk Vermij and Hiro Hirai, eds., 'Early Science and Medicine. The Marginalization of Astrology' 22, no. 5–6 (2017); and Michelle Pfeffer, 'Reassessing the Marginalization of Astrology in the Early Modern World', *The Historical Journal*, 6 September 2023, 1–25.

4   *Tetrabilos* I.1, Ptolemy, *Tetrabiblos*, trans. F.E. Robbins (Cambridge, Mass.; London: Harvard University Press, 1940), 3.

5   Muḥammad ibn Aḥmad Bīrūnī, *The Book of Instruction in the Elements of the Art of Astrology*, trans. Robert Ramsay Wright (London: Luzac & co, 1934).

prognosticatory astrology or astronomy, which corresponds to what is currently recognized as astrology.[6]

2 Quantification in Astrological Judgement

In addition to the mathematical and astronomical computations necessary for the construction of an astrological figure, classical and medieval astrological doctrines and judgements are dependent on the configuration of planets and their complex interrelations as delineated by their sign and house placements, rulerships, significations, and aspects. Quantification methods are employed exclusively in specialised judgements, such as life expectancy or the calculation of the most influential planet in a chart: the almuten or lord of the chart.[7] By the end of the fifteenth century and perhaps more notably during the sixteenth century, some judgement methods began to employ more mathematical and quantifiable approaches. One notable example is the judgement of temperament, which shifts from a general assessment of the significators of complexion to a more structured computation, applying tables and calculating by summing the contributions one by one.[8] Another aspect, which will be examined in detail within this paper, pertains to the development of a new methodology for attributing a certain amount of strength or weakness to the planets. This ultimately resulted in a numerical quantification of each planet's significance within an astrological chart. Implementing this quantification trans-

---

6 As late as the early seventeenth century, the Jesuit mathematician and astronomer, Christopher Clavius, used the terms interchangeably, giving preference to the term 'astrology' (*astrologia*). Ribeiro, *Jesuit Astrology*, 106–108. On the history of the terminological distinction between astrology and astronomy, see Charles Burnett, 'Ptolemy's Differentiation between Astronomy and Astrology in the Greek-Arabic-Latin Tradition', *Cahiers de Recherches Médiévales et Humanistes—Journal of Medieval and Humanistic Studies* 1, no. 47 (2024): 373–403; as well as, André Le Bœuffle, *Astronomie, astrologie. Lexique latin* (Paris: Picard, 1987); Wolfgang Hübner, *Die Begriffe 'Astrologie' und 'Astronomie' in der Antike: Wortgeschichte und Wissenschaftssystematik; mit einer Hypothese zum Terminus 'Quadrivium'*, vol. 1989, 7 (Stuttgart: Steiner, 1990); Max Lejbowicz, 'Les antécédents de la distinction isidorienne: astrologia/astronomia.', in *Observer, lire, écrire le ciel au Moyen Âge*, 1991, 173–212.

7 On life span and astrology, see Helena Avelar, 'Who Wants to Live Forever? Astrological Methods for Calculating Lifespan in Western Culture and Perspectives on Determinism in Astrology', *International Journal of Divination and Prognostication* 2, no. 2 (5 October 2021): 161–188. On the almutem of the chart refer to chapter 2 by David Juste.

8 On this matter see Francisco Malta Romeiras, Luís Campos Ribeiro, and Elisa Frei, 'Physiognomy, Complexion, and Ingenuity: The Management of Talent in the Society of Jesus, 1540–1773', *Early Science and Medicine* 30, no. 1 (6 March 2025): 93–100.

formed what was previously a predominantly subjective evaluation into an objective and established methodology that could be articulated mathematically. This transformation aligns with the increasing significance of mathematics in early modern scientific thought, of which astrology was a component, thereby becoming a fundamental element of early modern astrological practice.

In astrological doctrine, the effectiveness of a planet is established by its essential dignity derived from its position in a sign, and its accidental conditions, which are primarily related to the planet's position relative to the horizon, its configuration with the Sun and planets, and movements in the celestial sphere. Some of these conditions strengthen the planet and provide it with prominence, while others debilitate its power and effectiveness in the chart. The essential dignities relate to the essence of the planet, its intrinsic qualities and how much they are reinforced in its expression. Greek authors established the primary system of essential dignities during the classical period, but most originated from the pre-classical astronomical and astrological corpus.[9] The classical essential dignities passed on to medieval and early modern astrology and consistently referred to, are five: domicile, fall, triplicity, term, and face. Domicile has detriment as its corresponding debility, and exaltation has fall as its equivalent debility. Each of these is equated to a state of expression of the planet's nature, for better or for worse.

Accidental conditions, however, relate mainly to the changes in the expression of the planet's nature beyond its essential qualities, i.e. its zodiacal position. In this sense, the essence of a planet cannot be changed; instead, it can be masked or conditioned according to its movement and position in the celestial sphere. Differently from essential dignities, there were many accidental conditions with different levels of impact on the planet's expression. Conditions such as the close conjunction with the Sun (combustion) and angularity (rising, culminating, or setting) were considered the most powerful—the first being a debility and the latter a strength. Others were of lesser importance, such as the planet's distance from the Earth or its movement towards a northern or southern latitude. They were typically used when more detail was needed in the astrological judgement.

---

9   See, for example, Alexander Jones and John Steele, 'A New Discovery of a Component of Greek Astrology in Babylonian Tablets: The "Terms"'., ISAW Papers, no. 1 (2011), http://dlib.nyu.edu/awdl/isaw/isaw-papers/1/; Markham J. Geller, *Melothesia in Babylonia: Medicine, Magic, and Astrology in the Ancient near East*, Science, Technology, and Medicine in Ancient Cultures, volume 2 (Boston: De Gruyter, 2014).

House placement was of paramount importance to astrological judgements. Houses established the main topics of life (the individual, the first house, resources, the second house, siblings, the third, etc.). A planet placed in a house or ruling it became a significator of the topics associated with the house. For example, if Mars was positioned in the seventh house or ruled it, it became a significator for opponents, associations, and marriage. However, the houses had another crucial role in judgements. They would also confer the planet a certain level of strength and visibility. The angular houses (first, tenth, seventh, and fourth) were the strongest position for a planet, followed by the succedent houses (eleventh, eighth, fifth, and second), with the weakest being the cadent houses (twelve, ninth, sixth, and third). This order was not always straightforward because other considerations were in place. For example, the eleventh and fifth houses were considered fortunate and thus conferred greater strength than the other succedent houses. Contrarily, the succedent eighth house was considered malefic and therefore weaker than some cadent houses, such as the ninth.

The proximity of a planet to the Sun was also a condition that empowered or weakened the planets considerably. Within this category fell the states related to the proximity to the Sun, of which the most damaging was combustion, that is, being within $8°$ or less of the Sun's position. The other two conditions were being under the rays, a distance between $8°$ and $16°$, and *cazimi*, which was defined as being within the heart of the Sun, $1°$ apart or, for early modern authors, $16'$ from the Sun's position. Another type of relationship was the rising before the Sun and the setting after the Sun. A planet that rose before the Sun was called oriental, a position that strengthened the superior planets but weakened the inferior. On the contrary, occidentality, i.e., setting after the Sun, empowered the inferior planets but diminished the superiors.

Another relevant category was that of the aspects, an essential element in the astrological relationship of the planets. Strength and weakness were measured by the existence of a good relationship between a planet and the benefics (Venus and Jupiter), which would empower it, or a bad relationship with the malefics (Mars and Saturn), which would damage the planets' strength. While conjunctions were the most potent aspects, their outcome depended on the type of planets involved. Trines ($120°$) and sextiles ($60°$) with Jupiter or Venus constituted empowering configurations for a planet. In comparison, oppositions ($180°$) and squares ($90°$) with Mars and Saturn weakened them, with oppositions and trines being stronger than squares and sextiles. A particularly damaging configuration was that of besiegement. This would apply to a planet that moved from a hard aspect (conjunction, opposition, and square) of one of the malefics to another hard aspect of the other malefic.

Motion was also relevant, particularly the planets' retrograde motion, which was considered to weaken their influence. Speed was also considered, but it was of less importance. A planet with a faster mean daily motion was more potent than a slower one.

The affinity of a planet with its celestial position was also considered, and in this category, there are many different conditions. The most common is that of *haiz*. This condition occurs when a planet's position by sign and in the chart agrees with its gender and sect. For example, Jupiter, a masculine and diurnal planet, will be in *haiz* if placed in a masculine sign and the same hemisphere (superior or inferior) as the Sun. In this state, the planet is considered strong. If the conditions are opposed to those of the planet's nature, they are said to be in contrariety of *haiz* and, thus, weakened. Other similar conditions are the place-ment in a quadrant of the same gender (conformity of quarter) and a complex condition called security or *dustoria*. The definition of the latter shows varia-tions according to different authors. Still, in the early modern period, it implies a planet being simultaneously angular, in square to the luminary of the hour (Sun by day, Moon by night), oriental to the Sun by day or occidental to the Moon by night, and in *haiz*.

The Moon had its specific set of conditions because of its status as a lumi-nary and the fastest celestial body. There are complete listings of such condi-tions, but the most common in tables of planetary strengths is the Moon in Gemini (the twelfth sign from its domicile, Cancer), at the end of a sign in terms of a malefic planet, and under the rays going to combustion, which for the Moon implies being less than 12° from the Sun.[10]

Conjunctions with fixed stars have also been added to some tables. These can be in a general form, indicating that conjunctions with stars of benefic nature strengthen the planet and those of malefic nature damage it. Later tables include only Regulus and Spica as benefic stars, with Algol as a malefic star. Particular degrees are also mentioned in some tables. A planet placed in a degree of increasing fortune or in a degree of the same gender was consid-ered strengthened, while a planet positioned in a void, smoky, dark, pitted, or *azemene* degree was considered weakened.

---

10   Such systematic listings for the Moon's conditions, as well as for the planets and Sun, can be found, in many astrological texts, as for example, in Abū Maʿšar, *The Great Intro-duction to Astrology*, ed. Keiji Yamamoto and Charles Burnett, vol. 1 (Leiden: Brill, 2019), 787–795.

3   The Becoming of a Method

The numerical measuring of the strength of a planet can be traced to Greek authors who advocate counting the number of dignities that a planet has in a given degree of the Zodiac in certain judgements. By the eighth century, the counting of dignities became more mathematical by applying a scoring system to essential dignities. This added a different weight to each essential condition, differentiating their power. The state of domicile is given a value of five dignities: exaltation, four dignities; triplicity, three; term, two; and face, one dignity. This system was generally applied by medieval authors, giving rise to a series of methodologies, such as determining the almuten of a house, a topic, or the almuten of the chart addressed by David Juste in chapter 2.

During the sixteenth century, the scoring system applied to the essential dignities of the planets was extended to the accidental conditions, becoming a standard method by the seventeenth century. The first instance of this table in print appears in 1539 in the *Opusculum astrologicum* by Johannes Schöner (1477–1547).[11] This introductory work defines the foundational principles of astrology, among which are planetary strength and debility. These are discussed in Canon 39, which begins by offering three key diagrams displaying the conditions of strength and debility for the Sun, the Moon, and the planets. Here, Schöner lists all the conditions affecting the luminaries and the planets, dividing them into those that make these celestial bodies fortunate, strong, unfortunate, or debilitated. Only afterwards does he present the scoring of these conditions. Schöner roughly groups the conditions into categories, and within each, the strengths are placed against their corresponding debility when one exists. He begins with house position (in angular, succedent, and cadent houses), followed by essential dignities and debilities. In addition to the common scores of the dignities, this category includes those for detriment (or exile), marked with two debilities, and fall, marked with five debilities. These were not included in his table of essential dignities and debilities (see Table 12.1). Then he lists proximity to the Sun, aspects with benefic or malefic planets, a mix of essential conditions and aspects (reception, void of course, and feral), followed by joy (*gaudium*), particular degrees of the zodiac, then orientality and occidentality, *hayz* and other states of conformity, speed, direction, and other facets of planetary movement. He finishes with conjunctions with fixed stars and particular conditions of the Moon (see Figure 12.2 and Table 12.1).

---

11   Johannes Schöner, *Opusculum Astrologicum ex diversorum libris summa cura pro studiosorum utilitate collectum* (Nuremberg: Iohan. Petreium, 1539), fol. H 4ᵛ.

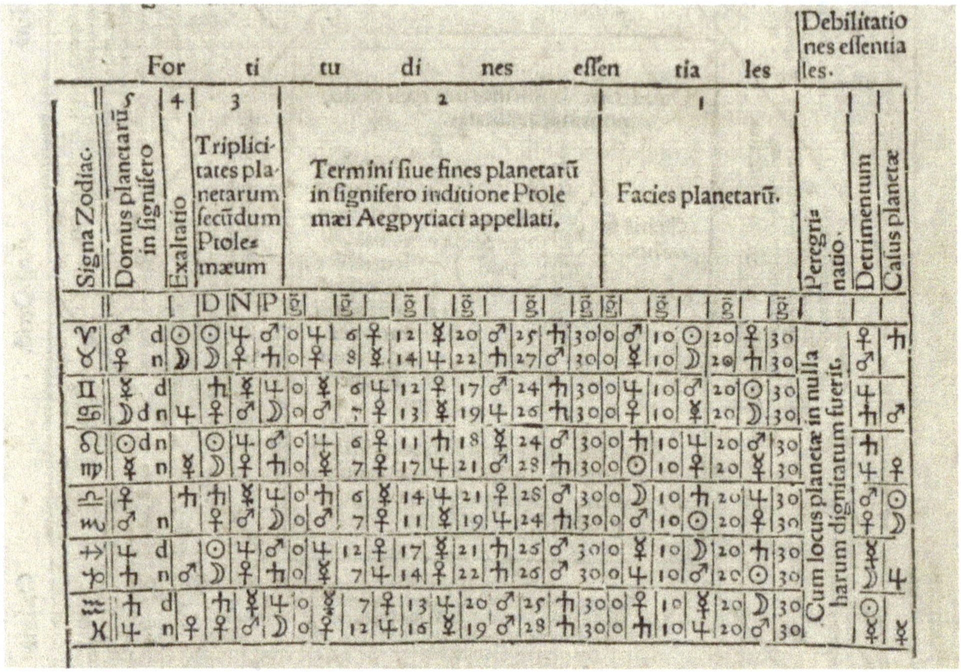

For	ti	tu	di	nes	essen	tia	les																		Debilitatio nes essentia les.		
	5		4	3				2										1									
Signa Zodiac.	Domus planetarũ in signifero		Exaltatio	Triplicitates planetarum secũdum Ptolemæum			Termini siue fines planetarũ in signifero inditione Ptolemæi Aegpytiaci appellati.											Facies planetarũ.							Peregrinatio.	Detrimentum	Casus planetæ
				D	N	P	g		g		g		g		g		g	g		g		g		g			
♈	♂	d	☉	☉	♃	♂	0	♃	6	♀	12	☿	20	♂	25	♄	30	0	♂	10	☉	20	♀	30	Cum locus planetæ in nulla harum dignitatum fuerit.	♀	♄
♉	♀	n	☽	☽	♀	♄	0	♀	8	☿	14	♃	22	♄	27	♂	30	0	☿	10	☽	20	♄	30		♂	
♊	☿	d		♄	☿	♃	0	☿	6	♃	12	♀	17	♂	24	♄	30	0	♃	10	♂	20	☉	30		♃	
♋	☽	d n	♃	♀	♂	☽	0	♂	7	♀	13	☿	19	♃	26	♄	30	0	♀	10	☿	20	☽	30		♄	♂
♌	☉	d n		☉	♃	♂	0	♃	6	♀	11	♄	18	☿	24	♂	30	0	♄	10	♃	20	♂	30		♄	
♍	☿	n	☿	☽	♀	♄	0	☿	7	♀	17	♃	21	♂	28	♄	30	0	☉	10	♀	20	☿	30		♃	♀
♎	♀		♄	♄	☿	♃	0	♄	6	☿	14	♃	21	♀	28	♂	30	0	☽	10	♄	20	♃	30		♂	☉
♏	♂	n		♀	♂	☽	0	♂	7	♀	11	☿	19	♃	24	♄	30	0	♂	10	☉	20	♀	30		♀	☽
♐	♃	d		☉	♃	♂	0	♃	12	♀	17	☿	21	♄	25	♂	30	0	☿	10	☽	20	♄	30		☿	
♑	♄	n	♂	☽	♀	♄	0	☿	7	♃	14	♀	22	♄	26	♂	30	0	♃	10	♂	20	☉	30		☽	♃
♒	♄	d		♄	☿	♃	0	☿	7	♀	13	♃	20	♂	25	♄	30	0	♀	10	☿	20	☽	30		☉	
♓	♃	n	♀	♀	♂	☽	0	♀	12	♃	16	☿	19	♂	28	♄	30	0	♄	10	♃	20	♂	30		☿	☿

FIGURE 12.1 Table of essential dignities and debilities from Johannes Schöner's Opusculum astrologicum (1539), Canon 4. The values for each dignity are noted at the top of the corresponding column (from top left to right: 5, 4, 3, 2, and 1).

After the table, Schöner offers an alternative method by John of Seville, which is simpler and focused on the main conditions, and is considered more adequate for beginners:

> John of Seville observes this more generally, which the novices commonly follow. Consider first if a planet is combust or not. Secondly, if it is direct or not, fast or slow. Third, if it is in some other of their dignities other than domicile or exaltation, i.e. triplicity, term, or face. In fourth place, if it is in a bad aspect with an infortune, or in a good aspect with a fortune, or not. Fifth and last, how it is placed in the celestial figure, whether in an angle, succedent, or cadent. The planets can be said to be powerful and strong when they are direct, in domicile or exaltation, in the angles or the succedent [houses], free from combustion, oriental, and unimpeded by the malefics. Their power and strength are increased if they aspect the benefics, or are conjunct to them, and when they are in their haiz, the superior (planets), oriental, the inferior (planets), occidental. They are said to be supremely damaged and unfortunate when retrograde,

PARS

¶Notandum tamen, quòd D. Anthonius de montulmo hanc rem de fortitudinibus & debilitatibus planetarum,numeris diftinxit, ut ex empli cauffa:Domus prima uel decima obtinet 5.eo quòd fortes funt ficut 5.id eft,in eadem fortitudine ,ficut eft planeta exiftens in fuo domicilio. Huius tabulam accipe fequentem.

Fortitudines planetarum.		Debilitates planetarum.	
5	Domus prima uel decima.	5	Domus duodecima.
4	Domus feptima uel quarta.	4	Domus octaua.
2	Domus nona.	3	Domus fexta.
3	Domus undecima uel quinta	2	Domus fecunda.
1	Domus tertia.	2	Dom. feptia à domo planetæ,id
5	Domicilium.		eft detrimentum.
4	Exaltatio.	5	Dom. feptia ab exaltatiõe.i.cafɡ.
3	Triplicitas.	6	Combuftio planetæ à Sole.
2	Terminus.	4	Sub radijs extra combuftionem.
1	Facies.	5	Obfeffio inter duas infortunas
5	Exiftentia in Cazimi.	3	Applicatio cum infortuna.
5	Coniunctio corpalis cũ fortũa	5	Coniunctio corpalis cũ infortũa
4	Applicatio cum fortuna ex △.	4	Applicatio cũ infortuna per ♂.
3	Applicatio cum fortuna ex ✳.	5	Applicatio corpalis cũ ftella de
5	Receptio.	5	Peregrinatio. (natura infortũæ
3	Gaudium ratione figni.	2	Euacuatio curfus.
2	Gaudiũ ratione domɡ figuræ.	3	Feralitas.
1	Gradus lucidi.	3	Gradus uacui uel fumofi.
1	Gradus augentes fortunam.	3	Gradɡ tenebrofi,putei,Azemene
1	Gradus conformis in fexu.	2	Occidentalitas trium fuperiorũ.
2	Orientalitas triũ fuperiorum.	2	Orientalitas inferiorum.
2	Occidentalitas inferiorum.	2	Contrarietas Hayz.
3	Hayz.	5	Retrogradatio.
2	Conformitas quartæ.	1	Tarditas curfus.
5	Securitas.	1	Minutio luminis.
4	Directio.	1	Minutio numeri.
1	Velocitas curfus.	2	Defcenfio in circulo augis.
1	Augmentum luminis.	2	Defcenfio in meridiem.
1	Augmentum numeri.	3	Coniunctio cum ☊
2	Afcenfio in circulo augis.	5	Coniunctio cum ☋
2	Afcenfio in feptentrionem.	2	Via combufta.
5	Coniunctio corporalis cũ ftella de natura fortunæ.	5	Eclipfis luminarum.
5	Exiftentia inter duas fortunas.	2	☽ in Ⅱ .uel in fine fignorum, in terminis malorum.
		4	Luminare infra terminos eclipfis
		4	Luna uadens ad combuftionem uel infra 12 gradus.

Ioannes

FIGURE 12.2   Table in *Opusculum astrologicum* (1539)

TABLE 12.1   Planetary strengths and debilities by Johannes Schöner (1539)

	Strengths		Debilities
5	First or tenth house	5	Twelfth house
4	Seventh or fourth house	4	Eight house
2	Nineth house.	3	Sixth house
3	Eleventh or fifth house	2	Second house
1	Third house		
5	Domicile	2	Detriment
4	Exaltation	5	Fall
3	Triplicity	6	Combust
2	Term	4	Under rays outside combustion
1	Face	5	Besieged by the two malefics
5	Cazimi.	3	Application to a malefic
5	Bodily conjunction with a benefic	5	Bodily conjunction with a malefic
4	Application with a benefic by △	4	Application with a malefic by ☍.
3	Application with a benefic by ✶	5	Corporeal conjunction with a star of malefic nature
5	Reception	5	Peregrine
3	Joy by sign	2	Void of course
2	Joy by house	3	Feral
1	Light degree	3	Void or smocky degree
1	Degree of incresing fortune	3	Dark, pitted, or azemene degree
1	Degree of the same gender	2	Occidentality of the three superiors
2	Orientality of the three superiors	2	Orientality of the inferiors
2	Occidentality of the inferiors	2	Contrarity of Hayz
3	Hayz	5	Retrogradation
2	Conformity of quarter	1	Slow
5	Security	1	Diminishing in light
4	Direct	1	Decreasing in number
1	Fast	2	Descending in the circle of the auge
1	Increasing in light	2	Descending towards south
1	Increasing in number	3	Conjunction with ☊
2	Ascending in the circle of the auge	5	Conjunction with ☋
2	Ascending towards north	2	Via combusta
5	Corporeal conjunction with a star of benefic nature	5	Eclipse of the luminaries
5	Between two benefic planets	3	☽ in ♊, or at the end of a sign in terms of malefic
		4	Luminary in terms of eclipse
		4	Moon going towards combustion under 12°

combust, falling from exaltation, in a cadent house, impeded by a conjunction, square, or opposition of a malefic, in the contrary of [their] *haiz*, southern
[in latitude]. And the greater number of bad testimonies they have, the more
unfortunate they are. Still, if they are partly in their dignity and strengths, and
partly in their debilities and depressions, they are said to be indifferent or
mediocre.[12]

Many other authors, such as Haly Abenragel, another highly disseminated
medieval source, not having a specific chapter on planetary strengths, offer only
a summary of the more important groupings in a similar fashion to that of John
of Seville:

> And the first of these dignities is that of the angles and the succedents,
> and noblest of the angles is the ascendant and then the midheaven. The
> other dignity is that [a planet] be in its dignity, and the noblest is domicile,
> and after it, exaltation because these as safe and clean; but the triplicity
> and the term can occur with detriment and fall. And the other dignity is
> *haiz* and it is best when it occurs above the earth. And the fourth dignity
> is direct. And the fifth is orientality. And each one has its contrary ... And
> the contraries are: the fall from the angle is the opposite of [being in an]
> angle, peregrination is the opposite of dignity, and not being in *haiz*, is
> the contrary of *haiz*, and the retrogradation is the opposite of direct, and
> occidentality the opposite of orientality.[13]

---

12 Ioannes Hispalen[sis] generaliora tantum ex illis obseruat, quem communiter sequuntur
    nouitij. Considerat primo, an planeta sit combustus an non. Secundo, an sit directus an
    non, seu uelox aut tardus. Tertio, an in aliqua suarum dignitatum fuerit, ut domo exal-
    tat[ione]. Triplicitate termino uel facie. Quarto, an sit in malo aspectu infortunarum, uel
    in bono aspectu fortunarum, an non. Quinto & ultimo, quomodo sit collocatus in figura
    coeli, an sit in ângulo uel succedenti, uel cadenti. Potentes igitur & fortes dicuntur plane-
    tae, cum sunt directi in domibus aut exaltationibus, in angulis uel succedentibus, liberi
    à combustione, orientales, non impediti à malis, sed potentia & fortitudo eorum aug-
    mentatur, si à fortunis aspiciuntur, aut eis coniunguntur, & qua[n]do sunt in Hayz suis,
    superiores orientales, inferiores occidentales. Supreme damnati & infortunati dicuntur,
    cum sunt retrogradi, combusti, cadentes ab exaltatione, in cadente, à malis impediti ♂,
    □ aut ☍, in contrario Hayz, meridionales. Et quanto plura malorum testimonia, tanto
    infortunatiores, sed partim in dignitatibus & fortitudinibus, partim uero in debilitatibus
    & depressionibus, indifferentes siue mediocres dicu[n]tur. Schöner, fol. 1 r.

13 E la vna d'estas dignidades es los angulas e los succedentes, e el mas noble de los angulas
    es el ascendente e depues el medio cielo. E la otra dignidat es que sea en su dignidat, e la
    mas noble d'ellas es la casa e pues la exaltacion, ca estas son saluas e linpias, mas la trip-
    licidat e el termino pueden acaecer con decaso e caemiento. E la otra dignidat es hayz.
    E la meior d'ellas es que sea sobre tierra. E la quarta dignidat es direction. E la quinta es
    orientalidat E cada vna d'estas a su contrario ... E los contrarios son estos: El caemiento de

TABLE 12.2   Accidental Strengths and Debilities by Johannes Schöner (1531)

Accidental strengths	Accidental debilities
Direct	Retrogradation
Increasing in light	Diminishing in light
Increasing in motion or speed	Diminishing in motion or slow
Northern	Southern
Orientality of the three superiors	Occidentality of the three superiors
Occidentality of the inferiors	Orientality of the superiors
Apperance	Combustion
Similarity or hayz	Dissimilitude or contrarity of hayz
Good configuration	Bad configuration
Ascending to the angles of the figure	Falling from the angles of the figure

This long-standing categorization of planetary conditions is clearly the basis for this new table of planetary strengths since it follows a similar arrangement. However, the addition of this new table by Schöner is curious because he does not seem to use it in his other astrological works. When addressing planetary strengths in his *Ephemeris*, published in 1531, part two, canon 14, Schöner offers only the standard table of essential dignities followed by a list of the main accidental strengths and debilities. This is much simpler than any of the tables and diagrams in the Opusculum and offers an interesting summary and wording of the chief accidental conditions. However, there is no numerical scoring see table 12.2, above.

The scoring table is also not present or applied in Schöner's text on nativities, *De iudiciis nativitatum libri tres*, published in 1545, where he again follows John of Seville when exemplifying the determination of planetary strength.[14] This seems to indicate that Schöner was not completely confident in scoring accidental conditions, since he does not apply it in his only astrology manual.

---

angulo contrario de angulo, e la peregrinacion contraria de la dignidat, e non seyendo en su ayz contraria de la ayz, e la retrogradacion contraria de la direction, e la occidentalidat contraria de la orientalidat. ʿAlī Abū al-Ḥasan al-šaybānī Ibn Abī al-Riǧāl, *El libro conplido en los iudizios de las estrellas*, ed. Gerold Hilty (Madrid: Real Academia Española, 1954), bk. 4, page 166.

14   Johannes Schöner, *De Iudiciis Nativitatum: Libri Tres* (Nuremberg: Montanus & Neuber, 1545), fol. B 2ᵛ.

In fact, in this form, this scoring method appears to be a complete novelty in astrological practice.

There are earlier instances of scoring of accidental conditions, but these follow a different mathematical arrangement. An example of this methodology appears in Abraham Ibn Ezra's (1089–1167) works:

⟨The planet⟩ that is in the first place has twelve portions of power; ⟨the planet that is⟩ in the tenth place ⟨has⟩ eleven ⟨portions of power⟩; in the eleventh place, ten; in the seventh place, nine; in the fourth, eight; in the fifth, seven; in the ninth, six; in the sixth, five; in the second, four; in the eighth, three; in the twelfth, two; in the sixth, one.

When Saturn, Jupiter and Mars are moving out from under the rays of the Sun and are oriental, they have twelve portions of power. ⟨When⟩ they are within 30° of the location of the Sun, ⟨they have⟩ eleven ⟨portions of power⟩. ⟨When⟩ they are within 60° ⟨of the Sun⟩ ⟨they have⟩ ten ⟨portions of power⟩. Within 70°, nine. Up to the first station, eight. In the second station, seven. Up to 90° from the Sun, six. If 60°, five. In the first station, four. In opposition to the Sun, three. When it is 30° from the Sun and occidental, two. If 15°, one. When it is under ⟨the rays of⟩ the Sun, it has no power. But Jupiter and Saturn, after leaving the domain of burning, meaning 6° from the Sun and oriental, are assigned six of the portions of power. If there are 10° between the Sun and Mars, but no less [i.e., at least 10° between them], and if it [Mars] is oriental, it [Mars] will be considered to be like the aforementioned [Saturn and Jupiter]. The method for ⟨assigning powers to⟩ Venus and Mercury is the same as for ⟨assigning⟩ the number of portions of power to the upper planets. There is no difference between them except when they [Venus and Mercury] are occidental, because when they are ⟨occidental⟩ they have great power.[15]

Here, there is no equivalence with the scoring of essential dignities. The accidental conditions are scored from 12 to 1 in decreasing number of strength. There is no debility value to subtract. Erza applies this to assess which planet is the dominant in a given chart, being that of a Jupiter-Saturn conjunction, an important moment in the study of the general conditions of the world, or in a nativity, as detailed by David Juste in chapter two. By the sixteenth century this system is mainly used in the computation of the almuten of the figure.

---

15   Shlomo Sela, ed., *Abraham Ibn Ezra Book of the World* (Leiden–Boston: Brill, 2009), 167–169.

Schöner's new table makes a considerable modification to this previous concept of scoring systems, not just in terms of simplicity but also highlighting the contrast between strength and debility. He also adds two important commentaries that subsequent authors will develop further. The first concerns the fortunate or unfortunate conditions of house cusps and parts in Canon 40. He points out that conjunctions, trines, and sextiles of benefic planets, as well as the presence of the North Node, bring fortune. In contrast, conjunctions, oppositions, and squares of the malefic planets and the South Node represent misfortune.

The second, and perhaps more relevant, regards the determination of the lord of the geniture, also known as the almuten of the chart or figure (as discussed in chapter 2). While the most common and traditional method involves the five *hylegical* points, Schöner suggests something different:

> The lord of the chart (*dux thematis*) is the one who holds the most powerful and numerous authorities in the entire chart, both essential and accidental. The essential authorities include domicile, exaltation, triplicity, term, and face. The accidental authorities are, for example, being in the Midheaven (12), the Ascendant (11), according to the sixth canon of this work. Therefore, the leader (*dux*) is the one who possesses more of these authorities and strengths.[16]

This definition of the lord of the geniture will become an important departure from tradition. Although Schöner does not directly link this to the table of planetary strengths, and the concept of the planet with the most essential and accidental strengths does not necessarily require a scoring system, it certainly helps the astrologer make a judgement. Thus, following the same logic as the essential dignity scoring system, the table attributes different values of strength and weakness for each accidental condition.

---

16   Dux autê thematis est, que in toto themate potiores & plures obtinet auctoritates cum
       essentiales tum accidentales. Sunt autem auctoritates essentiales. Domus exaltat, triplici-
       tas. Terminus & facies. Accidentales autê ut in M.C. 12. in ascendente 11: juxta canonem sex-
       tum huius. Dux igitur is est, qui plures ex iis obtinet auctoritares ac fortitudines. Schöner,
       Opusculum Astrologicum, fol. 1 v. The sixth canon refers to the complexions, strengths,
       colours and joys of the planets in the twelve houses (fol. F 2ʳ).

3.1 *Unclear Origins*

As to the origins of this table, while Schöner is certainly its disseminator, he is not its creator, at least not entirely. In the *Opusculum*, he offers important clues regarding its origin. Before presenting the table, he states that:

> However, it should be noted that in this matter concerning the strengths and debilities of the planets, D. Antonio of Montulmo distinguished them by numbers. For example, the first and tenth houses obtain a score of five. That is, in the same strength as a planet in its domicile. This is illustrated in the following table.[17]

From this statement, two important pieces of information emerge: 1) the Italian astrologer Antonius of Montulmo (fl. 1360–1393) is Schöner's source of this scoring, and 2) the reasoning underlying the numeric values of the table is reliant on equating the strongest essential dignity, domicile, with the angular position of a planet, one of the strongest and most straightforward accidental conditions.

The latter is quite interesting since a quick study of the table shows the numerical values used for scoring are inspired by the five-to-one scoring system used for the essential dignities. Although other scoring forms exist that use higher numerical values, as mentioned above, using the same values of essential dignities provides a certain mathematical equivalence and allows for a straightforward combination of essential and accidental conditions. The only exception is the debility value for combustion, which is scored as six, reflecting the high level of debility inflicted on the planet by this condition. All subsequent versions of this table, studied below, follow this premise, and the scoring never surpasses the value of six. It must be noted that, in the essential scoring system, a planet can accumulate more than five points of strength or debility when placed in a sign or degree with more than one dignity. For example, Mars, positioned in the first degrees of Scorpio, possesses domicile, triplicity, term, and face, culminating in a total strength score of eleven. By contrast, Mercury, in most degrees of Pisces, amasses the debility of detriment and fall, receiving a score of nine debilities. Therefore, in the same way that the different scores of essential dignities and debilities help the astrologer to differentiate between

---

17   Notandum tamen, quòd D. Anthonius de montulmo hanc rem de fortitudinibus & debilitatibus planetarum, numeris distinxit, ut exempli caussa: Domus prima uel decima obtinet 5. Eo quòd fortes sunt sicut 5. Id est, in eadem fortitudine, sicut est planeta existens in suo domicilio. Huius tabulam accipe sequentem. Schöner, fol. H 4ᵛ.

various levels of power, the different scoring of accidental conditions will operate regarding accidental conditions.

The attribution to Montulmo, although significant, offers an interesting
problem. Only one of Montulmo's astrological texts was ever circulated in
print. This was the *De iudiciis nativitatum liber praeclarissimus*, annotated
by Regiomontanus and printed in Nuremberg a few years after the *Opusculum* in 1540.[18] However, it offers neither a table nor a discussion of planetary
strengths. The table or any mention of scoring is also absent from the manuscript source of this printed text, Vienna, Österreichische Nationalbibliothek,
Cod. 5335, fol. 61^r–96^v, as well as in other fragments of Montulmo's that belong
to Regiomontanus in Vienna, Österreichische Nationalbibliothek, Cod. 10745.[19]

The table only appears in the manuscript Nürnberg, Stadtbibliothek, MS
Cent. V 85, which contains a copy of Leopold of Austria's *De astrorum scientia* and Ptolemy's *Quadripartitum*. At the end of this manuscript, on folio 78^v,
there is a two-column table entitled '*Antonii de monte vlmi / Fortitudines planetarum Debilitaciones planetarum*'.[20] This table is identical to the one presented
by Schöner in the *Opusculum*, with a few minor differences in wording and
content, such as the omission of 'joy by house' (see Tables 12.3A and B). Since
nothing like it can be found in the known texts by Montulmo and this copy
belonged to Regiomontanus, it would be tempting to attribute the authorship
of the table to Regiomontanus. Yet, he does not indicate the text from which
he extracted the table. Regiomontanus appears to have been quite familiar
with Montulmo's work. In a letter of 1465, Regiomontanus cites another work
by Montulmo on revolutions, which appears to have been circulated only in
manuscript form.[21] Therefore, the table could have come from a manuscript by

---

18   This work is included in Luca Gaurico, Antonio di Montulmo, and Johannes Camillus
      Regiomontanus, *Tractatvs Astrologiae Ivdiciariae De Nativitatibus Virorvm & mulierum,
      compo situs per D. Lucam Gauricum Neapolitanum, ex Ptolemæo & alijs autoribus dignis-
      simis, cum multis aphorismis expertis & comprobatis ab eodem. Addito in fine libello Antonij
      de Montulmo, de eadem re, cum annotationibus Ioannis de Regiomonte, hactenus nusque
      impresso.* (apud Iohan. Petreium, 1540).

19   On Montulmo and its work, see Stephan Heilen, *Konjunktionsprognostik in der Frühen
      Neuzeit. Band 1. Die Antichrist-Prognose des Johannes von Lübeck (1474) zur Saturn-Jupiter-
      Konjunktion von 1504 und ihre frühneuzeitliche Rezeption*, vol. 1 (Baden-Baden: Valentin
      Koerner, 2020), 302–309.

20   My thanks to David Juste for calling my attention to this manuscript.

21   On Regiomontanus's life, sources, and manuscripts, see Ernst Zinner, *Regiomontanus, His
      Life and Work*, vol. 1, Studies in the History and Philosophy of Mathematics (Amster-
      dam / New York: North-Holland, 1990). Regiomontanus's copy of this text, *De revolution-
      ibus annorum* can be found in Vienna, Österreichische Nationalbibliothek, Cod. 10745,
      fols. 39^v–43^v. This codex also has as notes from Montulmo's *De nativitatibus* in fols. 37^v–39^v.

Montulmo that has yet to be unidentified. It must be noted that this type of table could have been easily compiled from his texts because Montulmo refers to some of them when discussing the strength of a planet. This occurs when he addresses topics such as the almuten, the *hyleg*, and the *alcochoden*. Regiomontanus could have tabulated the various conditions mentioned by Montulmo, which would explain the attribution to him. However, whether the scoring comes from Montulmo or is an innovation by Regiomontanus remains unclear. The table is clearly in Regiomontanus's hand, the same as is found in other manuscripts of his.

Whatever the case, after Regiomontanus' death, the Nürnberg Cent. v 85 manuscript containing the table of planetary strengths came into Schöner's possession, and he followed Regiomontanus' reference to Montulmo. This table is the oldest known version of this scoring of planetary strengths. Unfortunately, the numbering in the table has been deliberately erased, making it impossible to reconstruct the scoring completely.[22] Only a few numbers can still be identified and appear identical to those in Schöner's *Opusculum* (see Table 12.3B). The fact that Schöner presents the scoring in the *Opusculum* suggests that, in his time, the manuscript still had the numeric values of strength and debility for each condition.

If Montulmo was the author, this method was devised sometime in the fourteenth century, but had no significant dissemination among astrologers until Schöner received it via Regiomontanus and decided to include it in the *Opusculum*. It was only after 1539 that this table began to appear in astrological treatises, and no older example is currently known.

Other known texts by Montulmo are *De occultis et manifestis, sive Liber intelligentiarum* and *Glosa super imagines duodecim signorum Hermetis* both extant in Paris, Bibliothèque Nationale de France, lat. 7337 and the latter also in Vatican, Biblioteca Apostolica Vaticana, Vat. lat. 4085. For a modern editions, see Nicolas Weill-Parot, 'Antonio Da Montolmo's De Occultis et Manifestis or Liber Intelligentiarum: An Annotated Critical Edition with English Translation and Introduction', in *Invoking Angels: Theurgic Ideas and Practices, Thirteenth to Sixteenth Centuries*, ed. Claire Fanger (University Park, PA: Penn State University Press, 2012), 219–293; Nicolas Weill-Parot, 'Antonio Da Montolmo et La Magie Hermétique', in *Hermetism from Late Antiquity to Humanism. La Tradizione Ermetica Dal Mondo Tardo- Antico All'umanesimo (Atti Del Convegno Internazionale Di Studi, Napoli, 20–24 Novembre 2001)*, ed. Paolo Lucentini, Ilaria Parri, and Vittoria Perrone Compagni (Turnhout: Brepols, 2003), 545–568.

22   A specialised infrared photograph might allow a complete reading of the scoring, but this was not possible at this time.

TABLE 12.3A   Planetary strengths and debilities attributed to Antonio of Montulmo by Regiomontanus (MS Cent. v 85)

Antonii de monte ulmi

Fortitudines planetaru[m]	Debiltac[i]ones
... Domus pri[m]a uel deci[m]a	... Domus duodeci[m]a
... Domus septi[m]a ut 4ta	... Domus octaua
... Domus nona	... Domus sexta
... Domus undeci[m]a ut 5ta	... Domus secunda
... Domus tertia	... Dom[us] 7ma a domo pl[neta]e
... Domiciliu[m]	... Dom[us] 7ma ab exaltat[i]one
... Exaltatio	... Combustio pl[neta]e a sole
... Triplicitas	... Sub radiis ex[tra] combustione[m]
... Termin[us]	... Obsession inter duas infortu[n]as
... Facies	... Applicatio cu[m] infortuna
... Existentia i[n] cazimj [margin:] i[n] vnitione cu[m] sole	
... Co[n]iu[n]ctio corp[or]alis cu[m] fortu[n]a	... Co[n]iu[n]ctio corp[or]alis cu[m] i[n]fortu[n]a
... Applicatio cu[m] fortu[n]a ex t[ri]no	... Applicatio cu[m] i[n]fortu[n]a p[er] oppo[sitionem]
... Applicatio cu[m] fortu[n]a ex sex[ti]li	... Applica[ti]o cor[pora]lis cu[m] stella de na[tura] i[n]fortu[n]ae
... Receptio	... Peregrinatio
... Gaudiu[m]	... Euacuatio cursus
... Gradus lucidi	... Feralitas
... Grad[us] augm[en]ta[n]tes fortuna[m]	... Gradus vacui uel fumosi
... Gradus conformis i[n] sexu	... Gradus tenebrosi, putei, et azemene
... Orientalitas triu[m] sup[er]ioru[m]	... Occidentalitas triu[m] sup[er]ioru[m]
... Occidentalitas inferioru[m]	... Orientalitas inferioru[m]
... Aiz	... Contrarietas aiz.
... Conformitas quartae	... Retrogradatio
... Securitas	... Tarditas cursus
... Directio	... Minutio lum[in]is
... Velocitas cursus	... Minutio numeri
... Augm[em]tu[m] lumi[n]is	... Descensio i[n] circulo augis
... Augm[em]tu[m] numeri	... Descensio i[n] meridiem

TABLE 12.3A   Planetary strengths and debilities attributed to Antonio of Montulmo (*cont.*)

Antonii de monte ulmi

Fortitudines planetaru[m]	Debiltac[i]ones
... Ascensio i[n] c[ir]culo augis	... Co[n]iu[n]ctio cu[m] capite
... Ascensio i[n] sept[em]trione[m]	... Co[n]iunctio cu[m] cauda
... [Coniuncti]o cor[pora]lis cu[m] stella de na[tura] fortu[n]ae	... Via combusta
... Existentia int[er] duas fortu[n]as	... Eclipsis lu[m]i[n]ariu[m]
	... Luna i[n] gemi[n]is, uel i[n] fi[n]e sig[n]oru[m] i[n] t[er]mi[n]is mal-oru[m]
	... Lumi[n]are infra termi[n]os eclipsis
	... Luna vade[n]s ad co[m]bustione[m] uel infra 12 gradus

TABLE 12.3B   Planetary strengths and debilities attributed to Antonio of Montulmo (translation)

Antonius of monte ulmi

Strengths of the planets	Debilitations of the planets
[...] First or tenth house	[...] Twelfth house
[...] Seventh or 4th house	[...] Eighth house
[...] Nineth house	[...] Sixth house
[...] Eleventh or 5th house	[2] Second house
[...] Third house	[...] Seventh house for the planet's domicile
[...] Domicile	[...] Seventh house from exaltatione
[...] Exaltation	[...] Combustion by the Sun
[...] Triplicity	[...] Under the rays free from combustion
[...] Term	[5] Besieged between two infortues
[1] Face	[...] Applying to an infortune
[...] In *Cazimi*	
[5] Corporal conjunction with a fortune	[...] Corporal conjunction with am infortune
[...] Application to fortune by trine	[...] Application to infortune by oposition
[...] Application to fortune by sextile	[...] Comporeal application with a star the nature of na infortune

TABLE 12.3B   Planetary strengths and debilities attributed to Antonio of Montulmo (*cont.*)

Antonius of monte ulmi

Strengths of the planets		Debilitations of the planets	
[...]	Reception	[...]	Peregrination
[...]	Joy	[...]	Void of course
[...]	Light degree	[...]	Feral
[1]	Degree of increasing fortune	[...]	Void or smoky degree
[1]	In a degree of the same gender	[...]	Dark / Pitted / and azemener degree
[...]	Orientality of the three superiors	[...]	Occidentality of the three superiors
[...]	Occidentality of the inferiors	[...]	Orientality of the inferiors
[...]	*Haiz*	[...]	Contrarity of *haiz*
[...]	Conformity of quarter	[...]	Retrogradation
[...]	Security	[1]	Slow
[...]	Direct	[1]	Diminishing in light
[...]	Fast	[1]	Diminishing in number
[...]	Increasing in light	[...]	Descending in the circle of its auge
[...]	Increasing in number	[...]	Descending to the south
[...]	Ascending in the circle of its auge	[...]	Conjuction with the head [of the dragon]
[...]	Ascending to the north	[...]	Conjuction with the tail [of the dragon]
[...]	Corporal conjunction with a fortunate star	[...]	Via combusta
[...]	Existing between two fortunes	[...]	Eclipse of the luminaries
		[...]	Moon in Gemini or at the end of a sign in term of malefic
		[...]	Luminary in the terms of eclipse
		[...]	Moon going to combustion or within 12 degrees

4   Transmission and Development

After Schöner, Cyprián Karásek Lvovický (1514–1574), commonly known by his Latinized name, Leovitus, appears to have been the first to follow the new table of planetary strengths. Born in Hradec Králové in Bohemia, Lvovický became one of the most influential astrological authors of the early modern period. His texts circulated widely and are cited by almost every subsequent author. One of the most significant of Lvovický's works is his nativity text, *Doctrina de iuditiis nativitatum*, which was included in his *Ephemeridum nouum opus* (1557).[23] The text teaches the principles of nativity judgement and is structured in a very helpful format for those learning astrology. It provides a step-by-step judgement of nativity using two charts as examples. This offers the student a demonstration of how to apply the rules in practice and a comparison of how the same rules would be used in different configurations. This text was so successful that it became a standard for nativity judgement, which testified in the many manuscript judgments of natal figures of the early modern period.

Among the methods presented is the scoring of planetary strengths and debilities. Here, Lvovický provides a table with the scoring of essential and accidental dignities in the same fashion as that of Schöner's *Opusculum*. The popularity of his works and methodologies certainly contributed to the widespread transmission of the table.

Lvovický's table is more condensed than Schöner's and presents noticeable differences. While the table does not include besiegement by the malefics, it is more specific when listing the aspects to the benefics and malefics. It leaves out increasing in number and only considers increasing in light for the Moon. It refers only to mutual receptions by domicile or exaltation, which are scored with the same value as that of the corresponding dignities. Also, detriment and fall are scored with a debility value equivalent to their dignity counterparts, i.e. five for detriment and four for fall instead of two and five. Special degrees, such as void, dark, and others, are left out. In the house position score, the eleventh, seventh and fourth have the same value of four dignities, the eighth and the sixth have the opposing score of four debilities, and the ninth and the third houses share the dignity of two. Unlike Schöner, the conjunction with the North Node is considered beneficial and given a score of three, while the conjunction with the South Node has the equivalent value of debility. The aspects to the benefic and malefic planets are scored if partile, that is, within one degree of exactness, while Schöner mostly considers applying (i.e. forming) aspects. Regarding fixed stars, Lvovický is more specific, listing just Regulus and Spica as benefic stars and only Algol as malefic.

---

23   Cyprian Leowitz, *Ephemeridum nouum atque insigne opus ab anno Domini 1556. usque in 1606. accuratissimè supputatum: cui praeter alia omnia in caeteris editionibus addi solita, etiam haec accesserunt.* (Augsburg: Philippus Ulhardus, 1557). This was later printed in London on its own under the title *Breuis et perspicua ratio iudicandi genituras ex physicis causis & vera experientia extructa* (1558).

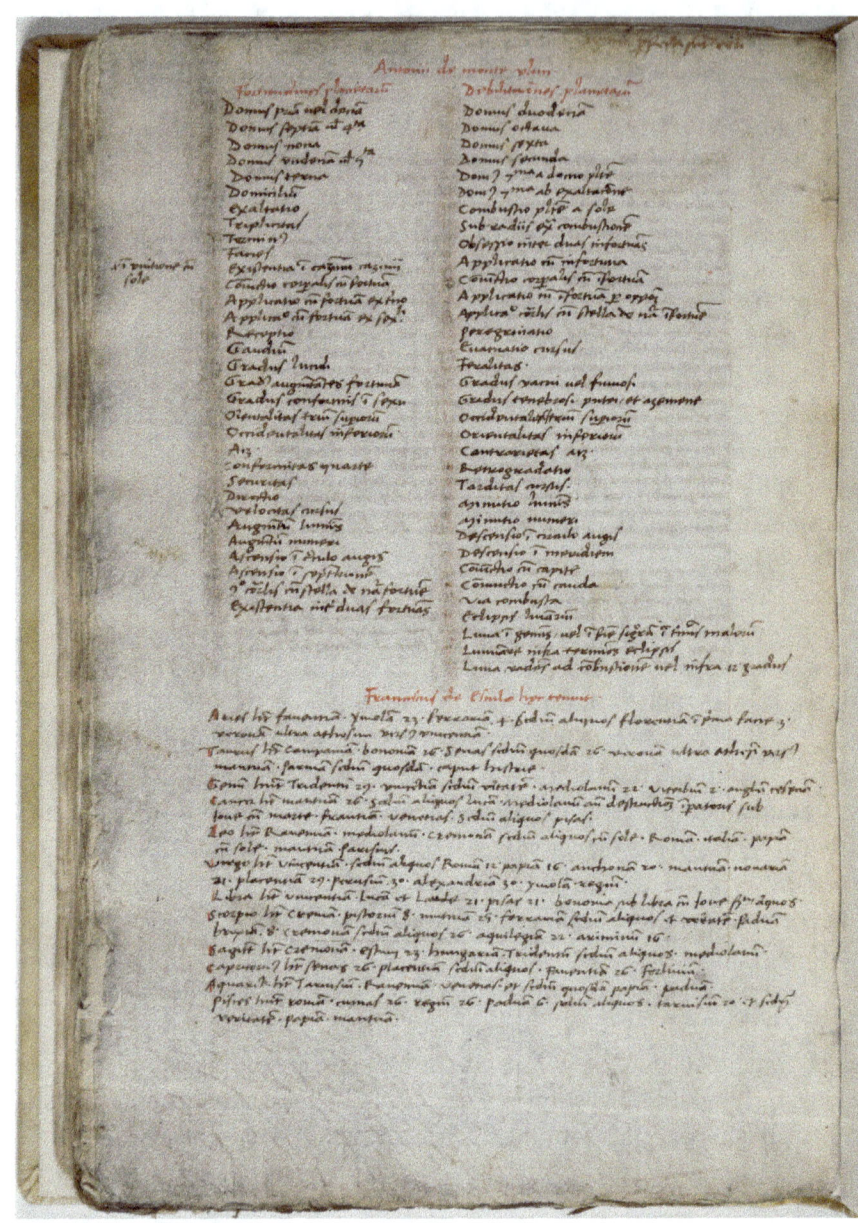

FIGURE 12.3   Table in MS Cent. V 85, fol. 78ᵛ

TABLE 12.4 Planetary strengths and debilities by Cyprián Lvovický (1557)

	Strengths		Debilities
5	Free from combustion and rays of the Sun	5	Combust
5	Cazimi (less than 16′ from Sun's degree)	4	Under the rays of the Sun
4	Direct (not including the Moon)	5	Retrograde
2	Orientality of the superiors	2	Occidentality of the superiors
2	Occidentality of the inferiors	2	Orientality of the inferiors
2	Moon increasing in light (from ☌ to ☍)	2	Moon decreasing in light (from ☍ to ☌)
5	In domicile or mutual reception by domicile	5	In detriment
2	Fast	2	Slow
4	In exaltation or mutual receptios by exaltation	4	In fall
3	In its own triplicity	5	Peregrine
2	In term		
1	In face		
5	On the midheaven or ascendant	5	In the twelfth house
4	In the seventh, fourth, or eleventh house	4	In the eight or sixth house
3	In the second or fifth house		
2	In the ninth or third house		
5	In partile ☌ with ♃ or ♀	5	In partile ☌ with ♄ or ♂
4	In partile △ with ♃ or ♀	4	In partile ☍ with ♄ or ♂
3	In partile ✶ with ♃ or ♀	3	In partile □ with ♄ or ♂
3	☌ ☊	3	☌ ☋
6	Conjunction with Regulus (5° before or after)	4	Conjunction with Algol (5° before or after)
5	Conjunction with Spica (5° before or after)		

The scoring seems more symmetrical than in Schöner's table, and the maximum value is five, even for combustion, except for the conjunction with Regulus, which is scored as six points of strength. Although Lvovický follows the same principles as Schöner, he chooses to score only the most necessary conditions. He introduces this idea at the beginning of the chapter on Planetary Strengths:

> This observation is very necessary and useful in the whole doctrine of judgments regarding the strength of the planets—namely, in which places in the heavens they are positioned, and how they exert their natural effects more forcefully, and, conversely, when and where they are

weaker. For whenever something must be pronounced regarding the conditions of a nativity, such as life, dignity, marriage, or similar matters, certain places must be inspected, which we commonly call significators. According to their constitution, mutual agreement in signification of the same event, nature, placement in the world and in the chart, movement, and their conjunction or configuration with other benefic or malefic stars, judgments about the proposed question are to be made. These considerations are to be made regarding the planets, then the fortune (Part of Fortune), and finally in the places or houses of the celestial figure.

In the planets, six conditions especially must be considered:

1. Whether the planet is combust or not.
2. Whether it is direct and fast or retrograde and slow.
3. Whether it is oriental or occidental.
4. Whether it is in one of its essential dignities, or peregrine, falling, or in detriment.
5. Whether it is configured with benefic planets in a favourable aspect, or with malefics in an adversarial one.
6. How it is positioned in the natal chart, whether in an angular, succedent, or cadent house.[24]

Cyprián Lvovický apparently adopted this methodology wholeheartedly, and he became the promoter of the new computation of the lord or almuten of the geniture, which as mentioned above became a significant change in the astrological methodology of the sixteenth century:

---

24   Admodum necessaria & vtilis est in tota iudiciorum doctrina hæc admonitio, de planetarum fortitudine, hoc est in quibus cœli locis & quomodo constituti suos naturales effectus vehementius exerant, & rursus quando & vbi sint imbecilliores. Quotiescunque enim aliquid de nati conditionibus utpote de vita, dignitate, coniugio aut similibus pronunciandum est, inspiciendi sunt certi loci, quos vsitate appellamus significatores, ac iuxta eorum constitutionem, mutuam conuenientiam in eiusdem euentus significatione, naturam, positum [sic] in mundo & in themate, motum & cum alijs benignis vel malignis stellis congressum & configurationem, iudicia de proposita quæstione sunt ferenda. Hæc considerantur. In planetis, deinde in *fortuna* postremo etiam in locis seu domibus figuræ cœlestis.

      In planetis præcipué sunt expendenda sex accidentia. 1. An planeta sit combustus necne. 2. An sit directus & velox vel retrogradus aut tardus. 3. An sit orientalis vel occidentalis. 4. An sit in aliqua suarum dignitatum essentialium vel peregrinus, cadens, aut in detrimento suo. 5. An sit beneficis planetis benigno aspectu configuratus, aut maleficis inimico. 6. Quomodo sit constitutus in figura natiuitatis, num in ângulo, succedente, vel cadente ab angulis domo. Leowitz, aa 4ᵛ.

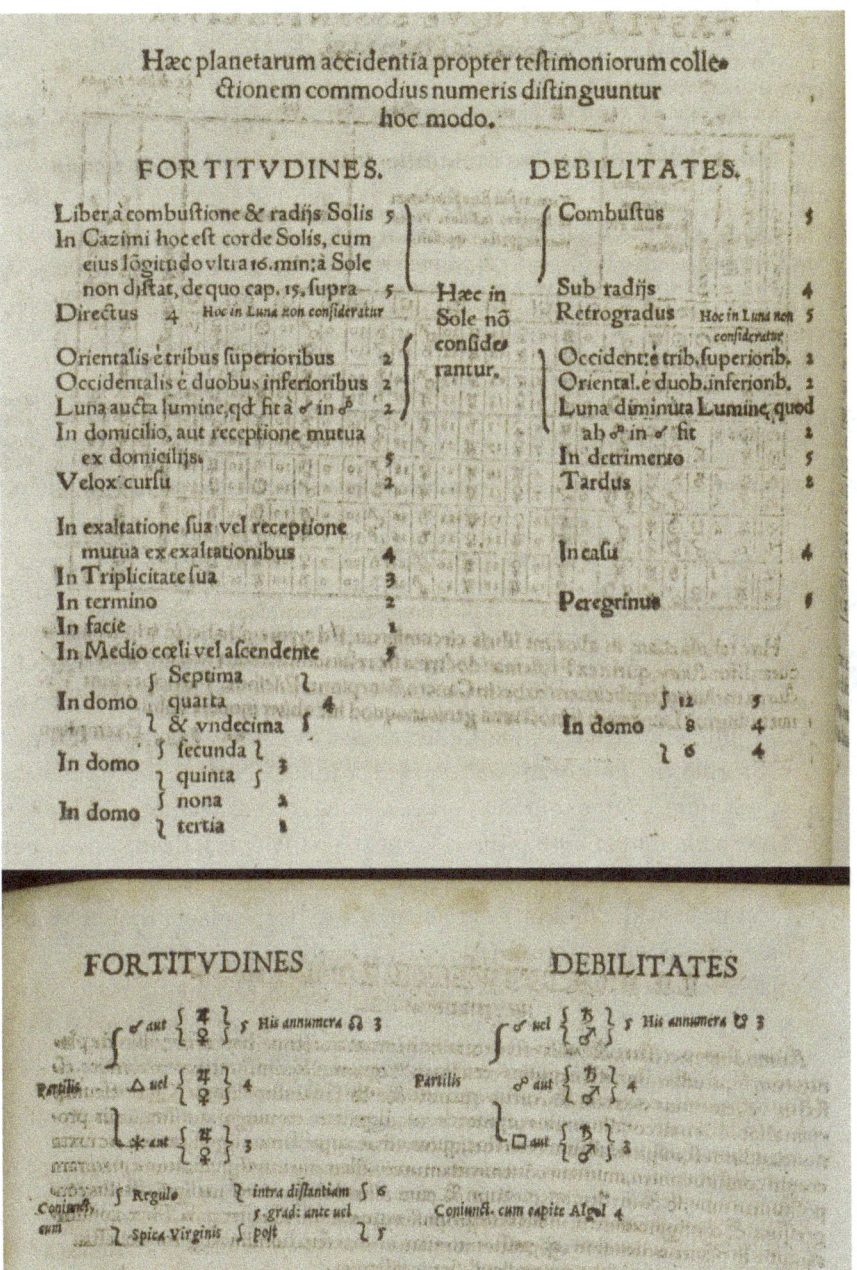

Hæc planetarum accidentia propter teſtimoniorum colle-
ctionem commodius numeris diſtinguuntur
hoc modo.

FORTITVDINES.   **DEBILITATES.**

FORTITVDINES		DEBILITATES	
Liber à combuſtione & radijs Solis	5	Combuſtus	5
In Cazimi hoc eſt corde Solis, cum eius lõgitudo vltra 16.min:à Sole non diſtat, de quo cap. 15. ſupra	5	Sub radijs	4
Directus 4 *Hoc in Luna non conſideratur*		Retrogradus *Hoc in Luna non conſideretur*	5
Orientalis è tribus ſuperioribus	2	Occident:è trib.ſuperiorib.	2
Occidentalis è duobus inferioribus	2	Oriental.è duob.inferionb.	2
Luna aucta lumine, qd fit à ☌ in ☍	2	Luna diminuta Lumine, quod ab ☌ in ☍ fit	2
In domicilio, aut receptione mutua ex domicilijs.	5	In detrimento	5
Velox curſu	2	Tardus	2
In exaltatione ſua vel receptione mutua ex exaltationibus	4	In caſu	4
In Triplicitate ſua	3		
In termino	2	Peregrinus	5
In facie	1		
In Medio cœli vel aſcendente	5		
In domo { Septima / quarta / & vndecima	4	In domo { 12 / 8 / 6	5 / 4 / 4
In domo { ſecunda / quinta	3		
In domo { nona / tertia	2 / 1		

(middle text: Hæc in Sole nõ conſide- rantur.)

FORTITVDINES   **DEBILITATES**

FIGURE 12.4   Table in Lvovický's *Ephemeridum nouum* (1557), aa 4ᵛ–aa 5ʳ

As David Juste demonstrated in chapter two, during the medieval and part of the early modern periods, the lord of the geniture was calculated as the planet having the greatest score of essential dignities in the five *hylegical* places: the Sun, the Moon, the Ascendant, the Part of Fortune, and the pre-natal syzygy. In the chapter 'On the Lord of the Geniture' (*De Domino Geniturae*), Lvovický explains that there are many ideas regarding its computation. First, he refers to earlier authorities, particularly the Roman astrologer Julius Firmicus Maternus (4th century), whose method he deems too simplistic. Next, he discusses the most widely used method concerning the *hylegical* points or places:

> There are various opinions among astrologers about the method of choosing the ruler of the nativity, and which of these is the most certain and supported by physical and astrological reasoning I will not dispute here. Instead, I will review the principal methods in such a way that everyone is free to follow whichever they prefer.
>
> Firmicus, who is the only ancient writer among the Latins whose astrological predictions have reached us, declares that the ruler of the nativity is the planet that governs the sign into which the Moon enters immediately after birth, with the exception of Leo and Cancer, which are ruled by the luminaries. For example, if the Moon at the time of someone's birth is in Scorpio, the ruler of the nativity will be Jupiter, because the Moon next moves from Scorpio into Sagittarius, and the ruler of Sagittarius is Jupiter. This method of choosing the ruler of the nativity is indeed simple, but how strong its reasoning is should be left to the judgment of others.
>
> Some consider the ruler of the nativity to be the planet that holds the most prominent and numerous essential dignities in the five *hylegical* places, namely the positions of the Sun, Moon, Ascendant, Part of Fortune, and the conjunction or opposition of the luminaries immediately preceding the nativity. Whoever finds this method appealing can follow it, and I do not criticise it.[25]

---

25   Variæ sunt Astrologorum opiniones de ratione eligendi dominum natiuitatis, quarum quæ certior sit, & physicis ac Astrologicis rationibus magis firmata, hoc loco non disputabo, Sed præcipuas ita recensebo, ut per me cuique liberrimum futurum sit sequi, quam velit quisque libentius, Firmicus qui apud latinos solus astrologicas prædictiones conscripsit ex veteribus qui ad nostram ætatem peruenerunt, pronunciat eum planetam genituræ dominum qui præest signo, quod luna proximé post natiuitatem ingreditur, Leone et Cancro exceptis, quibus luminaria præsunt: Exempli causa. Si luna tempore alicuius natiuitatis sit in Scorpione, dominus natiuitatis erit Iupiter, quia Luna proximé ex Scorpione in Sagittarium transit, cuius signi dominus est Iupiter. Hic modus eligendi dominum natiui-

However, in the face of this new scoring method, Lvovický proposes an alternative computation using the new table. Thus, he introduces the concept that the planet with the greatest number of essential dignities and accidental strengths is the lord of the geniture and shows the application of the method in his two example charts:

> However, this is my approach: I designate as the ruler of the nativity that planet which is the most powerful both in terms of essential dignity and celestial position. But if it happens that a planet possesses only one of these qualifications—either essential dignity or a strong position in the celestial figure—then it is necessary to associate with it another planet, which is stronger in terms of its position in the celestial figure. This reasoning has, among other considerations, these particular grounds: the planet that is thus positioned in the radix and is the most powerful among the others cannot, by any fair and reasonable judgment, be removed from this administration.[26]

While Schöner had already suggested this methodology after presenting his table, Lvovický enhances its relevance by contextualising it and contrasting it with other more common methods. Furthermore, he demonstrates its application through his examples. Yes, despite the differences in methodology, the function of this significator remains unchanged. Lvovický is not creating a new concept but offering a new line of reasoning regarding its determination:

> Moreover, the nature of the ruler of the nativity provides a general basis for judging the entire life, character, and physical constitution or temperament of the native. This is because, in shaping the body, the ruler of the nativity, in conjunction with the luminaries, exerts a dominant influence.[27]

---

tatis facilis quidem est, sed quam firmis rationibus nitatur aliorum esto iudicium. Leowitz, aa 8ᵛ.

26 Cui hæc ratio placet, is eam poterit sequi: neque ego repræhendo eam. Mea hæc est ratio, & hunc planetam præficio dominio genituræ qui & respectu essentialis dignitatis & simul loci cœlestis est potentior. Quod si alterutrum tantum vni alicui planeta acciderit, ut sit quidem in essentiali dignitate, sed tamen non in potenti loco figure colestis, tum necesse est ei associari alterum quendam, qui respectu loci figure cœli potentior fit. Huius rationis cum alias, tum præcipué has causas habeo, quod is planeta qui sic constitutus est in radice & reliquorum potentissimus, non videat iure merito posse ab hac administratione remoueri. Leowitz, aa 8ᵛ.

27 Porro iuxta naturam domini natiuitatis generaliter iudicatur de tota vita, moribus & com-

The computation of the lord of the geniture is not the only innovation that Lvovický presents. He also extends this scoring to the Part of Fortune, the most significant of the so-called parts or lots, which provide additional meaning in an astrological judgement. Therefore, to assess the strength of the Part of Fortune, he proposes the following:

> Ptolemy considers the Part of Fortune no less than any planet. However, it must be observed that aspects are not assigned to it, except insofar as it is aspected by planets, because it is merely a place in the heavens where the rays of the Sun and Moon converge. Its strengths and weaknesses must also be diligently examined, which are primarily derived from the signs in which it is positioned. Then, from the aspects of the planets. Thirdly, from the location within the celestial figure (the house it occupies). Fourthly, from the fixed royal stars, etc. These are distinguished by their respective numbers as follows.[28]

This table follows the same logic as the one for planetary strengths and utilizes the same values for similar conditions, including house placement, aspects to planets, the nodes and fixed stars, and proximity to the Sun. It does not incorporate essential dignities, as those do not apply to the Part of Fortune. Instead, these are substituted with sign placements where the part is considered strengthened or weakened. The signs ruled by benefic planets and the luminaries are rated high in strength, while those governed by Mercury, a neutral planet, remain positive but are weaker. After presenting this scoring system, Lvovický states that it is also to be applied in house cusps, but he does not provide examples of its application.

> In the very same way, the strengths and weaknesses of the individual celestial houses should be evaluated, just as with the Part of Fortune. It should only be noted that intercepted signs within the houses must also be included in the assessment. Everything else is simple and does not require further elaboration.[29]

---

plexione seu temperamento corporis nati, quia in constitutione corporis secundum luminaria præcipuam vim habet dominus genituræ. Leowitz, aa 8ᵛ.

28　Partem fortunæ Ptolemæus nonminus planetam aliquem considerat, hoc tamen observando, quo ei non tribuuntur aspectus, nisi quatenus à planetis aspicitur, quia est tantum locus cœli in quo Solis & Lunæ radij concurrunt. Eius fortitudines & debilitates quoque diligenter examinandæ sunt, quæ sumuntur primum à signis, in quibus constituitur. Deinde ab aspectibus planetarum. Tertio a loco figuræ cœlestis. Quarto à stellis fixis regijs etc. Distinguuntur autem numeris suis hoc pacto. Leowitz, aa 7ʳ⁻ᵛ.

29　Eadem prorsus ratione fortitudines ac debilitates singularum domorum cœlestium

TABLE 12.5 Strengths and debilities for the Part of Fortune and Cusps by Cyprián Lvovický (1557)

	Strengths		Debilities
5	In ♉ or ♓	5	♍ ☌ ♏
4	In ♎ ♐ ♋ ♌	0	♈
3	In ♊		
2	In ♍		
2	In the terms of ♃ or ♀[30]		
5	Conjunction with ♃ or ♀	5	Conjunction with ♄ or ♂
3	Conjunction with ☊	3	Conjunction with ☋
4	Trine to ♃ or ♀	4	Opposition to ♄ or ♂
3	Sextile to ♃ or ♀	3	Square to ♄ or ♂
		2	In terms of ♄ or ♂
5	In the first or tenth house	5	In the twelfth house
4	In the seventh, fourth, or eleventh house	4	In the eighth house
3	In the second or fifth house	4	In the sixth house
2	In the ninth house		
1	In the third house		
6	Conjunct Regulus	4	Conjunct Algol
5	Conjunct Spica virginis		
5	Neiter combust nor under rays	5	Combust
		4	Under the rays

This methodology is not in Schöner's work, but it follows the same principle of beneficial and harmful aspects that he mentions in cannon 40 regarding house cusps and parts while extending it to conditions beyond the aspects:

> Cusps and beginnings of the houses of the heavens: likewise, planets and significations of the parts, are made fortunate by conjunctions, all aspects of benefic planets, and by the favourable aspects of the mediocre planets, when they observe the same places or are in conjunction with them by halves, or within half of their orbs. For example, if 14° Taurus is the cusp of

---

examinandæ sunt, ut partis fortuna. Hoc tantum obseruandum est, simul etiam in iudi-tium adhiberi oportere signa in domibus intercepta. Reliqua omnia sunt facilia, neque opus est prolixiore explicatione. Leowitz, *Ephemeridum nouum opus*, aa 7ᵛ.

30 While in the 1557 table it is not clear if he means 'in Virgo in the terms of Jupiter or Venus' or if these are two different conditions, the 1558 table clearly states them as independent.

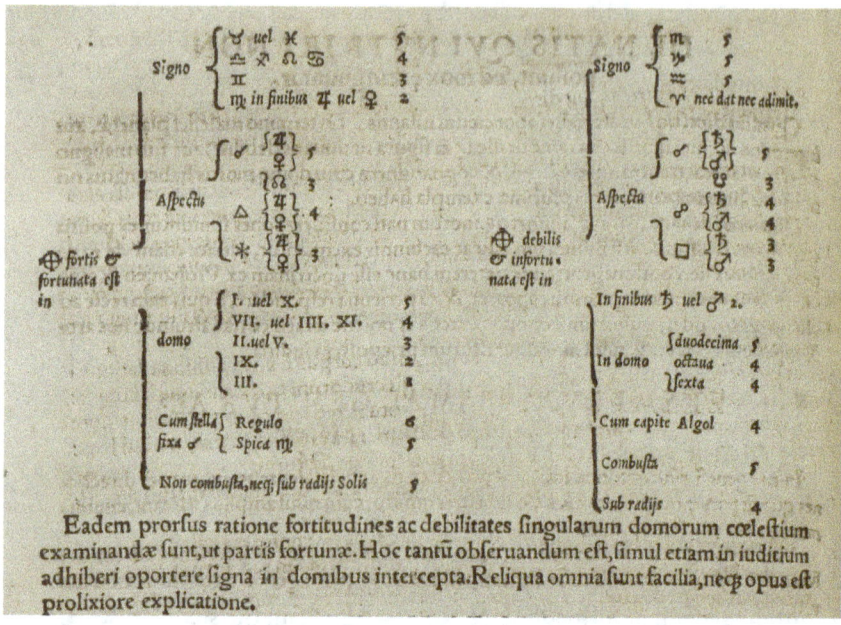

FIGURE 12.5 Lot of Fortune table in Lvovický's *Ephemeridum nouum* (1557), aa 7ᵛ

the second house of the celestial figure, and Jupiter is at 23° Taurus. Thus, Jupiter, by its presence in the second house, from half of its orb, which is 9 degrees, would fortify the cusp of the second house. This would also apply to any intermediate degree. In the same manner, aspects are to be observed: if 14° Taurus is, as before, the cusp of the second house, and Jupiter is at 23° Virgo, observing the cusp by trine, from half of its orb, which would thereby fortify the cusp of the second house, as well as any intermediate degree within half of its orb. In this way, understand also the misfortunes and afflictions of the aforementioned places. For the malefic planets, by conjunction, opposition, and square, and the mediocre planets, by their opposition and square, afflict the places of benefic planets, the cusps of houses, and the significations of the parts from half and within the halves of their orbs. The North Node, by its presence, fortifies and increases whatever place it occupies. Therefore, the good is with the good, and evil with the evil, as [it happens] with Mercury. The South Node weakens and diminishes, being good with the evil and evil with the good.[31]

---

31   Cuspides & initia domorum celi: Item planeta & partes significatorum, fortunantur per ♂,

By presenting and discussing the uses of the two scoring tables, Cyprián Lvovický seems to be the primary, or one of the primary, divulgers of the methodology reservedly offered by Schöner in the *Opusculum*. He strongly contributed to its establishment as a standard practice in early modern astrology, at least by the seventeenth century. However, the transmission of this table was not a completely straightforward process.

After Lvovický, the table is mentioned in 1558 by the mathematician Giovanni Battista Carelli (fl. 1550) in his *Ephemerides*. The table is equivalent to Schöner's in the order of the conditions and their scores, except with the omission of fall.[32] A similar table is published a year later by the astrologer and mathematician Jean Taisnier (1508–1562) in his text *Astrologiae iudiciariae ysagogica, et totius divinatricis artis encomia* (1559).[33] Taisnier's offers not a table, but a list of scorings in a section of the treatise discussing the various dignities, debilities, and planetary conditions. He closely follows Schöner's table rather than Lvovický's. Indeed, the entire section is quite similar to the *Opusculum*, further indicating that Taisnier sourced his table directly from Schöner's text. His listing of dignities is not as organised as in the previous authors. It is incomplete, presents some printing errors in the glyphs, and does not display the usual strength-debility mirroring. For example, it lacks

---

& omnes aspectus bonorum planetarum, & per bonos aspectus mediocrium Planetarum, cum eade[m] loca aspiciunt uel ♂ illis fuerint ex medietate, uel intra medietates orbium eorum, ut si 14 ♉ esset cuspis secunda domus figurae coeli, & ♃ in 23 ♉. Sic ♃ per sua praesentia in secu[n]da domo, ex medietate orbis sui, qui est 9 graduum, fortunaret cuspidem secunda domus. Hoc idem etiam faceret in quolibet gradu intermedio. Sic pari uia aspectus oserua[n]di, ut sit 14 ♉, ut prius cuspis secundae domus, & ♃ in 23 gradu ♍, aspiciens cuspidem △, ex medietate orbis sui, q[ue]m sic fortunaret culpidem secunda, sic etia[m] in quolibet gradu intermedio sub medietate orbis sui. Isto modo intellige etiam infortunationes & damnationes praedictoru[m] locorum. Nam mali planetae per ♂ ☍ & □, & mediocres planeta per eorum ☍ & □, infortunant loca planetarum bonorum, & cuspides domorum, ac partes significatorum ex medietare, & intra medietates orbium eoru[m]. ☌ cum sua praesentia, fortunat & augmentat, quemlibet locum in quo est. Quare bonum cum bonis, & malum cum malis, sicut ☋. ☊ infortunat & minuit, quare bona cum malis, & cum bonis mala. Schöner, *Opusculum Astrologicum*, fol. I.

32 Giovanni Battista Carelli, *Ephemerides Io. Baptistae Carelli Placentini ad annos XVIII incipientes ab anno Christi* MDLXIII *usque ad annum* MDLXXX. *Meridiano inclitae vrbis Venetiarum diligentissime supputatae* (Venice: Vincentium Valgrisium, & haeredes Baldassaris Constantini, 1558), fig. C 2ʳ.

33 Joannes Taisnier, *Astrologiae ivdiciariae ysagogica et totius divinatricis artis encomia, cum nonnullis Habrahami Iudęi et Lucae Gaurici dictis* (Cologne: Arnold Birckmann, 1559). Later reproduced in his *Opus Mathematicum octo libros complectens* (Cologne: apud Ioannem Birckmannum & Wernerum Richsimom, 1562).

the house's strengths despite listing the corresponding debilities. However, in explaining the various planetary conditions in the following chapter, Taisnier again offers points of dignity and debility. Despite its inconsistencies and lacunae, the full text allows an approximate reconstruction of his scoring system (see table 12.6, below).

Taisnier does not have a specific section discussing the lord of the geniture and its calculation. However, he appears to follow the same idea as Lvovický. Just before he discusses the planetary strengths, he states:

> Therefore, each place and the rulers of the domains of the places are examined individually, proceeding from the horoscope through the succession of the 12 houses, for it matters greatly in which places, houses, and zodiac signs the planets shine upon themselves with various aspects, so that a true judgment may be made. Therefore, it is fundamental to note the dignities and debilities of the planets so that the one who is more dignified and powerful in dignities may be recognised in the governance and rule of the native.[34]

His statement is not conclusive as to the method he used, but it does suggest that he considers the strongest planet to be the ruler of the nativity, like Lvovický. Afterwards, he confirms this by saying that the most dignified planet becomes the lord of the geniture, which he names as the rector of the figure or ruler of the native (*rector thematis & nati dominator*):

> A planet that holds several of these dignities in the natal chart is the ruler of the chart and the master of the native, who often follows and is inclined toward its nature. However, a planet disturbed by debilities brings nothing good to the native.[35]

---

34   Examinanda igitur sunt sigillatim quelibet loca & locorum dominia possessores ab horoscopo per 12 domorum successionem procedendo, multum enim re fert quibus locis ac? domibus zodiacique signis planeta diuersis aspectibus sese irradiant, ut verum fiat iudicium. Imprimis ergo notanda sunt planetarum dignitates & debilitates, ut dignior & potentior in dignitatibus in gubernatione & regimine nati dinoscatur. Taisnier, *Astrologiae ivdiciariae ysagogica*, fol. C4ʳ.

35   Planeta in natalicio themate plures ex his obtinens dignitates, rector est thematis & nati dominator, qui illius naturam non rarò sequitur & inclinatur, planeta vero debilitatibus turbatus, nato nil boni confert. Taisnier, fig. C4ᵛ.

TABLE 12.6 Planetary strengths and debilities by Jean Taisnier (1559)

Strengths		Debilities	
5	*First or tenth house*	5	Twelfth house
4	*Seventh or fourth house*	4	Eighth house
3	*Eleventh or fifth house*	3	Sixth house
2	*Nineth or third house*	2	Second house
5	Domicile	5	Seventh house from planet's domicile, i.e. detriment
4	Exaltation	4	Seventh house from planet's exaltation, i.e. fall
3	Triplicity	5	Peregrine
2	Term		
1	Face		
3	Joy by sign		
5	Received [mutually by domicile?][36]		
5	Cazimi	5	Combust by the Sun [*6 debilities in later explanation*]
		4	Under the rays outside combustion
5	Between the two benefics	5	Besiedge between two malefics
5	Conjunction *with Jupiter or Venus*	3	Application to a malefic
4	Application *by trine to Jupiter or Venus*	5	Bodily ♂ with a malefic
3	*Application by sextile with Jupiter or Venus*	4	Application with malefic by ☍
5	Conjunct a star of its nature / *of a benefic nature*	5	Bodily application to a star of malefic nature
		3	Conjunction with ☋
		5	♂ ☊
		2	Void of course
		3	Feral
3	Joy by house		
1	In lucid degree	3	In void or smoky degrees
1	In degree of increasing fortune	3	In dark, pitted, or azemene degrees
1	In degree of the same gender		
2	Orientality of the three superior	2	*Occidentality of the three superiors*
2	*Occidentality of the inferiors*	2	Orientality of the inferiors
3	Haiz	2	Contrarity of Haiz
2	Conformity of quadrant		
5	Security		
4	Direct	5	Retrograde
1	Fast	1	Slow
1	Increasing in light	1	Decreasing in light
1	Increasing in number	1	Decreasing in number
2	Ascending in the circle of its auge	2	Descending in the circle of its auge
2	Ascending in northern [latitude?]	2	Descendign to southern [latitude?]

36   He is not clear as to scoring in his explanation.

TABLE 12.6   Planetary strengths and debilities by Jean Taisnier (1559) (*cont.*)

Strengths	Debilities
	2 Via combusta [any planet]
	5 Eclipse of the luminaries
	2 ☽ in ♊ or at the end of the sign in terms of a malefic
	4 Luminary in the terms of an eclipse
	4 ☽ going to combustion under 12°

By 1563, Giuseppe Moletti (1531–1588) published a table of strengths and debilities of the planets in his ephemeris. This version is identical to Schöner's and Taisnier's but in Italian.[37] However, he does not mention its use in calculating the lord of the geniture.

Ten years later, a version close to that of Lvovický's table appears in the work of another influential author for late sixteenth-century astrology, Francesco Giuntini (1523–1590). In his popular *Speculum astrologiae* (1573), he offers a list of scores of planetary strengths and debilities identical to Lvovický's, excluding the conjunction with lunar nodes, which is absent.[38] Like Lvovický, Giuntini also includes the table with the scoring for the Part of Fortune..[39] Lvovický's table appears again in Henri de Lintaut (fl. 17th century) in his *Introductio in physicam iudiciariam* (1597) with no changes, while in 1589, the ephemeris by Giuseppe Scala (1556–1585) offers a copy of Schöner's table.[40]

In 1598 the table appeared in English in a translation of Claude Dariot's (1533–1594) *Ad astrorum judicia facilis introductio* (1557).[41] Although the original Latin text does not include the table, the translation offers a mixed version

---

37   Giuseppe Moleti, *L'efemeridi di m. Gioseppe Moleto matematico*. (Venice: appresso Vincenzo Valgrisio, 1563), 175.

38   Francesco Giuntini, *Speculum Astrologiae, quod attinet ad iudiciariam rationem natiuitatum atque annuarum reuolutionum, cum nonnullis approbatis astrologorum sententiis* (Lyon: Philippi Tinghi Florentini, 1573), 215ᵛ–216.

39   Giuntini, fol. 216ᵛ. These tables also appear in different formatting in the 1580 edition of the *Speculum*—Francesco Giuntini, *Speculum Astrologiae universam mathematicam scientiam in certas classes digestam complectens* (Florence: Phil. Tinghius, 1581), 1146–1147.

40   Henricus a Lindhout, *Introductio in physicam iudiciariam* (Hamburg: Philippum de Ohr, 1597), 117–118; Giuseppe Scala, *Ephemerides Iosephi Scalae Siculi Noetini Art. & Med. Doc. Ad annos duodecim, incipientes ab anno Domini 1589*. (Venice: appresso i Giunti, 1589), 83.

41   Claude Dariot, *Ad astrorum iudicia facilis introductio* (Lugduni: Apud Mauricium Roy & Ludouicum Pesnot, 1557).

of Schöner's and Lvovický's tables, including some unique elements such as application to a benefic planet and being in terms of a malefic. The edition also includes a shorter version of the table for the Part of Fortune from Lvovický. The translator likely introduced this unusual combination.[42]

Considering the evidence, it becomes clear that, by the end of the sixteenth century, there were two versions of the table of planetary strengths and debilities in circulation: one based on Schöner's *Opusculum* and another proposed by Lvovický in his *Ephemeridum nouum opus*. Schöner's table, based on Regiomontanus's notes and allegedly based on Montulmo, includes more conditions and has a more medieval tone. It includes astronomical conditions such as rising or decreasing in number or in its auge and more specialised degrees, dark, void, masculine, feminine, etc., which are less used in everyday practice.

Lvovický's table, although based on the same principles and scoring values, offers a more abridged version which focuses on the fundamental conditions, such as essential dignities, house position, aspects, orientality, etc. In a certain sense, it is more modern than Schöner's.

5   Variation and Continuity

At the end of the century, David Origanus (David Tost, 1558–1628), another very influential author, published his ephemeris, which included a complete introduction to astrology entitled *De effectibus*.[43] Here, Origanus offers a list of planetary strengths and debilities, following, for the most part, Lvovický's fundamental scoring rationale. The exception is the scoring of planetary aspects, where he expands the scoring by attributing numerical values to all aspects and not just the easy aspects from the benefics and the hard aspects from the malefics.[44]

His following of Lvovický's table becomes more evident when he discusses the computation of the lord of the geniture. Like his predecessors, he begins by introducing the ideas of the ancients (i.e., the Greeks) and offering the

---

42   Claude Dariot, *A Briefe and Most Easie Introduction to the Astrologicall Iudgement of the Starres Whereby the Diligent Reader with Easie Laboure May Giue a Certen, True, and Determinate Iudgement to Any Question Demanded, Vpon the Naturall Causes Thereof.* (London: Printed by Thomas Purfoot, 1598), fol. K 1ʳ⁻ᵛ.

43   David Origanus, *Ephemerides Novae Annorum XXXVI, Incipientes Ab Anno Chrisogeneseos 1595, Quo Ioannis Stadii Maxime Aberrare Incipiunt, & Desinentes in Annum 1630* (Frankfurt (Oder): Andreae Eichornii, 1599).

44   Origanus, 267–270.

TABLE 12.7 Planetary strengths and debilities by David Origanus (1599)

	Strengths		Debilities
5	Domicile	5	Exile
4	Exaltation	4	Fall
3	Triplicity	5	Peregrine
2	Term		
1	Face		
1	Joy by sign		
5	Mutual reception by domicile		
4	Mutual reception by exaltation		
5	Cazimi or heart of the Sun	5	Combust
5	Free from combustion and rays	4	Under the rays
2	Moon increasing in light	2	Moon decreasing in light
2	Orientality of the three superior planets	2	Occidentality of the superiors
2	Occidentality if the inferior planets	2	Orientality of the inferiors
4	Direct	5	Retrograde
2	Fast	2	Slow
5	Conjunction with ♃ or ♀	5	Conjunction with ♄ or ♂
		5	☽ ☌ ♂
4	☌ ♃☉, ♃☿, ♃☽, ☉♀, ☿♀, ♀☽	4	☌ ♄☉, ♂☉, ♄☽, ☉☽
3	☌ ☿☽	3	☌ ☉☿
1	☌ ♃♂, ♃♄, ♂♀	1	☌ ♄♀, ♄☿, ♂☿
4	△ ♃♀	4	□ ♄♂, ☽♂
3	△ ♃☿, ♀☿, ☉♃, ☉♀ [sic], ♃☽	3	□ ☉☽, ♄☉, ♂☉
2	△ ☿☽, ♄♀, ♀☽	2	□ ♄☽, ☉☿ [sic]
1	△ ♃♂, ♃♄, ♂♀, ♄☽	1	□ ☽☿
3	⚹ ♃♀	4	☍ ☉☽
2	⚹ ♃☿, ♀☿, ☉♃, ☉♀ [sic], ♃☽	3	☍ ♄♂
1	⚹ ☿☽, ☉☽	2	☍ ♄☿, ♂☽
6	Conjunct Regulus (5° before or after)	5	Conjunct Algol
5	Conjunct Spica (5° before or after)		
5	In the midheaven or ascendant	5	In the 12th house
4	In the 7th, 4th, or 11th	4	In the 8th or 6th
3	In the 2nd or 5th		
2	In the 9th		
1	In the 3rd		

example of Firmicus Maternus. Then, he addresses the leading opinions of the astrologers:

> II. The common opinion among astrologers is that the ruler of the nativity is the planet that is the lord or almuten of the Ascendant.
>
> III. Most of the more recent authorities follow Ptolemy, who, in Book 3 of the *Tetrabiblos*, chooses the ruler of the nativity from five *hylegical* or life-giving points. The planet that holds the most essential dignities in the Ascendant, the Midheaven, the position of the Sun, the position of the Moon, and the Part of Fortune is to be established as the ruler of the nativity. However, the one with the next highest dignities will share in this rulership. If two or three planets have an equal number of dignities, all of them will be considered rulers of the nativity.
>
> IV. Cyprian Leovitius assigns as the ruler of the nativity that planet which, in terms of essential dignities, is more powerful than the others and at the same time holds the most dignified position in the chart.
>
> However, if no single planet possesses both conditions—namely, surpassing the others in essential dignity and occupying the most powerful position in the heavens—preference should be given to the one superior in essential dignities. Yet, the planet holding a stronger position in the chart should also be considered.
>
> It is probable and entirely reasonable that the one excelling in multiple positional strengths and dignities is preferable to another planet with only one advantage, even if that planet surpasses others in a single respect. This is because it may be significantly weaker than the other planets in other dignities and conditions. The planet that is most potent and well-positioned at the root (i.e., in the nativity) will exert its influence more evidently on the native than one with weaker powers.
>
> Which planet is the most powerful in the chart is determined by collecting the testimonies of each planet, as discussed in the previous chapter. The order of houses to determine which planet is strongest in terms of celestial position is as follows: 10, 1, 11, 7, 4, 5, 2, 9, 3, 8, 6, 12. For example, the 10th house takes precedence over the 1st, the 1st over the 11th, and so on.
>
> V. In this diversity of opinion, we consider it safest to choose two rulers of the nativity: first, the ruler of the ascendant, according to the common method; second, the most fortunate and prosperous planet in the nativity, according to the method of Cyprian.[45]

---

45   II. Vulgus Asrologorum dominum geniturae existimat illum esse, qui & Dominus seu almuten est horoscopi.

Thus, not only does Origanus support the concept of the overall strongest planet in an astrological figure proposed by Lvovický, but it also reconciles this with the usual importance given to the ruler of the ascendant. This endorsement of Lvovický's ideas is further supported by his promotion of Lvovický's table for the Part of Fortune, like Giunctini.

In the seventeenth century, the table became a frequent feature in astrological treatises. Generally speaking, the simpler and more modern version proposed by Lvovický became the standard model, although with some changes. While the complex scoring of the aspects proposed by Origanus does not seem to have continued in subsequent authors' tables, it does appear to have had some acceptance from practitioners, as testified by some astrologer's notes, the most famous of which are those of Galileo Galilei.[46]

In this example, regarding the nativity of his daughter Virginia (1600–1634), Galileo weighed the strengths and weaknesses of all seven planets, including scores for planetary aspects as observed in Origanus's table (Figure 12.6).[47]

III. Recentiores plerique Ptolomaeum sequuntur, qui lib. 3 quadrip. eligit Dominum geniturae ex quinque locis hylegialibus seu Apheticis. Qui enim plurimas dignitates essentiales habuerit in ascendente, Medio caeli, loco solis, loco lunam, & loco fortuna is geniturae Dominus constituendus erit. Particeps autem dominii erit qui proximas dignitates possederit. Quod si duo aut tres pari numero dignitates habeant, hi omnes Domini nativitatis dicentur.

IV. Cyprianus Leouicius eum Planetam dominio geniturae praeficit, qui & respectu et essentialium dignitatum reliquis potentior est, & simul locum in figura dignissimum obtinet.

Quod si veró uni alicui planeta hac duo simul non accidant, ut videlicet & valore ex dignitatibus essentialibus contracto, reliquos vincat & superet, & simul coeli locum potentiorem occupet, praeferendus quidem reliquum omnibus erit, qui essentialibus dignitatibus alios antecellit: sed tamen ipsi in hoc munere associandus est, qui respectu loci figurae caelestum potentior existit. Probabile est enim, & omnino verissimile, eum qui in pluribus loci viribus plus valet, & dignitate praeferendum esse ei qui unica tantum praerogativa caeteros anteit: ubi fieri potest, ut aliis dignitatibus & dispositionibus caeteris planetis longe sit inferior. Qui enim reliquis potentissimus est in radice, & optime constitutus, manifestius suas vires in natum exerit, quam alius, cuius vires debiliores suns. Quis autem Planeta sit in themate potentissimus, cognoscitur ex collectione testimoniorum singulorum planetarum, de qua praecedenti capite monuimus. Ordo verò locorun, unde qui Planeta respectu loci figurae coelestis potentior sit, cognoscitur, hic est: 10, 1, 11, 7, 4, 5, 2, 9, 3, 8, 6, 12. Praefertur enim domus 10 prima, prima undecimae, &c.

v. Nos in hac opinionum diversitate, tutissimum esse judicamus, si duos nativitatis dominos eligamus: Primo quidem dominum horoscopi, juxta modum vulgarem, alterum felicissimum & fortunatissimum in nativitate juxta modum Cypriani. Origanus, 328–329.

46   For example, in Galileo Galilei's 'Astrological Nonnulla', Florence, Biblioteca nazionale centrale, Ms Gal. 81, fols. 4, 13, 23 (among others).

47   Ms Gal. 81, fol. 25r

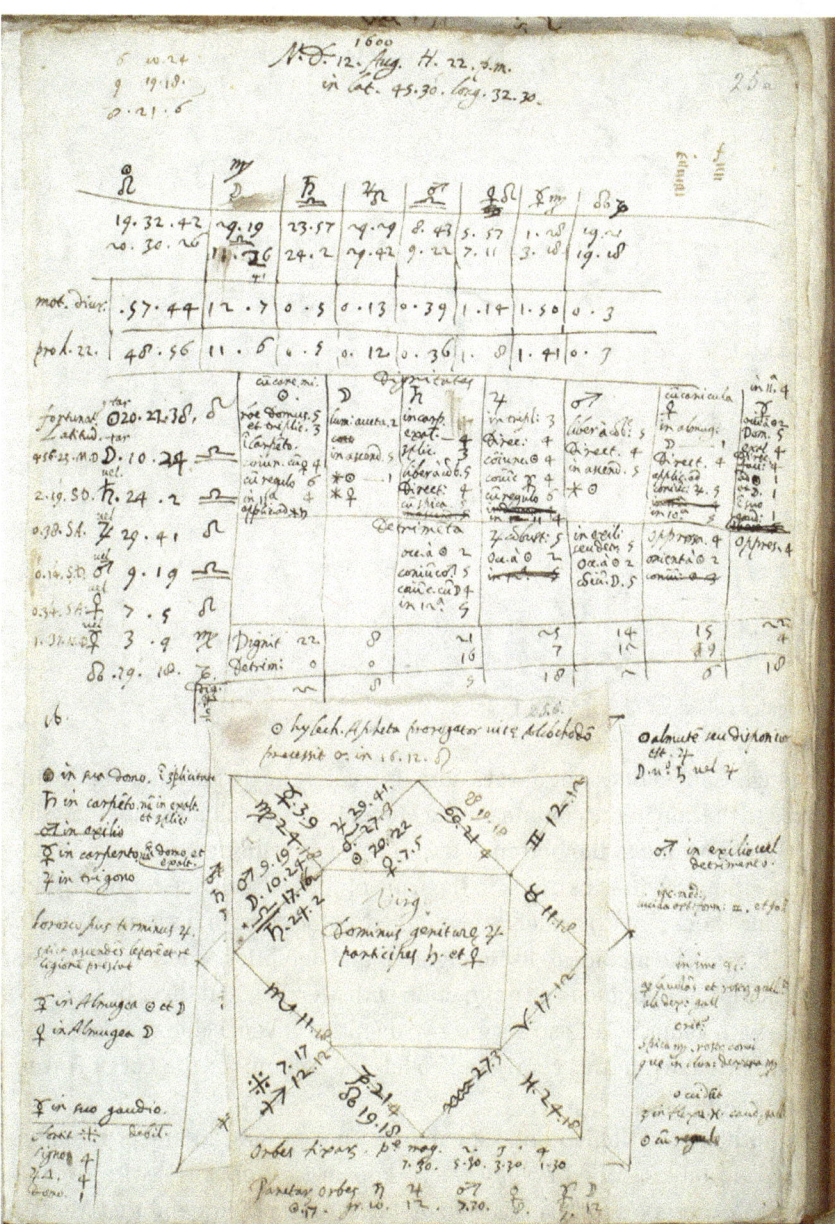

FIGURE 12.6 Galileo's chart for Virginia, Ms Gal. 81, fol. 25ʳ

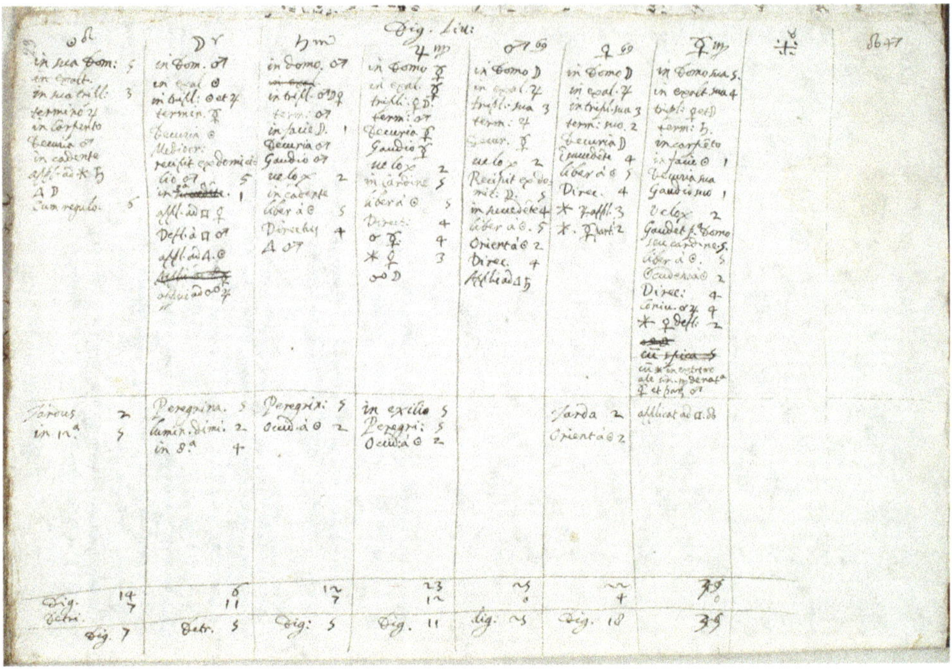

FIGURE 12.7 Galileo's chart for Livia, Ms Gal. 81, fol. 23ʳ

Although Galileo does not always note the scores, he assigns one dignity to a sextile to the Sun in the column for the Moon. He also evaluates the strength of the Lot of Fortune at the bottom left of the page, awarding it four dignities by sign position (Sagittarius), four to the trine of Jupiter, and one for house position (third house), with no debilities marked. In the chart of his other daughter, Livia (b. 1601), he includes a list of dignities and debilities, where he notes four dignities for Jupiter due to a conjunction with Mercury, and three because of a sextile with Venus.[48] He also assigns two dignities to Venus due to a partile sextile with Mercury. In this chart, Galileo left the column for the Lot of Fortune blank (Figure 12.7).

In both charts, Galileo notes a condition not present in any of the aforementioned tables, called *almugea*, also known as Proper Face. In Virginia's nativity, he observes that Venus is in *almugea* to the Moon and that Mercury is in *almugea* to both the Sun and the Moon (noted in the table and on to the left of the figure). In Livia's table, he notes that Mercury is in *almugea* to the Sun, while Saturn is in *almugea* to the Moon. This condition is scored with one dignity.

---

48   Ms Gal. 81, fol. 23ʳ

In 1607 Christoph Pezel's (1539–1604) *Precepta genethliaca* of 1607 lists this same condition giving it the same score.[49] Pezel also offers the table for the Part of Fortune, which he states is to be applied to the house cusps. Like Origanus before, he favours the use of the table to access the lord of the geniture. Curiously enough, he also makes an observation that helps to understand why the method of the *hylegical* point was put aside in favour of the new method:

> The Arabs, followed by many contemporary astrologers, determine the ruler of the nativity from five hylegical points: the Ascendant, the position of the Sun, the position of the Moon, the Part of Fortune, and the place of the preceding conjunction or opposition. The planet that has the most essential dignities in these five points is declared the ruler of the nativity.
>
> We, however, believe this method of selecting the ruler of the nativity to be the strongest of all, as it relies on more probable causes aligned with natural principles. Therefore, the planet that is the strongest in essential dignities and simultaneously occupies the best position in the sky should be established as the ruler of the nativity.[50]

Since the *hylegical* points method was attributed to the Arabs, the reluctance of early modern authors regarding Arabic authors and the search for natural causes for astrology might have been behind the abandonment of the older method.

---

49   Christoph Pezel, *D. Christophori Pezelii Praecepta genethliaca siue de prognosticandis hominum natiuitatibus commentarius eruditissimus, in quo non solum astrologiae praecepta & certa istius fundamenta demonstrantur, verum etiam varii casus, historiae, euentus & exempla lepidissima proponuntur. Omnibus et singulis cuiuscunque facultatis studiosis lectu iucundus & scitu necessarius* (Frankfurt: typis Wolfgangi Richteri, impensis Johan. Thebaldi Schonvvetteri & Cunradi Meulii, consortorum, 1607), 47–49.

50   Arabes vero, quos multi hoc tempore Astrologi [sic] sequuntur, Dominum genituræ ex quinque locis Hylegialibus (de quibus paulo post dicemus) nativitatis extrahunt, videlicet ex ascendente seu horoscopo, ex loco Solis, ex loco Lunæ, ex loco Fortunæ, & ex loco conjunctionis aut oppositionis nativitatem proxime præcedentis. Quicunque igitur plures dignitates essentiales in his quinque locis obtinuerit, illum genituræ dominum esse pronunciant. Nos vero eam rationem eligendi Dominum genituræ reliquis omnibus firmiorem credimus, quæ probabilioribus causis cum ipsa natura congruentibus nititur. Atque hac ratione is Planeta Dominus genituræ constituendus est, qui respectu dignitatum essentialium fortior est reliquis, & simul cæli locum optimum occupat. Pezel, fol. G 3^r.

TABLE 12.8   Planetary Strengths and Debilities by Christoph Pezel (1607)

	Strengths		Debilities
5	In domicile or [mutual] reception by domicile	5	In its detriment
4	In exaltation or mutual] reception by exaltation	4	In fall
3	In triplicity and participation	5	Peregrine
2	In term		
1	In joy (by sign)		
1	In Almugea of either ☽ or ☉		
5	In the Midheaven or 10th house		
5	In the Horoscope (Ascendant / 1st house)	5	In the 12th house
4	In the 7th or 4th house	4	In the 8th or 6th house
3	In the 5th or 11th house		
2	In the 2nd or 9th house		
1	In the 3rd house		
5	In Cazimi	5	Combust
5	Free from combustion or rays	4	Under the rays ☉
4	Direct	5	Retrograde
2	Fast	2	Slow
2	Oriental	2	Occidental
2	☽ increasing in light	2	☽ decreasing in light
5	Partile ☌ ♃ or ♀	5	Partile ☌ ♄ or ♂
4	Partile ☌ ☊	4	Partile ☌ ☋
		5	Besiedged by ♄ and ♂
4	Partile △ ♃ or ♀	4	Partile ☍ ♄ or ♂
3	Partile ✶ ♃ or ♀	2	Partile □ ♄ or ♂
5	☌ with Regulus (5° before or after)	5	☌ with Algol (5° before or after)
5	☌ with Spica ♍ (5° before or after)		

Redento Baranzano (Giovanni Antonio Baranzano 1590–1622), in his *Urano-scopia* (1617), also favours the strongest planet in the chart as the lord of the geniture. He offers a list similar to Pezel's, but with some modifications in the scoring, as well as the list for Part of Fortune and house cusps.[51]

---

51   Redento Baranzano, *Uranoscopia, seu de Coelo* (Genève: apud Petrum & Jacobum Chouët, 1617), 66–71.

In the first half of the seventeenth century, the table appears in several vernacular astrological texts. In 1624, Antoine de Villon (fl. 1620s) offered the table in French with the same features as Lvovický's, including the table for the Part of Fortune, although with some differences in the scoring.[52]

The table was published in Spanish in 1632 by Portuguese author António de Najera (fl. 1630s) in *Summa astrologica*.[53] His table also follows Lvovický's for the most part, but includes several elements from Schöner's table: the dignities of Joy by sign, joy by house, *haiz*, conformity of quarter, *ductoria*, ascending in its auge, ascending to a northern latitude, and the debilities of void of course, feral, contrariety of *haiz*, descension in its auge, descension to mid-day, *via combusta*, eclipses of the luminaries, the Moon in Gemini or at the end of the signs, and luminaries in the bounds of eclipses.[54] These additions are enough to make it a hybrid version. A copy of this table can be found in the manuscript lessons of Luís Gonzaga SJ (1666–1747) written in 1702.[55] Earlier, however, other tables were considered by Portuguese astrologers such as João Delgado SJ (1553–1612), who, in 1607, offered his students the table by Origanus. He considered the lord of the geniture to be the planet with the greatest strength, but in the case of a close scoring, he gave precedence to the planet that also had the most significant number of essential dignities in the five *hylegical* places, showing that the older method still had some validity among practitioners.[56]

In 1647, the table appeared again in English in William Lilly's (1602–1681) influential *Christian Astrology*, but he closely followed Lvovický's version instead of Schöner's.[57] Lilly also includes the table for the Part of Fortune. This same model of the table was followed by subsequent English authors such as Henry Coley (1633–1704), John Gadbury (1627–1704), and William Ramesey (1627–c.1676).[58]

---

52   Antoine de Villon, *L'usage des éphémérides, avec la méthode de dresser et corriger toute sorte de figures coelestes et juger par le moyen d'icelles des diverses constitutions des temps et saisons de l'Annee, et de toutes les autres choses qui en dépendent*, vol. 2 (Paris: Iean Moreau, 1624), 517–528.

53   Antonio de Najera, *Summa astrologica y arte para enseñar hazer pronosticos de los tiempos* (Lisboa: Antonio Alvarez, 1632).

54   Najera, 99–100.

55   Ribeiro, *Jesuit Astrology*, 479–480.

56   Ribeiro, 450–451.

57   William Lilly, *Christian Astrology Modestly Treated in Three Books*, 1st ed. (London: Tho. Brudenelle, 1647).

58   William Ramesey, *Astrologia Restaurata or, Astrologie Restored* (London: Robert White, 1653), 66–67; John Gadbury, *Genethlialogia, or, The Doctrine of Nativities Containing the Whole Art of Directions and Annual Revolutions* (London: Ja. Cottrel, 1658), 88–89; Henry Coley, *Clavis Astrologiæ Elimata, or, A Key to the Whole Art of Astrologie New Filed and Polished in Three Parts*. (London: Benj. Tooke and The Sawbridge, 1676), 88–89.

TABLE 12.9   Planetary strengths and debilities by Antonio de Najera (1632)

	Strengths		Debilities
5	First or tenth house	5	Twelfth house
4	Seventh, fourth or elevent house	4	Eighth house
3	Second or fifth house	3	Sixth house
2	Nineth house		
1	Third house		
5	In domicile or mutual reception by domicile	5	Detriment
4	In exaltation or mutual receptios by exaltation	4	Fall
3	Triplicity	5	Peregrine
2	Term		
1	Face		
5	Cazimi	5	Combustion
5	Free from combustion and beams	4	Under the Sun's beams
5	Conjunction with benefic		
4	Application by trine to benefic		
3	Application by sextile to benefic	3	Application to malefic by opposition
3	Joy by sign		
3	Joy by house		
2	Orientality of the superiors	2	Occidentality of the superiors
2	Occidentality of the inferiors	2	Orientality of the inferiors
3	Haiz	2	Contrary of Haiz
2	Conformity of quadrant		
5	*Ductoria* or Security		
4	Direct	5	Retrograde
1	Fast	1	Slow
1	Moon increasing in light	1	Moon decreasing in light
2	Ascending in the circle of its auge	2	Descending in the circle of its auge
2	Ascending in northern latitude	2	Descending to southern latitude
5	Assistence between the two benefics	5	Besieged between two malefics
		2	Void of course
		3	Feral
		5	Eclipse of the luminaries
		2	Moon in Gemini or at the end of the sign in terms of a malefic
		4	Luminary in the terms of an eclipse
		4	Moon going to combustion under 12°

TABLE 12.9 Planetary strengths and debilities by Antonio de Najera (1632) (*cont.*)

Strengths	Debilities
	2 Via combusta
5 Conjunction with Regulus (5° before or after)	5 Conjunction with Algol (5° before or after)
5 Conjunction with Spica (5° before or after)	

6   Final Considerations

From its origin and in the latter examples the table of planetary strengths follows the same scheme. It combines both essential and accidental states of the
planets, offering a scoring from one to five, occasionally six (usually applied to
the conjunction with Regulus and the debility of combustion), and rarely zero
(i.e. a condition that gives neither strength nor debility). The different conditions of strength and debility are grouped according to their type. Thus, essential dignities come together in the list, as well as house placement, aspects,
position regarding the Sun, movement, and others. However, this grouping is
not always consistent in the various authors. The groups do not appear in the
same sequence in different tables, and often, some conditions are outside their
expected group. Usually, the conditions of strength are listed side by side with
their counterpart debilities, when such equivalence exists. Yet, some authors
provide two separate lists, one with the planetary strengths and another with
the debilities. This appears to be mostly conditioned by the printing process.

The grouping of planetary conditions by type, as displayed in the table, is not
in itself an innovation. Many medieval sources present them in such a fashion.
Popular medieval texts such as The *Great Introduction* by Albumasar and The
Introduction by Alcabitius discuss the various essential and accidental conditions defining each according to type. In part seven of the *Great Introduction*,
Albumasar explains the various conditions (chapters one to five), and then in
chapter six, he lists the main strengths and weaknesses of the planets, including
many of the conditions mentioned in the Montulmo/Regiomontanus/Schöner
table.[59] There are, however, no numerical values attributed to the planetary
strengths, at least not in such a systematic and comprehensive way. The scorings offered by medieval authors such as Abraham Ibn Ezra not only follow a

---

59   Abū Ma'šar, *The Great Introduction to Astrology*, 1:787–793.

different rationale but also do not seem to have been so widely applied, except in specific computations such as the almuten of the figure. With respect to the conditions of strength and debility, their grouping, and classification, the table is clearly a derivative work of such texts, only innovating by attributing a numeric value to the accidental conditions in a similar fashion to that of essential dignities.

Although its exact origin is not completely clear, this innovation is concurrent with a time when natural and mathematical thinking was being increasingly valued. Therefore, this mathematical approach to the determination of planetary strength was quickly accepted by most authors, giving rise to a complete transformation in the method of computation of the lord of the geniture, a planet which had profound signification over the native's life. Another of its appeals was likely the fact that such a table contributed, at least in theory, to a uniformity of practice needed to counter several of the anti-astrological arguments.

The creation of this method is not the only example of the transformation of astrology in the early modern period. The new mathematical complexity of prediction methods, both in nativities and general affairs, the search for precise tables and the methodology for determining the native's temperament are other examples. Nonetheless, something so essential as the measure of planetary effectiveness and strength provides an excellent example of the attempts by practitioners of this period to make astrology more rational and scientific.

CAMPOS RIBEIRO

TABLE 12.10   Planetary conditions and their scoring in different authors

	Johannes Schöner (1539)	Cyprián Lvovický (1557)	Giovanni B. Carelli (1558)	Jean Taisnier (1559)	Giuseppe Moletti (1563)	Francesco Giuntini (1573)
DIGNITIES						
First house	5	5	5	5	5	5
Tenth house	5	5	5	5	5	5
Seventh house	4	4	4	4	4	4
Fourth house	4	4	4	4	4	4
Eleventh house	3	4	3	3	3	4
Fifth house	3	3	3	3	3	3
Second house	[deb.]	3	[deb.]	[deb.]	[deb.]	3
Ninth house	2	2	2	2	–	2
Third house	1	2	1	2	1	1
Domicile	5	5	5	5	5	5
Exaltation	4	4	4	4	4	4
Triplicity	3	3	3	3	3	3
Term	2	2	2	2	2	2
Face	1	1	1	1	1	1
Reception by domicile	–	5	–	–	–	5
Reception by exaltation	–	4	–	–	–	4
Reception (not specified)	5	–	5	5	5	–
Joy by sign	3	–	3	3	3	–
Joy by house	2	–	2	3	2	–
Almugea of Sun or Moon	–	–	–	–	–	–
Cazimi	5	5	5	5	5	5
Free of combustion and beams	–	5	–	–	–	5
Conjunction with benefics [partile for some]	5	5	5	5	5	5
Application with a benefic by △ [partile to some]	4	–	4	4	4	–
△ ♃ or ♀ [partile for some]	–	4	–	–	–	4
Application with a benefic by ✶ [partile to some]	3	–	3	3	3	–
✶ ♃ or ♀ [partile to some]	–	3	–	–	–	3
Between two benefic planets (assistance)	5	–	5	5	5	–
Application to benefic	–	–	–	–	–	–
♂ ☌	[deb.]	3	[deb.]	[deb.]	[deb.]	–
♂ ♃☉, ♃♂, ♃☽, ☉♀, ☿♀, ♀☽	–	–	–	–	–	–
♂ ☿☽	–	–	–	–	–	–
♂ ♃♂, ♃♄, ♂♀	–	–	–	–	–	–
△ ♃♂, ♀♂, ☉♃, ♃☽	–	–	–	–	–	–

Claude Dariot (1598)	David Origanus (1599)	Christoph Pezel (1601)	Redento Baranzano (1617)	Antoine de Villon (1624)	António de Najera (1632)	William Lilly (1647)
5	5	5	3 [?]	5	5	5
5	5	5	5	5	5	5
4	4	4	4	4	4	4
4	4	4	4	4	4	4
4	4	3	3	4	4	4
3	3	3	3	3	3	3
3	3	2	2	3	3	3
2	2	2	2	2	2	2
1	1	1	1	1	1	1
5	5	5	5	5	5	5
4	4	4	4	5	4	4
3	3	3	3	3	3	3
2	2	2	2	2	2	2
1	1	1	1	1	1	1
5	5	5	5	5	5	5
4	4	4	4	5	4	4
–	–	–	–	–	–	-
3	1	1	1	–	3	-
3	–	–	–	–	3	-
–	–	1	1	–	–	-
5	5	5	5	5	5	5
5	5	5	5	5	5	5
5	5	5	5	5	5	5
–	–	–	–	–	4	-
4	4	4	3	4	–	4
–	–	–	–	–	3	-
3	3	3	–	3	–	3
5	–	–	–	–	5	-
3	–	–	–	–	–	-
3	–	4	4	4	–	4
–	4	–	–	–	–	-
–	3	–	–	–	–	-
–	1	–	–	–	–	-
–	3	–	–	–	–	-

TABLE 12.10   Planetary conditions and their scoring in different authors (*cont.*)

	Johannes Schöner (1539)	Cyprián Lvovický (1557)	Giovanni B. Carelli (1558)	Jean Taisnier (1559)	Giuseppe Moletti (1563)	Francesco Giuntini (1573)
DIGNITIES						
△ ☿☽, ♄♀, ♀☽	–	–	–	–	–	–
△ ♃♂, ♃♄, ♂♀, ♄☽	–	–	–	–	–	–
✶ ♃♀, ♀♀, ☉♃, ♃☽	–	–	–	–	–	–
✶ ☿☽, ☉☽	–	–	–	–	–	–
Orientality of superiors	2	2	2	2	2	2
Occidentality of inferiors	2	2	2	2	2	2
Oriental	–	–	–	–	–	–
Hayz	3	–	3	3	3	–
Conformity of quarter	2	–	2	2	2	–
Security or dustoria	5	–	5	5	5	–
Direct	4	4	4	4	4	4
Fast	1	2	1	1	1	2
Increasing in light	1	–	1	1	1	–
Moon increasing in light	–	2	–	–	–	2
Increasing in number	1	–	1	1	1	–
Ascending in the circle of its auge	2	–	2	2	2	–
Ascending to north in Lat.	2	–	2	2	2	–
Light degree	1	–	1	1	–	–
Degree of increasing fortune	1	–	1	1	–	–
Degree of the same gender	1	–	1	1	–	–
Conjunction with a benefic star	5	–	5	?	5	–
Conjunction with a star of its nature	–	–	–	5	–	–
Conjunction with Regulus	–	6	–	–	–	6
Conjunction with Spica	–	5	–	–	–	5
DEBILITIES						
Twelve house	5	5	5	5	5	5
Eight house	4	4	4	4	4	4
Sixth house	3	4	3	3	3	4
Second house	2	–	2	2	2	[dig.]
Exile or detriment	2	5	2	5	2	5
Fall	5	4	–	4	5	4
Peregrine	5	5	5	5	5	5
Combustion.	6	5	6	5 / 6	6	5
Under Sun's beams	4	4	4	4	4	4

Claude Dariot (1598)	David Origanus (1599)	Christoph Pezel (1601)	Redento Baranzano (1617)	Antoine de Villon (1624)	António de Najera (1632)	William Lilly (1647)
–	2	–	–	–	–	-
–	1	–	–	–	–	-
–	2	–	–	–	–	-
–	1	–	–	–	–	-
2	2	–	–	2	2	2
2	2	–	–	2	2	2
–	–	2	2	–	–	-
3	–	–	–	–	3	-
2	–	–	–	–	2	-
5	–	–	–	–	5	-
4	4	4	4	4	4	4
2	2	2	2	2	1	2
2	–	–	–	–	–	-
–	2	2	–	2	1	2
2	–	–	–	–	–	-
–	–	–	–	–	2	-
–	–	–	–	–	2	-
1	–	–	–	–	–	-
1	–	–	–	–	–	-
1	–	–	–	–	–	-
5	–	–	–	–	–	-
–	–	–	–	–	–	-
–	6	5	5	5	5	6
–	5	5	5	5	5	5
5	5	5	4 [?]	5	5	5
4	4	4	4	4	4	2
3	4	4	4	4	3	2
[dig.]	[dig.]	[dig.]	[dig.]	[dig.]	[dig.]	[dig.]
5	5	5	5	5	5	5
4	4	4	5[?]	5	4	4
5	5	5	5	5	5	5
5	5	5	5	5	5	5
5	4	4	4	4	4	4

TABLE 12.10 Planetary conditions and their scoring in different authors (*cont.*)

	Johannes Schöner (1539)	Cyprián Lvovický (1557)	Giovanni B. Carelli (1558)	Jean Taisnier (1559)	Giuseppe Moletti (1563)	Francesco Giuntini (1573)
DEBILITIES						
Conjunction with malefic [partile to some]	5	5	5	5	5	5
Application to a malefic	3	–	3	3	3	–
Application with a malefic by ☍ [partile to some]	4	–	4	4	–	–
☍ ♄ or ♂ [partile to some]	–	4	–	–	4	4
Application with a benefic by □ [partile to some]	–	–	–	–	–	–
□ ♄ or ♂ [partile to some]	–	3	–	–	–	3
Besiedged by malefics	5	–	5	5	5	–
Void of course	2	–	2	2	–	–
Feral	5	–	3	3	3	–
☌ ☊ [partile to some]	3	[dig.]	3	3	3	–
☌ ☋ [partile to some]	5	3	5	5	5	–
☽ ☌ ♂	–	–	–	–	–	–
☌ ♄☉, ♂☉, ♄☽, ☉☽	–	–	–	–	–	–
☌ ☉☿	–	–	–	–	–	–
☌ ♄♀, ♄☿, ♂☿	–	–	–	–	–	–
□ ☽♂	–	–	–	–	–	–
□ ☉☽, ♄☉, ♂☉	–	–	–	–	–	–
□ ♄☽	–	–	–	–	–	–
□ ☽☿	–	–	–	–	–	–
☍ ☉☽	–	–	–	–	–	–
☍ ♄☿, ♂☽	–	–	–	–	–	–
Occidentality of superiors	2	2	2	2	2	2
Orientality of inferiors	2	2	2	2	2	2
Occidentality	–	–	–	–	–	–
Contrarity of hayz	2	–	2	2	2	–
Contrarity of quarter	–	–	–	–	–	–
Retrograde	5	5	5	5	5	5
Slow	1	2	2	1	1	2
Diminishing in light	1	–	1	1	1	–
Moon decreasing in light	–	–	–	–	–	2
Decreasing in number	1	–	1	1	1	
Descending in the circle of its auge	2	–	2	2	2	–
Descending to south in Lat.	2	–	2	2	–	–
Via combusta	2	–	2	2	2	–
Eclipse of the luminaries	5	–	5	5	5	–

Claude Dariot (1598)	David Origanus (1599)	Christoph Pezel (1601)	Redento Baranzano (1617)	Antoine de Villon (1624)	António de Najera (1632)	William Lilly (1647)
5	5	5	5	5	–	5
4	–	–	–	–	–	-
–	–	–	–	–	3	-
4	3	4	4	4	–	4
–	–	–	–	–	–	-
3	4	2	2	3	–	3
5	–	5	4	4	5	5
2	–	–	–	–	2	-
5	–	–	–	–	3	-
[dig.]	–	[dig.]	–	[dig.]	–	[dig.]
3	–	4	–	4	–	4
–	5	–	–	–	–	-
–	4	–	–	–	–	-
–	3	–	–	–	–	-
–	1	–	–	–	–	-
–	4	–	–	–	–	-
–	3	–	–	–	–	-
–	2	–	–	–	–	-
–	1	–	–	–	–	-
–	4	–	–	–	–	-
–	2	–	–	–	–	-
2	2	–	–	2	2	2
2	2	–	–	2	2	2
–	–	2	2	–	–	-
3	–	–	–	–	2	-
2	–	–	–	–	–	-
5	5	5	5	5	5	5
2	2	2	2	2	1	2
2	–	–	–	–	–	-
–	2	2	2	2	1	2
2	–	–	–	–	–	-
–	–	–	–	–	2	-
–	–	–	–	–	2	-
2	–	–	–	–	2	-
5	–	–	–	–	5	-

TABLE 12.10   Planetary conditions and their scoring in different authors (*cont.*)

	Johannes Schöner (1539)	Cyprián Lvovický (1557)	Giovanni B. Carelli (1558)	Jean Taisnier (1559)	Giuseppe Moletti (1563)	Francesco Giuntini (1573)
DEBILITIES						
☽ in ♊, or at the end of a sign in terms of malefic	2	–	2	2	2	–
Luminary in terms of eclipse	4	–	4	4	4	–
Moon going to combustion below 12°	4	–	4	4	4	–
In void or smoky degrees	3	–	3	3	–	–
In dark, pitted, or azemene degrees	3	–	3	3	–	–
In terms of malefics	–	–	–	–	–	–
Bodily application to a star of malefic nature	5	–	5	5	5	–
Conjunction with Algol	–	4	–	–	–	4

Claude Dariot (1598)	David Origanus (1599)	Christoph Pezel (1601)	Redento Baranzano (1617)	Antoine de Villon (1624)	António de Najera (1632)	William Lilly (1647)
	–	–	–	–	2	-
–	–	–	–	–	4	-
–	–	–	–	–	4	-
1	–	–	–	–	–	-
1	–	–	–	–	–	-
2	–	–	–	–	–	-
5	–	–	–	–	–	-
–	5	5	[5?]	5	5	5

Acknowledgements

I would like to thank David Just for his valuable insights on improving this paper, as well as Christine Sauer and Susanne Edelmann of the Nürnberg Stadtbibliothek for their assistance in enhancing the photo of MS Cent. V 85. Research financed by FCT—Fundação para a Ciência e a Tecnologia, project 2023.06562.CEECIND/CP2831/CT0016. DOI: https://doi.org/10.54499/2023.0656 2.CEECIND/CP2831/CT0016.

Bibliography

Manuscripts

Florence, Biblioteca nazionale centrale, Gal. 81.
Nürnberg, Stadtbibliothek, MS Cent. V 85.
Paris, Bibliothèque Nationale de France, lat. 7337.
Vatican, Biblioteca Apostolica Vaticana, Vat. lat. 4085.
Vienna, Österreichische Nationalbibliothek, Cod. 10745.
Vienna, Österreichische Nationalbibliothek, Cod. 5335.

Printed Works

Abū Maʿšar. *The Great Introduction to Astrology*. Edited by Keiji Yamamoto and Charles Burnett. Vol. 1. 2 vols. Leiden: Brill, 2019.

Antoine de Villon. *L'usage des éphémérides, avec la méthode de dresser et corriger toute sorte de figures coelestes et juger par le moyen d'icelles des diverses constitutions des temps et saisons de l'Annee, et de toutes les autres choses qui en dépendent*. Vol. 2. 2 vols. Paris: Iean Moreau, 1624.

Avelar, Helena. 'Who Wants to Live Forever? Astrological Methods for Calculating Lifespan in Western Culture and Perspectives on Determinism in Astrology'. *International Journal of Divination and Prognostication* 2, no. 2 (5 October 2021): 161–188. https://doi.org/10.1163/25899201-12340018.

Baranzano, Redento. *Uranoscopia, seu de Coelo*. Genève: apud Petrum & Jacobum Chouët, 1617.

Bīrūnī, Muḥammad ibn Aḥmad. *The Book of Instruction in the Elements of the Art of Astrology*. Translated by Robert Ramsay Wright. London: Luzac & co, 1934.

Bœuffle, André Le. *Astronomie, astrologie. Lexique latin*. Paris: Picard, 1987.

Burnett, Charles. 'Ptolemy's Differentiation between Astronomy and Astrology in the Greek-Arabic-Latin Tradition'. *Cahiers de Recherches Médiévales et Humanistes— Journal of Medieval and Humanistic Studies* 1, no. 47 (2024): 373–403.

Carelli, Giovanni Battista. *Ephemerides Io. Baptistae Carelli Placentini ad annos XVIII incipientes ab anno Christi* MDLXIII *usque ad annum* MDLXXX. *Meridiano inclitae vrbis Venetiarum diligentissime supputatae.* Venice: Vincentium Valgrisium, & haeredes Baldassaris Constantini, 1558.

Clavius, Christophorus. *In Sphaeram Ioannis de Sacro Bosco commentarius.* Roma: ex officina Dominici Basae, 1585.

Coley, Henry. *Clavis Astrologiæ Elimata, or, A Key to the Whole Art of Astrologie New Filed and Polished in Three Parts.* London: Benj. Tooke and The Sawbridge, 1676.

Dariot, Claude. *A Briefe and Most Easie Introduction to the Astrologicall Iudgement of the Starres Whereby the Diligent Reader with Easie Laboure May Giue a Certen, True, and Determinate Iudgement to Any Question Demanded, Vpon the Naturall Causes Thereof.* London: Printed by Thomas Purfoot, 1598.

Dariot, Claude. *Ad astrorum iudicia facilis introductio.* Lugduni: Apud Mauricium Roy & Ludouicum Pesnot, 1557.

Gadbury, John. *Genethlialogia, or, The Doctrine of Nativities Containing the Whole Art of Directions and Annual Revolutions.* London: Ja. Cottrel, 1658.

Gaurico, Luca, Antonio di Montulmo, and Johannes Camillus Regiomontanus. *Tractatvs Astrologiae Ivdiciariae De Nativitatibus Virorvm & mulierum, compo situs per D. Lucam Gauricum Neapolitanum, ex Ptolemæo & alijs autoribus dignissimis, cum multis aphorismis expertis & comprobatis ab eodem. Addito in fine libello Antonij de Montulmo, de eadem re, cum annotationibus Ioannis de Regiomonte, hactenus nusque impresso.* apud Iohan. Petreium, 1540.

Geller, Markham J. *Melothesia in Babylonia: Medicine, Magic, and Astrology in the Ancient near East.* Science, Technology, and Medicine in Ancient Cultures, volume 2. Boston: De Gruyter, 2014.

Giuntini, Francesco. *Speculum Astrologiae, quod attinet ad iudiciariam rationem natiuitatum atque annuarum reuolutionum, cum nonnullis approbatis astrologorum sententiis.* Lyon: Philippi Tinghi Florentini, 1573.

Giuntini, Francesco. *Speculum Astrologiae universam mathematicam scientiam in certas classes digestam complectens.* Florence: Phil. Tinghius, 1581.

Heilen, Stephan. *Konjunktionsprognostik in der Frühen Neuzeit. Band 1. Die Antichrist-Prognose des Johannes von Lübeck (1474) zur Saturn-Jupiter-Konjunktion von 1504 und ihre frühneuzeitliche Rezeption.* Vol. 1. Baden-Baden: Valentin Koerner, 2020.

Hübner, Wolfgang. *Die Begriffe 'Astrologie' und 'Astronomie' in der Antike: Wortgeschichte und Wissenschaftssystematik; mit einer Hypothese zum Terminus 'Quadrivium'.* Vol. 1989, 7. Stuttgart: Steiner, 1990.

Isidore. *The etymologies of Isidore of Seville.* Edited by Stephen A. Barney. Cambridge, UK; New York: Cambridge University Press, 2006.

Jones, Alexander, and John Steele. 'A New Discovery of a Component of Greek Astrology in Babylonian Tablets: The 'Terms'', *ISAW Papers*, no. 1 (2011). http://dlib.nyu.edu/awdl/isaw/isaw-papers/1/.

Lejbowicz, Max. 'Les antécédents de la distinction isidorienne: astrologia/astronomia', In *Observer, lire, écrire le ciel au Moyen Âge*, 173–212, 1991.

Leowitz, Cyprian. *Ephemeridum nouum atque insigne opus ab anno Domini 1556. usque in 1606. accuratissimè supputatum: cui praeter alia omnia in caeteris editionibus addi solita, etiam haec accesserunt*. Augsburg: Philippus Ulhardus, 1557.

Lilly, William. *Christian Astrology Modestly Treated in Three Books*. 1st ed. London: Tho. Brudenelle, 1647.

Lindhout, Henricus a. *Introductio in physicam iudiciariam*. Hamburg: Philippum de Ohr, 1597.

Manilius, Marcus. *Astronomica*. Translated by George Patrick Goold. Cambridge, Mass: Harvard University Press, 1977.

Moleti, Giuseppe. *L'efemeridi di m. Gioseppe Moleto matematico*. Venice: appresso Vincenzo Valgrisio, 1563.

Najera, Antonio de. *Summa astrologica y arte para enseñar hazer pronosticos de los tiempos*. Lisboa: Antonio Alvarez, 1632.

Origanus, David. *Ephemerides Novae Annorum XXXVI, Incipientes Ab Anno Chrisogeneseos 1595, Quo Ioannis Stadii Maxime Aberrare Incipiunt, & Desinentes in Annum 1630*. Frankfurt (Oder): Andreae Eichornii, 1599.

Pezel, Christoph. *D. Christophori Pezelii Praecepta genethliaca siue de prognosticandis hominum natiuitatibus commentarius eruditissimus, in quo non solum astrologiae praecepta & certa istius fundamenta demonstrantur, verum etiam varii casus, historiae, euentus & exempla lepidissima proponuntur. Omnibus et singulis cuiuscunque facultatis studiosis lectu iucundus & scitu necessarius*. Frankfurt: typis Wolfgangi Richteri, impensis Johan. Thebaldi Schonvvetteri & Cunradi Meulii, consortorum, 1607.

Pfeffer, Michelle. 'Reassessing the Marginalization of Astrology in the Early Modern World'. *The Historical Journal*, 6 September 2023, 1–25. https://doi.org/10.1017/S0018 246X23000328.

Ptolemy. *Tetrabiblos*. Translated by F.E. Robbins. Cambridge, Mass.; London: Harvard University Press, 1940.

Ramesey, William. *Astrologia Restaurata or, Astrologie Restored*. London: Robert White, 1653.

Ribeiro, Luís Campos. *Jesuit Astrology: Prognostication and Science in Early Modern Culture*. Leiden; Boston: Brill, 2023.

Riğāl, 'Alī Abū al-Ḥasan al-šaybānī Ibn Abī al-. *El libro conplido en los iudizios de las estrellas*. Edited by Gerold Hilty. Madrid: Real Academia Española, 1954.

Romeiras, Francisco Malta, Luís Campos Ribeiro, and Elisa Frei. 'Physiognomy, Complexion, and Ingenuity: The Management of Talent in the Society of Jesus, 1540–1773'. *Early Science and Medicine* 30, no. 1 (6 March 2025): 59–104. https://doi.org/10.1163/15733823-20251335.

Scala, Giuseppe. *Ephemerides Iosephi Scalae Siculi Noetini Art. & Med. Doc. Ad annos duodecim, incipientes ab anno Domini 1589*. Venice: appresso i Giunti, 1589.

Schöner, Johannes. *De Iudiciis Nativitatum: Libri Tres*. Nuremberg: Montanus & Neuber, 1545.

Schöner, Johannes. *Opusculum Astrologicum ex diversorum libris summa cura pro studiosorum utilitate collectum*. Nuremberg: Iohan. Petreium, 1539.

Sela, Shlomo, ed. *Abraham Ibn Ezra Book of the World*. Leiden–Boston: Brill, 2009.

Sempill, Hugh. *De mathematicis disciplinis Libri duodecim*. Antwerp: Balthasar Moreti, 1635.

Taisnier, Joannes. *Astrologiae ivdiciariae ysagogica et totius divinatricis artis encomia, cum nonnullis Habrahami Iudęi et Lucae Gaurici dictis*. Cologne: Arnold Birckmann, 1559.

Taisnier, Joannes. *Opus Mathematicum octo libros complectens*. Cologne: apud Ioannem Birckmannum & Wernerum Richwimom, 1562.

Vermij, Rienk, and Hiro Hirai, eds. 'Early Science and Medicine. The Marginalization of Astrology' 22, no. 5–6 (2017).

Weill-Parot, Nicolas. 'Antonio Da Montolmo et La Magie Hermétique'. In *Hermetism from Late Antiquity to Humanism. La Tradizione Ermetica Dal Mondo Tardo- Antico All'umanesimo (Atti Del Convegno Internazionale Di Studi, Napoli, 20–24 Novembre 2001)*, edited by Paolo Lucentini, Ilaria Parri, and Vittoria Perrone Compagni, 545–568. Turnhout: Brepols, 2003.

Weill-Parot, Nicolas. 'Antonio Da Montolmo's De Occultis et Manifestis or Liber Intelligentiarum: An Annotated Critical Edition with English Translation and Introduction'. In *Invoking Angels: Theurgic Ideas and Practices, Thirteenth to Sixteenth Centuries*, edited by Claire Fanger, 219–293. University Park, PA: Penn State University Press, 2012.

Zinner, Ernst. *Regiomontanus, His Life and Work*. Vol. 1. Studies in the History and Philosophy of Mathematics. Amsterdam / New York: North-Holland, 1990.

CHAPTER 13

The Private Workings of a Very Public Astrologer: William Lilly (1602–1681)

Susan Ward

Abstract

This paper explores the private astrological practice of William Lilly (1602–1681), one of the most renowned astrologers of seventeenth-century England. By closely examining his manuscripts—particularly his practice books—it sheds light on the practical, day-to-day workings of an astrologer in early modern England. While much scholarly attention has been devoted to Lilly's published works and his role in public life, this study delves into his private consultations, his clientele, and the technical aspects of his astrological practice. The analysis reveals patterns in his record-keeping, the types of questions posed by clients, and his methods of calculation, often conducted under considerable time constraints. The paper also addresses broader historiographical issues, including misconceptions about Lilly's political stance and his association with figures such as Jane Whorwood during the British Civil Wars. Additionally, new findings regarding Lilly's consultation fees and his adaptation to periods of crisis, including the plague, highlight the complexity of his role in both public and private spheres. By reassessing Lilly's manuscripts in this way, this study contributes to a deeper understanding of astrology as both a technical discipline and a social practice in seventeenth-century England.

Keywords

William Lilly – client records – early modern astrology – Jane Whorwood – Charles I's captivity

1 Introduction

The difficulty in working with astrological manuscripts is, of course, the technical complexities of the subject and this paper will demonstrate the benefits that can be elicited from such manuscripts through a close examination enlightened by limited knowledge of that technical language. Some features of the private practices of this published astrologer will be examined, and, whilst prose notation in these manuscripts, even when abbreviated, is interesting and informative, the non-textual can be revealing too. A wider lens is used to examine William Lilly's place in the historiography and is discussed in one particular respect, that of the well-known figure of the British civil wars (1642–1651): Jane Whorwood (1612–1684). Some time is spent here because this episode bridges his public and private work, and because Whorwood's presence highlights the way in which Lilly is sometimes portrayed in the historiography and how that can lead to errors and oversights. A narrower lens is then used to focus on further aspects of Lilly's client work found in his practice books where he kept his astrological figures, calculations, and sometimes his notes.

A great deal of research has been undertaken into who astrologers worked for and for what purposes, who they themselves were, and their place in their respective cultural and political frames, but less is known about what they actually did in practical, everyday terms.[1] All of which are interesting in their own right, of course, but an exception is the work done by Helena Avelar de Carvalho in her investigation of the work of a medieval French astrologer.[2] Although there is little to show a difference in the astrological system and method applied by Belle and Lilly, the latter was practising with several clients on most work days, which is somewhat different from Belle's practice, at least as far as his notebooks are concerned.[3] By examining that very feature—astrology in action almost by pen stroke—a number of interesting and novel factors arise, some of which are included here in a fairly wide-ranging review of this selection of manuscripts. By so doing an image is sketched of the man behind the manuscripts, and, in Lilly's case, behind the autobiography on which so many historians and commentators have relied.

---

1 For example, in terms of private practice, although of an earlier period, case studies by Lauren Kassell, *Medicine and Magic in Elizabethan London: Simon Forman Astrologer, Alchemist, and Physician* (Oxford: Oxford University Press, 2005); 'The Casebooks Project' itself lists the client/patient work of Simon Forman (1552–1611) and Richard Napier (1559–1634), https://casebooks.lib.cam.ac.uk; Sophie Page, 'Richard Trewythian and the Uses of Astrology in Late Medieval England', *Journal of the Warburg and Courtauld Institutes*, vol. 64 (2001), 193–228; Benjamin N. Dykes, 'Practice and Counsel in Guido Bonatti', in Wiebke Deimann and David Juste, eds, *Astrologers and Their Clients in Medieval and Early Modern Europe*, (Cologne: Böhlau, 2015), 29–42.

2 Helena Avelar de Carvalho, *An Astrologer at Work in Late Medieval France: The Notebooks of S. Belle* (Leiden: Brill, 2021).

3 Avelar de Carvalho, *An Astrologer at Work*.

The manuscripts referred to here are from the practice books of a busy astrologer.[4] William Lilly is a very well-known practitioner, author, and almanac compiler working in England in the mid- to late seventeenth century. He rose to prominence in London during the years of the British civil wars, the subsequent Commonwealth, and Protectorate (1642–1660). Most of his writings had their genesis following his return to London in the late summer of 1641 from the countryside, where he had lived in semi-retirement for five years. With the outbreak of the first of the British civil wars in the following year, a sense of urgency may have informed his motivation. He had correctly perceived that there was a need for more commentary and, perhaps, reassurance through the use of the predictive capacity of astrology. As Charles I (1600–1649) left London with his family in 1642, confusion and fear drove the demand for news when the need to find order from the chaos of life, and the breakdown of monarchy and the Church was never more severe. Though complex, astrology was orderly; it had a system and a method; it 'was the most systematic attempt to explain natural phenomena according to rigorous scientific laws'.[5] For many people, through the private consultation, astrology filled the need for certainty and information in individual lives, and for the wider reading public there were the astrological almanacs with their prognostications for the forthcoming year.

Bernard Capp suggests that astrologers and almanacs were mutually beneficial, each raising the profile of the other.[6] Lilly's arrival in London coincided with the breakdown of the censorship of the press, noted in the historiography as the print explosion.[7] 'The golden age of English almanacs, however, was from 1640 to 1700, when they plunged into political, social, and religious controversies'.[8] As an illustration of the vastly increased output of the printers, it is noted that George Thomason, a bookseller, had bought twenty-two titles in 1640, but over two thousand in 1642.[9] His collection of twenty-two thousand pamphlets

---

4   Using the term 'practice-books' as applied by Elias Ashmole (1617–1692) when adding them to his collection. See William Henry Black, *A Descriptive, Analytical, and Critical Catalogue of the Manuscripts Bequeathed unto the University of Oxford by Elias Ashmole, Esq., M.D., F.R.S., Windsor Herald* (Oxford: Oxford University Press, 1845), for example, 127.

5   Bernard Capp, *Astrology and the Popular Press: English Almanacs 1500–1800* (London: Faber, 1979), 15.

6   Capp, *Astrology and the Popular Press*, 20.

7   For example, Joad Raymond, 'Seventeenth-Century Print Culture', in *History Compass*, 2, no. 1, 2004, 5; and Sharon Achinstein, 'Texts in conflict: the Press and the Civil War', in *The Cambridge Companion to Writing of the English Revolution* (Cambridge: Cambridge University Press, 2006), 51. *Cambridge Companions Online*, https://doi.org/10.1017/CCOL0521642523.004.

8   Capp, *Astrology and the Popular Press*, 24.

9   Sharon Achinstein, 'Texts in Conflict:', 51. The huge Thomason collection of texts is now in the possession of the British Library.

was made between 1640 and 1660, which provides a sketch of the situation in England. Sharon Achinstein goes on to note the comparison of printed texts in 1600 (two hundred and fifty-nine items) with those in 1642 by which time the number had risen to 2958. With the instability of the times coinciding with the relaxing of censorship, the astrological almanac fitted the need perfectly. There was still censorship though and Lilly complains in his 'Life' about the deletions made to his first *Merlin* of 1644.[10] As Capp notes, their popularity would have promoted his private work; his practice books attest to this showing possibly up to nineteen consultations in any one day.

He began his published career in 1644 with his first almanac and three treatises: one dedicated to the prophecy of 'the White King and the Dreadfull Dead-man'; one to the heavenly phenomena of that year and a particular astrological configuration; one to the doctrine of Jupiter-Saturn conjunctions;[11] and that first almanac. The practice books preserved by Ashmole and now in the Bodleian Library at Oxford also begin in March 1644.[12] As previously mentioned, this is the same year that he began to publish his work. This may well mark the beginning of a 'professional' career as an astrologer, rather than as a gentleman-astrologer. Indeed, the horary chart on folio 1 is that found in his seminal work *Christian Astrology*.[13] It refers to a battle on 29 March 1644 (the battle of Cheriton) and the figure is dated 29 March 1644 at 10.12 am. He had bought the book itself on 26 March 1644, so this figure is the first use of the book for his private work; a time that is likely to have been significant to Lilly. It was never intended that these practice books should be made public; this would be especially the case in view of possible sensitivities regarding the identification of some of his higher-profile clients, some evidence of that perhaps being the enciphering of certain clients' names as illustrated below. Lilly is often writing at speed and not always it seems on a fixed surface (perhaps standing as he wrote), which makes the palaeography difficult at times with few details to provide context.

---

10   William Lilly, 'The Life of William Lilly student in Astrology wrote by himselfe in the 66th year of his age, at Hersham in the parish of Walton uppon Thames in the County of Surrey: propria manu', Oxford, Bodleian Library MS Ashmole 421, fol. 205ᵛ, in Susan Ward, ed., *William Lilly (1602–1681) the Astrologer: A Book of Sources*, vol. 1 (Lisbon: Prisma Edições, 2024), 9–91. (Referred to hereafter as his 'Life'.); William Lilly, *Merlinus Anglicus Junior: The English Merlin Revived* (London, 1644), subscribed 'June 12th'.

11   William Lilly, 'England's Propheticall Merline', in Ward, *William Lilly (1602–1681) the Astrologer*, vol. 1, 249–415.

12   Oxford, Bodleian MS Ashmole 184, 30 March 1644 to 4 June 1645. (Hereafter, Bod. MS Ashm.).

13   William Lilly, *Christian Astrology*, Facsimile Edition (Exeter: Regulus, 1985), 399.

2   Client Records

The manuscripts mentioned here are Oxford, Bodleian Library, Ashmole 420, April 1647 to September 1648, and MS Ashmole 210, 30 July to 30 October 1649. A selection of astrological figures from these two ledger-like books was chosen because they were some of the few that were annotated. These notes referred to the status of the client, sometimes a physical description, the nature of the question being asked, and, occasionally, his response. The notes are in English and in Latin, and, sometimes, a mixture of both. The figures themselves take the form of a stamped chart square completed as required for the day. It is clear that in preparation for work on 16 June 1647, he stamped the recto four times, then closed the book the previous evening before the ink had dried completely transferring the wet ink to the previous verso.[14] The earlier of the two practice books is usually stamped with two squares on the verso and four on the recto; in 1649, there are usually six squares on the verso and four slightly larger squares on the recto. His practice had obviously increased, and it is also noticeable that his handwriting had changed accordingly, perhaps with the pressure of work and the need for speed.

The books are not completely systematic, but neither are they commonplace books, even though figures are occasionally found out of chronological order; presumably he would take whatever space was available when he needed it. Most of the figures relate to questions, otherwise known as horaries, with an occasional birth chart, seemingly as an adjunct to a horary, as shown in the example below.[15] It is hand-drawn, that is, not a pre-stamped chart, suggesting that there was no prior notice of this nativity and that it was generated spontaneously. This might be the result of a question relating to having children or to marriage. If the horary had been read in the negative, the nativity could be examined for the potential in the longer term. The questions were generally wide-ranging, covering almost every possible contingency from crime to love, from career to journeys, and all stops in between.

It appears that he often drew up a new chart for each client even when there were only a few minutes separating the figures and little astrological difference would have been found. It is unclear why he did this; in many cases it would have been unnecessary since little would have changed in astronomical and mathematical terms between the two times. For example, on 29 August 1649 Lilly received two clients at 9 am and 9.15 am: the former was 'Dˢ Robinson

---

14   Bod. MS Ashm. 420, fol. 44ʳ. All figures are reproduced by kind permission of the Bodleian Library.
15   Bod. MS Ashm. 420, fol. 36ʳ.

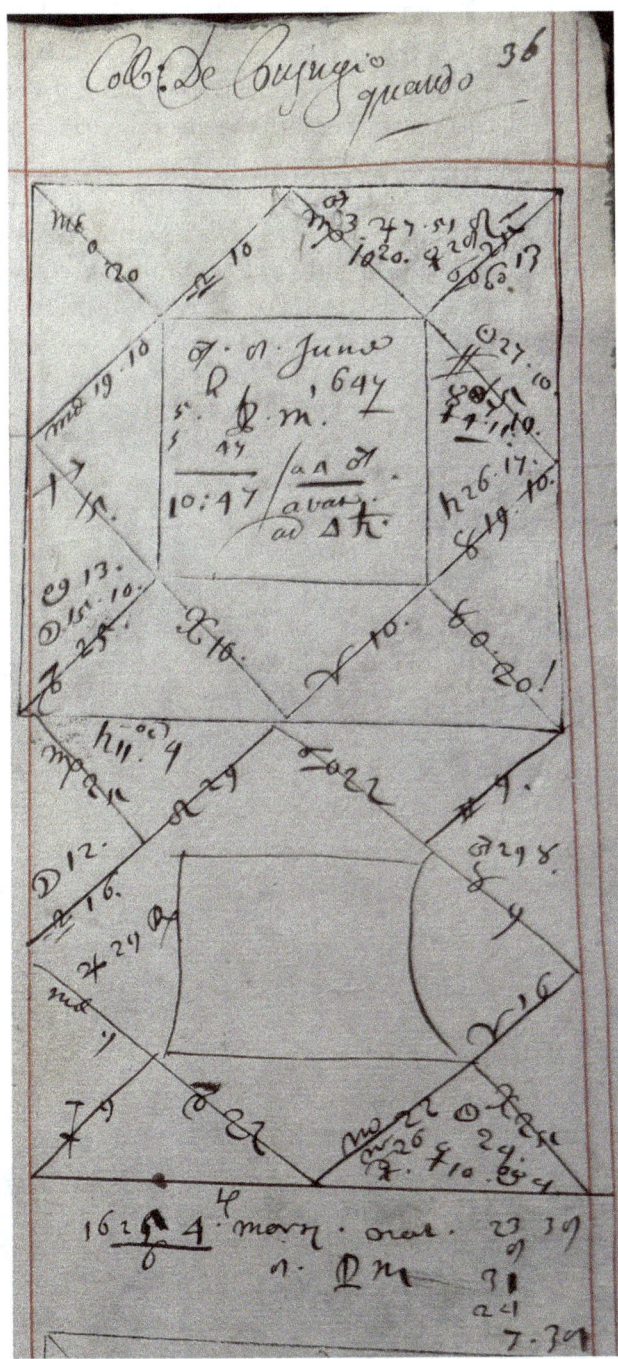

FIGURE 13.1 Above horary about marriage with nativity below

[enciphered]', the latter 'Sutor [a tailor]'. The earlier question was about career; the latter about wealth.[16] Clearly, there is no similarity between the two, and yet the two sets of calculations are very similar, but not identical, because he was not simply copying over those details from the earlier figure. He really did recalculate the second chart, although this is not to suggest that this was always the case. It might be speculated that the second client in this case was somewhat knowledgeable in astrology and expected a new chart to be calculated. There are also a few occasions where two clients had arrived at exactly the same time and in those cases both questions were applied to the same astrological figure.[17]

There is no intention here to provide a detailed statistical study of these practice books partly because the sample is so small, but the following will give some idea of the nature and number of these charts; a more complete study of Lilly's practice books is forthcoming. Of these 210 figures, only eight are nativities, with one possible election, that is, the choosing of an auspicious time for a particular activity. It was possible to draw this conclusion because a hand-drawn chart was attached (as in Figure 1) to a figure for 5.07 PM on 19 May 1648; the remaining charts immediately following this were charts for the 20 and 22 May. The chart was erected, cast forward, for 9.30 am on 22 May 1648, so it would seem to be for an election.[18] Eighteen questions have the client's name encoded, eleven of which range from fairly to very clear. Of these, 104 have a given status of some kind, and over a hundred have significant marks, often of emphasis, some of which will be discussed later. Of the seventy-nine figures in 1649, forty-three have a fee ascribed to them, again discussed later.

3   Practice Books or Casebooks?

While Lauren Kassell refers to casebooks in regard to Simon Forman (1552–1611) and Richard Napier (1559–1634), Lilly's practice books do not appear to fall into her definition of a casebook exactly: 'Casebooks are serial records of practice. When written by physicians, surgeons and apothecaries, they contain records of medical consultations. Astrological casebooks are related, but distinct. They record medical questions alongside consultations about, for instance, marital fortune and the identity of a thief'.[19] Whilst parts of Lilly's practice books do

16   Bod. MS Ashm. 210, fol. 118ᵛ.
17   Bod. MS Ashm. 420, fol. 288ʳ.; Bod. MS Ashm. 210, fol. 118ᵛ, & fol. 146ᵛ.
18   Bod. MS Ashm. 420, fol. 288ᵛ.
19   Lauren Kassell, 'Casebooks in Early Modern England: Medicine, Astrology, and Written

seem to agree with this definition, that agreement is not consistent, particularly when client name or purpose is not noted in so many instances. For a practising astrologer, an essential resource was somewhere to make calculations and review the result. This would seem to be the sole purpose of Lilly's practice books, although there might also have been times when he needed to refer back to previous charts. There are suggestions that some figures were worthy of note and it may have been his intention to use them again in one of his publications.[20] However, these are rare and it seems more likely that the practice books were simply a more secure and practical solution than were individual pieces of paper. There were times, naturally, when he needed to erect a chart when away from home and without his practice book to hand. There is an example of this where a chart has been drawn on a scrap of paper and then bound within the practice book.[21]

Unlike Forman, Lilly seems to have had no didactic or professional ambitions or uses for these practice books. His teaching was done either in person or through the auspices of his textbook *Christian Astrology*; his professional aspirations were satisfied by the popularity of his *Merlins* and other writings and his wide associations and influence; it is unlikely that his legacy was to be contained within these practice books. However, the first two volumes do seem to have more detail within them, but this might simply be because he had more time during this period.[22] These documents do not represent any form of diary or journal as found elsewhere, which, in at least two cases, are not the records of professional astrologers in any case.[23]

For all of these reasons, the manuscripts clearly represent the working day and are simply more secure than loose leaves; another convenience of the bound ledger was that it was securely portable. It is not known where in his house in London Lilly entertained clients, although he once mentions receiving a client at the front door and then going 'upp', presumably upstairs to his

Records', *Bulletin of the History of Medicine* 88, no. 4 (2014), 600; Kassell, *Medicine and Magic in Elizabethan London*, 137.

20 For example, Bod. MS Ashm. 185, fol. 211ʳ. This is the very well-known horary from his *Christian Astrology*, 439, 'If Presbytery shall stand?'.

21 Bod. MS Ashm. 420, fol. 230ʳ.

22 Bod. MSS Ashm. 184 & 185.

23 Samuel Jeake, *An Astrological Diary of the Seventeenth Century: Samuel Jeake of Rye, 1652–1699*, eds. Michael Hunter and Annabel Gregory (Oxford: Clarendon Press, 1988); Jeremy Roch, 'Hieron Roch J. His Journal of Some Remarkable Voyages and Adventures at Sea in the Years 1665, 1666 and 1667', in *Three Sea Journals of Stuart Times*, ed. Bruce S. Ingram (London: Constable & Co. Ltd., 1936), 29–139.

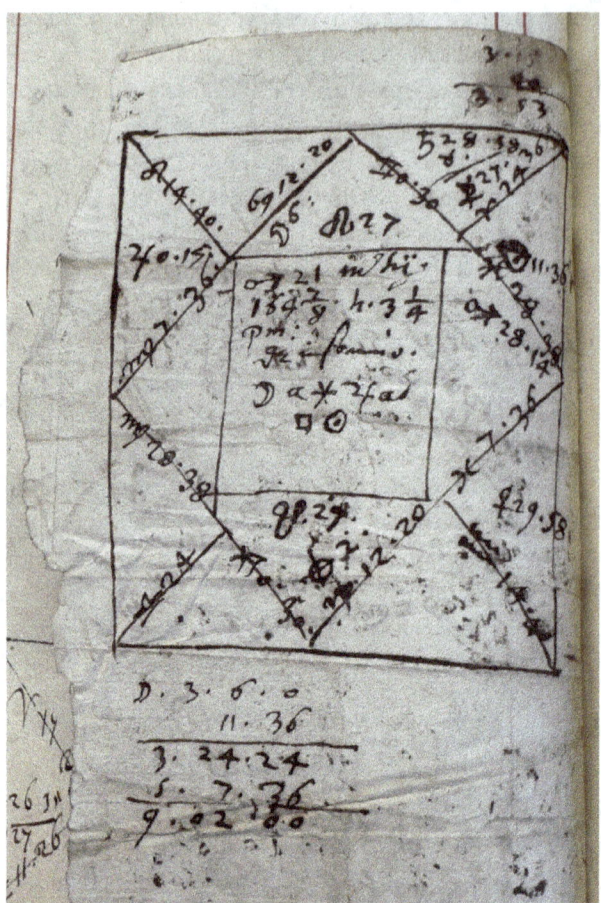

FIGURE 13.2
Interleaved chart

study.[24] Given the number of clients he had in any one day, sometimes two arriving at once or within a few minutes of each other, and from various social groups, being able to pick up practice book, quill, and ink and go to the front door or near it would seem convenient. This becomes even more reasonable as a suggestion when examining a period of plague covered by the manuscripts, when infected clients would stand back from Lilly as they gave him their samples of urine, as pointed out below. There are no other examples of where Lilly entertained clients other than these and whilst it might be expected that a servant would answer the door, this does not appear to have been the case here. It is unlikely that all clients would have gone upstairs to his study; perhaps there

---

24   Lilly, 'Life', MS Ashm. 421, fol. 205ᵛ, in Ward, *William Lilly (1602–1681) the Astrologer*, vol. 1, 53.

was an area nearer to the front door where Lilly carried out his business. It is also possible that Lilly may have carried on business as a shop with clients entering the house once he had put out his shingle for the day.

Lilly lived in the Strand area of London in a house that he had bought with some others in 1634.[25] It seems to have been one of the better areas of London, popular for fabric and clothing; being near to Drury Lane, theatres, and coffee houses added to the vibrancy of the area.[26] The political situation had been and remained unstable; having lost the first civil war and escaped from Oxford, King Charles had been handed over by the Scots to the English in January 1647. It was widely anticipated that there would be a settlement with the king and, as will be shown, Lilly's sentiments record this.[27] In August of that year, the king was moved to Hampton Court Palace via Holdenby House in Northamptonshire to continue his captivity. However, he escaped in November. Shortly after, he surrendered to the governor of the Isle of Wight, only to discover the governor's loyalty to Parliament, resulting in Charles being placed under arrest. Other escape attempts failed, even though he had been planning a military intervention by the Scots. As a result, by February 1648, England was again embroiled in war, this time against English and Welsh insurgents and, a little later, the Scots who had engaged for the king.[28] Clearly, the added uncertainties of living in London at such a time might well affect an astrologer's business, but life went on it seems and questions about love, marriage, money, business, career, illness, losses, theft, and travel continued much as they always had.

4   Lilly's Politics

There was one element of the period that stands out as unusual, if fairly well known, and that could hardly have arisen at any other time. But first it needs to be stated that Lilly, the parliamentary supporter, was never against monarchy. This should come as no surprise since such apparent ambivalence was the view of the majority after the fall of the king's war capital, Oxford, in 1646; a situation that had persisted among parliamentarians since the beginning of the war in 1642.[29]

---

25   William Lilly, *Christian Astrology*, 219 and 221.
26   Peter Earle, *A City Full of People* (London, 1994), 14.
27   Philip Baker, 'The Regicide', in *The Oxford Handbook of the English Revolution*, ed. Michael J. Braddick (Oxford: Oxford University Press, 2015), 157.
28   Sean Kelsey, 'The Trial of Charles I', *The English Historical Review*, 118, no. 477 (2003), 584.
29   Rachel Foxley, 'Varieties of Parliamentarianism', in *The Oxford Handbook of the English Revolution*, ed. Michael J. Braddick (Oxford: Oxford University Press, 2015), 421 and 426.

I highly prize Monarchy, and extremely respect the Majestie and Honour
attending it. I have just cause, and I do cordially esteem His Majestie now
living, and His posterity: the War he maintains and countenanceth against
His English and Scotish Subjects, I totally abhor: the end will be bitter.[30]

Indeed, the title of this piece alone describes Lilly's politics, which never
wavered from this moderate position. In his almanac for 1648 (inscribed 'Nov:
8th 1647'), he states his case again, '*Anglicus* is yet for Monarchy, as most con-
sonant to English constitutions', and further on, 'I desire his Majesty should
be restored, (but herein I submit to the decree of the almighty)'; 'that I loved
Monarchy, [but] took part with the English Parliament against oppressions'.[31]
Of note is that this is dated three days before Charles I escaped captivity at
Hampton Court, and Lilly invokes Providence, which became almost a byword
for the trial and execution of the king.[32] These expressions of loyalty to both
the king and parliament are indicative of the feelings and opinions of many
in the country.[33] It is reasonable to assume that he would not have wanted to
alienate his readership in any case. His views might, of course, have attracted
criticism, but the ease with which he expresses them suggests that they were
readily accepted by, and resonated with, his readers. Even Oliver Cromwell
(1599–1658), eventually Lord Protector, it has been argued, had been 'a bitter
opponent of Charles, a reluctant regicide, and a firm monarchist'.[34]

It is of note that, relying on Lilly's 'Life' as their source, some authors still have
difficulty believing what he writes about his political position. The reason for
exploring that position in a little detail is that in discussing a negative contemporary comment about Jane Whorwood (1614/15–1684), John Fox writes: 'yet
she, the king and others did commit one major continuing folly which helped
undo them: they confided continuously in William Lilly'.[35] He provides no evidence of this and continues to use the 'Life' as a main source for this period of
Jane's life. Inaccuracies are also found there, for example, when discussing John

---

30   William Lilly, 'To all of the English Nation that are Lovers of Astrologie, His Majestie, the
      Privileges of Parliament, just Liberties of the City London and Commonalty of England',
      Anglicus, Peace or No Peace. 1645 (London, 1645), no pagination.
31   William Lilly, 'To the Reader', *Merlini Anglici Ephemeris 1648* (London, 1648), no pagina-
      tion.
32   Baker, 'The Regicide', 155.
33   Baker, 'The Regicide', 166.
34   John Morrill and Philip Baker, 'Oliver Cromwell, the Regicide and the Sons of Zeruiah', in
      Jason Peacey, ed., *Regicides and the Execution of Charles I* (London, Springer, 2001), 14.
35   John Fox, *The King's Smuggler: Jane Whorwood Secret Agent to Charles I* (Stroud: The His-
      tory Press, 2010), 80 and 114 for example.

Gadbury (1627–1704) as Lilly's rival 'for the role of national astrologer'; again no source is provided.[36] Such a statement assumes that Gadbury could rival Lilly, which is open to question, and the latter never was a 'national astrologer', and in any case ignores the very popular John Booker (1603–1667).[37] Nadine Akkerman repeats some of Fox's research and attention is drawn to her opinion below.[38]

Apart from the paucity of appropriate source referencing, there is the question of the type of source used. To find biographical information about Lilly requires that all of his printed works are examined because it is there that he offers information that is not in his 'Life'.[39] Whilst accusing Lilly of 'humbug innuendo' Fox goes on to quote Lilly's description of King Charles's extramarital activities. Fox's source for this is given in endnote 11, page 161, as 'William Lilly, *Observations on the Life and Death of King Charles I* (1651), 185'; clearly, Charles could not be Charles I until 1660 when his son Charles took the throne. The italicized title implies that it is a book, but it is actually an extract from a collection of texts about the civil wars published in 1815. Even so, the given page number is inaccurate; it should be page 142 (no edition is mentioned in Fox's reference above and there appears to be no more than one).[40] The original is entitled 'Severall Observations on the Life and Death of Charles Late King of England', which forms part of Lilly's treatise *Monarchy or No Monarchy*.[41] Since Lilly repeats his position in the same way many times before the Restoration of 1660, a position that was common before the second civil war of 1648, some caution at least should be applied before implying that he was a dishonourable double-agent of some kind.

By June 1648 at the latest, Lilly was already dismissing the possibility of the king's execution, stating that the army had 'no intention (I hope) to destroy Monarchy as is falsely suggested, but to regulate it and obtain those just rights we were borne unto'.[42] This might be taken as a summary of the opinions of

---

36 Fox, *The King's Smuggler*, 84.

37 For the detail of Gadbury's attacks on Lilly and its chronology: P. Stockinger & S. Ward, 'Monster of Ingratitude', *The Tradition Journal*, no. 3 (Autumn 2009), 5–36, http://www.th etraditionjournal.com/.

38 Nadine Akkerman, *Invisible Agents: Women and Espionage in Seventeenth-Century Britain* (Oxford: Oxford University Press, 2018), 36–37.

39 Included as 'Additional Autobiographical Information', in Ward, ed., *William Lilly (1602–1681) the Astrologer*, vol. 1, 171–181.

40 Francis Maseres, ed., *Select Tracts Relating to the Civil Wars in England, in the Reign of Charles the First* (London, 1815), 137–182.

41 William Lilly, 'Several Observations on the Life and Death of Charles Late King of England', in *Monarchy or No Monarchy* (London, 1651), 74–120.

42 William Lilly, *A peculiar Prognostication Astrologically predicted according to Art: Whether, or No, His Majestie Shall suffer Death this present yeere 1649* (London, 1649), no pagination.

many people even after the vicious fighting of 1648 that had almost destroyed royalist forces. When King Charles had been executed at the end of January 1649, Lilly addressed this in his almanac for 1650 (inscribed 'Novemb. 1649').[43] His 'Letter to the Reader' opens with 'Albus Rex mortuus. *the White King is now dead*', referring to the prophecy in his earlier treatise *A Prophecy of the White King and Dreadfull Dead-Man Explaned*.[44] Thus the prophecy had been fulfilled.[45] This opening provides the context for the interrogation at the pamphlet's end: 'If King Charles should live or dye', which was 'strongly propounded by a Royalist' on 19 January 1648/9. So, even at this late date, Lilly mixed with royalists and was trusted by at least some of them and he publishes that—not the kind of openness to be expected from a 'double-agent'. He published this contact to a wide readership and his memoir of this episode was intended for publication so it is more likely that his position could be taken at face value.

There are a number of points found in the historiography that can be questioned in the context of this chapter. Akkerman notes, when dealing with the Whorwood episode involving Lilly, 'Some of those women might have visited Lilly, like Jane—on 13 June [1647] the astrologist summarizes the consultation as "*d[omin]a ex Oxford de amico* [[a] mistress/lady from Oxford about her friend]"'.[46] She gives no indication as to her reason for assuming that this was Jane Whorwood. The chart she seems to be referring to is for 5.48 PM, Thursday 3 June 1647 (OS): 'D[omi]na ex Oxfordsh[ire] de amico'. There is another, confusing, note but it is not clear in which order it should be read: 'Saturn [glyph] erat' and 'a virij allus [*sic*]'.[47] This lady was from Oxfordshire the county, not Oxford the town and the additional note seems to imply that there was more than one man being enquired after, not relating to the alleged affair with the king. After the fall of Oxford in June 1646, it would be reasonable to assume that, having followed the king there, large numbers of people would have returned to their homes, or sought new ones in London. It is not perhaps surprising that '*ex Oxford*', should crop up at this time. Clearly, an examination of the archives is always recommended, but it does need to be done with some sensitivity to get the most from that effort. Jane Whorwood is well known as is her relationship with Lilly, but there was a much more interesting and, perhaps, more impor-

43   William Lilly, 'To the Reader', *Merlini Anglici Ephemeris* (London, 1650), no pagination.
44   William Lilly, *A Prophecy of the White King and Dreadfull Dead-Man Explaned* (London, 1644).
45   Lilly, 'To the Reader', *Merlini Anglici Ephemeris* (London, 1650), no pagination.
46   Akkerman, *Invisible Agents*, 41.
47   Bod. MS Ashm. 420, fol. 31ʳ. This might possibly read: 'Saturn erat a viri alius'—Saturn was another man.

tant question put to Lilly, probably by Jane, which will be addressed further on. It is from the same archive but in this case the palaeography is more difficult.

5   The Working Day

Moving on to a closer examination of this astrologer's work and some of its details, some comments regarding the practicalities are offered, which also provide a slightly more intimate introduction to Lilly's working day. At a little after 4.30 PM on Friday 4 June 1647, Lilly closed his practice book for the day with the ink not completely dry. He had added the status of the client at the end of the consultation: 'Comitt', which transferred to the opposite page.[48] Had he written the note at the time of the consultation, the ink would have had time to dry as had the rest of the figure. It provides a little evidence that, at least, in some cases, the notes were made after the client had left. It might also explain why Lilly sometimes confused one chart with another, because he had had to return to it a little afterwards, perhaps after dealing with another client. The cipher he used does not stand up to any kind of close examination in most cases but would be enough to hide the name from being overlooked, particularly upside down, that is, from the point of view of the client. It might also have reassured the anonymized client that his or her identity was being protected. An example can be seen at Figure 3. Such small points, seemingly unimportant and often going unnoticed, add to a fuller understanding of the manner of working and of the man himself.

There appear to have been two kinds of delineation of nativities: the very detailed delineation often including several years of prediction and kept as a separate, single document.[49] This was presented to the client and would have cost a considerable sum of money to commission. The other type was as found in these manuscripts: quickly worked to answer a particular question in terms of a clarification of or support to the horary chart. This might be the case, as mentioned, in a question of marriage or childbirth; the horary might answer the question in the negative in the short term, but the nativity might be used for the longer-term capacity of the client, particularly in terms of whether either was ever achievable. In Figure 1 for example, where the question referred to marriage, the question was extended into the nativity. It would not always have been necessary to do this except in certain questions of a longer-term nature;

---

48   Bod. MS Ashm. 420, fol. 32ʳ.
49   See four examples of this type of extended client work in Ward, ed., *William Lilly (1602–1681) Astrologer*, vol. 2.

fertility would be another such example where the nativity might be of use. However, few people knew their birth times, essential for the calculation of a nativity; some hardly knew their birth date. Where a full delineation of the nativity was required, it would be done as a separate task, taking a considerable length of time and making it correspondingly costly.

As noted, of the 210 charts in this selection, over one hundred seem to have deliberate marks and emphases, either within the figure itself or, where there are noted details, within those notes. It is possible, of course, that some of those marks were not deliberate or were otherwise not meaningful. However, many are deliberate, as will be illustrated. These marks are frequently highlighting significant astrological configurations by underscoring, that is, planets representing the matters contained within the question or problem are highlighted. Less frequently, these marks point to the house division under examination, or a mathematical point such as the Part of Fortune. In almost all charts, the immediate aspects that the Moon is making, or has made, are noted; sometimes one of these will be emphasized. In some instances, points within the question are underscored and not just to indicate the end of a sentence.

As a demonstration, the two figures below contain such marks or emphases; one has the question noted, one has not.[50] The former will act as a guide to the latter.

To give a simplified review of this figure Lilly's own primer is used as a reference for the astrological technicalities. The annotation here reads 'M[rs.] Bridges [enciphered] fre[i]nd *de conjugio/*', he had dotted a non-existent 'i', but this is his usual spelling of the word 'friend'. As an interrogation, the questioner and quesited must be identified before a judgement can be made. The querent is always signified by the rising sign and its planetary ruler. In this case, Sagittarius rises on the eastern horizon, which has Jupiter as its lord or ruler. The question is about marriage, '*de conjugio*', and so the quesited is signified by the sign on the 7th house cusp, Gemini, and its ruler Mercury.[51] As the significator of marriage is the ruler of the sign on the 7th house cusp, Mercury is, of course,

50 Bod. MS Ashm. 210, fol. 132[v] and 163[r], resp.
51 Lilly, *Christian Astrology*, 50 and 54. Information regarding the signs of the Zodiac can be found at 93–99. The time of the horary question is taken by the astrologer and, with the date and place, an astrological chart is then erected from those data. The path of the Sun, the ecliptic, is divided into the twelve signs of the Zodiac; the heavens are further divided into the twelve mundane houses which relate to the various people and situations of life. The first division relates to the horizon east to west which results in the ascendant and descendant—the cusps of the 1st and 7th houses respectively. The second division, south to north, results in the Midheaven or Medium Cælum (M.C.) and the Nadir or Imum Cælum—the cusps of the 10th and 4th houses respectively.

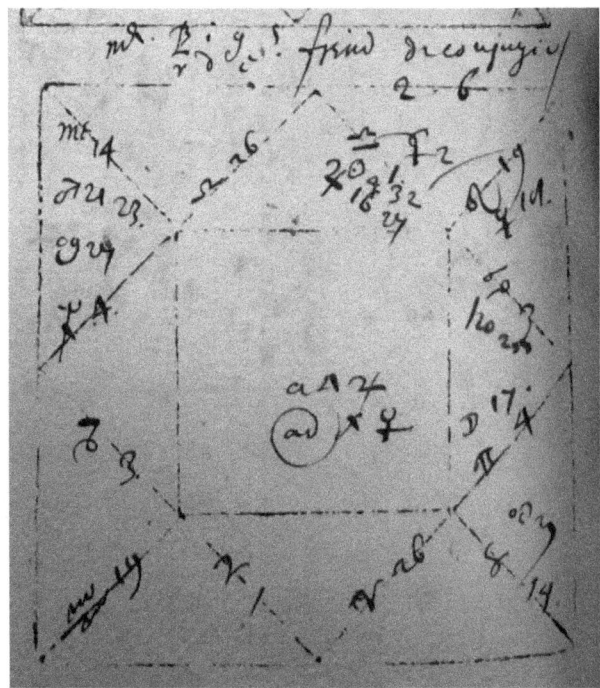

FIGURE 13.3
Showing question and
emphasis
Note: Erected for
17 September 1649 at
11.50 am. Bod. MS Ashm.
210, fol. 131ᵛ

important for making a judgement. Here Lilly has underscored Mercury which
is in 2° of the sign of Libra and in the 10th house at 1° Libra relating to honour
and by extension to success (he has written it in the 9th house because of lack of
space, but also demonstrating that Mercury was calculated after the others).[52]
It might also have described the desired party, in this case Mercury, as a person
of elevated social standing. Both Jupiter and the Sun are also placed in the 10th
house of which Lilly writes: 'either Jupiter or the Sun doe much Fortunate this
House when they are posited therein'.[53] It can be conjectured that this client
received a positive judgement.

As there are no annotations associated with the next figure, it might be useful to note the emphases within and conjecture the subject matter from them.
The Moon is placed at 13°50′ of Capricorn, the Sun is placed at 16° Scorpio, both
are underlined, and the 2nd house is scored through (the pen pressure is similar to that of the end stroke following the aspects noted in the centre square).
By marking the 2nd house, the querent's finances are brought into focus; this

52   Lilly, *Christian Astrology*, 55.
53   Lilly, *Christian Astrology*, 55.

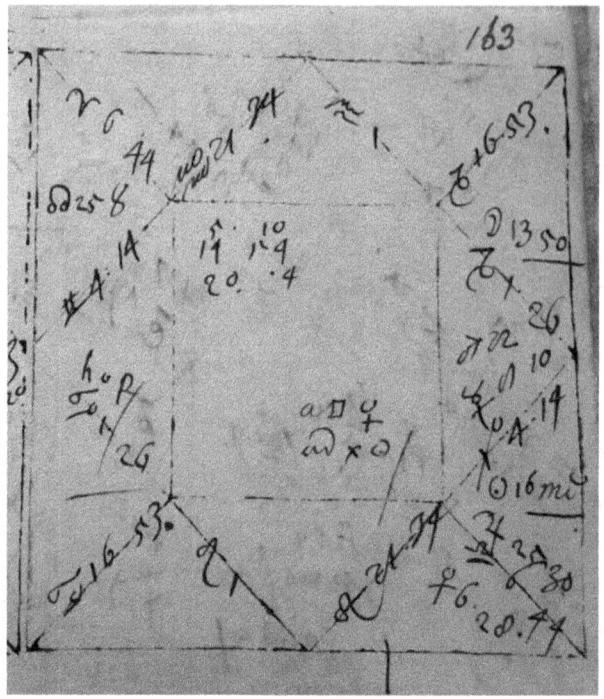

FIGURE 13.4
Showing emphasis but
not the question
Note: Erected for
29 October 1649 at
5.10 PM. Bod. MS Ashm.
210, fol. 163ʳ

house has Cancer on its cusp, a sign ruled by the Moon, hence the Moon is underscored.[54] It is placed in the 8th house of, among other things, legacies and inheritances.[55] The reason for choosing this signification over any other is that the Sun is also underscored which is the ruler of the sign of Leo. The 4th house has Leo on its cusp making the Sun the significator of the matters of that house (it also rules the 5th house and this house may also be emphasized). The 4th house rules the father and property, as in real estate, given that the 8th house is emphasized by the Moon's position there, it would not be unreasonable to assume that the question is about inheritance. This might especially be so since the Sun-ruled 5th house is significant of the father's money and possessions. The oblique following the Moon's aspects listed in the centre square is showing an end stop implying that he will not look any further than this even though there is another possible aspect to Jupiter. The cross-stroke near the 'R' next to 'ℏ' [Saturn] near the 2nd house cusp is the vertical stroke for 'R' meaning retrograde. So, these marks seem to illustrate what the astrologer is examining and

---

54   Lilly, *Christian Astrology*, 51–52.
55   Lilly, *Christian Astrology*, 54.

what he is stressing in his judgement. In another chart, a line in the 2nd house of the client's finances is found in a question about lost money, and the Part of Fortune—usually significant in financial matters—is underscored.[56] In yet another, the Part of Fortune is in the 1st house of the client, and there is a line drawn in the 2nd house possibly underscoring the north lunar node, a significator of good fortune. A larger sample, as in the forthcoming study, would answer any doubts but the following discovery perhaps indicates the advantage of further closer research.

In the sample of sixty-nine figures from 28 August to 29 October 1649, Lilly had begun to note down the fee he had been paid. It is not known if this has been noticed before. Many researchers rely upon Keith Thomas's *Religion and the Decline of Magic* for their information regarding the working practices of astrologers.[57] Thomas's work is, of course, essential reading in this field and it mentions Lilly many times, particularly in the section frequently favoured by those researchers.[58] He offers a suggestion or two about the kind of consultation fees charged by various astrologers, naming one John Vaux as charging according to the type of question that was asked: for a question relating to the theft of a horse, he had charged one shilling, but four shillings for the loss of a mare and foal.[59] In the selection in this manuscript, this does not appear to be what Lilly does, but he seems to vary the fee according to the status of the client and thus their ability to pay rather than the type of question. In two charts, one each on 29 August 1649 and 3 September 1649, the fee was one shilling and two shillings and sixpence respectively, yet both referred to a journey, '*de itinere*'.[60]

Finding what appear to be the fees became obvious when it was clear that these were extraneous numbers that seemed to have nothing to do with the astrological figure (see also Figure 3). The illustrations show four examples of this notation and the fourth strongly suggests that this is monetary notation since pricing was often shown in that way, for example, 4/6 or 4/6d would be a common way of labelling a price of four shillings and sixpence. Remembering Lewis Carroll's *Alice In Wonderland*, the Mad Hatter in all visual representations whether engraving, film, or animation always show him with the price label still in his hat band as 10/6, or ten shillings and sixpence; one shilling would often

---

56 Bod. MS Ashm. 420, fol. 115ʳ.

57 For example, Patrick Curry, *Prophecy and Power: Astrology in Early Modern England* (Princeton: Princeton University Press, 1989), 28.

58 Keith Thomas, *Religion and the Decline of Magic: Studies in Popular Beliefs in Sixteenth- and Seventeenth-Century England* (Harmondsworth: Penguin, 1973), 362–382.

59 Thomas, *Religion and the Decline of Magic*, 382.

60 Bod. MS Ashm. 210, fols. 118ʳ and 119ᵛ.

be noted as 1/-. This practice continued in the UK until the decimalization of currency in 1971.[61]

A fee is not noted on every chart, leaving only speculation to explain that lack, but it is possible that he either did not charge the person if they were very poor, attested to by the quotation from Ashmole's addenda to Lilly's 'Life' quoted below, accepted payment in kind, or, of course, simply forgot to note it. Forty-four fees are apparent; twice there are two sums on one figure where, on one occasion, he appears to have had two clients who had arrived at exactly the same time and so there had been two questions, but it is unclear why two sums were noted on the other chart.[62]

In the charts for 17 and 18 September 1649 the first working day begins at 9.07 am and ends at 5.20 PM; the second begins at 7.57 am ending at 7 PM—at least these are the times of the figures therein.[63] The first day was the busier day, showing eleven figures; even so, there was a long gap between the chart for 12.04 PM and that for 4.07 PM. Of these eleven charts, ten have fees noted (one figure has two fees as explained above), three are of one shilling, one is for two shillings, six are for two shillings and sixpence, and one is for five shillings. Of those noted with questions, none is the same, so here at least there is no suggestion that he charged according to the type of question. The next day, there were only seven clients and three have a fee noted: one shilling, two shillings, and two shillings and sixpence. As explained, the fees reflect the coinage available at the time and in most cases would not have required Lilly to give change. That said, there are two figures that do not conform to this pattern: on 9 October 1649, Lilly received two sums, one in the morning and one in the afternoon, of one shilling and five pence, and one shilling and eleven pence.[64] These each fall short of the usual fee by one penny: one shilling and six pence and two shillings, respectively. Although to happen twice in one day is unusual, it is reasonable to conjecture that the clients simply had no more money with them, or at all.

Supporting evidence of fees can be found from Lilly himself in one of his letters to his close friend Elias Ashmole (1617–1692). On 29 May 1671, Lilly wrote to Ashmole, amongst other things, to thank the Ashmoles for a cloak they had

---

61   A note here about the coinage used in England at this time and to which the above refers: the penny was the standard; a sixpence—six pennies, half a shilling; one shilling worth twelve pennies, twenty shillings to the pound; two-shilling piece; half a crown worth two shillings and sixpence; a crown worth five shillings. The pricing of goods was often done to accommodate the coinage, reducing the need to give change.

62   Bod. MS Ashm. 210, fols. 132ʳ and 163ᵛ, respectively.

63   Bod. MS Ashm. 210, fols. 132ʳ and 133ʳ.

64   Bod. MS Ashm. 210, fol. 146ʳ.

given him for his weekly rides into Kingston upon Thames (near to his home then at Hersham) where he would hold a type of clinic for those who were sick.[65] On 10 August 1671, he reported that during his usual Saturday visit to Kingston he was paid four sums of money for 'Astrologicall Questions': ten shillings, five shillings, one shilling, and sixpence for 'physick'.[66] These first two are large sums of money which argues again for the variety of social class in Lilly's clientele. But Ashmole himself reports, in his addenda to Lilly's 'Life' that 'every Saterday [he] rode to Kingston, where the poorer sort flockt to him from severall parts & received much benefit by his advice & prescriptions, which he gave them freely & without money; from those that were more able he now & then received a Shilling, & sometimes an halfe Crowne, if they offered it to him, otherwise he demanded nothing',[67]

So, there is support for the numbers in the corners of the figures being sums of money or fees and of their being varied according to the client's ability to pay by social status. One other point of note is that, whilst space is restricted around some of these figures, Lilly has chosen to write the fee overhanging the space on the chart that is the 9th house, that is, the house of religion and God. It is clear that there was space near some of the charts for him to have written these numbers elsewhere had he so chosen. Lilly was devout and it might be speculated that this was his way of calling to mind that he had received that money by the Grace of God and perhaps this notation was recognizing that.

Another feature of life in London was the outbreaks of plague. One of the main methods of dealing with epidemics was household isolation whereby the external doors of a house could be nailed shut or padlocked when infection had occurred within. This isolation could last for forty days and may have increased following subsequent infections.[68] Lilly recounts that on 4 August 1647 his servant was buried following the plague; he buried a second servant from the plague on 28 August 1647.[69] Presumably, this led to a second period of isolation which would have ended on about 7 October, six days after he

---

65 C.H. Josten, ed., *Elias Ashmole (1617–1692) His Autobiographical and Historical Notes, his Correspondence, and Other Contemporary Sources Relating to his Life and Work: with a Biographical Introduction by C.H. Josten*, vol. III. 5 vols (Oxford: Clarendon Press, 1966), 1217.

66 Josten, ed., *Elias Ashmole (1617–1692) His Autobiographical and Historical Notes*, vol. III, 1222.

67 Josten, ed., *Elias Ashmole (1617–1692) His Autobiographical and Historical Notes*, vol. III, 1197.

68 Paul Slack, *The Impact of Plague in Tudor and Stuart England* (Oxford: Clarendon Press, 1990), 211, 223, and 298.

69 Lilly, 'To the Reader', in *Christian Astrology*, no pagination.

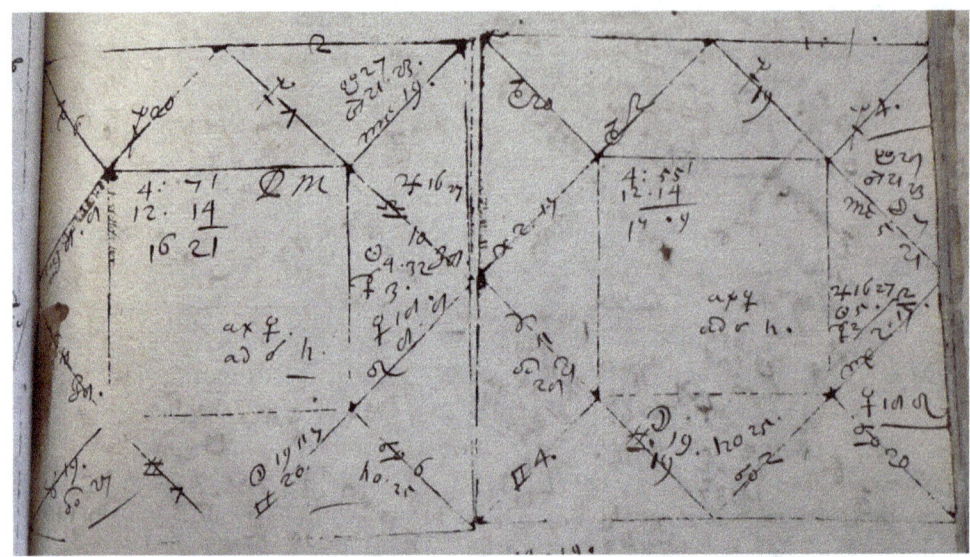

FIGURE 13.5 Left: fee of 2—two shillings; right: 1:/.—one shilling. (Bod. MS Ashm. 210, fol. 132ʳ.)

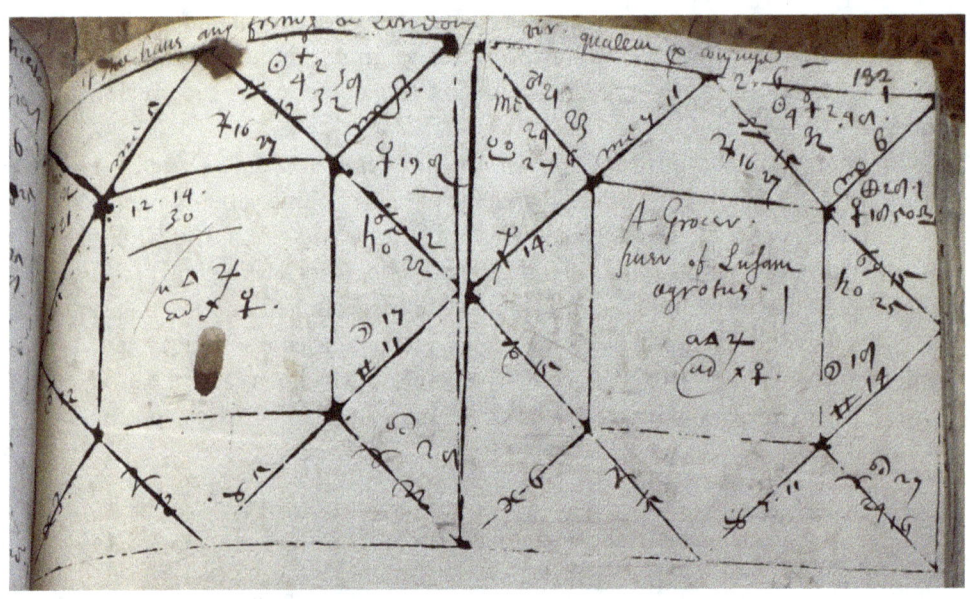

FIGURE 13.6 Left having no fee; right showing fees of 2:6—two shillings and sixpence, and 1—one shilling. (Bod. MS Ashm. 210, fol. 132ʳ.)

completed *Christian Astrology*.[70] However much he, like many others, suffered from this isolation with 'abundant sorrow and perplexity', he managed to keep working for at least part of this period.[71] In this selection there are six charts for 30 August 1647, one for the following day, four for the 3 September 1647, and two for the following day: the period of isolation.[72] Of these thirteen clients, four were designated 'Dns' (dominus) or 'Dna' (domina), each of their names being encrypted, which would suggest at least a tolerance for his working even from a more influential class. There is no suggestion that any one of these clients entered his house, as he says of his experience of the Great Plague of 1665 'I had, before I came away, very many people of the poorer sort frequented my lodging, many whereof wear so civill as when they brought water, viz: Urine, from infected people, would stand purposely at a distance'.[73] Although there was no infection in his house that time, visitors were concerned to keep at a distance to protect him, and this may well be what occurred when Lilly was himself in isolation.

Perhaps the law, or its enforcement, was more flexible than is often assumed. As already noted, for example, Akkerman reproduces one of Lilly's astrological figures which was a question put by Jane Whorwood.[74] It was set for 2 May 1647 at 5.45 PM, which was a Sunday. In the selection considered in this essay, of the 210 figures only one was erected on a Sunday (19 December 1647) at 5.30 PM. Of course, this selection is not always contiguous by day, but there are enough to show that working on a Sunday was unusual, and it, too, was labelled 'Comitt'.[75] On that Sunday, Lilly's taking a question at 5.30 PM, meant that he had probably already been to church, nevertheless working on the Sabbath was prohibited.[76] On the next day, Lilly took one question at 8.10 am then appears to have stopped work until the following Monday at 1.20 PM—20 to 26 December, the Christmas period.[77] Celebrating Christmas Day had been forbidden by ordinance in the previous June and it was to be considered an ordinary working day.[78] This is

---

70   William Lilly, *Christian Astrology*, closing, no pagination.
71   Lilly, 'To the Reader', in *Christian Astrology*, no pagination.
72   Bod. MS Ashm. 420, fol. 82^r & fol. 85^r resp.
73   Lilly, 'Life', Bod. MS Ashm. 421 fol. 218^v, in *William Lilly (1602–1681) the Astrologer*, ed. Ward, vol. 1, 76.
74   Akkerman, *Invisible Agents*, 36. Akkerman as Fox, *The King's Smuggler*, 114. A subject can be inferred from the non-textual marks within the figure, and thus the question could well relate to the king's captivity, who was at that time being held at Holdenby House.
75   Bod. MS Ashm. 420, fol. 154^v.
76   Bod. MS Ashm. 420, fol. 154^v. It is tempting to make more of the similarity of day and time between these two questions.
77   Bod.MS Ashm. 420, fol. 155^r.
78   'June 1647: An Ordinance for the enabling the Committee of the Militia of London to

not to suggest that Lilly was rebelling in any way, but it seems he might present an example of how people perhaps resisted, avoided, or ignored such unpopular strictures which may well have been tolerated by the authorities when it posed no threat to public order.[79]

6   The Case of Jane Whorwood

However, there was someone who did not keep a distance, who had no fear of the plague, and who did not keep the Sabbath either. As mentioned earlier, Lilly recounts the story of Jane Whorwood upon which the historiography largely depends. She visited Lilly at his house in London on 11 November 1647 when he reports the following:

> uppon the Kings intention to escape, and with his consent, Madam W[horwood]: ... came to receive my judgment, viz: in what quarter of this Nation hee might bee most safe, and not to bee discovered, until himselfe pleased. I told her I would not let her come in, for I buried a mayd servant of the plague very lately; I fear not the plague but the Pox, quoth shee, so upp wee went; after erection of my figure, I told her about twenty miles or thereabouts from London and in Essex, I was certain hee might continue undiscovered:[80]

The escape he mentions referred to the king's detention at Hampton Court Palace. The incidents which Lilly recounts are a few of a number of attempts that Whorwood made to secure the king's escape.[81] In 1648, around the time of another attempt described by Lilly, there was a letter warning the governor of the Isle of Wight, Colonel Robert Hammond (1621–1654), that a ship was leaving the Thames to effect the king's escape. Its interest here is that having added that she was aboard that ship, she was described as 'a tall, well-fashioned, and well-languaged gentlewoaman [sic], with a round visage and pockholes in her face',

make Searches, and to raise Horses'., in C H. Firth and R S. Rait, eds, Acts and Ordinances of the Interregnum, 1642–1660, (London: H.M. Stationery Office, 1911). British History Online: http://www.british-history.ac.uk/no-series/acts-ordinances-interregnum/pp 954-956 [accessed 11 July 2021].

79   Christopher Hill, *The Century of Revolution, 1603–1714*, 2nd ed, (Walton-on-Thames: Thomas Nelson & Sons, 1981), 147–148.

80   Lilly, 'Life', Bod. MS Ashm. 421 fol. 205ᵛ, in *William Lilly (1602–1681) the Astrologer*, ed. Ward, vol. 1, 53.

81   Fox, *The King's Smuggler*, 16.

and Anthony Wood (1632–1695) adds that she had red hair.[82] This is likely to be the 'pox' to which she refers, smallpox, which of course results in scarring. From Whorwood's stated fear of the pox and Lilly's subsequent statement, Akkerman extrapolates: 'Whether Lilly made a move on Jane is pure speculation'.[83] She provides no evidence to support such speculation and there is nothing within the 'Life' to support it either. She also wrote 'Lilly advised Jane on how best to get the king out of Hampton Court' when that is clearly not what was asked or advised.[84] Otherwise, she appears to follow Fox's account of this episode and Lilly's involvement in Whorwood's life.[85]

Presumably Whorwood would have given Lilly's advice to the king to go east to Essex and hide himself there for a time, except that the king had escaped that same night and travelled west, and later handed himself over to the governor of the Isle of Wight. Far from being safe, the king had taken himself into captivity from which he would never extricate himself despite further attempts by Whorwood and others.

A closer examination of Lilly's practice book reveals a much more important horary question and figure. It might well have been Whorwood who asked the question regarding Charles's escape from Carisbrooke Castle: 'de an exibit ex Isle of Wighte', ('About the king. Whether he will escape from the Isle of Wight'.)[86] This figure appears not to have been published before. It was erected on Tuesday 14 December 1647 at 1.20 PM (the first of the day and just thirteen minutes before the next client) when Charles had been a prisoner there from November 1647.

It is possible to check this hypothesis using Lilly's methodology as explained in his primer. The rising sign, its ruler and the 1st house signify the querent. In this case, the rising sign is Taurus and its ruler Venus is in Sagittarius in the 7th house. Using Lilly's textbook, it is possible that the querent was a woman because the representative planet is Venus, which is a feminine planet and naturally, that is, by its nature or always, signifies women. It is placed in the fiery sign of Sagittarius which is a masculine sign possibly adding to Whorwood's bravery, and possibly her red hair.[87] The Moon is the significator of the question

---

82   John Fox, 'Whorwood [née Rider], Jane (1614/15–1684)', Oxford Dictionary of National Biography, (2007) https://doi.org/10.1093/ref:odnb/29341; C.H. Firth, 'Whorwood, Jane (fl. 1648)', Dictionary of National Biography, (1900) https://doi.org/10.1093/odnb/9780192683120.013.29341.

83   Akkerman, Invisible Agents, 42.

84   Akkerman, Invisible Agents, 42.

85   Fox, The King's Smuggler, 35, for example.

86   Bod. MS Ashm. 420, fol. 149ᵛ.

87   Lilly, Christian Astrology, 72–73 and 97–98.

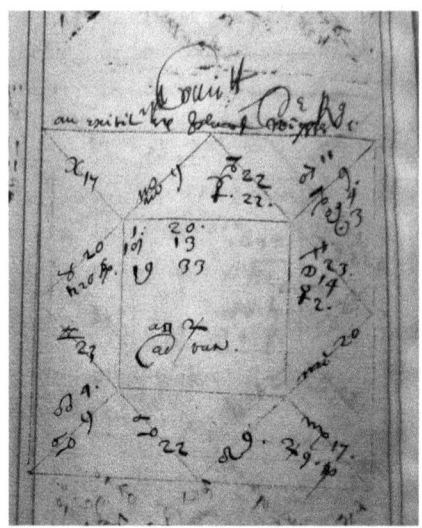

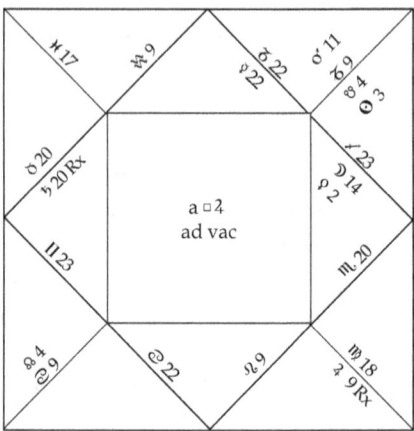

FIGURE 13.7
If escape from the Isle of Wight

FIGURE 13.8
Representation of the figure left for clarity

itself, and because of that it is also a secondary significator of the querent.[88] It is also in the 7th house and in the sign of Sagittarius; this might be taken as supporting the previous statement regarding the description offered by the querent's primary significator.

The king is represented by the 10th house having Capricorn on its cusp, with the planet Mercury placed exactly on that cusp.[89] Capricorn is ruled by the planet Saturn, which is placed in the 1st house of the querent and is retrograde.[90] Lilly says of this, 'if Saturn be in the Ascendant, especially Retrograde, the matter of the Question seldome or never comes to good'.[91] Whilst keeping this overview brief and simple, the Moon's aspects at least must also be considered.[92] In this case, the Moon is separating from the square aspect of Jupiter at 9° Virgo (90°, or three signs apart) but cannot apply to another planet. The

---

88   Lilly, *Christian Astrology*, 182.
89   Lilly, *Christian Astrology*, 55.
90   Retrograde is the apparent backward motion of a planet: Lilly, *Christian Astrology*, 114.
91   Lilly, *Christian Astrology*, 122.
92   Aspects: these are mathematical relationships between planets and planets and points. Each planet has its own unique virtue or characteristics that radiate from it on its light or rays. This light extends around the planet (here including the luminaries as planets) measured in degrees of zodiacal longitude and those distances vary by planet. Traditionally, these aspects are: conjunction 0°, sextile 60°, square 90°, trine 120°, opposition 180°. For ease, these can be expressed as being so many zodiacal signs apart: none, two, three,

next planet is Mercury, but it is too far away for the Moon currently to make an aspect with it, the same can be said of Saturn. Therefore, the Moon is described as void of course; nothing can happen if the Moon is inactive in this way. Lilly describes the condition thus:

> All manner of matters goe hardly on (except the principall significators be very strong) when the Moon is voyd of course; yet somewhat she performes if voyd of course, and be in either Taurus, Cancer, Sagittarius or Pisces.[93]

So it might be possible to find some effect from this figure since the Moon in Sagittarius is one of those exceptions. However, with the Moon inactive and Saturn going backwards, it would be difficult to judge an escape. However, Lilly must have found some hope from this chart since he was again assisting Whorwood the following year, in which, he says that he provided a hacksaw and nitric acid to the king, or was effective in their provision.[94] This was connected with the famous escape attempt in the following March when Charles became stuck in the window as he tried to climb out.

7   Conclusion

Bringing this review to an end, it is clear that working through Lilly's household isolation, the plague, Christmas, his fees, where and how he worked, idiosyncrasies that revealed further information, and personal politics in action, understanding of the astrologer himself has been augmented, without recourse to very detailed technical explanations. These are among the features found in this research and which justify and encourage further investigations into such manuscripts, and this astrologer's work in particular, quite apart from comparisons of his application of astrological method with that of others. Although most information about William Lilly is found through his published work, little enough has been examined closely, including these manuscript sources which offer a way of discovering much more. However, there is enough

---

four, six. Aspects can be exact, but more often the faster moving planet 'separates' from a slower planet, and 'applies' to the next slower planet, but always within the extent of their rays.

93   Lilly, *Christian Astrology*, 122.
94   Lilly, 'Life', Bod. MS Ashm. 421, fol. 206ʳ, in *William Lilly (1602–1681) the Astrologer*, ed. Ward, vol. 1, 54.

known to preclude the kind of weaknesses in the historiography that have been pointed out here. This review has demonstrated the kind of information that can be discovered by approaching such manuscripts with and without a degree of technical knowledge. Most of the detail of these findings seems never to have been published before, even though the manuscripts themselves have been handled a number of times by researchers. A thorough examination and analysis of Lilly's practice books is required and will be done in the forthcoming study.

Bibliography

Manuscripts

Lilly, William, 'The Life of William Lilly student in Astrology wrote by himselfe in the 66th year of his age, at Hersham in the parish of Walton uppon Thames in the County of Surrey: propria manu', Oxford, Bodleian Library, MS Ashmole 421 fols. 178^v–224.

Oxford, Bodleian Library, MS Ashmole 184.

Oxford, Bodleian Library, MS Ashmole 185.

Oxford, Bodleian Library, MS Ashmole 210.

Oxford, Bodleian Library, MS Ashmole 420.

Oxford, Bodleian Library, MS Ashmole 421.

Printed Works

Achinstein, Sharon. 'Texts in conflict: the press and the Civil War'. In *The Cambridge Companion to Writing of the English Revolution*. Cambridge: Cambridge University Press, 2006. *Cambridge Companions Online*, https://doi.org/10.1017/CCOL052164252 3.004

Akkerman, Nadine. *Invisible Agents: Women and Espionage in Seventeenth-Century Britain*. Oxford: Oxford University Press, 2018.

Avelar de Carvalho, Helena. *An Astrologer at Work in Late Medieval France: the Notebooks of S. Belle*. Leiden: Brill, 2021.

Baker, Philip. 'The Regicide'. In *The Oxford Handbook of the English Revolution*, edited by Michael J. Braddick, 154–169. Oxford: Oxford University Press, 2014.

Black, William Henry. *A Descriptive, Analytical, and Critical Catalogue of the Manuscripts Bequeathed unto the University of Oxford by Elias Ashmole, Esq., M.D., F.R.S., Windsor Herald*. Oxford: Oxford University Press, 1845.

Capp, Bernard. *Astrology and the Popular Press: English Almanacs 1500–1800*. London: Faber, 1979.

Casebooks Project, https://casebooks.lib.cam.ac.uk.

Curry, Patrick. *Prophecy and Power: Astrology in Early Modern England*. Princeton: Princeton University Press, 1989.

Deimann, Wiebke & David Juste (eds). *Astrologers and Their Clients in Medieval and Early Modern Europe*. Cologne: Böhlau, 2015.

Dykes, Benjamin N. 'Practice and Counsel in Guido Bonatti'. In *Astrologers and Their Clients in Medieval and Early Modern Europe*, edited by Wiebke Deimann and David Juste, 29–42. Cologne: Böhlau, 2015.

Earle, Peter. *A City Full of People: Men and Women of London, 1650–1750*. London: Methuen, 1994.

Firth, C.H. 'Whorwood, Jane (fl. 1648)', *Dictionary of National Biography*, (1900). https://doi.org/10.1093/odnb/9780192683120.013.29341

Fox, John. 'Whorwood [*née* Rider], Jane (1614/15–1684)', *Oxford Dictionary of National Biography*, (2007), https://doi.org/10.1093/ref:odnb/29341

Fox, John. *The King's Smuggler: Jane Whorwood Secret Agent to Charles I*. Stroud: The History Press, 2010.

Foxley, Rachel. 'Varieties of Parliamentarianism'. In *The Oxford Handbook of the English Revolution*, edited by Michael J. Braddick. Oxford: Oxford University Press, 2015, 414–429.

Hill, Christopher. *The Century of Revolution, 1603–1714*. Walton-on-Thames: Norton, 1981.

Ingram, Bruce S., ed. *Three Sea Journals of Stuart Times*. London: Constable & Co. Ltd, 1936.

Jeake, Samuel. *An Astrological Diary of the Seventeenth Century: Samuel Jeake of Rye, 1652–1699*, edited by Michael Hunter and Annabel Gregory. Oxford: Clarendon Press, 1988.

Josten, C.H., ed. *Elias Ashmole (1617–1692) His Autobiographical and Historical Notes, his Correspondence, and Other Contemporary Sources Relating to his Life and Work: with a Biographical Introduction by C.H. Josten*, 5 vols. Oxford, Clarendon Press 1966.

'June 1647: An Ordinance for the enabling the Committee of the Militia of London to make Searches, and to raise Horses'. In *Acts and Ordinances of the Interregnum, 1642–1660*, edited by C.H. Firth and R.S. Rait. London: H.M. Stationery Office, 1911. *British History Online*: http://www.british-history.ac.uk/no-series/acts-ordinances-interregnum/pp954-956 [accessed 11 July 2021].

Kassell, Lauren. *Medicine and Magic in Elizabethan London Simon Forman: Astrologer, Alchemist, and Physician*. Oxford: Oxford University Press, 2005.

Kassell, Lauren. 'Casebooks in Early Modern England: Medicine, Astrology, and Written Records'. *Bulletin of the History of Medicine* 88, no. 4 (2014): 595–625.

Kelsey, Sean. 'The Trial of Charles I', *The English Historical Review*, 118, no. 477 (2003), 583–616.

Lilly, William. *Merlinus Anglicus Junior: The English Merlin Revived*. London, 1644.

Lilly, William. *England's Propheticall Merline*. London, 1644.

Lilly, William. *A Prophecy of the White King and Dreadfull Dead-Man Explaned*. London, 1644.

Lilly, William. *Anglicus, Peace or No Peace. 1645*. London, 1645.

Lilly, William. *Merlini Anglici Ephemeris 1648*. London, 1648.

Lilly, William. *A peculiar Prognostication Astrologically predicted according to Art: Whether, or No, His Majestie Shall suffer Death this present yeere 1649*. London, 1649.

Lilly, William. *Merlini Anglici Ephemeris*. London, 1650.

Lilly, William. *Monarchy or No Monarchy*. London, 1651.

Lilly, William. *Merlini Anglici Ephemeris 1656*. London, 1656.

Lilly, William. *Christian Astrology*. Facsimile Edition. Exeter: Regulus, 1985.

Maseres, Francis, ed. *Select Tracts Relating to the Civil Wars in England, in the Reign of Charles the First*. London: Printed by R. Wilks, 1815.

Morrill, John and Philip Baker. 'Oliver Cromwell, the Regicide and the Sons of Zeruiah'. In *Regicides and the Execution of Charles I*, edited by Jason Peacey, 14–35. New York: Palgrave, 2001.

Page, Sophie. 'Richard Trewythian and the Uses of Astrology in Late Medieval England'. *Journal of the Warburg and Courtauld Institutes*, vol. 64 (2001), 193–228.

Raymond, Joad. 'Seventeenth-Century Print Culture'. *History Compass* 2, no. 1 (2004): 1–12.

Roch, Jeremy. 'Hieron Roch J. His Journal of Some Remarkable Voyages and Adventures at Sea in the Years 1665, 1666 and 1667,' in *Three Sea Journals of Stuart Times*, edited by Bruce S. Ingram, 29–139. London: Constable & Co. Ltd., 1936.

Slack, Paul. *The Impact of Plague in Tudor and Stuart England*. Oxford: Clarendon, 1990.

Stockinger, Peter and Susan Ward. 'Monster of Ingratitude', *The Tradition Journal*, no. 3 (Autumn 2009), http://thetraditionjournal.com.

Thomas, Keith. *Religion and the Decline of Magic: Studies in Popular Beliefs in Sixteenth- and Seventeenth-Century England* (Harmondsworth: Penguin, 1973).

Ward, Susan (ed.). *William Lilly, the Astrologer (1602–1681): A Book of Sources*. Vol. 1 & 2. Lisbon: Prisma Edições, 2024–2025. (vols 3 *in progress*).

Helena Avelar (1964–2021)

Helena Avelar de Carvalho was born in 1964 in Lisbon. After a successful career in journalism, she turned her lifelong passion for astrology into a new professional path. By 2000, she had developed a keen interest in traditional astrological practices and began researching historical Portuguese astrological documents alongside her partner, Luís Ribeiro. This growing interest led her to pursue formal academic study, and in 2008 she earned a degree in history from Nova University of Lisbon.

She continued her education with a Master's in medieval history, focusing on the history of astrology in Portugal. Her dissertation, 'Vir Sapiens Dominabitur Astris: Astrological Knowledge and Practices in the Portuguese Medieval Court (King João I to King Afonso V)' (2011), examined astrological narratives in Portuguese chronicles and demonstrated the importance of astrological practice in fourteenth- and fifteenth-century Portugal. It was the first academic study in Portugal devoted entirely to the history of astrology.

In 2014, Helena was accepted into the doctoral programme at The Warburg Institute, where she continued her research under the supervision of Professor Charles Burnett. Her thesis, 'The Making of an Astrologer in Fifteenth-Century France: The Notebooks of S. Belle (Lisbon, MS 1711 and Paris, NAL 398)' (2018), explored the education and working methods of a late medieval French astrologer. This accomplishment made Helena the first Portuguese historian of astrology.

Helena co-founded the Astra Project with Luís Ribeiro in 2018, a research initiative dedicated to the study of historical astrological practices and techniques. The project quickly built a collaborative network of scholars in the field. In 2020, she held a short-term postdoctoral position at the IKGF—the International Consortium for Research in the Humanities 'Fate, Freedom and Prognostication' at the University of Erlangen-Nuremberg. There, she studied astrological doctrines concerning the human lifespan. This research culminated in her final publication: the paper 'Who Wants to Live Forever? Astrological Methods for Calculating Lifespan in Western Culture and Perspectives on Determinism in Astrology' in the International Journal of Divination and Prognostication (October 2021). She was also part of the Institute for Medieval Studies (Nova University of Lisbon) and the Interuniversity Centre for the History of Science and Technology (CIUHCT, University of Lisbon).

Although she began her academic journey later in life, Helena was deeply committed to advancing the field of the history of astrology. She left a lasting impression on those who knew her and worked because of her passion and generosity. Tragically, her academic career was cut short by her sudden passing in March 2021. Her final major contribution was the book based on her doctoral research, *An Astrologer at Work in Late Medieval France: The Notebooks of S. Belle*, published posthumously by Brill in 2021, five months after her death.

As a trailblazer in Portugal, her legacy will certainly continue more widely to inspire future generations of researchers.

Academic Publications by Helena Avelar

Avelar de Carvalho, Helena. 'Who Wants to Live Forever? Astrological Methods for Calculating Lifespan in Western Culture and Perspectives on Determinism in Astrology'. *International Journal of Divination and Prognostication* 2, no. 2 (5 October 2021): 161–188. https://doi.org/10.1163/25899201-12340018.

Avelar de Carvalho, Helena. *An Astrologer at Work in Late Medieval France: The Notebooks of S. Belle. An Astrologer at Work in Late Medieval France*. Leiden–Boston: Brill, 2021.

Avelar de Carvalho, Helena. 'Ibn Ezra from Hebrew to Latin'. *Journal for the History of Astronomy* 52, no. 2 (2021): 242–243. https://doi.org/10.1177/0021828621995307.

Avelar de Carvalho, Helena. 'Libro de Las Suertes: An Example of Inter-Cultural Exchanges in Late-Medieval Iberia'. In *Prognostication in the Medieval World: A Handbook*, edited by Matthias Heiduk, Klaus Herbers, and Hans-Christian Lehner, 849–851. Berlin–Boston: De Gruyter, 2020.

Avelar de Carvalho, Helena. 'Preludes to the Inquisition: Self-Censorship in Medieval Astrological Discourse'. *Annals of Science* 77, no. 1 (2020): 10–25.

Avelar de Carvalho, Helena. 'The Heavens on Earth. An Overview of Astrological Geography'. In *Spreading Knowledge in a Changing World*, edited by Charles Burnett and Pedro Mantas-España, 225–245. Córdoba: UCOPress, 2019.

Avelar de Carvalho, Helena. 'The Making of an Astrologer in Fifteenth-Century France. The Notebooks of S. Belle: Lisbon, MS 1711 and Paris, NAL 398'. PhD thesis, University of London, The Warburg Institute, 2018. https://sas-space.sas.ac.uk/9460/.

Avelar de Carvalho, Helena. 'Astrology and Sarcasm in Three Medieval Portuguese Songs of Mockery'. *Culture and Cosmos* 22, no. 1 (2018): 47–55.

Avelar de Carvalho, Helena. 'Prophecy and Divination in the Portuguese Royal Court'. In *Secrets and Discovery in the Middle Ages: Proceedings of the 5th European Congress of the Fédération Internationale Des Instituts d'Études Médiévales*, edited by José Francisco Meirinhos, Celia López Alcalde, and João Rebalde. 90. Barcelona-Roma: Brepols, 2017.

Avelar de Carvalho, Helena. 'Vícios e virtudes na teoria e na prática astrológica medieval: exemplos portugueses da dinastia de Avis (século XV)'. Edited by Hélène

Thieulin-Pardo. *e-Spania. Revue interdisciplinaire d'études hispaniques médiévales et modernes*, no. 22 (31 October 2015). https://doi.org/10.4000/e-spania.24859.

Avelar de Carvalho, Helena. 'D. Duarte e a Astrologia Na Corte de Avis'. In *D. Duarte e a Sua Época. Arte, Cultura, Poder e Espiritualidade*, edited by Catarina Fernandes Barreira and Miguel Metelo de Seixas, 235–248. Lisboa: Instituto de Estudos Medievais, Centro Lusíada de Estudos Genealógicos, Heráldicos e Históricos, 2014.

Avelar de Carvalho, Helena. 'Vir Sapiens Dominabitur Astris: Astrological Knowledge and Practices in the Portuguese Medieval Court (King João I to King Afonso v)'. Universidade Nova de Lisboa–Faculdade de Ciências Sociais e Humanas, 2011. http://run.unl.pt/handle/10362/6672.

Avelar de Carvalho, Helena, and Luís Campos Ribeiro. 'As práticas astrológicas em Portugal'. In *Ciência, Tecnologia e Medicina na construção de Portugal*, edited by Antonio Sánchez, Palmira Fontes da Costa, and Henrique Leitão, 1:373–392. Lisboa: Tinta-da-China, 2021.

Avelar de Carvalho, Helena, and Luís Campos Ribeiro. 'Manuscripts and Evidences of Jewish Astrology and Medicine in Fifteenth-Century Portugal: An Overview'. In *Sephardic Book Art of the 15th Century*, edited by Luis U. Afonso and Tiago Moita, 145–156. Turnhout: Harvey Miller Publishers, 2019.

Avelar de Carvalho, Helena, and Luís Campos Ribeiro. 'Fisionomia e astrologia: o manuscrito de Rolando de Lisboa'. In *Luz, Cor e Ouro. Estudos sobre manuscritos iluminados*, edited by Catarina Fernandes Barreira, 235–248. Lisboa: Biblioteca Nacional de Portugal. Instituto de Estudos Medievais, 2016.

Avelar de Carvalho, Helena, and Luís Campos Ribeiro. 'A Ciência Judaica Em Portugal No Século xv'. In *O Livro e a Iluminura Judaica Em Portugal No Final Da Idade Média*, edited by Luís Urbano Afonso and Maria Adelaide Miranda, 87–91. Lisboa: Biblioteca Nacional Portugal, 2015.

Burnett, Charles, and Helena Avelar de Carvalho. 'The Interpretation of a Horoscope Cast by Abraham the Jew in Be'ziers for a Child Born on 29 November 1135: An Essay in Understanding a Medieval Astrologer'. *Culture and Cosmos* 18, no. 2 (2014): 19–40.

Ribeiro, Luís Campos, Helena Avelar de Carvalho, and Samuel Gessner. 'Astrology and Astronomy in the Court Culture of the Avis Dynasty'. In *Philippa of Lancaster and the Court Culture of Medieval Portugal*, edited by Tiago Viúla De Faria, 99–121. The New Middle Ages. Cham: Springer Nature Switzerland, 2025. https://doi.org/10.1007/978-3-031-65560-9.

General Index

References to footnotes are indicated by '*n*' following the page number.